4/96

A Bibliographical Guide

to the Study of

Western American Literature

A Bibliographical Guide to the Study of

SECOND EDITION

Western American Literature

Edited by
Richard W. Etulain
and
N. Jill Howard

University of New Mexico Press
Albuquerque
in cooperation with
the University of New Mexico
Center for the American West

WILL JAMES. '30

Library of Congress Cataloging-in-Publication Data

Etulain, Richard W.
A bibliographical guide to the study
of Western American literature / edited by Richard W. Etulain
and N. Jill Howard.—2nd ed.
p.   cm.
Includes bibliographical references and index.
1. American literature—West (U.S.)—History and
criticism—Bibliography.
2. West (U.S.) in literature—Bibliography.
3. West (U.S.)—Bibliography.
I. Howard, N. Jill (Nancy Jill), 1959–   .
II. Title.
ISBN 0-8263-1644-1
Z1251.W5E8 1995
YPS271"
016.8109'978—dc20   95-4418
CIP

Designed by Emmy Ezzell

Title page illustration from Will James, *Lone Cowboy: My Life Story*
(Charles Scribner, 1930)

CONTENTS

WORKS ON INDIVIDUAL AUTHORS

PREFACE TO THE SECOND EDITION

This second edition of a standard reference work in western American literature, in addition to including most of the items listed in the first edition published in 1982, also lists the most important essays and books in the field published from 1981 through 1994. It likewise illustrates shifting scholarly trends in the study of Western American literature. Increasing numbers of specialists are now at work on the American literary West, with this expanded and updated edition demonstrating their mounting interest in the field.

In preparing this second edition, we have followed the format of the earlier version. Thus, this bibliography not only includes listings of significant articles and volumes published on general western literary topics since the early 1980s, it also provides useful checklists of scholarship on more than 300 western writers. Reluctantly, in this revision we have omitted nearly all master's theses, dozens of briefer essays and introductions, and a few older volumes to make room for the blizzard of publications appearing since the first edition.

We have made other revisions to reflect recent changes in western literary studies. To survey the flood of new publications on women and western literature and the environment and western literature, we have added separate sections on those notable topics. Also more than three dozen new writers whose works have already elicited critical commentary appear in this edition. We have likewise broadened our coverage to include several additional nature writers, historians, and children's authors.

This new edition reveals a good deal about recent major trends in western literature scholarship. Still, even though listings on new authors such as Louise Erdrich, Marilynne Robinson, Michael Dorris, and Ursula Le Guin indicate mounting interest in ethnic and women writers in western literature, the most extensive listings remain those on Willa Cather, Samuel Clemens, James Fenimore Cooper, Jack London, and John Steinbeck. At the same time, much of the recent scholarship represents new approaches to these western giants as well as to other authors like Mari Sandoz, Wallace

Stegner, Larry McMurtry, N. Scott Momaday, or Sam Shepard, authors whose careers ended recently or who have now reached full stride. Revealingly, fewer scholars seem at work on Hamlin Garland, Bret Harte, Robinson Jeffers, and William Stafford.

Along the way, we have made other changes to aid readers. To provide additional consistency, we have placed all listings after an author's birth rather than pen name. That is, in addition to locating Mark Twain materials under Samuel Clemens and Luke Short under Frederick Glidden, for instance, readers will find essays and books about Nathanael West under Nathan Wallenstein Weinstein and items about Mourning Dove under Christine Quintasket. Since limited space necessitated fewer crosslistings in this edition, users should closely examine, for example, bibliographical, general, and Native American sections for items on Indian writers and Native American literature. The same is true for other ethnic topics and for coverage of gender-related and environmental topics.

We would like to thank those groups and persons who have aided us in the preparation of this second edition. First of all, former Dean B. Hobson Wildenthal and History Department Chair Jonathan Porter provided financial support through the College of Arts and Sciences and the Center for the American West that made possible our work. The Research Allocations Committee at the University of New Mexico also funded some of the costs for the preparation of this manuscript. Along the way, staff members at the Center for the American West, most notably Jon Hunner, Traci Hukill, David Key, and Florence Goulesque, devoted many valuable hours to the preparation of manuscript drafts and to checking the accuracy of our listings. Pat Devejian and Jackie Etulain Partch prepared bibliographical cards and checked citations, and David Null, former director of reference services, and his reference desk staff at the Zimmerman Library at University of New Mexico were unstintingly helpful and courteous in their assistance.

Also of great help were several specialists in western American literature who reviewed topical and author sections, suggesting changes and additions and correcting errors and oversights. In this regard, we would like to thank Barbara Howard Meldrum, Fred Erisman, Forrest Robinson, James Maguire, Gary Scharnhorst, Susan Rosowski, Glen Love, Louis Owens, and Lee Nash for their assistance. Special thanks go to Dick Harrison for aiding us with the section on Canadian western literature. Finally, Barbara Guth and David Holtby at the University of New Mexico Press encouraged and supported our work when this project seemed impossible. To all these persons we are especially grateful.

PREFACE TO THE FIRST EDITION

The recentness of most listings in this bibliography illustrates the growing interest in western literature in the last decades. Although the first significant interpretations of the literary West by Ralph Leslie Rusk, Dorothy Dondore, and Lucy Lockwood Hazard appeared in the 1920s, Franklin Walker's notable works in the 1930s and 1940s, and Henry Nash Smith's indispensable *Virgin Land* in 1950, these pioneer studies did not spawn immediate interest in western writing. Not until the 1960s did a growing number of students and scholars begin systematic study of western literature.

Much of this earliest commentary dealt with nineteenth-century writers like James Fenimore Cooper, Bret Harte, and Joaquin Miller and later interpretations of such authors as Owen Wister, Eugene Manlove Rhodes, and Sinclair Lewis. While interest in some of these writers has declined, critics continue to deal extensively with the life and writings of Hamlin Garland, Frank Norris, Willa Cather, and John Steinbeck. And an increasing number of essay and books have been written about Jack London, Robinson Jeffers, Larry McMurtry, N. Scott Momaday, and post-Beat writers Ken Kesey, Gary Snyder, Richard Brautigan, and Joan Didion.

At the same time, scholars have been paying increased attention to several topics. Regionalism, the formula Western, the Beats, and the Western film as literature are popular subjects; and women writers and western heroines, Mormons, images of Indians and Chicanos, and Canadian western literature are subjects receiving additional notice. While such well-known critics as John R. Milton, Don D. Walker, and Max Westbrook have advanced tentative overviews of western American literature, their broader interpretations are exceptions, for most western literary commentary is narrowly focused or limited to single works. In addition, several popular approaches in American literary criticism have not been applied to western writing and writers. This being the case, western American literature, though benefitting from the increased attention it has received in the last twenty years or so, remains a field ripe with possibilities for literary critics and historians.

To take into account the growing and diversified interest in western literature, this bibliography updates, enlarges, and reorganizes *Western American Literature: A Bibliography of Interpretive Books and Articles* (Vermillion, S. Dak.: Dakota Press, 1972). Intended as handy guides to the major interpretive works about western literature, as well as those on numerous individual authors, the following lists are not exhaustive, but they are comprehensive and bring together in one volume the most important research on the literature of the American West. Recent work is stressed, including material published through 1981.

This checklist is divided into five major sections: (1) bibliographies listing research on western American literature; (2) anthologies of western literature; (3) general works, divided into two categories: (a) books, dissertations, and theses; and (b) essays; (4) listings of research dealing with seven important aspects of western literature: (a) local color and regionalism; (b) popular western literature: dime novels and the Western; (c) Western films as literature; (d) Indian literature and Indians in literature; (e) Mexican-American literature; and (5) essays and books on more than three hundred fifty writers.

Limited primarily to those authors who were born and reared in the trans-Mississippi West or who spent large portions of their lives in the West, this listing also includes items on writers like Cooper, Washington Irving, Stephen Crane, Owen Wister, Nathanael West, and Thomas Berger, whose works have influenced western literature. Major emphasis is placed on writers of fiction and poetry, but some books and articles dealing with notable western historians and well-known nonfiction writers are also noted.

I have included listings on this large and varied region and group of writers because I want this bibliography to be as comprehensive as possible. To move in the other direction—to narrow the definition of "western," to omit the Beats and such contemporary writers as Kesey, Brautigan, and Tom Robbins, and to leave out non-Westerners who have written notable books about the West—is to become too exclusive and to amputate the meaning of the region. Still, authors such as Thomas Mann, Henry Miller, Ursula LeGuin, and others who lived (or have lived) long periods in the West, are not included because they have not written about the West. Literary critics and historians must utilize definitions sufficiently broad and flexible to cover the varied kinds of literature about the West, by insid-

4

ers and outsiders. I have used this broader definition of the West and "western" literature in compiling this bibliography.

Users should note other aspects of the organization of this volume. Because so much has been written about Cooper, Clemens, Cather, and Steinbeck, these sections are particularly selective, although I have tried to include all major books and essays about these authors, as well as the most useful bibliographical references. Though the table of contents lists official and pen names of several authors, items are listed under their given names. Thus, for example, books and essays about Mark Twain are under Clemens, items about Max Brand under Frederick Faust, and those about Artemus Ward under Charles Farrar Browne. On a few occasions autobiographical books and essays are noted when they add information not otherwise available on that writer's life and works. Finally, the index is a guide only to authors of the books and essays listed here; it is not a subject index.

Scholars interested in additional bibliographical materials about western writers and writings should consult the yearly bibliographies in winter issues of *Western American Literature*. Also helpful are the annual *MLA International Bibliography*, bibliographical listings in *American Literature* and *Western Historical Quarterly*, and bibliographies appended to volumes and pamphlets in the Twayne United States Authors Series and the Boise State Western Writers Series.

A number of persons helped in the preparation of this volume. At Idaho State University, Sherrill and John Redd, Barb Herrbach, and Andy Dredge typed and double-checked endless 4-by 6-inch cards. At the University of New Mexico, Avis and Jo Lou Trujillo and Anabelle Oczon typed the manuscript and helped prepare the index. My daughter, Jackie, proofread numerous entries. The Research Allocation Committee of the University of New Mexico provided partial funding for typing the manuscript. John R. Milton encouraged the preparation of the earlier version of this bibliography.

BIBLIOGRAPHIES AND REFERENCE VOLUMES

1. Abajian, James de T. *Blacks and Their Contributions to the American West: A Bibliography....* Boston: G.K. Hall, 1974.
2. Adams, Ramon F. *Burs Under the Saddle: A Second Look at Books and Histories of the West.* Norman: University of Oklahoma Press, 1964, 1989.
3. ———. *More Burs Under the Saddle: Books and Histories of the West.* Norman: University of Oklahoma Press, 1979, 1989.
4. Allen, James Paul, and Eugene James Turner. *We the People: An Atlas of America's Ethnic Diversity.* New York: Macmillan, 1988.
5. Alsmeyer, Henry L., Jr. "A Preliminary Southwestern Reconnaisance." *Southwestern American Literature* 1 (May 1971): 67–71. Lists literary guides of the Southwest.
6. *American Literary Scholarship: An Annual.* Durham, N.C.: Duke University Press, 1965–. Yearly collection that summarizes and analyzes literary scholarship.
7. Anderson, John Q., Edwin W. Gaston, Jr., and James W. Lee, eds. *Southwestern American Literature: A Bibliography.* Chicago: Swallow Press, 1980.
8. "Annual Bibliography of Studies in Western American Literature." *Western American Literature*, 1966–. Issued each year in the Winter issue.
9. Ballou, Patricia K. *Women: A Bibliography of Bibliographies.* 2d ed. Boston: G. K. Hall, 1986.
10. Biblowitz, Iris, et al. *Women and Literature: An Annotated Bibliography of Women Writers.* 3d ed. Cambridge, Mass.: Women and Literature Collective, 1976. American writers, 1–93.
11. Blanck, Jacob, comp. *Bibliography of American Literature. 8 vols.* New Haven: Yale University Press, 1955–1989.
12. ———, and Michael Winship, comps. *Bibliography of American Literature, Vol. 9: Edward Noyes Westcott to Elinore Wylie.* New Haven: Yale University Press, 1991.

13. Bowman, John S., ed. *The World Almanac of the American West*. New York: World Almanac, 1986.
14. Bragin, Charles. *Dime Novels: Bibliography, 1860–1928*. Brooklyn: C. Bragin, 1938.
15. Brenni, Vito Joseph. *The Bibliographic Control of American Literature 1920–1975*. Metuchen, N.J.: Scarecrow Press, 1975.
16. Brooker–Bowers, Nancy. *The Hollywood Novel and Other Novels about Film, 1912–1982: An Annotated Bibliography*. New York: Garland, 1985.
17. Browning, James A. *The Western Reader's Guide: A Selected Bibliography of Nonfiction Magazines, 1953–91*. Stillwater, Okla.: Barbed Wire Press, 1992.
18. Bruccoli, Matthew J., ed. *Dictionary of Literary Biography*. Detroit: Gale Research, 1978–.
19. ———, and Judith S. Baughman, eds. *Facts on File Bibliography of American Fiction: 1919–1988*. 2 vols. New York: Facts on File, 1991.
20. Brye, David L., ed. *European Immigration and Ethnicity in the United States and Canada: A Historical Bibliography*. Santa Barbara, Calif.: ABC-Clio, 1983.
21. Bryer, Jackson R., ed. *Fifteen Modern American Authors: A Survey of Research and Criticism*. Durham, N.C.: Duke University Press, 1969. Contains sections on Cather and Steinbeck.
22. ———. *Sixteen Modern American Authors: A Survey of Research and Criticism*. Rev ed. Durham, N.C.: Duke University Press, 1974.
23. ———. *Sixteen Modern American Authors, Volume 2, A Survey of Research and Criticism Since 1972*. Durham, N.C.: Duke University Press, 1990.
24. Camarillo, Albert, ed. *Latinos in the United States: A Historical Bibliography*. Santa Barbara, Calif.: ABC-Clio, 1986.
25. Cancellari, Mike. *Checklist of Western and Northern Fiction*. New York: Cancellari, 1986.
26. Carpenter, Allan. *The Encyclopedia of the Central West*. New York: Facts on File, 1990.
27. ———. *The Encyclopedia of the Far West*. New York: Facts on File, 1991.
28. ———. *The Encyclopedia of the Midwest*. New York: Facts on File, 1989.
29. Carpenter, Charles A. "American Drama: A Bibliographical Essay." *American Studies International* 21 (April 1983): 3–52.
30. ———. "Modern Drama Studies: An Annual Bibliography." *Modern Drama* 26 (June 1983): 150–233.

31. Carson, W. G. B. "The Theatre of the American Frontier: A Bibliography." *Theatre Research* 1 (March 1958): 14–23.
32. Chan, Sucheng. "Asian Americans: A Selected Bibliography of Writings Published since the 1960s." *Reflections on Shattered Windows: Promises and Prospects for Asian American Studies.* Eds. Gary Y. Okihiro, et al. Pullman: Washington State University Press, 1988, 214–37.
33. Cheung, King-Kok, and Stan Yogi. *Asian American Literature: An Annotated Bibliography.* New York: Modern Language Association of America, 1988.
34. Clark, Beverly Lyon. "American Children's Literature: Background and Bibliography." *American Studies International* 30 (April 1992): 4–40.
35. Coan, Otis W., and Richard G. Lillard. *American Fiction: An Annotated List of Novels that Interpret Aspects of Life in the U.S.* 5th ed. Palo Alto, Calif.: Pacific Books, 1967.
36. Cole, Wendell. "Early Theatre West of the Rockies: A Bibliographical Essay." *Theatre Research* 4 (No. 1, 1962): 36–45.
37. Coleman, Rufus A., ed. *Northwest Books: First Supplement.* Lincoln: University of Nebraska Press, 1949.
38. Collins, James L., ed. *The Western Writer's Handbook.* Boulder, Colo.: Johnson Books, 1987.
39. Colonnese, Tom, and Louis Owens. *American Indian Novelists: An Annotated Critical Bibliography.* New York: Garland, 1985.
40. Cortina, Lynn Ellen Rice. *Spanish–American Women Writers: A Bibliographical Research Checklist.* New York: Garland, 1983.
41. Cronin, Gloria L., Blaine H. Hall, and Connie Lamb, eds. *Jewish American Fiction Writers: An Annotated Bibliography.* New York: Garland, 1991.
42. Davidson, Levette Jay. *Rocky Mountain Life in Literature: A Descriptive Bibliography.* Denver: University of Denver Book Store, 1936.
43. *Dictionary of Literary Biography.* Detroit: Gale, 1978–.
44. Di Pietro, Robert J., and Edward Ifkovic, eds. *Ethnic Perspectives in American Literature: Selected Essays on the European Contribution: A Source Book.* New York: Modern Language Association, 1983.
45. Dobie, J. Frank. *Guide to Life and Literature of the Southwest.* Rev ed. Dallas: Southern Methodist University Press, 1952.
46. Donelson, Kenneth L. "Some Adolescent Novels About the West: An Annotated Bibliography." *Elementary English* 49 (May 1972): 735–39.

47. Drew, Bernard Alger. *Western Series and Sequels.* 2d ed. New York: Garland, 1993.

48. Dykes, Jeff C. *Western High Spots: Reading and Collecting Guides.* [Flagstaff, Ariz.]: Northland Press, 1977.

49. Eichelberger, Clayton L., comp. *A Guide to Critical Reviews of United States Fiction, 1870–1910.* 2 vols. Metuchen, N.J.: Scarecrow Press, 1971, 1974.

50. Elliot, Emory, ed. *Columbia Literary History of the United States.* New York: Columbia University Press, 1988.

51. Erisman, Fred. "American Regional Juvenile Literature, 1870–1910: An Annotated Bibliography." *American Literary Realism 1870–1910* 6 (Spring 1973): 109–22.

52. ———, and Richard W. Etulain, eds. *Fifty Western Writers: A Bio-Bibliographical Sourcebook.* Westport, Conn.: Greenwood Press, 1982.

53. Etulain, Jacqueline J., comp. *Mexican Americans in the Twentieth-Century American West: A Bibliography.* Occasional Papers, No. 3. Albuquerque: Center for the American West, University of New Mexico, 1990.

54. Etulain, Richard W. "The American Literary West and Its Interpreters: The Rise of a New Historiography." *Pacific Historical Review* 45 (August 1976): 311–48.

55. ———. *A Bibliographical Guide to the Study of Western American Literature.* Lincoln: University of Nebraska Press, 1982. First edition of this volume.

56. ———. "Novelists of the Northwest: Needs and Opportunities for Research." *Idaho Yesterdays* 17 (Summer 1973): 24–32.

57. ———. "Research Opportunities in Western Literary History." *Western Historical Quarterly* 4 (July 1973): 263–72.

58. ———. "The Twentieth-Century American West: A Selective Bibliography." *The Twentieth-Century West: Historical Interpretations.* Albuquerque: University of New Mexico Press, 1989, 421–46.

59. ———. "Western American Literature: A Selective Annotated Bibliography." *Rendezvous* 7 (Winter 1972): 67–78.

60. ———. "Western Literary History: A Brief Bibliographical Essay." *Journal of the West* 19 (January 1980): 71–73.

61. Eysturoy, Annie O., and José Antonio Gurpegui. "Chicano Literature: Introduction and Bibliography." *American Studies International* 28 (April 1990): 48–82.

62. Fairbanks, Carol, and Sara Brooks Sundberg. *Farm Women on the Prairie Frontier: A Sourcebook for Canada and the United States.* Metuchen, N.J.: Scarecrow Press, 1983.

63. Fleck, Richard F., and Robert A. Campbell. "A Selective Literary Bibliography of Wyoming." *Annals of Wyoming* 46 (Spring 1974): 75–112; 47 (Fall 1975): 232.

64. Fullerton, B. M. *Selective Bibliography of American Literature 1775–1900: A Brief Estimate of the More Important American Authors and a Description of Their Representative Works.* Woodbridge, Conn.: Ox Bow Press, 1989.

65. Gale, Steven H., ed. *Encyclopedia of American Humorists.* New York: Garland, 1988.

66. Gaston, Edwin W., Jr. *The Early Novel of the Southwest.* Albuquerque: University of New Mexico Press, 1961, 195–302.

67. *Gem State Authors: A Bio-Bibliography.* [Pocatello: Idaho State Library, 1978].

68. Gerhardstein, Virginia Brokaw, ed. *Dickinson's American Historical Fiction*, 5th ed. Metuchen, N.J.: Scarecrow Press, 1986.

69. Gerstenberger, Donna, and George Hendrick. *The American Novel 1789–1959: A Checklist of Twentieth-Century Criticism.* Denver: Alan Swallow, 1961.

70. ———. *The American Novel: A Checklist of Twentieth Century Criticism on Novels Since 1789. Volume II: Criticism Written 1960–1968.* Chicago: Swallow Press, 1970.

71. Gohdes, Clarence. *Literature and Theatre of the States and Regions of the U.S.A.: An Historical Bibliography.* Durham, N.C.: Duke University Press, 1967. Excellent listing for each western state and other lists for the Western and regionalism; very useful.

72. ———, and Sanford E. Marovitz. *Bibliographical Guide to the Study of the Literature of the U.S.A.* 5th ed., rev. Durham, N.C.: Duke University Press, 1984.

73. Green, Rayna. *Native American Women: A Contextual Bibliography.* Bloomington: Indiana University Press, 1983.

74. Hand, Richard A. *A Bookman's Guide to the Indians of the Americas: A compilation of over 10,000 catalogue entries with prices and annotations, both bibliographical and descriptive.* Metuchen, N.J.: Scarecrow Press, 1989.

75. Hanna, Archibald. "Western Americana Collectors and Collections." *Western Historical Quarterly* 2 (October 1971): 401–4.

76. Harbert, Earl N., and Robert A. Rees, eds. *Fifteen American Authors Before 1900*. Rev ed. Madison: University of Wisconsin Press, 1984.

77. Harrison, Cynthia E., ed. *Women in American History: A Bibliography*. 2 vols. Santa Barbara, Calif.: ABC-Clio, 1979, 1985.

78. Hart, James D., ed. *The Oxford Companion to American Literature*. 5th ed. New York: Oxford University Press, 1983.

79. Harvey, Alice G. *Nebraska Writers*. Rev ed. Omaha: The Author, 1964.

80. Henderson, Lesley, and Noelle Watson, eds. *Contemporary Novelists*. 5th ed. Chicago: St. James Press, 1991.

81. Hill, Gertrude. "The Southwest in Verse: A Selective Bibliography of Arizona and New Mexican Poetry." *Arizona Quarterly* 23 (Winter 1967): 306–12.

82. Hotchkiss, Jeanette. *American Historical Fiction and Biography for Children and Young People*. Metuchen, N.J.: Scarecrow Press, 1973.

83. Jacobson, Angeline, comp. *Contemporary Native American Literature: A Selected and Partially Annotated Bibliography*. Metuchen, N.J.: Scarecrow Press, 1977.

84. Jones, Howard Mumford. *Guide to American Literature and Its Backgrounds since 1890*. 4th ed., rev and enl. Cambridge, Mass.: Harvard University Press, 1972.

85. Kanellos, Nicolás. *The Hispanic-American Almanac: A Reference Work on Hispanics in the United States*. Detroit: Gale Research, 1993.

86. Kibler, James E., ed. *American Novelists Since World War II*. 2d Ser. Detroit: Gale, 1980.

87. Kim, Hyung-chan, ed. *Asian American Studies: An Annotated Bibliography and Research Guide*. New York: Greenwood Press, 1989.

88. Kirby, David K. *American Fiction to 1900: A Guide to Information Sources*. Detroit: Gale Research, 1975.

89. Kirkpatrick, D. L., ed. *Reference Guide to American Literature*. 2d ed. Chicago: St. James Press, 1987.

90. Klein, Barry T., ed. *Reference Encyclopedia of the American Indian*. 5th ed. West Nyack, N.Y.: Todd Publications, 1990.

91. Kolin, Philip C., ed. *American Playwrights Since 1945: A Guide to Scholarship, Criticism, and Performance*. Westport, Conn.: Greenwood Press, 1989.

92. Kuehl, Warren F. *Dissertations in History: An Index to Dissertations Completed in History Departments of United States and Canadian Universities 1873–1960.* Lexington: University Press of Kentucky, 1965; *1961–June 1970.* Lexington: University Press of Kentucky, 1972; *1970–June 1980.* Santa Barbara, Calif.: ABC-Clio, 1985.

93. Lamar, Howard R., ed. *The Reader's Encyclopedia of the American West.* New York: Thomas Y. Crowell, 1977.

94. Landrum, Larry N. *American Popular Culture: A Guide to Information Sources.* Detroit: Gale Research, 1982.

95. Leary, Lewis. *American Literature: A Study and Research Guide.* New York: St. Martin's Press, 1976.

96. ———. *Articles on American Literature, 1950–1967.* Durham, N.C.: Duke University Press, 1970.

97. ———. *Articles on American Literature, 1968–1975.* Durham, N.C.: Duke University Press, 1979.

98. Lewis, Tom. *Storied New Mexico: An Annotated Bibliography of Novels with New Mexico Settings.* Albuquerque: University of New Mexico Press, 1991.

99. "A List of Dissertations." *Western Historical Quarterly.* This listing of recent dissertations in western history appears each year in the July issue of the *Quarterly.*

100. Littlefield, Daniel F., Jr., and James W. Parins. *A Bibliography of Native American Writers, 1772–1924.* Metuchen, N.J.: Scarecrow Press, 1981.

101. Logasa, Hannah. *Regional United States: A Subject List.* Boston: Faxon, 1942.

102. McNamee, Lawrence F. *Dissertations in English and American Literature ... 1865–1964.* New York: R. R. Bowker, 1968; *Supplement One ... 1964–1968,* 1969; *Supplement Two....1969–1973,* 1974.

103. McPheron, William, and Jocelyn Sheppard. *The Bibliography of Contemporary American Fiction, 1945–1988: An Annotated Checklist.* Westport, Conn.: Meckler, 1989.

104. Maguire, James H. "A Selected Bibliography of Western American Drama." *Western American Literature* 14 (Summer 1979): 149–63.

105. Mainiero, Lina, ed. *American Women Writers: A Critical Reference Guide. From Colonial Times to the Present.* 4 vols. New York: Ungar, 1979–1982.

106. Major, Mabel, and T. M. Pearce. *Southwest Heritage: A Literary History with Bibliographies.* 3d ed., rev and enl. Albuquerque: University of New Mexico Press, 1972.

107. Malone, Michael P., ed. *Historians and the American West.* Lincoln: University of Nebraska Press, 1983.

108. Marken, Jack W., comp. *The American Indian: Language and Literature.* Arlington Heights, Ill.: AHM Publishing, 1978.

109. Martínez, Julio A., ed. *Chicano Scholars and Writers: A Bio-Bibliographical Directory.* Metuchen, N.J.: Scarecrow Press, 1979.

110. ———, and Francisco A. Lomelí, eds. *Chicano Literature: A Reference Guide.* Westport, Conn.: Greenwood Press, 1985.

111. Mead, S. Jean. *Maverick Writers: Candid Comments from Fifty-Two of the Best.* Caldwell, Idaho: Caxton, 1989.

112. Meyer, Roy W. "An Annotated Bibliography of Middle Western Farm Fiction, 1891–1962." *The Middle Western Farm Novel in the Twentieth Century.* Lincoln: University of Nebraska Press, 1965, 200–242.

113. *MLA International Bibliography.* Published annually in hard covers and includes a large section on American literature. Now available on CD-ROM. Bronx, N.Y.: H.W. Wilson, 1988–.

114. Morris, Mary Lee. *Southwestern Fiction 1960–1980: A Classified Bibliography.* Albuquerque: University of New Mexico Press, 1986.

115. Nagel, James, and Gwen L. Nagel, eds. *Facts on File Bibliography of American Fiction: 1866–1918.* New York: Facts on File, 1993.

116. Nemanic, Gerald, ed. *A Bibliographical Guide to Midwestern Literature.* Iowa City: University of Iowa Press, 1981.

117. Nichols, Roger L., ed. *American Frontier and Western Issues: A Historiographical Review.* Westport, Conn.: Greenwood Press, 1986.

118. Nilon, Charles H. *Bibliography of Bibliographies in American Literature.* New York: R. R. Bowker, 1970.

119. Nomura, Gail M., et al., eds. *Frontiers of Asian American Studies: Writing, Research, and Commentary.* Pullman: Washington State University Press, 1989.

120. *Northwest Books.* Portland, Oreg.: Binfords and Mort, 1942.

121. Oaks, Priscilla. *Minority Studies: A Selective Annotated Bibliography.* Boston: G. K. Hall, 1976.

122. Paluka, Frank. *Iowa Authors: A Bio-Bibliography of Sixty Native Writers.* Iowa City: Friends of the University of Iowa Libraries, 1967.

123. Paul, Rodman W., and Richard W. Etulain. *The Frontier and the American West.* Goldentree Bibliographies in American History. Arlington Heights, Ill.: AHM Publishing, 1977.

124. Peavy, Charles D. *Afro-American Literature and Culture since World War II: A Guide to Information Sources.* Detroit: Gale Research, 1979.

125. Peck, David R. *American Ethnic Literatures: Native American, African American, Chicano/Latino, and Asian American Writers and their Backgrounds: An Annotated Bibliography.* Pasadena, Calif.: Salem Press, 1992.

126. Polk, Noel, comp. "Guide to Dissertations on American Literary Figures, 1870–1910: Part One." *American Literary Realism 1870–1910* 8 (Summer 1975): 177–280.

127. Pollard, Lancaster. "A Check List of Washington Authors." *Pacific Northwest Quarterly* 31 (1940): 3–96; 35 (1944): 233–66.

128. Powell, Lawrence Clark. *Land of Fiction: Thirty-two Novels and Stories About Southern California from <u>Ramona</u> to "The Loved One": A Bibliographical Essay.* Los Angeles: Historical Society of Southern California, 1991.

129. Pownall, David. *Articles on Twentieth-Century Literature: An Annotated Bibliography, 1954 to 1970.* 7 vols. New York: Kraus-Thomson, 1973–80.

130. "Recent Articles." *Western Historical Quarterly.* This listing of recent essays in western history appears in each issue of the journal.

131. Redfern, Bernice. *Women of Color in the United States: A Guide to the Literature.* New York: Garland, 1989.

132. "Research in Western American Literature." *Western American Literature,* 1974– . Appears annually in the Winter issue and lists theses and dissertations completed or in progress on western American literature.

133. Robbins, J. Albert, et al., comps. *American Literary Manuscripts: A Checklist of Holdings in Academic, Historical, and Public Libraries, Museums, and Authors' Homes in the United States.* 2d ed. Athens: University of Georgia Press, 1977. Lists the major manuscript collections of the leading western writers.

134. Rock, Roger O. *The Native American in American Literature: A Selectively Annotated Bibliography.* Westport, Conn.: Greenwood Press, 1985.

135. Rosa, Alfred F., and Paul A. Eschholz. *Contemporary Fiction in America and England, 1950–1970: A Guide to Information Sources.* Detroit: Gale Research, 1976.

136. Rubin, Louis D., ed. *A Bibliographical Guide to the Study of Southern Literature.* Baton Rouge: Louisiana State University Press, 1969.

137. Ruoff, A. LaVonne Brown. *American Indian Literatures: An Introduction, Bibliographic Review, and Selected Bibliography.* New York: Modern Language Association, 1990.

138. Sackett, S. J., comp. "Master's Theses in Literature." *Lit* 8 (November 1967): 45–174.

139. Sadler, Geoff, ed. *Twentieth-Century Western Writers.* 2d ed. Chicago and London: St. James Press, 1991. Immensely useful reference work.

140. Salzman, Jack, ed. *American Studies: An Annotated Bibliography.* 3 vols. New York: Cambridge University Press, 1986.

141. ———, ed. *Cambridge Handbook of American Literature.* New York: Cambridge University Press, 1986.

142. Singh, Jane, et al., eds. *South Asians in North America: An Annotated and Selected Bibliography.* Berkeley: Center for South and Southeast Asian Studies, University of California, Berkeley, 1988.

143. Smith, Dwight La Vern, ed. *The American and Canadian West: A Bibliography.* Santa Barbara, Calif.: ABC-Clio, 1979.

144. ———. *Indians of the United States and Canada: A Bibliography.* Santa Barbara, Calif.: ABC-Clio, 1974.

145. Steiner, Michael, and Clarence Mondale. *Region and Regionalism in the United States: A Source Book for the Humanities and Social Sciences.* New York: Garland, 1988.

146. Stoddard, Ellwyn R., Richard L. Nostrand, and Jonathan P. West, eds. *Borderlands Sourcebook: A Guide to the Literature on Northern Mexico and the American Southwest.* Norman: University of Oklahoma Press, 1983.

147. Taylor, J. Golden, Thomas J. Lyon, et al., eds. *A Literary History of the American West.* Fort Worth: Texas Christian University Press, 1987. A major reference volume.

148. Thernstrom, Stephan, ed. *Harvard Encyclopedia of American Ethnic Groups.* Cambridge, Mass.: Harvard University Press, 1980.

149. Thrapp, Dan L. *Encyclopedia of Frontier Biography.* 3 vols. Glendale, Calif.: Arthur H. Clark, 1988.

150. ———. *Encyclopedia of Frontier Biography.* Volume 4. Supplemental volume. Spokane, Wash.: Arthur H. Clark, 1994.

151. Tonsfeldt, Ward, comp. "The Pacific Northwest: A Selected and Annotated Bibliography." *Northwest Perspectives: Essays on the Culture of the Pacific Northwest.* Eds. Edwin R. Bingham and Glen A. Love. Seattle: University of Washington Press, 1979, 219–35. Lists primary and secondary literary items.

152. Tuska, Jon, and Vicki Piekarski, eds. *Encyclopedia of Frontier and Western Fiction.* New York: McGraw-Hill, 1983.

153. ———, and Paul J. Blanding, eds. *The Frontier Experience: A Reader's Guide to the Life and Literature of the American West.* Jefferson, N.C.: McFarland, 1984.

154. Underwood, June O. "Plains Women, History and Literature: A Selected Bibliography." *Heritage of the Great Plains* 16 (Summer 1983): 41–46.

155. Uzendoski, Emily Jane. "A Handlist of Nebraska Authors." Doctoral dissertation, University of Nebraska, Lincoln, 1976.

156. Van Derhoff, Jack. *A Bibliography of Novels Related to American Frontier and Colonial History.* Troy, N.Y.: Whitston Publishing, 1971.

157. Vinson, James, ed. *Twentieth-Century Western Writers.* Detroit: Gale Research, 1982.

158. Wagner, H. R. *The Plains and the Rockies: A Bibliography of Original Narratives of Travel and Adventure, 1800–1865.* San Francisco, 1921; 3d ed. rev by Charles L. Camp. Columbus, Ohio: Long's College Book Company, 1953.

159. Weber, F. J. "A Bibliography of California Bibliographies." *Southern California Quarterly* 50 (March 1968): 5–32.

160. Weixlmann, Joe. *American Short-Fiction Criticism and Scholarship, 1959–1977: A Checklist.* Chicago: Swallow Press, 1982.

161. Wertheim, Arthur Frank, ed. *American Popular Culture: A Historical Bibliography.* Santa Barbara, Calif.: ABC-Clio, 1984.

162. West, Ray B. *Writing in the Rocky Mountains with a Bibliography by Nellie Cliff.* Lincoln: University of Nebraska Press, 1947.

163. Wheeler, Eva F. "A Bibliography of Wyoming Writers." *University of Wyoming Publications* 6 (1939): 11–37.

164. White, Richard. "Race Relations in the American West." *American Quarterly* 38 (Bibliography 1986): 396–416.

165. Wilkinson, Charles F. *The American West: A Narrative Bibliography and a Study in Regionalism.* Niwot: University Press of Colorado, 1989.

166. Wilson, Charles Reagan, and William Ferris, eds. *Encyclopedia of Southern Culture.* Chapel Hill: University of North Carolina Press, 1989. Includes material on the trans-Mississippi West.

167. Wilson, Clyde N., ed. *American Historians, 1607–1865.* Detroit: Gale Research, 1984.

168. Woodress, James. *American Fiction, 1900–1950: A Guide to Information Sources.* Detroit: Gale Research, 1974.

169. ———. *Dissertations in American Literature 1891–1966*. Rev and enl. with assistance of Marian Koritz. Durham, N.C.: Duke University Press, 1968.

170. ———, ed. *Eight American Authors*. Rev ed. New York: W. W. Norton, 1972.

171. Wunder, John R., ed. *Historians of the American Frontier: A Bio-Bibliographical Sourcebook*. Westport, Conn.: Greenwood Press, 1988.

ANTHOLOGIES

172. Apple, Max, ed. *Southwest Fiction.* New York: Bantam Books, 1980, 1981.
173. Barclay, Donald A., James H. Maguire, and Peter Wild, eds. *Into the Wilderness Dream: Exploration Narratives of the American West, 1500–1805.* Salt Lake City: University of Utah Press, 1994.
174. Bergon, Frank, and Zeese Papanikolas, eds. *Looking Far West: The Search for the American West in History, Myth, and Literature.* New York: New American Library, 1978.
175. Blackburn, Alexander, and C. Kenneth Pellow, eds. *Higher Elevations: Stories for the West.* Athens: Ohio University and Swallow Press, 1993.
176. Blacker, Irwin R. *The Old West in Fiction.* New York: I. Obolensky, 1961.
177. Botkin, Benjamin Albert, ed. *A Treasury of Western Folklore.* Rev ed. New York: Bonanza Books, 1975, 1980.
178. Boyer, Mary G. *Arizona in Literature.* Glendale, Calif.: Arthur H. Clark, 1934.
179. Brown, Lois, comp. *Tales of the Wild West: An Illustrated Collection of Adventure Stories.* New York: Rizzoli; Oklahoma City: National Cowboy Hall of Fame, 1993.
180. Cárdenas de Dwyer, Carlota, ed. *Chicano Voices.* Boston: Houghton Mifflin, 1975.
181. Carlson, Roy, ed. *Contemporary Northwest Writing: A Collection of Poetry and Fiction.* Corvallis: Oregon State University Press, 1979.
182. Castañeda Shular, Antonia, Tomás Ybarra-Frausto, and Joseph Sommers. *Literatura chicana: texto y contexto.* Englewood Cliffs, N.J.: Prentice-Hall, 1972.
183. Caughey, John, and La Ree Caughey, eds. *California Heritage.* Los Angeles: Ward Ritchie Press, 1962; rev ed., Itasca, Ill.: F. E. Peacock, 1971.

184. Chan, Jeffrey Paul, Frank Chin, Lawson Fusao Inada, and Shawn Wong, eds. *The Big Aiiieeeee! An Anthology of Chinese American and Japanese American Literature.* New York: Penguin, 1991.

185. Coggeshall, William T. *The Poets and Poetry of the West.* Columbus: Follett, Foster, 1860.

186. Coleman, Rufus A. *The Golden West in Story and Verse.* New York: Harper, 1932.

187. Davidson, Levette J. *Poems of the Old West: A Rocky Mountain Anthology.* Denver: University of Denver Press, 1951.

188. ———, and Forrester Blake. *Rocky Mountain Tales.* Norman: University of Oklahoma Press, 1947.

189. ———, and Prudence Bostwick. *The Literature of the Rocky Mountain West, 1803–1903.* Caldwell, Idaho: Caxton, 1939.

190. Day, A. Grove. *The Sky Clears: Poetry of the American Indians.* Lincoln: University of Nebraska Press, 1964.

191. Dodds, Gordon B., ed. *Varieties of Hope: An Anthology of Oregon Prose.* Corvallis: Oregon State University Press, 1993.

192. Dow, Philip. *19 New American Poets of the Golden Gate.* San Diego: Harcourt Brace Jovanovich, 1984.

193. Durham, Philip, and Everett L. Jones, eds. *The Frontier in American Literature.* New York: Odyssey Press, 1969.

194. ———. *The Western Story: Fact, Fiction and Myth.* New York: Harcourt Brace Jovanovich, 1975.

195. Elder, Gary, ed. *The Far Side of the Storm: New Ranges of Western Fiction.* Los Cerillos, N. Mex.: San Marcos Press, 1975.

196. Flanagan, John T., ed. *America is West: An Anthology of Middlewestern Life and Literature.* Minneapolis: University of Minnesota Press, 1945.

197. Frederick, John T., ed. *Out of the Midwest: An Anthology of Midwestern Writing.* New York: Whittlesey House, 1944.

198. Gallagher, William D. *Selections from the Poetical Literature of the West.* Cincinnati: U.P. James, 1841.

199. Green, Rayna, ed. *That's What She Said: Contemporary Poetry and Fiction by Native American Women.* Bloomington: Indiana University Press, 1984.

200. Greenway, John. *Folklore of the Great West.* Palo Alto, Calif.: American West, 1969.

201. Gregg, John J., and Barbara Gregg, eds. *Best Loved Poems of the American West.* Garden City, N.Y.: Doubleday, 1980.

202. Griego y Maestas, José. *Cuentos: Tales from the Hispanic Southwest.* Trans. Rudolfo A. Anaya. Santa Fe: Museum of New Mexico, 1980.

203. Griffin, Shaun T., ed. *Desert Wood: An Anthology of Nevada Poets.* Reno: University of Nevada Press, 1991.

204. Hagedorn, Jessica, ed. *Charlie Chan Is Dead: An Anthology of Contemporary Asian American Fiction.* New York: Penguin Books, 1993.

205. Haslam, Gerald, ed. *Many Californias: Literature from the Golden State.* Reno: University of Nevada Press, 1992.

206. ———, and James D. Houston, eds. *California Heartland: Writing from the Great Central Valley.* Santa Barbara, Calif.: Capra Press, 1978.

207. Hillerman, Tony, ed. *The Best of the West: An Anthology of Classic Writing from the American West.* New York: HarperCollins, 1991.

208. Holbrook, Stewart H., ed. *Promised Land: A Collection of Northwest Writing.* New York: Whittlesey House, 1945.

209. Jackson, Joseph Henry, ed. *Continent's End: A Collection of California Writing.* New York: Whittlesey House, 1944.

210. [Kanellos, Nicolás, ed.] *Short Fiction by Hispanic Writers of the United States.* Houston: Arte Público, 1993.

211. Kittredge, William, ed. *Montana Spaces: Essays and Photographs in Celebration of Montana.* New York: Lyons and Binford, 1988.

212. ———, and Annick Smith, eds. *The Last Best Place: A Montana Anthology.* Helena: Montana Historical Society Press, 1988.

213. Kopp, Karl, and Jane Kopp, eds. *Southwest: Towards the Twenty-First Century.* Corrales, N.Mex.: Red Earth Press, 1981.

214. ———, and Bart Lanier Stafford, III. *Southwest: A Contemporary Anthology.* Albuquerque: Red Earth Press, 1977.

215. Larson, Clinton, and William Stafford, eds. *Modern Poetry of Western America.* Provo, Utah: Brigham Young University Press, 1975.

216. Lee, Charles, ed. *North, East, South, West: A Regional Anthology of American Writing.* New York: Howell, Soskin, 1945.

217. Lee, W. Storrs, ed. *California: A Literary Chronicle.* New York: Funk and Wagnalls, 1969.

218. ———. *Colorado: A Literary Chronicle.* New York: Funk and Wagnalls, 1970.

219. ———. *Washington State: A Literary Chronicle.* New York: Funk and Wagnalls, 1969.

220. Lerner, Andrea, ed. *Dancing on the Rim of the World: An Anthology of Contemporary Northwest Native American Writing.* Tucson: University of Arizona Press, 1990.

221. Lesley, Craig, and Katheryn Stavrakis, eds. *Dreamers and Desperadoes: Contemporary Short Fiction of the American West.* New York: Laurel, 1993.

222. Lewis, Jon E. *The Mammoth Book of the Western.* New York: Carroll and Graf, 1991.

223. Lomax, John A., coll. *Cowboy Songs and Other Frontier Ballads.* New York: Macmillan, 1927.

224. Love, Glen A., ed. *The World Begins Here: An Anthology of Oregon Short Fiction.* Corvallis: Oregon State University Press, 1993.

225. Lucia, Ellis. *This Land Around Us: A Treasury of Pacific Northwest Writing.* Garden City, N.Y.: Doubleday, 1969.

226. Lyons, Richard, ed. *Poetry North.* Fargo: North Dakota Institute for Regional Studies, 1970.

227. McFarland, Ronald E., and William Studebaker, eds. *Idaho's Poetry: A Centennial Anthology.* Moscow: University of Idaho Press, 1988.

228. McNamee, Gregory, ed. *Named in Stone and Sky: An Arizona Anthology.* Tucson: University of Arizona Press, 1993.

229. Maguire, James H., ed. *The Literature of Idaho: An Anthology.* Boise, Idaho: Boise State University, 1986.

230. Major, Mabel, and Thomas M. Pearce, eds. *Signature of the Sun: Southwest Verse 1900–1950.* Albuquerque: University of New Mexico Press, 1950.

231. Martin, Russell, ed. *New Writers of the Purple Sage: An Anthology of Contemporary Western Writing.* New York: Penguin, 1992.

232. ———, and Marc Barasch, eds. *Writers of the Purple Sage: An Anthology of Recent Western Writing.* New York: Viking, 1984.

233. Maule, Harry E., ed. *Great Tales of the American West.* New York: Modern Library, 1945.

234. Meltzer, David, ed. *The San Francisco Poets.* New York: Ballantine Books, 1971.

235. Miller, John, and Genevieve Anderson, eds. *Southwest Stories: Tales from the Desert.* San Francisco: Chronicle Books, 1993.

236. Milton, John R., ed. *The Literature of South Dakota.* Vermillion: University of South Dakota Press, 1976.

237. Muller, Marcia, and Bill Pronzini, eds. *She Won the West: An Anthology of Western and Frontier Stories.* New York: Morrow, 1985.

238. Ortego y Gasca, Philip D., ed. *We Are Chicanos: An Anthology of Mexican-American Literature.* New York: Washington Square Press, 1973.

239. Pearce, Thomas M., and A.P. Thomason, eds. *Southwesterners Write.* Albuquerque: University of New Mexico Press, 1947.

240. ———, and Telfair Hendon, eds. *America in the Southwest: A Regional Anthology.* Albuquerque: University of New Mexico Press, 1933.

241. Perry, George Sessions, ed. *Roundup Time: A Collection of South-Western Writing.* New York: Whittlesey House, 1943.

242. Peyer, Bernd C., ed. *The Singing Spirit: Early Short Stories by North American Indians.* Tucson: University of Arizona Press, 1989.

243. Rebolledo, Tey Diana, and Eliana S. Rivero, eds. *Infinite Divisions: An Anthology of Chicana Literature.* Tucson: University of Arizona Press, 1993.

244. Rosen, Kenneth, ed. *The Man to Send Rain Clouds: Contemporary Stories by American Indians.* New York: Penguin, 1992.

245. Shockley, Martin, ed. *Southwest Writers Anthology.* Austin, Tex.: Steck-Vaughn, 1967.

246. Silber, Irwin. *Songs of the Great American West.* New York: Macmillan, 1967.

247. Simmen, Edward, ed. *North of the Rio Grande: The Mexican-American Experience in Short Fiction.* New York: Mentor Books, 1992.

248. Sonnichsen, C. L. *The Southwest in Life and Literature.* New York: Devin-Adair, 1962.

249. ———, comp. and ed. *The Laughing West: Humorous Western Fiction Past and Present: An Anthology.* Athens: Swallow Press and Ohio University Press, 1988.

250. ———, ed. *Texas Humoresque: Lone Star Humorists From Then Till Now: An Anthology.* Fort Worth: Texas Christian University Press, 1990.

251. Soto, Gary, ed. *Pieces of the Heart: New Chicano Fiction.* San Francisco: Chronicle Books, 1993.

252. Sterling, George, et al. *Continent's End.* San Francisco: J. H. Nash, 1925.

253. Stevens, A. Wilbur, ed. *Poems Southwest.* Prescott, Ariz.: Prescott College Press, 1968.

254. Strelow, Michael, et al. *An Anthology of Northwest Writing 1900–1950.* Eugene, Oreg.: Northwest Review Books, 1979.

255. *Tales of the Wild West: An Illustrated Collection of Adventure Stories.* New York: Rizzoli International; Oklahoma City: National Cowboy Hall of Fame, 1993.

256. Targ, William, ed. *Western Story Omnibus.* Cleveland: World, 1945.

257. Tatum, Charles. *New Chicana-Chicano Writing.* Tucson: University of Arizona Press, 1992.

258. Tatum, Stephen. "Literature Out-of-Doors." *American Literary History* 5 (Summer 1993): 294–313. Essay review of James Work's anthology, *Prose and Poetry of the American West* (1990).

259. Taylor, J. Golden, ed. *Great Western Short Stories.* Palo Alto, Calif.: American West, 1967.

260. ———, ed. *The Literature of the American West.* Boston: Houghton Mifflin, 1971.

261. Thomas, James, and Denise Thomas, eds. *Best of the West: New Short Stories From the Wide Side of the Missouri.* Salt Lake City: Peregrine Smith Books, 1988.

262. ———. *The Best of the West 2: New Short Stories From the Wide Side of the Missouri.* Salt Lake City: Peregrine Smith Books, 1989.

263. ———. *The Best of the West 3: New Short Stories From the Wide Side of the Missouri.* Salt Lake City: Peregrine Smith Books, 1990.

264. ———. *The Best of the West 4: New Short Stories From the Wide Side of the Missouri.* New York: W. W. Norton, 1991.

265. ———. *The Best of the West 5: New Stories From the Wide Side of the Missouri.* New York: W. W. Norton, 1992.

266. Thorp, N. Howard ("Jack"). *Songs of the Cowboys.* Eds. Austin E. Fife and Alta S. Fife. New York: Clarkson N. Potter, 1966.

267. Trusky, A. Thomas. *Women Poets of the West: An Anthology, 1850–1950.* Boise, Idaho: Ahsahta Press, 1978.

268. Tuska, Jon, ed. *The American West in Fiction.* New York: New American Library, 1982.

269. Vinz, Mark, and Thom Tammaro, eds. *Inheriting the Land: Contemporary Voices from the Midwest.* Minneapolis: University of Minnesota Press, 1993.

270. Walker, Dale, ed. *The Golden Spurs: The Best of Western Short Fiction.* New York: TOR, 1991.

271. West, Ray B., ed. *The Rocky Mountain Reader.* New York: E. P. Dutton, 1946.

272. *A Western Sampler: Nine Contemporary Poets.* Georgetown, Calif.: Talisman, 1963.

273. Winters, Yvor. *Poets of the Pacific, Second Series.* Stanford, Calif.: Stanford University Press, 1949.

274. Work, James C., ed. *Prose and Poetry of the American West.* Lincoln: University of Nebraska Press, 1990.

GENERAL WORKS: BOOKS AND DISSERTATIONS

275. Ahearn, Kerry D. "Aspects of the Contemporary American Western Novel." Doctoral dissertation, Ohio University, 1974.

276. Ahnebrink, Lars. *The Beginnings of Naturalism in American Fiction: A Study of the Works of Hamlin Garland, Stephen Crane, and Frank Norris.* Cambridge, Mass.: Harvard University Press, 1950.

277. Allen, Martha Mitten. "Women in the West: A Study of Booklength Travel Accounts by Women Who Traveled in the Plains and Rockies, with Special Attention to General Concepts that Women Applied to the Plains, the Mountains, Westerners and the West in General." Doctoral dissertation, University of Texas, Austin, 1972.

278. Alter, Judith. "The Western Myth in American Painting and Fiction of the Late 19th and Early 20th Centuries." Doctoral dissertation, Texas Christian University, 1970.

279. Andrews, Clarence A. *A Literary History of Iowa.* Iowa City: University of Iowa Press, 1972.

280. Athearn, Robert G. *The Mythic West in Twentieth-Century America.* Lawrence: University Press of Kansas, 1986.

281. Backes, Clarus, ed. *Growing Up Western: Recollections.* New York: Knopf, 1990. Autobiographical sketches of seven western writers.

282. Baker, Houston A., Jr., ed. *Three American Literatures: Essays in Chicano, Native American, and Asian-American Literature for Teachers of American Literature.* New York: Modern Language Association, 1982.

283. Balassi, William, John F. Crawford, and Annie O. Eysturoy, eds. *This is About Vision: Interviews with Southwestern Writers.* Albuquerque: University of New Mexico Press, 1990.

284. Barnes, Michael John. "Trends in Texas Theatre History." Doctoral dissertation, University of Texas, 1993.

285. Barnett, Louise K. *The Ignoble Savage: American Literary Racism, 1790–1890.* Westport, Conn.: Greenwood Press, 1975.

286. Barsness, John A. "The Breaking of the Myth: A Study of the Cultural Implications in the Western Novel in the Twentieth Century." Doctoral dissertation, University of Minnesota, 1966.

287. Bartlett, Lee. *The Sun Is But A Morning Star: Studies in West Coast Poetry and Poetics.* Albuquerque: University of New Mexico Press, 1989.

288. Bevis, William W. *Ten Tough Trips: Montana Writers and the West.* Seattle: University of Washington Press, 1990.

289. Billington, Ray Allen. *Land of Savagery/Land of Promise: The European Image of the American Frontier in the Nineteenth Century.* New York: W. W. Norton, 1981.

290. Bingham, Edwin R., and Glen A. Love, eds. *Northwest Perspectives: Essays on the Culture of the Pacific Northwest.* Seattle: University of Washington Press, 1979.

291. Blaine, Harold A. "The Frontiersman in American Prose and Fiction, 1800–1860." Doctoral dissertation, Western Reserve University, 1936.

292. Blair, Walter, and Franklin J. Meine. *Half Horse, Half Alligator: The Growth of the Mike Fink Legend.* Chicago: University of Chicago Press, 1956.

293. Blatt, Muriel Rosen. "Making California American: Poetry and Culture, 1866–1925." Doctoral dissertation, University of California, Irvine, 1977.

294. Blevins, Winfred. *Dictionary of the American West.* New York: Facts on File, 1993.

295. Boatright, Mody C. *Folk Laughter on the American Frontier.* New York: Collier Books, 1961.

296. Bogard, William J. "The West as Cultural Image at the End of the Nineteenth Century." Doctoral dissertation, Tulane University, 1970.

297. Bold, Christine. *Selling the Wild West: Popular Western Fiction, 1860 to 1960.* Bloomington: Indiana University Press, 1987.

298. Boynton, Percy H. *The Rediscovery of the Frontier.* Chicago: University of Chicago Press, 1931.

299. Branch, E. Douglas. *The Cowboy and His Interpreters.* New York: D. Appleton, 1926; New York: Cooper Square, 1961.

300. Bredahl, A. Carl, Jr. *New Ground: Western American Narrative and the Literary Canon.* Chapel Hill: University of North Carolina Press, 1989.

301. Brenner, Gerald J. "The New Western: Studies in Modern Western American Literature." Doctoral dissertation, University of New Mexico, 1969.

302. Brown, Sharon Rogers. "American Travel Narratives as a Literary Genre from 1542–1832: The Art of Perpetual Journey." Doctoral dissertation, State University of New York, Stony Brook, 1990.

303. Bucco, Martin. *Western American Literary Criticism*. Western Writers Series, No. 62. Boise, Idaho: Boise State University, 1984.

304. Butler, Michael D. "The Literary Landscape of the Trans-Mississippi West: 1826–1902." Doctoral dissertation, University of Illinois, 1971.

305. Calder, Jenni. *There Must Be a Lone Ranger: The American West in Film and in Reality*. New York: Taplinger, 1974.

306. Campbell, Walter S. *The Book Lover's Southwest*. Norman: University of Oklahoma Press, 1955.

307. Castanier, Chris. "'Roadworks': The Open Frontier in American Literature of Travel." Doctoral dissertation, Wayne State University, 1992.

308. Chittick, V. L. O., ed. *Northwest Harvest: A Regional Stocktaking*. New York: Macmillan, 1948.

309. Clevenger, Darnell Haines. "A Comparative Study of the Frontier in the Literatures of Spanish America and the United States." Doctoral dissertation, Indiana University, 1974.

310. Clifford, Craig, and Tom Pilkington, eds. *Range Wars: Heated Debates, Sober Reflections, and Other Assessments of Texas Writing*. Dallas: Southern Methodist University Press, 1989.

311. Clifford, John. "Social and Political Attitudes of Fiction of Ranch and Range." Doctoral dissertation, University of Iowa, 1954.

312. Clough, Wilson O. *The Necessary Earth: Nature and Solitude in American Literature*. Austin: University of Texas Press, 1964.

313. Collins, James L., ed. *The Western Writer's Handbook*. Boulder, Colo.: Johnson Books, 1987.

314. Collins, Mark Leonard. "Wolfish Festivity: The Humor of American Frontier Literature." Doctoral dissertation, University of Illinois, Urbana-Champaign, 1987.

315. Colquitt, Betsy F. *A Part of Space: Ten Texas Writers*. Fort Worth: Texas Christian University Press, 1969.

316. Conder, John J. *Naturalism in American Fiction: The Classic Phase*. Lexington: University Press of Kentucky, 1984.

317. Crow, Charles L., ed. *Itinerary: Criticism, Essays on California Writers*. Bowling Green, Ohio: University Press, 1978.

318. Crowley, Frank Edward. "The American Dream as Cultural Archetype: The Myth of the West as a Twentieth-Century Literary Phenomenon." Doctoral dissertation, State University of New York, Buffalo, 1978.

319. Davis, Robert Murrray. *Playing Cowboys: Low Culture and High Art in the Western.* Norman: University of Oklahoma Press, 1992.

320. DeMenil, Alexander Nicholas. *The Literature of the Louisiana Territory.* St. Louis: St. Lewis News, 1904.

321. Dobie, J. Frank. *Guide to Life and Literature of the Southwest.* Dallas: Southern Methodist University Press, 1943, 1952.

322. Dondore, Dorothy. *The Prairie and the Making of Middle America.* Cedar Rapids, Iowa: Torch Press, 1926.

323. Durham, Philip, and Everett L. Jones. *The Negro Cowboys.* New York: Dodd, Mead, 1965.

324. Emmons, David M. *Garden in the Grasslands: Boomer Literature of the Central Great Plains.* Lincoln: University of Nebraska Press, 1971.

325. Erben, Rudolf. "Western American Drama and the Myth of the Changing West, 1890–1990." Doctoral dissertation, University of New Mexico, 1990.

326. Erisman, Fred, and Richard W. Etulain, eds. *Fifty Western Writers: A Bio-Bibliographical Sourcebook.* Westport, Conn.: Greenwood Press, 1982.

327. Etulain, Richard W., ed. *The American Literary West.* Manhattan, Kans.: Sunflower University Press, 1980. Reprints *Journal of the West,* January 1980.

328. ———, ed. *Writing Western History: Essays on Major Western Historians.* Albuquerque: University of New Mexico Press, 1991.

329. Evans, James Leroy. "The Indian Savage, the Mexican Bandit, the Chinese Heathen — Three Popular Stereotypes." Doctoral dissertation, University of Texas, 1967.

330. Everson, William. *Archetype West: The Pacific Coast as a Literary Region.* Berkeley, Calif.: Oyez, 1976.

331. Farah, Cynthia. *Literature and Landscape: Writers of the Southwest.* El Paso: Texas Western Press, 1988.

332. Faulkner, Virginia, ed., with Frederick C. Luebke. *Vision and Refuge: Essays on the Literature of the Great Plains.* Lincoln: University of Nebraska Press, 1982.

333. Fender, Stephen. *Plotting the Golden West.* New York: Cambridge University Press, 1981.

334. Ferlinghetti, Lawrence, and Nancy J. Peters. *Literary San Francisco: A Pictorial History from the Beginnings to the Present Day.* San Francisco: City Lights Books and Harper and Row, 1980.

335. Fiedler, Leslie. *The Return of the Vanishing American.* New York: Stein and Day, 1968.

336. Fielding, Lavina. "Attitudes Toward Experience in Western Travel Narratives." Doctoral dissertation, University of Washington, 1975.

337. Fine, David, ed. *Los Angeles in Fiction: A Collection of Original Essays.* Albuquerque: University of New Mexico Press, 1984.

338. Fitzmaurice, James Earl. "Migration Epics of the Trans-Mississippi West." Doctoral dissertation, University of Maryland, 1974.

339. Fleck, Byron Y. "The West as Viewed by Foreign Travelers, 1783–1840." Doctoral dissertation, University of Iowa, 1950.

340. Folsom, James K. *The American Western Novel.* New Haven, Conn.: College and University Press, 1966.

341. ———, ed. *The Western: A Collection of Critical Essays.* Englewood Cliffs, N.J.: Prentice-Hall, 1979.

342. Franklin, Wayne. *Discoverers, Explorers, Settlers: The Diligent Writers of Early America.* Chicago: University of Chicago Press, 1979.

343. Frantz, Joe B., and Julian E. Choate, Jr. *The American Cowboy: The Myth and the Reality.* Norman: University of Oklahoma Press, 1955.

344. Fussell, Edwin. *Frontier: American Literature and the American West.* Princeton, N.J.: Princeton University Press, 1965.

345. Gaston, Edwin W., Jr. *The Early Novel of the Southwest.* Albuquerque: University of New Mexico Press, 1961.

346. Goetzmann, William H., and William N. Goetzmann. *The West of the Imagination.* New York: Norton, 1986.

347. Gottfried, Herbert Wilson. "Spatiality and the Frontier: Spatial Themes in Western American Painting and Literature." Doctoral dissertation, Ohio University, 1974.

348. Graham, Don, James W. Lee, and William T. Pilkington, eds. *The Texas Literary Tradition: Fiction, Folklore, History.* Austin: University of Texas and the Texas State Historical Association, 1983.

349. "Great Historians of the Great Plains: Special Theme Issue." *Heritage of the Great Plains* 22 (Fall 1989).

350. Green, Martin. *The Great American Adventure.* Boston: Beacon Press, 1984.

351. Gregory, James N. *American Exodus: The Dust Bowl Migration and Okie Culture in California.* New York: Oxford University Press, 1989.

352. Gurian, Jay. *Western American Writing: Tradition and Promise.* Deland, Fla.: Everett/Edwards, 1975.

353. Gustafson, Antoinette McCloskey. "The Image of the West in American Popular Performance." Doctoral dissertation, New York University, 1988.

354. Hafer, John William. "The Sea of Grass: The Image of the Great Plains in the American Novel." Doctoral dissertation, Northern Illinois University, 1975.

355. Hairston, Joel Beck. "Westerner's Dilemma: A Study of Modern Western Fiction." Doctoral dissertation, University of Minnesota, 1971.

356. Hamilton, Ian. *Writers in Hollywood, 1915–1951.* New York: Harper and Row, 1990.

357. Hardwick, Bonnie Skell. "Science and Art: The Travel Writings of the Great Surveys of the American West after the Civil War." Doctoral dissertation, University of Pennsylvania, 1977.

358. Harriott, Esther. *American Voices: Five Contemporary Playwrights in Essays and Interviews.* Jefferson, N.C.: McFarland, 1988.

359. Hart, James D. *A Companion to California.* Rev and exp. Berkeley: University of California Press, 1987.

360. Haslam, Gerald, ed. *Western Writing.* Albuquerque: University of New Mexico Press, 1974.

361. Hazard, Lucy Lockwood. *The Frontier in American Literature.* New York: Thomas Y. Crowell, 1927; New York: Ungar, 1961.

362. Hazel, Erik R. "The Hollywood Image: An Examination of the Literary Perspective." Doctoral dissertation, Case Western Reserve University, 1974.

363. Herron, Ima Honaker. *The Small Town in American Literature.* Durham, N.C.: Duke University Press, 1939.

364. Heyne, Eric, ed. *Desert, Garden, Margin, Range: Literature on the American Frontier.* New York: Twayne, 1992.

365. Hilfer, Anthony Channell. *The Revolt from the Village, 1915–1930.* Chapel Hill: University of North Carolina Press, 1969.

366. Hodgins, Francis E., Jr. "The Literary Emancipation of a Region: The Changing Image of the American West in Fiction." Doctoral dissertation, Michigan State University, 1957.

367. Howard, Richard. *Alone with America: Essays on the Art of Poetry in the United States.* New York: Atheneum, 1969.

368. Hubbell, Jay B. *South and Southwest: Literary Essays and Reminiscences.* Durham, N.C.: Duke University Press, 1965.

369. Hudson, Ruth, et al. *Studies in Literature of the West: University of Wyoming Publications*. Laramie: University of Wyoming, 1956.

370. Hume, Kathryn. *Fantasy and Mimesis: Response to Reality in Western Literature*. New York: Methuen, 1984.

371. Hurst, Mary Jane. *The Voice of the Child in American Literature: Linguistic Approaches to Fictional Child Language*. Lexington: University Press of Kentucky, 1990.

372. Huseboe, Arthur R., and William Geyer, eds. *Where the West Begins: Essays on the Middle Border and Siouxland Writing, in Honor of Herbert Krause*. Sioux Falls, S. Dak.: Center for Western Studies Press, 1978.

373. Hyde, Stuart Wallace. "The Representation of the West in American Drama from 1849–1917." Doctoral dissertation, Stanford University, 1954.

374. *Interpretive Approaches to Western American Literature*. Pocatello: Idaho State University Press, 1972. Reprints *Rendezvous* 7 (Winter 1972).

375. Jacobs, Elijah L., and Forrest E. Wolverton. *Missouri Writers: A Literary History of Missouri, 1780–1955*. St. Louis: State Publishing, 1955.

376. Johannsen, Albert. *The House of Beadle and Adams and Its Dime and Nickel Novels*. 2 vols. Norman: University of Oklahoma Press, 1950; supplement, 1962.

377. Jones, Howard Mumford. *The Frontier in American Fiction: Four Lectures on the Relation of Landscape to Literature*. Jerusalem: Magness Press, Hebrew University, 1956.

378. Jones, Joel M. "Everyman's Usable Past: The American Historical Novel." Doctoral dissertation, University of New Mexico, 1966.

379. Karolides, Nicholas J. *The Pioneer in the American Novel: 1900–1950*. Norman: University of Oklahoma Press, 1967.

380. Kawaharada, Dennis. "The Rhetoric of Identity in Japanese American Writings, 1948–1988." Doctoral dissertation, University of Washington, 1988.

381. Kay, Arthur M. "The Epic Intent and the American Dream: The Westering Theme in Modern American Poetry." Doctoral dissertation, Columbia University, 1961.

382. Keiser, Albert. *The Indian in American Literature*. New York: Oxford University Press, 1933.

383. Kim, Elaine H. *Asian American Literature, An Introduction to the Writings and Their Social Context*. Philadelphia: Temple University Press, 1982.

384. Koon, Helene Wickham. *How Shakespeare Won the West: Players and Performances in America's Gold Rush, 1849–1865.* Jefferson, N.C.: McFarland, 1989.

385. Krupat, Arnold. *Ethnocriticism: Ethnography, History, Literature.* Berkeley: University of California Press, 1992.

386. Lai, Him Mark, Genny Lim, and Judy Yung. *Island: Poetry and History of Chinese Immigrants on Angel Island, 1910–1940.* San Francisco, Calif.: HOC-DOI Project, 1980.

387. Lamar, Howard R., ed. *The Reader's Encyclopedia of the American West.* New York: Thomas Y. Crowell, 1977.

388. Lawlor, Mary. "Fin de siècle Representations: Naturalism and the American West." Doctoral dissertation, New York University, 1989.

389. Leach, Joseph. *The Typical Texan: Biography of an American Myth.* Dallas: Southern Methodist University Press, 1952.

390. Lee, Lawrence L., and Merrill E. Lewis, eds. *Women, Women Writers, and the West.* Troy, N.Y.: Whitston, 1978.

391. Lee, Robert Edson. *From West to East: Studies in the Literature of the American West.* Urbana: University of Illinois Press, 1966.

392. Lewis, Merrill E. "American Frontier History as Literature: Studies in Historiography of George Bancroft, Frederick Jackson Turner, and Theodore Roosevelt." Doctoral dissertation, University of Utah, 1968.

393. ———, and L. L. Lee, eds. *The Westering Experience in American Literature: Bicentennial Essays.* Bellingham: Bureau for Faculty Research, Western Washington University, 1977.

394. Limerick, Patricia Nelson. *Legacy of Conquest: The Unbroken Past of the American West.* New York: Norton, 1987.

395. ———, Clyde A. Milner, II, and Charles E. Rankin, eds. *Trails: Toward a New Western History.* Lawrence: University Press of Kansas, 1991.

396. Lin, Mao-Chu. "Identity and Chinese-American Experience: A Study of Chinatown American Literature Since World War II." Doctoral dissertation, University of Minnesota, 1987.

397. Love, Glen A. *New Americans: The Westerner and the Modern Experience in the American Novel.* Lewisburg, Penn.: Bucknell University, 1981.

398. Lutwack, Leonard. *The Role of Place in Literature.* Syracuse: Syracuse University Press, 1984.

399. McKelly, James Crisley. "True Wests: Twentieth Century Portraits of the Artist as a Young American." Doctoral dissertation, Indiana University, 1990.

400. McMurtry, Larry. *In a Narrow Grave: Essays on Texas.* Austin, Tex.: Encino Press, 1968.

401. Mahon, Robert Lee. "The Use of Adam and Eve as Conventions in the American Western Novel of the Twentieth Century." Doctoral dissertation, University of Notre Dame, 1975.

402. Marovitz, Sanford E. "Frontier Conflicts, Villains, Outlaws, and Indians in Selected Western Fiction, 1799–1860." Doctoral dissertation, Duke University, 1968.

403. Meldrum, Barbara Howard, ed. *Old West–New West: Centennial Essays.* Moscow: University of Idaho Press, 1993.

404. ———, ed. *Under The Sun: Myth and Realism in Western American Literature.* Troy, N.Y.: Whitston, 1985.

405. Meyer, Roy W. *The Middle Western Farm Novel in the Twentieth Century.* Lincoln: University of Nebraska Press, 1965.

406. Miles, Elton. *Southwestern Humorists.* Southwest Writers Series, No. 26. Austin, Tex.: Steck-Vaughn, 1969.

407. Milner, Clyde A., Carol A. O'Connor, and Martha A. Sandweiss, eds. *The Oxford History of the American West.* New York: Oxford University Press, 1994.

408. Milton, John R. *The Novel of the American West.* Lincoln: University of Nebraska Press, 1980.

409. Mitchell, Lee Clark. *Witness to a Vanishing America: The Nineteenth-Century Response.* Princeton, N.J.: Princeton University Press, 1981.

410. Mogen, David Lee. *Frontier Themes in Science Fiction.* Boulder: University of Colorado, 1977.

411. ———, ed. *Wilderness Visions: The Western Theme in Science Fiction,* 2d ed. San Bernardino, Calif.: Borgo Press, 1990.

412. ———, Mark Busby, and Paul Bryant, eds. *The Frontier Experience and the American Dream: Essays on American Literature.* College Station: Texas A & M University Press, 1989.

413. ———, Scott P. Sanders, and Joanne B. Karpinski, eds. *Frontier Gothic: Terror and Wonder at the Frontier in American Literature.* Rutherford, N.J.: Fairleigh Dickinson University Press, 1993.

414. Morgan, H. Wayne. *American Writers in Rebellion from Twain to Dreiser.* New York: Hill and Wang, 1965.

415. Morris, Wright. *The Territory Ahead.* New York: Harcourt, Brace and World, 1958.

416. Morrow, Patrick D. *The Popular and the Serious in Select Twentieth-Century American Novels.* Lewiston, N.Y.: E. Mellen, 1992.

417. Mossberg, Christer Lennart. "The Emigrant Voice as American Literature: Scandinavian Emigrant Fiction of the American West." Doctoral dissertation, Indiana University, 1979.

418. ———. *Scandinavian Immigrant Literature.* Western Writers Series, No. 47. Boise, Idaho: Boise State University, 1981.

419. Nash, Gerald D. *Creating the West: Historical Interpretations, 1890–1990.* Albuquerque: University of New Mexico Press, 1991.

420. Nelson, Barney. *Voices and Visions of the American West.* Austin: Texas Monthly Press, 1986.

421. Nelson, Herbert B. *The Literary Impulse in Pioneer Oregon.* Corvallis: Oregon State College Press, 1948.

422. Nelson, Solveig Leraas. "Mountain Man: Fact and Fiction." Doctoral dissertation, Duke University, 1978.

423. Noble, David W. *The Eternal Adam and the New World Garden: The Central Myth in the American Novel Since 1830.* New York: George Brazillier, 1968.

424. Noel, Mary. *Villains Galore...the Heyday of the Popular Story Weekly.* New York: Macmillan, 1954.

425. O'Connell, Nicholas. *At the Field's End: Interviews with Twenty Pacific Northwest Writers.* Seattle: Madrona Publishers, 1987.

426. Ogden, Dunbar H., Douglas McDermott, and Robert K. Sarlós. *Theatre West: Image and Impact.* Amsterdam: Rodopi, 1990.

427. Padget, Martin. "Cultural Geographies: Travel Writing in the Southwest, 1869–1897." Doctoral dissertation, University of California, San Diego, 1993.

428. Payne, Leonidas W. *A Survey of Texas Literature.* New York: Rand McNally, 1928.

429. Pearce, Roy Harvey. *The Savages of America: A Study of the Indian and the Idea of Civilization.* Baltimore: The Johns Hopkins Press, 1953.

430. Peng Bisiar, Nan. "Beyond Virtue and Vice: The Literary Self in Chinese-American Literature." Doctoral dissertation, Bowling Green State University, 1990.

431. Peterson, Levi. "The Ambivalence of Alienation: The Debate Over Frontier Freedom in the Quality Western Novel of the Twentieth Century." Doctoral dissertation, University of Utah, 1965.

432. Pilkington, William T. *Imagining Texas: The Literature of the Lone Star State.* Boston: American Press, 1981.

433. ———. *My Country's Blood: Studies in Southwestern Literature.* Fort Worth: Texas Christian University Press, 1973.

434. ———, ed. *Critical Essays on the Western American Novel.* Boston: G. K. Hall, 1980.

435. Pizer, Donald. *Realism and Naturalism in Nineteenth-Century American Literature.* Rev ed. Carbondale: Southern Illinois University Press, 1984.

436. Potter, Richard Harold. "Rural Life in Populist America: A Study of Short Fiction as Historical Evidence." Doctoral dissertation, University of Maryland, 1971.

437. Poulsen, Richard Carl. *The Landscape of the Mind: Cultural Transformations of the American West.* New York: Peter Lang, 1992.

438. ———. "The Mountainman Vernacular: Its Historical Roots, Its Linguistic Nature, and Its Literary Uses." Doctoral dissertation, University of Utah, 1976.

439. Powell, Lawrence Clark. *California Classics: The Creative Literature of the Golden State.* Los Angeles: Ward Ritchie Press, 1971.

440. ———. *Southwest Classics: The Creative Literature of the Arid Lands: Essays on the Books and Their Writers.* Los Angeles: Ward Ritchie Press, 1974.

441. Powers, Alfred. *History of Oregon Literature.* Portland: Metropolitan Press, 1935.

442. Prassel, Frank Richard. *The Great American Outlaw: A Legacy of Fact and Fiction.* Norman: University of Oklahoma Press, 1993.

443. *Prose and Poetry of the Livestock Industry of the United States.* Denver: National Live Stock Historical Association, 1905.

444. Pugh, David William. "A Study in Literary, Social, and University History: The Life and Often Hard Times of the *New Mexico Quarterly,* 1931–1969." Doctoral dissertation, University of New Mexico, 1975.

445. Reddin, Paul Laverne. "Wild West Shows: A Study in the Development of Western Romanticism." Doctoral dissertation, University of Missouri, Columbia, 1970.

446. Reeve, Kay Aiken. "The Making of An American Place: The Development of Santa Fe and Taos, New Mexico, As An American Cultural Center, 1898–1942." Doctoral dissertation, Texas A & M University, 1977.

447. ———. *Santa Fe and Taos, 1898–1942: An American Cultural Center.* El Paso: Texas Western Press, 1982.

448. Robinson, Cecil. *Mexico and the Hispanic Southwest in American Literature.* Tucson: University of Arizona Press, 1977. Revised and enlarged edition of *With the Ears of Strangers,* 1963.

449. ———. *No Short Journeys: The Interplay of Cultures in the History and Literature of the Borderlands.* Tucson: University of Arizona Press, 1992.

450. Rodgers, John William. *Finding Literature on the Texas Plains.* Dallas: Southwest Press, 1931.

451. Rolfe, Lionel. *Literary L. A.* San Francisco: Chronicle Books, 1981.

452. Rosenberg, Bruce A. *The Code of the West.* Bloomington: Indiana University Press, 1982.

453. Ruoff, A. LaVonne Brown, and Jerry W. Ward, Jr., eds. *Redefining American Literary History.* New York: Modern Language Association of America, 1990.

454. Rusk, Ralph Leslie. *The Literature of the Middle Western Frontier.* 2 vols. New York: Columbia University Press, 1925.

455. Russell, Sharman Apt. *Kill the Cowboy: A Battle of Mythology in the New West.* Reading, Mass.: Addison-Wesley, 1993.

456. Saciuk, Olena H. "A Comparative Study of the Cowboy, Gaucho, and Kozak as Protagonists in Selected Novels." Doctoral dissertation, University of Illinois, Urbana-Champaign, 1973.

457. Savage, William W., Jr. *The Cowboy Hero: His Image in American History and Culture.* Norman: University of Oklahoma Press, 1979. The best study of the subject.

458. Scheckel, Susan Elizabeth. "Shifting Boundaries: The Poetics and Politics of the American Frontier, 1820–1850." Doctoral dissertation, University of California, Berkeley, 1992.

459. Schmitt, Peter J. *Back to Nature: The Arcadian Myth in Urban America.* New York: Oxford University Press, 1969.

460. See, Carolyn P. "The Hollywood Novel: An Historical and Critical Study." Doctoral dissertation, University of California, Los Angeles, 1963.

461. Seelye, John., ed. *Stories of the Old West: Tales of the Mining Camp, Cavalry Troop, & Cattle Ranch.* New York: Penguin, 1994.

462. Seller, Maxine Schwartz, ed. *Ethnic Theatre in the United States.* Westport, Conn.: Greenwood Press, 1983.

463. Silver, Marilyn Brick. "The Farmer in American Literature, 1608–1864." Doctoral dissertation, Ohio State University, 1976.

464. Simonson, Harold P. *Beyond the Frontier: Writers, Western Regionalism, and a Sense of Place.* Fort Worth: Texas Christian University Press, 1989.

465. ———. *The Closed Frontier: Studies in American Literary Tragedy.* New York: Holt, Rinehart and Winston, 1970.

466. Skårdal, Dorothy Burton. *The Divided Heart: Scandinavian Immigrant Experience Through Literary Sources.* Lincoln: University of Nebraska Press, 1974. Contains extensive bibliography.

467. Slotkin, Richard. *The Fatal Environment: The Myth of the Frontier in the Age of Industrialism, 1800–1890.* New York: Atheneum, 1985.

468. ———. *Gunfighter Nation: The Myth of the Frontier in Twentieth-Century America.* New York: Atheneum, 1992.

469. ———. *Regeneration Through Violence: The Myth of the American Frontier, 1600–1860.* Middletown, Conn.: Wesleyan University Press, 1973.

470. Smith, Caroline. "The Literary Image of Daniel Boone: A Changing Heroic Ideal in Nineteenth- and Twentieth-Century Popular Literature." Doctoral dissertation, University of Utah, 1974.

471. Smith, Henry Nash. *Virgin Land: The American West as Symbol and Myth.* Cambridge: Harvard University Press, 1950, 1970. A classic study.

472. Smith, Richard Cándida. "Margins of the Modern: Aesthetics and Subjectivity in California Art and Poetry Movements, 1925–1975." Doctoral dissertation, University of California, Los Angeles, 1992.

473. Sonnichsen, C. L. *Cowboys and Cattle Kings.* Norman: University of Oklahoma Press, 1950.

474. ———. *From Hopalong to Hud: Thoughts on Western Fiction.* College Station: Texas A & M University Press, 1978.

475. "Special Theme Issue: Great Historians of the Great Plains, II." *Heritage of the Great Plains* 23 (Winter 1990): 2–49.

476. Sper, Felix. *Native Roots: A Panorama of Our Regional Drama.* Caldwell, Idaho: Caxton, 1948.

477. Spotts, Carl B. "The Development of Fiction on the Missouri Frontier (1830–1860)." Doctoral dissertation, Pennsylvania State University, 1934.

478. Stafford, William. *Writing the Australian Crawl: Views on the Writer's Vocation.* Ann Arbor: University of Michigan Press, 1978.

479. Starr, Kevin. *Americans and the California Dream: 1850–1915.* New York: Oxford University Press, 1973.

480. ———. *Inventing the Dream: California Through the Progressive Era.* New York: Oxford University Press, 1985.

481. ———. *Material Dreams: Southern California Through the 1920s.* New York: Oxford University Press, 1990.

482. Stauffer, Helen Winter, and Susan J. Rosowski, eds. *Women and Western American Literature.* Troy, N.Y.: Whitston, 1982.

483. Stearns, Peter N. *Meaning Over Memory: Recasting the Teaching of Culture and History.* Chapel Hill: University of North Carolina Press, 1993.

484. Stegner, Wallace. *The American West as Living Space.* Ann Arbor: University of Michigan Press, 1987.

485. ———. *The Sound of Mountain Water.* Garden City, N.Y.: Doubleday, 1969.

486. ———. *Where the Bluebird Sings to the Lemonade Springs.* New York: Random House, 1992.

487. Stein, Rita. *A Literary Tour Guide to the United States: West and Midwest.* New York: William Morrow, 1979.

488. Stuhr, Margaret D. "The Middle West and the American Imagination, 1890–1940." Doctoral dissertation, Northwestern University, 1983.

489. Sullivan, Leslie Noelle. "On the Western Stage: Theatre in Montana, 1880–1920." Master's thesis, University of New Mexico, 1990.

490. Sullivan, Tom R. *Cowboys and Caudillos: Frontier Ideology of the Americas.* Bowling Green, Ohio: Bowling Green State University Popular Press, 1990.

491. Taft, Robert. *Artists and Illustrators of the Old West.* New York: Charles Scribner's Sons, 1953.

492. Tatum, Stephen. *Inventing Billy the Kid: Visions of the Outlaw in America, 1881–1981.* Albuquerque: University of New Mexico Press, 1982.

493. Taylor, J. Golden, and Thomas J. Lyon, et al., eds., *A Literary History of the American West.* Fort Worth: Texas Christian University Press, 1987.

494. Tebbel, John. *Fact and Fiction Problems of the Historical Novelist.* Lansing: Historical Society of Michigan, 1962.

495. Temple, Judy Nolte, ed. *Open Spaces, Open Places: Contemporary Writers on a Changing Southwest.* Tuscon: University of Arizona Press, 1994.

496. Thacker, Robert. *The Great Prairie Fact and Literary Imagination.* Albuquerque: University of New Mexico Press, 1989.

497. Tinker, Edward Larocque. *The Horsemen of the Americas and the Literature They Inspired.* Austin: University of Texas Press, 1967.

498. Todd, Edgeley W. "Literary Interest in the Fur Trade and Fur Trappers of the Trans-Mississippi West." Doctoral dissertation, Northwestern University, 1952.

499. Tooker, Dan, and Roger Hofheins. *Fiction: Interviews with Northern California Novelists.* New York: Harcourt Brace Jovanovich, 1976. Interviews with Stegner, J. West, Janet Lewis, and others.

500. Tuska, Jon, Vicki Piekarski, and Paul J. Blanding, eds. *The Frontier Experience: A Reader's Guide to the Life and Literature of the American West.* Jefferson, N.C.: McFarland, 1984.

501. Venable, William H. *Beginnings of Literary Culture in the Ohio Valley.* Cincinnati: Robert Clarke, 1891.

502. Von Frank, Albert James. "Frontier Consciousness in American Literature." Doctoral dissertation, University of Missouri, 1976.

503. ———. *The Sacred Game: Provincialism and Frontier Consciousness in American Literature, 1630–1860.* New York: Cambridge University Press, 1985.

504. Vorda, Allan. *A Conscientious Recorder: Interviews with Contemporary Novelists.* Houston: Rice University Press, 1993. Includes interviews with several western writers.

505. Walker, Dale L. *Mavericks: Ten Uncorralled Westerners.* Phoenix: Golden West Publishers, 1989.

506. Walker, Don D. *The Adventures of Barney Tullus.* Albuquerque: University of New Mexico Press, 1988. Humorous commentary on, and fiction about western literature.

507. ———. *Clio's Cowboys: Studies in the Historiography of the Cattle Trade.* Lincoln: University of Nebraska Press, 1981.

508. Walker, Franklin. *A Literary History of Southern California.* Berkeley: University of California Press, 1950.

509. ———. *San Francisco's Literary Frontier.* New York: Knopf, 1939; Seattle: University of Washington Press, 1969.

510. ———. *The Seacoast of Bohemia.* Santa Barbara, Calif.: Peregrine Smith, 1973. Supplements Book Club of California edition in 1966.

511. Watkins, Eric. "The Mississipi River as Image and Symbol in American Literature, 1820–1936." Doctoral dissertation, University of Minnesota, 1972.

512. Weber, Harley R. "Midwestern Farm Writing in the Late Nineteenth Century: A Study in Changing Attitudes." Doctoral dissertation, University of Minnesota, 1968.

513. Weigle, Marta, and Kyle Fiore. *Santa Fe and Taos: The Writer's Era, 1916–1941.* Santa Fe: Ancient City Press, 1982.

514. "Western Literary History." *Pacific Historical Review* 45 (August 1976): 311–432. Special issue.

515. White, G. Edward. *The Eastern Establishment and the Western Experience: The West of Frederic Remington, Theodore Roosevelt, and Owen Wister.* New Haven: Yale University Press, 1968.

516. White, Richard. *"It's Your Misfortune and None of My Own": A History of the American West.* Norman: University of Oklahoma Press, 1991.

517. Wilson, Edmund. *The Boys in the Backroom: Notes on California Novelists.* San Francisco: Ridgeway Books, 1941.

518. Winston, Robert Paul. "From Farmer James to Natty Bumppo: The Frontier and the Early American Romance." Doctoral dissertation, University of Wisconsin, Madison, 1979.

519. Wolfe, Hilton John. "Alaskan Literature: The Fiction of America's Last Wilderness." Doctoral dissertation, Michigan State University, 1973.

520. Wrobel, David M. *The End of American Exceptionalism: Frontier Anxiety from the Old West to the New Deal.* Lawrence: University Press of Kansas, 1993.

521. Wu, William F. "The Yellow Peril: Chinese-Americans in American Fiction, 1850–1940." Doctoral dissertation, University of Michigan, 1979.

GENERAL WORKS: ARTICLES

522. Adams, Andy. "Western Interpreters." *Southwest Review* 10 (October 1924): 70–74.

523. Altrocchi, J.C. "California Biography in Poetry." *Pacific Historian* 15 (Winter 1971): 1–12.

524. Anderson, John Q. "Scholarship in Southwestern Humor: Past and Present." *Mississippi Quarterly* 17 (1964): 67–86.

525. Arrington, Leonard, and Jon Haupt. "Community and Isolation: Some Aspects of 'Mormon Westerns.'" *Western American Literature* 8 (Spring–Summer 1973): 15–31.

526. ———. "Intolerable Zion: The Image of Mormonism in Nineteenth Century American Literature." *Western Humanities Review* 22 (Summer 1968): 243–60.

527. Ashliman, D. L. "The American West in Twentieth-Century Germany." *Journal of Popular Culture* 2 (Summer 1968): 81–92.

528. ———. "The Novel of Western Adventure in Nineteenth-Century Germany." *Western American Literature* 3 (Summer 1968): 133–45.

529. Athearn, Robert. "The American West: An Enduring Mirage?" *Colorado Quarterly* 26 (Autumn 1977): 3–16.

530. ———. "The Ephemeral West." *Colorado Quarterly* 28 (Autumn 1979): 5–13.

531. Atherton, L. E. "The Midwestern Country Town–Myth and Reality." *Agricultural History* 26 (July 1952): 73–80.

532. Attebery, Louis. "The American West and the Archetypal Orphan." *Western American Literature* 5 (Fall 1970): 205–17.

533. Autor, Hans. "Alaskan Poetry." *Alaska Review* 1 (Spring 1964): 48–55.

534. Banks, Loy Otis. "The Credible Literary West." *Colorado Quarterly* 8 (Summer 1959): 28–50.

535. Baritz, Loren. "The Idea of the West." *American Historical Review* 66 (April 1961): 618–40.

536. Barnes, Robert. "Novels of the Oil Industry in the Southwest." *Southwestern American Literature* 2 (Fall 1972): 74–82.

537. Barsness, John. "Creativity Through Hatred–and a Few Thoughts on the Western Novel." *Western Review* 6 (Winter 1969): 12–17.

538. Bashford, Herbert. "The Literary Development of the Pacific Coast." *Atlantic Monthly* 92 (July 1903): 1–9.

539. Baurecht, William C. "Romantic Male Deviance: Myth of Freedom in the West." *Southwest Images and Trends.* Eds. Suzanne M. Owings and Helen M. Bannan. Las Cruces: New Mexico State University, 1979, 160–70.

540. Billington, Ray A. "The Plains and Deserts through European Eyes." *Western Historical Quarterly* 10 (October 1979): 467–87. European literature about the American West.

541. Bingham, Edwin R. "American Wests Through Autobiography and Memoir." *Pacific Historical Review* 56 (February 1987): 1–24.

542. Boag, Peter G. "Overlanders and the Snake River Region: A Case Study of Popular Landscape Perception in the Early West." *Pacific Northwest Quarterly* 84 (October 1993): 122–29.

543. Boatright, Mody C. "The American Myth Rides the Range." *Southwest Review* 36 (Summer 1951): 157–63.

544. ———. "The Beginnings of Cowboy Fiction." *Southwest Review* 51 (Winter 1966): 11–28.

545. ———. "The Formula in Cowboy Fiction and Drama." *Western Folklore* 28 (April 1969): 136–45.

546. ———. "Literature in the Southwest." *Sul Ross State College Bulletin* (June 1, 1953): 1–32.

547. ———. "The Myth of Frontier Individualism." *Southwestern Social Science Quarterly* 22 (June 1941): 14–32.

548. Bold, Christine. "How the Western Ends: Fenimore Cooper to Frederic Remington." *Western American Literature* 17 (Summer 1982): 117–35.

549. Bracher, Frederick. "California's Literary Regionalism." *American Quarterly* 7 (Fall 1955): 275–84.

550. Brashear, Minnie M. "Missouri Literature Since the First World War: Part III– The Novel." *Missouri Historical Review* 41 (April 1947): 241–65.

551. Bredahl, A. Carl. "Valuing Surface." *Western American Literature* 24 (August 1989): 113–20.

552. Bredeson, Robert C. "Landscape Description in Nineteenth-Century American Travel Literature." *American Quarterly* 20 (Spring 1968): 86–94.

553. Brenner, Jack. "Imagining the West." *The Westering Experience in American Literature: Bicentennial Essays.* Eds. Merrill Lewis and L. L. Lee. Bellingham: Bureau for Faculty Research, Western Washington University, 1977, 32–47.

554. Brown, Richard Maxwell. "Western Violence: Structure, Values, Myth." *Western Historical Quarterly* 24 (February 1993): 5–20.

555. Brunvand, Jan Harold. "As the Saints Go Marching By: Modern Jokelore Concerning Mormons." *Journal of American Folklore* 83 (January–March 1970): 53–60.

556. Bryant, Paul T. "Western Literature: A Window on America." *CEA Critic* 40 (March 1978): 6–13.

557. Butler, Michael D. "Kansas Novels." *The Kansas Art Reader.* Ed. Jonathan Wesley Bell. Lawrence: University of Kansas, 1976, 299–322.

558. ———. "Sons of Oliver Edwards; or, The Other American Hero." *Western American Literature* 12 (May 1977): 53–66.

559. Byington, Robert. "The Frontier Hero: Refinement and Definition." *Publications of the Texas Folklore Society* 30 (1960): 140–55.

560. *BYU Studies* 14 (Winter 1974). Special issue on Mormons and literature.

561. Carstensen, Vernon. "Making Use of the Frontier and the American West." *Western Historical Quarterly* 13 (January 1982): 5–16.

562. ———. "Remarks on the Literary Treatment of the American Westward Movement." *Moderna Sprak* 51 (1957): 275–87.

563. Carter, Harvey C., and Marcia C. Spencer. "Stereotypes of the Mountain Man." *Western Historical Quarterly* 6 (January 1975): 17–32.

564. Carver, Wayne. "Literature, Mormon Writers, and the Powers that Be." *Dialogue* 4 (August 1969): 65–73.

565. Caughey, John W. "Shaping a Literary Tradition." *Pacific Historical Review* 8 (June 1939): 201–14. California literature.

566. Cawelti, John. "Cowboys, Indians, Outlaws." *American West* 1 (Spring 1964): 28–35, 77–79.

567. ———. "Prolegomena to the Western." *Western American Literature* 4 (Winter 1970): 259–71.

568. Christensen, J. A. "Poetry in Its Western Setting." *Western Review* 7 (1970): 10–19.

569. Cleaver, J.D. "L. Samuel and the *West Shore:* Images of a Changing Pacific Northwest." *Oregon Historical Quarterly* 94 (Summer–Fall 1993): 167–224.

570. Clements, William M. "Savage, Pastoral, Civilized: An Ecology Typology of American Frontier Heroes." *Journal of Popular Culture* 8 (Fall 1974): 254–66.

571. Clough, Wilson O. "The Cult of the Bad Man of the West." *Texas Quarterly* 5 (Autumn 1962): 11–20.

572. Cohen, B. J. "Nativism and Western Myth: The Influence of Nativist Ideas on American Self-Image." *Journal of American Studies* 8 (April 1974): 23–40.

573. Commager, Henry Steele. "The Literature of the Pioneer West." *Minnesota History* 8 (December 1927): 319–28.

574. Cook, Nancy. "More Names on Inscription Rock: Travel Writers on the Great Plains in the 1980s." *Great Plains Quarterly* 11 (Spring 1991): 113–26.

575. Corning, Howard M. "The Prose and Poetry of It." *Oregon Historical Quarterly* 74 (September 1973): 244–67. Oregon writers in the 1920s and 30s.

576. Cracroft, Richard H. "The American West of Karl May." *American Quarterly* 19 (Summer 1967): 249–58.

577. ———. "World Westerns: The European Writer and the American West." *Western American Literature* 20 (August 1985): 111–32.

578. Current-Garcia, E. "Writers in the 'Sticks.'" *Prairie Schooner* 12 (Winter 1938): 294–309.

579. Dale, Edward E. "The Frontier Literary Society." *Nebraska History* 31 (1950): 167–82.

580. Davidson, Levette J. "Early Fiction of the Rocky Mountain Region." *Colorado Magazine* 10 (September 1933): 161–72.

581. ———. "Fact or Formula in 'Western' Fiction." *Colorado Quarterly* 3 (Winter 1955): 278–87.

582. ———. "Folk Elements in Midwestern Literature." *Western Humanities Review* 3 (July 1949): 187–95.

583. ———. "The Literature of Western America." *Western Humanities Review* 5 (Spring 1951): 165–73.

584. Davis, David B. "Ten-Gallon Hero." *American Quarterly* 6 (Summer 1954): 111–25.

585. Davis, Robert Murray. "Playing Cowboys: The Paradoxes of Genre." *Heritage of Kansas* 12 (Spring 1979): 3–8.

586. Davis, Ronald L. "Culture on the Frontier." *Southwest Review* 53 (Autumn 1968): 383–403. Western drama.

587. Day, Robert. "Some Western Fiction of the 1970s." *Kansas Quarterly* 10 (Fall 1978): 99–103.

588. de Graaf, Lawrence B. "Recognition, Racism, and Reflections on the Writing of Western Black History." *Pacific Historical Review* 44 (February 1975): 22–51.

589. Deringer, Ludwig. "The Pacific Northwest in American and Canadian Literature since 1776: The Present State of Scholarship." *Oregon Historical Quarterly* 90 (Fall 1989): 305–27.

590. Dessain, Kenneth. "Once in the Saddle: The Memory and Romance of the Trail Driving Cowboy." *Journal of Popular Culture* 4 (Fall 1970): 464–96.

591. Deverell, William. "Fighting Words: The Significance of the American West in the History of the United States." *Western Historical Quarterly* 25 (Summer 1994): 185–206.

592. Dippie, Brian W. "American Wests: Historiographical Perspectives." *American Studies International* 27 (October 1989): 3–25.

593. ———. "Bards of the Little Big Horn." *Western American Literature* 1 (Fall 1966): 175–95.

594. Dobie, J. Frank. "Cow Country Tempo." *Texas Quarterly* 7 (Spring 1964): 30–36.

595. Donald, David, and Frederick A. Palmer. "Toward a Western Literature, 1820–1860." *Mississippi Valley Historical Review* 35 (December 1948): 413–28.

596. Dondore, Dorothy. "Points of Contact Between History and Literature in the Mississippi Valley." *Mississippi Valley Historical Review* 11 (September 1924): 227–36.

597. Donelson, Kenneth L. "A Fistful of Southwestern Books for Students and Teachers." *Arizona English Bulletin* 13 (April 1971): 71–76.

598. ———. "The Southwest in Literature and Culture: A New Horizon for the English Class." *English Journal* 61 (February 1972): 193–204.

599. Durham, Philip. "The Lost Cowboy." *Midwest Journal* 7 (1955): 176–82.

600. ———. "The Negro Cowboy." *American Quarterly* 7 (Fall 1955): 291–301.

601. Dykes, J. C. "Dime Novel Texas; or, the Sub-Literature of the Lone Star State." *Southwestern Historical Quarterly* 49 (January 1946): 327–40.

602. Eifner, Walter H. "The Kansas *Agora*: A Forum for Literature." *Markham Review* 8 (Fall 1978): 11–15.

603. Elliott, William D. "Poets of the Moving Frontier: Bly, Whittemore, Wright, Berryman, McGrath and Minnesota North Country Poetry." *Midamerica* 3 (1976): 17–38.

604. England, Eugene. "A Modern Act of the Apostles, 1840: Mormon Literature in the Making." *Brigham Young University Studies* 27 (Spring 1987): 79–95.

605. Erben, Rudolf. "The Western Holdup Play: The Pilgrimage Continues." *Western American Literature* 23 (Winter 1989): 311–22.

606. Erisman, Fred. "Growing up with the Country in Young Adult Fiction." *Roundup Quarterly* 4 (Winter 1991): 5–14.

607. ———. "Western Writers and the Literary Historian." *North Dakota Quarterly* 47 (Autumn 1979): 64–69.

608. ———. "'Where We Plan to Go': The Southwest in Utopian Fiction." *Southwestern American Literature* 1 (September 1971): 137–43.

609. Erno, Richard B. "The New Realism in Southwestern Literature." *Western Review* 7 (Spring 1970): 50–54.

610. Etulain, Richard W. "The American Literary West and Its Interpreters: The Rise of a New Historiography." *Pacific Historical Review* 45 (August 1976): 311–48.

611. ———. "The Basques in Western American Literature." *Anglo-American Contributions to Basque Studies....* Eds. William A. Douglass, et al. Reno: Desert Research Institute Publications in the Social Sciences, 1977, 7–18.

612. ———. "Contours of Culture in Arizona and the Modern West." *Arizona at Seventy-Five: The Next Twenty-Five Years.* Eds. Beth Luey and Noel J. Stowe. Tucson: Arizona Historical Society, 1987, 11–53.

613. ———. "Farmers in Southwestern Fiction." *Southwestern Agriculture: Pre-Columbian to Modern.* Eds. Henry C. Dethloff and Irvin M. May, Jr. College Place: Texas A & M University Press, 1982, 28–46.

614. ———. "Main Currents in Modern Western Literature." *Journal of American Culture* 3 (Summer 1980): 374–88.

615. ———. "Novelists of the Northwest: Needs and Opportunities for Research." *Idaho Yesterdays* 17 (Summer 1973): 24–32. Includes extended bibliography.

616. ———. "Research Opportunities in Western Literary History." *Western Historical Quarterly* 4 (July 1973): 263–72.

617. ———. "Shifting Interpretations of Western American Cultural History." *Historians and the American West.* Ed. Michael P. Malone. Lincoln: University of Nebraska Press, 1983, 414–32.

618. ———. "Western Fiction and History: A Reconsideration. *The American West: New Perspectives, New Dimensions.* Ed. Jerome O. Steffen. Norman: University of Oklahoma Press, 1979, 152–74.

619. Fadiman, Clifton. "Party of One–The Literature of the Rockies." *Holiday* 34 (August 1963): 10, 12–17.

620. Fender, Stephen. "The Western and the Contemporary." *Journal of American Studies* 6 (April 1972): 97–108.

621. Fife, Austin, and Alta Fife. "Spurs and Saddlebags: Ballads of the Cowboy." *American West* 7 (September 1970): 44–47.

622. Fisher, Vardis. "The Western Writer and the Eastern Establishment." *Western American Literature* 1 (Winter 1967): 244–59.

623. Fishwick, Marshall W. "The Cowboy: America's Contribution to the World's Mythology." *Western Folklore* 11 (April 1952): 77–92.

624. "Five Historians of the American West." *Pacific Historical Review* 56 (November 1987): 481–560. Special issue.

625. Flanagan, John T. "A Half-Century of Middlewestern Fiction." *Critique* 2 (Winter 1959): 16–34.

626. ———. "Literary Protests in the Midwest." *Southwest Review* 34 (Spring 1948): 148–57.

627. ———. "The Middle Western Farm Novel." *Minnesota History* 23 (June 1942): 113–47.

628. ———. "Thirty Years of Minnesota Fiction." *Minnesota History* 31 (September 1950): 129–47.

629. Flores, Vetal. "Literature for Frontier Children." *Southwestern American Literature* 2 (Fall 1972): 65–73.

630. Folsom, James K. "English Westerns." *Western American Literature* 2 (Spring 1967): 3–13.

631. ———. "'Western' Themes and Western Films." *Western American Literature* 2 (Fall 1967): 195–203.

632. Frederick, John T. "Early Iowa in Fiction." *Palimpsest* 36 (October 1955): 389–420.

633. ———. "The Farm in Iowa Fiction." *Palimpsest* 32 (March 1951): 124–52.

634. ———. "Town and City in Iowa Fiction." *Palimpsest* 35 (February 1954): 49–96.

635. Freeman, Martha Doty. "New Mexico in the Nineteenth Century: The Creation of an Artistic Tradition." *New Mexico Historical Review* 49 (Janaury 1974): 5–26.

636. French, Carol Anne. "Western Literature and the Myth-Makers." *Montana: The Magazine of Western History* 22 (April 1972): 76–81.

637. French, Warren. "The Cowboy in the Dime Novel." *Texas Studies in English* (1951): 219–34.

638. Furness, Edna L. "Image of the Schoolteacher in Western Literature." *Arizona Quarterly* 18 (Winter 1962): 346–57.

639. Fuson, Ben W. "Prairie Dreamers of 1890: Three Kansas Utopian Novels and Novelists." *Kansas Quarterly* 5 (Fall 1973): 63–77.

640. Gard, Wayne. "A Tale of the Old Days: Buffalo Bill Comes to Town." *Southwest Review* 69 (Winter 1984): 54–77.

641. Garland, Hamlin. "Literary Emancipation of the West." *Forum* 16 (1893): 156–66.

642. ———. "The West in Literature." *Arena* 6 (1892): 669–76.

643. Gaston, Edwin W., Jr. "Travel Accounts of the Southern Plains: 1800–1850." *Texas Journal of Science* 11 (March 1959): 3–16.

644. Geary, Edward A. "Mormondom's Lost Generation: The Novelists of the 1940's." *BYU Studies* 18 (Fall 1977): 89–98.

645. ———. "The Poetics of Provincialism: Mormon Regional Fiction." *Dialogue* 11 (Summer 1978): 15–24.

646. Gilliard, Frederick W. "Theatre in Early Idaho: A Brief Review and Appraisal." *Rendezvous* 8 (Summer 1973): 25–31.

647. Gillis, Everett A. "Southwest Literature: Perspectives and Prospects." *Southwestern American Literature* 2 (Spring 1972): 1–7.

648. Gillmor, Frances. "Southwestern Chronicle from Report to Literature." *Arizona Quarterly* 12 (Winter 1956): 344–51.

649. Goetzmann, William H. "Mountain Man Stereotypes: Notes and Reply." *Western Historical Quarterly* 6 (July 1975): 295–302. Reply by Harvey L. Carter, 301–2.

650. Goodwyn, Frank. "The Frontier in American Fiction." *Revista Interamericana de Bibliografía* 10 (1960): 356–69.

651. Gordon-McCutchan, R.C. "Revising the Revisionists: Manifesto of the Realist Western Historians." *Journal of the West* 33 (July 1994): 3–7.

652. Graham, Don. "Is Dallas Burning? Notes on Recent Texas Fiction." *Southwestern American Literature* 4 (1974): 68–73.

653. Green, Douglas B. "The Singing Cowboy in American Culture." *Heritage of Kansas* 9 (Fall 1976): 3–9.

654. Green, Timothy, and Jack Schneider. "In Defense of the Southwestern Ethos: The Literature of Reaction." *RE: Artes Liberales* 5 (Fall 1978): 1–15.

655. Gressley, Gene M. "The West: Past, Present, and Future." *Western Historical Quarterly* 17 (July 1986): 5–23.

656. ———. "Whither American History? Speculations on a Direction." *Pacific Historical Review* 53 (November 1984): 493–501.

657. Gurian, Jay. "The Possibility of a Western Poetics." *Colorado Quarterly* 15 (Summer 1966): 69–85.

658. ———. "Sweetwater Journalism and Western Myth." *Annals of Wyoming* 36 (April 1964): 79–88.

659. ———. "The Unwritten West." *American West* 2 (Winter 1965): 59–63.

660. Guthrie, Alfred B., Jr. "The Historical Novel." *Montana: Magazine of History* 4 (Fall 1954): 1–8.

661. ———. "Why Write About the West?" *Western American Literature* 7 (Fall 1972): 163–69.

662. Haslam, Gerald. "Alternative Publishing in the West." *Western American Literature* 19 (August 1984): 85–92.

663. ———. American Literature: Some Forgotten Pages." *ETC* 17 (June 1970): 221–38.

664. ———. "The Other Literary West." *Arizona Quarterly* 38 (Autumn 1982): 197–202.

665. ———. "Predators in Literature." *Western American Literature* 11 (August 1977): 123–31.

666. ———, ed. *Western American Writers.* Cassette Series. Deland, Fla.: Everett/Edwards, 1974.

667. Hauptman, Laurence M. "Mythologizing Westward Expansion: Schoolbooks and the Image of the American Frontier Before Turner." *Western Historical Quarterly* 7 (July 1977): 269–82.

668. Heatherington, Madelon E. "Romance Without Women: The Sterile Fiction of the American West." *Georgia Review* 33 (Fall 1979): 643–56.

669. Heilman, Robert B. "The Western Theme: Exploiters and Explorers." *Northwest Review* 4 (Fall–Winter 1960): 5–14.

670. Hertzel, Leo J. "What About Writers in the North?" *South Dakota Review* 5 (Spring 1967): 3–19.

671. "Historians of the Northern Plains," and "Historians of the Southern Plains." *Great Plains Journal* 18 (1979). Essays on major historians of the Great Plains.

672. Hitt, Helen. "History in Pacific Northwest Novels Written Since 1920." *Oregon Historical Quarterly* 51 (September 1950): 180–206.

673. Holbrook, Stewart H. *Far Corner: A Personal View of the Pacific Northwest.* New York: Macmillan, 1952, 220–30.

674. Horgan, Paul. "The Cowboy Revisited." *Southwest Review* 39 (Autumn 1954): 285–97.

675. Hornberger, Theodore. "The Self-Conscious Wests." *Southwest Review* 26 (July 1941): 428–48.

676. Hough, Emerson. "The West, and Certain Literary Discoveries." *Century* 59 (February 1900): 506–11.

677. Howard, Leon. "Literature and the Frontier." *English Literary History* 7 (1940): 68–82.

678. Hubbell, Jay B. "The Frontier in American Literature." *Southwest Review* 10 (January 1925): 84–92.

679. Hunsaker, Kenneth B. "Mid-Century Mormon Novels." *Dialogue* 4 (Autumn 1969): 123–28.

680. Hurst, Mary Jane. "Linguistic Innovation and Conservatism: Dialect in Cowboy Poetry." *New Mexico Humanities Review* 36 (1992): 103–12.

681. Hutchinson, W. H. *The Cowboy in Literature.* Cassette. Deland, Fla.: Everett/Edwards, 1974.

682. ———. "Packaging the Old West in Serial Form." *Westways* 65 (February 1973): 18–23.

683. ———. "Virgins, Villains, and Varmints." *Huntington Library Quarterly* 16 (August 1953): 381–92.

684. ———. "The 'Western Story' as Literature." *Western Humanities Review* 3 (January 1949): 33–37.

685. "Issue on Mormons and Literature." *BYU Studies* 14 (Winter 1974).

686. Iverson, Peter. "Cowboys, Indians and the Modern West." *Arizona and the West* 28 (Summer 1986): 107–24.

687. James, Stuart B. "Western American Space and the Human Imagination." *Western Humanities Review* 24 (Spring 1970): 147–55.

688. Jewett, Isaac Appleton. "Themes for Western Fiction." *Western Monthly Magazine* 1 (December 1833): 574–88.

689. Jones, Harry H. "The Mining Theme in Western Fiction." *Studies in the Literature of the West.* Laramie: University of Wyoming, 1956, 101–29.

690. Jones, Howard Mumford. "The Allure of the West." *Harvard Library Bulletin* 28 (January 1980): 19–32. Early nineteenth-century narratives.

691. Jones, Margaret Ann. "The Cowboy and Ranching in Magazine Fiction, 1901–1910." *Studies in the Literature of the West.* Laramie: University of Wyoming, 1956, 57–74.

692. Jordan, Roy A. "Myth and the American West." *American Renaissance and the American West....* Eds. Christopher S. Durer, et al. Laramie: University of Wyoming, 1982, 141–48.

693. Jorgensen, B. W. "Imperceptive Hands: Some Recent Mormon Verse." *Dialogue* 5 (Winter 1970): 23–34.

694. Juricek, John T. "American Usage of the Word 'Frontier' from Colonial Times to Frederick Jackson Turner." *Proceedings of the American Philosophical Society* 110 (February 18, 1966): 10–34.

695. Kedro, M. James. "Literary Boosterism: The Great Divide." *Colorado Magazine* 52 (Summer 1975): 200–224.

696. Keeler, Clinton. "Children of Innocence: The Agrarian Crusade in Fiction." *Western Humanities Review* 6 (Autumn 1952): 363–76.

697. Keim, Charles J. "Writing the Great Alaska Novel." *Alaska Review* 4 (Fall–Winter 1969): 47–51.

698. Keller, Karl. "On Words and the Word of God: The Delusions of a Mormon Literature." *Dialogue* 4 (Autumn 1969): 13–20.

699. Kimball, Stanley B. "The Captivity Narrative on Mormon Trails, 1846–1865." *Dialogue* 18 (Winter 1985): 81–88.

700. King, James T. "The Sword and the Pen: The Poetry of the Military Frontier." *Nebraska History* 47 (September 1966): 229–45.

701. Kittredge, William, and Steven M. Krauzer. "Writers of the New West." *TriQuarterly* 48 (Spring 1980): 5–14.

702. Klotman, Phyllis R. "The Slave and the Western: Popular Literature of the Nineteenth Century." *North Dakota Quarterly* 41 (Autumn 1973): 40–54.

703. Kolodny, Annette. "Letting Go Our Grand Obsessions: Notes Toward a New Literary History of the American Frontiers." *American Literature* 64 (March 1992): 1–18.

704. Kowalewski, Michael. "Imagining the California Gold Rush: The Visual and Verbal Legacy." *California History* 71 (Spring 1992): 60–73.

705. Krause, Herbert. "Myth and Reality on the High Plains." *South Dakota Review* 1 (December 1963): 3–20.

706. Krupat, Arnold. "American Autobiography: The Western Tradition." *Georgia Review* 35 (1981): 307–17.

707. Kuhlman, Thomas A. "Warner's History of Dakota County, Nebraska: The Western County History as a Literary Genre." *Western Review* 9 (Winter 1972): 57–64.

708. Lamar, Howard R. "Much to Celebrate: The Western History Association's Twenty-Fifth Birthday." *Western Historical Quarterly* 17 (October 1986): 397–416.

709. Lambert, Neal E. "Freedom and the American Cowboy." *BYU Studies* 8 (Autumn 1967): 61–71.

710. ———. "The Representation of Reality in Nineteenth Century Mormon Autobiography." *Dialogue* 11 (Summer 1978): 63–74.

711. ———. "Saints, Sinners and Scribes: A Look at the Mormons in Fiction." *Utah Historical Quarterly* 36 (Winter 1968): 63–76.

712. Lambert, Patricia J. B. "The Western Hero Grows Narcissistic." *Heritage of Kansas* 12 (Winter 1979): 7–13.

713. Lavender, David. "The Petrified West and the Writer." *American Scholar* 37 (Spring 1968): 293–306.

714. Leach, Joseph. "The Paper-Back Texan: Father of the American Western Hero." *Western Humanities Review* 11 (Summer 1957): 267–75.

715. Lee, Hector. *The Roots of Western Literature.* Cassette. Deland, Fla.: Everett/Edwards, 1974.

716. ———. "Tales and Legends in Western American Literature." *Western American Literature* 9 (February 1975): 239–54.

717. Lee, James Ward. "Texas Fiction at the End of the Century." *Roundup Quarterly* 3 (Spring 1991): 20–28.

718. Lee, L. L. "Western Myth, Mormon Society." *Under the Sun: Myth and Realism in Western American Literature.* Ed. Barbara Howard Meldrum. Troy, N.Y.: Whitston, 1985, 64–72.

719. Leithead, J. Edward. "The Saga of Young Wild West." *American Book Collector* 19 (March 1969): 17–22.

720. Lewandowska, M. L. "Feminism and the Emerging Woman Poet: Four Bay Area Poets." *Itinerary: Criticism, Essays on California Writers.* Ed. Charles L. Crow. Bowling Green, Ohio: University Press, 1978, 123–41.

721. Lewis, Marvin. "A Free Life in the Mines and on the Range." *Western Humanities Review* 12 (Winter 1958): 87–95.

722. Limerick, Patricia Nelson. "The Case of the Premature Departure: The Trans-Mississippi West and American History Textbooks." *Journal of the American West* 78 (March 1992): 1380–94.

723. ———. "The Trail to Santa Fe: The Unleashing of the Western Public Intellectual." Eds. Patricia Nelson Limerick, et al. *Trails: Toward a New Western History.* Lawrence: University Press of Kansas, 1991, 59–77, 224–26.

724. ———. "What on Earth Is the New Western History?" *Montana: The Magazine of Western History* 40 (Summer 1990): 61–64.

725. Lindstrom, Naomi. "The Novel in Texas: How Big a Patrimony?" *Texas Quarterly* 21 (Summer 1978): 73–83.

726. Lojek, Helen. "Reading the Myth of the West." *South Dakota Review* 28 (Spring 1990): 46–61.

727. Love, Glen A. "The Pacific Northwest: Regional Literacy and the Great Tradition." *Pacific Northwest Forum* 6 (Summer 1981): 22–31.

728. Loy, R. Philip. "Saints or Scoundrels: Images of Mormons in Literature and Film about the American West." *Journal of the American Studies Association of Texas* 21 (October 1990): 57–74.

729. Lyon, Thomas J. "Western Poetry." *Journal of the West* 19 (January 1980): 45–53.

730. McDowell, Tremaine. "Regionalism in the United States." *Minnesota History* 20 (June 1939): 105–18.

731. McMurtry, Larry. "How the West Was Won or Lost." *New Republic* 203 (October 22, 1990): 32–38.

732. ———. "Take My Saddle from the Wall." *Harper's* 237 (September 1968):37–46. Cowboy myth and modern cattlemen.

733. McReynolds, Douglas J. "American Literature, American Frontier, All American Girl." *Heritage of Kansas* 10 (Spring 1977): 25–33.

734. McWilliams, Carey. "Myths of the West." *North American Review* 232 (November 1931): 424–32.

735. ———. "The West: A Lost Chapter." *Frontier* 12 (November 1932): 15–24.

736. Maguire, James H. "The Canon and the 'Diminished Thing.'" *American Literature* 60 (December 1988): 643–52.

737. ———. "Fiction of the West." Eds. Emory Elliott, et al. *The Columbia History of the American Novel.* New York: Columbia University Press, 1991, 437–64.

738. Malone, Michael P. "Beyond the Last Frontier: Toward a New Approach to Western American History." *Western Historical Quarterly* 20 (November 1989): 409–27.

739. ———. "The West in American Historiography." *The American West, as Seen by Europeans and Americans.* Ed. Rob Kroes. Amsterdam: Free University Press, 1989, 1–18.

740. Manfred, Frederick. *Writing in the West.* Cassette. Deland, Fla.: Everett/Edwards, 1974.

741. Marchand, Ernest. "Emerson and the Frontier." *American Literature* 3 (May 1931): 149–74.

742. Marks, Barry. "The Concept of Myth in *Virgin Land.*" *American Quarterly* 5 (Spring 1953): 71–76.

743. Marovitz, Sanford E. "Bridging the Continent with Romantic Western Realism." *Journal of the West* 19 (January 1980): 17–28.

744. ———. "Myth and Realism in Recent Criticism of the American Literary West." *Journal of American Studies* 15 (April 1981): 95–114.

745. ———. "Romance or Realism? Western Periodical Literature: 1893–1902." *Western American Literature* 10 (May 1975): 45–58.

746. Marshall, Ian. "The Easterner in Western Literature–And in the Western Literature Association." *Western American Literature* 26 (November 1991): 229–35.

747. Meldrum, Barbara Howard. "The Agrarian versus Frontiersman in Midwestern Fiction." *Heritage of Kansas* 11 (Summer 1978): 3–18.

748. ———. "Images of Women in Western American Literature." *Midwest Quarterly* 17 (Spring 1976): 252–67.

749. ———. "Western Writers and the River: Guthrie, Fisher, Stegner." *Pacific Northwest Forum* 4 (Summer 1979): 21–26.

750. Melling, Philip H. "The West in Fiction." *Nothing Else to Fear: New Prospectus on America in the Thirties*. Eds. Stephen Baskerville and Ralph Willett. Manchester, Engl.: Manchester University Press, 1985, 104–31.

751. Meyer, Roy W. "Character Types in Literature About the American West." *Opinion* 13 (December 1969): 21–29.

752. ———. "Naturalism in American Farm Fiction." *Journal of the Central Mississippi Valley American Studies Association* 2 (Spring 1961): 27–37.

753. ———. "The Outback and the West: Australian and American Frontier Fiction." *Western American Literature* 6 (Spring 1971): 3–19.

754. ———. "The Scandinavian Immigrant in American Farm Fiction." *American Scandinavian Review* 47 (September 1959): 243–49.

755. Miles, Elton. "Mencken's *Mercury* and the West." *Southwestern American Literature* 3 (1973): 39–48.

756. Miles, Josephine. "Pacific Coast Poetry, 1947." *Pacific Spectator* 2 (Spring 1948): 134–50.

757. Milner, Clyde A., II. "The Shared Memory of Montana's Pioneers." *Montana: The Magazine of Western History* 37 (Winter 1987): 2–13.

758. Milton, John R. "The American Novel: The Search for Home, Tradition, and Identity." *Western Humanities Review* 16 (Spring 1962): 169–80.

759. ———. "The American West: A Challenge to the Literary Imagination." *Western American Literature* 1 (Winter 1967): 267–84.

760. ———. "The Dakota Image." *South Dakota Review* 8 (Autumn 1970): 7–26.

761. ———. "Inside the *South Dakota Review*." *Midcontinent American Studies Journal* 10 (Fall 1969): 68–78.

762. ———. "The Novel in the American West." *South Dakota Review* 2 (Autumn 1964): 56–76.

763. ———. "Two Wests." *Antaeus* 25/26 (Spring/Summer 1977): 93–98.

764. ———. "The West and Beyond: *South Dakota Review*." *South Dakota History* 13 (Winter 1983): 332–51.

765. ———. "The Western Novel: Sources and Forms." *Chicago Review* 16 (Summer 1963): 74–100.

766. ———. "The Western Novel: Whence and What?" *Rendezvous* 7 (Winter 1972): 7–21.

767. ———. "The Writer's West." *Antaeus* 29 (Spring 1978): 76–87.

768. ———, ed. "Conversations with Distinguished Western American Novelists." *South Dakota Review* 9 (Spring 1971): 15–57.

769. ———, ed. "Special Topic: Which Three Novels of the American West Do You Consider Best?" *South Dakota Review* 29 (Autumn 1991): 3–102.

770. ———, ed. "The Western Novel–A Symposium." *South Dakota Review* 2 (Autumn 1964): 3–36.

771. Morgan, Dale L. "Literature in the History of the Church: The Importance of Involvement." *Dialogue* 4 (Autumn 1969): 26–32.

772. Morley, S. Griswold. "Cowboy and Gaucho Fiction." *New Mexico Quarterly* 16 (Autumn 1946): 253–67.

773. Moss, George. "Silver Frolic: Popular Entertainment in Virginia City, Nevada, 1859–1863." *Journal of Popular Culture* 22 (Fall 1988): 1–31.

774. Mossberg, Christer Lennart. "Notes Toward an Introduction to Scandinavian Immigrant Literature on the Pioneer Experience." *Proceedings of the Pacific Northwest Conference on Foreign Languages* 28 (1977): 112–17.

775. ———. "Shucking the Pastoral Ideal: Sources and Meaning of Realism in Scandinavian Immigrant Fiction About the Pioneer Farm Experience." *Where the West Begins*. Eds. Arthur R. Huseboe and William Geyer. Sioux Falls, S. Dak.: Center for Western Studies Press, 1978, 42–50.

776. Nash, Gerald D. "European Images of America: The West in Historical Perspective." *Montana: The Magazine of Western History* 42 (Spring 1992): 2–16.

777. ———. "The Great Adventure: Western History, 1890–1990." *Western Historical Quarterly* 22 (February 1991): 5–18.

778. ———. "New Approaches to the American West." *Old West–New West: Centennial Essays.* Ed. Barbara Howard Meldrum. Moscow: University of Idaho Press, 1993, 15–27.

779. ———. "The West as Utopia and Myth." *Montana: The Magazine of Western History* 41 (Winter 1991): 69–75.

780. Nelson, F. C. "The Norwegian-American's Image of America." *Illinois Quarterly* 36 (April 1974): 5–23.

781. Nicholl, James R. "Dust in the Air: Narratives of Actual Versus Fictional Trail Drives." *Heritage of Kansas* 12 (Winter 1979): 14–24.

782. Nomura, Gail M. "Significant Lives: Asia and Asian Americans in the History of the U.S. West." *Western Historical Quarterly* 25 (Spring 1994): 69–88.

783. Norell, Irene P. "Prose Writers of North Dakota." *North Dakota Quarterly* 26 (Winter 1958): 1–36.

784. O'Connell, Nick. "Interviews with Northwest Writers." *Seattle Review* 10 (Fall 1987): 5–16.

785. Oliver, Egbert S. "The Pig-Tailed China Boys Out West." *Western Humanities Review* 12 (Spring 1958): 159–78.

786. Olson, James C. "The Literary Tradition in Pioneer Nebraska." *Prairie Schooner* 24 (Summer 1950): 161–68.

787. Olson, Paul A. "The Epic and Great Plains Literature: Rølvaag, Cather, and Neihardt." *Prairie Schooner* 55 (Spring/Summer 1981): 263–85.

788. Owens, William A. "The Golden Age of Texas Scholarship: Webb, Dobie, Bedichek, and Boatright." *Southwest Review* 60 (Winter 1975): 1–14.

789. Packer, Warren M. "Color Me Gray, Dobie, or Sandoz." *Arizona English Bulletin* 13 (April 1971): 23–31. Teaching western American Literature.

790. Paine, Gregory. "The Frontier in American Literature." *Sewanee Review* 36 (April 1928): 225–36.

791. Paul, Rodman W., and Michael P. Malone. "Tradition and Challenge in Western Historiography." *Western Historical Quarterly* 16 (January 1985): 27–53.

792. Pearce, T. M. "The 'Other' Frontiers of the American West." *Arizona and the West* 4 (Summer 1962): 105–12.

793. Peters, J. U. "The Los Angeles Anti-Myth." *Itinerary: Criticism, Essays on California Writers.* Ed. Charles L. Crow. Bowling Green, Ohio: University Press, 1978, 21–34.

794. Peterson, Levi S. "The Primitive and the Civilized in Western Fiction." *Western American Literature* 1 (Fall 1966): 197–207.

795. ———. "Tragedy and Western American Literature." *Western American Literature* 6 (Winter 1972): 243–49.

796. Peyroutet, Jean A. "The North Dakota Farmer in Fiction." *North Dakota Quarterly* 39 (Winter 1971): 59–71.

797. Phillips, James E. "Arcadia on the Range." *Themes and Directions in American Literature: Essays in Honor of Leon Howard.* Eds. Ray B. Browne and Donald Pizer. Lafayette, Ind.: Purdue University Studies, 1969, 108–29.

798. Pickens, Donald K. "Westward Expansion and the End of American Exceptionalism: Sumner, Turner, and Webb." *Western Historical Quarterly* 12 (October 1981): 409–18.

799. Pilkington, W. T. "Aspects of the Western Comic Novel." *Western American Literature* 1 (Fall 1966): 209–17.

800. ———. "The Recent Southwestern Novel." *Southwestern American Literature* 1 (January 1971): 12–15.

801. Pollard, Lancaster. "Washington Literature: A Historical Sketch." *Pacific Northwest Quarterly* 29 (July 1938): 227–54.

802. Polos, Nicholas C. "Early California Poetry." *California Historical Society Quarterly* 48 (September 1969): 243–55.

803. Pomeroy, Earl. "Old Lamps for New: The Cultural Lag in Pacific Coast Historiography." *Arizona and the West* 2 (Summer 1960): 107–26.

804. ———. "Rediscovering the West." *American Quarterly* 12 (Spring 1960): 20–30.

805. ———. "Toward a Reorientation of Western History: Continuity and Environment." *Mississippi Valley Historical Review* 41 (March 1955): 579–600.

806. ———. "What Remains of the West?" *Utah Historical Quarterly* 35 (Winter 1967): 37–55.

807. Popper, Frank J. "The Strange Case of the Contemporary American Frontier." *Yale Review* 76 (Autumn 1986): 101–21.

808. Poulsen, Richard C. "The Trail Drive Novel: A Matter of Balance." *Southwestern American Literature* 4 (1974): 53–61.

809. Putnam, Jackson K. "Historical Fact and Literary Truth: The Problem of Authenticity in Western American Literature." *Western American Literature* 15 (May 1980): 17–23.

810. Quantic, Diane Dufva. "The Ambivalence of Rural Life in Prairie Literature." *Kansas Quarterly* 12 (Spring 1980): 109–19.

811. ———. "The Revolt from the Village and Middle Western Fiction 1870–1915." *Kansas Quarterly* 5 (Fall 1973): 5–16.

812. ———. "The Unifying Thread: Connecting Place and Language in Great Plains Literature." *American Studies* 32 (Spring 1991): 67–83.

813. Ricou, Laurie. "Prairie Poetry and Metaphors of Plain/s Space." *Great Plains Quarterly* 3 (Spring 1983): 109–19.

814. Ridge, Martin. "The American West: From Frontier to Region." *New Mexico Historical Review* 64 (April 1989): 125–41.

815. Riley, Glenda. "Writing, Teaching, and Recreating Western History through Intersections and Viewpoints." *Pacific Historical Review* 62 (August 1993): 339–57.

816. Robbins, William G. "Laying Siege to Western History: The Emergence of New Paradigms." *Reviews in American History* 19 (September 1991): 313–31.

817. ———. "The 'Plundered Province' Thesis and the Recent Historiography of the American West." *Pacific Historical Review* 55 (November 1986): 577–97.

818. ———. "Western History: A Dialectic on the Modern Condition." *Western Historical Quarterly* 20 (November 1989): 429–49.

819. Robertson, Kirk. "Unknown Diversity: Little Magazines and Small Presses of the West, 1960–1980." *Western American Literature* 19 (August 1984): 125–34.

820. Robinson, Forrest G. "The New Historicism and the Old West." *Western American Literature* 25 (Summer 1990): 103–23.

821. Robinson, John W. "High Sierra Classics." *Book Club of California Quarterly Newsletter* 42 (Winter 1976): 3–20.

822. Rodenberger, Lou. "'The Gen-u-wine Stuff': Character Makes the Difference in the Trail-Drivin' Novel." *Heritage of Kansas* 11 (Winter 1978): 3–12.

823. Ronda, James P. "Dreams and Discoveries: Exploring the American West, 1760–1815." *William and Mary Quarterly* 46 (January 1989): 145–62.

824. Rudolph, Earle Leighton. "The Frontier in American Literature." *Jahrbuch, für Amerikastudien* 7 (1962): 77–91.

825. Rusch, Lana Koepp. "The American Dream in Selected South Dakota Novels." *South Dakota Review* 12 (Autumn 1974): 58–72.

826. Sage, Leland L. "Iowa Writers and Painters: An Historical Survey." *Annals of Iowa* 42 (Spring 1974): 241–70.

827. San Juan, E., Jr. "Mapping the Boundaries: The Filipino Writer in the U.S.A." *Journal of Ethnic Studies* 19 (Spring 1991): 117–31.

828. Saucerman, James R. "A Critical Approach to Plains Poetry." *Western American Literature* 15 (Summer 1980): 93–102.

829. Savage, William W., Jr. "Western Literature and Its Myths: A Rejoinder." *Montana: The Magazine of Western History* 22 (October 1972): 78–81.

830. Schroeder, Fred E. H. "The Development of the Super-Ego on the American Frontier." *Soundings* 57 (1974): 189–205.

831. Schwartz, Joseph. "The Wild West Show: 'Everything Genuine.'" *Journal of Popular Culture* 3 (Spring 1970): 656–66.

832. Sellars, Richard West. "The Interrelationship of Literature, History and Geography in Western Writing." *Western Historical Quarterly* 4 (April 1973): 171–85.

833. Shadoian, Jack. "Yuh Got Pecos: Doggone, Belle, Yuh're As Good as Two Men." *Journal of Popular Culture* 12 (Spring 1979): 721–36.

834. Shaul, Lawana J. "The West in Magazine Fiction, 1870–1900." *Studies in the Literature of the West*. Laramie: University of Wyoming, 1956, 29–56.

835. Sherman, Caroline B. "The Development of American Rural Fiction." *Agricultural History* 12 (January 1938): 67–76.

836. ———. "Farm Life Fiction." *South Atlantic Quarterly* 27 (July 1928): 310–24.

837. ———. "Rural Literature Faces Peace." *South Atlantic Quarterly* 42 (January 1943): 59–71.

838. Simonson, Harold P. "Pacific Northwest Literature–Its Coming of Age." *Pacific Northwest Quarterly* 71 (October 1980): 146–51.

839. ———. "The West as Archetype." *Under the Sun: Myth and Realism in Western American Literature*. Ed. Barbara Howard Meldrum. Troy, N.Y.: Whitston, 1985, 20–28.

840. Singer, Barnett. "Toward the Great Northwest Novel." *Research Studies* 43 (1975): 55–69.

841. Skårdal, Dorothy Burton. "The Scandinavian Immigrant Writer in America." *Norwegian-American Studies* 21 (1962): 14–53.

842. Smith, Edwin B. "'The Confused West': A Literary Forecast." *Essays and Addresses*. Chicago: A. C. McClurg, 1909, 360–76.

843. Smith, Goldie Capers. "*The Overland Monthly*: Landmark in American Literature." *New Mexico Quarterly* 33 (Autumn 1963): 333–40.

844. Smith, Henry Nash. "The Dime Novel Heroine." *Southwest Review* 34 (Spring 1949): 182–88.

845. ———. "The Frontier Hypothesis and the Myth of the West." *American Quarterly* 2 (Spring 1950): 3–11.

846. ———. "Kit Carson in Books." *Southwest Review* 28 (Winter 1943): 164–90.

847. ———. "Origins of Native American Literary Tradition." *The American Writer and the European.* Eds. Margaret Denny and William H. Gibson. Minneapolis: University of Minnesota Press, 1959, 63–77.

848. ———. "*Virgin Land* Revisited." *Indian Journal of American Studies* 3 (1973): 83–90.

849. ———. "The West as an Image of the American Past." *University of Kansas City Review* 18 (Autumn 1951): 29–40.

850. ———. "Western Chroniclers and Literary Pioneers." *Literary History of the United States.* Eds. Robert E. Spiller, et al. 3 vols. New York: Macmillan, 1948.

851. ———. "The Western Farmer in Imaginative Literature, 1818–1891." *Mississippi Valley Historical Review* 36 (December 1949): 479–90.

852. ———. "The Western Hero in the Dime Novel." *Southwest Review* 33 (Summer 1948): 276–84.

853. Smorkaloff, Pamela Maria. "Shifting Borders, Free Trade, and Frontier Narratives: U.S., Canada, and Mexico." *American Literary History* 6 (Spring 1994): 88–102.

854. Snyder, Gary. "The Incredible Survival of Coyote." *Western American Literature* 9 (February 1975): 255–72.

855. Sondrup, Steven P. "Literary Dimensions of Mormon Autobiography." *Dialogue* 11 (Summer 1978): 75–80.

856. Sonnichsen, C. L. "Fat Man and the Storytellers: Los Alamos in Fiction." *New Mexico Historical Review* 65 (January 1990): 49–71.

857. ———. "Laughter and History: Humorous Fiction of the American West." *Western Historical Quarterly* 16 (January 1985): 5–14.

858. ———. "The New Style Western." *South Dakota Review* 4 (Summer 1966): 22–28.

859. ———. "Tombstone in Fiction." *Journal of Arizona History* 9 (Summer 1968): 58–76.

860. ———. "The Two Black Legends." *Southwestern American Literature* 3 (1973): 5–21; with bibliography "Fiction of the Spanish-American Southwest, A Selection," 22–26.

861. ———. "The West That Wasn't: Some Observations on Our Dual Citizenship in the Wests of Myth and Reality." *American West* 14 (November–December 1977): 8–15.

862. ———. "The Wyatt Earp Syndrome." *American West* 7 (May 1970): 26–28, 60–62.

863. "Special Issue: Five Historians of the American West." *Pacific Historical Review* 56 (November 1987): 481–560.

864. Steckmesser, Kent L. "Custer in Fiction." *American West* 1 (Fall 1964): 47–52, 63–64.

865. ———. "Paris and the Wild West." *Southwest Review* 54 (Spring 1969): 168–74.

866. Steensma, Robert C. "'Stay Right There and Tough It Out': The American Homesteader as Autobiographer." *Western Review* 6 (Spring 1969): 10–18.

867. Stegner, Wallace. "Born a Square—The Westerner's Dilemma." *Atlantic* 213 (January 1964): 46–50.

868. ———. "History, Myth, and the Western Writer." *American West* 4 (May 1967): 61–62, 76–79.

869. Steinmetz, Lee. "Immortal Youth Astride a Dream: The Cowboy in Western American Poetry." *Books at Brown* 29–30 (1982–1983): 129–57.

870. Stevenson, Dorothy. "The Battle for Buckshot Basin." *New Mexico Quarterly* 33 (Autumn 1963): 315–24.

871. Stewart, George R. "The West as Seen from the East (1800–1850)." *Pacific Spectator* 1 (Spring 1947): 188–95.

872. Stouck, David. "The Art of the Mountain Man Novel." *Western American Literature* 20 (November 1985): 211–22.

873. Straight, Michael. "Truth and Formula for the Western Novel." *South Dakota Review* 2 (Autumn 1964): 88–93.

874. Swallow, Alan. "A Magazine for the West?" *Inland* 1 (Autumn 1957): 3–6.

875. ———. "The Mavericks." *Critique* 2 (Winter 1959): 74–92.

876. ———. "Poetry of the West." *South Dakota Review* 2 (Autumn 1964): 77–87.

877. Szasz, Ferenc M. "The Cultures of Modern New Mexico, 1940–1990." *Contemporary New Mexico, 1940–1990.* Ed. Richard W. Etulain. Albuquerque: University of New Mexico Press, 1994, 159–200.

878. Tate, George S. "Halldór Laxness, the Mormons and the Promised Land." *Dialogue* 11 (Summer 1978): 25–37.

879. Taylor, J. Golden. "The Western Short Story." *South Dakota Review* 2 (Autumn 1964): 37–55.

880. Taylor, Samuel W. "Peculiar People, Positive Thinkers and the Prospect of Mormon Literature." *Dialogue* 2 (Summer 1967): 17–31.

881. Tenefelde, Nancy L. "New Frontiers Revisited." *Midwest Review* 4 (1962): 54–62.

882. Todd, Edgeley W. "James Hall and the Hugh Glass Legend." *American Quarterly* 7 (Winter 1955): 363–70.

883. Tompkins, Jane. "West of Everything." *South Atlantic Quarterly* 86 (Fall 1987): 357–77.

884. Tyler, Daniel. "Barbecueing a 'Paleo-Liberal': Western Historians React to Patricia Nelson Limerick's *The Legacy of Conquest: The Unbroken Past of the American West." Gateway Heritage* 9 (Winter 1988/89): 38–42.

885. Van Doren, Mark. "Repudiation of the Pioneer." *English Journal* 17 (October 1928): 616–23.

886. Venn, George. "Continuity in Northwest Literature." *Northwest Perspectives: Essays on the Culture of the Pacific Northwest.* Eds. Edwin R. Bingham and Glen A. Love. Seattle: University of Washington Press, 1979, 99–118.

887. Veysey, Laurence R. "Myth and Reality in Approaching American Regionalism." *American Quarterly* 12 (Spring 1960): 31–43.

888. Waldmeir, J. J. "The Cowboy, Knight and Popular Taste." *Southern Folklore* Quarterly 22 (September 1958): 113–20.

889. Walker, Don D. "Can the Western Tell What Happens?" *Rendezvous* 7 (Winter 1972): 33–47.

890. ———. "Criticism of the Cowboy Novel: Retrospect and Reflections." *Western American Literature* 11 (February 1977): 275–96.

891. ———. "Freedom and Destiny in the Myth of the American West." *New Mexico Quarterly* 33 (Winter 1963–64): 381–87.

892. ———. "History and Imagination: The Prose and the Poetry of the Cattle Industry, 1895–1905." *Pacific Historical Review* 45 (August 1976): 379–97.

893. ———. "The Minimal Western." *Western American Literature* 23 (Summer 1988): 121–27.

894. ———. "The Mountain Man as Literary Hero." *Western American Literature* 1 (Spring 1966): 15–25.

895. ———. "The Mountain Man Journal: Its Significance in a Literary History of the Fur Trade." *Western Historical Quarterly* 5 (July 1974): 307–18.

896. ———. "Philosophical and Literary Implications in the Historiography of the Fur Trade." *Western American Literature* 9 (Summer 1974): 79–104.

897. ———. "Plains and Prairie: Space, History, and the Literary Imagination, in Australia and the United States." *Great Plains Quarterly* 14 (Winter 1994): 29–48.

898. ———. "Reading on the Range: The Literary Habits of the American Cowboy." *Arizona and the West* 2 (Winter 1960): 307–18.

899. ———. "Riders and Reality: A Philosophical Problem in the Historiography of the Cattle Trade." *Western Historical Quarterly* 9 (April 1978): 163–79.

900. ———. "The Rise and Fall of Barney Tullus." *Western American Literature* 3 (Summer 1968): 93–102.

901. ———. "Who Is Going to Ride Point?" *The Westering Experience in American Literature: Bicentennial Essays.* Eds. Merrill Lewis and L. L. Lee. Bellingham: Bureau for Faculty Research, Western Washington University, 1977, 23–31. Reality in cowboy fiction.

902. Walker, Franklin. "On Writing Literary History." *Pacific Historical Review* 45 (August 1976): 349–56.

903. Walker, Robert H. "The Poets Interpret the Western Frontier." *Mississippi Valley Historical Review* 47 (March 1961): 619–35.

904. Walker, William S. "Buckskin West: Leatherstocking at High Noon." *New York Folklore Quarterly* 24 (June 1968): 88–102.

905. Warren, Sidney. *Farthest Frontier: The Pacific Northwest.* New York: Macmillan, 1949, 242–74.

906. Webb, Walter P. "The American West: Perpetual Mirage." *Harper's* 214 (May 1957): 25–31.

907. ———. "The Great Frontier and Modern Literature." *Southwest Review* 37 (Spring 1952): 85–100.

908. Weber, David J. "The Spanish Legacy in North America and the Historical Imagination." *Western Historical Quarterly* 23 (February 1992): 5–24.

909. West, Elliott. "A Longer, Grimmer, but More Interesting Story." *Montana: The Magazine of Western History* 40 (Summer 1990): 72–76.

910. West, Ray B., Jr. "Four Rocky Mountain Novels." *Rocky Mountain Review* 10 (Autumn 1945): 21–28.

911. Westbrook, Max. "The Authentic Western." *Western American Literature* 13 (Fall 1978): 213–25.

912. ———. "Conservative, Liberal and Western: Three Modes of American Realism." *South Dakota Review* 4 (Summer 1966): 3–19.

913. ———. "Mountain Home: The Hero in the American West." *The Western Experience in American Literature: Bicentennial Essays.* Eds. Merrill Lewis and L. L. Lee. Bellingham: Bureau for Faculty Research, Western Washington University, 1977, 9–18.

914. ———. "Myth, Reality, and the American Frontier." *Under the Sun: Myth and Realism in Western American Literature.* Ed. Barbara Howard Meldrum. Troy, N.Y.: Whitston, 1985, 10–19.

915. ———. "The Ontological Critic." *Rendezvous* 7 (Winter 1972): 49–66.

916. ———. "The Practical Spirit: Sacrality and the American West." *Western American Literature* 3 (Fall 1968): 193–205.

917. ———. "The Themes of Western Fiction." *Southwest Review* 43 (Summer 1958): 193–205.

918. Westermeier, Clifford P. "The Cowboy–His Pristine Image." *South Dakota History* 8 (Winter 1977): 1–23.

919. "Western State Historiography: A Status Report." *Pacific Historical Review* 50 (November 1981): 387–525. A collection of several essays.

920. Whisenhunt, Donald W. "The Bard in the Depression: Texas Style." *Journal of Popular Culture* 2 (Winter 1968): 370–86.

921. Wilgus, D. K. "The Individual Song: 'Billy the Kid.'" *Western Folklore* 30 (July 1971): 226–34.

922. Williams, John. "The 'Western': Definition of the Myth." *Nation* 193 (November 18, 1961): 401–6.

923. Willson, Lawrence. "The Transcendentalist View of the West." *Western Humanities Review* 14 (Summer 1960): 183–91.

924. Wilson, Christopher P. "American Naturalism and the Problem of Sincerity." *American Literature* 54 (December 1982): 511–27.

925. Winther, Sophus Keith. "The Emigrant Theme." *Arizona Quarterly* 34 (Spring 1978): 31–43.

926. Wolf, Bobi. "Westerns in Eastern Europe." *Pacific Historian* 21 (Spring 1977): 29–35.

927. Worster, Donald, et al. "*The Legacy of Conquest,* by Patricia Nelson Limerick: A Panel of Appraisal." *Western Historical Quarterly* 20 (August 1989): 303–22.

928. "Writing in the West and Midwest." *Critique* 2 (Winter 1959): 1–97.

929. Wylder, Delbert E. "Professor Tully Barnhous Teaches the Mountain Man Novel." *South Dakota Review* 29 (Winter 1991): 158–68.

930. ———. "Recent Western Fiction." *Journal of the West* 19 (January 1980): 62–70.

931. ———. "The Western Hero From a Strange Perspective." *Rendezvous* 7 (Winter 1972): 23–32.

932. Yoder, John A. "Miscegenation in Our Virgin Land." *South Dakota Review* 12 (Winter 1974–75): 102–10.

933. Young, Vernon. "An American Dream and Its Parody." *Arizona Quarterly* 6 (Summer 1950): 112–23.

934. Zanger, Jules. "The Frontiersman in Popular Fiction." *The Frontier Reexamined.* Ed. John Francis McDermott. Urbana: University of Illinois Press, 1968.

SPECIAL TOPICS:
LOCAL COLOR AND REGIONALISM

935. Allen, Barbara, and Thomas J. Schlereth, eds. *Sense of Place: American Regional Cultures.* Lexington: University Press of Kentucky, 1990.
936. Allen, Charles. "Regionalism and the Little Magazines." *College English* 7 (October 1945): 10–16.
937. Anderson, David Louis. "The American Dream in Twentieth-Century California Fiction." Doctoral dissertation, Carnegie-Mellon University, 1983.
938. Armitage, Shelley. "New Mexico's Literary Heritage." *El Palacio* 90 (1984): 20–31.
939. Austin, Mary. "Regionalism in American Fiction." *English Journal* 21 (February 1932): 97–107.
940. Baker, Joseph E. "Four Arguments for Regionalism." *Saturday Review* 15 (November 28, 1936): 3–4, 14.
941. ———. "Provinciality." *College English* 1 (March 1940): 488–94.
942. ———. "Regionalism in the Middle West." *American Review* 4 (March 1935): 603–14.
943. ———. "Western Man Against Nature." *College English* 4 (October 1942): 19–26.
944. Barclay, Donald A. "*The Laughing Horse*: A Literary Magazine of the American West." *Western American Literature* 24 (May 1992): 47–55.
945. Bartlett, Lee. "From Waldport to San Francisco: Art Politics Make Peace." *Literary Review* 32 (Fall 1988): 9–15.
946. Beggs, Nancy Marie Kyker. "Development of the Regional American Short Story." Doctoral dissertation, East Texas State University, 1980.
947. Bennett, Patrick. *Talking With Texas Writers: Twelve Interviews.* College Station: Texas A & M University Press, 1980.
948. Benson, Peter Edward. "Regional Realism and Regional Magazines in the American 1890s." Doctoral dissertation, State University of New York, Stony Brook, 1978.

949. Benton, Thomas H. "American Regionalism: A Personal History of the Movement." *University of Kansas City Review* 17 (Autumn 1951): 41–75.

950. Bingham, Edwin R., and Glen A. Love, eds. and comps. *Northwest Perspectives: Essays on the Culture of the Pacific Northwest.* Seattle: University of Washington Press, 1978.

951. Blouet, Brian W., and Frederick C. Luebke, eds. *The Great Plains: Environment and Culture.* Lincoln: University of Nebraska Press, 1979.

952. Bonora, Diane Christine. "The Hollywood Novel of the 1930's and 1940's." Doctoral dissertation, State University of New York, Buffalo, 1983.

953. Botkin, Benjamin A. "Regionalism: Cult or Culture?" *English Journal* 25 (March 1936): 181–85.

954. ———. "We Talk about Regionalism — North, East, South, and West." *Frontier* 13 (May 1933): 286–96.

955. Bracher, Frederick. "California's Literary Regionalism." *American Quarterly* 7 (Fall 1955): 275–84.

956. Bradshaw, Michael. *Regions and Regionalism in the United States.* Jackson: University Press of Mississippi, 1988.

957. Brashear, Minnie M. "Missouri Literature Since the First World War: Part III – The Novel." *Missouri Historical Review* 41 (April 1947): 241–65.

958. Brooker-Bowers, Nancy. "The Hollywood Novel: An American Literary Genre." Doctoral dissertation, Drake University, 1983.

959. ———. *The Hollywood Novel and Other Novels about Film, 1912–1982: An Annotated Bibliography.* New York: Garland, 1985.

960. Brooks, Cleanth. "Regionalism in American Literature." *Journal of Southern History* 26 (Fall 1960): 35–43.

961. Brown, Richard Maxwell. "The Enduring Frontier: The Impact of Weather on South Dakota History and Literature." *South Dakota History* 15 (Spring–Summer 1985): 26–57.

962. ———. "The New Regionalism in America, 1970–1981." *Regionalism and the Pacific Northwest.* Eds. William G. Robbins, et al. Corvallis: Oregon State University Press, 1983, 37–96.

963. Burke, John Gordon, ed. *Regional Perspectives: An Examination of America's Literary Heritage.* Chicago: American Library Association, 1973. Midwest, Southwest, and frontier; also includes a bibliography on regionalism.

964. Chametzky, Jules. "Regional Literature and Ethnic Realities." *Antioch Review* 31 (Fall 1971): 385–96.

965. Chipman, Bruce Lewis. "America's Dream-Dump: A Study of the American Hollywood Novel." Doctoral dissertation, Tufts University, 1981.

966. Chittick, V. L. O., ed. *Northwest Harvest: A Regional Stocktaking.* New York: Macmillan, 1948.

967. Christensen, Paul. "From Cowboys to Curanderas: The Cycle of Texas Literature." *Southwest Review* 73 (Winter 1988): 10–29.

968. Clifford, Craig Edward. *In the Deep Heart's Core: Reflections on Life, Letters, and Texas.* College Station: Texas A & M University Press, 1985.

969. ———, and Tom Pilkington, eds. *Range Wars: Heated Debates, Sober Reflections, and Other Assessments of Texas Writing.* Dallas: Southern Methodist University Press, 1989.

970. Coleman, Rufus A. "Literature and the Region." *Pacific Northwest Quarterly* 39 (October 1948): 312–18.

971. Colquitt, Betsy. *A Part of Space: Ten Texas Writers.* Fort Worth: Texas Christian University Press, 1969.

972. Crawford, John F., William Balassi, and Annie O. Eysturoy, eds. *This is About Vision: Interviews with Southwestern Writers.* Albuquerque: University of New Mexico Press, 1990.

973. Crow, Charles L. "Homecoming in the California Visionary Romance." *Western American Literature* 24 (May 1989): 3–19.

974. Davidson, Donald. "Regionalism and Nationalism in American Literature." *American Review* 5 (April 1935): 48–61.

975. Deringer, Ludwig. "The Pacific Northwest in American and Canadian Literature since 1776: The Present State of Scholarship." *Oregon Historical Quarterly* 90 (Fall 1989): 305–27.

976. Dike, Donald A. "Notes on Local Color and Its Relation to Realism." *College English* 14 (November 1952): 81–88.

977. Dobie, J. Frank. "The Writer and His Region." *Southwest Review* 35 (Spring 1950): 81–87.

978. Dondore, Dorothy. "Points of Contact Between History and Literature in the Mississippi Valley." *Mississippi Valley Historical Review* 11 (September 1924): 227–36.

979. Dorman, Robert Lee. *Revolt of the Provinces: The Regionalist Movement in America, 1920–1945.* Chapel Hill: University of North Carolina Press, 1993.

980. DuBois, Arthur E. "Among the Quarterlies: The Question of 'Regionalism.'" *Sewanee Review* 45 (April–June 1937): 216–27.

981. Dunlop, Mary Helen. "Midwestern Landscapes: Nineteenth-Century Literature of the American Prairie." Doctoral dissertation, George Washington University, 1982.

982. Erisman, Fred. "The Changing Face of Western Literary Regionalism." *The Twentieth-Century West: Historical Interpretations.* Eds. Gerald D. Nash and Richard W. Etulain. Albuquerque: University of New Mexico Press, 1989, 361–81.

983. ———. "Literature and Place: Varieties of Regional Experience." *Journal of Regional Cultures* 1 (Fall–Winter 1981): 144–53.

984. ———. "Regionalism in American Children's Literature." *Society and Children's Literature.* Ed. James H. Fraser. Boston: David R. Godine, 1978, 53–75.

985. ———. "'This is the Place': A Regional Approach to Western Literature." *Cross Timbers Review* 1 (1984): 41–51.

986. ———. "Western Literary Regionalism: A Status Report." *Regionalism and the Female Imagination* 4 (1978): 14–18.

987. ———. "Western Regional Writers and the Uses of Place." *Journal of the West* 19 (January 1980): 36–44.

988. ———. "Western Writers and the Literary Historian." *North Dakota Quarterly* 47 (Autumn 1979): 64–69.

989. Etulain, Richard W. "Frontier and Region in Western Literature." *Southwestern American Literature* 1 (September 1971): 121–28.

990. Everson, William. *Archetype West: The Pacific Coast as a Literary Region.* Berkeley, Calif.: Oyez, 1976.

991. Faulkner, Virginia, and Frederick C. Luebke, eds. *Vision and Refuge: Essays on the Literature of the Great Plains.* Lincoln: University of Nebraska Press, 1982.

992. Fender, Stephen. *Plotting the Golden West: American Literature and the Rhetoric of the California Trail.* Cambridge: Cambridge University Press, 1981.

993. Fine, David. "Running out of Space: Vanishing Landscapes in California Novels." *Western American Literature* 26 (November 1991): 209–18.

994. ———, ed. *Los Angeles in Fiction: A Collection of Original Essays.* Albuquerque: University of New Mexico Press, 1984.

995. Fisher, Vardis. "The Novelist and His Background." *Western Folklore* 12 (January 1953): 1–8.

996. Fishwick, Marshall. "What Ever Happened to Regionalism?" *Southern Humanities Review* 2 (Fall 1968): 393–401.

997. Flanagan, John. "The Middle Western Farm Novel." *Minnesota History* 23 (June 1942): 113–47.

998. ———. Middlewestern Regional Literature." *Research Opportunities in American Cultural History.* Ed. John Francis McDermott. Lexington: University of Kentucky Press, 1961, 124–39.

999. ———. "Some Middlewestern Literary Magazines." *Papers on Language and Literature* 3 (Summer 1967): 237–57.

1000. French, Warren. *The San Francisco Poetry Renaissance, 1955–1960.* Boston: Twayne Publishers, 1991.

1001. Gastil, Raymond D. *Cultural Regions of the United States.* Seattle: University of Washington Press, 1975.

1002. Geary, Edward A. "Women Regionalists of Mormon Country." *Kate Chopin Newsletter* 2 (1976): 20–26.

1003. Gohdes, Clarence. "Exploitation of the Provinces." *The Literature of the American People....* Ed. Arthur H. Quinn. New York: Appleton-Century-Crofts, 1951, 639–60.

1004. Graham, Don. *Texas: A Literary Portrait.* San Antonio: Corona Publishing, 1985.

1005. ———, James W. Lee, and William T. Pilkington, eds. *The Texas Literary Tradition: Fiction, Folklore, History.* Austin: College of Liberal Arts, University of Texas, 1983.

1006. Gressley, Gene M. "Regionalism and the Twentieth-Century West." *The American West: New Perspectives, New Dimensions.* Ed. Jerome O. Steffen. Norman: University of Oklahoma Press, 1979, 197–234.

1007. Griffith, Thomas. "The Pacific Northwest." *Atlantic Monthly* 237 (April 1976): 47–93.

1008. Gwynn, R. S., Jan Epton Seale, Naomi Shihab Nye, and William Virgil Davis. *Texas Poets in Concert: A Quartet.* Denton: North Texas State University Press, 1990.

1009. Hakac, John. "Southwestern Regional Material in a Literature Class." *Western Review* 7 (Spring 1970): 12–18.

1010. Hamalian, Linda. "The Genesis of the San Francisco Renaissance: Literary and Political Currents, 1945–1955." *Literary Review* 32 (Fall 1988): 5–8.

1011. Haslam, Gerald. "California's Last Vaquero." *Western American Literature* 21 (August 1986): 123–30.

1012. ———. "California Writing and the West." *Western American Literature* 18 (November 1983): 209–22.

1013. ———. "Literary California: 'The Ultimate Frontier of the Western World.'" *California History* 68 (Winter 1989/90): 188–95.

1014. ———. *The Other California: The Great Central Valley in Life and Letters.* Santa Barbara: Joshua Odell Editions, 1990.

1015. Holman, David Marion. "A House Divided: Regionalism and the Form of Midwestern and Southern Fiction, 1832–1925." Doctoral dissertation, University of Michigan, 1983.

1016. Horgan, Paul. "The Pleasures and Perils of Regionalism." *Western American Literature* 8 (Winter 1974): 167–71.

1017. Hubbell, Jay B. "The Decay of the Provinces...." *Sewanee Review* 35 (October 1927): 473–87.

1018. Hudson, Wilson M. "Adams, Dobie, and Webb on the Use of Regional Material." *American Bypaths: Essays in Honor of E. Hudson Long.* Eds. Robert G. Collmer and Jack W. Herring. Waco, Tex.: Markham Press Fund, 1980, 57–78.

1019. Jensen, Merrill, ed. *Regionalism in America.* Madison: University of Wisconsin Press, 1951, 1965.

1020. Jessup, Emily Decker Lardner. "Embattled Landscapes: Regionalism and Gender in Midwestern Literature, 1915–1941." Doctoral dissertation, University of Michigan, 1985.

1021. Johnson, Thomas. "Regionalism and Local Color." *Literary History of the U.S.* Eds. Robert E. Spiller, et al. New York: Macmillan, 1948, Vol. 3, 304–25; 3d ed., 1963, Vol. 2, 304–25.

1022. Jones, Margaret Catherine. "Prophets in Babylon: Four California Novelists in the 1930s: Steinbeck, Huxley, West, Armstrong." Doctoral dissertation, Purdue University, 1989.

1023. Jordan, Terry G. "The Concept and Method." *Regional Studies: The Interplay of Land and People.* Ed. Glen E. Lich. College Station: Texas A & M University Press, 1992, 8–24.

1024. Kehde, Martha, comp. "Regionalism in American Literature: A Bibliography." *Regional Perspectives: An Examination of America's Literary Heritage.* Ed. John G. Burke. Chicago: American Library Association, 1973, 307–10.

1025. Kellock, Katharine. "The WPA Writers: Portraitists of the United States." *American Scholar* 9 (Autumn 1940): 473–82.

1026. Kelton, Elmer. "Fact, Folklore and Fiction – Regional Writing." *Texas Library Journal* 52 (May 1976): 47–51.

1027. King, Kimball. "Local Color and the Rise of the American Magazine." *Essays Mostly on Periodical Publishing in America: A Collection in Honor of Clarence Gohdes.* Eds. James Woodress, et al. Durham, N.C.: Duke University Press, 1973, 121–33.

1028. Lamar, Howard R. "Regionalism and the Broad Methodological Problem." *Regional Studies: The Interplay of Land and People.* Ed. Glen E. Lich. College Station: Texas A & M University Press, 1992, 25–44.

1029. ———. "Seeing More Than Earth and Sky: The Rise of a Great Plains Aesthetic." *Great Plains Quarterly* 9 (Spring 1989): 69–77.

1030. LaPresto, Brigitte Loos. "Agricultural Promise and Disillusionment in the California Novel: Frank Norris, John Steinbeck, Raymond Barrio." Doctoral dissertation, Bowling Green State University, 1987.

1031. Lawson, Benjamin S., Jr. "American Local Color in the British Isles." Doctoral dissertation, Bowling Green State University, 1972.

1032. Lee, James Ward. *Classics of Texas Fiction.* Dallas: E-Heart Press, 1987.

1033. ———. "Texas Fiction at the End of the Century." *Roundup Quarterly* 3 (Spring 1991): 20–28.

1034. ———. *Texas, My Texas.* Denton: University of North Texas Press, 1993.

1035. ———, ed. "Texans Speak Out on Writing and Texas Literature." *Roundup Quarterly* 1 (September 1988): 2–10.

1036. Lensink, Judy Nolte, ed. *Old Southwest/New Southwest: Essays on a Region and Its Literature.* Tucson: Tucson Public Library, 1987.

1037. Lewis, Merrill. "Discovering Pacific Northwest Writing." *Western American Literature* 15 (Winter 1981): 297–300.

1038. Lewis, Nathaniel. "Stone-Eyed Griffons: Mythology in Contemporary Montana Fiction." *Old West–New West: Centennial Essays.* Ed. Barbara Howard Meldrum. Moscow: University of Idaho Press, 1993, 199–212.

1039. Lich, Glen E., ed. *Regional Studies: The Interplay of Land and People.* College Station: Texas A & M University Press, 1992.

1040. Looney, Sandra, Arthur R. Husboe and Geoffrey Hunt, eds. *The Prairie Frontier.* [Sioux Falls, S.D.]: Nordland Heritage Foundation, 1984.

1041. Love, Glen A. "The Pacific Northwest: Regional Literacy and the Great Tradition." *Pacific Northwest Forum* 6 (Summer 1981): 22–32.

1042. Luebke, Frederick C. "Regionalism and the Great Plains: Problems of Concept and Method." *Western Historical Quarterly* 15 (January 1984): 19–38.

1043. Luther, T. N. *Collecting Taos Authors.* Albuquerque: New Mexico Book League, 1993.

1044. Lutwack, Leonard. *The Role of Place in Literature.* Syracuse: Syracuse University Press, 1984.

1045. Mabie, Hamilton W. "Provincialism in American Life." *Harper's* 134 (March 1917): 575–84.

1046. McCue, Frances. "Interviews with Northwest Writers." *Seattle Review* 10 (Fall 1987): 73–80.

1047. McDowell, Tremaine. "Regionalism in American Literature." *Minnesota History* 20 (June 1939): 105–18.

1048. Macleod, Norman, et al. "Regionalism: A Symposium." *Sewanee Review* 39 (October–December 1931): 456–83.

1049. McWilliams, Carey. "Localism in American Criticism, a Century and a Half of Controversy." *Southwest Review* 19 (1934): 410–28.

1050. ———. *The New Regionalism in American Literature.* Seattle: University of Washington Book Store, 1930.

1051. Martin, Stoddard. *California Writers: Jack London, John Steinbeck, the Tough Guys.* New York: St. Martin's Press, 1983.

1052. Mawer, Randall Ray. "Cosmopolitan Characters in Local Color Fiction." Doctoral dissertation, University of Pennsylvania, 1976.

1053. Meinig, D. W. "American Wests: Preface to a Geographical Introduction." *Annals of the Association of American Geographers* 62 (June 1972): 159–84.

1054. Milner, Clyde A., II. "The View From Wisdom: Region and Identity in the Minds of Four Westerners." *Montana: The Magazine of Western History* 41 (Summer 1991): 2–17.

1055. Milton, John R. "Materialism and Mysticism in Great Plains Literature." *Vision and Refuge: Essays on the Literature of the Great Plains.* Eds. Virginia Faulkner with Frederick C. Luebke. Lincoln: University of Nebraska Press, 1982, 31–43.

1056. ———. "Plains Landscapes and Changing Visions." *Great Plains Quarterly* 2 (Winter 1982): 55–62.

1057. Mondale, Clarence. "Concepts and Trends in Regional Studies." *American Studies International* 27 (April 1989): 13–37.

1058. Morrow, Patrick D. "Parody and Parable in Early Western Local Color Writing." *Journal of the West* 19 (January 1980): 9–16.

1059. Neinstein, Raymond L. "Neo-Regionalism in America." Doctoral dissertation, State University of New York, Buffalo, 1977.

1060. O'Connell, Nicholas. *At the Field's End: Interviews with Twenty Pacific Northwest Writers.* Seattle: Madrona Publishers, 1987.

1061. Odum, Howard W., and Harry Estill Moore. *American Regionalism.* New York: Henry Holt, 1938.

1062. Oldenburg, Ray. *The Great Good Place: Cafes, Coffee Shops, Community Centers, Beauty Parlors, General Stores, Bars, Hangouts, and How They Get You Through the Day.* New York: Paragon House, 1989.

1063. Oldham, John N. "Anatomy of Provincialism." *Sewanee Review* 44 (1936): 68–75, 145–52, 296–302.

1064. Petry, Alice Hall. "Local Color Fiction 1879–1910." Doctoral dissertation, Brown University, 1979.

1065. ———. "Universal and Particular: The Local-Color Phenomenon Reconsidered." *American Literary Realism 1870–1910* 12 (Spring 1979): 111–26.

1066. Quantic, Diane Dufva. "Learning to Live on the Land: Theories of Land and Society in Great Plains Literature." *Platte Valley Review* 17 (Winter 1989): 17–32.

1067. Radke, Merle L. "Local-Color Fiction in Middle-Western Magazines, 1865–1900." Doctoral dissertation, Northwestern University, 1965.

1068. Ransom, John C. "The Aesthetic of Regionalism." *American Review* 2 (January 1934): 290–310.

1069. Rathmell, George. "*The Overland Monthly*: California's Literary Treasure." *The Californians* 8 (March/April 1991): 12–21.

1070. Raymond, Catherine E. "'Down to Earth': Sense of Place in Midwestern Literature." Doctoral dissertation, University of Pennsylvania, 1979.

1071. "The Realities of Regionalism: A Symposium." *South Dakota Review* 18 (Winter 1981). Special issue.

1072. Reigelman, Milton M. *The Midland: A Venture in Literary Regionalism.* Iowa City: University of Iowa Press, 1975.

1073. Reynolds, Clay. "Texas Fiction in the Nineties: A Formula for the Twenty-first Century." *Cimarron Review* 94 (January 1991): 113–22.

1074. Rhode, Robert D. *Setting in the American Short Story of Local Color.* The Hague: Mouton, 1975.

1075. Ridge, Martin. "The American West: From Frontier to Region." *New Mexico Historical Review* 64 (April 1989): 125–41.

1076. Robbins, William G., Robert J. Frank and Richard E. Ross, eds. *Regionalism and the Pacific Northwest*. Corvallis: Oregon State University Press, 1983.

1077. Rolfe, Lionel. *In Search of Literary L.A.* Los Angeles: California Classic Books, 1991.

1078. Ronald, Ann. "Why Don't They Write About Nevada?" *Western American Literature* 24 (November 1989): 213–24.

1079. Rovit, Earl H. "The Regions versus the Nation: Critical Battle of the Thirties." *Mississippi Quarterly* 13 (Spring 1960): 90–98.

1080. Royce, Josiah. "Provincialism: Based upon a Study of Early Conditions in California." *Putnam's Magazine* 7(November 1909): 232–40.

1081. Saum, L. O. "The Success Theme in Great Plains Realism." *American Quarterly* 18 (Winter 1966): 579–98.

1082. Savage, George M., Jr. "Regionalism in the American Drama." Doctoral dissertation, University of Washington, 1935.

1083. Shortridge, James R. *The Middle West: Its Meaning in American Culture*. Lawrence: University Press of Kansas, 1989.

1084. Simonson, Harold P. *Beyond the Frontier: Writers, Western Regionalism, and a Sense of Place*. Fort Worth: Texas Christian University Press, 1989.

1085. Simpson, Claude M., ed. *The Local Colorists: American Short Stories, 1857–1900*. New York: Harper and Brothers, 1960.

1086. Skårdal, Dorothy Burton. "Life on the Great Plains in Scandinavian-American Literature." *Vision and Refuge: Essays on the Literature of the Great Plains*. Eds. Virginia Faulkner with Frederick C. Luebke. Lincoln: University of Nebraska Press, 1982, 71–92.

1087. Skelley, Grant Teasdale. "The *Overland Monthly* under Millicent Washburn Shinn, 1883–1894: A Study of Regional Publishing." Doctoral dissertation, University of California, Berkeley, 1968.

1088. Sloan, Karin Ramspeck. "Trading the Pen for the Spade: 19th-century German Immigrant Literature in Texas." Doctoral dissertation, Texas A & I University, 1990.

1089. "The Southwest: A Regional View." *New America* 3 (Spring 1979). Special topic issue.

1090. Spencer, Benjamin T. "Nationality During the Interregnum." *American Literature* 32 (January 1961): 434–45.

1091. ———. *The Quest for Nationality: An American Literary Campaign*. Syracuse, N.Y.: Syracuse University Press, 1957.

1092. ———. "Regionalism in American Literature." *Regionalism in America*. Ed. Merrill Jensen. Madison: University of Wisconsin Press, 1952, 219–60.

1093. Stafford, William, Lois Hudson, Frederick Manfred, and Gilbert Fite. "Panel: The Realities of Regionalism." *South Dakota Review* 26 (Winter 1988): 77–91.

1094. Stegner, Wallace. *The American West as Living Space*. Ann Arbor: University of Michigan Press, 1987.

1095. ———, and Page Stegner. "Rocky Mountain Country." *Atlantic Monthly* 241 (April 1978): 44–91.

1096. Steiner, Michael C. "Regionalism in the Great Depression." *Geographical Review* 73 (October 1983): 430–46.

1097. Stewart, George R. "The Regional Approach to Literature." *College English* 9 (April 1948): 370–75.

1098. Stratton, David H. "Hells Canyon: The Missing Link in Pacific Northwest Regionalism." *Idaho Yesterdays* 28 (Fall 1984): 3–9.

1099. Suckow, Ruth. "Middle Western Literature." *English Journal* 21 (March 1932): 175–82.

1100. Taber, Ronald Warren. "The Federal Writers' Project in the Pacific Northwest: A Case Study." Doctoral dissertation, Washington State University, 1969.

1101. Tate, Allen. "The New Provincialism...." *Virginia Quarterly Review* 21 (1945): 262–72.

1102. Thacker, Robert. *The Great Prairie Fact and Literary Imagination*. Albuquerque: University of New Mexico, 1989.

1103. Thomas, John L. "The Uses of Catastrophism: Lewis Mumford, Vernon L. Parrington, Van Wyck Brooks, and the End of American Regionalism." *American Quarterly* 42 (June 1990): 223–51.

1104. Thompson, Joyce. "Seeing Through the Veil: Concepts of Truth in Two West Texas Novels." *Journal of American Culture* 14 (Summer 1991): 69–74.

1105. Tuan, Yi-Fu. *Space and Place: The Perspective of Experience*. Minneapolis: University of Minnesota Press, 1977.

1106. ———. *Topophilia: A Study of Environmental Perception, Attitudes, and Values*. Englewood Cliffs, N.J.: Prentice-Hall, 1974.

1107. Tuppet, Mary M. "A History of *The Southwest Review*: Toward an Understanding of Regionalism." Doctoral dissertation, University of Illinois, 1966.

1108. Venis, Linda. "L.A. Novels and the Hollywood Dream Factory: Popular Art's Impact on Los Angeles Literature in the 1940s." *Southern California Quarterly* 69 (Winter 1987): 349–69.

1109. Veysey, Lawrence R. "Myth and Reality in Approaching American Regionalism." *American Quarterly* 12 (Spring 1960): 31–43.

1110. Wakoski, Diane. "The Birth of San Francisco Renaissance: Something Now Called the Whitman Tradition." *Literary Review* 32 (Fall 1988): 36–41.

1111. Walcutt, Charles C. "The Regional Novel and Its Future." *Arizona Quarterly* 1 (Summer 1945): 17–27.

1112. ———. "Regionalism – Practical or Aesthetic?" *Sewanee Review* 49 (1941): 165–72.

1113. Walterhouse, Roger R. *Bret Harte, Joaquin Miller, and the Western Local Color Story: A Study in the Origins of Popular Fiction.* Chicago: University of Chicago Libraries, 1939.

1114. Warfel, Harry R., and G. Harrison Orians, eds. *American Local-Color Stories.* New York: American Book, 1941.

1115. Warren, Robert P. "Some Don'ts for Literary Regionalists." *American Review* 8 (December 1936): 142–50.

1116. Weathers, Winston. "The Writer and His Region." *Southwestern American Literature* 2 (Spring 1972): 25–32.

1117. Webb, Walter Prescott. "The American West, Perpetual Mirage." *Harper's Magazine* 214 (May 1957): 25–31.

1118. ———. *Divided We Stand: The Crisis of a Frontierless Democracy.* New York: Farrar and Rinehart, 1937.

1119. Wells, Walter. *Tycoons and Locusts: A Regional Look at Hollywood Fiction of the 1930s.* Carbondale: Southern Illinois University Press, 1973.

1120. Williams, Cecil B. "The American Local Color Movement and Its Cultural Significance." *Oklahoma State University Publications* 48 (September 30, 1951): 5–13.

1121. ———. "Regionalism in American Literature." *Geist Einer Freien Gesellschaft.* Heidelberg: Verlag Quelle and Meyer, 1962, 331–87.

1122. Winther, Sophus K. "The Limits of Regionalism." *Arizona Quarterly* 8 (Spring 1952): 30–36.

1123. Worster, Donald. "New West, True West: Interpreting the Region's History." *Western Historical Quarterly* 18 (April 1987): 141–56.

1124. Wright, Barbara Herb. "'Golden Dreams and Leaden Realities': A Study of the American Mining Frontier Romance, 1849–1915." Doctoral dissertation, University of Colorado, Boulder, 1989.
1125. Wyatt, David. *The Fall into Eden: Landscape and Imagination in California.* New York: Cambridge University Press, 1986.
1126. Zelinsky, Wilbur. *The Cultural Geography of the United States.* Englewood Cliffs, N.J.: Prentice-Hall, 1973.

POPULAR WESTERN LITERATURE:
DIME NOVELS AND THE WESTERN

1127. Agnew, Seth M. "Destry Goes on Riding – or Working – the Six-Gun Lode." *Publisher's Weekly* 162 (August 23, 1952): 746–51.

1128. Arbuckle, Donald Redmond. "Popular Western: The History of a Commercial Literary Formula." Doctoral dissertation, University of Pennsylvania, 1977.

1129. Armitage, Shelley. "Rawhide Heroines: The Evolution of the Cowgirl and the Myth of America." *The American Self: Myth, Ideology, and Popular Culture.* Ed. Sam B. Girgus. Albuquerque: University of New Mexico Press, 1981, 166–81.

1130. Bakker, Jan. "The Popular Western – Window to the American Spirit?" *The American West as Seen by Europeans and Americans.* Ed. Rob Kroes. Amsterdam, Neth.: Free University Press, 1989, 237–51.

1131. ———. "The Western: Can It Be Great?" *Dutch Quarterly Review of Anglo-American Letters* 14 (No. 2, 1984): 138–63.

1132. Barker, Warren J., M.D. "The Stereotyped Western Story: Its Latent Meaning and Psychoeconomic Function." *Psychoanalytic Quarterly* 24 (April 1955): 270–80.

1133. Bennett, M. H. "The Scenic West: Silent Mirage." *Colorado Quarterly* 8 (Summer 1959): 15–25.

1134. Blackburn, Alexander. "A Western Renaissance." *Western American Literature* 29 (May 1994): 51–62.

1135. Bloodworth, William. "Literary Extensions of the Formula Western." *Western American Literature* 14 (Winter 1980): 287–96.

1136. Bluestone, George. "The Changing Cowboy: From Dime Novel to Dollar Film." *Western Humanities Review* 14 (Summer 1960): 331–37.

1137. Boatright, Mody C. "The American Myth Rides the Range." *Southwest Review* 36 (Summer 1951): 157–63.

1138. ———. "The Beginnings of Cowboy Fiction." *Southwest Review* 51 (Winter 1966): 11–28.

1139. ———. "The Formula in Cowboy Fiction and Drama." *Western Folklore* 28 (April 1969): 136–45.

1140. Bold, Christine. "Popular Forms I." *The Columbia History of the American Novel.* Eds. Emory Elliott, et al. New York: Columbia University Press, 1991, 285–305. Dime novels.

1141. ———. *Selling the Wild West: Popular Western Fiction, 1860 to 1960.* Bloomington: Indiana University Press, 1987.

1142. ———. "The Voice of the Fiction Factory in Dime and Pulp Westerns." *Journal of American Studies* 17 (April 1983): 29–46.

1143. Branch, Edward Douglas. *The Cowboy and His Interpreters.* New York: D. Appleton, 1926.

1144. Brashers, Howard C. "The Cowboy Story from Stereotype to Art." *Moderna Sprak* 57 (1963): 290–99.

1145. Braun, Matt. *How to Write Western Novels.* Cincinnati: Writer's Digest Books, 1988.

1146. Brown, Bill. "Popular Forms II." *The Columbia History of the American Novel.* Eds. Emory Elliott, et al. New York: Columbia University Press, 1991, 355–79. Popular Westerns.

1147. Buscombe, Edward, ed. *The BFI Companion to the Western.* New York: Atheneum, 1988.

1148. Calder, Jenni. *There Must Be a Lone Ranger: The American West in Film and in Reality.* New York: Taplinger, 1975.

1149. Capps, Benjamin. "The Promise of Western Fiction." *Roundup* 17 (October 1969): 1–2, 20; (November 1969): 2, 4, 14; (December 1969): 6, 8, 24.

1150. Carr, Nick, ed. *The Western Pulp Hero.* Mercer Island, Wash.: Starmont House, 1989.

1151. Cawelti, John G. *Adventure, Mystery, and Romance: Formula Stories as Art and Popular Culture.* Chicago: University of Chicago Press, 1976.

1152. ———. "Cowboys, Indians, Outlaws: The West in Myth and Fantasy." *American West* 1 (Spring 1964): 28–35, 77–79.

1153. ———. "The Gunfighter and Society: Good Guys, Bad Guys, Deviates, and Compulsives: A View of the Adult Western." *American West* 5 (March 1968): 30–35, 76–78.

1154. ———. "Prolegomena to the Western." *Western American Literature* 6 (Winter 1970): 259–71.

1155. ———. "Recent Trends in the Study of Popular Culture." *American Studies: An International Newsletter* 10 (Winter 1971): 23–37. Includes helpful bibliography.

1156. ———. *The Six-Gun Mystique*. Bowling Green, Ohio: Bowling Green University Popular Press, [1971]; 2d ed., 1984.

1157. Cleary, Michael. "Saddle Sore: Parody and Satire in the Contemporary Western Novel." Doctoral dissertation, Middle Tennessee State University, 1978.

1158. Clements, William M. "Savage, Pastoral, Civilized: An Ecology Typology of American Frontier Heroes." *Journal of Popular Culture* 8 (Fall 1974): 254–66.

1159. Cook, Michael L. *Dime Novel Roundup: Annotated Index 1931–1981*. Bowling Green, Ohio: Bowling Green University Popular Press, 1983.

1160. Curti, Merle. "Dime Novels and the American Tradition." *Yale Review* 26 (Summer 1937): 761–78.

1161. Daly, David, and Joel Persky. "The West and the Western." *Journal of the West* 29 (April 1990): 3–64.

1162. Davidson, Levette J. "Fact or Formula in 'Western' Fiction." *Colorado Quarterly* 3 (Winter 1955): 278–87.

1163. Davis, David B. "Ten-Gallon Hero." *American Quarterly* 6 (Summer 1954): 111–25.

1164. Davis, Kenneth W. "Splendid Spurs to the Imagination: Qualities of Modern Popular Western Fiction." *Roundup Quarterly* 1 (Summer 1989): 2–8.

1165. Davis, Robert Murray. *Playing Cowboys: Low Culture and High Art in the Western*. Norman: University of Oklahoma Press, 1991.

1166. Denning, Michael. *Mechanic Accents: Dime Novels and Working-Class Culture in America*. New York: Verso, 1987.

1167. DeVoto, Bernard. "Birth of an Art." *Harper's* 221 (December 1955): 8–9, 12, 14, 16.

1168. ———. "Phaëthon on Gunsmoke Trail." *Harper's* 209 (December 1954): 10–11, 14, 16.

1169. Dinan, John A. *The Pulp Western: A Popular History of the Western Fiction Magazine in America*. San Bernardino, Calif.: Borgo Press, 1983.

1170. Drew, Bernard A., Martin H. Greenberg, and Charles G. Waugh. *Western Series and Sequels: A Reference Guide*. New York: Garland, 1986.

1171. Durham, Philip. "The Cowboy and the Myth Makers." *Journal of Popular Culture* 1 (Summer 1967): 58–62.

1172. ———. "Dime Novels: An American Heritage." *Western Humanities Review* 9 (Winter 1954–55): 33–43.

1173. ———. "Riders of the Plains: American Westerns." *Neuphilogische Mitteilungen* 58 (November 1957): 22–38.

1174. ———, and Everett L. Jones. "The West as Fiction." *The Negro Cowboys.* New York: Dodd, Mead, 1965, 220–30.

1175. Dykes, J.C. "High Spots of Western Fiction: 1902–1952." *Westerners Brand Book* 12 (September 1955): 49–56.

1176. Estleman, Loren D. *The Wister Trace: Classic Novels of the American Frontier.* Ottawa, Ill.: Jameson Books, 1987.

1177. Etulain, Richard W. "The Historical Development of the Western." *Journal of Popular Culture* 7 (Winter 1973): 717–26.

1178. ———. "Literary Historians and the Western." *Journal of Popular Culture* 4 (Fall 1970): 518–26.

1179. ———. "Origins of the Western." *Journal of Popular Culture* 6 (Spring 1972): 799–805.

1180. ———. "The Western." *Handbook of American Popular Culture.* Vol. 1. Ed. M. Thomas Inge. Westport, Conn.: Greenwood Press, 1978, 355–76.

1181. ———, and Michael T. Marsden, eds. *The Popular Western: Essays Toward a Definition.* Bowling Green, Ohio: Bowling Green University Popular Press, 1974. Reprints *Journal of Popular Culture* 7 (Winter 1973).

1182. Fishwick, Marshall W. "The Cowboy: America's Contribution to the World's Mythology." *Western Folklore* 11 (April 1952): 77–92.

1183. ———. "Daniel Boone and the Pattern of the Western Hero." *Filson Club Historical Quarterly* 27 (1953): 119–38.

1184. Folsom, James K. *The American Western Novel.* New Haven, Conn.: College and University Press, 1966.

1185. Frederick, John T. "Worthy Westerns." *English Journal* 43 (September 1954): 281–86, 296.

1186. French, Warren. "The Cowboy in the Dime Novel." *Texas Studies in English* 30 (1951): 219–34.

1187. Gardner, Erle Stanley. "My Stories of the Wild West." *Atlantic Monthly* 218 (July 1966): 60–62.

1188. Garfield, Brian. "What Is the 'Formula'?" *Roundup* 13 (August 1965): 1–2.

1189. Garrett, Greg. "The American West and the American Western: Printing the Legend." *Journal of American Culture* 14 (Summer 1991): 99–105.

1190. Gibson, Michael D. "The Western: A Selective Bibliography." *Journal of Popular Culture* 7 (Winter 1973): 743–48.

1191. Gleason, G. Dale. "Attitudes Toward Law and Order in the American Western." Doctoral dissertation, Washington State University, 1978.

1192. Goodykoontz, Colin B. "The Wild West or Beadle's Dime Novels." *The Westerner Brand Book 1945.* Ed. Herbert O. Brayer. Denver: The Westerners, 1946, 25–37.

1193. Goulart, Ron. *Cheap Thrills: An Informal History of the Pulp Magazines.* New Rochelle, N.Y.: Arlington House, 1972.

1194. Gregory, Horace. "Guns of the Roaring West." *Avon Book of Modern Writing No. 2.* New York, 1954, 217–35.

1195. Gruber, Frank. *The Pulp Jungle.* Los Angeles: Sherbourne Press, 1967.

1196. Hamilton, Cynthia. *Western and Hardboiled Detective Fiction in America: From High Noon to Midnight.* London: Macmillan, 1987.

1197. Harris, Charles W., and Buck Rainey, eds. *The Cowboy: Six-Shooters, Songs, and Sex.* Norman: University of Oklahoma Press, 1976.

1198. Harvey, Charles M. "The Dime Novel in American Life." *Atlantic Monthly* 100 (July 1907): 37–45.

1199. Horton, Andrew S. "Ken Kesey, John Updike and the Lone Ranger." *Journal of Popular Culture* 8 (Winter 1974): 570–78.

1200. Hutchinson, W. H. "Grassfire on the Great Plains." *Southwest Review* 41 (Spring 1956): 181–85.

1201. ———. "Virgins, Villains, and Varmints." *Huntington Library Quarterly* 16 (August 1953): 381–92.

1202. Jacobson, Larry King. "Mythic Origins of the Western." Doctoral dissertation, University of Minnesota, 1973.

1203. Johannsen, Albert. *The House of Beadle and Adams and Its Dime and Nickel Novels.* 2 vols. Norman: University of Oklahoma Press, 1950; supplement, 1962.

1204. Jones, Daryl E. "Blood'n Thunder: Virgins, Villains, and Violence in the Dime Novel Western." *Journal of Popular Culture* 4 (Fall 1970): 507–17.

1205. ———. "Clenched Teeth and Curses: Revenge and the Dime Novel Outlaw Hero." *Journal of Popular Culture* 7 (Winter 1973): 652–65.

1206. ———. *The Dime Novel Western.* Bowling Green, Ohio: Bowling Green State University Popular Press, 1978. The best study of this topic.

1207. Kelton, Elmer. "The Myth of the Mythical West." *Western American Literature* 26 (May 1991): 3–8.

1208. ———. "The Trail Drive in Western Fiction." *Roundup Quarterly* 3 (Spring 1991): 6–19.

1209. Kent, Thomas L. "The Formal Conventions of the Dime Novel." *Journal of Popular Culture* 16 (Summer 1982): 37–47.

1210. Klaschus, Candy. "You Can't Keep a Good Man Down: Sex in the Popular Western." *Roundup Quarterly* 4 (Fall 1991): 27–36.

1211. Leach, Joseph. "The Paper-Back Texan: Father of the Western Hero." *Western Humanities Review* 11 (Summer 1957): 267–76.

1212. Leithead, J. Edward. "The Klondike Stampede in Dime Novels." *American Book Collector* 21 (1971): 23–29.

1213. Marsden, Michael T. "The Modern Western." *Journal of the West* 19 (January 1980): 54–61.

1214. ———. "Savior in the Saddle: The Sagebrush Testament." *Illinois Quarterly* 36 (December 1973): 5–15.

1215. Miller, Alexander. "The 'Western' – A Theological Note." *Christian Century* 74 (November 27, 1956): 1409–10.

1216. Milton, John R. *The Novel of the American West.* Lincoln: University of Nebraska Press, 1980, 1–40.

1217. Monaghan, Jay. *The Great Rascal: The Life and Adventures of Ned Buntline.* New York: Bonanza Books, 1951.

1218. Munden, Kenneth J., M.D. "A Contribution to the Psychological Understanding of the Origins of the Cowboy and His Myth." *American Image* 15 (Summer 1958): 103–48.

1219. Nesbitt, John D. "Literary Convention in the Classic Western Novel." Doctoral dissertation, University of California, Davis, 1980.

1220. ———. "A New Look at Two Popular Western Classics." *South Dakota Review* 18 (Spring 1980): 30–42.

1221. Nussbaum, Martin. "The 'Adult Western' as an American Art Form." *Folklore* 70 (September 1959): 460–67.

1222. ———. "Sociological Symbolism in the 'Adult Western.'" *Social Forces* 39 (October 1960): 25–28.

1223. Nye, Russel. *The Unembarrassed Muse: The Popular Arts in America.* New York: Dial Press, 1970, 280–304.

1224. Pearson, Edmund. *Dime Novels; or, Following an Old Trail in Popular Literature.* Boston: Little, Brown, 1929.

1225. Percy, Walker. "Decline of the Western." *Commonweal* 68 (May 16, 1958): 181–83.

1226. Primeau, Ronald. "Slave Narrative Turning Westward: Deadwood Dick Rides into Difficulties." *Midamerica* (1974): 16–35.

1227. Reynolds, Quentin. *The Fiction Factory.* New York: Random House, 1955.

1228. Roberts, Thomas J. "*Gold Bullet Sport,* a Dime Novel by Buffalo Bill; or, A Record of an Expedition into the Great American Desert." *Texas Studies in Literature and Language* 33 (Fall 1991): 403–44.

1229. Robinson, Forrest G. *Having It Both Ways: Self-Subversion in Western Popular Classics.* Albuquerque: University of New Mexico Press, 1993.

1230. Rosenberg, Betty. "The Poor, Lonesome, Unreviewed Cowboy." *Library Journal* 85 (December 15, 1960): 4432–33.

1231. *Roundup Quarterly.* The monthly publication of the Western Writers of America. Each issue contains useful information on the Western. Continues *The Roundup.*

1232. Settle, William A., Jr. "Literature as History: The Dime Novel as an Historian's Tool." *Literature and History.* Ed. I. E. Cadenhead, Jr. University of Tulsa Monograph Series, No. 9. Tulsa: University of Tulsa, 1970, 9–20.

1233. Simmons, Michael K. "The Dime Novel and the American *Zeitgeist* 1860–1910: A Question of Influence." Doctoral dissertation, Indiana University of Pennsylvania, 1973.

1234. "The Six-Gun Galahad." *Time* 73 (March 30, 1959): 52–60.

1235. Skjelver, Mabel R. "William Wallace Cook: Dime Novelist." *Annals of Wyoming* 49 (Spring 1977): 109–30.

1236. Smith, Henry Nash. *Virgin Land: The American West as Symbol and Myth.* Cambridge, Mass.: Harvard University Press, 1950, 1970.

1237. Snell, Joseph W. "The Wild and Wooly West of the Popular Writer." *Nebraska History* 48 (Summer 1967): 141–53.

1238. Sonnichsen, C. L. *From Hopalong to Hud: Thoughts on Western Fiction.* College Station: Texas A & M University Press, 1978.

1239. ———. "Gene Rhodes and the Decadent West." *Roundup Quarterly* 4 (Fall 1991): 17–26.

1240. Steckmesser, Kent Ladd. *The Western Hero in History and Legend.* Norman: University of Oklahoma Press, 1965.

1241. Straight, Michael. "Truth and Formula for the Western Novel." *South Dakota Review* 2 (Autumn 1964): 88–93.

1242. Tompkins, Jane. "West of Everything." *South Atlantic Quarterly* 86 (Fall 1987): 357–77.

1243. ———. *West of Everything: The Inner Life of Westerns.* New York: Oxford University Press, 1992.

1244. Topping, Gary. "The Rise of the Western." *Journal of the West* 19 (January 1980): 29–35.

1245. Turner, E. S. *Boys Will Be Boys.* London, 1948; 2d ed., rev. London: Joseph Michael, 1957.

1246. Walker, Don D. "The Minimal Western." *Western American Literature* 23 (August 1988): 121–27.

1247. ———. "Notes Toward a Literary Criticism of the Western." *Journal of Popular Culture* 7 (Winter 1973): 728–41.

1248. ———. "Wister, Roosevelt, and James: A Note on the Western." *American Quarterly* 12 (Fall 1960): 358–66.

1249. Williams, John. "The 'Western': Definitions of the Myth." *Nation* 193 (November 18, 1961): 401–6.

1250. Wilson, Daniel J. "Nature in Western Popular Literature from the Dime Novel to Zane Grey." *North Dakota Quarterly* 44 (Spring 1976): 41–50.

1251. Wylder, Delbert E. "The Popular Western Novel: An Essay Review." *Western American Literature* 14 (Winter 1970): 299–303.

1252. ———. *Popular Westerns.* Cassette. Deland, Fla.: Everett/Edwards, 1974.

WESTERN FILM

1253. Adams, Les, and Buck Rainey. *Shoot-em-Ups: The Complete Reference Guide to Westerns of the Sound Era.* Metuchen, N.J.: Scarecrow Press, 1985.

1254. Aleiss, Angela Maria. "From Adversaries to Allies: The American Indian in Hollywood Films, 1930–1950." Doctoral dissertation, Columbia University, 1991.

1255. Astre, Georges-Albert, and Albert-Patrick Hoarau. *Univers du Western.* Paris: Éditions Seghers, 1973.

1256. Balio, Tino. *Grand Design: Hollywood as a Modern Business Enterprise, 1930–1939.* New York: Scribner, 1993.

1257. Barsness, John A. "A Question of Standard." *Film Quarterly* 21 (Fall 1967): 32–37.

1258. Bazin, André. *What is Cinema?* Vol. 2. Trans. Hugh Gray. Berkeley: University of California Press, 1971.

1259. Bluestone, George. "The Changing Cowboy: From Dime Novel to Dollar Film." *Western Humanities Review* 14 (Summer 1960): 331–37.

1260. Boatright, Mody C. "The Cowboy Enters the Movies." *The Sunny Slopes of Long Ago.* Eds. Wilson M. Hudson and Allen Maxwell. Dallas: Southern Methodist University Press, 1966, 51–69.

1261. ———. "The Morality Play on Horseback: Tom Mix." *Tire Shrinker to Dragster.* Publications of the Texas Folklore Society, 34. Austin: Encino Press, 1968, 63–71.

1262. Bogdanovich, Peter. *John Ford.* London: Studio Vista, 1967.

1263. Bowser, Eileen. *The Transformation of Cinema, 1907–1915.* New York: Maxwell Macmillan International, 1990.

1264. Brauer, Ralph. "Who Are Those Guys? The Movie Western During the TV Era." *Journal of Popular Culture* 2 (Fall 1973): 389–404.

1265. ——— (with Donna Brauer). *The Horse, The Gun and The Piece of Property: Changing Images of the TV Western.* Bowling Green, Ohio: Bowling Green University Popular Press, 1975.

1266. Brownlow, Kevin. *The War, The West and The Wilderness.* New York: Alfred A. Knopf, 1979.

1267. Bukalski, Peter J. *Film Research: A Critical Bibliography.* Boston: G.K. Hall, 1972.

1268. Buscombe, Edward, ed. *The BFI Companion to the Western.* New York: Atheneum, 1988.

1269. Calder, Jenni. *There Must Be a Lone Ranger: The American West in Film and in Reality.* New York: Taplinger, 1975.

1270. Cawelti, John G. *Adventure, Mystery, and Romance: Formula Stories as Art and Popular Culture.* Chicago: University of Chicago Press, 1976.

1271. ———. "God's Country, Las Vegas and the Gunfighter: Differing Visions of the West." *Western American Literature* 9 (February 1975): 273–83.

1272. ———. "The Gunfighter and the Hard-boiled Dick: Some Ruminations on American Fantasies of Heroism." *American Studies* 16 (Fall 1975): 49–65.

1273. Cleary, Michael. "*True Grit*: Parody, Formula, Myth." *North Dakota Quarterly* 54 (Winter 1986): 72–86.

1274. Daly, David, and Joel Persky. "The West and the Western." *Journal of the West* 29 (April 1990): 3–64.

1275. Davis, Ronald L. *Hollywood Beauty: Linda Darnell and the American Dream.* Norman: University of Oklahoma Press, 1991.

1276. Engel, Leonard. "Space and Enclosure in Cooper and Peckinpah: Regeneration in the Open Spaces." *Journal of American Culture* 14 (Summer 1991): 86–93.

1277. ———, ed. *The Big Empty: Essays on Western Landscapes as Narratives.* Albuquerque: University of New Mexico Press, 1994.

1278. Esselman, Kathryn C. "When the Cowboy Stopped Kissing His Horse." *Journal of Popular Culture* 6 (Fall 1972): 337–49.

1279. Etulain, Richard W. "Changing Images: The Cowboy in Western Films." *Colorado Heritage* 1 (1981): 37–55.

1280. ———. "Recent Interpretations of Western Films: A Bibliographical Essay." *Journal of the West* 22 (October 1983): 72–81.

1281. ———, ed. *Western Films: A Brief History.* Manhattan, Kans.: Sunflower University Press, 1983.

1282. Evans, Max. *Sam Peckinpah: Master of Violence.* Vermillion, S. Dak.: Dakota Press, 1972.

1283. Everson, William K. *American Silent Film.* New York: Oxford University Press, 1978.

1284. Fender, Stephen. "The Western and the Contemporary." [British] *Journal of American Studies* 6 (April 1972): 97–108.

1285. Fenin, George N., and William K. Everson. *The Western: From Silents to the Seventies.* New York: Grossman Publishers, 1973. Updates the authors' *The Western: From Silents to Cinerama,* 1962.

1286. Fielding, Raymond. *A Bibliography of Theses and Dissertations on the Subject of Film: 1916–1979.* Houston: University Film Association, 1979. Lists nearly 1,500 unannotated items.

1287. Folsom, James K. "'Western' Themes and Western Film." *Western American Literature* 2 (Fall 1967): 195–203.

1288. Foote, Cheryl J. "Changing Images of Women in the Western Film." *Journal of the West* 22 (October 1983): 64–71.

1289. Ford, Charles. *Historie du Western.* Paris: Editions Pierre Horay, 1964.

1290. Frayling, Christopher. *Spaghetti Westerns: Cowboys and Europeans from Karl May to Sergio Leone.* London: Routledge and Kegan Paul, 1981.

1291. French, Philip. *Westerns: Aspects of a Movie Genre.* Rev ed. New York: Oxford University Press, 1977.

1292. Friar, Ralph E., and Natasha A. Friar. *The Only Good Indian...The Hollywood Gospel.* New York: Drama Book Specialists, 1972.

1293. Gallagher, Tag. *John Ford: The Man and His Films.* Berkeley: University of California Press, 1986.

1294. García, Juan R. "Hollywood and the West: Mexican Images in American Films." *Old Southwest/New Southwest: Essays on a Region and Its Literature.* Ed. Judy Nolte Lensink. Tucson: Tucson Public Library, 1987, 75–90.

1295. Garfield, Brian. *Western Films: A Complete Guide.* New York: Rawson Associates, 1982.

1296. Georgakas, Dan. "They Have Not Spoken: American Indians in Film." *Film Quarterly* 25 (Spring 1972): 26–32.

1297. Goetzmann, William H., and William N. Goetzmann. *The West of the Imagination.* New York: Norton, 1986.

1298. Goldstein, Bernice, and Robert Perucci. "The TV Western and the Modern American Spirit." *Southwest Social Science Quarterly* 43 (March 1963): 357–66.

1299. Graham, Don. *Cowboys and Cadillacs: How Hollywood Looks at Texas.* Austin: Texas Monthly, 1983.

1300. ———. "Moo-vie Cows: The Trail to Hollywood." *Southwestern American Literature* 18 (Fall 1992): 1–11.

1301. ———. *No Name on the Bullet: A Biography of Audie Murphy.* New York: Viking, 1989.

1302. Hardy, Phil. *The Western: The Film Encyclopedia.* New York: William Morrow, 1983.

1303. Harrington, John. "Understanding Hollywood's Indian Rhetoric." *Canadian Review of American Studies* 8 (Spring 1977): 77–88.

1304. Hart, William S. *My Life East and West.* Boston: Houghton Mifflin, 1929; New York: Benjamin Blom, 1966.

1305. Hilger, Michael. *The American Indian in Film.* Metuchen, N.J.: Scarecrow Press, 1986.

1306. Homans, Peter. "Puritanism Revisited: An Analysis of the Contemporary Screen-Image Western." *Studies in Public Communication* 3 (1961): 73–84.

1307. Howze, William Clell. "The Influence of Western Painting and Genre Painting on the Films of John Ford." Doctoral dissertation, University of Texas, Austin, 1986.

1308. Hoy, Jim. "Rodeo in American Film." *Heritage of the Great Plains* 23 (Spring 1990): 26–32.

1309. Hutton, Paul Andrew. "The Celluloid Alamo." *Arizona and the West* 28 (Spring 1986): 5–22.

1310. ———. "The Celluloid Custer." *Red River Valley Historical Review* 4 (Fall 1979): 20–43.

1311. ———. "Celluloid Lawman: Wyatt Earp Goes to Hollywood." *American West* 21 (May/June 1984): 58–65.

1312. ———. "'Correct in Every Detail': General Custer in Hollywood." *Montana: The Magazine of Western History* 41 (Winter 1991): 28–57.

1313. ———. "Dreamscape Desperado." *New Mexico Magazine* 68 (June 1990): 44–57. Billy the Kid films.

1314. ———. "From Little Big Horn to Little Big Man: The Changing Image of a Western Hero in Popular Culture." *Western Historical Quarterly* 7 (January 1976): 19–45. General Custer.

1315. Jefchak, Andrew. "Prostitutes and Schoolmarms: An Essay on Women in Western Films." *Heritage of the Great Plains* 16 (Summer 1983): 19–26.

1316. Kaminsky, Stuart M. *Clint Eastwood.* New York: Signet Books, 1974.

1317. Kitses, Jim. *Horizons West... Studies of Authorship Within the Western.* Bloomington: Indiana University Press, 1969.

1318. Koszarski, Diane Kaiser. *The Complete Films of William S. Hart: A Pictorial Record.* New York: Dover, 1980.

1319. Koszarski, Richard. *An Evening's Entertainment: The Age of the Silent Feature Picture, 1915–1928.* New York: Charles Scribner's Sons, 1991.

1320. Lahmen, Peter Robert. "John Ford and the Auteur Theory." Doctoral dissertation, University of Wisconsin, Madison, 1978.

1321. Langman, Larry. *A Guide to Silent Westerns.* Westport, Conn.: Greenwood Press, 1992.

1322. Lenihan, John H. "Classics and Social Commentary: Postwar Westerns, 1946–1960." *Journal of the West* 22 (October 1983): 34–42.

1323. ———. *Showdown: Confronting Modern America in the Western Film.* Urbana: University of Illinois Press, 1980.

1324. Leong, Russell, ed. *Moving the Image: Independent Asian Pacific American Media Arts.* Seattle: University of Washington Press, 1991.

1325. *Le Western: Sources, Thèmes, mythologies, auteurs, acteurs, filmographies.* Paris: Union Générale d'Editions, 1966.

1326. McBride, Joseph. *John Ford.* New York: Da Capo Press, 1975.

1327. ———, ed. *Focus on Howard Hawks.* Englewood Cliffs, N.J.: Prentice-Hall, 1972.

1328. McCarthy, John Alan. "Sam Peckinpah and *The Wild Bunch.*" *Film Heritage* 5 (Winter 1969–70): 1–10, 32.

1329. McDonald, Archie P., ed. *Shooting Stars: Heroes and Heroines of Western Film.* Bloomington: Indiana University Press, 1987.

1330. Maciel, David R. *El Norte: The U.S.–Mexican Border in Contemporary Cinema.* Institute for Regional Studies of the Californias. San Diego: San Diego State University, 1990.

1331. McKinney, Doug. *Sam Peckinpah.* Boston: G. K. Hall, 1979.

1332. McMurtry, Larry. "Cowboys, Movies, Myths, and Cadillacs: Realism in the Western." *Man in the Movies.* Ed. W. R. Robinson. Baltimore: Penguin Books, 1967.

1333. Manchel, Frank. *Cameras West.* Englewood Cliffs, N.J.: Prentice-Hall, 1971.

1334. Marsden, Michael T. "The Rise of the Western Movie: From Sagebrush to Screen." *Journal of the West* 22 (October 1983): 17–23.

1335. ———. "Savior in the Saddle: The Sagebrush Testament." *Illinois Quarterly* 36 (December 1973): 5–15.

1336. Marshall, Susan Elaine. "Within the Moral Eye – Peckinpah's Art of Visual Narration." Doctoral dissertation, University of Florida, 1984.

1337. Mass, Roslyn. "Values in Film: A Comparison of Selected American Western Films of the 1940s and the 1970s." Doctoral dissertation, New York University, 1978.

1338. Meyer, William R. *The Making of the Great Westerns.* New Rochelle, N.J.: Arlington House, 1979.

1339. Money, Mary Alice. "Evolutions of the Popular Western in Novels, Films, and Television." Doctoral dissertation, University of Texas, Austin, 1975.

1340. Mortimer, Barbara Anne. "From Monument Valley to Vietnam: Revisions of the American Captivity Narrative in Hollywood Film." Doctoral dissertation, Emory University, 1990.

1341. Movshovitz, Howard. "The Still Point: Women in the Westerns of John Ford." *Frontiers* 7 (No. 3, 1984): 68–72.

1342. Musser, Charles. *The Emergence of Cinema: The American Screen to 1907.* New York: Charles Scribner's Sons, 1991.

1343. Nachbar, Jack. "Horses, Harmony, Hope and Hormones: Western Movies, 1930–1946." *Journal of the West* 22 (October 1983): 24–33.

1344. ———, ed. *Focus on the Western.* Englewood Cliffs, N.J.: Prentice-Hall, 1974.

1345. ———, ed. *Western Films: An Annotated Critical Bibliography.* New York: Garland, 1975.

1346. ———, Jackie R. Donath, and Chris Foran. *Western Films 2: An Annotated Critical Bibliography from 1974 to 1987.* New York: Garland, 1988.

1347. O'Connor, John E. *The Hollywood Indian: Stereotypes of Native Americans in Films.* Trenton: New Jersey Museum, 1980.

1348. Palmieri, Rory Albert Joseph. "The Old West and the Modern World: Western Attributes in the Western and Non-Western Films of Sam Peckinpah." Doctoral dissertation, Brown University, 1984.

1349. Parkhurst, Donald B. "Broncho Billy and Niles, California: A Romance of the Early Movies." *Pacific Historian* 26 (Winter 1982): 1–22.

1350. Pauly, Thomas H. "The Cold War Western." *Western Humanities Review* 33 (Summer 1979): 257–73.

1351. ———. "What's Happened to the Western Movie?" *Western Humanities Review* 28 (Summer 1974): 260–69.

1352. Pettit, Arthur G. "Nightmare and Nostalgia: The Cinema West of Sam Peckinpah." *Western Humanities Review* 29 (September 1975): 10–15.

1353. ———. (with Dennis E. Showalter). *Images of the Mexican-American in Fiction and Film.* College Station: Texas A & M University Press, 1980.

1354. Phillips, Robert W. *Silver Screen Cowboys.* Layton, Utah: Peregrine Smith Books, 1993.

1355. Pilkington, William T., and Don Graham, eds. *Western Movies*. Albuquerque: University of New Mexico Press, 1979.

1356. Pitts, Michael R. *Western Movies: A TV and Video Guide to 4,200 Genre Films*. Jefferson, N.C.: McFarland, 1986.

1357. Place, J. A. *The Western Films of John Ford*. Secaucus, N.J.: Citadel Press, 1974.

1358. Putnam, Ann. "The Bearer of the Gaze in Ridley Scott's *Thelma and Louise*." *Western American Literature* 27 (February 1993): 291–302.

1359. Rainey, Buck. *The Shoot-em-Ups Ride Again. A Supplement*. Metuchen, N.J.: Scarecrow Press, 1990.

1360. Réyes, Luis, and Peter Rubie. *Hispanics in Hollywood: An Encyclopedia*. New York: Garland, 1994.

1361. Rieupeyrout, Jean-Louis. *La grande adventure du western: du Far West á Hollywood, 1894–1963*. Paris: Éditions du Cerf, 1964.

1362. ———. *Le western; ou, Le cinéma américain par excellence*. Paris: Éditions du Cerf, 1953.

1363. Robertson, Richard. "New Directions in Westerns of the 1960s and 70s." *Journal of the West* 22 (October 1983): 43–52.

1364. Sarf, Wayne Michael. *God Bless You, Buffalo Bill: A Layman's Guide to History and the Western Film*. New York: Cornwall Books, 1983.

1365. Sarris, Andrew. "*Stagecoach* in 1939 and in Retrospect." *Action* 6 (September–October 1971): 30–33.

1366. Saxton, Christine. "Illusions of Grandeur: The Representation of Space in the American Western Films." Doctoral dissertation, University of California, Berkeley, 1984.

1367. Schackel, Sandra Kay. "Women in Western Films: The Civilizer, the Saloon Singer, and Their Modern Sister." *Shooting Stars: Heroes and Heroines of Western Film*. Ed. Archie P. McDonald. Bloomington: Indiana University Press, 1987, 196–217.

1368. Schein, Harry. "The Olympian Cowboy." *American Scholar* 24 (Summer 1955): 309–20.

1369. Sennett, Ted. *Great Hollywood Westerns*. New York: Abrams, 1990.

1370. Seydor, Paul. *Peckinpah: The Western Films*. Urbana: University of Illinois Press, 1980.

1371. Shadoian, Jack. "Yuh Got Pecos! Doggone, Belle, Yuh're As Good As Two Men!" *Journal of Popular Culture* 12 (Spring 1979): 721–36.

1372. Shiveley, JoEllen. "Cowboys and Indians: The Perception of Western Films among American Indians and Anglo-Americans." Doctoral dissertation, Stanford University, 1990.

1373. Silver, Charles. *The Western Film.* New York: Pyramid Productions, 1976.

1374. Simons, John L. "The Tragedy of Love in *The Wild Bunch.*" *Western Humanities Review* 39 (Spring 1985): 1–19.

1375. Sinclair, Andrew. *John Ford: The Waning of the Great West, A Biography.* New York: Dial Press, 1979.

1376. Slotkin, Richard. *Gunfighter Nation: The Myth of the Frontier in Twentieth-Century America.* New York: Atheneum, 1992.

1377. Smith, Paul. *Clint Eastwood: A Cultural Production.* Minneapolis: University of Minnesota Press, 1993.

1378. Sonnichsen, C. L. "The West that Wasn't." *American West* 14 (November–December 1977): 8–15.

1379. Spears, Jack. "Hollywood's Oklahoma." *Chronicles of Oklahoma* 67 (Winter 1989/90): 340–81.

1380. ———. "The Indian on the Screen." *Films in Review* 10 (January 1959): 18–35.

1381. Stedman, Raymond William. *Shadows of the Indian: Stereotypes in American Culture.* Norman: University of Oklahoma Press, 1982.

1382. Stekler, Paul. "Essays on the West: Custer and Crazy Horse Ride Again. . . And Again, and Again: Filmmaking and History at the Little Bighorn." *Montana: The Magazine of Western History* 42 (Autumn 1992): 63–72.

1383. Stowell, Peter. *John Ford.* Boston: Twayne, 1986.

1384. Tatum, Stephen. "The Western Film Critic as 'Shootist'." *Journal of Popular Film and Television* 11 (Fall 1983): 114–21.

1385. Tompkins, Jane. *West of Everything: The Inner Life of Westerns.* New York: Oxford University Press, 1992.

1386. Trimmer, Joseph F. "*The Virginian*: Novel and Films." *Illinois Quarterly* 35 (December 1972): 5–18.

1387. Tuska, Jon. *The American West in Film: Critical Approaches to the Western.* Westport, Conn.: Greenwood Press, 1985

1388. ———. *The Filming of the West.* Garden City, N.Y.: Doubleday, 1976.

1389. ———. *A Variable Harvest: Essays and Reviews of Film and Literature.* Jefferson, N.C.: McFarland, 1990.

1390. Warshow, Robert. "Movie Chronicle: The Westerner." *The Immediate Experience.* Garden City, N.Y.: Doubleday, 1962, 135–54. First appeared in *Partisan Review* 21 (March–April 1954): 190–203.

1391. Welsh, Michael. "Origins of Western Film Companies, 1887–1920." *Journal of the West* 22 (October 1983): 5–16.

1392. West, Elliott. "An End to Dreaming: The American Vision in Recent Westerns." *Red River Valley Historical Review* 5 (Summer 1980): 22–39.

1393. ———. "Shots in the Dark: Television and the Western Myth." *Montana: The Magazine of Western History* 38 (Spring 1988): 72–76.

1394. Westbrook, Max. "Flag and Family in John Wayne's Westerns: The Audience as Co-Conspirator." *Western American Literature* 29 (May 1994): 25–40.

1395. ———. "The Night John Wayne Danced with Shirley Temple." *Western American Literature* 25 (Summer 1990): 157–69.

1396. Whitehall, Richard. "The Heroes Are Tired." *Film Quarterly* 20 (Winter 1966–67): 12–24.

1397. Willett, Ralph. "The American Western: Myth and Anti-Myth." *Journal of Popular Culture* 4 (Fall 1970): 455–63.

1398. Winkler, Martin M. "Classical Mythology and the Western Film." *Comparative Literature Studies* 22 (Winter 1985): 516–40.

1399. Wood, Robin. *Howard Hawks.* Garden City, N.Y.: Doubleday, 1968.

1400. Wright, Will. *SixGuns and Society: A Structural Study of the Western.* Berkeley: University of California Press, 1975.

1401. Young, Vernon. "The West in Celluloid: Hollywood's Lost Horizons." *Southwest Review* 28 (Spring 1953): 126–34.

1402. Zolotow, Maurice. *Shooting Star: A Biography of John Wayne.* New York: Simon and Schuster, 1974.

INDIAN LITERATURE AND INDIANS
IN WESTERN LITERATURE

1403. Allen, Paula Gunn. "The Mythopoeic Vision in Native American Literature: The Problem of Myth." *American Indian Culture and Research Journal* 1 (1974): 3–13.

1404. ———. *The Sacred Hoop: Recovering the Feminine in American Indian Traditions.* Boston: Beacon, 1986.

1405. ———, ed. *Studies in American Indian Literature: Critical Essays and Course Designs.* New York: Modern Language Association, 1983.

1406. ———, ed. *Voice of the Turtle: American Indian Literature.* New York: Ballantine Books, 1994.

1407. Allen, T. D. *The Whispering Wind: Poetry of Young American Indians.* Garden City, N.Y.: Doubleday, 1972.

1408. Anderson, Vicki. *Native Americans in Fiction: A Guide to 765 Books, K-9, For Librarians and Teachers.* Jefferson, N.C.: McFarland, 1994.

1409. Austin, Mary. *American Rhythm: Studies and Reexpressions of American Indian Songs.* 1930; New York: Cooper Square, 1972.

1410. Ballinger, Franchot. "Living Sideways: Social Themes and Social Relationships in Native American Trickster Tales." *American Indian Quarterly* 13 (Winter 1989): 15–30.

1411. ———. "The Responsible Center: Man and Nature in Pueblo and Navaho Ritual Songs and Prayers." *American Quarterly* 30 (Spring 1978): 90–107.

1412. Ballotti, Geno A. "The Southwest Indian in Fiction." *Studies in the Literature of the West.* Laramie: University of Wyoming, 1956, 130–56.

1413. Barnett, Louise K. *The Ignoble Savage: American Literary Racism, 1790–1890.* Westport, Conn.: Greenwood Press, 1975.

1414. ———. "Nineteenth-Century Indian Hater Fiction: A Paradigm for Racism." *South Atlantic Quarterly* 74 (1975): 224–36.

1415. Bataille, Gretchen M., ed. *Native American Women: A Biographical Dictionary.* New York: Garland, 1993.

1416. ———, and Kathleen Mullen Sands. *American Indian Women, Telling Their Lives*. Lincoln: University of Nebraska Press, 1984.

1417. Beidler, Peter G. "Animals and Human Development in the Contemporary American Indian Novel." *Western American Literature* 14 (Summer 1979): 133–48.

1418. ———, and Marion F. Egge. *The American Indian in Short Fiction: An Annotated Bibliography*. Metuchen, N.J.: Scarecrow Press, 1979.

1419. Berkhofer, Robert F., Jr. *The White Man's Indian: Images of the American Indian from Columbus to the Present*. New York: Alfred A. Knopf, 1978.

1420. Berkman, Brenda. "The Vanishing Race: Conflicting Images of the American Indian in Children's Literature, 1880–1930." *North Dakota Quarterly* 44 (Spring 1966): 31–40.

1421. Bevis, William. "American Indian Verse Translations." *College English* 35 (March 1974): 693–703.

1422. Bishop, Elizabeth. "Reshaping Ethnicity: The Half-Blood as Shaman in Native American Literature." Doctoral dissertation, Bowling Green State University, 1992.

1423. Bloodworth, William. "Neihardt, Momaday, and the Art of Indian Autobiography." *Where the West Ends*. Eds. Arthur R. Huseboe and William Geyer. Sioux Falls, S. Dak.: Center for Western Studies Press, 1978, 152–60.

1424. ———. "Varieties of American Indian Autobiography." *MELUS* 5 (Fall 1978): 67–81.

1425. Brandon, William, ed. *The Magic World: American Indian Songs and Poems*. New York: William Morrow, 1971; Athens: Ohio University Press, 1991.

1426. Brant, Beth, ed. *A Gathering of Spirit: Writing and Art by North American Indian Women*. Rockland, Maine: Sinister Wisdom, 1984.

1427. Brayboy, Mary Elizabeth Jones. "Voices of Indianness: The Lived World of Native American Women." Doctoral dissertation, University of North Carolina, Greensboro, 1990.

1428. Brenzo, Rich[ard Allen]. "American Indians vs. American Writers." *Margins* 14 (October/November 1974): 40–45, 88.

1429. ———. "Civilization Against the Savage: The Destruction of Indians in American Novels, 1823–1854." Doctoral dissertation, University of Wisconsin, Milwaukee, 1973.

1430. Brotherston, Gordon. *The Book of the Fourth World: Reading the Native Americans Through Their Literature*. New York: Cambridge University Press, 1993.

1431. Bruchac, Joseph. "The Many Roots of Song: Influences on Native American Literature, Past, and Present." *North Dakota Quarterly* 53 (Spring 1985): 28–35.

1432. ———. *Survival This Way: Interviews with American Indian Poets.* Tucson: University of Arizona Press, 1987.

1433. Brumble, H. David, III. *American Indian Autobiography.* Berkeley: University of California Press, 1988.

1434. ———. *An Annotated Bibliography of American Indian and Eskimo Autobiographies.* Lincoln: University of Nebraska Press, 1981.

1435. Buller, Galen Mark. "Comanche Oral Narratives." Doctoral dissertation, University of Nebraska, Lincoln, 1977.

1436. ———. "New Interpretations of Native American Literature: A Survival Technique." *American Indian Culture and Research Journal* 4 (1980): 165–77.

1437. Bulow, Ernie. "Native Americans in American Literature." *Roundup Quarterly* 5 (Spring 1993): 24–29.

1438. ———. "The New Warpath: Native American Literature." *Roundup Quarterly* 5 (Summer 1993): 23–29.

1439. Burns, Glen. "Indian Madness." *Amerikastudien/American Studies* 22 (1977): 90–106.

1440. Carey, Larry Lee. "A Study of the Indian Captivity Narrative as a Popular Literary Genre, ca. 1675–1875." Doctoral dissertation, Michigan State University, 1978.

1441. Carver, Nancy Lynn. "Stereotypes of American Indians in Adolescent Literature." *English Journal* 77 (September 1988): 25–32.

1442. Castro, Michael Edward. *Interpreting the Indian: Twentieth-Century Poets and the Native American.* Norman: University of Oklahoma Press, 1991.

1443. Churchill, Ward. "Literature and the Colonization of the American Indian." *Journal of Ethnic Studies* 9 (Fall 1982): 37–56.

1444. Clark, LaVerne Harrell. "An Introduction to the Hopi Indians and Their Mythology." *Arizona English Bulletin* 13 (April 1971): 1–14.

1445. Colonnese, Tom, and Louis Owens. *American Indian Novelists: An Annotated Critical Bibliography.* New York: Garland, 1985.

1446. Coltelli, Laura. *Winged Words: American Indian Writers Speak.* Lincoln: University of Nebraska Press, 1990.

1447. ———, ed. *Native American Literatures.* Pisa, Italy: SEU, 1989, 1992.

1448. Davidson, Levette J. "White Versions of Indian Myths and Legends." *Western Folklore* 7 (April 1948): 115–28.

1449. Davis, Mary B., ed. *Native America in the Twentieth Century: An Encyclopedia.* New York: Garland, 1994.

1450. Davis, Randall Craig. "Firewater Myths: Alcohol and Portrayals of Native Americans in American Literature." Doctoral dissertation, Ohio State University, 1991.

1451. Day, A. Grove. *The Sky Clears: Poetry of the American Indian.* Lincoln: University of Nebraska Press, 1964.

1452. DeFlyer, Joseph Eugene. "Partition Theory: Patterns and Partitions of Consciousness in Selected Works of American and American Indian Authors." Doctoral dissertation, University of Nebraska, Lincoln, 1974.

1453. Derounian-Stodola, Kathryn Zabelle, and James Arthur Levernier. *The Indian Captivity Narrative, 1550–1900.* Boston: Twayne, 1993.

1454. Dockstader, Frederick J., and Alice W. Dockstader. *The American Indian in Graduate Studies: A Bibliography of Theses and Dissertations.* Parts 1 and 2. New York: Museum of the American Indian, Heye Foundation, 1973, 1974.

1455. Dorris, Michael. "Native American Literature in an Ethnohistorical Context." *College English* 41 (October 1979): 147–62.

1456. Drinnon, Richard. *Facing West: The Metaphysics of Indian-Hating and Empire Building.* Minneapolis: University of Minnesota Press, 1980.

1457. Easy, Peter. "The Treatment of American Indian Materials in Contemporary American Poetry." *Journal of American Studies* 12 (April 1978): 81–98.

1458. Edmonds, Margot, and Ella E. Clark. *Voices of the Winds: Native American Legends.* New York: Facts on File, 1989.

1459. Espey, David B. "Endings in Contemporary American Indian Fiction." *Western American Literature* 13 (Summer 1978): 113–39.

1460. Evers, Lawrence J. "'Further Survivals of Coyote.'" *Western American Literature* 10 (1975): 233–36.

1461. ———. "The Literature of the Omaha." Doctoral dissertation, University of Nebraska, Lincoln, 1972.

1462. ———. "Native American Oral Literatures in the College English Classroom: An Omaha Example." *College English* 36 (February 1975): 649–62.

1463. Fast, Robin Riley. "Outside Looking In: Nonnatives and American Indian Literature." *American Quarterly* 46 (March 1994): 62–76.

1464. Fiedler, Leslie A. *The Return of the Vanishing American.* New York: Stein and Day, 1968.

1465. Fields, Kenneth. "Seventh Wells: Native American Harmonies." *Parnassus* 2 (Spring–Summer 1974): 172–98.

1466. Fisher, Laura. "All Chiefs, No Indians: What Children's Books Say About American Indians." *Elementary English* 51 (February 1974): 185–89. Includes a bibliography.

1467. Fleck, Richard F. *Henry Thoreau and John Muir Among the Indians.* Hamden, Conn.: Archon Books, 1985.

1468. ———, ed. *Critical Perspectives on Native American Fiction.* Washington, D. C.: Three Continents, 1993.

1469. Friar, Ralph E. and Natasha A. Friar. *The Only Good Indian... The Hollywood Gospel.* New York: Drama Books, 1973.

1470. Fullerton, Mary Elizabeth. "Reception and Representation: The Western Vision of Native American Performance on the Northwest Coast." Doctoral dissertation, University of Washington, 1986.

1471. Gill, Sam D., and Irene F. Sullivan. *Dictionary of Native American Mythology.* Santa Barbara, Calif.: ABC-Clio, 1992.

1472. Green, Rayna. *Native American Women: A Contextual Bibliography.* Bloomington: Indiana University Press, 1983.

1473. ———. "The Pocahontas Perplex: The Image of Indian Women in American Culture." *Massachusetts Review* 16 (Autumn 1975): 698–714.

1474. Hamilton, W. I. "The Correlation between Social Attitudes and Those of American Authors Depicting the American Indian." *American Indian Quarterly* 1 (1974): 1–26.

1475. Hanson, Elizabeth I. *The American Indian in American Literature: A Study in Metaphor.* Lewiston, N.Y.: E. Mellen, 1988.

1476. ———. *Forever There: Race and Gender in Contemporary Native American Fiction.* New York: Peter Lang, 1989.

1477. Haslam, Gerald. *American Indian Literature.* Cassette. Deland, Fla.: Everett/Edwards, 1974.

1478. ———. "American Indians: Poets of the Cosmos." *Western American Literature* 5 (Spring 1970): 15–29.

1479. ———. "American Oral Literature: Our Forgotten Heritage." *English Journal* 60 (September 1971): 709–23.

1480. ———. "The Light That Fills the World: Native American Literature." *South Dakota Review* 11 (Spring 1973): 27–41.

1481. ———. "Literature of *The People*: Native American Voices." *CLA Journal* 15 (December 1971): 153–70.

1482. Hegeman, Susan. "Native American 'Texts' and the Problem of Authenticity." *American Quarterly* 41 (June 1989): 265–83.

1483. Henley, Joan Asher. "Native American Life Stories: Problems and Opportunities for Literary Study." Doctoral dissertation, American University, 1976.

1484. Henry, Jeannette. *The American Indian Reader: Literature.* San Francisco: Indian Historian Press, 1973.

1485. Highwater, Jamake. *Arts of the Indian Americas: Leaves From the Sacred Tree.* New York: Harper and Row, 1983.

1486. Hirschfelder, Arlene B. *American Indian and Eskimo Authors: A Comprehensive Bibliography.* New York: Association on American Indian Affairs, 1973.

1487. Hobson, Geary. "Indian Country: A Critical Examination of Native American Literature Since 1968." Doctoral dissertation, University of New Mexico, 1986.

1488. Howard, Helen Addison. *American Indian Poetry.* Boston: Twayne, 1979.

1489. ———. "Literary Translators and Interpreters of Indian Songs." *Journal of the West* 12 (April 1973): 212–28.

1490. Hunter, Carolyn Berry. "Ten Southwestern Captivity Narratives." Doctoral dissertation, Northern Arizona University, 1992.

1491. Hymes, Dell. "Particle, Pause and Pattern in American Indian Narrative Verse." *American Indian Culture and Research Journal* 4 (No. 4, 1980): 7–51.

1492. Jamison, Blanche Noma Miller. "The Western American Indian: Cross-Cultural Literacy Attitudes." Doctoral dissertation, East Texas State University, 1978.

1493. Kaufman, Donald L. "The Indian as a Media Hand-Me-Down." *Colorado Quarterly* 23 (Spring 1975): 489–504.

1494. Keiser, Albert. *The Indian in American Literature.* New York: Oxford University Press, 1933; New York: Farrar, Straus and Giroux, 1975.

1495. Keller, Betty. *Black Wolf: The Life of Ernest Thompson Seton.* Vancouver: Douglas and McIntyre, 1984.

1496. King, Thomas Hunt. "Inventing the Indian: White Images, Native Oral Literature, and Contemporary Native Writers." Doctoral dissertation, University of Utah, 1986.

1497. Klein, Barry T. *Reference Encyclopedia of the American Indian.* Santa Barbara, Calif.: ABC-CLIO, 1992.

1498. Krupat, Arnold. *Ethnocriticism: Ethnography, History, Literature.* Berkeley: University of California Press, 1992.

1499. ———. *For Those Who Come After: A Study of Native American Autobiography.* Berkeley: University of California Press, 1985.

1500. ————. "Scholarship and Native American Studies: A Response to Daniel Littlefield, Jr." *American Studies* 34 (Fall 1993): 81–100.

1501. ————. *The Voice in the Margin: Native American Literature and the Canon.* Berkeley: University of California Press, 1989.

1502. ————, ed. *New Voices in Native American Literary Criticism.* Washington, D.C.: Smithsonian, 1993.

1503. Lang, Nancy Helene. "Through Landscape Toward Story/Through Story Toward Landscape: A Study of Four Native American Women Poets." Doctoral dissertation, Indiana University of Pennsylvania, 1991.

1504. Larson, Charles R. *American Indian Fiction.* Albuquerque: University of New Mexico Press, 1978.

1505. Levernier, James A. "Indian Captivity Narratives: Their Functions and Forms." Doctoral dissertation, University of Pennsylvania, 1975.

1506. ————, and Hennig Cohen, eds. *The Indians and Their Captives.* Contributions in American Studies, No. 31. Westport, Conn.: Greenwood Press, 1977.

1507. Levine, Richard. "Indians, Conversation, and George Bird Grinnell." *American Studies* 28 (Fall 1987): 41–55.

1508. Lincoln, Kenneth. *Indi'n Humor: Bicultural Play in Native America.* New York: Oxford University Press, 1992.

1509. ————. "Native American Poetries." *Southwest Review* 63 (Autumn 1978): 367–84.

1510. ————. *Native American Renaissance.* Berkeley: University of California Press, 1983.

1511. ————. "Native American Tribal Poetics." *Southwest Review* 60 (Spring 1975): 101–16.

1512. ————. "Tai-Me to Rainy Mountain: The Makings of American Indian Literature." *American Indian Quarterly* 10 (Spring 1986): 101–17.

1513. Linden, George W. "Dakota Philosophy." *American Studies* 13 (Fall 1977): 17–43.

1514. Littlefield, Daniel F., Jr. *Alex Posey: Creek Poet, Journalist, and Humorist.* Lincoln: University of Nebraska Press, 1992.

1515. ————. "American Indians, American Scholars and the American Literary Canon." *American Studies* 33 (Fall 1993): 95–111.

1516. ————, and James W. Parins. *A Biobibliography of Native American Writers, 1772–1924.* Metuchen, N.J.: Scarecrow Press, 1981; *Supplement,* 1985.

1517. ———, and Lonnie Underhill. "Renaming the American Indian: 1890–1913." *American Studies* 12 (Fall 1971): 33–45.

1518. Lowie, Robert H. *Myths and Traditions of the Crow Indians.* Lincoln: University of Nebraska Press, 1993.

1519. Ludovici, Paola. "The Struggle for an Ending: Ritual and Plot in Recent American Indian Literature." Doctoral dissertation, American University, 1979.

1520. McAllister, H. S. "'The Language of Shamans': Jerome Rothenberg's Contributions to American Indian Literature." *Western American Literature* 10 (February 1976): 293–309.

1521. McTaggart, Fred. "Native American Literature: Teachings for the Self." *English Education* 6 (October/November 1974): 3–10.

1522. Marken, Jack W., comp. *The American Indian: Language and Literature.* Arlington Heights, Ill.: AHM Publishing Corporation, 1978.

1523. ———. *The Indians and Eskimos of North America: A Bibliography of Books in Print through 1972.* Vermillion, S. Dak.: Dakota Press, 1973.

1524. Merriam, C. Hart, ed. *The Dawn of the World: Myths and Tales of the Miwok Indians of California.* Lincoln: University of Nebraska Press, 1993.

1525. Miller, Jay, ed. *Mourning Dove: A Salishan Autobiography.* Lincoln: University of Nebraska Press, 1990.

1526. Milton, John R., ed. *The American Indian Speaks,* in *South Dakota Review* 7 (Summer 1969); reprinted Vermillion, S. Dak.: Dakota Press, 1969.

1527. ———. *American Indian II,* in *South Dakota Review* (Summer 1971); reprinted Vermillion, S. Dak.: Dakota Press, 1971.

1528. Momaday, Natachee Scott. *American Indian Authors.* Boston: Houghton Mifflin, 1972.

1529. Moseley, Mary Jean. "American Indian Oral Tradition Preservation, Protection, and Public Domain." Doctoral dissertation, University of North Dakota, 1985.

1530. Moser, Janette Irene. "Balancing the World: Spatial Design in Contemporary Native American Novels." Doctoral dissertation, University of North Carolina, Chapel Hill, 1992.

1531. Murray, David. *Forked Tongues: Speech, Writing, and Representation in North American Indian Texts.* Bloomington: Indiana University Press, 1991.

1532. Niatum, Duane, ed. *Harper's Anthology of 20th Century Native American Poetry.* San Francisco: Harper and Row, 1988.

1533. Nichols, Roger L. "Printer's Ink and Red Skins: Western Newspapers and Indians." *Kansas Quarterly* 3 (Fall 1971): 82–87.

1534. Oaks, Priscilla. "The First Generation of Native American Novelists." *MELUS* 5 (1978): 57–65.

1535. O'Brien, Lynne Woods. *Plains Indian Autobiographies.* Western Writers Series, No. 10. Boise, Idaho: Boise State College, 1973.

1536. Oliva, Leo E. "The American Indian in Recent Historical Fiction: A Review Essay." *Prairie Scout* 1 (1973): 95–120.

1537. Ortiz, Simon J., ed. *Earth Power Coming: Short Fiction in Native American Literature.* Tsaile, Ariz.: Navajo Community College Press, 1983.

1538. Osborne, Stephen Douglas. "Indian-Hating in American Literature, 1682–1857." Doctoral dissertation, University of Washington, 1989.

1539. Owens, Louis. *Other Destinies: Understanding the American Indian Novel.* Norman: University of Oklahoma Press, 1992.

1540. Pearce, Roy Harvey. *Savagism and Civilization: A Study of the Indian and the American Mind.* Baltimore: Johns Hopkins Press, 1965. Appeared as *The Savages of America: A Study of the Indian and the Idea of Civilization,* 1953.

1541. Peek, Charles A. "A Song Not-So-Plain, Not-So-Unknown." *Southwestern American Literature* 18 (Spring 1993): 7–18.

1542. Peyer, Bernd C., ed. *The Singing Spirit: Early Short Stories by North American Indians.* Tucson: University of Arizona Press, 1989.

1543. Porter, Mark. "Mysticism of the Land and the Western Novel." *South Dakota Review* 11 (Spring 1973): 79–91.

1544. Povey, John. "My Proud Headdress: New Indian Writing." *Southwest Review* 57 (Autumn 1972): 265–80.

1545. ———. "A New Second-Language Indian Literature." *Alaska Review* 4 (Fall–Winter 1969): 73–78.

1546. Ramsey, Jarold. "The Bible in Western Indian Mythology." *Journal of American Folklore* 90 (October–December 1977): 442–54.

1547. ———. "From 'Mythic' to 'Fictive' in a Nez Perce Orpheus Myth." *Western American Literature* 13 (Summer 1978): 119–31.

1548. ———. "The Indian Literature of Oregon." *Northwest Perspectives: Essays on the Culture of the Pacific Northwest.* Eds. Edwin R. Bingham and Glen A. Love. Seattle: University of Washington Press, 1979, 2–19.

1549. ———. *Reading the Fire: Essays in the Traditional Indian Literatures of the Far West.* Lincoln: University of Nebraska Press, 1983.

1550. ———. "The Wife Who Goes Out Like a Man Comes Back as a Hero: The Art of Two Oregon Indian Narratives." *PMLA* 92 (January 1977): 9–18.

1551. ———, ed. *Coyote Was Going There: Indian Literature of the Oregon Country.* Seattle: University of Washington, 1977. Anthology and commentary.

1552. Rans, Geoffrey. "Inaudible Man: The Indian in the Theory and Practice of White Fiction." *Canadian Review of American Studies* 8 (Fall 1977): 103–15.

1553. Redekip, Ernest. "The Redman: Some Representations of Indians in American Literature Before the Civil War." *Canadian Association for American Studies Bulletin* 3 (Winter 1968): 1–44.

1554. Rice, Julian. "Encircling Ikto: Incest and Avoidance in *Dakota Texts.*" *South Dakota Review* 22 (Winter 1984): 92–103.

1555. Rock, Roger O. *The Native American in American Literature: A Selectively Annotated Bibliography.* Westport, Conn.: Greenwood Press, 1985.

1556. Roemer, Kenneth M. "Bear and Elk: The Nature(s) of Contemporary Indian Poetry." *Journal of Ethnic Studies* 5 (Summer 1977): 69–79.

1557. Rosen, Kenneth. "American Indian Literature: Current Condition and Suggested Research." *American Indian Culture and Research Journal* 3 (1979): 57–66.

1558. ———, ed. and intro. *The Man to Send Rain Clouds: Contemporary Stories by American Indians.* New York: Vintage Books, 1975.

1559. ———, ed. *Voices of the Rainbow: Contemporary Poetry by American Indians.* New York: Viking, 1975.

1560. Rothenberg, Jerome. "American Indian Workings." *Poetry Review* 63 (1972): 17–29.

1561. ———, ed. *Shaking the Pumpkin: Traditional Poetry of the Indian North Americas.* Rev ed. Albuquerque: University of New Mexico Press, 1991.

1562. Ruoff, A. LaVonne Brown. *American Indian Literatures: An Introduction, Bibliographic Review, and Selected Bibliography.* New York: Modern Language Association, 1990.

1563. Ruppert, James. "Henry Rowe Schoolcraft: The Indian Expert and American Literature." *Platte Valley Review* 19 (Winter 1991): 99–128.

1564. ———. "Mediation and Multiple Narrative in Contemporary Native American Fiction." *Texas Studies in Literature and Language* 28 (Summer 1986): 209–25.

1565. ————. "The Uses of Oral Tradition in Six Contemporary Native American Poets." *American Indian Culture and Research Journal* 4 (No. 4, 1980): 87–110.

1566. Sarris, Greg. *Keeping Slug Woman Alive: A Holistic Approach to American Indian Texts.* Berkeley: University of California Press, 1993.

1567. ————, ed. *The Sound of Rattles and Clappers: A Collection of New California Indian Writing.* Sun Tracks, Vol. 26. Tucson: University of Arizona Press, 1994.

1568. Saunders, Thomas E. "Tribal Literature: Individual Identity and the Collective Unconscious." *College Composition and Communication* 24 (October 1973): 256–66.

1569. ————, and Walter W. Peek, eds. *Literature of the American Indian.* Abr. ed. Beverly Hills, Calif.: Glencoe; London: Collier Macmillan, 1976.

1570. Schneider, Jack W. "The New Indian: Alienation and the Rise of the Indian Novel." *South Dakota Review* 17 (Winter 1979–80): 67–76.

1571. ————. "Patterns of Cultural Conflict in Southwestern Indian Fiction." Doctoral dissertation, Texas Tech University, 1977.

1572. Schöler, Bo, ed. *Coyote Was Here: Essays on Contemporary Native American Literary and Political Mobilization.* Aarhus, Denmark: SEKLOS, 1984.

1573. Sevillano, Mando. "Interpreting Native American Literature: An Archetypal Approach." *American Indian Culture and Research Journal* 10 (No. 1, 1986): 1–12.

1574. Shames, Priscilla. "The Long Hope: A Study of American Indian Stereotypes in American Popular Fiction, 1890–1950." Doctoral dissertation, University of California, Los Angeles, 1969.

1575. Smith, Dwight L. *Indians of the United States and Canada.* Santa Barbara, Calif.: ABC-Clio, 1974.

1576. Smith, William F., Jr. "American Indian Autobiographies." *American Indian Quarterly* 2 (1975): 237–45.

1577. Sonnichsen, C. L. "The Ambivalent Apache." *Western American Literature* 10 (August 1975): 99–114.

1578. Standiford, Lester A. "Worlds Made of Dawn: Characteristic Image and Incident in Native American Imaginative Literature." *Proceedings of the Comparative Literature Symposium* (Lubbock, Tex.) 9 (1978): 327–52.

1579. Steinberg, Alan L. "The Popular Western and the Indian." *South Dakota Review* 28 (Autumn 1990): 104–12.

1580. Stensland, Anna Lee. "American Indian Culture: Promises, Problems, and Possibilities." *English Journal* 60 (December 1971): 1195–1200.

1581. ———. *Literature by and about the American Indian: An Annotated Bibliography.* 2d ed. Urbana, Ill.: National Council of Teachers of English, 1979.

1582. ———. "Traditional Poetry of the American Indian." *English Journal* 64 (September 1975): 41–47.

1583. Sullivan, Sherry Ann. "The Indian in American Fiction 1820–1850." Doctoral dissertation, University of Toronto, 1979.

1584. Sundquist, Åsebrit. *Sacajawea & Co.: The Twentieth-Century Fictional American Indian Woman and Fellow Characters: A Study of Gender and Race.* Oslo: Solum Forlag, 1991.

1585. Swann, Brian, ed. *Smoothing the Ground: Essays on Native American Oral Literature.* Berkeley: University of California Press, 1983.

1586. ———, and Arnold Krupat, eds. *I Tell You Now: Autobiographical Essays by Native American Writers.* Lincoln: University of Nebraska Press, 1987.

1587. Szasz, Margaret C., and Ferenc M. Szasz. "The American Indian and the Classical Past." *Midwest Quarterly* 17 (1975): 58–70.

1588. Taigue, Michelle. "'Never Again I': Death and Beauty in Yaqui Stories." Doctoral dissertation, University of Arizona, 1990.

1589. Turner, Frederick W., III, ed. *The Portable North American Indian Reader.* New York: Penguin, 1977.

1590. Tyree, Donald W. "Northwest Indian Poets." *Portland Review Magazine* 20 (March 1974): 39–56.

1591. VanDerBeets, Richard. *The Indian Captivity Narrative: An American Genre.* Lanham, Md.: University Press of America, 1984.

1592. ———. "The Indian Captivity Narrative as Ritual." *American Literature* 43 (January 1971): 548–62.

1593. Velie, Alan R. *Four American Indian Literary Masters: N. Scott Momaday, James Welch, Leslie Silko, and Gerald Vizenor.* Norman: University of Oklahoma Press, 1982.

1594. ———, ed. *American Indian Literature: An Anthology.* Rev ed. Norman: University of Oklahoma Press, 1991.

1595. ———, ed. *The Lightning Within: An Anthology of Contemporary American Indian Fiction.* Lincoln: University of Nebraska Press, 1991.

1596. Vizenor, Gerald. *Manifest Manners: Postindian Warriors of Survivance.* Hanover: University Press of New England, 1994.

1597. ———, ed. *Narrative Chance: Postmodern Discourse on Native American Indian Literature.* Albuquerque: University of New Mexico Press, 1989.

1598. Walters, Anna Lee, ed. *Neon Powwow: New Native American Voices of the Southwest.* Flagstaff, Ariz.: Northland Publishers, 1993.

1599. Waters, Frank. "Crossroads: Indians and Whites." *South Dakota Review* 11 (Autumn 1973): 28–38.

1600. Wiget, Andrew. *Native American Literature.* Boston: Twayne, 1985.

1601. ———. "The Oral Literature of Native North America: A Critical Anthology." 2 vols. Doctoral dissertation, University of Utah, 1977.

1602. ———. "Sending a Voice: The Emergence of Contemporary Native American Poetry." *College English* 46 (October 1984): 598–609.

1603. ———, ed. *Critical Essays on Native American Literature.* Boston: G. K. Hall, 1985.

1604. ———, ed. *Dictionary of Native American Literature.* New York: Garland, 1994.

1605. Williamson, Ray A., and Claire R. Farrer, eds. *Earth and Sky: Visions of the Cosmos in Native American Folklore.* Albuquerque: University of New Mexico Press, 1992.

1606. Wilmeth, Don B. "Tentative Checklist of Indian Plays." *Journal of American Drama and Theatre* 1 (Fall 1989): 34–54.

1607. Wilson, Norma Jean Clark. "The Spirit of Place in Contemporary American Indian Poetry." Doctoral dissertation, University of Oklahoma, 1978.

1608. Witt, Shirley Hill, and Stan Steiner, eds. *The Way: An Anthology of American Indian Literature.* New York: Alfred A. Knopf, 1972.

1609. Wong, Hertha Dawn. *Sending My Heart Back Across the Years: Tradition and Innovation in Native American Autobiography.* New York: Oxford University Press, 1992.

1610. Zolla, Elémire. *The Writer and the Shaman: A Morphology of the American Indian.* New York: Harcourt Brace Jovanovich, 1969, 1973.

MEXICAN-AMERICAN LITERATURE AND CHICANOS IN WESTERN LITERATURE

1611. Anaya, Rudolfo A. "The Myth of Quetzalcoatl in a Contemporary Setting: Mythical Dimensions/Political Reality." *Western American Literature* 23 (November 1988): 195–200.

1612. ———, and Francisco A. Lomelí. *Aztlán: Essays on the Chicano Homeland.* Albuquerque: University of New Mexico Press, 1991.

1613. Bain, Joe Staten, III. "Mexican Americans in Modern American Fiction." Doctoral dissertation, University of California, San Diego, 1983.

1614. Baker, Houston A., Jr., ed. *Three American Literatures: Essays in Chicano, Native American, and Asian American Literature for Teachers of American Literature.* New York: Modern Language Association, 1982.

1615. Bruce-Novoa, [Juan]. *Chicano Authors: Inquiry by Interview.* Austin: University of Texas Press, 1980.

1616. ———. *Chicano Poetry: A Response to Chaos.* Austin: University of Texas Press, 1982.

1617. ———. "History as Content, History as Act: The Chicano Novel." *Aztlán* 18 (Spring 1987): 29–44.

1618. ———. "Interview with José Antonio Villarreal." *Revista Chicano-Riqueña* 4 (Spring 1976): 40-48.

1619. ———. "*Pocho* as Literature." *Aztlán* 7 (Spring 1976): 65–77.

1620. ———. *RetroSpace: Collected Essays on Chicano Literature, Theory, and History.* Houston: Arte Público Press, 1990.

1621. ———. "The Space of Chicano Literature." *De Colores* 3 (1975): 22–42.

1622. ———, and David Valentin. "Revolutionizing the Popular Image: Essay on Chicano Theatre." *Latin American Literary Review* 5 (Spring–Summer 1977): 42–50.

1623. Candelaria, Cordelia. *Chicano Poetry: A Critical Introduction.* Westport, Conn.: Greenwood Press, 1986.

1624. Cantú, Roberto. "Estructura y sentido de lo onírico en *Bless Me, Ultima*." *Mester* 5 (November 1974): 27–41.

1625. Cárdenas de Dwyer, Carlota. "Chicano Literature, 1965–1975: The Flowering of the Southwest." Doctoral dissertation, State University of New York, Stony Brook, 1976.

1626. ———. "Cultural Regionalism and Chicano Literature." *Western American Literature* 15 (Fall 1980): 187–94.

1627. ———, ed. *Chicano Voices*. Boston: Houghton Mifflin, 1975.

1628. Carrillo, Loretta. "The Search for Selfhood and Order in Contemporary Chicano Fiction." Doctoral dissertation, Michigan State University, 1979.

1629. Castañeda Shular, Antonia, Tomás Ybarra-Frausto, and Joseph Sommers, eds. *Literatura chicana: texto y contexto*. Englewood Cliffs, N.J.: Prentice-Hall, 1972.

1630. Castillo-Speed, Lillian. "Chicano Studies: A Selected List of Materials since 1980." *Frontiers* 11 (No. 1, 1990): 66–84.

1631. Chabram, Angie C. "Chicano Literary Criticism: Directions and Development of an Emerging Critical Discourse." Doctoral dissertation, University of California, San Diego, 1986.

1632. Chávez, John R. *The Lost Land: The Chicano Image of the Southwest*. Albuquerque: University of New Mexico Press, 1984.

1633. "Chicano Literature and Criticism." *De Colores* 3 (1977). An important special issue.

1634. Clegg, J. Halvor. "Languages and Dialects." *Borderlands Sourcebook: A Guide to the Literature on Northern Mexico and the American Southwest*. Eds. Ellwyn R. Stoddard, et al. Norman: University of Oklahoma Press, 1983, 268–71.

1635. Cortés, Carlos E., et al., eds. *The Chicano Heritage: Aspects of the Mexican-American Experience*. New York: Arno Press, 1976.

1636. Del Castillo, Adelaida R., ed. *Between Borders: Essays on Mexicana/Chicana History*. Encino, Calif.: Floricanto Press, 1990.

1637. Dowell, Faye Nell. "The Chicano Novel: A Study of Self-Definition." Doctoral dissertation, University of Cincinnati, 1979.

1638. Eger, Ernestina N. *A Bibliography of Criticism of Contemporary Chicano Literature*. Berkeley, Calif.: Chicano Studies Library Publications, 1982.

1639. Elizondo, Sergio D. "Myth and Reality in Chicano Literature." *Latin American Literary Review* 5 (Spring–Summer 1977): 23–31.

1640. Etulain, Jacqueline J., comp. *Mexican Americans in the Twentieth-Century American West.* Occasional Papers, No. 3. Albuquerque: Center for the American West, University of New Mexico, 1990. Contains nearly 900 items.

1641. Eysturoy, Annie O., and José Antonio Gurpegui. "Chicano Literature: Introduction and Bibliography." *American Studies International* 27 (April 1990): 48–82.

1642. Fabre, Genevieve, ed. *European Perspectives on Hispanic Literature of the United States.* Houston: Arte Público Press, 1988.

1643. Fallis, Guadalupe Valdés. "Metaphysical Anxiety and the Existence of God in Contemporary Chicano Fiction." *Revista Chicano-Riqueña* 3 (Winter 1975): 26–33.

1644. Fernandez, Celestino, and James E. Officer. "The Lighter Side of Mexican Immigration: Humor and Satire in the Mexican *Corrido.*" *Journal of the Southwest* 31 (Winter 1989): 471–96.

1645. Garcia, Ricardo. "Multi-Ethnic Literature in America: Overview of Chicano Folklore." *English Journal* 65 (February 1976): 83–87.

1646. García-Girón, Edmundo. "The Chicanos: An Overview." *Proceedings of the Comparative Literature Symposium* (Lubbock, Tex.) 9 (1978): 87–119.

1647. Gonzáles, Sylvia A. "National Character vs. Universality in Chicano Poetry." *De Colores* 1 (1975): 10–21.

1648. Gonzales-Berry, Erlinda. "Chicano Literature in Spanish: Roots and Content." Doctoral dissertation, University of New Mexico, 1978.

1649. ———, ed. *Pasó por Aquí: Critical Essays on the New Mexican Literary Tradition, 1542–1988.* Albuquerque: University of New Mexico Press, 1989.

1650. Gonzalez, Maria Carmen. "Toward a Feminist Identity: Contemporary Mexican-American Women Novelists." Doctoral dissertation, Ohio State University, 1991.

1651. Grajeda, Rafael Francisco. "The Figure of the Pocho in Contemporary Chicano Fiction." Doctoral dissertation, University of Nebraska, Lincoln, 1974.

1652. Gutiérrez, David G. "Significant to Whom?: Mexican Americans and the History of the American West." *Western Historical Quarterly* 24 (November 1993): 519–39.

1653. Gutiérrez, Ramón, and Genaro Padilla, eds. *Recovering the U.S. Hispanic Literary Heritage.* Houston: Arte Público Press, 1993.

1654. Hancock, Joel. "The Emergence of Chicano Poetry: A Survey of Sources, Themes, and Techniques." *Arizona Quarterly* 29 (Spring

1973): 57–73.

1655. Haslam, Gerald. "¡Por La Causa! Mexican-American Literature." *College English* 31 (April 1970): 695–709.

1656. Hernandez, Guillermo E. *Chicano Satire: A Study in Literary Culture.* Austin: University of Texas Press, 1991.

1657. Herrera-Sobek, María, ed. *Reconstructing a Chicano/a Literary Heritage: Hispanic Colonial Literature of the Southwest.* Tucson: University of Arizona Press, 1993.

1658. ———, and Helena Maria Viramontes, eds. *Chicana Creativity and Criticism: Charting New Frontiers in American Literature.* Houston: Arte Público Press, 1988.

1659. Hinojosa, Rolando. "Mexican-American Literature: Toward an Identification." *Books Abroad* 49 (Summer 1975): 422–30.

1660. Horno-Delgado, Asuncion, et al. *Breaking Boundaries: Latina Writings and Critical Readings.* Amherst: University of Massachusetts Press, 1989.

1661. Huerta, Jorge A. *Chicano Theater: Themes and Forms.* Ypsilanti, Mich.: Bilingual Press, 1982.

1662. ———. *Necessary Theatre: Six Plays About the Chicano Experience.* Houston: Arte Público Press, 1989.

1663. Jiménez, Francisco, ed. *The Identification and Analysis of Chicano Literature.* New York: Bilingual Press, 1979.

1664. Kanellos, Nicolás. *Hispanic Theatre in the United States.* Houston: Arte Público Press, 1984.

1665. ———. *A History of Hispanic Theatre in the United States: Origins to 1940.* Austin: University of Texas Press, 1990.

1666. ———. *Two Centuries of Hispanic Theatre in the Southwest.* [Houston]: Revista Chicano-Riqueña, 1982.

1667. ———, ed. *Mexican Theatre: Then and Now.* Houston: Arte Público Press, 1989.

1668. ———, and Jorge A. Huerta, eds. *Nuevos Pasos: Chicano and Puerto Rican Drama.* Houston: Arte Público Press, 1989.

1669. Lattin, Vernon E. "The City in Contemporary Chicano Fiction." *Studies in American Fiction* 6 (1978): 93–100.

1670. ———. "The Quest for Mythic Vision in Contemporary Native American and Chicano Fiction." *American Literature* 50 (January 1979): 625–40.

1671. ———, ed. *Contemporary Chicano Fiction: A Critical Survey.* Binghamton, N.Y.: Bilingual, 1986.

1672. Leal, Luis. "Américo Paredes and Modern Mexican American Scholarship." *Ethnic Affairs* 1 (Fall 1987): 1–11.

1673. ———. "Mexican American Literature: A Historical Perspective." *Revista Chicano-Riqueña* 1 (Spring 1973): 32–44.

1674. Leff, Gladys Ruth. "George I. Sanchez: Don Quixote of the Southwest." Doctoral dissertation, University of North Texas, 1976.

1675. [Lewis, Tom J., ed.]. "Fiesta of the Living: A Chicano Symposium." *Books Abroad* 49 (Summer 1975): 422–58.

1676. Lomelí, Francisco A., and Carl R. Shirley, eds. *Chicano Writers: First Series. Dictionary of Literary Biography, Vol. 82.* Detroit: Gale Research, 1989.

1677. ———, and Donaldo W. Urioste. *Chicano Perspectives in Literature: A Critical and Annotated Bibliography.* Albuquerque: Pajarito Publications, 1976.

1678. Ludwig, Edward W., and James Santibanez, eds. *The Chicanos: Mexican American Voices.* New York: Penguin Books, 1971.

1679. McGinity, Sue Simmons. "The Image of the Spanish-American Woman in Recent Southwestern Fiction." Doctoral dissertation, East Texas State University, 1968.

1680. Madrid-Barela, Arturo. "In Search of the Authentic Pachuco: An Interpretive Essay." *Aztlán* 4 (Spring 1973): 31–60.

1681. Mares, E. A. "Myth and Reality: Observations on American Myths and the Myth of Aztlán." *El Cuaderno* 3 (Winter 1973): 35–50.

1682. Márquez, Antonio C. "Richard Rodriguez's *Hunger of Memory* and the Poetics of Experience." *Arizona Quarterly* 40 (Summer 1984): 130–41.

1683. Márquez, María Teresa. "A Selected Bibliography of New Mexican Hispanic Literature." *Pasó por Aquí: Critical Essays on the New Mexican Literary Tradition, 1542–1988.* Ed. Erlinda Gonzales-Berry. Albuquerque: University of New Mexico Press, 1989, 297–316.

1684. Martínez, Julio A., ed. *Chicano Scholars and Writers: A Bio-Bibliographical Directory.* Metuchen, N.J.: Scarecrow Press, 1979.

1685. ———, and Francisco A. Lomelí, eds., *Chicano Literature: A Reference Guide.* Westport, Conn.: Greenwood Press, 1985.

1686. Monahan, Helena. "The Chicano Novel: Toward a Definition and Literary Criticism." Doctoral dissertation, St. Louis University, 1972.

1687. Montes de Oca Ricks, Maria Helena. "Mediating the Past: Continuity and Diversity in the Chicano Literary Tradition." Doctoral dissertation, University of South Carolina, 1991.

1688. Ortega, Adolfo. "Of Social Politics and Poetry: A Chicano Perspective." *Latin American Literary Review* 5 (Spring–Summer 1977):

32–41.

1689. Ortego, Philip D. "Backgrounds of Mexican-American Literature." Doctoral dissertation, University of New Mexico, 1971.

1690. ———. "Chicano Poetry: Roots and Writers." *Southwestern American Literature* 2 (Spring 1972): 8–24.

1691. ———, ed. *We are Chicanos: An Anthology of Mexican-American Literature.* New York: Washington Square Press, 1973.

1692. Ortego y Gasca, Felipe de. "An Introduction to Chicano Poetry." *Modern Chicano Writers.* Eds. Joseph Sommers and Tomás Ybarra-Frausto. Englewood Cliffs, N.J.: Prentice-Hall, 1979, 108–16.

1693. Osborn, M. Elizabeth, ed. *On New Ground: Contemporary Hispanic-American Plays.* New York: Theatre Communications Group, 1987.

1694. Otero, Rosalie. "Ethnicity: Cooperation and Conflict in Modern New Mexico as Reflected in Literature and Art." *Contemporary New Mexico, 1940–1990.* Ed. Richard W. Etulain. Albuquerque: University of New Mexico Press, 1994, 119–58.

1695. Padilla, Genaro M. *My History, Not Yours: The Formation of Mexican American Autobiography.* Madison: University of Wisconsin Press, 1993.

1696. ———. "The Progression from Individual to Social Consciousness in Two Chicano Novelists: José Antonio Villareal and Oscar Zeta Acosta." Doctoral dissertation, University of Washington, 1981.

1697. Paredes, Américo. "The Folk Base of Chicano Literature." *Modern Chicano Writers.* Eds. Joseph Sommers and Tomás Ybarra-Frausto. Englewood Cliffs, N.J.: Prentice-Hall, 1979, 4–17.

1698. ———. *"With His Pistol in His Hand": A Border Ballad and Its Hero.* Austin: University of Texas Press, 1958.

1699. ———, and Raymund Paredes, comps. *Mexican-American Authors.* Boston: Houghton Mifflin, 1972.

1700. Paredes, Raymund A. "The Evolution of Chicano Literature." *MELUS* 5 (Summer 1978): 71–110.

1701. ———. "The Image of the Mexican in American Literature." Doctoral dissertation, University of Texas, Austin, 1973.

1702. Parr, Carmen Salazar. "Current Trends in Chicano Literary Criticism." *Latin American Literary Review* 5 (Spring–Summer 1977): 8–15.

1703. Pettit, Arthur G. *Images of the Mexican American in Fiction and Film.* Ed. Dennis E. Showalter. College Station: Texas A & M University Press, 1980.

1704. Pino, Frank. "Chicano Poetry: A Popular Manifesto." *Journal of Popu-*

lar Culture 6 (Spring 1973): 718–30.

1705. ———. *Mexican Americans: A Research Bibliography.* 2 vols. East Lansing: Michigan State University, 1974. See especially Vol. 2, 98–232.

1706. ———, ed. "In-depth Section [on Chicano Culture]." *Journal of Popular Culture* 13 (Spring 1980): 488–574.

1707. Rabasa, Jose. *Inventing America: Spanish Historiography and the Formation of Ethnocentrism.* Norman: University of Oklahoma Press, 1993.

1708. Ramírez, Elizabeth C. *Footlights Across the Border: A History of Spanish-Language Professional Theatre on the Texas Stage.* New York: Peter Lang, 1990.

1709. Rebolledo, Tey Diana. "Hispanic Women Writers of the Southwest: Tradition and Innovation." *Old Southwest, New Southwest: Essays on a Region and Its Literature.* Ed. Judy Nolte Lensink. Tucson: Tucson Public Library, 1987, 49–61.

1710. ———. "Tradition and Mythology: Signatures of Landscapes in Chicana Literature." *The Desert is No Lady: Southwestern Landscapes in Women's Writing and Art.* Eds. Vera Norwood and Janice Monk. New Haven: Yale University Press, 1987, 96–124.

1711. ———, and Eliana S. Rivero, eds. *Infinite Divisions: An Anthology of Chicana Literature.* Tucson: University of Arizona Press, 1993.

1712. Réyes, Luis, and Peter Rubie. *Hispanics in Hollywood: An Encyclopedia.* New York: Garland, 1994.

1713. Rivera, Tomás. "Chicano Literature: Fiesta of the Living." *Books Abroad* 49 (Summer 1975): 439–53.

1714. ———. "The Great Plains as Refuge in Chicano Literature." *Vision and Refuge: Essays on the Literature of the Great Plains.* Ed. Virginia Faulkner with Frederick C. Luebke. Lincoln: University of Nebraska Press, 1982, 126–40.

1715. ———. "Into the Labyrinth: The Chicano in Literature." *Southwestern American Literature* 2 (Fall 1972): 90–97.

1716. Robinson, Barbara J., and J. Cordell Robinson. *The Mexican American: A Critical Guide to Research Aids.* Greenwich, Conn.: JAI Press, 1980.

1717. Robinson, Cecil. "The Extended Presence: Mexico and Its Culture in North American Writing." *MELUS* 5 (1978): 3–15.

1718. ———. *Mexico and the Hispanic Southwest in American Literature.* Tucson: University of Arizona Press, 1977. Updates *With the Ears of Strangers: The Mexican in American Literature* (Tucson: University of

Arizona Press, 1963).

1719. ———. *No Short Journeys: The Interplay of Cultures in the History and Literature of the Borderlands.* Tucson: University of Arizona Press, 1992.

1720. Rocard, Marcienne. *The Children of the Sun: Mexican-Americans in the Literature of the United States.* Tucson: University of Arizona Press, 1989.

1721. Rodríguez, Raymond J. "A Few Directions in Chicano Literature." *English Journal* 62 (May 1973):724–29.

1722. ———. "Notes on the Evolution of Chicano Prose Fiction." *Modern Chicano Writers.* Eds. Joseph Somers and Tomás Ybarra-Frausto. Englewood Cliffs, N.J.: Prentice-Hall, 1979, 67–73.

1723. Salazar Parr, Carmen. "Current Trends in Chicano Literary Criticism." *Latin American Literary Review* 5 (Spring–Summer 1977): 8–15.

1724. Saldívar, Ramón. "The Borderlands of Culture: Américo Paredes's *George Washington Gómez* and Chicano Literature at the End of the Twentieth Century." *American Literary History* 5 (Summer 1993): 272–93.

1725. ———. *Chicano Narrative: The Dialectics of Difference.* Madison: University of Wisconsin Press, 1990.

1726. ———. "A Dialectic of Difference: Towards a Theory of the Chicano Novel." *MELUS* 6 (Fall 1979): 73–92.

1727. Salinas, Judy. "The Image of Woman in Chicano Literature." *Revista Chicano-Riqueña* 4 (Fall 1976): 139–48.

1728. ———. "Recommended Resources for Teaching Chicano Literature and Culture." *Popular Culture Association Newsletter* 6 (March 1977): 62–75.

1729. Salinas, Luis Omar, and Lillian Faderman, eds. *From the Barrio: A Chicano Anthology.* San Francisco: Canfield Press, 1973.

1730. Sanchez, George I. "Pachucos in the Making." *Common Ground* 4 (Fall 1943): 13–20.

1731. Sanchez, Marta Ester. *Contemporary Chicana Poetry: A Critical Approach to an Emerging Literature.* Berkeley: University of California Press, 1985.

1732. Sánchez, Rosaura. "Postmodernism and Chicano Literature." *Aztlán* 18 (Fall 1987): 1–14.

1733. Segade, Gustavo. "Toward a Dialectic of Chicano Literature." *Mester* 4 (November 1973).

1734. Shirley, Carl R., and Francisco A. Lomelí, eds. *Chicano Writers.* Detroit: Gale Research, 1992.

1735. ———, and Paula W. Shirley. *Understanding Chicano Literature.* Columbia: University of South Carolina Press, 1988.

1736. Simmen, Edward. "'We Must Make This Beginning': The Chicano Leader Image in the Short Story." *Southwest Review* 57 (Spring 1972): 126–33.

1737. ———, ed. *North of the Rio Grande: The Mexican-American Experience in Short Fiction.* New York: Penguin, 1992.

1738. Smith, Norman David. "Stereotypical Enemies: American Frontiersman and Mexican Caricatures in the Literature of an Expanding White Nation." Doctoral dissertation, Oklahoma State University, 1975.

1739. Sommers, Joseph. "From the Critical Premise to the Product: Critical Modes and Their Applications to a Chicano Literary Text." *New Scholar* 6 (1977): 51–80.

1740. ———, and Tomás Ybarra-Frausto, eds. *Modern Chicano Writers: A Collection of Critical Essays.* Englewood Cliffs, N.J.: Prentice-Hall, 1979.

1741. Sonnichsen, C. L. "The Two Black Legends." *Southwestern American Literature* 3 (1973): 5–21.

1742. "Special Issue of Chicano Literature." *Latin American Literary Review* 5 (Spring–Summer 1977): 5–141.

1743. Tatum, Charles M. *Chicano Literature.* Boston: Twayne, 1982.

1744. ———. "Contemporary Chicano Prose Fiction: A Chronicle of Misery." *Latin American Literary Review* 1 (Spring 1973): 7–17.

1745. ———. "Contemporary Chicano Prose Fiction: Its Ties to Mexican Literature." *Books Abroad* 49 (Summer 1975): 431–39.

1746. ———, ed. *New Chicana/Chicano Writing.* Tucson: University of Arizona Press, 1993.

1747. ———, ed. *A Selected and Annotated Bibliography of Chicano Studies.* 2d ed. Lincoln, Nebr.: Society of Spanish and Spanish-American Studies, 1979.

1748. Torres, Luis Angel. "From Imitation to Diversification: Nineteenth Century California Pre-Chicano Poetry." Doctoral dissertation, University of Washington, 1989.

1749. Tovar, Ines Hernandez. "Sara Estela Ramirez: The Early Twentieth Century Texas-Mexican Poet." Doctoral dissertation, University of Houston, 1984.

1750. Trejo, Arnulfo D. *Bibliografia Chicana: A Guide to Information*

Sources. Detroit: Gale Research, 1975.

1751. Trujillo, Robert G., and Andrés Rodriguez. *Literatura Chicana: Creative and Critical Writings Through 1984.* Oakland, Calif.: Floricanto, 1985.

1752. Ulibarrí, Sabine R., and Dick Gerdes. "Mexican Literature and Chicano Literature: A Comparison." *Proceedings of the Comparative Literature Symposium* (Lubbock, Tex.) 10 (1978): 149–67.

1753. Urioste, Donald W. "The Child Protagonist in Chicano Fiction." Doctoral dissertation, University of New Mexico, 1985.

1754. Vaca, Nick Corona. "Sociology through Literature: The Case of the Mexican-American." Doctoral dissertation, University of California, Berkeley, 1976.

1755. Valdes, Ricardo. "Defining Chicano Literature, or The Perimeters of Literary Space." *Latin American Literary Review* 5 (Spring–Summer 1977): 16–22.

1756. Valdez, Luis, and Stan Steiner, eds. *Aztlán: An Anthology of Mexican American Literature.* New York: Vintage, 1972.

1757. Vallejos, Thomas. "Mestizaje: The Transformations of Ancient Indian Religious Thought in Contemporary Chicano Fiction." Doctoral dissertation, University of Colorado, Boulder, 1980.

1758. Woods, Richard D. "The Chicano Novel: Silence after Publication." *Revista Chicano-Riqueña* 4 (Summer 1976): 42–47.

1759. Ybarra-Frausto, Tomás. "The Chicano Movement and the Emergence of a Chicano Poetic Consciousness." *New Scholar* 6 (1977): 81–109.

1760. Zamora, Beatrice B. Ortiz. "Mythopoeia of Chicano Poetry: An Introduction to Cultural Archetypes." Doctoral dissertation, Stanford University, 1986.

THE ENVIRONMENT AND
WESTERN LITERATURE

1761. Applewhite, James. "Postmodernist Allegory and the Denial of Nature." *Kenyon Review*, New Series 11 (Winter 1989): 1–17.

1762. Bergon, Frank, ed. *The Wilderness Reader*. New York: New American Library, 1980.

1763. Bredahl, A. Carl. "Landscape: The Perceiver and the Coursing of Human Events." *The Big Empty: Essays on Western Landscapes as Narratives*. Ed. Leonard Engel. Albuquerque: University of New Mexico Press, 1994, 303–18.

1764. Brooks, Paul. *Speaking for Nature: How Literary Naturalists from Henry Thoreau to Rachel Carson Have Shaped America*. San Francisco: Sierra Club Books, 1983.

1765. Buell, Lawrence. "American Pastoral Ideology Reappraised." *American Literary History* 1 (Spring 1989): 1–29.

1766. Burgess, Cheryll Anne. "Out-of-Doors: Representations of Nature in Sarah Orne Jewett, Willa Cather, and Eudora Welty." Doctoral dissertation, Cornell University, 1990.

1767. Campbell, SueEllen. "Feasting in the Wilderness: The Language of Food in American Wilderness Narratives." *American Literary History* 6 (Spring 1994): 1–23.

1768. ———. "The Land and Language of Desire: Where Deep Ecology and Post-Structuralism Meet." *Western American Literature* 24 (November 1989): 199–211.

1769. Cheney, Jim. "Eco-feminism and Deep Ecology." *Environmental Ethics* 9 (Summer 1987): 115–45.

1770. Culmsee, Carlton F. *Malign Nature and the Frontier*. Logan: Utah State University Press, 1959.

1771. Diamond, Irene, and Gloria Feman Orenstein, eds. *Reweaving the World: The Emergence of Ecofeminism*. San Francisco: Sierra Club Books, 1990.

1772. Doughty, Robin W. *At Home in Texas: Early Views of the Land*. College Station: Texas A & M Press, 1987.

1773. Elder, John. *Imagining the Earth: Poetry and the Vision of Nature.* Urbana: University of Illinois Press, 1985.

1774. Engel, Leonard, ed. *The Big Empty: Essays on Western Landscapes as Narratives.* Albuquerque: University of New Mexico Press, 1994.

1775. Erisman, Fred. "The Environmental Crisis and Present-Day Romanticism: The Persistence of an Idea." *Rocky Mountain Social Science Journal* 10 (January 1973): 7–14.

1776. ———. "Western Fiction as an Ecological Parable." *Environmental Review* 2 (Spring 1978): 14–23.

1777. Ettin, Andrew V. *Literature and the Pastoral.* New Haven: Yale University Press, 1984.

1778. Ewan, Joseph. "San Francisco as a Mecca for Nineteenth Century Naturalists." *A Century of Progress in the Natural Sciences, 1853–1953.* Eds. Ernest B. Babcock, J. Wyatt Durham, and George S. Myers. San Francisco: California Academy of Sciences, 1955, 1–63.

1779. Farris, Sara. "Women Writing Nature: Creating an Ecofeminist Praxis." Doctoral dissertation, Miami University, 1992.

1780. Finch, Robert, and John Elder, eds. *The Norton Book of Nature Writing.* New York: W. W. Norton, 1990.

1781. Frazier, Charles Robinson. "The Geography of Possibility: Man in the Landscape in Recent Western Fiction." Doctoral dissertation, University of South Carolina, 1986.

1782. Fritzell, Peter A. *Nature Writing and America: Essays Upon a Cultural Type.* Ames: Iowa State University Press, 1990.

1783. Garber, Frederick. "Pastoral Spaces." *Texas Studies in Literature and Language* 30 (Fall 1988): 431–60.

1784. Gill, Sam D. *Mother Earth: An American Story.* Chicago: University of Chicago Press, 1987.

1785. Gould, Lewis L. *Lady Bird Johnson and the Environment.* Lawrence: University Press of Kansas, 1988.

1786. Greiner, Patricia. "Radical Environmentalism in Recent Literature Concerning the American West." *Rendezvous* 19 (Fall 1983): 8–15.

1787. Griffin, Susan. *Woman and Nature: The Roaring Inside Her.* London: Women's Press, 1984.

1788. Grossman, Mark. *The Clio Companion to the Environmental Movement.* Santa Barbara, Calif.: ABC-CLIO, 1994.

1789. Haines, John. *Living Off the Country: Essays on Poetry and Place.* Ann Arbor: University of Michigan Press, 1981.

1790. Harwell, Albert Brantley. "Writing the Wilderness: A Study of Henry Thoreau, John Muir, and Mary Austin." Doctoral dissertation, University of Tennessee, 1992.

1791. Haslam, Gerald. "Who Speaks for the Earth?" *English Journal* 63 (January 1973): 42–48. Ecology and literature. Includes selected bibliography of American Indian, western American, and nature literature.

1792. Heyne, Eric. *Desert, Garden, Margin, Range: Literature on the American Frontier.* New York: Twayne, 1992.

1793. Huth, Hans. *Nature and the American: Three Centuries of Changing Attitudes.* Berkeley: University of California Press, 1957.

1794. Ingham, Zita. "Reading and Writing a Landscape: A Rhetoric of Southwest Desert Literature." Doctoral dissertation, University of Arizona, 1991.

1795. Jeffrey, Julie Roy. "'There is Some Splendid Scenery': Women's Responses to the Great Plains Landscape." *Great Plains Quarterly* 8 (Spring 1988): 69–78.

1796. Johnson, Kenneth. "The Lost Eden: The New World in American Nature Writing." Doctoral dissertation, University of New Mexico, 1973.

1797. Knowles, Karen, ed. *Celebrating the Land: Women's Nature Writing 1850–1991.* Flagstaff, Ariz.: Northland, 1992.

1798. Lankford, Scott. "John Muir and the Nature of the West: An Ecology of American Life, 1864–1914." Doctoral dissertation, Stanford University, 1991.

1799. Limerick, Patricia Nelson. *Desert Passages: Encounters with the American Deserts.* Albuquerque: University of New Mexico Press, 1985.

1800. Lopez, Barry. *Crossing Open Ground.* New York: Vintage, 1988.

1801. Love, Glen A. "Ecology in Arcadia." *Colorado Quarterly* 21 (Autumn 1972): 175–85.

1802. ———. "*Et in Arcadia Ego*: Pastoral Theory Meets Ecocriticism." *Western American Literature* 27 (Fall 1992): 195–207.

1803. ———. "Revaluing Nature: Toward an Ecological Criticism." *Western American Literature* 25 (November 1990): 201–15.

1804. Lueders, Edward, ed. *Writing Natural History: Dialogues with Authors.* Salt Lake City: University of Utah Press, 1989.

1805. Lyon, Thomas J. "The Nature Essay in the West." *A Literary History of the American West.* Eds. J. Golden Taylor, Thomas J. Lyon, et al. Fort Worth: Texas Christian University Press, 1987, 221–65.

1806. ———, ed. *This Incomparable Lande. A Book of American Nature Writing.* Boston: Houghton Mifflin, 1989.

1807. ———, and Peter Stine, eds. *On Nature's Terms: Contemporary Voices.* College Station: Texas A & M University Press, 1992.

1808. McDowell, Michael J. "Finding Tongues in Trees: Dialogical and Ecological Landscapes in Henry David Thoreau, Robinson Jeffers, and Leslie Marmon Silko." Doctoral dissertation, University of Oregon, 1992.

1809. Martin, Calvin. "The American Indian as Miscast Ecologist." *History Teacher* 14 (February 1981): 243–52.

1810. Marx, Leo. *The Machine in the Garden: Technology and the Pastoral Ideal in America.* New York: Oxford University Press, 1964.

1811. Merchant, Carolyn. *The Death of Nature: Women, Ecology, and the Scientific Revolution.* San Francisco: Harper & Row, 1980.

1812. ———. *Ecological Revolutions.* Chapel Hill: University of North Carolina Press, 1989.

1813. Miller, David S. "The Silence of Nature." *Sewanee Review* 92 (Winter 1984): 160–67.

1814. Nash, Roderick. *The Rights of Nature: A History of Environmental Ethics.* Madison: University of Wisconsin Press, 1989.

1815. ———. *Wilderness and the American Mind.* 3d ed. New Haven: Yale University Press, 1982.

1816. Nordstrom, Lars. *Theodore Roethke, William Stafford, and Gary Snyder: The Ecological Metaphor as Transformed Regionalism.* Stockholm: Uppsala, 1989.

1817. Norwood, Vera. *Made From This Earth: American Women and Nature.* Chapel Hill: University of North Carolina Press, 1993.

1818. ———. "The Photographer and the Naturalist: Laura Gilpin and Mary Austin in the Southwest." *Journal of American Culture* 5 (Summer 1982): 1–28.

1819. ———, and Janice Monk, eds. *The Desert Is No Lady: Southwestern Landscapes in Women's Writing and Art.* New Haven: Yale University Press, 1987.

1820. Nunnally, Patrick DeWitt. "Visions of Sustainable Place: Voice, Land, and Culture in Rural America." Doctoral dissertation, University of Iowa, 1989.

1821. Oelschlaeger, Max. *The Idea of Wilderness: From Prehistory to the Age of Ecology.* New Haven: Yale University Press, 1991.

1822. Paul, Sherman. *For Love of the World: Essays on Nature Writers.* Iowa City: University of Iowa Press, 1992.

1823. ————, and Don Scheese, eds. "Nature Writers/Nature Writing."
North Dakota Quarterly 59 (Spring 1991). Special issue.

1824. Poland, Tim. "'A Relative to All That Is': The Eco-Hero in Western
American Literature." *Western American Literature* 26 (November
1991): 195–208.

1825. Porter, Mark. "Mysticism of the Land and the Western Novel." *South
Dakota Review* 11 (Spring 1973): 79–91.

1826. Quantic, Diane Dufva. "The Unifying Thread: Connecting Place and
Language in Great Plains Literature." *American Studies* 32 (Spring
1991): 67–83.

1827. Raglon, Rebecca Sue. "American Nature Writing in the Age of Ecology: Changing Perceptions, Changing Forms." Doctoral dissertation,
Queen's University of Kingston (Canada), 1990.

1828. Robbins, William G. "Narrative Form and Great River Myths: The
Power of Columbia River Stories." *Environmental History Review* 17
(Summer 1993): 1–22.

1829. Robertson, David. *West of Eden: A History of the Art and Literature of
Yosemite.* [Yosemite National Park, Calif.]: Yosemite Natural History
Association: Wilderness Press, 1984.

1830. Ronald, Ann. "Why Don't They Write About Nevada?" *Western
American Literature* 24 (November 1989): 213–24.

1831. ————, ed. *Words for the Wild: The Sierra Club Trailside Reader.* San
Francisco: Sierra Club Books, 1987.

1832. Ronda, James P. "Dreaming the Pass: The Western Imagination and
the Landscape of South Pass." *The Big Empty: Essays on Western
Landscapes as Narratives.* Ed. Leonard Engel. Albuquerque: University of New Mexico Press, 1994, 7–25.

1833. Rueckert, William. "Literature and Ecology: An Experiment in
Ecocriticism." *Iowa Review* 9 (Winter 1978): 71–86.

1834. Seelye, John. "Some Green Thoughts on a Green Theme."
TriQuarterly 23–24 (Winter–Spring 1972): 576–638.

1835. Shepard, Paul. *Nature and Madness.* San Francisco: Sierra Club
Books, 1982.

1836. Slotkin, Richard. *The Fatal Environment: The Myth of the Frontier in
the Age of Industrialization, 1800–1890.* New York: Atheneum, 1985.

1837. Slovic, Scott Harlan. *Seeking Awareness in American Nature Writing:
Henry Thoreau, Annie Dillard, Edward Abbey, Wendell Berry, and
Barry Lopez.* Salt Lake City: University of Utah Press, 1992.

1838. Smith, Patricia Clark, and Paula Gunn Allen. "Earthy Relations, Carnal Knowledge: Southwestern American Indian Women Writers and the Landscape." *The Desert Is No Lady: Southwestern Landscapes in Women's Writing and Art*. Eds. Vera Norwood and Janice Monk. New Haven: Yale University Press, 1987, 174–96.

1839. Snyder, Gary. *The Practice of the Wild*. San Francisco: North Point Press, 1990.

1840. Stegner, Wallace. *The American West as Living Space*. Ann Arbor: University of Michigan Press, 1987.

1841. ———. *The Sound of Mountain Water*. Garden City, N.Y.: Doubleday, 1969.

1842. ———. *Where the Bluebird Sings to the Lemonade Springs: Living and Writing in the West*. New York: Random House, 1992.

1843. ———, Madison Jones, Rudolfo A. Anaya, Ross Macdonald, Thomas E. Sanders (Nippawanock), and Robert Roripaugh. "The Writer's Sense of Place." *South Dakota Review* 26 (Winter 1988): 93–120.

1844. Trimble, Stephen, ed. *Words From the Land: Encounters with Natural History Writing*. Layton, Utah: Peregrine Smith Books, 1988.

1845. Turner, Frederick. *Spirit of Place: The Making of an American Literary Landscape*. San Francisco: Sierra Club Books, 1989.

1846. White, Donald W. "'It's a Big Country': A Portrait of the American Landscape after World War II." *Journal of the West* 26 (January 1987): 80–86.

1847. Wiget, Andrew. "Wonders of the Visible World: Changing Images of the Wilderness in Captivity Narratives." *The Westering Experience in American Literature: Bicentennial Essays*. Eds. Merrill Lewis and L. L. Lee. Bellingham: Bureau for Faculty Research, Western Washington University, 1977, 69–84.

1848. Witkowsky, Paul. "If Prairies Had Trees: East, West, Environmentalist Fiction, and the Great Plains." *Western American Literature* 28 (November 1993): 195–207.

1849. Worster, Donald. *Nature's Economy: A History of Ecological Ideas*. New York: Cambridge University Press, 1977, 1985.

1850. ———. *The Wealth of Nature: Environmental History and the Ecological Imagination*. New York: Oxford University Press, 1993.

1851. Wyatt, David. *The Fall into Eden: Landscape and Imagination in California*. Cambridge: Cambridge University Press, 1986

WOMEN, FAMILIES,
AND WESTERN LITERATURE

1852. Alexander, Ruth Ann. "South Dakota Women Writers and the Blooming of the Pioneer Heroine, 1922–1939." *South Dakota History* 14 (Winter 1984): 281–307.

1853. ———. "South Dakota Women Writers and the Emergence of the Pioneer Heroine." *South Dakota History* 13 (Fall 1983): 177–205.

1854. Allen, Martha Mitten. *Traveling West: 19th Century Women on the Overland Routes.* El Paso: Texas Western Press, 1987.

1855. ———. "Women in the West: A Study of Booklength Travel Accounts by Women Who Traveled in the Plains and Rockies with Special Attention to General Concepts that Women Applied to the Plains, the Mountains, Westerners and the West in General." Doctoral dissertation, University of Texas, Austin, 1972.

1856. Armitage, Shelley. "Rawhide Heroines: The Evolution of the Cowgirl and the Myth of America." *The American Self: Myth, Ideology, and Popular Culture.* Ed. Sam B. Girgus. Albuquerque: University of New Mexico Press, 1981, 166–81.

1857. ———. "Western Heroines: Real and Fictional Cowgirls." *Heritage of Kansas* 12 (Spring 1979): 12–20.

1858. Armitage, Susan. "Through Women's Eyes: A New View of the West." *The Women's West.* Eds. Susan Armitage and Elizabeth Jameson. Norman: University of Oklahoma Press, 1987, 9–18.

1859. ———. "Women's Literature and the American Frontier: A New Perspective on the Frontier Myth." *Women, Women Writers, and the West.* Eds. Lawrence L. Lee and Merrill E. Lewis. Troy, N.Y.: Whitston, 1978.

1860. ———, and Elizabeth Jameson, eds. *The Women's West.* Norman: University of Oklahoma Press, 1987.

1861. ———, et al., eds. *Women in the West: A Guide to Manuscript Sources.* New York: Garland, 1991.

1862. Atkins, Annette. "Women on the Farming Frontier: The View from Fiction." *Midwest Review* 3 (Spring 1981): 1–10.

1863. Ballou, Patricia K. *Women: A Bibliography of Bibliographies.* 2d ed. Boston: G. K. Hall, 1986.

1864. Bangs, Carol Jane. "Women Poets and the 'Northwest School.'" *Women, Women Writers, and the West.* Eds. Lawrence L. Lee and Merrill E. Lewis. Troy, N.Y.: Whitston, 1978.

1865. Banta, Martha. *Imaging American Women: Idea and Ideals in Cultural History.* New York: Columbia University Press, 1987.

1866. Barnard, Ann. "A North American Connection: Women in Prairie Novels." *Great Plains Quarterly* 14 (Winter 1994): 21–28.

1867. Biblowitz, Iris, et al. *Women and Literature: An Annotated Bibliography of Women Writers.* 3d ed. Cambridge, Mass.: Women and Literature Collective, 1976. American writers, 1–93.

1868. Billick, David J. "Women in Hispanic Literature: A Checklist of Doctoral Dissertations and Master's Theses, 1905–1975." *Women Studies Abstracts* 6 (Summer 1977): 1–11.

1869. Blend, Benay. "Mary Austin and the Western Conservation Movement: 1900–1927." *Journal of the Southwest* 30 (Spring 1988): 12–34.

1870. Bouquet, Sarah. "Voices from the Southwest." *Voices from the Southwest: A Gathering in Honor of Lawrence Clark Powell.* Eds. Donald C. Dickinson, W. David Laird, and Margaret F. Maxwell. Flagstaff, Ariz.: Northland Press, 1976, 33–44. Accounts by women.

1871. Bradsher, Frieda Katherine. "Women in the Works of James Fenimore Cooper." Doctoral dissertation, University of Arizona, 1979.

1872. Castiglia, Christopher Dean. "Captive Subjects: The Captivity Narrative and American Women's Writing." Doctoral dissertation, Columbia University, 1991.

1873. Davis, Gayle R. "Women's Frontier Diaries: Writing for Good Reason." *Women's Studies* 14 (July 1987): 5–14.

1874. Dearborn, Mary V. *Pocahontas's Daughters: Gender and Ethnicity in American Culture.* New York: Oxford University Press, 1986.

1875. Downey, Betsy. "Battered Pioneers: Jules Sandoz and the Physical Abuse of Wives on the American Frontier." *Great Plains Quarterly* 12 (Winter 1992): 31–49.

1876. Egli, Ida Rae, ed. *No Rooms of Their Own: Women Writers of Early California, 1848–1869.* Berkeley, Calif.: Heyday Books in association with Rick Heide, 1992.

1877. Exley, Jo Ella Powell. *Texas Tears and Texas Sunshine: Voices of Frontier Women.* College Station: Texas A & M University Press, 1985.

1878. Fairbanks, Carol. *Prairie Women: Images in American and Canadian Fiction*. New Haven: Yale University Press, 1986.

1879. ———, and Sara Brooks Sundberg. *Farm Women on the Prairie Frontier: A Sourcebook for Canada and the United States*. Metuchen, N.J.: Scarecrow Press, 1983.

1880. Farris, Sara. "Women Writing Nature: Creating an Ecofeminist Praxis." Doctoral dissertation, Miami University, 1992.

1881. Fishburn, Katherine. *Women in Popular Culture: A Reference Guide*. Westport, Conn.: Greenwood Press, 1982.

1882. Foote, Cheryl J. "Changing Images of Women in the Western Film." *Journal of the West* 22 (October 1983): 64–71.

1883. Frost-Knappman, Elizabeth. *The Clio Companion to Women's Progress in America*. Santa Barbara, Calif.: ABC-CLIO, 1993.

1884. Furlong, Leslie Anne. "Gold-Dust and Buckskins: An Analysis of Calamity Jane as a Symbol of Luck and Womanhood in the Black Hills." Doctoral dissertation, University of Virginia, 1991.

1885. Gelfant, Blanche H. "'Lives' of Women Writers: Cather, Austin, Porter/and Willa, Mary, Katherine Anne." *Novel: A Forum on Fiction* 18 (Fall 1984): 64–80.

1886. Gilbert, Sandra M., and Susan Gubar. *No Man's Land: The Place of the Woman Writer in the Twentieth Century; Volume 1: The War of the Words*. New Haven: Yale University Press, 1987.

1887. Gilbert, V. F., and D. S. Tatla. *Women's Studies: A Bibliography of Dissertations, 1870–1982*. New York: Basil Blackwell, 1985.

1888. Gladstein, Mimi Reisel. *The Indestructible Woman in Faulkner, Hemingway, and Steinbeck*. Ann Arbor, Mich.: UMI Research Press, 1986.

1889. Graulich, Melody. "Violence Against Women in Literature of the Western Family." *Frontiers* 7 (No. 3, 1984): 14–20.

1890. Green, Rayna. *Native American Women: A Contextual Bibliography*. Bloomington: Indiana University Press, 1983.

1891. ———, ed. *That's What She Said: Contemporary Poetry and Fiction by Native American Women*. Bloomington: Indiana University Press, 1984.

1892. Griffin, Susan. *Woman and Nature: The Roaring Inside Her*. London: Women's Press, 1984.

1893. Grover, Dorys Crow. "The Pioneer Women in Fact and Fiction." *Heritage of Kansas* 10 (Spring 1977): 35–44.

1894. Hampsten, Elizabeth. *Read This Only to Yourself: The Private Writings of Midwestern Women, 1880–1910.* Bloomington: Indiana University Press, 1982.

1895. ———. *Settlers' Children: Growing Up on the Great Plains.* Norman: University of Oklahoma Press, 1991.

1896. Harline, Paula Kelly. "Polygamous yet Monogamous: Cultural Conflict in the Writings of Mormon Polygamous Wives." *Old West–New West: Centennial Essays.* Ed. Barbara Howard Meldrum. Moscow: University of Idaho Press, 1993, 115–32.

1897. Harrison, Cynthia E., ed. *Women in American History: A Bibliography.* 2 vols. Santa Barbara, Calif.: ABC-Clio, 1979, 1985.

1898. Heatherington, Madelon E. "Romance Without Women: The Sterile Fiction of the American West." *Georgia Review* 33 (Fall 1979): 643–56.

1899. Heil, Patricia Leeuwenburg. "The Frontier Heroine in American Literature." Doctoral dissertation, University of Illinois, Urbana-Champaign, 1983.

1900. Jeffrey, Julie Roy. "'There is Some Splendid Scenery': Women's Responses to the Great Plains Landscape." *Great Plains Quarterly* 8 (Spring 1988): 69–78.

1901. Johnson, Susan Lee. "'A memory sweet to soldiers': The Significance of Gender in the History of the 'American West.'" *Western Historical Quarterly* 24 (November 1993): 495–517.

1902. Kaye, Frances Weller. "The Roles of Women in the Literature of the Post Civil War American Frontier." Doctoral dissertation, Cornell University, 1973.

1903. Kennedy, Patricia. "The Pioneer Woman in Middle Western Fiction." Doctoral dissertation, University of Illinois, Urbana-Champaign, 1968.

1904. Kimble, Mary Ellen. "Literary Presentations of Pioneer Women in Kansas and Neighboring States." *Kansas Quarterly* 18 (Summer 1986): 105–20.

1905. Koehler, Lyle. "Native Women of the Americas: A Bibliography." *Frontiers* 6 (Fall 1981): 73–101.

1906. Kolodny, Annette. *The Land Before Her: Fantasy and Experience of the American Frontiers, 1630–1860.* Chapel Hill: University of North Carolina Press, 1984.

1907. ———. *The Lay of the Land: Metaphor as Experience and History in American Life and Letters.* Chapel Hill: University of North Carolina Press, 1975.

1908. Lee, Lawrence L., and Merrill E. Lewis, eds. *Women, Women Writers, and the West.* Troy, N.Y.: Whitston, 1978.

1909. Leoffelholz, Mary. *Experimental Lives: Women and Literature 1900–1945.* New York: Twayne, 1992.

1910. Lewandowska, M. L. "Feminism and the Emerging Woman Poet: Four Bay Area Poets." *Itinerary: Criticism, Essays on California Writers.* Ed. Charles L. Crow. Bowling Green, Ohio: University Press, 1978, 123–41.

1911. MacDonald, Alan. "Saying Something for Nothing: Attitudes of Some American Women Writers to the Romance of Open Space (Chopin, Robinson, Plath, Mason)." Doctoral dissertation, University of York (United Kingdom), 1989.

1912. McElhiney, Annette Bennington. "The Image of the Pioneer Woman in the American Novel." Doctoral dissertation, University of Denver, 1978.

1913. McKnight, Jeannie. "American Dream, Nightmare Underside: Diaries, Letters and Fiction of Women on the American Frontier." *Women, Women Writers, and the West.* Eds. Lawrence L. Lee and Merrill E. Lewis. Troy, N.Y.: Whitston, 1978.

1914. Mainiero, Lina, ed. *American Women Writers: A Critical Reference Guide from Colonial Times to the Present.* 4 vols. New York: Ungar, 1979–1982.

1915. Maples, Donna Elaine. "Building a Literary Heritage: A Study of Three Generations of Pioneer Women, 1880–1930." Doctoral dissertation, University of Missouri, Columbia, 1988.

1916. Meldrum, Barbara. "Images of Women in Western American Literature." *Midwest Quarterly* 17 (Spring 1976): 252–67.

1917. ———. "Women in Western American Fiction: Images or Real Women?" *Women and Western American Literature.* Eds. Helen Winter Stauffer and Susan J. Rosowski. Troy, N.Y.: Whitston, 1982, 55–69.

1918. Murphy, John J. "The Virginian and Antonia Shimerda: Different Sides of the Western Coin." *Women and Western American Literature.* Eds. Helen Winter Stauffer and Susan J. Rosowski. Troy, N.Y.: Whitston, 1982, 162–78.

1919. Namias, June. *White Captives: Gender and Ethnicity on the American Frontier.* Chapel Hill: University of North Carolina Press, 1993.

1920. Nelson, Doris. "Women in Early Western Drama." *Arizona Quarterly* 38 (Winter 1982): 347–64.

1921. Nesbitt, John D. "Uncertain Sex in the Sagebrush." *South Dakota Review* 23 (Autumn 1985): 15–27.

1922. Norwood, Vera, and Janice Monk, eds. *The Desert Is No Lady: Southwestern Landscapes in Women's Writing and Art.* New Haven: Yale University Press, 1987.

1923. Patterson-Black, Sheryll, and Gene Patterson-Black. *Western Women: In History and Literature.* Crawford, Nebr.: Cottonwood Press, 1978. Extensive bibliographies.

1924. Pearlman, Mickey, ed. *American Women Writing Fiction: Memory, Identity, Family, Space.* Lexington: University Press of Kentucky, 1989. Includes sections on Joan Didion and Louise Erdrich.

1925. ———, ed. *Mother Puzzles: Daughters and Mothers in Contemporary American Literature.* Westport, Conn.: Greenwood Press, 1989.

1926. Person, Leland S., Jr. "The American Eve: Miscegenation and a Feminist Frontier Fiction." *American Quarterly* 37 (Winter 1985): 668–85.

1927. Peterson, Levi S. *Juanita Brooks: Mormon Woman Historian.* Salt Lake City: University of Utah Press, 1988.

1928. Powell, Jo Ella, ed. *Texas Tears and Texas Sunshine: Voices of Frontier Women.* College Station: Texas A & M University Press, 1985.

1929. Pryse, Marjorie. "'Distilling Essences': Regionalism and 'Women's Culture.'" *American Literary Realism, 1870–1910* 25 (Winter 1993): 1–15.

1930. Quinn, Roland Joseph. "The Modest Seduction: The Experience of Pioneer Women on the Trans-Mississippi Frontier." Doctoral dissertation, University of California, Riverside, 1977.

1931. Rainwater, Catherine, and William J. Scheick, eds. *Contemporary American Women Writers: Narrative Strategies.* Lexington: University Press of Kentucky, 1985.

1932. Rebolledo, Tey Diana, Erlinda Gonzales-Berry, and Teresa Márquez. *Las Mujeras Hablan: An Anthology of Nuevo Mexicana Writers.* Albuquerque: Academia/El Norte Publications, 1988.

1933. Redfern, Bernice. *Women of Color in the United States: A Guide to the Literature.* New York: Garland, 1989.

1934. Remley, David. "Sacajawea of Myth and History." *Women and Western American Literature.* Eds. Helen Winter Stauffer and Susan J. Rosowski. Troy, N.Y.: Whitston, 1982, 70–89.

1935. Riley, Glenda. *Inventing the American Woman: A Perspective on Women's History 1865 to the Present.* Arlington Heights, Ill.: Harlan Davidson, 1986.

1936. ———. "Kansas Frontierswomen Viewed Through Their Writings." *Kansas History* 9 (Spring 1986): 2–9.

1937. Romero, Lora. "Vanishing Americans: Gender, Empire, and New Historicism." *American Literature* 63 (September 1991): 385–404.

1938. Ronald, Ann. "The Tonopah Ladies." *Women, Women Writers, and the West.* Eds. Lawrence L. Lee and Merrill E. Lewis. Troy, N.Y.: Whitston, 1978.

1939. Rosowski, Susan J. "Margaret Fuller, an Engendered West, and *Summer on the Lakes.*" *Western American Literature* 25 (August 1990): 125–44.

1940. Rubenstein, Roberta. *Boundaries of the Self: Gender, Culture, Fiction.* Urbana: University of Illinois Press, 1987.

1941. Sage, Frances. "Contemporary Women Poets of Texas." *Texas Quarterly* 21 (Summer 1978): 84–108.

1942. St. Laurent, Maureen Ellen. "American Women's Travel Narratives: Gender and Genre." Doctoral dissertation, Vanderbilt University, 1992.

1943. Saldivar-Hull, Sonia. "Feminism on the Border: From Gender Politics to Geopolitics." Doctoral dissertation, University of Texas, Austin, 1990.

1944. Sallquist, Sylvia Lea. "The Image of the Hired Girl in Literature: The Great Plains, 1860 to World War I." *Great Plains Quarterly* 4 (Summer 1984): 166–77.

1945. Santelmann, Patricia Kelly. "Fantasy Themes in Nineteenth-Century Women's Diaries and Women's Fiction: Women's Voice in Nineteenth-Century America." Doctoral dissertation, University of Minnesota, 1987.

1946. Schlissel, Lillian. *Diaries of the Westward Journey.* New York: Schocken, 1982, 1992.

1947. ———. "Women's Diaries on the Western Frontier." *American Studies* 18 (Spring 1977): 87–100.

1948. Schwartz, Narda Lacey. *Articles on Women Writers: A Bibliography.* 2 vols. Santa Barbara, Calif.: ABC-Clio, 1977, 1986. A very useful listing.

1949. Showalter, Elaine, Lea Baechler, and A. Walton Litz, eds. *Modern American Women Writers.* New York: Scribner's, 1991.

1950. Simmons, Marc. "Women on the Santa Fe Trail: Diaries, Journals, Memoirs. An Annotated Bibliography." *New Mexico Historical Review* 61 (July 1986): 233–43.

1951. Smith, Patricia Clark, and Paula Gunn Allen. "Earthy Relations, Carnal Knowledge: Southwestern American Indian Women Writers and the Landscape." *The Desert Is No Lady: Southwestern Landscapes in Women's Writing and Art.* Eds. Vera Norwood and Janice Monk. New Haven: Yale University Press, 1987, 174–96.

1952. Springer, Marlene, and Haskell Springer, eds. *Plains Woman: The Diary of Martha Farnsworth, 1882–1922.* Bloomington: Indiana University Press, 1986.

1953. Stauffer, Helen Winter, and Susan J. Rosowski, eds. *Women and Western American Literature.* Troy, N.Y.: Whitston, 1982.

1954. Sweeney, Patricia E. *Biographies of American Women: An Annotated Bibliography.* Santa Barbara, Calif.: ABC-CLIO, 1990.

1955. Thacker, Robert. "'twisting toward insanity': Landscape and Female Intrapment in Plains Fiction." *North Dakota Quarterly* 52 (Summer 1984): 181–94.

1956. Trusky, A. Thomas, ed. *Women Poets of the West: An Anthology, 1850–1950.* 2d ed. Boise, Idaho: Ahsahta Press, 1979.

1957. Underwood, June O. "Men, Women, and Madness: Pioneer Plains Literature." *Under the Sun: Myth and Realism in Western American Literature.* Ed. Barbara Howard Meldrum. Troy, N. Y.: Whitston, 1985, 50–62.

1958. ———. "Plains Women, History, and Literature: A Selected Bibliography." *Heritage of the Great Plains* 16 (Summer 1983): 41–46.

1959. ———. "Western Women and True Womanhood: Culture and Symbol in History and Literature." *Great Plains Quarterly* 5 (Spring 1985): 93–106.

1960. Ward, Kathryn Ann. "Clients, Colleagues, and Consorts: Roles of Women in American Hardboiled Detective Fiction and Film." Doctoral dissertation, Ohio State University, 1988.

1961. Western Writers of America. *The Women Who Made the West.* Garden City, N.Y.: Doubleday, 1980.

1962. Wherry, Peg. "At Home on the Range: Reactions of Pioneer Women to the Kansas Plains Landscape." *Kansas Quarterly* 18 (Summer 1986): 71–79.

1963. White, Barbara A. *American Women Writers: An Annotated Bibliography of Criticism.* New York: Garland, 1977.

1964. Winsbro, Bonnie C. "Supernatural Forces: Belief, Difference, and Power in Contemporary Works by Ethnic Women." Doctoral dissertation, University of Tennessee, 1992.

1965. *Women and Literature: An Annotated Bibliography of Women Writers.* 3d ed. Cambridge, Mass.: Women and Literature Collective, 1976. American writers, 1–93.

1966. "Women's Culture in the Great Plains." *Great Plains Quarterly* 8 (Spring 1988): 67–119. Special theme issue.

1967. Wood, Ann D. "The Literature of Impoverishment: The Women Local Colorists in America, 1865–1914." *Women's Studies* 1 (1972): 3–46.

1968. Yalom, Marilyn, ed. *Women Writers of the West Coast: Speaking of Their Lives and Careers.* Santa Barbara, Calif.: Capra Press, 1983.

THE BEATS

1969. Allan, Blaine. "The New American Cinema and the Beat Generation, 1956–1960." Doctoral dissertation, Northwestern University, 1984.

1970. Ardinger, Richard K., ed. *An Annotated Bibliography of Works by John Clellon Holmes.* Pocatello: Idaho State University, 1979.

1971. Bartlett, Lee, ed. *The Beats: Essays in Criticism.* Jefferson, N.C.: McFarland, 1981.

1972. Bingham, June. "The Intelligent Square's Guide to Hippieland." *New York Times Magazine* 6 (September 24, 1967): 25, 68–73, 76–84.

1973. Butler, Frank A. "On the Beat Nature of Beat." *American Scholar* 30 (Winter 1960–61): 79–92.

1974. Cassady, Carolyn. *Off the Road: My Years With Cassady, Kerouac, and Ginsberg.* New York: William Morrow, 1990.

1975. Charters, Ann. *Beats & Company: A Portrait of a Literary Generation.* Garden City, N.Y.: Doubleday, 1987.

1976. ———, ed. *The Beats: Literary Bohemians in Postwar America.* 2 vols. Detroit: Gale Research, 1983.

1977. ———, ed. *The Portable Beat Reader.* New York: Viking, 1992.

1978. ———, ed. *Scenes Along the Road: Photographs of the Desolation Angels, 1944–1960.* New York: Gotham Book Mart, 1970.

1979. Cook, Bruce. *The Beat Generation.* New York: Charles Scribner's Sons, 1971.

1980. Davidson, Michael. *The San Francisco Renaissance: Poetics and Community at Mid-Century.* New York: Cambridge University Press, 1989.

1981. Everson, William. *Archetype West: The Pacific Coast as Literary Region.* Berkeley, Calif.: Oyez, 1976.

1982. Feldman, Gene, and Max Gartenberg, eds. *The Beat Generation and the Angry Young Men.* New York: Citadel Press, 1958.

1983. Ferlinghetti, Lawrence, ed. *Beatitude Anthology.* San Francisco: City Lights Books, 1960.

1984. Fleischmann, Wolfgang B. "A Look at the 'Beat Generation' Writers." *Carolina Quarterly* 9 (Spring 1959): 13–20.

1985. Foster, Edward Halsey. *Understanding the Beats*. Columbia: University of South Carolina Press, 1992.

1986. French, Warren. *The San Francisco Poetry Renaissance, 1955–1960*. Boston: Twayne, 1991.

1987. Gebhardt, Eike. "Strategic Anomie and Contingent Valuation: Three Writers of Non-Political Dissent." Doctoral dissertation, Yale University, 1973. Kerouac, Burroughs, and Ferlinghetti.

1988. Goldman, Harold Raymond. "In the American Grain: A Definition of the Beat Sensibility." Doctoral dissertation, State University of New York, Stony Brook, 1984.

1989. Harney, Steve. "Ethnos and the Beat Poets." *Journal of American Studies* 25 (December 1991): 363–80.

1990. Holmes, John Clellon. *Nothing More to Declare*. New York: Scribner's, 1952.

1991. Huebel, Harry. "A Study of the Beat Generation and Its Effect on American Culture." Doctoral dissertation, Washington State University, 1971.

1992. Jackson, Carl T. "The Counterculture Looks East: Beat Writers and Asian Religion." *American Studies* 29 (Spring 1988): 51–70.

1993. Johnson, Joyce. *Minor Characters*. Boston: Houghton Mifflin, 1983.

1994. Kherdian, David. *Six Poets of the San Francisco Renaissance*. Fresno, Calif.: Giligia Press, 1967.

1995. Knight, Arthur Winfield, and Glee Knight, eds. *The Beat Book*. California, Penn., 1974.

1996. ———, and Kit Knight, eds. *The Beat Diary*. California, Pa: A. & K. Knight, 1977.

1997. Kodama, Sanehide. *American Poetry and Japanese Culture*. Hamden, Conn.: Archon Books, 1984.

1998. Krim, [Seymour]. "A Backward Glance o'er Beatnik Roads." *Tri-Quarterly* 43 (1978): 324–37.

1999. ———, ed. *The Beats*. New York: Fawcett Publications, 1960.

2000. Lipton, Lawrence. *The Holy Barbarians*. New York: Julian Messner, 1959.

2001. Mailer, Norman. "The White Negro: Superficial Reflections on the Hipster." *Dissent* 4 (Summer 1957): 276–93.

2002. Maynard, John Arthur. *Venice West: The Beat Generation in Southern California*. New Brunswick, N.J.: Rutgers University Press, 1991.

2003. Meltzer, David, ed. *The San Francisco Poets.* New York: Ballantine, 1971.

2004. Ossman, David. *The Sullen Art.* New York: Corinth Books, 1963. Includes interviews with Rexroth and Ginsberg.

2005. Parkinson, Thomas. "After the Beat Generation." *Colorado Quarterly* 17 (Summer 1968): 45–56.

2006. ———, ed. *A Casebook on the Beat.* New York: Thomas Y. Crowell, 1961.

2007. Podhoretz, Norman. "The Know-Nothing Bohemians." *Partisan Review* 25 (Spring 1958): 305–11, 313–16, 318.

2008. *Poets of the Cities: New York and San Francisco, 1950–1965.* New York: E. P. Dutton, 1974.

2009. Poland, Timothy Craig. "'Exuberance is Beauty': Method and Meaning in Beat Literature and Beyond." Doctoral dissertation, Georgia State University, 1987.

2010. Rao, Vimala C. "Oriental Influence on the Writings of Jack Kerouac, Allen Ginsberg, and Gary Snyder." Doctoral dissertation, University of Wisconsin, Milwaukee, 1974.

2011. Rexroth, Kenneth. *The Alternative Society: Essays from the Other World.* New York: Herder and Herder, 1970.

2012. ———. "Disengagement: The Art of the Beat Generation." *New World Writing No. 11.* New York: New American Library, 1957.

2013. ———. "San Francisco's Mature Bohemians." *Nation* 184 (February 23, 1957): 157–62.

2014. Robertson, David. "Real Matter, Spiritual Mountain: Gary Snyder and Jack Kerouac on Mt. Tamalpais." *Western American Literature* 17 (Fall 1992): 209–26.

2015. Saroyan, Aram. *Genesis Angels: The Saga of Lew Welch and the Beat Generation.* New York: William Morrow, 1979.

2016. Schwartz, Marilyn M. "From Beat to Beatific: Religious Ideas in the Writings of Kerouac, Ginsberg, and Corso." Doctoral dissertation, University of California, Davis, 1976.

2017. Scott, James F. "Beat Literature and the American Teen Cult." *American Quarterly* 14 (Summer 1962): 150–60.

2018. Skau, Michael Walter. "Themes, Things, and Movements in the Literature of the Beats." Doctoral dissertation, University of Illinois, Champaign-Urbana, 1973.

2019. Stephenson, Gregory. *The Daybreak Boys: Essays on the Literature of the Beat Generation.* Carbondale: Southern Illinois University Press, 1990.

2020. Tytell, John. "The Beat Generation and the Continuing American Revolution." *American Scholar* 42 (Spring 1973): 308–17.

2021. ———. *Naked Angels: The Lives and Literature of the Beat Generation.* New York: McGraw-Hill, 1976.

2022. Wallenstein, Barry. "The Beats." *Contemporary Literature* 18 (Autumn 1977): 542–51.

2023. Widmer, Kingsley. "The Beat in the Rise of Popular Culture." *The Fifties: Fiction, Poetry, and Drama.* Ed. Warren French. Deland, Fla.: Everett/Edwards, 1970, 155–73.

2024. Wilentz, Elias, ed. *The Beat Scene.* New York: Citadel Press/Corinth Books, 1960.

CANADIAN WESTERN LITERATURE

2025. Blodgett, E. D. "Fictions of Ethnicity in Prairie Writing." *Configuration: Essays on the Canadian Literatures*. Downsview, Ontario: ECW Press, 1982, 85–111.

2026. ———. "Gone West to Geometry's Country." *Configuration: Essays on the Canadian Literatures*. Downsview, Ontario: ECW Press, 1982, 187–218.

2027. Bringhurst, Robert. "That Also Is You: Some Classics of Native Canadian Literature." *Canadian Literature* 124–25 (Spring/Summer 1990): 32–47.

2028. Brown, Russell M. *Borderlines and Borderlands in English Canada: The Written Line*. Borderlands Monograph Series #4. [Orono, Maine]: Borderlands, 1990.

2029. Bukoski, Anthony. "The Canadian Writer and the Iowa Experience." *Canadian Literature* 101 (Summer 1984): 15–34.

2030. Cameron, Donald. *Conversations with Canadian Novelists*. 2 vols. Toronto: Macmillan, 1973.

2031. Carpenter, David. "Alberta in Fiction." Doctoral dissertation, University of Alberta, 1973.

2032. Collins, R. G., and Kenneth McRobbie, eds. "Manitoba in Literature: An Issue on Literary Environment." *Mosaic* 3 (Spring 1970). Special issue.

2033. Cooley, Dennis. "The Real Thing: In Search of a Prairie Aesthetic." *Essays on Canadian Writing* 50 (Fall 1993): 75–82.

2034. Dagg, Melvin Harold. "Beyond the Garrison: A Study of the Image of the Indian in Canadian Literature." Doctoral dissertation, University of New Brunswick, 1983.

2035. Davey, Frank. "The Explorer in Western Canadian Literature." *Studies in Canadian Literature* 4 (Summer 1979): 91–100.

2036. ———. *Surviving the Paraphrase: Eleven Essays On Canadian Literature*. Winnipeg: Turnstone Press, 1983.

2037. Davidson, Arnold E. *Coyote Country: Fictions of the Canadian West.* Durham, N.C.: Duke University Press, 1994.

2038. ———, ed. *Studies on Canadian Literature: Introductory and Critical Essays.* New York: Modern Language Asociation, 1990.

2039. Doyle, James. "American Literary Images of the Canadian Prairies, 1860–1910." *Great Plains Quarterly* 3 (Winter 1983): 30–38.

2040. ———. "The Post-Ultimate Frontier: American Authors in the Canadian West, 1885–1900." *Essays on Canadian Writing* 22 (Summer 1981): 14–26.

2041. Dyck, Edward Frank. "Topos and the Rhetoric of Prairie Poetry." Doctoral dissertation, University of Manitoba, 1988.

2042. ———, ed. *Essays on Saskatchewan Writing.* Regina: Saskatchewan Writers Guild, 1986.

2043. Eggleston, Wilfrid. *The Frontier and Canadian Letters.* Toronto: Ryerson, 1957.

2044. Engel, Mary Frances. "Bankrupt Dreams: The Isolated and the Insulated in Selected Works of Canadian and American Prairie Literature." Doctoral dissertation, Kent State University, 1978.

2045. Fairbanks, Carol. *Prairie Women: Images in American and Canadian Fiction.* New Haven: Yale University Press, 1986.

2046. Fraser, Janet. *Canadian Literature Index: A Guide to Periodicals and Newspapers.* Toronto: ECW Press, 1979–.

2047. Fraser, Wayne. *The Dominion of Women: The Personal and the Political in Canadian Women's Literature.* New York: Greenwood Press, 1991.

2048. Goldie, Terry. *Fear and Temptation: The Image of the Indigene in Canadian, Australian and New Zealand Literatures.* Montreal: McGill-Queens University Press, 1993.

2049. Grace, Sherrill E. "Comparing Mythologies: Ideas of West and North." *Borderlands: Essays in Canadian-American Relations.* Ed. Robert Lecker. Toronto: ECW Press, 1991, 293–362.

2050. Greene, Donald. "Western Canadian Literature." *Western American Literature* 2 (Winter 1968): 257–80.

2051. Harrison, Dick. "'Across the Medicine Line: Problems in Comparing Canadian and American Western Fiction.'" *The Westering Experience in American Literature: Bicentennial Essays.* Eds. Merrill Lewis and L. L. Lee. Bellingham: Bureau for Faculty Research, Western Washington University, 1977, 48–56.

2052. ———. "Fictions of the American and Canadian Wests." *Prairie Forum* 8 (Spring 1983): 89–97.

2053. ———. "Popular Fiction of the Canadian Prairies: Autopsy on a Small Corpus." *Journal of Popular Culture* 14 (Fall 1980): 326–32.

2054. ———. *Unnamed Country: The Struggle for a Canadian Prairie Fiction.* Edmonton: University of Alberta Press, 1977.

2055. ———, ed. *Best Mounted Police Stories.* Edmonton: University of Alberta Press, 1978.

2056. ———, ed. *Crossing Frontiers: Papers in American and Canadian Western Literature.* Edmonton: University of Alberta Press, 1979.

2057. Hin-Smith, Joan. *Three Voices: The Lives of Margaret Laurence, Gabrielle Roy, Frederick Philip Grove.* Toronto: Clarke Irwin, 1975.

2058. Howells, Coral Ann. *Private and Fictional Words: Canadian Women Novelists of the 1970s and 1980s.* New York: Methuen, 1987.

2059. Hoy, Helen Elizabeth. "The Portrayal of Women in Recent English-Canadian Fiction." Doctoral dissertation, University of Toronto, 1977.

2060. Hughes, Kenneth James, ed. *Contemporary Manitoba Writers: New Critical Studies.* Winnipeg: Turnstone Press, 1990.

2061. Hunt, Patricia. "North American Pastoral: Contrasting Images of the Garden in Canadian and American Literature." *American Studies* 23 (Spring 1982): 39–68.

2062. Kaye, Frances W. "Canadian-American Prairie-Plains: Literature in English." *Borderlands: Essays in Canadian-American Relations.* Ed. Robert Lecker. Toronto: ECW Press, 1991, 222–42.

2063. Keith, W. J. *A Sense of Style: Studies in the Art of Fiction in English-Speaking Canada.* Toronto: ECW Press, 1989.

2064. King, Thomas, ed. *All My Relations: An Anthology of Contemporary Canadian Native Fiction.* Norman: University of Oklahoma Press, 1992.

2065. Kreisel, Henry. "The Prairie: A State of Mind." *Transactions of the Royal Society of Canada,* 4th ser., 6 (June 1968): 171–80.

2066. Leckcr, Robert, and Jack David. *The Annotated Bibliography of Canada's Major Authors.* Toronto: ECW Press, 1979–.

2067. McCourt, Edward. *The Canadian West in Fiction.* Rev ed. Toronto: Ryerson, 1970.

2068. McLay, Catherine. "Crocus, Saskatchewan: A Country of the Mind." *Journal of Popular Culture* 14 (Fall 1980): 333–43. W. O. Mitchell.

2069. McLean, Kenneth Hugh. "The Treatment of History in Canadian Fiction." Doctoral dissertation, York University, 1980.

2070. McLeod, Gordon Duncan. "A Descriptive Bibliography of the Canadian Prairie Novel 1871–1970." Doctoral dissertation, Lakehead University, Ontario, 1974.

2071. Mandel, Eli. "Images of Prairie Man." *Another Time.* Ed. Eli Mandel. Erin, Ontario: Press Porcepic, 1977, 45–53.

2072. ———. "Romance and Realism in Western Canadian Fiction." *Prairie Perspectives 2.* Eds. A. W. Rasporich and H. C. Klassen. Toronto: Holt, Rinehart and Winston, 1973.

2073. ———. "Writing West: On the Road to Wood Mountain." *Another Time.* Ed. Eli Mandel. Erin, Ontario: Press Porcepic, 1977, 68–78.

2074. Morton, W. L. "Seeing an Unliterary Landscape." *Mosaic* 3 (Spring 1970): 1–10.

2075. New, W. H. *Articulating West: Essays on Purpose and Form in Modern Canadian Literature.* Toronto: New Press, 1972.

2076. ———. *A History of Canadian Literature.* New York: New Amsterdam Books, 1989.

2077. ———, ed. *Native Writers and Canadian Writing: Canadian Literature: Special Issue.* Vancouver: University of British Columbia Press, 1990.

2078. O'Conner, John Joseph William. "The Last Three Steppes: The Canadian West as 'Frontier' in Prairie Literature." Doctoral dissertation, University of Toronto, 1977.

2079. Petrone, Penny. *Native Literature in Canada: From the Oral Tradition to the Present.* Toronto: Oxford University Press, 1990.

2080. Pritchard, Allan. "West of the Great Divide: A View of the Literature of British Columbia." *Canadian Literature* 94 (Autumn 1982): 96–112.

2081. Probert, Kenneth G., ed. *Writing Saskatchewan: 20 Critical Essays.* Regina: Canadian Plains Research Centre, 1989.

2082. Rasky, Frank. *The Taming of the Canadian West.* Toronto: McClelland and Stewart, 1967.

2083. Rees, Ronald. "Nostalgic Reaction and the Canadian Prairie Landscape." *Great Plains Quarterly* 2 (Summer 1982): 157–67.

2084. Ricou, Laurence R. "Crossing Borders in the Literature of the Pacific Northwest." *Borderlands: Essays in Canadian-American Relations.* Ed. Robert Lecker. Toronto: ECW Press, 1991, 286–308.

2085. ———. *Vertical Man/Horizontal World.* Vancouver: University of British Columbia Press, 1973.

2086. Sproxton, Birk, ed. *Trace: Prairie Writers on Writing.* Winnipeg: Turnston Press, 1986.

2087. Stegner, Wallace. "Letter from Canada: A Son of the West Looks at His Native Region in Light of Today's Growing Canadian Nationalism." *American West* 11 (January 1974): 28–30.

2088. Stephens, D. G., ed. *Writers of the Prairies.* Vancouver: University of British Columbia Press, 1973.

2089. Stevens, Peter. "Explorer/Settler/Poet." *The Westering Experience in American Literature: Bicentennial Essays.* Eds. Merrill Lewis and L. L. Lee. Bellingham: Bureau for Faculty Research, Western Washington University, 1977, 189–98.

2090. Stich, Klaus Peter. "Immigration and the Canadian West From Propaganda to Fiction." Doctoral dissertation, York University, 1974.

2091. Story, Norah. *The Oxford Companion to Canadian History and Literature.* Toronto: Oxford University Press, 1967.

2092. Stouck, David. *Major Canadian Authors.* 2d ed., rev, exp. Lincoln: University of Nebraska Press, 1988.

2093. Tallman, Warren. "Wolf in the Snow: Part One, Four Windows on to Landscapes." *Canadian Literature* 5 (Summer 1960): 7–20.

2094. ———. "Wolf in the Snow: Part Two, The House Repossessed." *Canadian Literature* 6 (Autumn 1960): 41–48.

2095. Thacker, Robert. *The Great Prairie Fact and Literary Imagination.* Albuquerque: University of New Mexico Press, 1989.

2096. Thompson, Elizabeth Helen. "The Pioneer Woman: A Canadian Character Type." Doctoral dissertation, University of Western Ontario, 1987.

2097. Thompson, Eric Callum. "Prairie Mosiac: The Immigrant Novel in the Canadian West." *Studies in Canadian Literature* 5 (Fall 1980): 236–59.

2098. ———. "The Prairie Novel in Canada: A Study in Changing Form and Perception." Doctoral dissertation, University of New Brunswick, 1974.

2099. Walden, Keith. *Visions of Order: The Canadian Mounties in Symbol and Myth.* Toronto: Butterworths, 1982.

2100. Wiebe, Rudy. "Western Canada Fiction: Past and Future." *Western American Literature* 6 (Spring 1971): 21–30.

2101. Wood, Susan. "God's Doormats: Women in Canadian Prairie Fiction." *Journal of Popular Culture* 14 (Fall 1980): 350–59.

2102. ———. "The Land in Canadian Prose, 1840–1945." Doctoral dissertation, University of Toronto, 1975.

2103. Woodcock, George. *The Meeting of Time and Space: Regionalism in Canadian Literature.* Edmonton: NeWest Institute for Western Canadian Studies, 1981.

WORKS ON INDIVIDUAL AUTHORS

EDWARD ABBEY

2104. Bryant, Paul T. "Echoes, Allusions, and 'Reality' in *Hayduke Lives!*" *Western American Literature* 25 (Winter 1991): 311–22.

2105.————. "Edward Abbey and Environmental Quixoticism." *Western American Literature* 24 (May 1989): 37–43.

2106. ————. "The Structure and Unity of *Desert Solitaire*." *Western American Literature* 28 (Spring 1993): 3–19.

2107. Dougherty, Jay. "'Once more, and once more again': Edward Abbey's Cyclical View of Past and Present in *Good News*." *Critique* 29 (Summer 1988): 223–32.

2108. Gamble, David E. "Into the Maze with Edward Abbey." *South Dakota Review* 26 (Spring 1988): 66–77.

2109. Hepworth, James, and Gregory McNamee, eds. *Resist Much, Obey Little: Some Notes on Edward Abbey.* Tucson: Harbinger House, 1989.

2110. Herndon, Jerry A. "'Moderate Extremism': Edward Abbey and 'The Moon-Eyed Horse.'" *Western American Literature* 16 (Summer 1981): 97–103.

2111. Loeffler, Jack. "Edward Abbey, Anarchism and the Environment." *Western American Literature* 28 (Spring 1993): 43–49.

2112. McCann, Garth. *Edward Abbey.* Western Writers Series, No. 29. Boise, Idaho: Boise State University, 1977.

2113. McClintock, James I. "Edward Abbey's 'Antidotes to Despair.'" *Critique* 31 (Fall 1989): 41–54.

2114. Morris, David Copland. "Celebration and Irony: The Polyphonic Voice of Edward Abbey's *Desert Solitaire*." *Western American Literature* 28 (Spring 1993): 21–32.

2115. Murray, John A. "The Hill Beyond the City: Elements of the Jeremiad in Edward Abbey's 'Down the River with Henry Thoreau.'" *Western American Literature* 22 (Winter 1988): 301–6.

2116. Petersen, David. "Cactus Ed's Moveable Feast: A Preview of *Confessions of a Barbarian: Pages from the Journals of Edward Abbey.*" *Western American Literature* 28 (Spring 1993): 33–41.

2117. Pilkington, William T. "Edward Abbey: Western Philosopher, or How to be a 'Happy Hopi Hippie.'" *Western American Literature* 9 (May 1974): 17–31.

2118. Powell, Lawrence Clark. "A Singular Ranger." *Westways* 66 (March 1974): 32–35, 64–65.

2119. Rea, Paul W. "Abbey's Country." *Journal of the Southwest* 31 (Summer 1989): 264–70.

2120. Ronald, Ann. "The Nevada Scene Through Edward Abbey's Eyes." *Nevada Historical Society Quarterly* 27 (Spring 1984): 3–12.

2121. ———. *The New West of Edward Abbey.* Reno: University of Nevada Press, 1988.

2122. Tatum, Stephen. "Closing and Opening Western American Fiction: The Reader in *The Brave Cowboy.*" *Western American Literature* 19 (November 1984): 187–203.

2123. Thurn, Thora Flack. "The Quest for Freedom in the Changing West of Edward Abbey and Larry McMurtry." Doctoral dissertation, Texas Christian University, 1990.

2124. Twining, Edward S. "Edward Abbey, American: Another Radical Conservative." *Denver Quarterly* 12 (Winter 1978): 3–15.

2125. Westrum, Dexter Lyle. "The Art of Survival in the Contemporary West: The Fictions of Thomas McGuane, James Welch, and Edward Abbey." Doctoral dissertation, University of Minnesota, 1985.

2126. Wylder, Delbert E. "Edward Abbey and the 'Power Elite.'" *Western Review* 6 (Winter 1969): 18–22.

LEE K. ABBOTT

2127. Ingersoll, Earl, and Stan Samuel Rubin. "'The Whole Reach and Tug of Passion': A Conversation with Lee K. Abbott." *Indiana Review* 11 (Winter 1987): 1–10.

OSCAR ZETA ACOSTA

2128. Padilla, Genaro Miguel. "The Progression from Individual to Social Consciousness in Two Chicano Novelists: José Antonio Villarreal and Oscar Zeta Acosta." Doctoral dissertation, University of Washington, 1981.

2129. Paredes, Raymund A. "Los Angeles from the Barrio: "Oscar Zeta Acosta's *The Revolt of the Cockroach People*." *Los Angeles in Fiction: A Collection of Original Essays*. Ed. David Fine. Albuquerque: University of New Mexico Press, 1984, 209–22.

2130. Smith, Norman D. "Buffaloes and Cockroaches: Acosta's Siege at Aztlán." *Latin American Literary Review* 5 (Spring–Summer 1977): 86–97.

ANDY ADAMS

2131. Brunvand, Jan H. "'Sailors' and 'Cowboys' Folklore in Two Popular Classics." *Southern Folklore Quarterly* 29 (December 1965): 266–83.

2132. Davidson, Levette J. "The Unpublished Manuscripts of Andy Adams." *Colorado Magazine* 28 (April 1951): 97–107.

2133. Dobie, J. Frank. "Andy Adams, Cowboy Chronicler." *Southwest Review* 11 (January 1926): 92–101.

2134. Graham, Don. "Old and New Cowboy Classics." *Southwest Review* 65 (Summer 1980): 293–303.

2135. Hudson, Wilson M. *Andy Adams: His Life and Writings*. Dallas: Southern Methodist University Press, 1964.

2136. ———. *Andy Adams: Storyteller and Novelist of the Great Plains*. Southwest Writers Series, No. 4. Austin, Tex.: Steck-Vaughn, 1967.

2137. ———, ed. *Why the Chisholm Trail Forks and Other Tales of the Cattle Country*. Austin: University of Texas Press, 1956.

2138. Molen, Dayle H. "Andy Adams: Classic Novelist of the Western Cattle Drive." *Montana: The Magazine of Western History* 19 (January 1969): 24–35.

2139. ———. "Andy Adams... Log of a Cowboy." *Persimmon Hill* 9 (1979): 48–57.

2140. Quissell, Barbara. "Andy Adams and the Real West." *Western American Literature* 7 (Fall 1972): 211–19.

2141. Taylor, Archer. "Americanisms in *The Log of the Cowboy*." *Western Folklore* 18 (January 1959): 39–41.

MAX ADELER

See Charles Heber Clark

NANNIE ALDERSON

2142. Bevis, William W. "Alderson's Bride Goes West." *Ten Tough Trips: Montana Writers and the West*. Seattle: University of Washington Press, 1990, 49–75.

BESS STREETER ALDRICH

2143. Foreman, Ruth Jeane. "The Fiction of Bess Streeter Aldrich." Doctoral dissertation, Drake University, 1982.

2144. Martin, Abigail Ann. *Bess Streeter Aldrich*. Western Writers Series, No. 104. Boise, Idaho: Boise State University, 1992.

2145. Meier, A. Mabel. "Bess Streeter Aldrich: A Literary Portrait." *Nebraska History* 50 (Spring 1969): 67–100.

CHARLES ALEXANDER

2146. Corning, Howard M. "Charles Alexander: Youth of the Oregon Mood." *Oregon Historical Quarterly* 74 (March 1973): 34–70.

HENRY WILSON ALLEN

(Clay Fisher, Will Henry)

2147. Blevins, Richard Lowell. "Henry (Will Henry) Allen's Use of Historical Sources in *From Where the Sun Now Stands*, a Novel of the American West." Doctoral dissertation, University of Pittsburgh, 1985.

2148. Falke, Anne. "The Art of Convention: Images of Women in the Modern Western Novels of Henry Wilson Allen." *North Dakota Quarterly* 42 (Spring 1974): 17–27.

2149. ———. "Clay Fisher or Will Henry? An Author's Choice of Pen Name." *Journal of Popular Culture* 7 (Winter 1973): 692–700.

2150. Gale, Robert L. *Will Henry/Clay Fisher*. Western Writers Series, No. 52. Boise, Idaho: Boise State University, 1982.

2151. ———. *Will Henry/Clay Fisher*. Boston: Twayne, 1984.

2152. Kroll, Keith. "Henry W. Allen (Will Henry/Clay Fisher): A Bibliography of Primary and Secondary Sources." *Bulletin of Bibliography* 44 (December 1987): 219–31.

2153. Walker, Dale L. "Introduction: Shadow Writer: In Appreciation of Will Henry." *Will Henry's West*. El Paso: Texas Western Press, 1984, ix–xxvii.

2154. Aal, Katharyn Machan. "Writing as an Indian Woman: An Interview with Paula Gunn Allen." *North Dakota Quarterly* 57 (Spring 1989): 148–61.

2155. Ballinger, Franchot, and Brian Swann. "A *MELUS* Interview: Paula Gunn Allen." *MELUS* 10 (1983): 3–25.

2156. Bruchac, Joseph. "I Climb the Mesas in My Dreams: An Interview with Paula Gunn Allen." *Survival This Way: Interviews with American Indian Poets.* Ed. Joseph Bruchac. Tucson: University of Arizona Press, 1987, 1–21.

2157. Hanson, Elizabeth I. *Paula Gunn Allen.* Western Writers Series, No. 96. Boise, Idaho: Boise State University, 1990.

2158. Jahner, Elaine. "A Laddered, Rain-bearing Rug: Paula Gunn Allen's Poetry." *Women and Western American Literature.* Eds. Helen Winter Stauffer and Susan J. Rosowski. Troy, N. Y.: Whitston, 1982, 311–26.

2159. Ruppert, Jim. "Paula Gunn Allen and Joy Harjo: Closing the Distance Between Personal and Mythic Space." *American Indian Quarterly* 7 (1983): 27–40.

ALURISTA

See Alberto Urista

RUDOLFO A. ANAYA

2160. Cantú, Roberto. "Estructura y sentido de lo onírico en *Bless Me, Ultima.*" *Mester* 5 (November 1974): 27–41.

2161. Carpenter, Lorene Hyde. "Maps for the Journey: Shamanic Patterns in Anaya, Asturias, and Castañeda." Doctoral dissertation, University of Colorado, Boulder, 1981.

2162. Clements, William M. "The Way to Individuation in Anaya's *Bless Me, Ultima.*" *Midwest Quarterly* 23 (Winter 1982): 131–43.

2163. Gonzalez-T., Cesar A. *Rudolfo A. Anaya: Focus on Criticism.* La Jolla, Calif.: Lalo Press, 1990.

2164. Malpezzi, Frances. "A Study of The Female Protagonist in Frank Waters' *People of the Valley* and Rudolfo Anaya's *Bless Me, Ultima.*" *South Dakota Review* 14 (Summer 1976): 102–10.

2165. Mitchell, Carol. "Rudolfo Anaya's *Bless Me, Ultima*: Folk Culture in Literature." *Critique* 22 (No. 1, 1980): 55–64.

2166. Rogers, Jane. "The Function of the *La Llorona* Motif in Rudolfo Anaya's *Bless Me, Ultima*." *Latin American Literary Review* 5 (Spring–Summer 1977): 64–69.

2167. Testa, Daniel. "Extensive/Intensive Dimensionality in Anaya's *Bless Me, Ultima*." *Latin American Literary Review* 5 (Spring–Summer 1977): 70–78.

2168. Vassallo, Paul, ed. *The Magic of Words: Rudolfo A. Anaya and His Writings*. Albuquerque: University of New Mexico Press, 1982.

2169. Waggoner, Amy. "Tony's Dreams–An Important Dimension in *Bless Me, Ultima*." *Southwestern American Literature* 4 (1974): 74–79.

EDWARD ANDERSON

2170. Bennett, Patrick. *Rough and Rowdy Ways: The Life and Hard Times of Edward Anderson*. College Station: Texas A M University Press, 1988.

BROTHER ANTONINUS

See William Everson

MAX APPLE

2171. Glausser, Wayne. "Spots of Meaning: Literary Allusions in Max Apple's 'Vegetable Love.'" *Studies in Short Fiction* 20 (Fall 1983): 255–63.

2172. Vorda, Allan. "An Interview with Max Apple." *Michigan Quarterly Review* 27 (Winter 1988): 69–78.

2173. Wilde, Alan. "Dayanu: Max Apple and the Ethics of Sufficiency." *Contemporary Literature* 26 (Fall 1985): 254–85.

RON ARIAS

2174. Lewis, Marvin A. "On the Road to Tamazunchale." *Revista Chicano-Riqueña* 5 (Fall 1978): 49–52.

2175. Marín, Mariana. "*The Road to Tamazunchale*: Fantasy or Reality." *De Colores* 3 (1977): 34–38.

2176. Martínez, Eliud. "Ron Arias' *The Road to Tamazunchale*: A Chicano Novel of the New Reality." *Latin American Literary Review* 5 (Spring–Summer 1977): 51–63.

GERTRUDE ATHERTON

2177. Bradley, Jennifer. "Woman at the Golden Gate: The Last Works of Gertrude Atherton." *Women's Studies* 12 (1986): 17–30.

2178. Forman, Henry James. "A Brilliant California Novelist." *California Historical Society Quarterly* 40 (March 1961): 1–10.

2179. Forrey, Carolyn. "Gertrude Atherton and the New Woman." *California Historical Quarterly* 55 (Fall 1976): 194–209.

2180. ———. "Gertrude Atherton and the New Woman." Doctoral dissertation, Yale University, 1971.

2181. Leider, Emily Wortis. *California's Daughter: Gertrude Atherton and Her Times.* Stanford, Calif.: Stanford University Press, 1991.

2182. McClure, Charlotte S. "A Checklist of the Writings of and About Gertrude Atherton." *American Literary Realism 1870–1910* 9 (Spring 1976): 103–62.

2183. ———. *Gertrude Atherton.* Western Writers Series, No. 23. Boise, Idaho: Boise State University, 1976.

2184. ———. *Gertrude Atherton.* Boston: Twayne, 1979.

2185. ———. "Gertrude Atherton's California Women: From Love Story to Psychological Drama." *Women, Women Writers, and the West.* Eds. L. L. Lee and Merrill Lewis. Troy, N.Y.: Whitston, 1978, 101–9.

2186. Richey, Elinor. "The Flappers Were Her Daughters: The Liberated Literary World of Gertrude Atherton." *American West* 11 (July 1974): 4–10, 60–63.

2187. Starr, Kevin. "Gertrude Atherton, Daughter of the Elite." *Americans and the California Dream, 1850–1915.* New York: Oxford University Press, 1973, 345–64.

2188. Weir, Sybil. "Gertrude Atherton: The Limits of Feminism in the 1890's." *San Jose Studies* 1 (February 1975): 24–31.

2189. Wheeler, Leslie. "Montana and the Lady Novelist." *Montana: The Magazine of Western History* 27 (Winter 1977): 40–51.

MARY AUSTIN

2190. Austin, Mary. *Earth Horizon: An Autobiography.* Boston: Houghton Mifflin, 1932.

2191. Baer, Morley. *Room and Time Enough: The Land of Mary Austin.* Flagstaff, Ariz.: Northland Press, 1979.

2192. Ballard, Rae Galbraith. "Mary Austin's *Earth Horizon*: The Imperfect Circle." Doctoral dissertation, Claremont Graduate School, 1977.

2193. Berry, J. Wilkes. "Mary Austin: Sibylic Gourmet of the Southwest." *Western Review* 9 (Winter 1972): 3–8.

2194. ———. "Mary Hunter Austin (1868–1934)." *American Literary Realism 1870–1910* 2 (Summer 1969): 125–31.

2195. Blend, Benay. "Mary Austin and the Western Conservation Movement: 1900–1927." *Journal of the Southwest* 30 (Spring 1988): 12–34.

2196. Church, Peggy Pond, and Shelley Armitage, eds. *Wind's Trail: The Early Life of Mary Austin.* Santa Fe: Museum of New Mexico Press, 1990.

2197. Doyle, Helen McKnight. *Mary Austin: Woman of Genius.* New York: Gotham House, 1939.

2198. Dubois, Arthur E. "Mary Hunter Austin, 1868–1934." *Southwest Review* 20 (April 1935): 231–64.

2199. Fink, Augusta. *I Mary: A Biography of Mary Austin.* Tucson: University of Arizona Press, 1983.

2200. Ford, Thomas W. "*The American Rhythm*: Mary Austin's Poetic Principle." *Western American Literature* 5 (Spring 1970): 3–14.

2201. Gaer, Joseph. *Mary Austin, Bibliography and Biographical Data.* Monograph No. 2. Berkeley, Calif.: Library Research Digest, 1934.

2202. Graulich, Melody. "Introduction," to *Western Trails: A Collection of Short Stories by Mary Austin.* Reno: University of Nevada Press, 1987, 1–28.

2203. Langlois, Karen S. "A Fresh Voice from the West: Mary Austin, California, and American Literary Magazines, 1892–1910." *California History* 69 (Spring 1990): 22–35.

2204. ———. "Mary Austin and Houghton Mifflin Company: A Case Study in the Marketing of a Western Writer." *Western American Literature* 23 (May 1988): 31–42.

2205. ———. "Mary Austin and the New Theatre: The 1911 Production of *The Arrow Maker*." *Theatre History Studies* 8 (1988): 71–87.

2206. Lyday, Jo W. *Mary Austin: The Southwest Works.* Southwest Writers Series, No. 16. Austin, Tex: Steck-Vaughn, 1968.

2207. *Mary Austin: A Memorial.* Ed. Willard Hougland. Santa Fe: Laboratory of Anthropology, 1944.

2208. Morrow, Nancy. "The Artist as Heroine and Anti-Heroine in Mary Austin's *A Woman of Genius* and Anne Douglas Sedgwick's *Tante.*" *American Literary Realism 1870–1910* 22 (Winter 1990): 17–29.

2209. O'Grady, John P. *Pilgrims to the Wild: Everett Ruess, Henry David Thoreau, John Muir, Clarence King, Mary Austin.* Salt Lake City: University of Utah Press, 1993.

2210. Pearce, T. M. *The Beloved House.* Caldwell, Idaho: Caxton Printers, 1940.

2211. ———. *Mary Hunter Austin*. New York: Twayne, 1965.

2212. ———, ed. *Literary America, 1903–1934: The Mary Austin Letters*. Westport, Conn.: Greenwood Press, 1979.

2213. Powell, Lawrence Clark. "A Dedication to the Memory of Mary Hunter Austin, 1868–1934." *Arizona and the West* 10 (Spring 1968): 1–4.

2214. ———. "Southwest Classics Reread: A Prophetic Passage." *Westways* 65 (February 1973): 60–65.

2215. Pryse, Marjorie. "Introduction," to Mary Austin, *Stories from the Country of Lost Borders*. New Brunswick, N.J.: Rutgers University Press, 1987, vii–xxxviii.

2216. Ringler, Donald P. *Mary Austin: Kern County Days*. Bakersfield, Calif.: Bear Mountain Books, 1963. First appeared in *Southern California Quarterly* 45 (March 1963): 25–63.

2217. Ruppert, James. "Mary Austin's Landscape Line in Native American Literature." *Southwest Review* 68 (Autumn 1983): 376–90.

2218. Scheick, William J. "Mary Austin's Disfigurement of the Southwest in *The Land of Little Rain*." *Western American Literature* 27 (May 1992): 37–46.

2219. Smith, Henry. "The Feel of the Purposeful Earth." *New Mexico Quarterly* I (February 1931): 17–33.

2220. Steffens, Lincoln. "Mary Austin and the Desert: A Portrait." *American Mercury* 72 (June 1911): 244–63.

2221. Stineman, Esther Lanigan. *Mary Austin: Song of a Maverick*. New Haven: Yale University Press, 1989.

2222. Taylor, Cynthia. "Claiming Female Space: Mary Austin's Western Landscape." *The Big Empty: Essays on Western Landscapes as Narratives*. Ed. Leonard Engel. Albuquerque: University of New Mexico Press, 1994, 119–32.

2223. Work, James C. "The Moral in Austin's *The Land of Little Rain*." *Women and Western American Literature*. Eds. Helen Winter Stauffer and Susan J. Rosowski. Troy, N.Y.: Whitston, 1982, 297–310.

2224. Wynn, Dudley. "A Critical Study of the Writings of Mary Hunter Austin, 1868–1934." Doctoral dissertation, New York University, 1940.

2225. ———. "Mary Austin, Woman Alone." *Virginia Quarterly Review* 13 (Spring 1937): 243–56.

2226. Young, Vernon. "Mary Austin and the Earth Performance." *Southwest Review* 35 (Summer 1959): 153–63.

MARGARET JEWETT BAILEY

2227. Duncan, Janice K. "'Ruth Rover'–Vindictive Falsehood or Historical Truth?" *Journal of the West* 12 (April 1973): 240–53.

2228. Leasher, Evelyn, and Robert J. Frank. "Introduction," to Margaret Jewett Bailey, *The Grains....* Corvallis: Oregon State University Press, 1986, 1–20.

2229. Nelson, Herbert B. *The Literary Impulse in Pioneer Oregon.* Corvallis: Oregon State University Press, 1948, 36–41.

2230. ————. "Ruth Rover's Cup of Sorrow." *Pacific Northwest Quarterly* 50 (July 1959): 91–98.

FREDERIC HOMER BALCH

2231. Ballou, Robert. *Early Klickitat Valley Days.* Goldendale, Wash., 1938, 433–43.

2232. Coon, Delia M. "Frederick [*sic*] Homer Balch." *Washington Historical Quarterly* 15 (January 1924): 32–43.

2233. Harris, Stephen L., ed. "A Northwest Tale: Frederic Homer Balch's 'Camas Prairie Girl.'" *Columbia* 7 (Spring 1993): 37–44.

2234. Powers, Alfred. *History of Oregon Literature.* Portland: Metropolitan Press, 1935, 317–32.

2235. Wiley, Leonard. *The Granite Boulder: A Biography of Frederic Homer Balch.* Portland, Oreg.: n.p., 1970.

EVE BALL

2236. Clayton, Lawrence. "An Interview with Eve Ball." *Journal of Big Bend Studies* 3 (1991): 125–38.

HUBERT HOWE BANCROFT

2237. Caughey, John. *Hubert Howe Bancroft: Historian of the West.* Berkeley: University of California Press, 1946.

2238. Clark, Harry. *A Venture in History: The Production, Publication, and Sale of the Works of Hubert Howe Bancroft.* Berkeley: University of California Press, 1973.

2239. Peterson, Charles S. "Hubert Howe Bancroft: First Western Regionalist." *Writing Western History: Essays on Major Western Historians.* Ed. Richard W. Etulain. Albuquerque: University of New Mexico Press, 1991, 43–70.

2240. Smith, David Douglas. "Hubert Howe Bancroft and American Social Science, 1874–1918." Doctoral dissertation, Northern Illinois University, 1973.

MARY BARNARD

2241. Helle, Anita. "The Odysseys of Mary Barnard." *An Anthology of Northwest Writing: 1900–1950.* Ed. Michael Strelow, et al. Eugene, Oreg.: Northwest Review Books, 1979, 227–32.

WILL CROFT BARNES

2242. White, John I. "Will Croft Barnes: Cowboy, Author, Conservationist." *American West* 16 (March–April 1979): 38–39.

RAYMOND BARRIO

2243. Geuder, Patricia. "Address Systems in the *Plum Plum Pickers.*" *Aztlán* 6 (Fall 1975): 341–46.

2244. LaPresto, Brigitte Loos. "Agricultural Promise and Disillusionment in the California Novel: Frank Norris, John Steinbeck, Raymond Barrio." Doctoral dissertation, Bowling Green State University, 1987.

2245. Lattin, Vernon. "Paradise and Plums: Appearance and Reality in Barrio's *The Plum Plum Pickers.*" *Critique* 19 (No. 1, 1977): 49–57.

L. FRANK BAUM

2246. Anderson, Celia Catlett. "The Comedians of Oz." *Studies in American Humor* 5 (Winter 1986–87): 229–42.

2247. Averill, Thomas Fox. "Oz and Kansas Culture." *Kansas History* 12 (Spring 1989): 2–12.

2248. Earle, Neil. *The Wonderful Wizard of Oz in American Popular Culture: Uneasy in Eden.* Lewiston, N.Y.: Edwin Mellen, 1993.

2249. Griswold, Jerry. "There's No Place but Home: *The Wizard of Oz.*" *Antioch Review* 45 (Fall 1987): 462–75.

2250. Hudlin, Edward W. "The Mythology of *Oz*: An Interpretation." *Papers on Language and Literature* 25 (Fall 1989): 443–62.

REX BEACH

2251. Ravitz, Abe C. *Rex Beach.* Western Writers Series, No. 113. Boise, Idaho: Boise State University, 1994.

PETER S. BEAGLE

2252. Van Becker, David. "Time, Space, and Consciousness in the Fantasy of Peter S. Beagle." *San Jose Studies* 1 (February 1975): 52–61.

ROY BEDICHEK

2253. Bedichek, Roy. "My Father and Then My Mother." *Southwest Review* 52 (1967): 324–42.

2254. Dugger, Ronnie, ed. *Three Men in Texas: Bedichek, Webb, and Dobie.* Austin: University of Texas Press, 1967.

2255. James, Eleanor. *Roy Bedichek.* Southwest Writers Series, No. 32. Austin, Tex.: Steck-Vaughn, 1970.

2256. Owens, William A. *Three Friends: Bedichek, Dobie, Webb.* Garden City, N.Y.: Doubleday, 1969.

EMERSON BENNETT-SIDNEY MOSS

2257. Mills, Randall V. "Emerson Bennett's Two Oregon Novels." *Oregon Historical Quarterly* 41 (December 1940): 367–81.

2258. Nelson, Herbert B. *The Literary Impulse in Pioneer Oregon.* Corvallis: Oregon State University Press, 1948, 44–51.

2259. Poulsen, Richard C. "Black George, Black Harris, and the Mountain Man Vernacular." *Rendezvous* 8 (Summer 1973): 15–23.

2260. Powers, Alfred. *History of Oregon Literature.* Portland: Metropolitan Press, 1935, 195–203.

THOMAS BERGER

2261. Betts, Richard A. "Thomas Berger's *Little Big Man*: Contemporary Picaresque." *Critique* 23 (Winter 1981/82): 85–96.

2262. Cleary, Michael. "Finding the Center of the Earth: Satire, History, and Myth in *Little Big Man.*" *Western American Literature* 15 (Fall 1980): 195–221.

2263. Dippie, Brian W. "Jack Crabb and the Sole Survivors of Custer's Last Stand." *Western American Literature* 4 (Fall 1969): 189–202.

2264. Fetrow, Fred M. "The Function of the External Narrator in Thomas Berger's *Little Big Man.*" *Journal of Narrative Technique* 5 (1975): 57–65.

2265. Galligan, Edward L. *The Comic Vision in Literature.* Athens: University of Georgia Press, 1984.

2266. Gurian, Jay. "Style in the Literary Desert: *Little Big Man.*" *Western American Literature* 3 (Winter 1969): 285–96.

2267. Landon, Brooks. "The Measure of *Little Big Man.*" *Studies in American Fiction* 17 (Autumn 1989): 131–42.

2268. ———. *Thomas Berger.* Boston: Twayne, 1989.

2269. Lee, L. L. "American, Western, Picaresque: Thomas Berger's *Little Big Man*." *South Dakota Review* 4 (Summer 1966): 35–42.

2270. Moore, Jean P. "The Creative Function of the Popular Arts in the Novels of Thomas Berger." Doctoral dissertation, University of South Florida, 1981.

2271. Oliva, Leo E. "Thomas Berger's *Little Big Man* as History." *Western American Literature* 8 (Spring–Summer 1973): 33–54.

2272. Turner, Frederick W., III. "Melville and Thomas Berger: The Novelist as Cultural Anthropologist." *Centennial Review* 13 (Winter 1969): 101–21.

2273. Wallace, Jon. "The Implied Author as Protagonist: A Reading of *Little Big Man*." *Western American Literature* 22 (February 1988): 291–99.

2274. Wylder, Delbert E. "Thomas Berger's *Little Big Man* as Literature." *Western American Literature* 3 (Winter 1969): 273–84.

DON BERRY

2275. Love, Glen A. *Don Berry.* Western Writers Series, No. 35. Boise, Idaho: Boise State University, 1978.

2276. Singer, Barnett. "Toward the Great Northwest Novel." *Research Studies* (Pullman, Wash.) 43 (March 1975): 55–69.

AMBROSE BIERCE

2277. Bahr, H. W. "Ambrose Bierce and Realism." *Southern Quarterly* 1 (July 1963): 309–33.

2278. Berkove, Lawrence I. "'Hades in Trouble': A Rediscovered Story by Ambrose Bierce." *American Literary Realism, 1870–1910* 25 (Winter 1993): 67–84.

2279. ———. "The Man With the Burning Pen: Ambrose Bierce as Journalist." *Journal of Popular Culture* 15 (Fall 1981): 34–40.

2280. ———. "Two Impossible Dreams: Ambrose Bierce on Utopia and America." *Huntington Library Quarterly* 44 (Autumn 1981): 283–92.

2281. Brazil, John R. "Behind the Bitterness: Ambrose Bierce in Text and Context." *American Literary Realism 1870–1910* 13 (Autumn 1980): 225–37.

2282. Davidson, Cathy N. *The Experimental Fictions of Ambrose Bierce: Structuring the Ineffable.* Lincoln: University of Nebraska Press, 1984.

2283. ———, ed. *Critical Essays on Ambrose Bierce.* Boston: G. K. Hall, 1982.

2284. Fatout, Paul. "Ambrose Bierce (1842–1914)." *American Literary Realism 1870–1910* 1 (Fall 1967): 13–19.

2285. ———. *Ambrose Bierce and the Black Hills.* Norman: University of Oklahoma Press, 1956.

2286. ———. *Ambrose Bierce: The Devil's Lexicographer.* Norman: University of Oklahoma Press, 1951.

2287. Fortenberry, George E., comp. and ed. "Ambrose Bierce (1842–1914?): A Critical Bibliography of Secondary Comment." *American Literary Realism 1870–1910* 4 (Winter 1971): 11–56.

2288. Gaer, Joseph, ed. *Ambrose Gwinett Bierce: Bibliography and Biographical Data.* Berkeley, Calif., 1935; New York: Burt Franklin, 1968.

2289. Goldstein, Jesse Sidney. "Edwin Markham, Ambrose Bierce, and 'The Man with the Hoe.'" *Modern Language Notes* 58 (March 1943): 165–75.

2290. Grattan, C. Hartley. *Bitter Bierce: A Mystery of American Life.* New York: Doubleday, Doran, 1929.

2291. Grenander, M. E. *Ambrose Bierce.* New York: Twayne, 1971.

2292. ———. "The Critical Theories of Ambrose Bierce." Doctoral dissertation, University of Chicago, 1948.

2293. Klein, Marcus. "San Francisco and Her Hateful Ambrose Bierce." *Hudson Review* 7 (August 1954): 392–407.

2294. McWilliams, Carey. *Ambrose Bierce: A Biography.* New York: A. and C. Boni, 1929; Hamden, Conn.: Archon Books, 1967.

2295. Neale, Walter. *Life of Ambrose Bierce.* New York: Walter Neale, 1929; New York: AMS Press, 1969.

2296. O'Connor, Richard. *Ambrose Bierce: A Biography.* Boston: Little, Brown, 1967.

2297. Oliver, Lawrence J., and Gary Scharnhorst. "Charlotte Perkins Gilman v. Ambrose Bierce: The Literary Politics of Gender in Fin-de-Siècle California." *Journal of the West* 32 (July 1993): 52–60.

2298. Pope, Bertha, ed. *The Letters of Ambrose Bierce.* San Francisco: Book Club of California, 1922; Gordian Press, 1967.

2299. Roth, Russell. "Ambrose Bierce's 'Detestable Creature.'" *Western American Literature* 9 (November 1974): 169–76.

2300. Rubens, Philip M., and Robert Jones. "Ambrose Bierce: A Bibliographic Essay and Bibliography." *American Literary Realism 1870–1910* 16 (Spring 1983): 73–91.

2301. Saunders, Richard. *Ambrose Bierce: The Making of a Misanthrope.* San Francisco: Chronicle Books, 1985.

2302. Sheller, Harry L. "The Satire of Ambrose Bierce: Its Objects, Forms, Devices, and Possible Origins." Doctoral dissertation, University of Southern California, 1945.

2303. Starrett, Vincent. *Ambrose Bierce.* Chicago: Walter M. Hill, 1920.

2304. ———. *A Bibliography of the Writings of Ambrose Bierce.* Philadelphia: Centaur Book Shop, 1929.

2305. Walker, Dale L. "A Last Laugh for Ambrose Bierce." *American West* 10 (November 1973): 34–39, 63.

2306. Walker, Franklin. *San Francisco's Literary Frontier.* New York: Alfred A. Knopf, 1939.

2307. Wiggins, Robert A. *Ambrose Bierce.* Minneapolis: University of Minnesota Press, 1964.

2308. ———. "Ambrose Bierce: A Romantic in an Age of Realism." *American Literary Realism 1870–1910* 4 (Winter 1971): 1–10.

2309. Woodruff, Stuart C. *The Short Stories of Ambrose Bierce: A Study in Polarity.* Pittsburgh: University of Pittsburgh Press, 1964.

RAY ALLEN BILLINGTON

2310. Limerick, Patricia Nelson. "Persistent Traits and the Persistent Historian: The American Frontier and Ray Allen Billington." *Writing Western History: Essays on Major Western Historians.* Ed. Richard W. Etulain. Albuquerque: University of New Mexico Press, 1991, 277–310.

2311. Oglesby, Richard E. "A Dedication to the Memory of Ray Allen Billington 1903–1981." *Arizona and the West* 28 (Summer 1986): 103–6.

2312. Ridge, Martin. "Frederick Jackson Turner, Ray Allen Billington, and American Frontier History." *Western Historical Quarterly* 19 (January 1988): 5–20.

2313. ———. "Ray Allen Billington, Western History, and American Exceptionalism." *Pacific Historical Review* 56 (November 1987): 495–511.

KATE BOYLES BINGHAM

2314. Alexander, Ruth Ann. "Fictionalizing South Dakota from a Feminist Point of View: The Western Novels of Virgil D. Boyles and Kate Boyles Bingham." *South Dakota History* 23 (Fall 1993): 244–63.

NICHOLAS BLACK ELK

2315. Black Elk, Wallace, and William S. Lyon. *Black Elk: The Sacred Ways of a Lakota*. New York: Harper Row, 1990.

2316. Bloodworth, William. "Neihardt, Momaday, and the Art of Indian Autobiography." *Where the West Begins*. Eds. Arthur R. Huseboe and William Geyer. Sioux Falls, S. Dak.: Center for Western Studies Press, 1978, 152–60.

2317. Copeland, Marion W. "*Black Elk Speaks* and Leslie Silko's *Ceremony*: Two Visions of Horses." *Critique* 24 (Spring 1985): 158–72.

2318. DeMallie, Raymond J., ed. *The Sixth Grandfather: Black Elk's Teachings Given to John Neihardt*. Lincoln: University of Nebraska Press, 1984.

2319. Dombrowski, Daniel A. "Black Elk's Platonism." *North Dakota Quarterly* 55 (Winter 1987): 56–64.

2320. McCluskey, Sally. "*Black Elk Speaks*: and So Does John Neihardt." *Western American Literature* 6 (Winter 1972): 231–42.

2321. Olson, Paul A. "*Black Elk Speaks* as Epic and Ritual Attempt to Reverse History." *Vision and Refuge: Essays on the Literature of the Great Plains*. Eds. Virginia Faulkner with Frederick C. Luebke. Lincoln: University of Nebraska Press, 1982, 3–27.

2322. Rice, Julian. *Black Elk's Story: Distinguishing Its Lakota Purpose*. Albuquerque: University of New Mexico Press, 1991.

2323. Steltenkamp, Michael F. *Black Elk: Holy Man of the Oglala*. Norman: University of Oklahoma Press, 1993.

FORRESTER BLAKE

2324. Legris, Maurice. "The Western World of Forrester Blake." *South Dakota Review* 13 (Winter 1975–76): 64–76.

MARY CLEARMAN BLEW

2325. Meldrum, Barbara Howard. "Creative Cowgirl: Mary Clearman Blew's Herstory." *South Dakota Review* 31 (Spring 1993): 63–72.

BRUCE BLIVEN

2326. Greb, Gordon. "Seven Million Words Later: An Interview with Bruce Bliven." *San Jose Studies* 2 (May 1976): 62–73.

JUDY BLUME

2327. Weidt, Maryann N. *Presenting Judy Blume*. Boston: Twayne, 1990.

ROBERT BLY

2328. Davis, William V. "Camphor and Gopherwood: Robert Bly's Recent Poems in Prose." *Modern Poetry Studies* 11 (1982): 88–102.

2329. ———. "'In a Low Voice to Someone He is Sure is Listening': Robert Bly's Recent Poems in Prose." *Midwest Quarterly* 25 (Winter 1984): 148–56.

2330. ———. *Understanding Robert Bly*. Columbia: University of South Carolina Press, 1988.

2331. Dodd, Wayne. "An Interview with Robert Bly." *Ohio Review* 19 (Fall 1978): 32–48.

2332. Faas, Ekbert. "Robert Bly." *Boundary* 4 (1976): 707–26. Preceded by an interview between Faas and Bly, 677–700.

2333. ———. *Towards a New Poetics: Essays and Interviews*. Santa Barbara, Calif.: Black Sparrow Press, 1978, 199–243.

2334. Gioia, Dana. "The Successful Career of Robert Bly." *Hudson Review* 40 (Summer 1987): 207–23.

2335. Hertzel, Leo J. "What About Writers in the North?" *South Dakota Review* 5 (Spring 1967): 3–19.

2336. Heyen, William. "Inward to the World: The Poetry of Robert Bly." *Far Point* 3 (1969): 42–50.

2337. Janssens, G. A. M. "The Present State of American Poetry: Robert Bly and James Wright." *English Studies* 51 (April 1970): 112–37.

2338. Jones, Richard, and Kate Daniels, eds. *Of Solitude and Silence: Writings on Robert Bly*. Boston: Beacon Press, 1981.

2339. Justin, Jeffrey Arthur. "Unknown Land Poetry: Walt Whitman, Robert Bly, and Gary Snyder." Doctoral dissertation, University of Michigan, 1973.

2340. Kalaidjian, Walter. "From Silence to Subversion: Robert Bly's Political Surrealism." *Modern Poetry Studies* 11 (1983): 289–306.

2341. Kramer, Lawrence. "A Sensible Emptiness: Robert Bly and the Poetics of Immanence." *Contemporary Literature* 24 (Winter 1983): 449–62.

2342. Lensing, George S., and Ronald Moran. *Four Poets and the Emotive Imagination: Robert Bly, James Wright, Louis Simpson, and William Stafford*. Baton Rouge: Louisiana State University Press, 1976.

2343. Lockwood, William J. "Robert Bly: The Point Reyes Poems." *Where the West Begins.* Eds. Arthur R. Huseboe and William Geyer. Sioux Falls, S. Dak.: Center for Western Studies Press, 1978, 128–34.

2344. Mitchell, Roger. "Robert Bly and the Trouble with American Poetry." *Ohio Review* 42 (1988): 86–92.

2345. Molesworth, Charles. *The Fierce Embrace: A Study of Contemporary American Poetry.* Columbia: University of Missouri Press, 1979.

2346. Myers, George, Jr. "'Iron John': An Interview with Robert Bly." *Literary Review* 35 (Spring 1992): 408–14.

2347. Nelson, Howard. *Robert Bly: An Introduction to the Poetry.* New York: Columbia University Press, 1984.

2348. ———. "Robert Bly's Thoreau Book." *Ohio Review* 42 (1988): 93–106.

2349. Peseroff, Joyce, ed. *Robert Bly: When Sleepers Awake.* Ann Arbor: University of Michigan Press, 1984.

2350. Piccione, Anthony. "Robert Bly and the Deep Image." Doctoral dissertation, Ohio University, 1969.

2351. Roberson, William H. *Robert Bly: A Primary and Secondary Bibliography.* Metuchen, N.J.: Scarecrow Press, 1986.

2352. Sage, Francis Kellogg. "Robert Bly: His Poetry and Literary Criticism." Doctoral dissertation, University of Texas, Austin, 1974.

2353. Sugg, Richard P. *Robert Bly.* Boston: Twayne, 1986.

MODY C. BOATRIGHT

2354. Speck, Ernest B. "Mody Boatright's Cowboy as Hero." *Southwest Review* 66 (Summer 1981): 268–76.

2355. ———. *Mody C. Boatright.* Southwest Writers Series. Austin, Tex.: Steck-Vaughn, 1971.

HERBERT EUGENE BOLTON

2356. Bannon, John Francis. *Herbert Eugene Bolton: The Historian and the Man.* Tucson: University of Arizona Press, 1978.

2357. Hurtado, Albert L. "Herbert E. Bolton, Racism, and American History." *Pacific Historical Review* 62 (May 1993): 127–42.

2358. Jacobs, Wilbur R., et al. *Turner, Bolton, and Webb: Three Historians of the Frontier.* Seattle: University of Washington Press, 1965, 1979.

2359. Magnaghi, R. M. "Herbert E. Bolton and Sources for American Indian Studies." *Western Historical Quarterly* 6 (January 1975): 33–46.

2360. Weber, David J. *Myth and the History of the Hispanic Southwest.* Albuquerque: University of New Mexico Press, 1988.

2361. ———. "Turner, the Boltonians, and the Spanish Borderlands." *American Historical Review* 91 (February 1986): 66–81.

2362. Worcester, Donald E. "Herbert Eugene Bolton: The Making of a Western Historian." *Writing Western History: Essays on Major Western Historians.* Ed. Richard W. Etulain. Albuquerque: University of New Mexico Press, 1991, 193–213.

HAL BORLAND

2363. Barry, Nora Baker. "The Bear's Son Folk Tale in *When the Legends Die* and *House Made of Dawn.*" *Western American Literature* 12 (Winter 1978): 275–87.

B. M. BOWER

(Bertha Muzzey Bower Sinclair Cowan)

2364. Bloodworth, William A., Jr. "Mulford and Bower: Myth and History in the Early Western." *Great Plains Quarterly* 1 (Spring 1981): 95–104.

2365. Davison, Stanley R. "*Chip of the Flying U*: The Author Was a Lady." *Montana: The Magazine of Western History* 23 (Spring 1973): 2–15.

2366. Engen, Orrin A. *Writer of the Plains.* Culver City, Calif.: Pontine Press, 1973.

2367. Meyer, Roy W. "B. M. Bower: The Poor Man's Wister." *Journal of Popular Culture* 7 (Winter 1973): 667–79.

VIRGIL D. BOYLES

2368. Alexander, Ruth Ann. "Fictionalizing South Dakota from a Feminist Point of View: The Western Novels of Virgil D. Boyles and Kate Boyles Bingham." *South Dakota History* 23 (Fall 1993): 244–63.

RICHARD BRADFORD

2369. Etulain, Richard W. "Richard Bradford's *Red Sky at Morning*: New Novel of the Southwest." *Western Review* 8 (Spring 1971): 57–62.

MAX BRAND

See Frederick Faust

2370. Gale, Robert L. *Matt Braun*. Western Writers Series, No. 92. Boise, Idaho: Boise State University, 1990.

RICHARD BRAUTIGAN

2371. Abbott, Keith. *Downstream from Trout Fishing in America: A Memoir of Richard Brautigan*. Santa Barbara, Calif.: Capra Press, 1989.

2372. Bales, Kent. "Fishing the Ambivalence, or, A Reading of *Trout Fishing in America*." *Western Humanities Review* 29 (Winter 1975): 29–42.

2373. Blakely, Carolyn F. "Narrative Technique in Brautigan's *In Watermelon Sugar*." *CLA Journal* 35 (December 1991): 150–58.

2374. Boyer, Jay. *Richard Brautigan*. Western Writers Series, No. 79. Boise, Idaho: Boise State University, 1987.

2375. Chenetier, Marc. *Richard Brautigan*. London and New York: Methuen, 1983.

2376. Crouch, Jeff. "Discontinuity in Richard Brautigan's *The Tokyo–Montana Express*." *Midwest Quarterly* 33 (Summer 1992): 393–402.

2377. Foster, Edward Halsey. *Richard Brautigan*. Boston: Twayne, 1983.

2378. Hackenberry, Charles. "Romance and Parody in Brautigan's *The Abortion*." *Critique* 23 (Winter 1981/82): 24–36.

2379. Hearron, Thomas. "Escape Through Imagination in *Trout Fishing in America*." *Critique* 16 (1974): 25–31.

2380. Hernlund, Patricia. "Author's Intent: *In Watermelon Sugar*." *Critique* 16 (No. 1, 1974): 5–17.

2381. Horvath, Brooke. "Richard Brautigan's Search for Control over Death." *American Literature* 57 (October 1985): 434–55.

2382. Iftekharuddin, Farhat Mohammed. "Richard Brautigan: A Critical Look at *Trout Fishing in America, In Watermelon Sugar*, and *The Abortion*." Doctoral dissertation, Oklahoma State University, 1989.

2383. Jones, Stephen R. "Richard Brautigan: A Bibliography." *Bulletin of Bibliography* 33 (January 1976): 53–59.

2384. Kern, Robert. "Williams, Brautigan, and the Poetics of Primitivism." *Chicago Review* 27 (Summer 1975): 47–57.

2385. Leavitt, Harvey. "The Regained Paradise of Brautigan's *In Watermelon Sugar*." *Critique* 16 (No. 1, 1974): 18–24.

2386. Malley, Terence. *Richard Brautigan*. New York: Warner Books, 1972.

2387. Manso, Peter, and Michael McClure. "Brautigan's Wake." *Vanity Fair* 48 (May 1985): 62–68, 112–16.

2388. Schmitz, Neil. "Richard Brautigan and the Modern Pastoral." *Modern Fiction Studies* 19 (Spring 1973): 109–25.

2389. Stull, William L. "Richard Brautigan's *Trout Fishing in America*: Notes of a Native Son." *American Literature* 56 (March 1984): 68–80.

2390. Vanderwerken, David L. "*Trout Fishing in America* and the American Tradition." *Critique* 16 (No. 1, 1974): 32–40.

2391. Willis, Lonnie L. "Brautigan's *The Hawkline Monster*: As Big as the Ritz." *Critique* 23 (Winter 1981/82): 37–47.

2392. Wright, Lawrence. "The Life and Death of Richard Brautigan." *Rolling Stone* (April 11, 1985): 29–31 ff.

BILL BRETT

2393. Graham, Don. "Mark Twain and the Vernacular Tradition in Texas: The Example of Bill Brett." *Southwestern American Literature* 15 (Fall 1989): 6–13.

DOROTHY E. BRETT

2394. Brett, Dorothy E. "Autobiography: My Long and Beautiful Journey." *South Dakota Review* 5 (Summer 1967): 11–71.

2395. Hignett, Sean. *Brett, From Bloomsbury to New Mexico: A Biography.* New York: Franklin Watts, 1985.

2396. Manchester, John. "Thoughts on Brett: 1967." *South Dakota Review* 5 (Summer 1967): 3–9.

2397. Morrill, Claire. "Three Women of Taos: Frieda Lawrence, Mabel Luhan, and Dorothy Brett." *South Dakota Review* 2 (Spring 1965): 3–22.

2398. Zytaruk, George J., ed. "Dorothy Brett's Letters to S. S. Kateliansky." *D. H. Lawrence Review* 7 (1974): 240–74.

CAROL RYRIE BRINK

2399. Reed, Mary E. *Carol Ryrie Brink.* Western Writers Series, No. 100. Boise, Idaho: Boise State University, 1991.

FRANK BRINK

2400. Petersen, Lance. "Alaskan Men of Letters: Frank Brink." *Alaska Review* 1 (Spring 1964): 36–39.

JUANITA BROOKS

2401. Peterson, Levi S. *Juanita Brooks: Mormon Woman Historian.* Salt Lake City: University of Utah Press, 1988.

DEE BROWN

2402. Brown, Dee Alexander. *When the Century Was Young: A Writer's Notebook.* Little Rock, Ark.: August House, 1993.

2403. Hagen, Lyman B. *Dee Brown.* Western Writers Series, No. 95. Boise, Idaho: Boise State University, 1990.

CHARLES FARRAR BROWNE

(Artemus Ward)

2404. Austin, James C. *Artemus Ward.* New York: Twayne, 1964.

2405. ———. "Charles Farrar Browne (1834–1867)." *American Literary Realism 1870–1910* 5 (Spring 1972): 151–65.

2406. Blair, Walter. *Native American Humor.* New York: American Book, 1937.

2407. Fatout, Paul. "Artemus Ward Among the Mormons." *Western Humanities Review* 14 (Spring 1960): 193–99.

2408. Hingston, Edward P. *The Genial Showman.* New York: Harper, 1870.

2409. Jaynes, Bryson L. "Artemus Ward Among the Mormons." *Research Studies of the State College of Washington* 25 (March 1957): 75–84.

2410. Lorch, Fred W. "Mark Twain's 'Artemus Ward' Lecture on the Tour of 1871–1872." *New England Quarterly* 25 (September 1952): 327–43.

2411. McKee, Irving. "Artemus Ward in California and Nevada, 1863–1864." *Pacific Historical Review* 20 (February 1951): 11–23.

2412. Pullen, John J. *Comic Relief: The Life and Laughter of Artemus Ward, 1834–1867.* Hamden, Conn.: Archon Books, 1983.

2413. Reed, John Q. "Artemus Ward: A Critical Study." Doctoral dissertation, State University of Iowa, 1955.

2414. Seitz, Don C. *Artemus Ward (Charles Farrar Browne): A Biography and Bibliography.* New York: Harper and Brothers, 1919.

2415. Williams, Stanley T. "Artemus the Delicious." *Virginia Quarterly Review* 28 (Spring 1952): 214–27.

J. ROSS BROWNE

2416. Browne, Lina Fergusson, ed. *J. Ross Browne: His Letters, Journals and Writings*. Albuquerque: University of New Mexico Press, 1969.

2417. Dillon, Richard H. *J. Ross Browne, Confidential Agent in Old California*. Norman: University of Oklahoma Press, 1965.

2418. Powell, Lawrence Clark. "J. Ross Browne's *Adventures in the Apache Country*." *Westways* 63 (October 1971): 18–21, 40–43.

2419. Rock, Francis John. *J. Ross Browne: A Biography*. Washington, D. C.: Catholic University of America, 1929.

2420. Walker, Franklin. *Irreverent Pilgrims: Melville, Browne, and Mark Twain in the Holy Land*. Seattle: University of Washington Press, 1974.

CARLOS BULOSAN

2421. San Juan, E[pifanio]. *Carlos Bulosan and the Imagination of Class Struggle*. Quezon City: University of the Philippines Press, 1972.

GELETT BURGESS

2422. Backus, Joseph M. "Gelett Burgess: A Biography of the Man Who Wrote 'The Purple Cow.'" Doctoral dissertation, University of California, Berkeley, 1961.

FRANCES HODGSON BURNETT

2423. Maher, Susan Naramore. "A Bridging of Two Cultures: Frances Hodgson Burnett and the Wild West." *Old West–New West: Centennial Essays*. Ed. Barbara Howard Meldrum. Moscow: University of Idaho Press, 1993, 146–53.

EDGAR RICE BURROUGHS

2424. Topping, Gary. "The Pastoral Ideal in Popular American Literature: Zane Grey and Edgar Rice Burroughs." *Rendezvous* 12 (Fall 1977): 11–25.

WILLIAM S. BURROUGHS

2425. Brown, William J. "'Lonesome Cowboy Bill': The Western in the Later Fiction of William S. Burroughs." Doctoral dissertation, State University of New York, Buffalo, 1990.

2426. Morgan, Ted. *Literary Outlaw: The Life and Times of William S. Burroughs.* New York: Holt, 1988.

2427. Skerl, Jennie. *William S. Burroughs.* Boston: Twayne, 1985.

STRUTHERS BURT

2428. Phillips, Raymond C., Jr. *Struthers Burt.* Western Writers Series, No. 56. Boise, Idaho: Boise State University, 1983.

WITTER BYNNER

2429. Colony, Horatio. "Witter Bynner—Poet of Today." *Literary Review* 3 (Spring 1960): 339–61.

2430. Flanner, Hildegarde. "Witter Bynner's Poetry." *University of Kansas City Review* 6 (June 1940): 269–74.

2431. Lindsay, Robert O. *Witter Bynner: A Bibliography.* Albuquerque: University of New Mexico, 1967.

ALVAR NUÑEZ CABEZA DE VACA

2432. Pilkington, William T. "The Journey of Cabeza de Vaca: An American Prototype." *South Dakato Review* 6 (Spring 1968): 73–82.

2433. Wild, Peter. *Alvar Nuñez Cabeza de Vaca.* Western Writers Series, No. 101. Boise, Idaho: Boise State University, 1991.

JAMES M. CAIN

2434. Fine, David. "Beginning in the Thirties: The Los Angeles Fiction of James M. Cain and Horace McCoy." *Los Angeles in Fiction: A Collection of Original Essays.* Ed. David Fine. Albuquerque: University of New Mexico Press, 1984, 43–66.

2435. ———. "James M. Cain and the Los Angeles Novel." *American Studies* 20 (Spring 1979): 25–34.

2436. Hoopes, Roy. *Cain.* New York: Holt, Rinehart, and Winston, 1982.

2437. Madden, David. *Cain's Craft.* Metuchen, N.J.: Scarecrow Press, 1985.

2438. ———. *James M. Cain.* New York: Twayne, 1970.

2439. Reck, Tom S. "J. M. Cain's Los Angeles Novels." *Colorado Quarterly* 22 (Winter 1974): 375–87.

2440. Skenazy, Paul. *James M. Cain.* New York: Continuum, 1989.

ROBERT CANTWELL

2441. Bowman, John Scott. "The Proletarian Novel in America." Doctoral dissertation, Pennsylvania State College, 1939.

2442. Conroy, Jack. "Robert Cantwell's 'Land of Plenty.'" *Proletarian Writers of the Thirties.* Ed. David Madden. Carbondale: Southern Illinois Press, 1968, 74–84.

2443. Lewis, Merrill. *Robert Cantwell.* Western Writers Series, No. 70. Boise, Idaho: Boise State University, 1985.

2444. Rideout, Walter B. *The Radical Novel in the United States.* Cambridge, Mass.: Harvard University Press, 1956, 174–78 ff.

BENJAMIN CAPPS

2445. Clayton, Lawrence. *Benjamin Capps and the South Plains: A Literary Relationship.* Denton: University of North Texas Press, 1990.

2446. Etulain, Richard W. *"The White Man's Road*: An Appreciation." *Southwestern American Literature* 1 (May 1971): 88–92.

2447. Graham, Don. "'Mesquite Country': Benjamin Capps's Unpublished First Novel." *Cross Timbers Review* 1 (May 1984): 32–40.

2448. ———. "Old and New Cowboy Classics." *Southwest Review* 65 (Summer 1980): 293–303.

2449. Sonnichsen, C. L. "The New Style Western." *South Dakota Review* 4 (Summer 1966): 22–28.

2450. Speck, Ernest B. *Benjamin Capps.* Western Writers Series, No. 49. Boise, Idaho: Boise State University, 1981.

SARAH ELIZABETH CARMICHAEL

2451. Murphy, Miriam B. "Sarah Elizabeth Carmichael: Poetic Genius of Pioneer Utah." *Utah Historical Quarterly* 43 (Winter 1975): 52–66.

ASA CARTER

(Forrest Carter)

2452. Clayton, Lawrence. "Forrest Carter/Asa Carter and Politics." *Western American Literature* 21 (May 1986): 19–26.

2453. ———. "The Theology of Survival: The Identity of Forrest/Asa Carter and Religion in His Fiction." *Southwestern American Literature* 19 (Spring 1994): 9–19.

2454. Alton, John. "What We Talk About When We Talk About Literature: An Interview with Raymond Carver." *Chicago Review* 36 (Autumn 1988): 4–21.

2455. Brown, Arthur A. "Raymond Carver and Postmodern Humanism." *Critique* 31 (Winter 1990): 125–36.

2456. Campbell, Ewing. *Raymond Carver: A Study of the Short Fiction.* New York: Twayne, 1992.

2457. Carver, Maryann. "Glimpses: Raymond Carver." *Paris Review* 118 (Spring 1991): 260–303.

2458. Gentry, Bruce, and William L. Stull, eds. *Conversations with Raymond Carver.* Jackson: University Press of Mississippi, 1990.

2459. Halpert, Sam, ed. *When We Talk About Raymond Carver.* Layton, Utah: Gibbs Smith, 1991.

2460. Meyer, Adam. "Now You See Him, Now You Don't, Now You Do Again: The Evolution of Raymond Carver's Minimalism." *Critique* 30 (Summer 1989): 239–51.

2461. Nesset, Kirk. "'This Word Love': Sexual Politics and Silence in Early Raymond Carver." *American Literature* 63 (June 1991): 292–313.

2462. Runyon, Randolph Paul. *Reading Raymond Carver.* Syracuse, N.Y.: Syracuse University Press, 1992.

2463. Saltzman, Arthur M. *Understanding Raymond Carver.* Columbia: University of South Carolina Press, 1988.

2464. Shute, Kathleen Westfall. "Finding the Words: The Struggle for Salvation in the Fiction of Raymond Carver." *Hollins Critic* 24 (December 1987): 1–9.

2465. Stull, William L. "Beyond Hopelessville: Another Side of Raymond Carver." *Philological Quarterly* 64 (Winter 1985): 1–15.

2466. ———, and Maureen P. Carroll, eds. *Remembering Ray: A Composite Biography of Raymond Carver.* Santa Barbara, Calif.: Capra, 1993.

2467. Weele, Michael Vander. "Raymond Carver and the Language of Desire." *Denver Quarterly* 22 (Summer 1987): 108–22.

ROBERT ORMOND CASE

2468. Newton, Dwight B. "Meet Robert Ormond Case." *Roundup* 4 (March 1956): 3–4.

BILL CASEY

2469. Turner, Steve. "Bill Casey: Jottings Before a Journey." *Southwestern American Literature* 1 (May 1971): 80–86.

NEAL CASSADY

2470. Cassady, Carolyn. *Heart Beat: My Life with Jack Neal.* Berkeley, Calif.: Creative Arts, 1976.

2471. ———. *Off the Road: My Years with Cassady, Kerouac, and Ginsberg.* New York: William Morrow, 1990.

2472. Gifford, Barry, ed. *The Collected Correspondence of Allen Ginsberg and Neal Cassady.* Berkeley, Calif.: Bookpeople, 1977.

2473. Huebel, Harry Russell. "The 'Holy Goof': Neal Cassady and the Post-War American Counter Culture." *Illinois Quarterly* 35 (April 1973): 52–61.

CARLOS CASTAÑEDA

2474. Brown, Carl R. V. "*Journey to Ixtlan*: Inside the American Indian Oral Tradition." *Arizona Quarterly* 32 (Summer 1976): 138–45.

2475. Clements, William M. "Carlos Castañeda's *The Teachings of Don Juan*: A Novel of Initiation." *Critique* 26 (Spring 1985): 122–30.

2476. Olson, Alan M. "From Shaman to Mystic: An Interpretation of the Castañeda Quartet." *Soundings* 61 (Spring 1978): 47–66.

WILLA CATHER

2477. Ambrose, Jamie. *Willa Cather: Writing at the Frontier.* New York: St. Martin's Press, 1989.

2478. Ammons, Elizabeth. "The Engineer as Cultural Hero and Willa Cather's First Novel, *Alexander's Bridge*." *American Quarterly* 38 (Winter 1986): 746–60.

2479. Apthorp, Elaine Sargent. "Speaking of Silence: Willa Cather and the 'Problem' of Feminist Biography." *Women's Studies* 18 (May 1990): 1–11.

2480. Arnold, Marilyn. "*One of Ours*: Willa Cather's Losing Battle." *Western American Literature* 13 (Fall 1978): 259–66.

2481. ———. *Willa Cather: A Reference Guide.* Boston: G. K. Hall, 1986.

2482. ———. *Willa Cather's Short Fiction.* Athens: Ohio University Press, 1984.

2483. Auchincloss, Louis. *Pioneers and Caretakers: A Study of Nine Ameri-*

can Women Novelists. Minneapolis: University of Minnesota Press, 1965.

2484. Bailey, Jennifer. "The Dangers of Femininity in Willa Cather's Fiction." *Journal of American Studies* 16 (December 1982): 391–406.

2485. Baker, Bruce P., II. "Nebraska Regionalism in Selected Works of Willa Cather." *Western American Literature* 3 (Spring 1968): 19–35.

2486. ———. "*O Pioneers!* The Problem of Structure." *Great Plains Quarterly* 2 (Fall 1982): 218–23.

2487. Bennett, Mildred R. "The Childhood Worlds of Willa Cather." *Great Plains Quarterly* 2 (Fall 1982): 204–9.

2488. ———. *The World of Willa Cather.* New York: Dodd, Mead, 1951; Lincoln: University of Nebraska Press, 1961.

2489. Bloom, Edward A., and Lillian D. Bloom. *Willa Cather's Gift of Sympathy.* Carbondale: Southern Illinois University Press, 1962.

2490. Bloom, Lillian D. "On Daring to Look Back with Wharton and Cather." *Novel: A Forum on Fiction* 10 (Winter 1977): 167–78.

2491. Bohling, Beth. "The Husband of *My Ántonia.*" *Western American Literature* 19 (May 1984): 29–39.

2492. Bohlke, L. Brent. "Beginnings: Willa Cather and 'The Clemency of the Court.'" *Prairie Schooner* 48 (Summer 1974): 134–44.

2493. ———. "Godfrey St. Peter and Eugène Delacroix: A Portrait of the Artist in *The Professor's House.*" *Western American Literature* 17 (Spring 1982): 21–38.

2494. ———. "'Seeking is Finding': Willa Cather and Religion." Doctoral dissertation, University of Nebraska, Lincoln, 1982.

2495. ———. "Willa Cather's Nebraska Priests and *Death Comes for the Archbishop.*" *Great Plains Quarterly* 4 (Fall 1984): 264–69.

2496. ———, ed. *Willa Cather in Person: Interviews, Speeches, and Letters.* Lincoln: University of Nebraska Press, 1986.

2497. Borgman, Paul. "The Dialectic of Willa Cather's Moral Vision." *Renascence* 27 (Spring 1975): 145–59.

2498. Bradford, Curtis. "Willa Cather's Uncollected Short Stories." *American Literature* 26 (January 1955): 537–51.

2499. Brennan, Joseph X. "Music and Willa Cather." *University Review* 31 (March 1965): 175–83; (June 1965): 257–64.

2500. Brienzo, Gary William. "Developments in Cather Scholarship." *Platte Valley Review* 19 (Spring 1991): 79–89.

2501. Brown, E. K. *Willa Cather: A Critical Biography.* New York: Alfred A. Knopf, 1953. Completed by Leon Edel.

2502. Brown, Marion Marsh, and Ruth Crone. *Willa Cather: The Woman and Her Works*. New York: Charles Scribner's Sons, 1970.

2503. Brown, Muriel. "Growth and Development of the Artist: Willa Cather's *My Ántonia*." *Midwest Quarterly* 33 (Autumn 1991): 93–107.

2504. Byrne, Kathleen D., and Richard C. Snyder. *Chrysalis: Willa Cather in Pittsburgh*. Pittsburgh: Historical Society of Western Pennsylvania, 1980.

2505. Callander, Marilyn Berg. *Willa Cather and the Fairy Tale*. Ann Arbor, Mich.: UMI Research Press, 1989.

2506. Carlin, Deborah. *Cather, Canon, and the Politics of Reading*. Amherst: University of Massachusetts Press, 1992.

2507. Carpenter, David A. "Why Willa Cather Revised 'Paul's Case': The Work in Art and Those Sunday Afternoons." *American Literature* 59 (December 1987): 590–608.

2508. Cather, Willa. *My Ántonia*. Eds. Susan J. Rosowski, Charles Mignon, and Kari Ronning. Lincoln: University of Nebraska Press, 1994.

2509. ———. *O Pioneers!* Eds. Susan J. Rosowski, Charles W. Mignon, and Kathleen Danker. Lincoln: University of Nebraska Press, 1992.

2510. Charles, Peter Damian. "*Death Comes for the Archbishop*: A Novel of Love and Death." *New Mexico Quarterly* 36 (Winter 1966–67): 389–403.

2511. ———. "*My Ántonia*: A Dark Dimension." *Western American Literature* 2 (Summer 1967): 91–108.

2512. Cherny, Robert W. "Willa Cather and the Populists." *Great Plains Quarterly* 3 (Fall 1983): 206–18.

2513. Chown, Linda. "'It Came Closer than That': Willa Cather's *Lucy Gayheart*." *Cather Studies, Volume 2*. Ed. Susan J. Rosowski. Lincoln: University of Nebraska Press, 1993, 118–39.

2514. Comeau, Paul. "The Fool Figure in Willa Cather's Fiction." *Western American Literature* 15 (February 1981): 265–78.

2515. ———. "Willa Cather's *Lucy Gayheart*: A Long Perspective." *Prairie Schooner* 55 (Spring/Summer 1981): 199–209.

2516. Crane, Joan. *Willa Cather: A Bibliography*. Lincoln: University of Nebraska Press, 1982.

2517. Curtin, William M. "Willa Cather and *The Varieties of Religious Experience*." *Renascence* 27 (Spring 1975): 115–23.

2518. ———, ed. *The World and the Parish: Willa Cather's Articles and Reviews, 1893–1902*. 2 vols. Lincoln: University of Nebraska Press, 1970.

2519. Daiches, David. *Willa Cather: A Critical Introduction.* Ithaca, N.Y.: Cornell University Press, 1951; New York: Collier Books, 1962.

2520. Dillman, Richard. "Tom Outland: Emerson's American Scholar in *The Professor's House.*" *Midwest Quarterly* 25 (Summer 1984): 375–85.

2521. Dinn, James M. "A Novelist's Miracle: Structure and Myth in *Death Comes for the Archbishop.*" *Western American LIterature* 7 (Spring 1972): 39–46.

2522. Ditsky, John. "'Listening with Supersensual Ear': Music in the Novels of Willa Cather." *Journal of Narrative Technique* 13 (Fall 1983): 154–63.

2523. ———. "Nature and Character in the Novels of Willa Cather." *Colby Literary Quarterly* 10 (September 1974): 391–412.

2524. Doane, Margaret. "In Defense of Lillian St. Peter: Men's Perceptions of Women in *The Professor's House.*" *Western American Literature* 18 (Winter 1984): 299–302.

2525. Donovan, Josephine. *After the Fall: The Demeter-Persephone Myth in Wharton, Cather, and Glasgow.* University Park: Pennsylvania State University Press, 1989.

2526. Dyck, Reginald. "The Feminist Critique of Willa Cather's Fiction: A Review Essay." *Women's Studies* 22 (No. 3, 1993): 263–79.

2527. ———. "Revisiting and Revising the West: Willa Cather's *My Ántonia* and Wright Morris' *Plains Song.*" *Modern Fiction Studies* 36 (Spring 1990): 25–38.

2528. Fetterley, Judith. "*My Ántonia*, Jim Burden and the Dilemma of the Lesbian Writer." *Gender Studies: New Directions in Feminist Criticism.* Ed. Judith Spector. Bowling Green, Ohio: Bowling Green State University Popular Press, 1986.

2529. Fischer, Mike. "Pastoralism and Its Discontents: Willa Cather and the Burden of Imperialism." *Mosaic* 23 (Winter 1990): 31–44.

2530. Fischer-Wirth, Ann W. "Dispossession and Redemption in the Novels of Willa Cather." *Cather Studies, Volume 1.* Ed. Susan J. Rosowski. Lincoln: University of Nebraska Press, 1990, 36–54.

2531. ———. "Out of the Mother: Loss in *My Ántonia.*" *Cather Studies, Volume 2.* Ed. Susan J. Rosowski. Lincoln: University of Nebraska Press, 1993, 41–71.

2532. Forman, H. J. "Willa Cather: A Voice from the Prairie." *Southwest Review* 47 (Summer 1962): 248–58.

2533. Fox, Maynard. "Proponents of Order: Tom Outland and Bishop Latour." *Western American Literature* 4 (Summer 1969): 107–15.

2534. ———. "Symbolic Representation in Willa Cather's *O Pioneers!*" *Western American Literature* 9 (November 1974): 187–96.

2535. Fryer, Judith. "Desert Rock, Shelter, Legend: Willa Cather's Novels of the Southwest." *The Desert Is No Lady: Southwestern Landscapes in Women's Writing and Art.* Eds. Vera Norwood and Janice Monk. New Haven, Conn.: Yale University Press, 1987, 27–46.

2536. ———. *Felicitous Space: The Imaginative Structures of Edith Wharton and Willa Cather.* Chapel Hill: University of North Carolina Press, 1986.

2537. Gale, Robert. "Willa Cather and the Usable Past." *Nebraska History* 42 (September 1961): 181–90.

2538. Geismar, Maxwell. "Willa Cather: Lady in the Wilderness." *The Last of the Provincials: The American Novel, 1915–1925.* Boston: Houghton Mifflin, 1947, 153–220.

2539. Gelfant, Blanche H. "The Forgotten Reaping-Hook: Sex in *My Ántonia.*" *American Literature* 43 (March 1971): 60–82.

2540. ———. "Movement and Melody: The Disembodiment of Lucy Gayheart." *Women Writing in America: Voices in Collage.* Hanover, N.H.: University Press of New England, 1984, 117–43.

2541. ———. "'What was it...?': The Secret of Family Accord in *One of Ours.*" *Modern Fiction Studies* 36 (Spring 1990): 61–78.

2542. Gerber, Philip. *Willa Cather.* Boston: Twayne, 1975.

2543. Giannone, Richard. *Music in Willa Cather's Fiction.* Lincoln: University of Nebraska Press, 1968.

2544. ———. "Willa Cather and the Unfinished Drama of Deliverance." *Prairie Schooner* 52 (Spring 1978): 25–46.

2545. Gleason, John B. "The 'Case' of Willa Cather." *Western American Literature* 20 (Winter 1986): 275–99.

2546. Grumbach, Doris. "A Study of the Small Room in *The Professor's House.*" *Women's Studies* 11 (1984): 327–45.

2547. Harrell, David. *From Mesa Verde to The Professor's House.* Albuquerque: University of New Mexico Press, 1992.

2548. Harris, Jeane. "A Code of Her Own: Attitudes Toward Women in Willa Cather's Short Fiction." *Modern Fiction Studies* 36 (Spring 1990): 81–89.

2549. Helmick, Evelyn Thomas. "The Broken World: Medievalism in *A Lost Lady.*" *Renascence* 28 (Autumn 1975): 39–48.

2550. ———. "The Mysteries of Ántonia." *Midwest Quarterly* 17 (Winter 1976): 173–85.

2551. ———. "Myth in the Works of Willa Cather." *Midcontinent American Studies Journal* 9 (Fall 1968): 63–69.

2552. Hicks, Granville. "The Case Against Willa Cather." *English Journal* 22 (November 1933): 703–10.

2553. Hinz, Evelyn J. "Willa Cather's Technique and the Ideology of Populism." *Western American Literature* 7 (Spring 1972): 47–61.

2554. Hutchinson, Phyllis Martin. "The Writings of Willa Cather: A List of Works by and about Her." *Bulletin of the New York Library* 60 (June 1956): 267–87; (July 1956): 338–56; (August 1956): 378–400.

2555. Irving, Katrina. "Displacing Homosexuality: The Use of Ethnicity in Willa Cather's *My Ántonia*." *Modern Fiction Studies* 36 (Spring 1990): 91–102.

2556. Kaye, Frances W. *Isolation and Masquerade: Willa Cather's Women.* New York: Peter Lang, 1993.

2557. Laird, David. "Willa Cather's Women: Gender, Place, and Narrativity in *O Pioneers!* and *My Ántonia*." *Great Plains Quarterly* 12 (Fall 1992): 242–53.

2558. Lambert, Deborah G. "The Defeat of Hero: Autonomy and Sexuality in *My Ántonia*." *American Literature* 53 (January 1982): 676–90.

2559. Lathrop, Jo Anna, comp. *Willa Cather: A Checklist of Her Published Writing.* Lincoln: University of Nebraska, 1975.

2560. Leddy, Michael. "Observation and Narration in Willa Cather's *Obscure Destinies*." *Studies in American Fiction* 16 (Autumn 1988): 141–53.

2561. ———. "*The Professor's House* and the Professor's Houses." *Modern Fiction Studies* 38 (Summer 1992): 444–54.

2562. Lee, Hermione. *Willa Cather: Double Lives.* New York: Pantheon Books, 1989.

2563. ———. *Willa Cather: A Life Saved Up.* London: Virago, 1989.

2564. Lee, Robert Edson. *From East to West.* Urbana: University of Illinois Press, 1965, 112–35.

2565. Lewis, Edith. *Willa Cather Living: A Personal Record.* New York: Alfred A. Knopf, 1953.

2566. Love, Glen A. "The Cowboy in the Laboratory: Willa Cather's Hesitant Moderns." *New Americans: The Westerner and the Modern Experience in the American Novel.* Lewisburg, Pa.: Bucknell University, 1982, 107–69.

2567. ———. "*The Professor's House*: Cather, Hemingway, and the Chastening of American Prose Style." *Western American Literature* 24 (February 1990): 295–311.

2568. McCabe, John D., ed. "Special Issue: Willa Cather." *Renascence* 27 (1975).

2569. McClure, Charlotte S. "Willa Cather." *American Literary Realism 1870–1910* 8 (Summer 1975): 209–20. Review of dissertations on Cather.

2570. McFarland, Dorothy Tuck. *Willa Cather.* New York: Frederick Ungar, 1972.

2571. McLay, Catherine M. "Religion in the Novels of Willa Cather." *Renascence* 27 (Spring 1975): 125–44.

2572. March, John. *A Reader's Companion to the Fiction of Willa Cather.* Eds. Marilyn Arnold and Debra Lynn Thornton. Westport, Conn.: Greenwood Press, 1993.

2573. Martin, Terence. "The Drama of Memory in *My Ántonia*." *PMLA* 84 (March 1969): 304–11.

2574. Mayberry, Susan Neal. "A New Heroine's Marriage: Willa Cather's *O Pioneers!*" *Old Northwest* 16 (Spring 1992): 37–59.

2575. Medoff, Jeslyn. "An Anglo-American Author Creates Anglo-American Villains." *Heritage of Kansas* 12 (Spring 1979): 31–39.

2576. Meyering, Sheryl L. *A Reader's Guide to the Short Stories of Willa Cather.* New York: G.K. Hall, 1994.

2577. Middleton, Jo Ann. *Willa Cather's Modernism: A Study of Style and Technique.* Rutherford, N.J.: Fairleigh Dickinson University Press, 1990.

2578. Miller, Bruce E. "The Testing of Willa Cather's Humanism: *A Lost Lady* and Other Cather Novels." *Kansas Quarterly* 5 (Fall 1973): 43–49.

2579. Miller, James E., Jr. "*My Ántonia*: A Frontier Drama of Time." *American Quarterly* 10 (Winter 1958): 476–84.

2580. ———. "*My Ántonia* and the American Dream." *Prairie Schooner* 48 (Summer 1974): 112–23.

2581. ———. "The Nebraska Encounter: Willa Cather and Wright Morris." *Prairie Schooner* 41 (Summer 1967): 165–67.

2582. ———. "Willa Cather Today." *Great Plains Quarterly* 4 (Fall 1984): 270–77.

2583. Moorhead, Elizabeth. *These Two Were Here: Louise Homer and Willa Cather.* Pittsburgh: University of Pittsburgh Press, 1950.

2584. Mosely, Ann. "The Dual Nature of Art in *The Song of the Lark*." *Western American Literature* 14 (Spring 1979): 19–32.

2585. ———. "The Pueblo Emergence Myth in Cather's *Death Comes for the Archbishop*." *Southwestern American Literature* 8 (Fall 1982): 27–35.

2586. ———. "The Voyage Perilous: Willa Cather's Mythic Quest." Doctoral dissertation, University of Oklahoma, 1974.

2587. Murphy, John J. "The Art of *Shadows on the Rock*." *Prairie Schooner* 50 (Spring 1976): 37–51.

2588. ———. "A Comprehensive View of Cather's *O Pioneers!*" *Critical Essays on Willa Cather*. Ed. John J. Murphy. Boston: G. K. Hall, 1984, 113–27.

2589. ———. "Cooper, Cather, and The Downward Path to Progress." *Prairie Schooner* 55 (Spring/Summer 1981): 168–84.

2590. ———. "Euripides' *Hippolytus* and Cather's *A Lost Lady*." *American Literature* 53 (March 1981): 72–86.

2591. ———. *My Ántonia: The Road Home*. Boston: Twayne, 1989.

2592. ———. "*One of Ours* as American Naturalism." *Great Plains Quarterly* 2 (Fall 1982): 232–38.

2593. ———. "Willa Cather and Catholic Themes." *Western American Literature* 17 (Spring 1982): 53–60.

2594. ———. "Willa Cather and Religion: Highway to the World and Beyond." *Literature and Belief* 4 (1984): 49–68.

2595. ———. "Willa Cather's Archbishop: A Western and Classical Perspective." *Western American Literature* 13 (Summer 1978): 141–50.

2596. ———, ed. *Critical Essays on Willa Cather*. Boston: G.K. Hall, 1984.

2597. ———, ed. *Five Essays on Willa Cather: The Merrimack Symposium*. North Andover, Mass.: Merrimack College, 1974.

2598. ———, ed. *Willa Cather: Family, Community, and History* (The BYU Symposium). Provo, Utah: Brigham Young University, 1990.

2599. Novak, Frank G., Jr. "Crisis and Discovery in *The Professor's House*." *Colby Library Quarterly* 22 (June 1986): 119–32.

2600. O'Brien, Sharon. "Becoming Noncanonical: The Case Against Willa Cather." *American Quarterly* 40 (March 1988): 110–26.

2601. ———. "'The Thing Not Named': Willa Cather as a Lesbian Writer." *Signs* 9 (Summer 1984): 576–99.

2602. ———. *Willa Cather: The Emerging Voice*. New York: Oxford University Press, 1987.

2603. O'Connor, Margaret Anne. "A Guide to the Letters of Willa Cather." *Resources for American Literary Studies* 4 (1974): 145–72.

2604. Oehlschlaeger, Fritz. "*Indisponibilité* and the Anxiety of Authorship in *The Professor's House.*" *American Literature* 62 (March 1990): 74–86.

2605. Ostwalt, Conrad E., Jr. *After Eden: The Secularization of American Space in the Fiction of Willa Cather and Theodore Dreiser.* Lewisburg, Pa.: Bucknell University Press, 1990.

2606. Peck, Demaree Catherine. "'Possession Granted by a Different Lease': Alexandra Bergson's Imaginative Conquest of Cather's Nebraska." *Modern Fiction Studies* 36 (Spring 1990): 5–22.

2607. Pers, Mona. *Willa Cather's Children.* Uppsala, Sweden: Almquist and Wiksell, 1975.

2608. Quirk, Tom. *Bergson and American Culture: The Worlds of Willa Cather and Wallace Stevens.* Chapel Hill: University of North Carolina Press, 1990.

2609. Randall, John H., III. *The Landscape and the Looking Glass: Willa Cather's Search for Value.* Boston: Houghton Mifflin, 1960.

2610. ———. "Willa Cather: The Middle West Revisited." *New Mexico Quarterly* 31 (Spring 1961): 25–36.

2611. Reynard, Grant. "Willa Cather's Advice to a Young Artist." *Prairie Schooner* 46 (Spring 1972): 111–24.

2612. Robertson, R.M. " Disinterring the 'Scandal' of Willa Cather: *Youth and the Bright Medusa.*" *Criticism* 32 (Fall 1990): 485–509.

2613. Robinson, Phyllis C. *Willa, The Life of Willa Cather.* Garden City, N. Y.: Doubleday, 1983.

2614. Rohrbach, Charlotte. "Willa Cather, An Historian of Western Webster County, Nebraska: An Inquiry." Doctoral dissertation, Saint Louis University, 1976.

2615. Romines, Ann. "After the Christmas Tree: Willa Cather and Domestic Ritual." *American Literature* 60 (March 1988): 61–82.

2616. ———. "Willa Cather and Women's Culture: 'Now I Know.'" *The Home Plot: Women Writing Domestic Ritual.* Amherst: University of Massachusetts Press, 1992, 151–91.

2617. ———. "Willa Cather: Repudiating Home Plots." *The Home Plot: Women Writing Domestic Ritual.* Amherst: University of Massachusetts Press, 1992, 128–50.

2618. Rosowski, Susan J. "The Pattern of Willa Cather's Novels." *Western American Literature* 15 (February 1981): 243–63.

2619. ———. "Recent Books on Willa Cather: An Essay Review." *Modern Fiction Studies* 36 (Spring 1990): 131–41.

2620. ———. *The Voyage Perilous: Willa Cather's Romanticism.* Lincoln: University of Nebraska Press, 1986.

2621. ———. "Willa Cather and the Fatality of Place; *O Pioneers!, My Ántonia,* and *A Lost Lady.*" *Geography and Literature: A Meeting of the Disciplines.* Eds. William E. Mallory and Paul Simpson-Housley. Syracuse: Syracuse University Press, 1987, 81–94.

2622. ———. "Willa Cather – A Pioneer in Art: *O Pioneers!* and *My Ántonia.*" *Prairie Schooner* 55 (Spring/Summer 1981): 141–54.

2623. ———. "Willa Cather: A Review Essay." *Modern Fiction Studies* 36 (Spring 1990): 131–41.

2624. ———. "Willa Cather's *A Lost Lady*: Art Versus the Closing Frontier." *Great Plains Quarterly* 2 (Fall 1982): 239–48.

2625. ———. "Willa Cather's *A Lost Lady*: The Paradoxes of Change." *Novel: A Forum on Fiction* 11 (Fall 1977): 51–62.

2626. ———. "Willa Cather's American Gothic: *Sapphira and the Slave Girl.*" *Great Plains Quarterly* 4 (Fall 1984): 220–30.

2627. ———. "Willa Cather's Female Landscapes: *The Song of the Lark* and *Lucy Gayheart.*" *Women's Studies* 11 (1984): 233–46.

2628. ———. "Willa Cather's Pioneer Women: A Feminist Interpretation." *Where the West Begins.* Eds. Arthur R. Huseboe and William Geyer. Sioux Falls, S.Dak.: Center for Western Studies Press, 1978, 135–42.

2629. ———. "Willa Cather's Subverted Endings and Gendered Time." *Cather Studies, Volume 1.* Ed. Susan J. Rosowski. Lincoln: University of Nebraska Press, 1990, 68–88.

2630. ———. "Willa Cather's Women." *Studies in American Fiction* 9 (Autumn 1981): 261–75.

2631. ———. "Writing Against Silences, Female Adolescent Development in the Novels of Willa Cather." *Studies in the Novel* 21 (Spring 1989): 60–77.

2632. ———, ed. *Approaches to Teaching Cather's My Antonia.* New York: Modern Language Association, 1989.

2633. ———, ed. *Cather Studies, Volume 1.* Lincoln: University of Nebraska Press, 1990.

2634. ———, ed. *Cather Studies, Volume 2.* Lincoln: University of Nebraska Press, 1993.

2635. Roulston, Robert. "The Contrapuntal Complexity of Willa Cather's *The Song of the Lark.*" *Midwest Quarterly* 17 (Summer 1976): 350–68.

2636. Ryder, Mary R. "Prosodic Variations in Willa Cather's Prairie Poems." *Western American Literature* 20 (November 1985): 223–37.

2637. ———. *Willa Cather and Classical Myth: The Search for a New Parnassus.* Lewiston, N.Y.: E. Mellen, 1990.

2638. Saposnik-Noire, Shelley. "The Silent Protagonist: The Unifying Presence of Landscape in Willa Cather's *My Ántonia.*" *Midwest Quarterly* 31 (Winter 1990): 171–79.

2639. Schneider, Lucy. "Artistry and Intuition: Willa Cather's 'Land Philosophy.'" *South Dakota Review* 6 (Winter 1968–69): 53–64.

2640. ———. "Cather's 'Land Philosophy' in *Death Comes for the Archbishop.*" *Renascence* 22 (Winter 1970): 78–86.

2641. ———. "Of Land and Light: Willa Cather's *Lucy Gayheart.*" *Kansas Quarterly* 5 (Fall 1973): 51–62.

2642. ———. "Willa Cather's Early Stories in Light of Her 'Land Philosophy.'" *Midwest Quarterly* 9 (August 1967): 75–93.

2643. Schroeter, James Marvin. *Willa Cather and Her Critics.* Ithaca, N.Y.: Cornell University Press, 1967.

2644. Schwind, Jean. "Latour's Schismatic Church: The Radical Meaning in the Pictorial Methods of *Death Comes for the Archbishop.*" *Studies in American Fiction* 13 (Spring 1985): 71–88.

2645. Seibel, George. "Miss Willa Cather from Nebraska." *New Colophon* 2 (September 1949): 195–208.

2646. Selzer, John L. "Jim Burden and the Structure of *My Ántonia.*" *Western American Literature* 24 (May 1989): 45–61.

2647. Sergeant, Elizabeth Shepley. *Willa Cather: A Memoir.* Philadelphia: Lippincott, 1953; Lincoln: University of Nebraska Press, 1963.

2648. Shaw, Patrick W. "*My Ántonia*: Emergence and Authorial Revelations." *American Literature* 56 (December 1984): 527–40.

2649. ———. *Willa Cather and the Art of Conflict: Re-Visioning Her Creative Imagination.* Troy, N. Y.: Whitston, 1992.

2650. Shively, James R., ed. *Writings from Willa Cather's Campus Years.* Lincoln: University of Nebraska Press, 1950.

2651. Skaggs, Merrill Maguire. *After the World Broke in Two: The Later Novels of Willa Cather.* Charlottesville: University Press of Virginia, 1990.

2652. ———. "*Death Comes for the Archbishop*: Cather's Mystery and Manners." *American Literature* 57 (October 1985): 395–406.

2653. Slote, Bernice. "Willa Cather." *Sixteen Modern American Authors: A Study in Research and Criticism.* Ed. Jackson Bryer. Durham, N.C.: Duke University Press, 1974, 29–73.

2654. ———. "Willa Cather and Plains Culture." *Vision and Refuge: Essays on the Literature of the Great Plains.* Ed. Virginia Faulkner with

Frederick C. Luebke. Lincoln: University of Nebraska Press, 1982, 93–105.

2655. ———. "Willa Cather and the Sense of History." *Women, Women Writers, and the West*. Eds. Lawrence L. Lee and Merrill E. Lewis. Troy, N.Y.: Whitston, 1978.

2656. ———. *Willa Cather: A Pictorial Memoir*. Lincoln: University of Nebraska Press, 1973.

2657. ———. "Willa Cather as a Regional Writer." *Kansas Quarterly* 2 (Spring 1970): 7–15.

2658. ———, ed. *The Kingdom of Art: Willa Cather's First Principles and Critical Statements, 1893–1896*. Lincoln: University of Nebraska Press, 1967.

2659. ———, and Virginia Faulkner, eds. *The Art of Willa Cather*. Lincoln: University of Nebraska Press, 1975.

2660. Stegner, Wallace. "The West Authentic: Willa Cather." *The Sound of Mountain Water*. Garden City, N.Y.: Doubleday, 1969, 237–49.

2661. ———. "Willa Cather, *My Ántonia*." *The American Novel from James Fenimore Cooper to William Faulkner*. Ed. Wallace Stegner. New York: Basic Books, 1965.

2662. Stineback, David C. "The Case of Willa Cather." *Canadian Review of American Studies* 15 (Winter 1984): 385–95.

2663. ———. "Willa Cather's Ironic Masterpiece." *Arizona Quarterly* 29 (Winter 1973): 316–30.

2664. Stouck, David. "Cather's *Archbishop* and Travel Writing." *Western American Literature* 17 (Spring 1982): 3–12.

2665. ———. "Marriage and Friendship in *My Ántonia*." *Great Plains Quarterly* 2 (Fall 1982): 224–31.

2666. ———. "*O Pioneers!*: Willa Cather and the Epic Imagination." *Prairie Schooner* 46 (Spring 1972): 23–34.

2667. ———. "Perspective as Structure and Theme in *My Ántonia*." *Texas Studies in Literature and Language* 12 (Summer 1970): 285–94.

2668. ———. "Willa Cather and *The Professor's House*: 'Letting Go With the Heart.'" *Western American Literature* 7 (Spring 1972): 13–24.

2669. ———. *Willa Cather's Imagination*. Lincoln: University of Nebraska Press, 1975.

2670. Stouck, Mary-Ann, and David Stouck. "Art and Religion in *Death Comes for the Archbishop*." *Arizona Quarterly* 29 (Winter 1973): 293–302.

2671. ———. "Hagiographical Style in *Death Comes for the Archbishop*." *University of Toronto Quarterly* 41 (Summer 1972): 293–307.

2672. Stout, Janis P. "Autobiography as Journey in *The Professor's House*." *Studies in American Fiction* 19 (Autumn 1991): 203–15.

2673. ————. *Strategies of Reticence: Silence and Meaning in the Works of Jane Austen, Willa Cather, Katherine Anne Porter, and Joan Didion.* Charlottesville: University Press of Virginia, 1990.

2674. Sullivan, Patrick J. "Willa Cather's Southwest." *Western American Literature* 7 (Spring 1972): 25–37.

2675. Swift, John N. "Memory, Myth, and *The Professor's House*." *Western American Literature* 20 (February 1986): 301–14.

2676. Thomas, Susie. *Willa Cather.* New York: Barnes and Noble, 1990.

2677. Thurin, Erik Ingvar. *The Humanization of Willa Cather: Classicism in an American Classic.* Lund, Sweden: Lund University Press, 1990.

2678. Turner, Frederick. *Spirit of Place: The Making of an American Literary Landscape.* San Francisco: Sierra Club Books, 1989.

2679. Van Ghent, Dorothy. *Willa Cather.* Minneapolis: University of Minnesota Press, 1964.

2680. Vigil, Ralph H. "Willa Cather and Historical Reality." *New Mexico Historical Review* 50 (April 1975): 123–38.

2681. Wagenknecht, Edward. *Willa Cather.* New York: Continuum, 1994.

2682. Walker, Don D. "The Western Humanism of Willa Cather." *Western American Literature* 1 (Summer 1966): 75–90.

2683. Wasserman, Loretta. "Cather's Semitism." *Cather Studies, Volume 2.* Ed. Susan J. Rosowski. Lincoln: University of Nebraska Press, 1993, 1–22.

2684. ————. "Is Cather's Paul a Case?" *Modern Fiction Studies* 36 (Spring 1990): 121–29.

2685. ————. *Willa Cather: A Study of the Short Fiction.* Boston: Twayne, 1991.

2686. ————. "Willa Cather's 'The Old Beauty' Reconsidered." *Studies in American Fiction* 16 (Autumn 1988): 217–27.

2687. Wiesenthal, C. Susan. "Female Sexuality in Willa Cather's *O Pioneers!* and the Era of Scientific Sexology: A Dialogue Between Frontiers." *Ariel* 21 (January 1990): 41–63.

2688. Wild, Barbara. "'The Thing Not Named' in *The Professor's House*." *Western American Literature* 12 (Winter 1978): 263–74.

2689. *Willa Cather: A Pictorial Memoir.* Photographs by Lucia Woods and others; text by Bernice Slote. Lincoln: University of Nebraska Press, 1973.

2690. *Willa Cather Issue. Great Plains Quarterly* 2 (Fall 1982): 193–248.

2691. "A Willa Cather Issue." *Western American Literature* 17 (May 1982): 3–60.

2692. Winters, Laura G. *Willa Cather: Landscape and Exile.* Selinsgrove, Pa.: Susquehanna University Press, 1993.

2693. Woodress, James. "Cather and Her Friends." *Critical Essays on Willa Cather.* Ed. John J. Murphy. Boston: G. K. Hall, 1984, 81–95.

2694. ———. "The Uses of Biography: The Case of Willa Cather." *Great Plains Quarterly* 2 (Fall 1982): 195–203.

2695. ———. "Willa Cather." *Sixteen Modern American Authors: Volume 2: A Survey of Research and Criticism.* Ed. Jackson R. Bryer. Durham, N.C.: Duke University Press, 1990, 42–72.

2696. ———. *Willa Cather: A Literary Life.* Lincoln: University of Nebraska Press, 1987.

2697. ———. "Willa Cather and History." *Arizona* Quarterly 34 (Autumn 1978): 239–54.

2698. ———. *Willa Cather: Her Life and Art.* New York: Pegasus, 1970.

2699. ———. "Writing Cather's Biography." *Cather Studies, Volume 1.* Ed. Susan J. Rosowski. Lincoln: University of Nebraska Press, 1990, 103–14.

2700. Work, James C. "Cather's Confounded Conundrums in *The Professor's House.*" *Western American Literature* 18 (Winter 1984): 303–12.

2701. ———. "Willa Cather's Archbishop and the Seven Deadly Sins." *Platte Valley Review* 14 (Spring 1986): 93–103.

2702. Yongue, Patricia Lee. "*A Lost Lady*: The End of the First Cycle." *Western American Literature* 7 (Spring 1972): 3–12.

2703. ———. "*The Professor's House* and 'Rip Van Winkle.'" *Western American Literature* 18 (Winter 1984): 281–97.

2704. ———. "Willa Cather's Aristocrats." *Southern Humanities Review* 14 (Winter 1980): 43–56; (Spring 1980): 111–25.

GEORGE CATLIN

2705. Dippie, Brian W. *Catlin and His Contemporaries: The Politics of Patronage.* Lincoln: University of Nebraska Press, 1990.

2706. McCracken, Harold. *George Catlin and the Old Frontier.* New York: Dial Press, 1959.

2707. Millichap, Joseph R. *George Catlin.* Western Writers Series, No. 27. Boise, Idaho: Boise State University, 1977.

2708. Ross, Marvin C., ed. *George Catlin.* Norman: University of Oklahoma Press, 1959.

JOHN CAUGHEY

2709. Beckham, Stephen Dow. "John Walton Caughey, Historian and Civil Libertarian." *Pacific Historical Review* 56 (November 1987): 481–93.

RAYMOND CHANDLER

2710. Babener, Liahna K. "Raymond Chandler's City of Lies." *Los Angeles in Fiction: A Collection of Original Essays.* Ed. David Fine. Albuquerque: University of New Mexico Press, 1984, 109–31.

2711. Clark, Al. *Raymond Chandler in Hollywood.* London: Proteus, 1982.

2712. Fontana, Ernest. "Chivalry and Modernity in Raymond Chandler's *The Big Sleep*." *Western American Literature* 19 (November 1984): 179–86.

2713. Kaye, Howard. "Raymond Chandler's Sentimental Novel." *Western American Literature* 10 (August 1975): 135–45.

2714. Limerick, Patricia Nelson. "What Raymond Chandler Knew and Western Historians Forgot." *Old West–New West: Centennial Essays.* Ed. Barbara Howard Meldrum. Moscow: University of Idaho Press, 1993, 28–39.

2715. MacShane, Frank. *The Life of Raymond Chandler.* New York: Dutton, 1976.

2716. Marling, William. *Raymond Chandler.* Boston: Twayne, 1986.

2717. Newlin, Keith. "Raymond Chandler: A Critical and Biographical Bibliography." *Clues* 6 (Fall–Winter 1985): 61–72.

2718. Porter, Joseph C. "The End of the Trail: The American West of Dashiell Hammett and Raymond Chandler." *Western Historical Quarterly* 6 (October 1975): 411–24.

2719. Skenazy, Paul. *The New Wild West: The Urban Mysteries of Dashiell Hammett and Raymond Chandler.* Western Writers Series, No. 54. Boise, Idaho: Boise State University, 1982.

2720. Skinner, Robert E. *The Hard-Boiled Explicator: A Guide to the Study of Dashiell Hammett, Raymond Chandler and Ross Macdonald.* Metuchen, N.J.: Scarecrow Press, 1985.

2721. Smith, Johanna M. "Raymond Chandler and the Business of Literature." *Texas Studies in Literature and Language* 31 (Winter 1989): 592–610.

2722. Speir, Jerry. *Raymond Chandler.* New York: Ungar, 1981.

2723. Tate, J. O. "Raymond Chandler's Shakespearean Touch." *Sewanee Review* 101 (Spring 1993): 257–68.

2724. Thorpe, Edward. *Chandlertown: The Los Angeles of Philip Marlowe.* New York: St. Martins, 1983.

2725. Wasserburg, Charles. "Raymond Chandler's Great Wrong Place." *Southwest Review* 74 (Autumn 1989): 534–45.

2726. Wolfe, Peter. *Something More Than Night: The Case of Raymond Chandler.* Bowling Green, Ohio: Bowling Green State University Popular Press, 1985.

J. SMEATON CHASE

2727. Dillon, Richard H. "Prose Poet of the Trail: J. Smeaton Chase." *Book Club of California Quarterly Newsletter* 35 (Spring 1970): 27–36.

DENISE CHÁVEZ

2728. Heard, Martha E. "The Theatre of Denise Chávez: Interior Landscapes with *Sabor Nuevomexicano.*" *Americas Review* 16 (Summer 1988): 83–91.

FRAY ANGELICO CHÁVEZ

2729. Morales, Phyllis S. *Fray Angelico Chávez: A Bibliography of His Published Writings, 1925–1978.* Santa Fe, N. Mex.: Lightning Tree Press, 1980.

2730. Padilla, Genaro Miguel. "A Reassessment of Fray Angelico Chávez's Fiction." *MELUS* 11 (Winter 1984): 31–45.

PEGGY POND CHURCH

2731. Armitage, Shelley. *Peggy Pond Church.* Western Writers Series, No. 108. Boise, Idaho: Boise State University, 1993.

2732. Baker, Gail. "The Art of *The House at Otowi Bridge.*" *New America* 3 (Summer–Fall 1977): 32–36.

ANN NOLAN CLARK

2733. Whitehouse, Jeanne Carolyn. "The Early Life of Ann Nolan Clark: A Contextual Biography." Doctoral dissertation, University of New Mexico, 1987.

BADGER CLARK

2734. Chenoweth, Richard R., ed. "Badger Clark as 'The Prisoner of Camaquey.'" *South Dakota History* 7 (Summer 1977): 271–90.

2735. Lee, Shebby. "Dakota Resources: Researching the Works of Badger Clark." *South Dakota History* 13 (Winter 1983): 388–94.

CHARLES HEBER CLARK

(Max Adeler)

2736. Dussere, David Philip. "A Critical Biography of Charles Heber Clark ('Max Adeler'): American Journalist and Humorist." Doctoral dissertation, University of Arkansas, 1974.

WALTER VAN TILBURG CLARK

2737. Alt, Jon [Harlan]. "*The City of Trembling Leaves*: Humanity and Eternity." *South Dakota Review* 17 (Winter 1979–80): 8–18.

2738. ———. "Walter Van Tilburg Clark: Humanity and Eternity." Doctoral dissertation, Kansas State University, 1977.

2739. Andersen, Kenneth. "Character Portrayal in *The Ox-Bow Incident*." *Western American Literature* 4 (Winter 1970): 287–98.

2740. ———. "Form in Walter Van Tilburg Clark's *The Ox-Bow Incident*." *Western Review* 6 (Spring 1969): 19–25.

2741. Bates, Barclay W. "Clark's Man for All Seasons: The Achievement of Wholeness in *The Ox-Bow Incident*." *Western American Literature* 3 (Spring 1968): 37–49.

2742. Bluestone, George. *Novels into Film.* Baltimore: The Johns Hopkins Press, 1957, 170–96.

2743. Carpenter, Frederic I. "The West of Walter Van Tilburg Clark." *College English* 13 (February 1952): 243–48.

2744. Cochran, Robert W. "Nature and the Nature of Man in *The Ox-Bow Incident*." *Western American Literature* 5 (Winter 1971): 253–64.

2745. Crain, Mary Beth. "*The Ox-Bow Incident* Revisited." *Literature/Film Quarterly* 4 (1976): 240–48.

2746. Eisinger, Chester E. *Fiction of the Forties.* Chicago: University of Chicago Press, 1963, 310–24.

2747. Etulain, Richard W. "Walter Van Tilburg Clark: A Bibliography." *South Dakota Review* 3 (Autumn 1965): 73–77.

2748. Gorrell, Robert. "Walter Van Tilburg Clark and Trembling Leaves: A Review Essay." *Nevada Historical Society Quarterly* 35 (Fall 1992): 149–61.

2749. Heilman, Robert B. "Clark's Western Incident: From Stereotype to Model." *Walter Van Tilburg Clark: Critiques.* Ed. Charlton Laird. Reno: University of Nevada Press, 1983, 79–104.

2750. Houghton, Donald E. "The Failure of Speech in *The Ox-Bow Incident*." *English Journal* 59 (December 1970): 1245–51.

2751. ———. "Man and Animals in 'The Indian Well.'" *Western American Literature* 6 (Fall 1971): 215–18.

2752. Kehde, Suzanne. "Walter Van Tilburg Clark and the Withdrawal of Landscape." *The Big Empty: Essays on Western Landscapes as Narratives*. Ed. Leonard Engel. Albuquerque: University of New Mexico Press, 1994, 133–45.

2753. Kiefer, Gordon B. "Walter Van Tilburg Clark's Fiction: A Study in Structure." Doctoral dissertation, Texas Tech University, 1979.

2754. Kleis, David John. "The God Becoming: Sensation of the Nuclear in Walter Van Tilburg Clark." Doctoral dissertation, University of Michigan, 1974.

2755. Laird, Charlton. "The Gospel According to the Trembling Leaves." *Walter Van Tilburg Clark: Critiques*. Ed. Charlton Laird. Reno: University of Nevada Press, 1983, 147–80.

2756. ———, ed. *Walter Van Tilburg Clark: Critiques*. Reno: University of Nevada Press, 1983.

2757. Lee, L. L. *Walter Van Tilburg Clark*. Western Writers Series, No. 8. Boise, Idaho: Boise State College, 1973.

2758. Milton, John R. "Conversation with Walter Van Tilburg Clark." *South Dakota Review* 9 (Spring 1971): 27–38; 26 (Winter 1988): 44–56.

2759. ———. *The Novel of the American West*. Lincoln: University of Nebraska Press, 1980, 195–229.

2760. Portz, John. "Idea and Symbol in Walter Van Tilburg Clark." *Accent* 17 (Spring 1957): 112–28.

2761. Rogers, Douglas G. "Man and Nature in Clark's *Track of the Cat*." *South Dakota Review* 12 (Winter 1974–75): 49–55.

2762. Ronald, Ann. "Walter Van Tilburg Clark's Brave Bird, 'Hook.'" *Studies in Short Fiction* 25 (Fall 1988): 433–39.

2763. Stegner, Wallace. "Walter Clark's Frontier." *Atlantic* 232 (August 1973): 94–98.

2764. Stein, Paul. "Cowboys and Unicorns: The Novels of Walter Van Tilburg Clark." *Western American Literature* 5 (Winter 1971): 265–75.

2765. Swallow, Alan. "The Mavericks." *Critique* 2 (Winter 1959): 74–92.

2766. West, Ray B., Jr. "The Use of Setting in 'The Wind and the Snow of Winter.'" *The Art of Writing Fiction*. New York: Thomas Y. Crowell, 1968, 181–87.

2767. Westbrook, Max. "The Archetypal Ethic of *The Ox-Bow Incident*." *Western American Literature* 1 (Summer 1966): 105–18.

2768. ———. "The Indian in the Mirror: Clark's *The Track of the Cat*." *Western American Literature* 20 (May 1985): 17–33.

2769. ———. "Internal Debate as Discipline: Clark's *The Watchful Gods.*" *Western American Literature* 1 (Fall 1966): 153–65.

2770. ———. "To Escape the Tiger: The Short Stories." *Walter Van Tilburg Clark: Critiques.* Ed. Charlton Laird. Reno: University of Nevada Press, 1983, 105–18.

2771. ———. *Walter Van Tilburg Clark.* New York: Twayne, 1969.

2772. Wilner, Herbert. "Walter Van Tilburg Clark." *Western Review* 20 (Winter 1956): 103–22.

2773. Young, Vernon. "An American Dream and Its Parody." *Arizona Quarterly* 6 (Summer 1950): 112–23.

2774. ———. "Gods Without Heroes: The Tentative Myth of Van Tilburg Clark." *Arizona Quarterly* 7 (Summer 1951): 110–19.

WILLIAM CLARK

(Lewis and Clark)

See Meriwether Lewis

BEVERLY CLEARY

2775. Pflieger, Pat. *Beverly Cleary.* Boston: Twayne, 1991.

SAMUEL L. CLEMENS

(Mark Twain)

2776. Baender, Paul. "The 'Jumping Frog' as a Comedian's First Virtue." *Modern Philology* 60 (February 1963): 192–200.

2777. Baldanza, Frank. *Mark Twain: An Introduction and Interpretation.* New York: Barnes and Noble, 1961.

2778. Bassett, John E. "*Life on the Mississippi*: Being Shifty in a New Country." *Western American Literature* 21 (May 1986): 39–45.

2779. ———. "*Roughing It*: Authority Through Comic Performance." *Nineteenth Century Literature* 43 (September 1988): 220–34.

2780. ———. "Tom, Huck, and the Young Pilot: Twain's Quest For Authority." *Mississippi Quarterly* 39 (Winter 1985–86): 3–19.

2781. Beaver, Harold. *Huckleberry Finn.* Boston: Allen and Unwin, 1987.

2782. Beidler, Philip D. "Realistic Style and the Problem of Context in *The Innocents Abroad* and *Roughing It.*" *American Literature* 52 (March 1980): 33–49.

2783. Bellamy, Gladys Carmen. *Mark Twain as a Literary Artist.* Norman: University of Oklahoma Press, 1950.

2784. Benson, Ivan. *Mark Twain's Western Years.* Stanford, Calif.: Stanford University Press, 1938.

2785. Blair, Walter. *Mark Twain and Huck Finn.* Berkeley: University of California Press, 1960.

2786. ———. "Mark Twain's Other Masterpiece: 'Jim Baker's Blue-Jay Yarn.'" *Studies in American Humor* 1 (January 1975): 132–47.

2787. ———, ed. *Mark Twain's West: The Author's Memoirs About His Boyhood, Riverboats and Western Adventures.* Chicago: Lakeside Press, 1983.

2788. ———, and Victor Fischer, eds. *Adventures of Huckleberry Finn: Tom Sawyer's Comrade.* Berkeley: University of California Press, 1985.

2789. Bloom, Harold, ed. *Mark Twain.* New York: Chelsea House, 1986.

2790. Branch, Edgar M. "A Chronological Bibliography of the Writings of Samuel Clemens to June 8, 1867." *American Literature* 18 (May 1946): 109–59.

2791. ———. "Fact and Fiction in the Blind Lead Episode of *Roughing It.*" *Nevada Historical Society Quarterly* 28 (Winter 1985): 234–48.

2792. ———. *The Literary Apprenticeship of Mark Twain.* Urbana: University of Illinois Press, 1950.

2793. ———. "Mark Twain Reports the Races in Sacramento." *Huntington Library Quarterly* 32 (Fall 1969): 179–86.

2794. ———. "'My Voice Is Still for Setchell': A Background Study of 'Jim Smiley and His Jumping Frog.'" *PMLA* 82 (December 1967): 591–601.

2795. ———. "'Old Times on the Mississippi': Biography and Craftsmanship." *Nineteenth-Century Literature* 45 (June 1990): 73–87.

2796. ———, ed. *Clemens of the "Call": Mark Twain in San Francisco.* Berkeley: University of California Press, 1969.

2797. ———, Michael B. Frank, and Kenneth M. Sanderson, eds. *Mark Twain's Letters, Volume I, 1853–1866.* Berkeley: University of California Press, 1988.

2798. Brazil, John R. "Perception and Structure in Mark Twain's Art and Mind: *Life on the Mississippi.*" *Mississippi Quarterly* 34 (Spring 1981): 91–112.

2799. Bridgman, Richard. *Traveling in Mark Twain.* Berkeley: University of California Press, 1987.

2800. Brooks, Van Wyck. *The Ordeal of Mark Twain.* Rev ed. New York: E.P. Dutton, 1933.

2801. Budd, Louis J. *Mark Twain: Social Philosopher.* Bloomington: Indiana University Press, 1962.

2802. ———. *Our Mark Twain: The Making of His Public Personality.* Philadelphia: University of Pennsylvania Press, 1983.

2803. ———, ed. *Critical Essays on Mark Twain, 1910–1980.* Boston: G.K. Hall, 1983.

2804. ———, ed. *New Essays on Adventures of Huckleberry Finn.* New York: Cambridge University Press, 1985.

2805. Burnet, R. A. "Mark Twain in the Northwest–1895." *Pacific Northwest Quarterly* 42 (July 1951): 187–202.

2806. Busskohl, James L. "'The Story of the Old Ram' and the Tenderfoot Writer." *Studies in American Fiction* 18 (Autumn 1990): 183–92.

2807. Camp, James E., and X. J. Kennedy, eds. *Mark Twain's Frontier: A Textbook of Primary Source Materials for Student Research and Writing.* New York: Holt, Rinehart, Winston, 1963.

2808. Canby, Henry Seidel. *Turn West, Turn East.* Boston: Houghton Mifflin, 1951.

2809. Cardwell, Guy. *The Man Who Was Mark Twain: Images and Ideologies.* New Haven: Yale University Press, 1991.

2810. ———. "Samuel Clemens' Magical Pseudonym." *New England Quarterly* 48 (June 1975): 175–93.

2811. Carstensen, Vernon. "The West Mark Twain Did Not See." *Pacific Northwest Quarterly* 55 (October 1964): 170–76.

2812. Carter, Paul J., Jr. "The Influence of the Nevada Frontier on Mark Twain." *Western Humanities Review* 13 (Winter 1959): 61–70.

2813. Clemens, Samuel L. *Roughing It.* Ed. with intro. and notes, Franklin R. Rogers. Berkeley: University of California Press, 1972.

2814. Coulson, David C. "Reporter Mark Twain: Missouri Son Rises in the West." *Mark Twain Journal* 21 (Winter 1981/82): 1–7.

2815. Covici, Pascal, Jr. *Mark Twain's Humor: The Image of a World.* Dallas: Southern Methodist University Press, 1962.

2816. Cox, James M. *Mark Twain: The Fate of Humor.* Princeton, N.J.: Princeton University Press, 1966.

2817. Cracroft, Richard H. "Distorting Polygamy for Fun and Profit: Artemas [sic] Ward and Mark Twain Among the Mormons." *BYU Studies* 14 (Winter 1974): 272–88.

2818. ———. "The Gentle Blasphemer: Mark Twain, Holy Scripture, and the Book of Mormon." *BYU Studies* 11 (Winter 1971): 119–40.

2819. Cunliffe, Marcus. "American Humor and the Rise of the West: Mark Twain." *The Literature of the United States.* London: Penguin Books, 1954, 151–69.

2820. Davis, Sara deSaussure, et al., eds. *The Mythologizing of Mark Twain.* University: University of Alabama Press, 1984.

2821. Delaney, Paul. "The Genteel Savage: A Western Link in the Development of Mark Twain's Transcendent Figure." *Mark Twain Journal* 21 (Spring 1983): 29–31.

2822. ———. "You Can't Go Back to the Raft Ag'in Huck Honey!: Mark Twain's Western Sequel to *Huckleberry Finn.*" *Western American Literature* 11 (November 1976): 215–29.

2823. Derwin, Susan. "Impossible Commands: Reading *Adventures of Huckleberry Finn.*" *Nineteenth-Century Literature* 47 (March 1993): 437–54.

2824. DeVoto, Bernard. *Mark Twain at Work.* Cambridge, Mass.: Harvard University Press, 1942.

2825. ———. *Mark Twain's America.* Boston: Little, Brown, 1932.

2826. Dolmetsch, Carl. "*Huck Finn*'s First Century: A Bibliographical Survey." *American Studies International* 22 (October 1984): 79–121.

2827. Ducey, Cathryn Annette. "The Development of a Frontier Thesis: Mark Twain, Domingo Faustino Sarmiento, and Frederick Jackson Turner." Doctoral dissertation, University of Hawaii, 1975.

2828. Duckett, Margaret. *Mark Twain and Bret Harte.* Norman: University of Oklahoma Press, 1964.

2829. Emerson, Everett. *The Authentic Mark Twain: A Literary Biography of Samuel L. Clemens.* Philadelphia: University of Pennsylvania Press, 1984.

2830. Fatout, Paul. *Mark Twain in Virginia City.* Bloomington: Indiana University Press, 1964.

2831. ———, ed. *Mark Twain Speaking.* Iowa City: University of Iowa Press, 1976.

2832. Fender, Stephen. "'The Prodigal in a Far Country Chawing of Husks': Mark Twain's Search for a Style in the West." *Modern Language Review* 71 (October 1976): 737–56.

2833. Fertel, R. J. "'Free and Easy'?: Spontaneity and the Quest for Maturity in *The Adventures of Huckleberry Finn.*" *Modern Language Quarterly* 44 (June 1983): 157–77.

2834. Fiedler, Leslie. "*Huckleberry Finn*: The Book We Love To Hate." *Proteus* 1 (Fall 1984): 1–8.

2835. Fischer, Victor. "Huck Finn Reviewed: The Reception of *Huckleberry Finn* in the United States, 1885–1897." *American Literary Realism 1870–1910* 16 (Spring 1983): 1–56.

2836. ———, Michael B. Frank, and Dahlia Armon, eds. *Mark Twain's Letters, Volume 3: 1869.* Berkeley: University of California Press, 1992.

2837. Fishkin, Shelley Fisher. *Was Huck Black? Mark Twain and African American Voices.* New York: Oxford University Press, 1993.

2838. Foner, Philip S. *Mark Twain: Social Critic.* New York: International Publishers, 1958.

2839. Fried, Martin B. "The Composition, Sources, and Popularity of Mark Twain's *Roughing It.*" Doctoral dissertation, University of Chicago, 1951.

2840. Gale, Robert L. *Plots and Characters in the Works of Mark Twain.* 2 vols. Hamden, Conn.: Archon, 1973.

2841. Geismar, Maxwell. *Mark Twain: An American Prophet.* Boston: Houghton Mifflin, 1970.

2842. Gerber, John C. *Mark Twain.* Boston: Twayne, 1988.

2843. Gernes, Sonia Grace. "The Relationship of Storyteller to Community in the Tales of the Southwest Humorists, Mark Twain and William Faulkner." Doctoral dissertation, University of Washington, 1975.

2844. Gibson, William M. *The Art of Mark Twain.* New York: Oxford University Press, 1976.

2845. Gillman, Susan. *Dark Twins: Imposture and Identity in Mark Twain's America.* Chicago: University of Chicago Press, 1989.

2846. Green, Martin. "Twain's *Roughing It.*" *The Great American Adventure.* Boston: Beacon Press, 1984, 133–50.

2847. Gribben, Alan. "Removing Mark Twain's Mask: A Decade of Criticism and Scholarship." *ESQ: A Journal of the American Renaissance* 26 (1980): 100–108, 149–71.

2848. Gunn, Drewey Wayne. "The Monomythic Structure of *Roughing It.*" *American Literature* 61 (December 1989): 563–85.

2849. Harris, Susan K. *Mark Twain's Escape from Time: A Study of Patterns and Images.* Columbia: University of Missouri Press, 1982.

2850. Hill, Hamlin. *Mark Twain: God's Fool.* New York: Harper and Row, 1973.

2851. ———. "Mark Twain's *Roughing It*: The End of the American Dream." *American Renaissance and American West: Proceedings of the Second University of Wyoming American Studies Conference.* Eds. Christopher S. Durer, et al. Laramie: University of Wyoming, 1982, 3–13.

2852. ———. "Who Killed Mark Twain?" *American Literary Realism 1870–1910* 7 (Spring 1974): 119–24.

2853. Howe, Lawrence. "Transcending the Limits of Experience: Mark Twain's *Life on the Mississippi*." *American Literature* 63 (September 1991): 420–39.

2854. Howell, Elmo. "Mark Twain's Arkansas." *Arkansas Historical Quarterly* 29 (August 1970): 195–208.

2855. Hudson, Ruth. "A Literary 'Area of Freedom' between Irving and Twain." *Western Humanities Review* 13 (Winter 1959): 46–60.

2856. Inge, M. Thomas, ed. *Huck Finn Among the Critics: A Centennial Selection.* Frederick, Md.: University Publications of America, 1985.

2857. James, G. W. "Mark Twain and the Pacific Coast." *Pacific Monthly* 24 (1910): 115–32.

2858. Kaplan, Justin. *Mr. Clemens and Mark Twain: A Biography.* New York: Simon and Schuster, 1966.

2859. Kime, Wayne R. "Huck Among the Indians: Mark Twain and Richard Irving Dodge's *The Plains of the Great West and Their Inhabitants.*" *Western American Literature* 24 (February 1990): 321–33.

2860. Kolb, Harold H., Jr. "Mark Twain and the Myth of the West." *The Mythologizing of Mark Twain.* Eds. Sara deSaussure Davis and Philip D. Beidler. University: University of Alabama Press, 1984, 119–35.

2861. Krause, S[ydney]. J. "The Art and Satire of Twain's 'Jumping Frog' Story." *American Quarterly* 16 (Winter 1964): 562–76.

2862. ———. "Cooper's Literary Offenses: Mark Twain in Wonderland." *New England Quarterly* 38 (September 1965): 291–311.

2863. ———. *Mark Twain as Critic.* Baltimore: Johns Hopkins Press, 1967.

2864. ———. "Steinbeck and Mark Twain." *Steinbeck Newsletter* 6 (Fall 1973): 104–11.

2865. Krauth, Leland. "Mark Twain: The Victorian of Southwestern Humor." *American Literature* 54 (October 1982): 368–84.

2866. Kruse, Horst H. *Mark Twain and "Life on the Mississippi."* Amherst: University of Massachusetts Press, 1981.

2867. Kuperman, David Arnold. "Travels and Travelers in the Writing of Mark Twain." Doctoral dissertation, Indiana University, 1975.

2868. Lauber, John. *The Inventions of Mark Twain.* New York: Hill and Wang, 1990.

2869. ———. *The Making of Mark Twain: A Biography.* New York: American Heritage, 1985.

2870. Lee, Robert Edson. *From West to East.* Urbana: University of Illinois Press, 1966, 82–111.

2871. LeMaster, J. R., and James D. Wilson, eds. *The Mark Twain Encyclopedia.* New York: Garland, 1993.

2872. Lennon, Nigey. *Mark Twain in California: The Turbulent California Years of Samuel Clemens.* San Francisco: Chronicle Books, 1982.

2873. ———. *The Sagebrush Bohemian: Mark Twain in California.* New York: Paragon House, 1990.

2874. Leonard James S., Thomas A. Tenney, and Thadious M. Davis, eds. *Satire or Evasion? Black Perspectives on Huckleberry Finn.* Durham, N. C.: Duke University Press, 1992.

2875. Long, E. Hudson. *Mark Twain Handbook.* New York: Hendricks House, 1957.

2876. ———, and J.R. LeMaster. *The New Mark Twain Handbook.* New York: Garland, 1985.

2877. Loomis, C. Grant. "Dan De Quille's Mark Twain." *Pacific Historical Review* 15 (September 1946): 336–47.

2878. Lorch, Fred W. *The Trouble Begins at Eight.* Ames: Iowa State University Press, 1968.

2879. Lowry, Richard Scott. "Plots and Counterplots: Parody and Cultural Authority in the Work of Mark Twain, 1869–1885." Doctoral dissertation, Yale University, 1988.

2880. Lynn, Kenneth S. *Mark Twain and Southwestern Humor.* Boston: Little, Brown, 1959.

2881. Machlis, Paul, ed. *A Union Catalog of Clemens Letters.* Berkeley: University of California Press, 1986.

2882. ———. *Union Catalog of Letters to Clemens.* Berkeley: University of California Press, 1992.

2883. Mack, Effie Mona. *Mark Twain in Nevada.* New York: Charles Scribner's Sons, 1947.

2884. McKee, John DeWitt. "*Roughing It* as Retrospective Reporting." *Western American Literature* 5 (Summer 1970): 113–19.

2885. McMahan, Elizabeth, ed. *Critical Approaches to Mark Twain's Short Stories.* Port Washington, N.Y.: Kennikat Press, 1981.

2886. Marks, Barry A. "The Huck Finn Swindle." *Western American Literature* 14 (Summer 1979): 115–32.

2887. Marotti, Maria Ornella. *The Duplicating Imagination: Twain and the Twain Papers.* University Park: Pennsylvania State University Press, 1990.

2888. Marx, Leo. "Mr. Eliot, Mr. Trilling, and Huckleberry Finn." *American Scholar* 22 (August 1953): 423–40.

2889. ———. "The Pilot and the Passenger: Landscape Conventions and the Style of *Huckleberry Finn.*" *American Literature* 28 (May 1956): 129–46.

2890. Meyer, Harold. "Mark Twain on the Comstock." *Southwest Review* 12 (April 1927): 197–207.

2891. Michelson, Bruce. "Ever Such a Good Time: The Structure of Mark Twain's *Roughing It.*" *Dutch Quarterly Review of Anglo-American Letters* 17 (No. 3, 1987): 182–99.

2892. Miller, Robert Keith. *Mark Twain.* New York: Ungar, 1983.

2893. Mitchell, Lee Clark. "Verbally *Roughing It*: The West of Words." *Nineteenth-Century Literature* 44 (June 1989): 67–92.

2894. Mobley, Lawrence E. "Mark Twain and the Golden Era." *Bibliographical Society of America, Papers* 58 (1964): 8–23.

2895. Moss, George. "Silver Frolic: Popular Entertainment in Virginia City, Nevada, 1859–1863." *Journal of Popular Culture* 22 (Fall 1988): 1–31.

2896. Nibbelink, Harman. "Mark Twain and the Mormons." *Mark Twain Journal* 17 (Winter 1973/74): 1–5.

2897. Paine, Albert Bigelow. *Mark Twain: A Biography.* 3 vols. New York: Harper, 1912.

2898. Pettit, Arthur G. "Mark Twain's Attitude Toward the Negro in the West, 1861–1867." *Western Historical Quarterly* 1 (January 1970): 51–62.

2899. Reed, J. Q. "Mark Twain: West Coast Journalist." *Midwest Journal* 1 (Winter 1960): 141–61.

2900. Robinson, Forrest G. "The Characterization of Jim in *Huckleberry Finn.*" *Nineteenth-Century Literature* 43 (December 1988): 361–91.

2901. ———. *In Bad Faith: The Dynamics of Deception in Mark Twain's America.* Cambridge: Harvard University Press, 1986.

2902. ———. "'Seeing the Elephant': Some Perspectives on Mark Twain's *Roughing It.*" *American Studies* 21 (Fall 1980): 43–64.

2903. ———. "The Silences in *Huckleberry Finn.*" *Nineteenth-Century Fiction* 37 (June 1982): 50–74.

2904. ———, and Susan Gillman, eds. *Mark Twain's Pudd'nhead Wilson: Race, Conflict and Culture.* Durham, N.C.: Duke University Press, 1990.

2905. Robinson, William Hedges, Jr. "Mark Twain: Senatorial Secretary." *American West* 10 (January 1973): 16–17, 60–62.

2906. Rodgers, Paul C., Jr. "Artemus Ward and Mark Twain's 'Jumping Frog.'" *Nineteeth-Century Fiction* 28 (December 1973): 273–86.

2907. Rodney, Robert M., comp. *Mark Twain International: A Bibliography and Interpretation of His Worldwide Popularity.* Westport, Conn.: Greenwood Press, 1982.

2908. Rogers, Franklin R. "The Road to Reality: Burlesque Travel Literature and Mark Twain's *Roughing It.*" *Bulletin of the New York Public Library* 67 (March 1963): 155–68.

2909. ———, ed. *The Pattern for Mark Twain's Roughing It.* Berkeley: University of California Press, 1961.

2910. Rowlette, Robert. "'Mark Twain on Artemus Ward': Twain's Literary Debt to Ward." *American Literary Realism 1870–1910* 6 (Winter 1973): 13–25.

2911. Ryan, Pat M., Jr. "Mark Twain: Frontier Theatre Critic." *Arizona Quarterly* 16 (August 1960): 197–209.

2912. Sanborn, Margaret. *Mark Twain: The Bachelor Years: A Biography.* New York: Doubleday, 1990.

2913. Sattelmeyer, Robert, and J. Donald Crowley, eds. *One Hundred Years of Huckleberry Finn: The Boy, His Book, and American Culture: Centennial Essays.* Columbia: University of Missouri Press, 1985.

2914. Schacht, Paul. "The Lonesomeness of Huckleberry Finn." *American Literature* 53 (May 1981): 189–201.

2915. Scharnhorst, Gary. *Critical Essays on The Adventures of Tom Sawyer.* New York: G.K. Hall, 1993.

2916. ———. "Mark Twain's Imbroglio with the San Francisco Police: Three Lost Texts." *American Literature* 62 (December 1990): 686–91.

2917. Sloane, David E. E. *Adventures of Huckleberry Finn: American Comic Vision.* Boston: Twayne, 1988.

2918. ———. *Mark Twain as a Literary Comedian.* Baton Rouge: Louisiana State University Press, 1979.

2919. Smith, Harriet Elinor, Richard Bucci, and Lin Salamo, eds. *Mark Twain's Letters, Volume 2: 1867–1868.* Berkeley: University of California Press, 1990.

2920. Smith, Henry Nash. *Mark Twain: The Development of a Writer.* Cambridge, Mass.: Harvard University Press, 1962.

2921. ———, and Frederick Anderson, eds. *Mark Twain of the Enterprise.* Berkeley: University of California Press, 1957.

2922. Solomon, Roger B. *Mark Twain and the Image of History.* New Haven, Conn.: Yale University Press, 1961.

2923. "Special Issue: Black Writers on *Adventures of Huckleberry Finn* One Hundred Years Later." *Mark Twain Journal* 22 (Fall 1984): 2–52.

2924. Steinbrink, Jeffrey. *Getting to Be Mark Twain.* Berkeley: University of California Press, 1991.

2925. Stone, Albert E., Jr. *The Innocent Eye: Childhood in Mark Twain's Imagination.* New Haven, Conn.: Yale University Press, 1961.

2926. Stonely, Peter. *Mark Twain and the Feminine Aesthetic*. New York: Cambridge University Press, 1992.

2927. Sundquist, Eric J., ed. *Mark Twain: A Collection of Critical Essays*. Englewood Cliffs, N.J.: Prentice-Hall, 1994.

2928. Taper, Bernard, ed. *Mark Twain's San Francisco*. New York: McGraw-Hill, 1963.

2929. Taylor, J. Golden. "Introduction to 'The Celebrated Jumping Frog of Calaveras County.'" *American West* 2 (Fall 1965): 73–76.

2930. Tenney, Thomas Asa. *Mark Twain: A Reference Guide*. Boston: G. K. Hall, 1977.

2931. ———. "Mark Twain: A Reference Guide First Annual Supplement." *American Literary Realism 1870–1910* 10 (August 1977): 327–412.

2932. ———. "Mark Twain: A Reference Guide: Second Annual Supplement." *American Literary Realism 1870–1910* 11 (Autumn 1978): 158–218.

2933. Thoreson, Trygve. "'Virtuous According to Their Lights': Women in Mark Twain's Early Work." *Mark Twain Journal* 21 (Fall 1983): 52–56.

2934. Towers, Tom H. "'Hateful Reality': The Failure of the Territory in *Roughing It*." *Western American Literature* 9 (May 1974): 3–15.

2935. Vallin, Marlene Boyd. *Mark Twain: Protagonist for the Popular Culture*. Westport, Conn.: Greenwood Press, 1992.

2936. Vorpahl, B.M. "'Very Much Like a Fire-Cracker': Owen Wister on Mark Twain." *Western American Literature* 6 (Summer 1971): 83–98.

2937. Wagenknecht, Edward. *Mark Twain: The Man and His Work*. Rev ed. Norman: University of Oklahoma Press, 1961.

2938. Walsh, Thomas M., and Thomas D. Zlatic. "Mark Twain and the Art of Memory." *American Literature* 53 (May 1981): 214–31.

2939. Warren, Robert Penn. "Mark Twain." *Southern Review* 8 (July 1972): 459–92.

2940. Watkins, T. H. "Mark Twain and His Mississippi." *American West* 10 (November 1973): 12–19.

2941. Wecter, Dixon. *Sam Clemens of Hannibal*. Ed. Elizabeth Wecter. Boston: Houghton Mifflin, 1952.

2942. Welland, Dennis. *The Life and Times of Mark Twain*. New York: Crescent Books, 1991.

2943. Wells, Daniel A. "Mark Twain in *The Overland Monthly* (1868–1900): An Annotated List of Citations." *American Literary Realism 1870–1910* 20 (Winter 1988): 85–92.

2944. West, Ray B., Jr. "Mark Twain's Idyl of Frontier America." *University of Kansas City Review* 15 (1948): 92–104.

2945. Wiggins, Robert A. *Mark Twain: Jackleg Novelist.* Seattle: University of Washington Press, 1964.

2946. Williams, George J., III. *Mark Twain: His Adventures at Aurora and Mono Lake.* Riverside, Calif.: Tree by the River, 1987.

2947. ————. *On the Road with Mark Twain in California and Nevada.* Carson City, Nev.: Tree by the River, 1993.

2948. Wilson, James D. "Religious and Esthetic Vision in Mark Twain's Early Career." *Canadian Review of American Studies* 17 (Summer 1986): 155–72.

2949. Wister, Owen. "In Homage to Mark Twain." *Harper's Magazine* 171 (October 1935): 547–66.

2950. Wonham, Henry B. *Mark Twain and the Art of the Tall Tale.* New York: Oxford University Press, 1992.

JAMES CLYMAN

2951. Walker, Don D. "James Clyman's 'Narrative': Its Significance in the Literature of the Fur Trade." *Possible Sack* 4 (May 1973): 1–8.

2952. Zochert, Donald. "'A View of the Sublime Awful': The Language of a Pioneer." *Western American Literature* 6 (Winter 1972): 251–57.

WALT COBURN

2953. Porter, Willard H. "Walt Coburn: Word Wrangler of the Old West." *Persimmon Hill* 8 (1978): 58–65.

WILLIAM T. COGGESHALL

2954. Andrews, William D. "William T. Coggeshall: 'Booster' of Western Literature." *Ohio History* 81 (Summer 1972): 210–20.

EMMETT COLEMAN

(Ishmael Reed)

2955. Boyer, Jay. *Ishmael Reed.* Western Writers Series, No. 110. Boise, Idaho: Boise State University, 1993.

2956. Fabre, Michel. "Postmodernist Rhetoric in Ishmael Reed's *Yellow Back Radio Broke Down (1969).*" *The Afro-American Novel Since 1960.* Eds. Peter Bruck and Wolfgang Karrer. Amsterdam: B. R. Grüner, 1982, 167–88.

2957. Hume, Kathryn. "Ishmael Reed and the Problematics of Control." *PMLA* 108 (May 1993): 506–18.

2958. Martin, Reginald. "An Interview with Ishmael Reed." *Review of Contemporary Fiction* 4 (Summer 1984): 176–87.

2959. Mason, Theodore O., Jr. "Performance, History, and Myth: The Problem of Ishmael Reed's *Mumbo-Jumbo*." *Modern Fiction Studies* 34 (Spring 1988): 97–109.

2960. Settle, Elizabeth A., and Thomas A. Settle. *Ishmael Reed: A Primary and Secondary Bibliography.* Boston: G.K. Hall, 1982.

WILL LEVINGTON COMFORT

2961. Powell, Lawrence Clark. "Southwest Classics Reread: Massacre and Vengeance in Apacheria." *Westways* 64 (May 1972): 55–59.

EVAN S. CONNELL

2962. Blaisdell, Gus. "After Ground Zero: The Writings of Evan S. Connell, Jr." *New Mexico Quarterly* 36 (Summer 1966): 181–207.

2963. Myers, Edward. "Notes from a Bottle Found on the Beach at Sausalito: An Interview with Evan S. Connell." *Literary Review* 35 (Fall 1991): 60–69.

INA COOLBRITH

2964. Graham, Ina Agnes. "My Aunt, Ina Coolbrith." *Pacific Historian* 17 (Fall 1973): 12–19.

2965. Hurst, Lannie. "Ina Coolbrith: Forgotten as Poet ... Remembered As Librarian." *PNLA Quarterly* 41 (Summer 1977): 4–11.

2966. Rhodelhamel, Josephine DeWitt, and Raymund F. Wood. *Ina Coolbrith: Librarian and Laureate of California.* Provo, Utah: Brigham Young University Press, 1973.

2967. Wood, Raymund F. "Librarian and Laureate: Ina Coolbrith of California." *Markham Review* 5 (1976): 35–39.

DANE COOLIDGE

2968. Ulph, Owen. "Dane Coolidge: An Introduction to the Work of a Now Obscure Western Writer and Photographer." *American West* 14 (November–December 1977): 32–47.

2969. Adams, Charles Hansford. *"The Guardian of the Law": Authority and Identity in James Fenimore Cooper.* University Park: Pennsylvania State University Press, 1990.

2970. Allen, Dennis W. "'By All the Truth of Signs': James Fenimore Cooper's *The Last of the Mohicans.*" *Studies in American Fiction* 9 (Autumn 1981): 159–79.

2971. Axelrad, Allan M. "History and Utopia: A Study of the World View of James Fenimore Cooper." Doctoral dissertation, University of Pennsylvania, 1974.

2972. ————. "The Order of the Leatherstocking Tales: D.H. Lawrence, David Noble, and the Iron Trap of History." *American Literature* 54 (May 1982): 189–211.

2973. Baym, Nina. "The Women of Cooper's Leatherstocking Tales." *American Quarterly* 23 (December 1971): 696–709.

2974. Beard, James Franklin. "James Fenimore Cooper." *Fifteen American Authors Before 1900: Bibliographic Essays on Research and Criticism.* Eds. Robert A. Rees and Earl N. Harbert. Madison: University of Wisconsin Press, 1971, 63–96.

2975. ————, ed. *The Letters and Journals of James Fenimore Cooper.* 6 vols. Cambridge, Mass.: Harvard University Press, 1960–68.

2976. Bewley, Marius. *The Eccentric Design.* New York: Columbia University Press, 1959, 47–100.

2977. Bier, Jesse. "Lapsarians on *The Prairie*: Cooper's Novel." *Texas Studies in Literature and Language* 4 (Spring 1962): 49–57.

2978. Burkhardt, Peggy Craven. "Fenimore Cooper's Literary Defenders." Doctoral dissertation, University of Iowa, 1971.

2979. Butler, Michael D. "Narrative Structure and Historical Process in *The Last of the Mohicans.*" *American Literature* 48 (May 1976): 117–39.

2980. Chase, Richard. *The American Novel and Its Tradition.* Garden City, N.Y.: Doubleday, 1957, 52–65.

2981. Clark, Robert, ed. *James Fenimore Cooper: New Critical Essays.* London: Vision Press, 1985.

2982. Cunningham, Mary, ed. *James Fenimore Cooper: A Re-Appraisal.* Cooperstown: New York State Historical Association, 1954.

2983. Darnell, Donald. *"The Deerslayer*: Cooper's Tragedy of Manners." *Studies in the Novel* 11 (Winter 1979): 406–15.

2984. Dekker, George. *James Fenimore Cooper: The Novelist.* London: Routledge and Kegan Paul, 1967.

2985. Engel, Leonard. "Space and Enclosure in Cooper and Peckinpah." *Journal of American Culture* 14 (Summer 1991): 86–93.

2986. Erwin, Robert. "The First of the Mohicans." *Antioch Review* 44 (Spring 1986): 149–60.

2987. Flanagan, John T. "The Authenticity of Cooper's *The Prairie.*" *Modern Language Quarterly* 2 (March 1941): 99–104.

2988. Franklin, Wayne. *The New World of James Fenimore Cooper.* Chicago: University of Chicago Press, 1982.

2989. Frederick, John T. "Cooper's Eloquent Indians." *PMLA* 71 (1956): 1004–17.

2990. Fussell, Edwin. *Frontier: American Literature and the American West.* Princeton, N.J.: Princeton University Press, 1965, 27–68.

2991. Gilbert, Susan Hull. "James Fenimore Cooper: The Historical Novel and the Critics." Doctoral dissertation, University of North Carolina, Chapel Hill, 1974.

2992. Gladsky, Thomas S. "The Beau Ideal and Cooper's *The Pioneers.*" *Studies in the Novel* 20 (Spring 1988): 43–54.

2993. ———. "James Fenimore Cooper and the Genteel Hero of Romance." Doctoral dissertation, University of North Carolina, Greensboro, 1975.

2994. Grossman, James. *James Fenimore Cooper.* New York: William Sloane, 1949.

2995. House, Kay Seymour. *Cooper's Americans.* Columbus: Ohio State University Press, 1965.

2996. Jones, Howard Mumford. *The Frontier in American Fiction.* Jerusalem: Magness, 1956, 26–50.

2997. Kaul, A. N. *The American Vision: Actual and Ideal in Nineteenth-Century Fiction.* New Haven, Conn.: Yale University Press, 1963, 84–138.

2998. Kelly, William P. "Inventing American History: Cooper and the Leatherstocking Tales." *CUNY English Forum* 1 (1985): 359–79.

2999. ———. *Plotting America's Past: Fenimore Cooper and the Leatherstocking Tales.* Carbondale: Southern Illinois University Press, 1983.

3000. Lawrence, D. H. *Studies in Classic American Literature.* New York: Thomas Seltzer, 1923, 50–92.

3001. Lewis, Merrill. "Lost-and-Found-in the Wilderness: The Desert Metaphor in Cooper's *The Prairie.*" *Western American Literature* 5 (Fall 1970): 195–204.

3002. Long, Robert Emmet. *James Fenimore Cooper.* New York: Crossroad/ Continuum, 1990.

3003. Lounsbury, Thomas R. *James Fenimore Cooper.* Boston: Houghton Mifflin, 1882.

3004. Martin, Terence. "Beginnings and Endings in the Leatherstocking Tales." *Nineteenth-Century Fiction* 33 (June 1978): 69–87.

3005. ————. "Surviving on the Frontier: The Doubled Consciousness of Natty Bumppo." *South Atlantic Quarterly* 75 (Autumn 1976): 447–59.

3006. May, Judith Stinson. "Family and Aggression in the Leatherstocking Series." Doctoral dissertation, University of Illinois, Urbana-Champaign, 1976.

3007. Melada, Ivan. "'Poor Little Talkative Christianity': James Fenimore Cooper and the Dilemma of the Christian on the Frontier." *Studies in the Novel* 18 (Fall 1986): 225–37.

3008. Merlock, Raymond J. "From Flintlock to Forty-Five: James Fenimore Cooper and the Popular Western Tradition in Fiction and Film." Doctoral dissertation, Ohio University, 1981.

3009. Meyer, William Claus. "The Development of Myth in the Leatherstocking Tales of James Fenimore Cooper." Doctoral dissertation, Ball State University, 1972.

3010. Mikkelsen, Hubert Aage. "James Fenimore Cooper's Fiction: Theory and Practice." Doctoral dissertation, St. John's University, 1976.

3011. Mills, Gordon. "The Symbolic Wilderness: James Fenimore Cooper and Jack London." *Nineteenth-Century Fiction* 13 (March 1959): 329–40.

3012. Motley, Warren. *The American Abraham: James Fenimore Cooper and the Frontier Patriarch.* New York: Cambridge University Press, 1987.

3013. Movalli, Charles Joseph. "Pride and Prejudice: James Fenimore Cooper's Frontier Fiction and His Social Criticism." Doctoral dissertation, University of Connecticut, 1972.

3014. Muszynska-Wallace, E. Soteris. "The Sources of *The Prairie.*" *American Literature* 21 (May 1949): 191–200.

3015. Nevius, Blake. *Cooper's Landscapes: An Essay on the Picturesque Vision.* Berkeley: University of California Press, 1976.

3016. Noble, David W. "Cooper, Leatherstocking and the Death of the American Adam." *American Quarterly* 16 (Fall 1964): 419–31.

3017. Øverland, Örm. *The Making and Meaning of an American Classic: James Fenimore Cooper's "The Prairie...."* New York: Humanities Press, 1973.

3018. Paine, Gregory. "The Indians of *The Leatherstocking Tales.*" *Studies in Philology* 23 (1926): 16–39.

3019. Pearce, Roy Harvey. "The Leatherstocking Tales Re-examined." *South Atlantic Quarterly* 46 (October 1947): 524–36.

3020. Peck, H. Daniel. *A World By Itself: The Pastoral Moment in Cooper's Fiction.* New Haven, Conn.: Yale University Press, 1977.

3021. Person, Leland S., Jr. "Cooper's Queen of the Woods: Judith Hutter in *The Deerslayer.*" *Studies in the Novel* 21 (Fall 1989): 253–67.

3022. Poulsen, Richard C. "Fenimore Cooper and the Exploration of the Great West." *Heritage of Kansas* 10 (Spring 1977): 15–24.

3023. Pound, Louise. "The Dialect of Cooper's Leatherstocking." *American Speech* 2 (1927): 479–88.

3024. Railton, Stephen. *Fenimore Cooper: A Study of His Life and Imagination.* Princeton, N.J.: Princeton University Press, 1978.

3025. Rans, Geoffrey. *Cooper's Leather-Stocking Novels: A Secular Reading.* Chapel Hill: University of North Carolina Press, 1991.

3026. Redekop, Ernest H., ed. "James Fenimore Cooper 1789–1989: Bicentennial Essays." *Canadian Review of American Studies* 20 (Winter 1989): 1–164.

3027. Ringe, Donald A. *James Fenimore Cooper.* Rev ed. Boston: Twayne, 1988.

3028. ———. *The Pictorial Mode: Space and Time in the Art of Bryant, Irving and Cooper.* Lexington: University Press of Kentucky, 1972.

3029. Robinson, Forrest G. "Uncertain Borders: Race, Sex, and Civilization in *The Last of the Mohicans.*" *Arizona Quarterly* 47 (Spring 1991): 1–28.

3030. Ross, Morton L. "Cooper's *The Pioneers* and the Ethnographic Impulse." *American Studies* 16 (Autumn 1975): 49–65.

3031. Rucker, Mary E. "Natural, Tribal and Civil Law in Cooper's *The Prairie.*" *Western American Literature* 12 (November 1977): 215–22.

3032. Russell, Jason A. "Cooper: Interpreter of the Real and Historical Indian." *Journal of American History* 23 (1930): 41–71.

3033. Schachterle, Lance, and Kent Ljungquist. "Fenimore Cooper's Literary Defenses: Twain and the Text of *The Deerslayer.*" *Studies in the American Renaissance.* Ed. Joel Myerson. Charlottesville: University Press of Virginia, 1988, 401–17.

3034. Sequeira, Isaac. "The Frontier Attack on Cooper, 1850–1900." *Indian Journal of American Studies* 8 (1978): 25–35.

3035. Sheppard, Keith S. "Natty Bumppo: Cooper's Americanized Adam." Doctoral dissertation, Wayne State University, 1973.

3036. Smith, Henry Nash. "Consciousness and Social Order: The Theme of Transcendence in the Leatherstocking Tales." *Western American Literature* 5 (Fall 1970): 177–94.

3037. ———. *Virgin Land: The American West as Symbol and Myth.* Cambridge, Mass.: Harvard University Press, 1950.

3038. Snook, Donald Gene. "Leadership and Order in the Border Novels of James Fenimore Cooper." Doctoral dissertation, University of North Carolina, Chapel Hill, 1974.

3039. Spiller, Robert E. *Fenimore Cooper: Critic of His Times.* New York: Minton, Balch, 1931.

3040. ———. *James Fenimore Cooper.* Minneapolis: University of Minnesota Press, 1965.

3041. Starobin, Christina Fijan. "Cooper's Critters: Animals in the Leatherstocking Tales." Doctoral dissertation, New York University, 1992.

3042. Stein, W. B. "*The Prairie*: A Scenario of the Wise Old Man." *Bucknell Review* 19 (Spring 1971): 15–36.

3043. Steinberg, Alan L. "James Fenimore Cooper: The Sentimental Frontier." *South Dakota Review* 15 (Spring 1977): 94–108.

3044. Suderman, Elmer F. "Cooper's Sense of Place in *The Prairie.*" *North Dakota Quarterly* 55 (Winter 1987): 159–64.

3045. Swann, Charles. "James Fenimore Cooper: Historical Novelist." *American Fiction: New Readings.* Ed. Richard Gray. Totowa, N.J.: Barnes Noble, 1983, 15–37.

3046. Test, George A., ed. *James Fenimore Cooper: His Country and His Art.* Oneonta: SUNY College of Oneonta, 1987.

3047. Tompkins, Jane P. "No Apologies for the Iroquois: A New Way to Read the Leatherstocking Novels." *Criticism* 23 (Winter 1981): 24–41.

3048. Twain, Mark. "Fenimore Cooper's Literary Offenses." *North American Review* 156 (1895): 1–12.

3049. Vance, William L. "'Man and Beast': The Meaning of Cooper's *The Prairie.*" *PMLA* 89 (1974): 323–31.

3050. Vlach, Gordon R. "Fenimore Cooper's Leatherstocking as Folk Hero." *New York Folklore Quarterly* 27 (December 1971): 323–38.

3051. Walker, Warren S. "Buckskin West: Leatherstocking at High Noon." *New York Folklore Quarterly* 24 (June 1968): 88–102.

3052. ———. *James Fenimore Cooper: An Introduction and Interpretation.* New York: Barnes and Noble, 1962.

3053. ————. *Plots and Characters in the Fiction of James Fenimore Cooper.* Hamden, Conn.: Shoe String Press, 1978.

3054. Wallace, James D. *Early Cooper and His Audience.* New York: Columbia University Press, 1986.

3055. Watts, Steven. "'Through a Glass Eye, Darkly': James Fenimore Cooper as Social Critic." *Journal of the Early Republic* 13 (Spring 1993): 55–74.

3056. West, Elliott. "James Fenimore Cooper and the Leatherstocking Saga." *American History Illustrated* 18 (May 1983): 8–15.

3057. Wilson, Jennie Lee. "The Heroes of James Fenimore Cooper." Doctoral dissertation, University of Kansas, 1975.

3058. Wyatt, Bryant N. "Cooper's Leatherstocking: Romance and the Limits of Character." *College Language Association Journal* 29 (March 1986): 295–308.

3059. Yasuna, Edward Carl. "The Power of the Lord in the Howling Wilderness: The Achievement of Thomas Cole and James Fenimore Cooper." Doctoral dissertation, Ohio State University, 1976.

3060. Zoellner, Robert H. "Conceptual Ambivalence in Cooper's Leatherstocking." *American Literature* 31 (January 1960): 397–420.

PAUL COREY

3061. McCown, Robert A. "Paul Corey's Mantz Trilogy." *Books at Iowa* 17 (November 1972): 15–19, 23–26.

EDWIN CORLE

3062. Beidler, Peter G. *Fig Tree John: An Indian in Fact and Fiction.* Tucson: University of Arizona Press, 1977.

3063. Shirley, Carl R. "Edwin Corle and the White Man's Indian." *Arizona Quarterly* 42 (Spring 1986): 68–76.

GREGORY CORSO

3064. Cook, Bruce. *The Beat Generation.* New York: Charles Scribner's Sons, 1971.

3065. Dullea, Gerard J. "Ginsberg and Corso: Image and Imagination." *Thoth* 2 (Winter 1971): 17–27.

3066. Howard, Richard. *Alone With America: Essays in the Art of Poetry in the United States.* New York: Atheneum, 1969, 57–64.

3067. Seigel, Catharine F. "Corso, Kinnell, and the Bomb." *University of Dayton Review* 18 (Summer 1987): 95–103.

3068. Skau, Michael. "'To Dream, Perchance to Be': Gregory Corso and Imagination." *University of Dayton Review* 20 (Summer 1989): 69–78.

3069. Wilson, Robert. *A Bibliography of Works by Gregory Corso.* New York: Phoenix Book Shop, 1966.

WILLIAM R. COX

3070. Garfield, Brian. "William R. Cox: A Profile." *Roundup Quarterly* 1 (December 1988): 7–11.

STEPHEN CRANE

3071. Beer, Thomas. *Stephen Crane: A Study in American Letters.* New York: Knopf, 1923.

3072. Bergon, Frank. *Stephen Crane's Artistry.* New York: Columbia University Press, 1975.

3073. ———, ed. *The Western Writings of Stephen Crane.* New York: New American Library, 1979.

3074. Berryman, John. *Stephen Crane.* New York: William Sloane, 1950.

3075. Burns, Shannon, and James A. Levernier. "Androgyny in Stephen Crane's 'The Bride Comes to Yellow Sky.'" *Research Studies* 45 (1977): 236–43.

3076. Cady, Edwin H. *Stephen Crane.* New York: Twayne, 1962.

3077. Cather, Willa. "When I Knew Stephen Crane." *Prairie Schooner* 23 (Fall 1949): 231–36.

3078. Church, Joseph. "The Determined Stranger in Stephen Crane's 'Blue Hotel.'" *Studies in the Humanities* 16 (December 1989): 99–110.

3079. Collins, Michael J. "Realism and Romance in the Western Stories of Stephen Crane." *Under the Sun: Myth and Realism in Western American Literature.* Ed. Barbara Howard Meldrum. Troy, N.Y.: Whitston, 1985, 138–48.

3080. Colvert, James B. *Stephen Crane.* San Diego: Harcourt Brace Jovanovich, 1984.

3081. Cook, Robert G. "Stephen Crane's 'The Bride Comes to Yellow Sky.'" *Studies in Short Fiction* 2 (Summer 1965): 368–69.

3082. Cox, James Trammell. "Stephen Crane as Symbolic Naturalist: An Analysis of 'The Blue Hotel.'" *Modern Fiction Studies* 3 (Summer 1957): 147–58.

3083. Deamer, Robert Glen. *The Importance of Place in the American Literature of Hawthorne, Thoreau, Crane, Adams, and Faulkner: American*

Writers, American Culture, and the American Dream. Lewiston, N.Y.: E. Mellen, 1990.

3084. ———. "Remarks on the Western Stance of Stephen Crane." *Western American Literature* 15 (Summer 1980): 123–41.

3085. ———. "Stephen Crane and Western Myth." *Western American Literature* 7 (Summer 1972): 11–23.

3086. Dean, James L. "The Wests of Howells and Crane." *American Literary Realism 1870–1910* 10 (Summer 1977): 254–66.

3087. Dooley, Patrick K. *Stephen Crane: An Annotated Bibliography of Secondary Scholarship.* New York: G.K. Hall, 1992.

3088. Feaster, John. "Violence and the Ideology of Capitalism: A Reconsideration of Crane's 'The Blue Hotel.'" *American Literary Realism, 1870–1910* 25 (Fall 1992): 74–94.

3089. Garland, Hamlin. "Stephen Crane as I Knew Him." *Yale Review* 3 (April 1914): 494–506.

3090. Gibson, Donald. *The Fiction of Stephen Crane.* Carbondale: Southern Illinois Press, 1968.

3091. Gross, David S. "The Western Stories of Stephen Crane." *Journal of American Culture* 11 (Winter 1988): 15–21.

3092. Halliburton, David. *The Color of Sky: A Study of Stephen Crane.* New York: Cambridge University Press, 1989.

3093. James, Overton Philip. "The 'Game' in 'The Bride Comes to Yellow Sky.'" *Xavier University Studies* 4 (March 1965): 3–11.

3094. Katz, Joseph, ed. *Stephen Crane in the West and Mexico.* Kent, Ohio: Kent State University Press, 1971.

3095. ———, ed. *Stephen Crane: The Blue Hotel.* Merrill Literary Casebook Series. Columbus, Ohio: Charles E. Merrill, 1970.

3096. Kinnamon, Jon M. "Henry James, the Bartender in Stephen Crane's 'The Blue Hotel.'" *Arizona Quarterly* 30 (Summer 1974): 160–66.

3097. Knapp, Bettina L. *Stephen Crane.* New York: Ungar, 1987.

3098. MacLean, H.N. "The Two Worlds of 'The Blue Hotel.'" *Modern Fiction Studies* 5 (Autumn 1959): 260–70.

3099. Marovitz, Sanford E. "Scratchy the Demon in 'The Bride Comes to Yellow Sky.'" *Tennessee Studies in English* 16 (1971): 137–40.

3100. Monteiro, George. "Stephen Crane's 'The Bride Comes to Yellow Sky.'" *Approaches to the Short Story.* Eds. Neil Isaacs and Louis Leiter. San Francisco: Chandler, 1963, 221–38.

3101. ———. "Stephen Crane's 'Yellow Sky' Sequel." *Arizona Quarterly* 30 (Summer 1974): 119–26.

3102. Paredes, Raymund A. "Stephen Crane and The Mexican." *Western American Literature* 6 (Spring 1971): 31–38.

3103. Robertson, Jamie. "Stephen Crane, Eastern Outsider in the West and Mexico." *Western American Literature* 13 (Fall 1978): 243–57.

3104. Satterwhite, Joseph N. "Stephen Crane's 'The Blue Hotel': The Failure of Understanding." *Modern Fiction Studies* 2 (Winter 1956–57): 238–41.

3105. Slote, Bernice. "Stephen Crane Willa Cather." *Serif* 6 (December 1969): 3–15.

3106. ———. "Stephen Crane in Nebraska." *Prairie Schooner* 43 (Summer 1969): 192–99.

3107. Solomon, Eric. *Stephen Crane: From Parody to Realism.* Cambridge, Mass.: Harvard University Press, 1967.

3108. Stallman, R. W. *Stephen Crane: A Biography.* New York: George Braziller, 1968.

3109. ———. *Stephen Crane: A Critical Bibliography.* Ames: Iowa State University Press, 1972.

3110. Sutton, Walter. "Pity and Fear in 'The Blue Hotel.'" *American Quarterly* 4 (Spring 1952): 73–78.

3111. Vorpahl, Ben M. "Murder by the Minute: Old and New in 'The Bride Comes to Yellow Sky.'" *Nineteenth–Century Fiction* 26 (September 1971): 196–218.

3112. West, Ray B., Jr. "The Use of Action in 'The Bride Comes to Yellow Sky.'" *The Art of Writing Fiction.* New York: Thomas Y. Crowell, 1968, 134–40.

3113. Wolford, Chester L. *The Anger of Stephen Crane: Fiction and the Epic Tradition.* Lincoln: University of Nebraska Press, 1983.

3114. ———. "Classic Myth Versus Realism in Crane's 'The Bride Comes to Yellow Sky.'" *Under the Sun: Myth and Realism in Western American Literature.* Ed. Barbara Howard Meldrum. Troy, N.Y.: Whitston, 1985, 128–36.

3115. ———. "The Eagle and the Crow: High Tragedy and Epic in 'The Blue Hotel.'" *Prairie Schooner* 51 (Fall 1977): 260–74.

3116. ———. *Stephen Crane: A Study of the Short Fiction.* Boston: Twayne, 1989.

3117. Wolter, Jürgen. "Drinking, Gambling, Fighting, Paying: Structure and Determinism in 'The Blue Hotel.'" *American Literary Realism 1870–1910* 12 (Autumn 1979): 295–98.

3118. Zanger, Jules. "Stephen Crane's 'Bride' as Countermyth of the West." *Great Plains Quarterly* 11 (Summer 1991): 157–65.

J. W. CRAWFORD

3119. Miller, Darlis A. *Captain Jack Crawford: Buckskin Poet, Scout, and Showman.* Albuquerque: University of New Mexico Press, 1993.

3120. Nolan, Paul T. "Captain Jack Crawford: Gold Searcher Turned Playwright." *Alaska Review* 1 (Spring 1964): 41–47.

3121. ———. "J. W. Crawford: Poet-Scout of the Black Hills." *South Dakota Review* 2 (Spring 1965): 40–47.

3122. ———. "J. W. Crawford's *The Dregs*: A New Mexico Pioneer in the Short Drama." *New Mexico Quarterly* 33 (Winter 1963–64): 388–403.

HOMER CROY

3123. O'Dell, Charles A. "Homer Croy, Maryville Writer: The First Forty Years 1883–1923." *Northwest Missouri State University Studies* 33 (August 1972): 3–59.

EUGENE CUNNINGHAM

3124. Pike, Donald G. "Eugene Cunningham: Realism and the Action Novel." *Western American Literature* 7 (Fall 1972): 224–29.

3125. Price, Carol. "The Novels of Eugene Cunningham: A Southwestern Perspective." *Southwest Heritage* 10 (Fall/Winter 1980–81).

J. V. CUNNINGHAM

3126. Kaye, Frances W. "The West as Desolation: J. V. Cunningham's *To What Strangers, What Welcome.*" *Southern Review* 11 (Autumn 1975): 820–24.

3127. Stall, Lindon. "The Trivial, Vulgar, and Exalted: The Poems of J. V. Cunningham." *Southern Review* 9 (October 1973): 1044–48.

3128. Stein, Robert A. "The Collected Poems and Epigrams of J. V. Cunningham." *Western Humanities Review* 27 (Winter 1973): 1–12.

JAMES OLIVER CURWOOD

3129. Elridge, Judith A. *James Oliver Curwood: God's Country and the Man.* Bowling Green, Ohio: Bowling Green State University Popular Press, 1993.

DAN CUSHMAN

3130. Beidler, Peter G. "The Popularity of Dan Cushman's *Stay Away, Joe* Among American Indians." *Arizona Quarterly* 33 (Autumn 1977): 216–40.

ELIZABETH CUSTER

3131. Leckie, Shirley A. *Elizabeth Bacon Custer and the Making of a Myth.* Norman: University of Oklahoma Press, 1993.

ROLLIN MALLORY DAGGETT

3132. Weisenburger, Francis Phelps. *Idol of the West: The Fabulous Career of Rollin Mallory Daggett.* Syracuse, N.Y.: Syracuse University Press, 1965.

RICHARD HENRY DANA

3133. Aaron, Daniel. "Two Boston Fugitives: Dana and Parkman." *American Literature, Culture, and Ideology: Essays in Memory of Henry Nash Smith.* Ed. Beverly R. Voloshin. New York: Peter Lang, 1990, 115–32.

3134. Allison, James. "Journal of a Voyage from Boston to the Coast of California by Richard Henry Dana, Jr." *American Neptune* 12 (July 1952): 177–86.

3135. Cox, James M. "Richard Henry Dana's *Two Years Before the Mast*: Autobiography Completing Life." *The Dialectic of Discovery: Essays on Teaching and Interpretation of Literature Presented to Lawrence E. Harvey.* Eds. John D. Lyons and Nancy J. Vickers. Lexington, Ky.: French Forum, 1984, 159–77.

3136. Egan, Hugh. "'One of Them': The Voyage of Style in Dana's *Two Years Before the Mast.*" *American Transcendental Quarterly* 2 (September 1988): 177–90.

3137. Gale, Robert L. *Richard Henry Dana.* New York: Twayne, 1969.

3138. Hart, James David. "Richard Henry Dana, Jr." Doctoral dissertation, Harvard University, 1936.

3139. Hill, Douglas B., Jr. "Richard Henry Dana, Jr. and *Two Years Before the Mast.*" *Criticism* 9 (Fall 1967): 312–25.

3140. Leverenz, David. "Hard, Isolate, Ruthless, and Patrician: Dana and Parkman." *Manhood and the American Renaissance.* Ithaca, N.Y.: Cornell University Press, 1989, 205–26.

3141. Lucid, Robert Francis. "The Composition, Reception, Reputation and Influence of *Two Years Before the Mast.*" Doctoral dissertation, University of Chicago, 1958.

3142. ———, ed. *The Journal of Richard Henry Dana, Jr.* 3 vols. Cambridge, Mass.: Belknap Press, 1968.

H. L. DAVIS

3143. Armstrong, George M. "H. L. Davis's *Beulah Land*: A Revisionist's Novel of Westering." *The Westering Experience in American Literature: Bicentennial Essays.* Eds. Merrill Lewis and L. L. Lee. Bellingham: Bureau for Faculty Research, Western Washington University, 1977, 144–53.

3144. ———. "An Unworn and Edged Tool: H. L. Davis's Last Word on the West, 'The Kettle of Fire.'" *Northwest Perspectives: Essays on the Culture of the Pacific Northwest.* Eds. Edwin R. Bingham and Glen A. Love. Seattle: University of Washington Press, 1979, 169–85.

3145. Bain, Robert. *H. L. Davis.* Western Writers Series, No. 11. Boise, Idaho: Boise State University, 1974.

3146. Brunvand, Jan Harold. "*Honey in the Horn* and 'Acres of Clams': The Regional Fiction of H. L. Davis." *Western American Literature* 2 (Summer 1967): 135–45.

3147. Bryant, Paul T. *H. L. Davis.* Boston: Twayne, 1978.

3148. ———. "H. L. Davis: Viable Uses for the Past." *Western American Literature* 3 (Spring 1968): 3–18.

3149. Clare, Warren L. "'Posers, Parasites, and Pismires': *Status Rerum*, by James Stevens and H. L. Davis." *Pacific Northwest Quarterly* 61 (January 1970): 22–30.

3150. Corning, Howard M. "The Prose and the Poetry of It." *Oregon Historical Quarterly* 74 (September 1973): 244–67.

3151. Corning, Richard H. "Unity and Point of View in *The Distant Music.*" *Western American Literature* 23 (August 1988): 113–20.

3152. Greiner, Francis F. "Voice of the West: Harold L. Davis." *Oregon Historical Quarterly* 66 (September 1965): 240–48.

3153. Hodgins, Francis E., Jr. "The Literary Emancipation of a Region." Doctoral dissertation, Michigan State University, 1957, 457–84.

3154. Jenkins, Eli Seth. "H. L. Davis: A Critical Study." Doctoral dissertation, University of Southern California, 1960.

3155. Jones, Phillip L. "The West of H. L. Davis." *South Dakota Review* 6 (Winter 1968–69): 72–84.

3156. Kellogg, George. "H. L. Davis, 1896–1960: A Bibliography." *Texas Studies in Language and Literature* 5 (Summer 1963): 294–303.

3157. Kohler, Dayton. "H. L. Davis: Writer in the West." *College English* 14 (December 1952): 133–40. Also in *English Journal* 41 (December 1952): 519–26.

3158. Potts, James T. "H. L. Davis' View: Reclaiming and Recovering the Land." *Oregon Historical Quarterly* 82 (Summer 1981): 117–51.

3159. ———. "The West of H. L. Davis." Doctoral dissertation, University of Arizona, 1977.

3160. Stevens, James. "'Bunk-Shanty Ballads and Tales': The Annual Society Address." *Oregon Historical Quarterly* 50 (December 1949): 235–42.

3161. ———. "The Northwest Takes to Poesy." *American Mercury* 16 (January 1929): 64–70.

ROBERT DAY

3162. Cansler, Loman D. "Last of the Big Cattle Drives." *Heritage of Kansas* 9 (Fall 1976): 10–19.

ANGIE DEBO

3163. McIntosh, Kenneth W. "Geronimo's Friend: Angie Debo and the New History." *Chronicles of Oklahoma* 66 (Summer 1988): 164–77.

WILLIAM DECKER

3164. Toth, Bill D. "The Fiction of William Decker: The Western Tradition in Context and Conflict." Doctoral dissertation, Union Institute, 1989.

JOANNE DE LONGCHAMPS

3165. Agonia, Barbara. "Nevada Images in the Poetry of Joanne de Longchamps." *Nevada Historical Society Quarterly* 28 (Spring 1985): 15–24.

ELLA DELORIA

3166. Deloria, Ella Cara, and Julian Rice. *Deer Women and Elk Men: The Lakota Narratives of Ella Deloria.* Albuquerque: University of New Mexico Press, 1992.

3167. Rice, Julian. *Deer Women and Elk Men: The Lakota Narratives of Ella Deloria.* Albuquerque: University of New Mexico Press, 1992.

3168. ———. *Ella Deloria's Iron Hawk.* Albuquerque: University of New Mexico Press, 1993.

3169. ———. *Ella Deloria's "The Buffalo People."* Albuquerque: University of New Mexico Press, 1994.

DAN DE QUILLE

3170. Berkove, Lawrence I. "The Literary Journalism of Dan De Quille." *Nevada Historical Society Quarterly* 28 (Winter 1985): 249–61.

3171. ———, ed. *The Fighting Horse of the Stanislaus.* Iowa City: University of Iowa Press, 1990.

3172. Dwyer, Richard A., and Richard E. Lingenfelter. *Dan De Quille, the Washoe Giant: A Biography and Anthology.* Reno: University of Nevada Press, 1990.

GEORGE H. DERBY

(John Phoenix)

3173. Stewart, George R. *John Phoenix, Esq., The Veritable Squibob: A Life of Captain George H. Derby, USA.* New York: Henry Holt, 1937; New York: Da Capo Press, 1969.

3174. Thompson, Mrs. Launt. "A Forgotten American Humorist." *United Service Magazine* (October 1902): 343–61.

BERNARD DEVOTO

3175. Bowen, Catherine Drinker, et al. *Four Portraits and One Subject: Bernard DeVoto.* Boston: Houghton Mifflin, 1963.

3176. Boyling, Mary Ellen F. "'No Mind is Ever of One Piece...': Bernard DeVoto's Literary Correspondence." Doctoral dissertation, Stanford University, 1973.

3177. Hacker, Peter R. "Shooting the Sheriff: A Look at Bernard DeVoto, Historian." *Utah Historical Quarterly* 58 (Summer 1990): 232–43.

3178. Jones, Alfred Haworth. "The Persistence of the Progressive Mind: The Case of Bernard DeVoto." *American Studies* 12 (Spring 1971): 37–48.

3179. Lee, Robert Edson. *From West to East.* Urbana: University of Illinois Press, 1966, 136–52.

3180. ———. "The Work of Bernard DeVoto, Introduction and Annotated Check List." Doctoral dissertation, State University of Iowa, 1957.

3181. Lemons, William Everett, Jr. "Western Historical Perspectives of DeVoto, Webb, Dobie, and Hyde." Doctoral dissertation, University of Minnesota, 1973.

3182. Rawls, James J. "Bernard DeVoto and the Art of Popular History." *Pacific Historian* 25 (Spring 1981): 46–51.

3183. Sawey, Orlan. *Bernard DeVoto*. New York: Twayne, 1969.

3184. Stegner, Wallace. "Bernard DeVoto." *Western American Literature* 20 (August 1985): 151–64.

3185. ———. "DeVoto's Western Adventures." *American West* 10 (November 1973): 20–27.

3186. ———. "Historian by Serendipity." *American Heritage* 24 (August 1973): 28–32.

3187. ———. *The Sound of Mountain Water*. Garden City, N.Y.: Doubleday, 1969, 202–22; New York: E.P. Dutton, 1980, 250–75.

3188. ———. *The Uneasy Chair: A Biography of Bernard DeVoto*. Garden City, N.Y.: Doubleday, 1974.

3189. ———, ed. *The Letters of Bernard DeVoto*. Garden City, N.Y.: Doubleday, 1975.

3190. W[alker], D[on] D. "The Dogmas of DeVoto." *Possible Sack* 2 (August 1971): 6–8; 3 (November 1971): 1–7; (February 1972): 1–4; (March 1972): 14–18.

AL DEWLEN

3191. Merren, John. "Character and Theme in the Amarillo Novels of Al Dewlen." *Western Review* 6 (Spring 1969): 3–9.

JOAN DIDION

3192. Brady, H. Jennifer. "Points West, Then and Now: The Fiction of Joan Didion." *Contemporary Literature* 20 (Autumn 1979): 452–70.

3193. Chabot, C. Barry. "Joan Didion's *Play It As It Lays* and the Vacuity of the 'Here and Now.'" *Critique* 21 (No. 3, 1981): 53–60.

3194. Coale, Samuel. "Didion's Disorder: An American Romancer's Art." *Critique* 25 (Spring 1984): 160–70.

3195. Felton, Sharon. "Joan Didion: A Writer of Scope and Substance." *Hollins Critic* 26 (October 1989): 1–10.

3196. ———, ed. *The Critical Response to Joan Didion*. Westport, Conn.: Greenwood Press, 1994.

3197. Friedman, Ellen G., ed. *Joan Didion: Essays and Conversations*. Princeton, N.J.: Ontario Review Press, 1984.

3198. Geherin, David J. "Nothingness and Beyond: Joan Didion's *Play It As It Lays*." *Critique* 16 (No. 1, 1974): 64–78.

3199. Henderson, Katherine Usher. *Joan Didion*. New York: Ungar, 1981.

3200. Loris, Michelle Carbone. *Innocence, Loss, and Recovery in the Art of Joan Didion*. New York: Peter Lang, 1989.

3201. Mallon, Thomas. "The Limits of History in the Novels of Joan Didion." *Critique* 21 (No. 3, 1981): 43–52.

3202. Mosley, Merritt. "Joan Didion's Symbolic Landscapes." *South Carolina Review* 21 (Spring 1989): 55–64.

3203. Muggli, Mark Z. "The Poetics of Joan Didion's Journalism." *American Literature* 59 (October 1987): 402–21.

3204. Olendorf, Donna. "Joan Didion: A Working Checklist, 1955–1980." *Bulletin of Bibliography* 38 (January–March 1981): 32–44.

3205. Stineback, David C. "On the Limits of Fiction." *Midwest Quarterly* 14 (Summer 1973): 339–48.

3206. Stout, Janis P. *Strategies of Reticence: Silence and Meaning in the Works of Jane Austen, Willa Cather, Katherine Anne Porter, and Joan Didion*. Charlottesville: University of Virginia, 1990.

3207. Winchell, Mark Royden. *Joan Didion*. Rev ed. Boston: Twayne, 1989.

3208. Wolff, Cynthia Griffin. "*Play It as It Lays*: Didion and the Diver Heroine." *Contemporary Literature* 24 (Winter 1983): 480–95.

ANNIE DILLARD

3209. Johnson, Sandra Humble. "Literary Epiphany in the Work of Annie Dillard." Doctoral dissertation, Bowling Green State University, 1989.

MAYNARD DIXON

3210. Starr, Kevin. "Painterly Poet, Poetic Painter: The Dual Art of Maynard Dixon." *California Historical Quarterly* 56 (Winter 1977–78): 290–309.

J. FRANK DOBIE

3211. Abernethy, Francis Edward. *J. Frank Dobie*. Southwest Writers Series, No. 1. Austin, Tex.: Steck-Vaughn, 1967.

3212. Alsmeyer, Henry Louis, Jr. "J. Frank Dobie's Attitude Towards Physical Nature." Doctoral dissertation, Texas A M University, 1973.

3213. Bode, Winston. *A Portrait of Pancho: The Life of a Great Texan, J. Frank Dobie*. Austin, Tex.: Pemberton Press, 1965.

3214. Dobie, Bertha. "Dobie's Sunday Pieces." *Southwest Review* 50 (Spring 1965): 114–19.

3215. Dykes, Jeff. "A Dedication to the Memory of James Frank Dobie, 1888–1964." *Arizona and the West* 8 (Autumn 1966): 203–6.

3216. Graham, Don. "J. Frank Dobie: A Reappraisal." *Southwestern Historical Quarterly* 92 (July 1988): 1–15.

3217. Hogue, Alexandre. "A Portrait of Pancho Dobie." *Southwest Review* 50 (Spring 1965): 101–13.

3218. McVicker, Mary Louis. *The Writings of J. Frank Dobie: A Bibliography.* Lawton, Okla.: Museum of the Great Plains, 1968.

3219. "Memories of J. Frank Dobie and Walter Prescott Webb." *Southwestern Historical Quarterly* 92 (July 1988). Special issue.

3220. Peterson, Vernon. "J. Frank Dobie as 'The Father of Song.'" *South Dakota Review* 13 (Summer 1975): 73–81.

3221. Pilkington, Tom. *The Works of J. Frank Dobie.* Cassette. Deland, Fla.: Everett/Edwards, 1974.

3222. Stone, Paul C. "Orality Against Text: The Central Tension in J. Frank Dobie's Literary Career." *Southwestern American Literature* 19 (Spring 1994): 45–52.

3223. Tinkle, Lon. *An American Original: The Life of Frank J. Dobie.* Boston: Little, Brown, 1978.

3224. White, Victor. "Paisano and a Chair." *Southwest Review* 56 (Spring 1971): 188–96.

3225. Yarborough, Ralph W. *Frank Dobie: Man and Friend.* Washington, D.C.: Potomac Corral of the Westerners, 1967.

E. L. DOCTOROW

3226. Arnold, Marilyn. "History as Fate in E. L. Doctorow's Tale of a Western Town." *South Dakota Review* 18 (Spring 1980): 53–63.

3227. Bevilacqua, Winifred Farrant. "The Revision of the Western in E. L. Doctorow's *Welcome to Hard Times.*" *American Literature* 61 (March 1989): 78–95.

3228. Emblidge, David. "Marching Backward into the Future." *Southwest Review* 62 (Autumn 1977): 397–409.

3229. Levine, Paul. *E. L. Doctorow.* New York: Methuen, 1985.

3230. Parks, John G. *E. L. Doctorow.* New York: Continuum, 1991.

3231. Shelton, Frank W. "E. L. Doctorow's *Welcome to Hard Times*: The Western and the American Dream." *Midwest Quarterly* 25 (Autumn 1983): 7–17.

3232. Tanner, Stephen L. "Rage and Order in Doctorow's *Welcome to Hard Times*." *South Dakota Review* 22 (Autumn 1984): 79–85.

3233. Thompson, James R., and Carol C. Harter. *E. L. Doctorow*. Boston: Twayne, 1990.

IVAN DOIG

3234. Bevis, William W. "Doig's House of Sky." *Ten Tough Trips: Montana Writers and the West*. Seattle: University of Washington Press, 1990, 161–70.

3235. Robbins, William G. "The Historian as Literary Craftsman: The West of Ivan Doig." *Pacific Northwest Quarterly* 78 (October 1987): 134–40.

3236. Simonson, Harold P. "At the Edge of America with James Swan and Ivan Doig." *Pacific Northwest Forum*, 2d Ser. 1 (Spring 1988): 3–9.

3237. Simpson, Elizabeth. "'Bring Forth the King's Remembrancer!': Folklore as History in the Work of Ivan Doig." *Old West–New West: Centennial Essays*. Ed. Barbara Howard Meldrum. Moscow: University of Idaho Press, 1993, 230–40.

3238. ———. *Earthlight, Wordfire: The Works of Ivan Doig*. Moscow: University of Idaho Press, 1992.

IGNATIUS DONNELLY

3239. Anderson, David D. *Ignatius Donnelly*. Boston: Twayne, 1980.

3240. Axelrad, Allan M. "Ideology and Utopia in the Works of Ignatius Donnelly." *American Studies* 12 (Fall 1971): 47–65.

3241. Baker, J. Wayne. "Populist Themes in the Fiction of Ignatius Donnelly." *American Studies* 14 (Fall 1973): 65–83.

3242. Bovee, John R. "Ignatius Donnelly as a Man of Letters." Doctoral dissertation, Washington State University, 1968.

3243. Patterson, John. "From Yoeman to Beast: Images of Blackness in *Caesar's Column*." *American Studies* 12 (Fall 1971): 21–31.

3244. Ridge, Martin. *Ignatius Donnelly: The Portrait of a Politician*. Chicago: University of Chicago Press, 1962.

3245. Wright, David E. "The Art and Vision of Ignatius Donnelly." Doctoral dissertation, Michigan State University, 1974.

ED DORN

3246. Alpert, Barry. "Ed Dorn: An Interview." *Vort* 1 (Fall 1972): 2–20.

3247. Davidson, Michael. "To Eliminate the Draw: Edward Dorn's *Slinger*." *American Literature* 53 (November 1981): 443–64.

3248. Doherty, Thomas. "Poetry and History: Ed Dorn's *Recollections of Gran Apacheria*." *Southwestern American Literature* 8 (Spring 1983): 12–20.

3249. Dresman, Paul C. "Between Here and Formerly: A Study of History in the Work of Edward Dorn." Doctoral dissertation, University of California, San Diego, 1980.

3250. Lockwood, William J. "Ed Dorn's Mystique of the Real: His Poems for North America." *Contemporary Literature* 19 (Winter 1978): 58–79.

3251. McPheron, William. *Edward Dorn*. Western Writers Series, No. 85. Boise, Idaho: Boise State University, 1988.

3252. Okada, Roy K. "An Interview with Edward Dorn." *Contemporary Literature* 15 (Summer 1974): 297–314.

3253. Paul, Sherman. *The Lost America of Love: Rereading Robert Creeley, Edward Dorn, and Robert Duncan*. Baton Rouge: Louisiana State University Press, 1981.

3254. Wesling, Donald. "A Bibliography on Edward Dorn for America." *Parnassus* 5 (Spring–Summer 1977): 142–60.

3255. ———, ed. *Internal Resistances: The Poetry of Edward Dorn*. Berkeley: University of California Press, 1985.

MICHAEL DORRIS

3256. Bonetti, Kay. "An Interview with Louise Erdrich and Michael Dorris." *Missouri Review* 11 (1988): 79–99.

3257. Chavkin, Allan, and Nancy Feye Chavkin, eds. *Conversations with Louise Erdrich and Michael Dorris*. Jackson: University Press of Mississippi, 1993.

3258. Matchie, Thomas. "Exploring the Meaning of Discovery in *The Crown of Columbus*." *North Dakota Quarterly* 59 (Fall 1991): 243–50.

J. HYATT DOWNING

3259. Wadden, Anthony T. "J. Hyatt Downing: The Chronicle of an Era." *Books at Iowa* (April 1968): 11–23.

3260. ———. "Late to the Harvest: The Fiction of J. Hyatt Downing." *Western American Literature* 6 (Fall 1971): 203–14.

GLENN WARD DRESBACH

3261. Ford, Edsel. "Glenn Ward Dresbach: The New Mexico Years, 1915–1920." *New Mexico Quarterly* 34 (Spring 1964): 78–96.

NORMAN DUBIE

3262. Fay, Julie, and David Wojahn. "Norman Dubie; Dark Spiraling Figures: An Interview." *American Poetry Review* 7 (July/August 1978): 7–11.

LOIS DUNCAN

3263. Kies, Cosette. *Presenting Lois Duncan*. New York: Twayne, 1993.

ROBERT DUNCAN

3264. Cooley, Dennis. "Keeping the Green: The Vegetation of Renewal in Robert Duncan's Poetry." Doctoral dissertation, University of Rochester, 1972.

3265. Davidson, Robert M. "Disorders of the Net: The Poetry of Robert Duncan." Doctoral dissertation, State University of New York, Buffalo, 1973.

3266. Faas, Ekbert. *Young Robert Duncan: Portrait of the Poet as Homosexual in Society*. Santa Barbara, Calif.: Black Sparrow Press, 1983.

3267. Finkelstein, Norman M. "Robert Duncan, Poet of the Law." *Sagetrieb* 2 (Spring 1983): 75–88.

3268. Johnson, Mark Andrew. *Robert Duncan*. Boston: Twayne, 1988.

3269. ———. "Robert Duncan's 'Momentous Inconclusions.'" *Sagetrieb* 2 (Summer/Fall 1984): 71–84.

3270. Paul, Sherman. *The Lost America of Love: Rereading Robert Creeley, Edward Dorn, and Robert Duncan*. Baton Rouge: Louisiana State University Press, 1981.

3271. "Robert Duncan." *Sagetrieb* 4 (Fall, Winter 1985). Special issue.

3272. "Robert Duncan: A Special Issue." *Ironwood 22* (1983).

3273. Robert Duncan issue. *Southern Review* 21 (January 1985): 1–62.

3274. Weber, Robert C. "Roots of Language: The Major Poetry of Robert Duncan." Doctoral dissertation, University of Wisconsin, 1973.

ABIGAIL SCOTT DUNIWAY

3275. Moynihan, Ruth Barnes. *Rebel for Rights: Abigail Scott Duniway*. New Haven, Conn.: Yale University Press, 1983.

3276. Ross, Nancy Wilson. *Westward the Women.* New York: Alfred A. Knopf, 1945, 137–54.

JOHN GREGORY DUNNE

3277. Winchell, Mark Royden. *John Gregory Dunne.* Western Writers Series, No. 76. Boise, Idaho: Boise State University, 1986.

JOHN C. DUVAL

3278. Anderson, John Q. *John C. Duval: First Texas Man of Letters.* Southwest Writers Series, No. 2. Austin, Tex.: Steck-Vaughn, 1967.
3279. Dobie, J. Frank. *John C. Duval: First Texas Man of Letters: His Life and Some of His Unpublished Writings.* Dallas: Southern Methodist University Press, 1939.

EVA EMERY DYE

3280. Ellingsen, Melva G. "Eva and Clio; or, the Muse Meets Its Mistress." *Call Number* 19 (Fall 1957): 17–22.
3281. Powers, Alfred. *History of Oregon Literature.* Portland: Metropolitan Press, 1935, 404–14.
3282. Swanson, Kimberly. "Eva Emery Dye and the Romance of Oregon History." *Pacific Historian* 29 (Winter 1985): 59–68.
3283. Taber, Ronald W. "Sacagawea and the Suffragettes: An Interpretation of a Myth." *Pacific Northwest Quarterly* 58 (January 1967): 7–13.

WILLIAM EASTLAKE

3284. Bamberger, W.C. *The Work of William Eastlake: An Annotated Bibliography and Guide.* Eds. Boden Clarke and Daryl F. Mallett. San Bernardino, Calif.: Borgo Press, 1993.
3285. Graham, Don. "William Eastlake's First Novel: An Account of the Making of *Go in Beauty.*" *Western American Literature* 16 (Spring 1981): 27–37.
3286. Haslam, Gerald. *William Eastlake.* Southwest Writers Series, No. 36. Austin, Tex.: Steck-Vaughn, 1970.
3287. ———. "William Eastlake: Portrait of the Artist as Shaman." *Western Review* 8 (Spring 1971): 2–13.
3288. Lewis, Linda K. "William Eastlake." *Bulletin of Bibliography* 41 (March 1984): 6–11.

3289. McCaffery, Larry. "Absurdity and Oppositions in William Eastlake's Southwestern Novels." *Critique* 19 (No. 2, 1977): 62–76.

3290. Milton, John R. "The Land as Form in Frank Waters and William Eastlake." *Kansas Quarterly* 2 (Spring 1970): 104–9.

3291. *Review of Contemporary Fiction* 3 (Spring 1983): 4–105. Special issue on William Eastlake.

3292. Wylder, Delbert E. "The Novels of William Eastlake." *New Mexico Quarterly* 34 (Summer 1964): 188–203.

CHARLES ALEXANDER EASTMAN

3293. Copeland, Marion W. *Charles Alexander Eastman (Ohiyesa).* Western Writers Series, No. 33. Boise, Idaho: Boise State University, 1978.

3294. O'Brien, Lynne Woods. *Plains Indian Autobiographies.* Western Writers Series, No. 10. Boise, Idaho: Boise State College, 1973.

3295. Stensland, Anna Lee. "Charles Alexander Eastman: Sioux Storyteller and Historian." *American Indian Quarterly* 3 (Autumn 1977): 199–208.

3296. Wilson, Raymond. *Ohiyesa: Charles Eastman, Santee Sioux.* Urbana: University of Illinois Press, 1983.

ELAINE GOODALE EASTMAN

3297. Alexander, Ruth Ann. "Elaine Goodale Eastman and the Failure of the Feminist Protestant Ethic." *Great Plains Quarterly* 8 (Spring 1988): 89–101.

3298. Graber, Kay, ed. *The Memoirs of Elaine Goodale Eastman, 1885–91.* Lincoln: University of Nebraska Press, 1978.

EDWARD EGGLESTON

3299. Randel, William Pierce. *Edward Eggleston.* Gloucester, Mass.: Peter Smith, 1962.

3300. ———. "Edward Eggleston (1837–1902)." *American Literary Realism 1870–1910* 1 (Fall 1967): 36–38.

3301. Roth, John D. "Down East and Southwestern Humor in the Western Novels of Edward Eggleston." Doctoral dissertation, University of Alabama, 1971.

3302. Morris, Gregory L. "When East Meets West: The Passions of Landscape and Culture in Gretel Ehrlich's *Heart Mountain.*" *Great Plains Quarterly* 12 (Winter 1992): 50–59.

3303. Wackett, James. "An Interview with Gretel Ehrlich." *North Dakota Quarterly* 58 (Summer 1990): 121–27.

LOREN EISELEY

3304. Brill, Naomi. "Loren Eiseley and the Human Condition." *Prairie Schooner* 61 (Fall 1987): 64–69.

3305. Carlisle, E. Fred. "The Literary Achievement of Loren Eiseley." *Prairie Schooner* 61 (Fall 1987): 38–45.

3306. ———. *Loren Eiseley, the Development of a Writer.* Urbana: University of Illinois Press, 1983.

3307. ———. "The Poetic Achievement of Loren Eiseley." *Prairie Schooner* 51 (Summer 1977): 111–29.

3308. Carrithers, Gale H., Jr. *Mumford, Tate, Eiseley: Watchers in the Night.* Baton Rouge: Louisiana State University Press, 1991.

3309. Christensen, Erleen J. "Loren Eiseley, Student of Time." *Prairie Schooner* 61 (Fall 1987): 28–37.

3310. Christianson, Gale E. *Fox at the Wood's Edge: A Biography of Loren Eiseley.* New York: Henry Holt, 1990.

3311. Franke, Robert G. "Blue Plums and Smoke: Loren Eiseley's Perception of Time." *Western American Literature* 24 (August 1989): 147–50.

3312. Gamble, David E. "Loren Eiseley: Wilderness and Moral Transcendence." *Midwest Quarterly* 33 (Autumn 1991): 108–23.

3313. Heidtmann, Peter. *Loren Eiseley: A Modern Ishmael.* Hamden, Conn.: Archon Books, 1991.

3314. Kassebaum, L. Harvey. "To Survive Our Century: The Narrative Voice of Loren Eiseley: An Essay in Appreciation." Doctoral dissertation, University of Pennsylvania, 1979.

3315. Schwartz, James M. "The 'Immense Journey' of an Artist: The Literary Technique and Style of Loren Eiseley." Doctoral dissertation, Ohio State University, 1977.

3316. ———. "Loren Eiseley: The Scientist as Literary Artist." *Georgia Review* 31 (Winter 1977): 855–71.

ANNE ELLIS

3317. Matlack, Anne. "The Spirit of Anne Ellis." *Colorado Quarterly* 4 (1955–56): 61–72.

RALPH ELLISON

3318. Bishop, Jack. *Ralph Ellison.* New York: Chelsea House, 1988.

3319. Bucco, Martin. "Ellison's Invisible West." *Western American Literature* 10 (November 1975): 237–38.

LOULA GRACE ERDMAN

3320. Sewell, Ernestine. "An Interview with Loula Grace Erdman." *Southwestern American Literature* 2 (Spring 1972): 33–41.

3321. ———. *Loula Grace Erdman.* Southwest Writers Series, No. 33. Austin, Tex.: Steck-Vaughn, 1970.

LOUISE ERDRICH

3322. Barry, Nora, and Mary Prescott. "The Triumph of the Brave: *Love Medicine*'s Holistic Vision." *Critique* 30 (Winter 1989): 123–38.

3323. Bonetti, Kay. "An Interview with Louise Erdrich and Michael Dorris." *Missouri Review* 11 (1988): 79–99.

3324. Catt, Catherine M. "Ancient Myth in Modern America: The Trickster in the Fiction of Louise Erdrich." *Platte Valley Review* 19 (Winter 1991): 71–81.

3325. Chavkin, Allan, and Nancy Feye Chavkin, eds. *Conversations with Louise Erdrich and Michael Dorris.* Jackson: University of Mississippi, 1993.

3326. DePriest, Maria. "Necessary Fictions: The Revisioned Subjects of Louise Erdrich and Alice Walker." Doctoral dissertation, University of Oregon, 1991.

3327. Flavin, Louise. "Louise Erdrich's *Love Medicine*: Loving Over Time and Distance." *Critique* 31 (Fall 1989): 55–64.

3328. Larson, Sidner. "The Fragmentation of a Tribal People in Louise Erdrich's *Tracks*." *American Indian Culture and Research Journal* 17 (No. 2, 1993): 1–13.

3329. Magalaner, Marvin. "Louise Erdrich: Of Cars, Time, and the River." *American Women Writing Fiction: Memory, Identity, Family, Space.* Ed. Mickey Pearlman. Lexington: University Press of Kentucky, 1989, 95–112.

3330. Matchie, Thomas. "Exploring the Meaning of Discovery in *The Crown of Columbus*." *North Dakota Quarterly* 59 (Fall 1991): 243–50.

3331. Rainwater, Catherine. "Reading between Worlds: Narrativity in the Fiction of Louise Erdrich." *American Literature* 62 (September 1990): 405–22.

3332. Ruppert, James. "Mediation and Multiple Narrative in *Love Medicine*." *North Dakota Quarterly* 59 (Fall 1991): 229–42.

3333. Woodward, Pauline Groetz. "New Tribal Forms: Community in Louise Erdrich's Fiction." Doctoral dissertation, Tufts University, 1991.

WINSTON ESTES

3334. Frye, Bob J. "Winston Estes' Minor Classic: *Another Part of the House*." *Southwestern American Literature* 15 (Fall 1989): 26–38.

3335. ———. *Winston M. Estes*. Western Writers Series, No. 103. Boise, Idaho: Boise State University, 1992.

HELEN EUSTIS

3336. Burns, Stuart L. "St. Petersburg Re-Visited: Helen Eustis and Mark Twain." *Western American Literature* 5 (Summer 1970): 99–112.

MAX EVANS

3337. Milton, John R., ed. *Three West: Conversations with Vardis Fisher, Max Evans, Michael Straight*. Vermillion, S.Dak.: Dakota Press, 1970.

WILLIAM EVERSON

(Brother Antoninus)

3338. Bartlett, Lee. *William Everson*. Western Writers Series, No. 67. Boise, Idaho: Boise State University, 1985.

3339. ———. *William Everson: The Life of Brother Antoninus.* New York: New Directions, 1988.

3340. ———, ed. *Benchmark and Blaze: The Emergence of William Everson.* Metuchen, N.J.: Scarecrow Press, 1979.

3341. Cargas, H.J. "An Interview with Brother Antoninus." *Renascence* 18 (Spring 1966): 137–45.

3342. Carpenter, David A. *The Rages of Excess: The Life and Poetry of William Everson*. Bristol, Ind.: Wyndham Hall Press, 1987.

3343. Dill, Vicky Schreiber. "The Books of William Everson." *Books of Iowa* 28 (1978): 9–24.

3344. Rizzo, Fred F. "A Study of the Poetry of William Everson." Doctoral dissertation, University of Oklahoma, 1966.

3345. Stafford, William E., ed. *The Achievement of Brother Antoninus: A Comprehensive Selection of His Poems with a Critical Introduction.* Glenview, Ill.: Scott, Foresman, 1967.

FREDERICK FAUST

(Max Brand)

3346. Bloodworth, William A., Jr. *Max Brand.* Boston: Twayne, 1993.

3347. ———. "Max Brand's West." *Western American Literature* 16 (Fall 1981): 177–91.

3348. Chapman, Edgar L. "The Image of the Indian in Max Brand's Pulp Western Novels." *Heritage of Kansas* 11 (Spring 1978): 16–45.

3349. Easton, Jane Faust. *Memories of the '20s and '30s: Growing up in Florence, New York & Los Angeles.* Santa Barbara, Calif.: Easton, 1979.

3350. Easton, Robert. *Max Brand: The Big "Westerner."* Norman: University of Oklahoma Press, 1970.

3351. Nolan, William F., ed. *Max Brand, Western Giant: The Life and Times of Frederick Schiller Faust.* Bowling Green, Ohio: Bowling Green State University Popular Press, 1985.

3352. Reynolds, Quentin. *The Fiction Factory.* New York: Random House, 1955.

3353. Richardson, Darrell C., ed and comp. *Max Brand: The Man and His Work.* Los Angeles: Fantasy, 1952.

3354. Schoolcraft, John, ed. *The Notebooks and Poems of "Max Brand."* New York: Dodd, Mead, 1957.

FREDERICK FEIKEMA

(Frederick Feikema Manfred)

3355. Arthur, Anthony. "Manfred, Neihardt, and Hugh Glass: Variations on an American Epic." *Where the West Begins.* Eds. Arthur R. Huseboe and William Geyer. Sioux Falls, S.Dak.: Center for Western Studies Press, 1978, 99–109.

3356. Austin, James C. "Legend, Myth and Symbol in Frederick Manfred's *Lord Grizzly.*" *Critique* 6 (Winter 1963–64): 122–30.

3357. Bebeau, Don. "A Search for Voice: A Sense of Place in *The Golden Bowl.*" *South Dakota Review* 7 (Winter 1969–70): 79–86.

3358. Byrd, Forrest Mickey. "Prologemenon to Frederick Manfred." Doctoral dissertation, University of Nebraska, Lincoln, 1975.

3359. Flora, Joseph. *Frederick Manfred.* Western Writers Series, No. 13. Boise, Idaho: Boise State University, 1974.

3360. ———. "Siouxland Panorama: Frederick Manfred's *Green Earth.*" *Midwestern Miscellany* 7 (1979): 56–63.

3361. Huseboe, Arthur R., and Nancy Owen Nelson, eds. *The Selected Letters of Frederick Manfred 1932–1954.* Lincoln: University of Nebraska Press, 1988.

3362. Lee, James W. "An Interview in Minnesota with Frederick Manfred." *Studies in the Novel* 5 (Fall 1973): 358–82.

3363. McAllister, Mick. "'Wolf That I Am...': Animal Symbology in *Lord Grizzly* and *Scarlet Plume.*" *Western American Literature* 18 (May 1983): 21–31.

3364. McCord, Nancy Nelson. "Manfred's Elof Lofblom." *Western American Literature* 16 (Summer 1981): 125–34.

3365. Manfred, Frederick. "On Being a Western American Writer." *Prime Fathers.* Salt Lake City: Howe Brothers, 1988, 122–38.

3366. Milton, John R. "Frederick Feikema Manfred." *Western Review* 22 (Spring 1958): 181–98.

3367. ———. "*Lord Grizzly*: Rhythm, Form and Meaning in the Western Novel." *Western American Literature* 1 (Spring 1966): 6–14.

3368. ———. *The Novel of the American West.* Lincoln: University of Nebraska Press, 1980, 160–94.

3369. ———, ed. *Conversations with Frederick Manfred.* Salt Lake City: University of Utah Press, 1974.

3370. Moen, Ole O. "The Voice of the Siouxland: Man and Nature in Frederick Manfred's Writing." Doctoral dissertation, University of Minnesota, 1978.

3371. Mulder, Rodney J., and John H. Timmerman. *Frederick Manfred: A Bibliography and Publishing History.* Sioux Falls, S. Dak.: Center for Western Studies, Augustana College, 1981.

3372. Nelson, Nancy Owen. "Frederick Manfred and the Anglo-Saxon Oral Tradition." *Western American Literature* 19 (February 1985): 263–74.

3373. ———. "Frederick Manfred: Bard of Siouxland." *The Prairie Frontier.* Eds. Sandra Looney, Arthur R. Huseboe and Geoffrey Hunt. [Sioux Falls, S.Dak.]: Nordland Heritage Foundation, 1984, 53–75.

3374. ———. "'Sweet Dakota Land': The Manfred Letters and the Inception of *The Golden Bowl.*" *South Dakota Review* 30 (Spring 1992): 61–70.

3375. Oppewall, Peter. "Manfred and Calvin College." *Where the West Begins.* Eds. Arthur R. Huseboe and William Geyer. Sioux Falls, S. Dak.: Center for Western Studies Press, 1978, 86–98.

3376. Quantic, Diane Dufva. "Frederick Manfred's *The Golden Bowl*: Myth and Reality in the Dust Bowl." *Western American Literature* 25 (February 1991): 297–309.

3377. Roth, Russell. "The Inception of a Saga: Frederick Manfred's 'Buckskin Man.'" *South Dakota Review* 7 (Winter 1969–70): 87–99.

3378. Smith, Robert W. "Frederick Manfred, Outsize Man and Writer." *North Dakota Quarterly* 55 (Spring 1987): 139–50.

3379. *South Dakota Review* 7 (Winter 1969–70). Special issue on Manfred.

3380. Spies, George H. "John Steinbeck's *The Grapes of Wrath* and Frederick Manfred's *The Golden Bowl*: A Comparative Study." Doctoral dissertation, Ball State University, 1973.

3381. Ter Matt, Cornelius John. "Three Novelists and a Community: A Study of American Novelists with Dutch Calvinist Origins." Doctoral dissertation, University of Michigan, 1963.

3382. Timmerman, John H. "Harmony in Dynamic Pattern: Frederick Manfred's Novelistic Art." *Southwest Review* 68 (Spring 1983): 153–61.

3383. "West of the Mississippi: An Interview with Frederick Manfred." *Critique* 2 (Winter 1959): 35–56.

3384. Westbrook, Max. "*Riders of Judgment*: An Exercise in Ontological Criticism." *Western American Literature* 12 (May 1977): 41–51.

3385. Whipp, Leslie. "Frederick Manfred's *The Golden Bowl*–The Novel and Novelist Emerging." *South Dakota Review* 27 (Autumn 1989): 54–73.

3386. ———. "Frederick Manfred's *The Wind Blows Free*: Autobiographical Mythology." *South Dakota Review* 27 (Summer 1989): 100–128.

3387. Wright, Robert C. *Frederick Manfred.* Boston: Twayne, 1979.

3388. Wylder, Delbert E. "Frederick Manfred: The Quest of an Independent Writer." *Books at Iowa* 31 (November 1979): 16–31.

3389. ———. "Manfred's Indian Novel." *South Dakota Reivew* 7 (Winter 1969–70): 100–109.

EDNA FERBER

3390. Brenni, Vito J., and Betty Lee Spencer. "Edna Ferber: A Selected Bibliography." *Bulletin of Bibliography* 22 (September–December 1958): 152–56.

3391. Gilbert, Julie Goldsmith. *Ferber: A Biography.* Garden City, N.Y.: Doubleday, 1978.

3392. Horowitz, Steven P., and Miriam J. Landsman. "The Americanization of Edna: A Study of Ms. Ferber's Jewish American Identity." *Studies in American Jewish Literature* 2 (1982): 69–80.

3393. Shaughnessy, Mary Rose. *Women and Success in American Society in the Works of Edna Ferber.* New York: Gordon, 1976.

ERNA FERGUSSON

3394. Powell, Lawrence C. "Erna Fergusson and *Dancing Gods.*" *Westways* 63 (March 1971): 13–17, 62.

3395. Remley, David A. *Erna Fergusson.* Southwest Writers Series, No. 24. Austin, Tex.: Steck-Vaughn, 1969.

HARVEY FERGUSSON

3396. Cohen, Saul. *Harvey Fergusson: A Checklist.* Los Angeles: University of California at Los Angeles Library, 1965.

3397. Folsom, James K. *Harvey Fergusson.* Southwest Writers Series, No. 20. Austin, Tex.: Steck-Vaughn, 1969.

3398. Gish, Robert F. *Frontier's End: The Life and Literature of Harvey Fergusson.* Lincoln: University of Nebraska Press, 1988.

3399. ———. "'Pretty, But is it History?' The Legacy of Harvey Fergusson's *Rio Grande.*" *New Mexico Historical Review* 60 (April 1985): 173–92.

3400. McGinity, Sue Simmons. "Harvey Fergusson's Use of Animal Imagery in Characterizing Spanish-American Women." *Western Review* 8 (Winter 1971): 46–50.

3401. Milton, John R. "Conversation with Harvey Fergusson." *South Dakota Review* 9 (Spring 1971): 39–45; 26 (Winter 1988): 56–63.

3402. ———. *The Novel of the American West.* Lincoln: University of Nebraska Press, 1980, 230–63.

3403. "Modern Man and Harvey Fergusson – A Symposium." *New Mexico Quarterly* 6 (May 1936): 123–35.

3404. Pearson, Lorene. "Harvey Fergusson and the Crossroads." *New Mexico Quarterly* 21 (Autumn 1951): 334–55.

3405. Pilkington, William T. *Harvey Fergusson.* Boston: Twayne, 1975.

3406. Powell, Lawrence Clark. "Southwest Classics Reread: *Wolf Song.*" *Westways* 64 (January 1972): 22–24, 41, 58–59. Reprinted in *Southwest Classics* (Los Angeles: Ward Ritchie Press, 1974).

3407. Robinson, Cecil. *With the Ears of Strangers: The Mexican in American Literature.* Tucson: University of Arizona Press, 1963; rev ed. *Mexico and the Hispanic Southwest in American Literature.* Tucson: University of Arizona Press, 1977.

LAWRENCE FERLINGHETTI

3408. Butler, J.A. "Ferlinghetti: Dirty Old Man?" *Renascence* 18 (Spring 1966): 115–23.

3409. Cherkovski, Neeli. *Ferlinghetti: A Biography.* Garden City, N.Y.: Doubleday, 1979.

3410. Cook, Bruce. *The Beat Generation.* New York: Charles Scribner's Sons, 1971.

3411. Ianni, L.A. "Lawrence Ferlinghetti's Fourth Person Singular and the Theory of Relativity." *Wisconsin Studies in Contemporary Literature* 8 (Summer 1967): 392–406.

3412. Lin, Maurice Yaofu. "Children of Adam: Ginsberg, Ferlinghetti and Snyder in the Emerson-Whitman Tradition." Doctoral dissertation, University of Minnesota, 1973.

3413. Morgan, Bill. *Lawrence Ferlinghetti: A Comprehensive Bibliography to 1980.* New York: Garland, 1982.

3414. Skau, Michael. *"Constantly Risking Absurdity": The Writings of Lawrence Ferlinghetti.* Troy, N.Y.: Whitston, 1989.

3415. ———, "The Poet as Poem: Ferlinghetti's Songs of Myself." *Concerning Poetry* 20 (1987): 57–71.

3416. Smith, Larry. *Lawrence Ferlinghetti: Poet at Large.* Carbondale: Southern Illinois University Press, 1983.

THOMAS HORNSBY FERRIL

3417. Elkins, Andrew. "The Ecological Vision of Thomas Hornsby Ferril." *Western American Literature* 27 (August 1992): 109–20.

3418. Firebaugh, Joseph J. "Pioneer in the Parlor Car: Thomas Hornsby Ferril." *Prairie Schooner* 21 (Spring 1947): 69–85.

3419. Richards, Robert F. "Literature and Politics." *Colorado Quarterly* 19 (Summer 1970): 97–106.

3420. ———. "The Long Dimension of Ferril's Poetry." *Colorado Quarterly* 3 (Summer 1954): 22–38.

3421. ———. "The Poetry of Thomas Hornsby Ferril." Doctoral dissertation, Columbia University, 1961.

3422. ———. "Thomas Hornsby Ferril: A Biographical Sketch." *Western American Literature* 9 (November 1974): 205–14.

3423. ———. "Thomas Hornsby Ferril and the Problems of the Poet in the West." *Kansas Quarterly* 2 (Spring 1970): 110–16.

3424. Saucerman, James R. "Alien Myth and Natural Myth in the Poetry of Thomas Hornsby Ferril." *Under the Sun: Myth and Realism in Western American Literature.* Ed. Barbara Howard Meldrum. Troy, N.Y.: Whitston, 1985, 106–26.

3425. Scherting, Jack. "An Approach to the Western Poetry of Thomas Hornsby Ferril." *Western American Literature* 7 (Fall 1972): 179–90.

3426. ———. *The Works of Thomas Hornsby Ferril.* Cassette. Deland, Fla.: Everett/Edwards, 1974.

3427. Trusky, A. Thomas. *Thomas Hornsby Ferril.* Western Writers Series, No. 6. Boise, Idaho: Boise State College, 1973.

LESLIE FIEDLER

3428. Bellman, S.I. "The American Artist as European Frontiersman: Leslie Fiedler's *The Second Stone.*" *Critique* 6 (Winter 1963): 131–43.

3429. ———. "The Frontiers of Leslie Fiedler." *Southwest Review* 48 (Winter 1963): 86–89.

3430. Bluefarb, Sam. "Pictures of the Anti-Stereotype: Leslie Fiedler's Triptych, The Last Jew in America." *College Language Association Journal* 18 (1975): 412–21.

3431. Larson, Charles R. "Leslie Fiedler: The Critic and the Myth, the Critic as Myth." *Literary Review* 14 (Winter 1970–71): 133–43.

3432. Schultz, Max F. *Radical Sophistication: Studies in Contemporary Jewish-American Novelists.* Athens: Ohio University Press, 1969, 154–72.

3433. Winchell, Mark Royden. *Leslie Fiedler.* Boston: Twayne, 1985.

EUGENE FIELD

3434. Conrow, Robert. *Field Days.* New York: Charles Scribner's Sons, 1974.

3435. Smith, Duane A. "Eugene Field: Political Satirist." *Colorado Quarterly* 22 (1974): 495–508.

CLAY FISHER

See Henry Wilson Allen

3436. *American Book Collector* 14 (September 1963): 7–39. Special Fisher number.

3437. Arrington, Leonard J., and Jon Haupt. "The Mormon Heritage of Vardis Fisher." *Brigham Young University Studies* 18 (Fall 1977): 27–47.

3438. Bishop, John Peale. "The Strange Case of Vardis Fisher." *The Collected Essays of John Peale Bishop.* New York: Charles Scribner's Sons, 1948, 56–65.

3439. Chatterton, Wayne. *Vardis Fisher: The Frontier and Regional Works.* Western Writers Series, No. 1. Boise, Idaho: Boise State College, 1972.

3440. Crandall, Allen. *Fisher of the Antelope Hills.* Manhattan, Kans.: Crandall Press, 1949.

3441. Davis, David Brion. "'Children of God': A Historian's Evaluation." *Western Humanities Review* 8 (Winter 1953): 49–56.

3442. Day, George F. *The Uses of History in the Novels of Vardis Fisher.* New York: Revisionist Press, 1976.

3443. Fisher, Vardis. "The Western Writer and the Eastern Establishment." *Western American Literature* 1 (Winter 1967): 244–59.

3444. Flora, Joseph M. "Concealment in Vardis Fisher's *Orphans in Gethsemane*." *Redneck Review of Literature* 18 (Spring 1990): 5–12.

3445. ———. *Vardis Fisher.* New York: Twayne, 1965.

3446. ———. "Vardis Fisher and the Mormons." *Dialogue* 4 (Autumn 1969): 48–55.

3447. ———. "Vardis Fisher and Wallace Stegner: Teacher and Student." *Western American Literature* 5 (Summer 1970): 121–28.

3448. ———. "Westering and Women: A Thematic Study of Kesey's *One Flew Over the Cuckoo's Nest* and Fisher's *Mountain Man*." *Heritage of Kansas* 10 (Spring 1977): 3–14.

3449. Grover, Dorys C. *A Solitary Voice: Vardis Fisher, A Collection of Essays.* New York: Revisionist Press, 1973.

3450. ———. "A Study of the Poetry of Vardis Fisher." Doctoral dissertation, Washington State University, 1970.

3451. ———. "Vardis Fisher: The Antelope People Sonnets." *Texas Quarterly* 17 (Spring 1974): 97–106.

3452. ———. *The Works of Vardis Fisher.* Cassette. Deland, Fla.: Everett/Edwards, 1974.

3453. Hunsaker, Kenneth B. "The Twentieth Century Mormon Novel." Doctoral dissertation, Pennsylvania State University, 1968.

3454. Kellogg, George. "Vardis Fisher: A Bibliography." *Western American Literature* 5 (Spring 1970): 45–64.

3455. McAllister, Mick. "You Can't Go Home: Jeremiah Johnson and the Wilderness." *Western American Literature* 13 (Spring 1978): 35–49.

3456. Meldrum, Barbara. "Vardis Fisher's Antelope People: Pursuing an Elusive Dream." *Northwest Perspectives: Essays on the Culture of the Pacific Northwest.* Eds. Edwin R. Bingham and Glen A. Love. Seattle: University of Washington Press, 1979, 153–66.

3457. ———. "Western Writers and the River: Guthrie, Fisher, Stegner." *Pacific Northwest Forum* 4 (Summer 1979): 21–26.

3458. Milton, John R. *The Novel of the American West.* Lincoln: University of Nebraska Press, 1980, 117–59.

3459. ———. *Three West: Conversations with Vardis Fisher, Max Evans, Michael Straight.* Vermillion, S. Dak.: Dakota Press, 1970.

3460. Morton, Beatrice K. "An Early Stage of Fisher's Journey to the East, *Passions Spin the Plot.*" *South Dakota Review* 18 (Spring 1980): 43–52.

3461. Rein, David. *Vardis Fisher: Challenge to Evasion.* Chicago: Black Cat Press, Normandie House, 1937.

3462. Snell, George. *Shapers of American Fiction.* New York: E.P. Dutton, 1943, 276–88.

3463. Sonnichsen, C. L. "Vardis Fisher and the WLA." *South Dakota Review* 28 (Summer 1990): 8–21.

3464. Strong, Lester. "Vardis Fisher Revisited." *South Dakota Review* 24 (Autumn 1986): 25–37.

3465. Taber, Ronald W. "Sacajawea and the Suffragettes: An Interpretation of a Myth." *Pacific Northwest Quarterly* 58 (January 1967): 7–13.

3466. ———. "Vardis Fisher and the *Idaho Guide*: Preserving Culture for the New Deal." *Pacific Northwest Quarterly* 59 (April 1968): 68–76.

3467. ———. "Vardis Fisher: March 31, 1895–July 9, 1968." *Idaho Yesterdays* 12 (Fall 1968): 2–8.

3468. ———. "Vardis Fisher: New Directions for the Historical Novel." *Western American Literature* 1 (Winter 1967): 285–96.

3469. Thomas, Alfred Krupp. "The Epic of Evolution, Its Etiology and Art: A Study of Vardis Fisher's *Testament of Man.*" Doctoral dissertation, Pennsylvania State University, 1967.

3470. Woodward, Tim. *Tiger on the Road: The Life of Vardis Fisher.* Caldwell, Idaho: Caxton, 1989.

JOHN FISKE

3471. Saum, Lewis O. "John Fiske and the West." *Huntington Library Quarterly* 48 (Winter 1985): 47–68.

F. SCOTT FITZGERALD

3472. Gross, Barry. "Back West: Time and Place in *The Great Gatsby.*" *Western American Literature* 8 (Spring–Summer 1973): 3–13.

3473. Reiter, Joan Govan. "F. Scott Fitzgerald: Hollywood as Literary Material." Doctoral dissertation, Northwestern University, 1972.

JOHN GOULD FLETCHER

3474. Aldrich, Ann R. "Regionalism in the Writings of John Gould Fletcher." Doctoral dissertation, University of Arkansas, 1975.

3475. Morton, Bruce. *John Gould Fletcher: A Bibliography.* Kent, Ohio: Kent State University Press, 1979.

3476. Stephens, Edna Buell. *John Gould Fletcher.* New York: Twayne, 1967.

TIMOTHY FLINT

3477. Flint, Timothy. *Recollections of the Last Ten Years.* Boston, 1826; New York: Alfred A. Knopf, 1932.

3478. Folsom, James K. *Timothy Flint.* New York: Twayne, 1965.

3479. Kirkpatrick, John Ervin. *Timothy Flint.* Cleveland: Arthur H. Clark, 1911

3480. Lee, Robert Edson. *From West to East.* Urbana: University of Illinois Press, 1966, 39–54.

3481. Morris, Robert L. "Three Arkansas Travelers." *Arkansas Historical Quarterly* 4 (Autumn 1945): 215–30.

3482. Turner, Arlin. "James K. Paulding and Timothy Flint." *Mississippi Valley Historical Review* 34 (June 1947): 105–11.

3483. Vorpahl, Ben Merchant. "The Eden Theme and Three Novels by Timothy Flint." *Studies in Romanticism* 10 (Spring 1971): 105–29.

ROBERT FLYNN

3484. Cleary, Michael. "The Western as Comic Literature: Robert Flynn's *North to Yesterday.*" *North Dakota Quarterly* 50 (Spring 1982): 14–29.

3485. Frye, Bob J. "An Artful Quest for *Humanitas*: Satire in the Fiction of Robert Flynn." *Southwestern American Literature* 17 (Fall 1991): 6–16.

3486. Holland, Richard A. "Archives of Southwestern Writers: Robert Flynn's *North to Yesterday* Correspondence." *Southwestern American Literature* 19 (Fall 1993): 7–26.

MARY HALLOCK FOOTE

3487. Armitage, Shelley. "The Illustrator as Writer: Mary Hallock Foote and the Myth of the West." *Under the Sun: Myth and Realism in Western American Literature*. Ed. Barbara Howard Meldrum. Troy, N.Y.: Whitston, 1985, 150–74.

3488. Benn, Mary Lou. "Mary Hallock Foote: Early Leadville Writer." *Colorado Magazine* 33 (April 1956): 93–103.

3489. ———. "Mary Hallock Foote in Idaho." *University of Wyoming Publications* 20 (July 1956): 157–78.

3490. Cragg, Barbara. "Mary Hallock Foote's Images of the Old West." *Landscape* 24 (Winter 1980): 42–47.

3491. Etulain, Richard W. "Mary Hallock Foote: A Checklist." *Western American Literature* 10 (May 1975): 59–65.

3492. ———. "Mary Hallock Foote (1847–1938)." *American Literary Realism 1870–1910* 5 (Spring 1972): 145–50.

3493. Johnson, Lee Ann. *Mary Hallock Foote*. Boston: Twayne, 1980.

3494. Maguire, James H. *Mary Hallock Foote*. Western Writers Series, No. 2. Boise, Idaho: Boise State College, 1972.

3495. Paul, Rodman W. "When Culture Came to Boise: Mary Hallock Foote in Idaho." *Idaho Yesterdays* 20 (Summer 1976): 2–12.

3496. ———, ed. *A Victorian Gentlewoman in the Far West: The Reminiscences of Mary Hallock Foote*. San Marino, Calif.: Huntington Library, 1972.

3497. Taft, Robert. *Artists and Illustrators of the Old West: 1850–1900*. New York: Charles Scribner's Sons, 1953, 172–75, 345–47.

GEORGE C. FRASER

3498. Jett, Stephen C. "The Journals of George C. Fraser '93: Early Twentieth-Century Travels in the South and Southwest." *Princeton University Library Chronicle* 35 (1974): 290–308.

JOHN CHARLES FRÉMONT

3499. Rolle, Andrew F. "Exploring an Explorer: Psychohistory and John Charles Frémont." *Pacific Historical Review* 51 (May 1982): 135–63.

3500. ———. *John Charles Frémont: Character as Destiny*. Norman: University of Oklahoma Press, 1991.

ANDREW GARCIA

3501. Bevis, William W. "Garcia's Tough Trip." *Ten Tough Trips: Montana Writers and the West*. Seattle: University of Washington Press, 1990, 36–48.

WAYNE GARD

3502. Adams, Ramon F. *Wayne Gard: Historian of the West*. Southwest Writers Series, No. 31. Austin, Tex.: Steck-Vaughn, 1970.

HAMLIN GARLAND

3503. Ahnebrink, Lars. *The Beginnings of Naturalism in American Fiction, 1891–1903*. Upsala, 1950, 63–89; New York: Russell Russell, 1961.

3504. Alsen, Eberhard. "Hamlin Garland's First Novel: *A Spoil of Office*." *Western American Literature* 4 (Summer 1969): 91–105.

3505. Arvidson, Lloyd A., ed. *Centennial Tributes and a Checklist of the Hamlin Garland Papers in the University of Southern California Library*. Los Angeles: University of Southern California Library, 1962.

3506. Bryer, Jackson R., and Eugene Harding. *Hamlin Garland and the Critics: An Annotated Bibliography*. Troy, N.Y.: Whitston, 1973.

3507. Carter, Joseph L. "Hamlin Garland and the Western Myth." Doctoral dissertation, Kent State University, 1973.

3508. ———. "Hamlin Garland's Liberated Women." *American Literary Realism 1870–1910* 6 (Summer 1973): 255–58.

3509. Clark, Michael. "Herbert Spencer, Hamlin Garland, and *Rose of Dutcher's Coolly*." *American Literary Realism* 1870–1910 17 (Autumn 1984): 203–8.

3510. Culbert, Gary Allen. "Hamlin Garland's Image of Woman: An Allegiance to Ideality." Doctoral dissertation, University of Wisconsin, Madison, 1974.

3511. Davis, Jack L. "Hamlin Garland's Indians and the Quality of Civilized Life." *Where the West Begins*. Eds. Arthur R. Huseboe and William Geyer. Sioux Falls, S.Dak.: Center for Western Studies Press, 1978, 51–62.

3512. Duffey, Bernard. "Hamlin Garland's 'Decline' from Realism." *American Literature* 25 (March 1953): 69–74.

3513. Evans, T. Jeff. "The Return Motif as a Function of Realism in *Main-Travelled Roads*." *Kansas Quarterly* 5 (Fall 1973): 33–40.

3514. Fite, Gilbert. "Hamlin Garland and the Farmers' Frontier." *Heritage of Kansas* 10 (Summer 1977): 3–9.

3515. Fleeger, Wayne Robert. "Garland's Middle Period: Romantic Fiction, 1898–1916." Doctoral dissertation, Drake University, 1977.

3516. French, Warren. "What Shall We Do About Hamlin Garland?" *American Literary Realism 1870–1910* 3 (Fall 1970): 283–89.

3517. Garland, Hamlin. "The West in Literature." *Arena* 6 (1892): 669–76.

3518. Gish, Robert F. "Desertion and Rescue on the Dakota Plains: Hamlin Garland in the Land of the Straddle-Bug." *South Dakota Review* 16 (Autumn 1978): 30–45.

3519. ————. "Hamlin Garland's Dakota: History and Story." *South Dakota History* 9 (Summer 1979): 193–209.

3520. ————. "Hamlin Garland's Northwest Travels: 'Camp' Westering." *The Westering Experience in American Literature: Bicentennial Essays.* Eds. Merrill Lewis and L.L. Lee. Bellingham: Bureau for Faculty Research, Western Washington University, 1977, 94–105.

3521. ————. *Hamlin Garland: The Far West.* Western Writers Series, No. 24. Boise, Idaho: Boise State University, 1976.

3522. Harrison, Stanley R. "Hamlin Garland and the Double Vision of Naturalism." *Studies in Short Fiction* 6 (Fall 1969): 548–56.

3523. Harver, Hyla Hope. "The Influence of Scientific Theories of Expression on Garland's *Main Travelled Roads*." Doctoral dissertation, University of Tulsa, 1973.

3524. Herrscher, Walter. "The Natural Environment in Hamlin Garland's *Main Travelled Roads*." *Old Northwest* 11 (Spring, Summer 1985): 35–50.

3525. Higgins, J. E. "A Man from the Middle Borders: Hamlin Garland's Diaries." *Wisconsin Magazine of History* 46 (Summer 1963): 295–302.

3526. Hiscoe, David W. "Feeding and Consuming in Garland's *Main-Travelled Roads*." *Western American Literature* 15 (May 1980): 3–15.

3527. Holloway, Jean. *Hamlin Garland: A Biography.* Austin: University of Texas Press, 1960.

3528. Holsinger, Paul M. "Hamlin Garland's Colorado." *Colorado Magazine* 44 (Winter 1967): 1–10.

3529. Jacobson, Marcia. "The Flood of Remembrance and the Stream of Time: Hamlin Garland's *Boy Life on the Prairie*." *Western American Literature* 17 (November 1982): 227–41.

3530. Kaye, Frances W. "Hamlin Garland: A Closer Look at the Later Fiction." *North Dakota Quarterly* 43 (1976): 45–56.

3531. ———. "Hamlin Garland and Frederick Philip Grove: Self-Conscious Chronicles of the Pioneers." *Canadian Review of American Studies* 10 (Spring 1979): 31–39.

3532. ———. "Hamlin Garland's Feminism." *Women and Western American Literature*. Eds. Helen Winter Stauffer and Susan J. Rosowski. Troy, N.Y.: Whitston, 1982, 135–61.

3533. Koerner, James D. "Comment on 'Hamlin Garland's "Decline" from Realism.'" *American Literature* 26 (November 1954): 427–32.

3534. Larkin, Sharon. "The Warning of the American Agrarian Myth: Garland and the Garden." *Heritage of Kansas* 9 (Spring 1976): 19–27.

3535. Love, Glen A. "Back-Trailing Toward the Future: The Progressive Hamlin Garland." *New Americans: The Westerner and the Modern Experience in the American Novel*. Lewisburg, Pa.: Bucknell University Press, 1982, 67–106.

3536. McCullough, Joseph B. *Hamlin Garland*. Boston: Twayne, 1978.

3537. MacDonald, Bonney. "Eastern Imaginings of the West in Hamlin Garland's 'Up the Coolly' and 'God's Ravens.'" *Western American Literature* 28 (November 1993): 209–30.

3538. Meyer, Roy W. "Hamlin Garland and the American Indian." *Western American Literature* 2 (Summer 1967): 109–25.

3539. Miller, Charles T. "Hamlin Garland's Retreat from Realism." *Western American Literature* 1 (Summer 1966): 119–29.

3540. Morgan, H. Wayne. *American Writers in Rebellion: From Mark Twain to Dreiser*. New York: Hill and Wang, 1965.

3541. Motley, Warren. "Hamlin Garland's *Under the Wheel*: Regionalism Unmasking America." *Modern Drama* 26 (December 1983): 477–85.

3542. Nagel, James, ed. *Critical Essays on Hamlin Garland*. Boston: G. K. Hall, 1982.

3543. Neumann, Edwin J. "Hamlin Garland and the Mountain West." Doctoral dissertation, Northwestern University, 1951.

3544. Pilkington, John. "Fuller, Garland, Taft, and the Art of the West." *Publications in Language and Literature* 8 (Fall 1972, supplement): 39–56.

3545. Pizer, Donald. "Hamlin Garland (1860–1940)." *American Literary Realism 1870–1910* 1 (Fall 1967): 45–51.

3546. ———. "Hamlin Garland's *A Son of the Middle Border*: An Appreciation." *South Atlantic Quarterly* 65 (Autumn 1966): 448–59.

3547. ———. "Hamlin Garland's *A Son of the Middle Border*: Autobiography as Art." *Essays in American and English Literature Presented to Bruce Robert McElderry, Jr.* Ed. Max F. Schultz, et al. Athens: Ohio University Press, 1967, 76–107.

3548. ———. *Hamlin Garland's Early Work and Career.* Berkeley: University of California Press, 1960.

3549. ———. "Hamlin Garland's *Main Travelled Roads* Revisited." *South Dakota Review* 29 (Spring 1991): 53–67.

3550. ———, ed. *Hamlin Garland's Diaries.* San Marino, Calif.: Huntington Library, 1968.

3551. Reamer, Owen J. "Garland and the Indians." *New Mexico Quarterly* 34 (Autumn 1964): 257–80.

3552. Rocha, Mark William. "The Feminization of Failure in American Historiography: The Case of the Invisible Drama in the Life of Hamlin Garland (1860–1940)." Doctoral dissertation, University of Southern California, 1988.

3553. Saum, Lewis O. "Hamlin Garland and Reform." *South Dakota Review* 10 (Winter 1972–73): 36–62.

3554. Savage, George Howard. "'Synthetic Evolution' and the American West: The Influence of Herbert Spencer on the Later Novels of Hamlin Garland." Doctoral dissertation, University of Tulsa, 1974.

3555. Silet, Charles L.P. *Henry Blake Fuller and Hamlin Garland–A Reference Guide.* Boston: G. K. Hall, 1977

3556. Simpson, Claude M., Jr. "Hamlin Garland's Decline." *Southwest Review* 26 (Winter 1941): 223–34.

3557. Taylor, Walter F. *The Economic Novel in America.* Chapel Hill: University of North Carolina Press, 1942, 148–83.

3558. Underhill, Lonnie E., and Daniel F. Littlefield, Jr., eds. *Hamlin Garland's Observations on the American Indian 1895–1905.* Tucson: University of Arizona Press, 1976.

3559. Wagner, William D. "The Short Stories of Hamlin Garland." Doctoral dissertation, Bowling Green State University, 1972.

3560. Walcutt, Charles Child. *American Literary Naturalism, A Divided Stream.* Minneapolis: University of Minnesota Press, 1956, 53–65 and passim.

3561. Whitford, Kathryn. "Crusader Without a Cause: An Examination of Hamlin Garland's Middle Border." *Midcontinent American Studies Journal* 6 (Spring 1965): 61–72.

HECTOR LEWIS GARRARD

(Lewis H. Garrard)

3562. Foster, Edward Halsey. *Josiah Gregg and Lewis H. Garrard.* Western Writers Series, No. 28. Boise, Idaho: Boise State University, 1977.

3563. Meyer, Roy W. "New Light on Lewis Garrard." *Western Historical Quarterly* 6 (July 1975): 261–78.

3564. Powell, Lawrence Clark. "Southwest Classics Reread: Two for the Santa Fe Trail." *Westways* 64 (October 1972): 56–59, 73–74.

FRIEDRICH GERSTÄCKER

3565. Bukey, E.B. "Frederick Gerstaecker and Arkansas." *Arkansas Historical Quarterly* 31 (Spring 1972): 3–14.

3566. Kolb, Alfred. "Friedrich Gerstäcker and the American Dream." *Modern Language Studies* 5 (1975): 103–8.

3567. ———. "Friedrich Gerstäcker and the American Frontier." Doctoral dissertation, Syracuse University, 1966.

3568. ———. "Gerstäcker's America." *Thoth* 7 (Winter 1966): 12–21.

3569. Steeves, Harrison R. "The First of the Westerns." *Southwest Review* 53 (Winter 1968): 74–84.

BREWSTER GHISELIN

3570. Raine, Kathleen. "Country of the Minotaur." *Sewanee Review* 79 (1971): 288–92.

3571. Smith, Dave. "The Poetry of Brewster Ghiselin." *Western Humanities Review* 35 (Summer 1981): 162–65.

ARCHER B. GILFILLAN

3572. Etulain, Richard W. "Introduction," to Archer B. Gilfillan, *Sheep: Life on the South Dakota Range.* Rpr. St. Paul: Minnesota Historical Society Press, 1993, vii–xxx.

3573. McLean, Austin J. "A Herder's Life in South Dakota: The Cipher Diary of Archer B. Gilfillan." *Where the West Begins.* Eds. Arthur R. Huseboe and William Geyer, Sioux Falls, S.Dak.: Center for Western Studies Press, 1978, 63–71.

3574. Golden, Catherine, ed. *The Captive Imagination: A Casebook on The Yellow Wallpaper.* New York: Feminist Press, 1992.

3575. Lane, Ann J. *To 'Herland' and Beyond: The Life and Work of Charlotte Perkins Gilman.* New York: Pantheon, 1990.

3576. Meyering, Sheryl L., ed. *Charlotte Perkins Gilman: The Woman and Her Work.* Ann Arbor, Mich.: UMI Research Press, 1989.

3577. Oliver, Lawrence J., and Gary Scharnhorst. "Charlotte Perkins Gilman v. Ambrose Bierce: The Literary Politics of Gender in *Fin-de-Siècle* California." *Journal of the West* 32 (July 1993): 52–60.

3578. Scharnhorst, Gary. *Charlotte Perkins Gilman.* Boston: Twayne, 1985.

3579. ———. *Charlotte Perkins Gilman: A Bibliography.* Metuchen, N.J.: Scarecrow Press, 1985.

3580. ———. "Charlotte Perkins Gilman's 'The Giant Wistaria': A Hieroglyph of the Female Frontier Gothic." *Frontier Gothic: Terror and Wonder at the Frontier in American Literature.* Eds. David Mogen, et al. Rutherford, N.J.: Fairleigh Dickinson University Press, 1993, 156–64.

3581. ———. "Reconstructing *Here Also*: On the Later Poetry of Charlotte Perkins Gilman." *Critical Essays on Charlotte Perkins Gilman.* Ed. Joanne Karpinski. New York: G.K. Hall, 1992, 249–68.

3582. Shumaker, Conrad. "Realism, Reform, and the Audience: Charlotte Perkins Gilman's Unreachable Wallpaper." *Arizona Quarterly* 47 (Spring 1991): 81–93.

3583. ———. "'Too Terribly Good to be Printed': Charlotte Gilman's 'The Yellow Wallpaper.'" *American Literature* 57 (December 1985): 588–99.

ALLEN GINSBERG

3584. Ball, Gordon, ed. *Allen Verbatim.* New York: McGraw-Hill, 1974.

3585. Cook, Bruce. *The Beat Generation.* New York: Charles Scribner's Sons, 1971.

3586. Ginsberg, Allen. *Journals: Early Fifties–Early Sixties.* New York: Grove Press, 1977.

3587. Hahn, Stephen. "The Prophetic Voice of Allen Ginsberg." *Prospects: An Annual of American Cultural Studies.* Vol 2. Ed. Jack Salzman. New York: Burt Franklin, 1976, 527–67.

3588. Hyde, Lewis, ed. *On the Poetry of Allen Ginsberg*. Ann Arbor: University of Michigan Press, 1984.

3589. Kramer, Jane. *Allen Ginsberg in America*. New York: Random House, 1968.

3590. Kraus, Michelle P. *Allen Ginsberg: An Annotated Bibliograpy*. Metuchen, N.J.: Scarecrow Press, 1980.

3591. Merrill, Thomas F. *Allen Ginsberg*. Rev ed. New York: Twayne, 1988.

3592. Miles, Barry. *Ginsberg: A Biography*. New York: Simon Schuster, 1989.

3593. Penglase, John Dols. "Allen Ginsberg: The Flowering Vision of the Heart." Doctoral dissertation, University of Wisconsin, Milwaukee, 1975.

3594. Portugés, Paul. *The Visionary Poetics of Allen Ginsberg*. Santa Barbara, Calif.: Ross-Erikson Publishers, 1978.

3595. Rumaker, Michael. "Allen Ginsberg's *Howl*." *Black Mountain Review* 7 (Autumn 1957): 228–37.

3596. Schumacher, Michael. *Dharma Lion: A Biography of Allen Ginsberg*. New York: St. Martin's Press, 1992.

3597. Stewart, Robert, and Rebekah Presson. "Sacred Speech: A Conversation with Allen Ginsberg." *New Letters* 54 (Fall 1987): 73–86.

3598. Trilling, Diana. "The Other Night at Columbia." *Partisan Review* 26 (Spring 1959): 214–30.

3599. Tytell, John. *Naked Angels: The Lives and Literature of the Beat Generation*. New York: McGraw-Hill, 1976.

FRED GIPSON

3600. Henderson, Sam H. *Fred Gipson*. Southwest Writers Series, No. 10. Austin, Tex.: Steck-Vaughn, 1967.

3601. Lich, Glen E. *Fred Gipson at Work*. College Station: Texas A M University Press, 1990.

FREDERICK GLIDDEN

(Luke Short)

3602. Gale, Robert L. *Luke Short*. Boston: Twayne, 1981.

3603. Olsen, T.V. "Luke Short, Writer's Writer." *Roundup* 21 (March 1973): 10–11, 13.

3604. Thomas, Phillip D. "The Paperback West of Luke Short." *Journal of Popular Culture* 7 (Winter 1973): 701–8.

MOLLY GLOSS

3605. Morris, Gregory. "*The Jump-Off Creek*: Molly Gloss' Novel of Frontier Manners." *South Dakota Review* 30 (Summer 1992): 128–42.

CAROLINE GORDON

3606. Rodenberger, M. Lou. "Folk Narrative in Caroline Gordon's Frontier Fiction." *Heritage of Kansas* 10 (Summer 1977): 32–40.

WILLIAM GOYEN

3607. Duncan, Erika. "Come a Spiritual Healer: A Profile of William Goyen." *Book Forum* 3 (1977): 296–303. Includes a bibliography.

3608. Gibbons, Reginald. *William Goyen: A Study of the Short Fiction.* Boston: Twayne, 1991.

3609. Gossett, Louise Y. "The Voices of Distance: William Goyen." *Violence in Recent Southern Fiction.* Durham, N.C.: Duke University Press, 1965, 131–45.

3610. Paul, Jay S. "'Marvelous Reciprocity': The Fiction of William Goyen." *Critique* 19 (No. 2, 1977): 77–92.

3611. Phillips, Robert. *William Goyen.* Boston: Twayne, 1979.

3612. Stern, Daniel. "On William Goyen's *The House of Breath.*" *Rediscoveries.* Ed. David Madden. New York: Crown, 1971, 256–69.

JOHN GRAVES

3613. Bradford, M.E. "Arden up the Brazos: John Graves and the Uses of Pastoral." *Southern Review* 8 (October 1972): 949–55. An essay review.

3614. ———. "In Keeping with the Way: John Graves's *Hard Scrabble.*" *Southwest Review* 60 (Spring 1975): 190–95.

3615. Grover, Dorys Crow. *John Graves.* Western Writers Series, No. 91. Boise, Idaho: Boise State University, 1989.

JOSIAH GREGG

3616. Foster, Edward Halsey. *Josiah Gregg and Lewis H. Garrard.* Western Writers Series, No. 28. Boise, Idaho: Boise State University, 1977.

3617. Gregg, Josiah. *Diary and Letters.* 2 vols. Ed. Maurice Garland Fulton. Norman: University of Oklahoma Press, 1941–44.

3618. Horgan, Paul. *Josiah Gregg and His Vision of the Early Far West.* New York: Farrar Straus and Giroux, 1979.

3619. Lee, John Thomas. "The Authorship of Gregg's *Commerce of the Prairies.*" *Mississippi Valley Historical Review* 16 (March 1930): 451–66.

3620. Powell, Lawrence C. "Josiah Gregg's *Commerce of the Prairies.*" *Westways* 63 (May 1971): 14–17, 68–70.

3621. Twitchell, Ralph Emerson. *Dr. Josiah Gregg: Historian of the Santa Fe Trail.* Santa Fe: Santa Fe New Mexican, 1924.

ZANE GREY

3622. Bloodworth, William. "Zane Grey's Western Eroticism." *South Dakota Review* 23 (Autumn 1985): 5–14.

3623. Cawelti, John G. *Adventure, Mystery, and Romance: Formula Stories as Art and Popular Culture.* Chicago: University of Chicago Press, 1976, 215–30.

3624. Etulain, Richard W. "A Dedication to... Zane Grey 1872–1939." *Arizona and the West* 12 (Autumn 1970): 217–20.

3625. Gentles, Ruth G. *The Zane Grey Omnibus.* New York: Harper and Brothers, 1943.

3626. Goble, Danney. "'The Days That Were No More': A Look at Zane Grey's West." *Journal of Arizona History* 14 (Spring 1973): 63–75.

3627. Grey, Loren. *Zane Grey: A Photographic Odyssey.* Dallas: Taylor Publishing, 1985.

3628. Grey, Zane. "Breaking Through: The Story of My Own Life." *American Magazine* 97 (July 1924): 11–13 ff.

3629. Gruber, Frank. *Zane Grey: A Biography.* New York: World, 1970.

3630. Hamilton, Cynthia S. *Western and Hard-Boiled Detective Fiction in America: From High Noon to Midnight.* Iowa City: University of Iowa Press, 1987.

3631. Jackson, Carlton. *Zane Grey.* Rev ed. Boston: Twayne, 1989.

3632. Kant, Candace C. *Zane Grey's Arizona.* Flagstaff, Ariz.: Northland, 1984.

3633. Karr, Jean. *Zane Grey: Man of the West.* New York: Greenberg, 1949.

3634. Kimball, Arthur G. *Ace of Hearts: The Westerns of Zane Grey.* Fort Worth: Texas Christian University Press, 1993.

3635. ———. "My Navajo Oasis: Irony in Grey's *Heritage of the Desert.*" *South Dakota Review* 28 (Summer 1990): 34–51.

3636. ———. "Silent Walls: 'Nature' in Grey's *The Vanishing American.*" *South Dakota Review* 26 (Spring 1988): 78–90.

3637. Loomis, Edward. "History and Fiction: *To the Last Man.*" *South Dakota Review* 23 (Autumn 1985): 28–32.

3638. Lutman, Richard A. "A Woman to Live in Your Heart Forever: The Women of Zane Grey's West." *Journal of the West* 32 (January 1993): 62–68.

3639. Meyer, William E.H., Jr. "Zane Grey and the American Hypervisual Tradition." *Journal of American Culture* 12 (Winter 1989): 59–69.

3640. Mitchell, Lee [Clark]. "White Slaves and Purple Sage: Plotting Sex in Zane Grey's West." *American Literary History* 6 (Summer 1994): 234–64.

3641. Nesbitt, John D. "Uncertain Sex in the Sagebrush." *South Dakota Review* 23 (Autumn 1985): 15–27.

3642. Oehlschlaeger, Fritz H. "Civilization as Emasculation: The Threatening Role of Women in the Frontier Fiction of Harold Bell Wright and Zane Grey." *Midwest Quarterly* 22 (Summer 1981): 346–60.

3643. Olafson, Robert B. "Zane Grey's Washington: *The Desert of Wheat.*" *Pacific Northwest Forum* 9 (Winter 1984): 26–33.

3644. Patrick, A. "Getting into Six Figures: Zane Grey." *Bookman* 60 (December 1924): 424–29.

3645. Powell, L. C. "Southwest Classics Reread: Writer of the Purple Sage." *Westways* 64 (August 1972): 50–55, 69.

3646. Ronald, Ann. *Zane Grey.* Western Writers Series, No. 17. Boise, Idaho: Boise State University, 1975.

3647. Schneider, Norris F. *Zane Grey....* Zanesville, Ohio: n.p., 1967.

3648. Scott, Kenneth W. *Zane Grey. Born to West: A Reference Guide.* Boston: G.K. Hall, 1979.

3649. Stott, Graham St. John. "Zane Grey and James Simpson Emmett." *Brigham Young University Studies* 18 (Summer 1978): 491–503.

3650. Topping, Gary. "The Pastoral Ideal in Popular American Literature: Zane Grey and Edgar Rice Burroughs." *Rendezvous* 12 (Fall 1977): 11–25.

3651. ———. "Zane Grey: A Literary Reassessment." *Western American Literature* 13 (Spring 1978): 51–64.

3652. ———. "Zane Grey in Zion: An Examination of His Supposed Anti-Mormonism." *Brigham Young University Studies* 18 (Summer 1978): 483–90.

3653. ———. "Zane Grey's West." *Journal of Popular Culture* 7 (Winter 1973): 681–89.

3654. ———. "Zane Grey's West: Essays in Intellectual History and Criticism." Doctoral dissertation, University of Utah, 1977.

3655. Tranquilla, Ronald. "Ranger and Mountie: Myths of National Identity in Zane Grey's *The Lone Star Ranger* and Ralph Connor's *Corporal Cameron*." *Journal of Popular Culture* 24 (Winter 1990): 69–80.

3656. Wheeler, Joseph Lawrence. "Zane Grey's Impact on American Life and Letters: A Study in the Popular Novel." Doctoral dissertation, George Peabody College for Teachers, 1975.

3657. Whipple, T.K. "American Sagas." *Study Out the Land*. Berkeley: University of California Press, 1943, 19–29.

3658. Wilson, Daniel J. "Nature in Western Popular Literature from the Dime Novel to Zane Grey." *North Dakota Quarterly* 44 (Spring 1976): 41–50.

3659. *Zane Grey, The Man and His Works*. New York: Harper Brothers, 1928.

JOHN HOWARD GRIFFIN

3660. Campbell, Jeff H. *John Howard Griffin*. Southwest Writers Series, No. 35. Austin, Tex.: Steck-Vaughn, 1970.

3661. Geismar, Maxwell. "John Howard Griffin: The Devil in Texas." *American Moderns*. New York: Hill and Wang, 1958, 251–65.

3662. McDonnell, Thomas P. "John Howard Griffin: An Interview." *Ramparts* 1 (January 1963): 6–16

A. B. GUTHRIE, JR.

3663. Allred, Jared Rulon. "A. B. Guthrie, Jr.: The Artist in the Wilderness." Doctoral dissertation, University of Utah, 1973.

3664. Apthorp, Elaine S. "Steinbeck, Guthrie, and Popular Culture." *San Jose Studies* 16 (Winter 1990); 19–39.

3665. Astro, Richard. "*The Big Sky* and the Limits of Western Fiction." *Western American Literature* 9 (August 1974): 105–14.

3666. Bevis, William W. "Guthrie's Big Sky." *Ten Tough Trips: Montana Writers and the West*. Seattle: University of Washington Press, 1990, 3–19.

3667. ———. "Guthrie's Dream of the West." *Ten Tough Trips: Montana Writers and the West*. Seattle: University of Washington Press, 1990, 20–35.

3668. Coon, Gilbert D. "A. B. Guthrie, Jr.'s Tetralogy: An American Synthesis." *North Dakota Quarterly* 44 (Spring 1976): 73–80.

3669. ———. "A Study of A. B. Guthrie, Jr., and His Tetralogy." Doctoral dissertation, Washington State University, 1972.

3670. Cracroft, Richard H. "*The Big Sky*: A. B. Guthrie's Use of Historical Sources." *Western American Literature* 6 (Fall 1971): 163–76.

3671. Erisman, Fred. "Coming of Age in Montana: The Legacy of A. B. Guthrie." *Montana: The Magazine of Western History* 43 (Summer 1993): 69–74.

3672. ———. "The Education of Jason Beard: A. B. Guthrie's Western Suspense Stories." *Clues* 1 (1980): 126–31.

3673. ———. "Historical Commentary: Coming of Age in Montana: The Legacy of A. B. Guthrie, Jr." *Montana: The Magazine of Western History* 43 (Summer 1993): 69–74.

3674. ———. "Western Fiction as an Ecological Parable." *Environmental Review* 2 (Spring 1978): 15–23.

3675. Etulain, Richard W. "A. B. Guthrie: A Bibliography." *Western American Literature* 4 (Summer 1969): 133–38.

3676. Folsom, James K. *The American Western Novel.* New Haven, Conn.: College and University Press, 1966, 64–76.

3677. Ford, Thomas W. *A. B. Guthrie, Jr.* Southwest Writers Series, No. 15. Austin, Tex.: Steck-Vaughn, 1968.

3678. ———. *A. B. Guthrie, Jr.* Boston: Twayne, 1981.

3679. ———. "A. B. Guthrie's *Fair Land, Fair Land*: A Requiem." *Western American Literature* 23 (May 1988): 17–30.

3680. Guthrie, A. B., Jr. *The Blue Hen's Chick.* New York: McGraw-Hill, 1965; Lincoln: University of Nebraska Press, 1993.

3681. Hairston, Joe B. "Community in the West." *South Dakota Review* 11 (Spring 1973): 17–26.

3682. Hodgins, Francis E., Jr. "The Literary Emancipation of a Region...." Doctoral dissertation, Michigan State University, 1957, 485–517.

3683. Hood, Charles F. "The Man and the Book: Guthrie's *The Big Sky*." *Montana Journalism Review* 14 (1971): 6–15.

3684. Kohler, Dayton. "A.B. Guthrie, Jr. and the West." *College English* 12 (February 1951): 249–56. Also in *English Journal* 40 (February 1951): 65–72.

3685. Milton, John R. *The Novel of the American West.* Lincoln: University of Nebraska Press, 1980, 160–94.

3686. Petersen, David, ed. *Big Sky, Fair Land: The Environmental Essays of A.B. Guthrie, Jr.* [Flagstaff, Ariz.]: Northland Press, 1988.

3687. Putnam, Jackson K. "Down to Earth: A.B. Guthrie's Quest for Moral and Historical Truth." *Essays on Western History....* Grand Forks: University of North Dakota Press, 1970, 51–61.

3688. Ray, Charles Eugene. "An Interdisciplinary Study Based on Four Selected Novels by A. B. Guthrie, Jr." Doctoral dissertation, Middle Tennessee State University, 1974.

3689. Simmons, Michael K. "Boone Caudill: The Failure of an American Primitive." *South Dakota Review* 22 (Autumn 1984): 38–43.

3690. Stewart, Donald C. "A. B. Guthrie's Vanishing Paradise: An Essay on Historical Fiction." *Journal of the West* 15 (July 1976): 83–96.

3691. ———. "The Functions of Bird and Sky Imagery in A.B. Guthrie's *The Big Sky*." *Critique* 19 (1977): 53–61.

3692. Stineback, David C. "On History and Its Consequences: A. B. Guthrie's *These Thousand Hills*." *Western American Literature* 6 (Fall 1971): 177–89.

3693. Walker, Don D. "The Indian in Him: A Note on the Conception of Evil in A. B. Guthrie's First Novel." *Possible Sack* 2 (May 1971): 11–13.

3694. ———. "The Mountain Man as Literary Hero." *Western American Literature* 1 (Spring 1966): 15–25.

3695. ———. "The Primitivistic and the Historical in Guthrie's Fiction." *Possible Sack* 2 (June 1971): 1–5.

3696. Williams, John. "The 'Western': Definition of the Myth." *Nation* 193 (November 18, 1961): 401–6.

3697. Young, Vernon. "An American Dream and Its Parody." *Arizona Quarterly* 6 (Summer 1950): 112–23.

JOHN HAINES

3698. Allen, Carolyn J. "Death and Dreams in John Haines' *Writers News*." *Alaska Review* 4 (Fall–Winter 1969): 28–36.

3699. Wild, Peter. *John Haines.* Western Writers Series, No. 68. Boise, Idaho: Boise State University, 1985.

3700. Wilson, James R. "Relentless Self-Scrutiny: The Poetry of John Haines." *Alaska Review* 4 (Fall–Winter 1969): 16–27.

J. EVETTS HALEY

3701. Bradford, M. E. "The Care and Keeping of Memory: J. Evetts Haley and Plutarchian Biography." *Southwestern American Literature* 3 (1973): 69–76.

3702. Robinson, Chandler A. *J. Evetts Haley: Cowman-Historian.* El Paso, Tex.: Carl Hertzog, 1967.

DICK WICK HALL

3703. Boyer, Mary G., ed. "Dick Wick Hall." *Arizona in Literature*. Glendale, Calif.: Arthur H. Clark, 1935, 495–511.

3704. Myers, Samuel L. "Dick Wick Hall: Humorist with a Serious Purpose." *Journal of Arizona History* 11 (Winter 1970): 255–78.

3705. Nutt, Francis Dorothy. *Dick Wick Hall: Stories from the Salome Sun by Arizona's Most Famous Humorist*. Flagstaff, Ariz.: Northland Press, 1968.

HAZEL HALL

3706. Matthews, Eleanor H. "Hazel Hall." *An Anthology of Northwest Writing: 1900–1950*. Ed. Michael Strelow, et al. Eugene, Oreg.: Northwest Review Books, 1979, 98–103.

JAMES HALL

3707. Donald, David. "The Autobiography of James Hall, Western Literary Pioneer." *Ohio State Archaeological and Historical Quarterly* 56 (1947): 295–304.

3708. Flanagan, John T. *James Hall, Literary Pioneer of the Ohio Valley*. Minneapolis: University of Minnesota Press, 1941.

3709. Randall, Randolph C. *James Hall, Spokesman of the New West*. Columbus: Ohio State University Press, 1964.

3710. Todd, Edgeley W. "The Authorship of 'The Missouri Trapper.'" *Missouri Historical Society Bulletin* 15 (April 1959): 194–200.

3711. ———. "James Hall and the Hugh Glass Legend." *American Quarterly* 7 (Winter 1955): 362–70.

OAKLEY HALL

3712. Davis, Robert Murray. "Oakley Hall's Westerns: A Sense of Period." *Southwest Review* 69 (Autumn 1984): 444–61.

3713. ———. "Time and Space in the Western: *Warlock* as Novel and Film." *South Dakota Review* 29 (Spring 1991): 68–75.

3714. Dmytryk, Edward. "*Warlock*." *South Dakota Review* 23 (Autumn 1985): 102–11.

3715. Work, James C. "The Violent God in Oakley Hall's Novel, *Warlock*." *South Dakota Review* 23 (Autumn 1985): 112–34.

SHARLOT HALL

3716. Maxwell, Margaret F. *A Passion for Freedom: The Life of Sharlot Hall.* Tucson: University of Arizona Press, 1982.

3717. Weston, James J. "Sharlot Hall: Arizona's Pioneer Lady of Literature." *Journal of the West* 4 (October 1965): 539–52.

DONALD HAMILTON

3718. Erisman, Fred. "Western Motifs in the Thrillers of Donald Hamilton." *Western American Literature* 10 (February 1976): 283–92.

DASHIELL HAMMETT

3719. Dooley, Dennis. *Dashiell Hammett.* New York: Ungar, 1984.

3720. Gregory, Sinda. *Private Investigations: The Novels of Dashiell Hammett.* Carbondale: Southern Illinois University Press, 1985.

3721. Johnson, Diane. *Dashiell Hammett: A Life.* New York: Random House, 1983.

3722. Layman, Richard. *Shadow Man: The Life of Dashiell Hammett.* New York: Harcourt Brace Jovanovich, 1981.

3723. Marling, William. *Dashiell Hammett.* Boston: Twayne, 1983.

3724. Porter, Joseph C. "The End of the Trail: The American West of Dashiell Hammett and Raymond Chandler." *Western Historical Quarterly* 6 (October 1975): 411–24.

3725. Ruehlmann, William. *Saint with a Gun.* New York: New York University Press, 1974.

3726. Skenazy, Paul. *The New Wild West: The Urban Mysteries of Dashiell Hammett and Raymond Chandler.* Western Writers Series, No. 54. Boise, Idaho: Boise State University, 1982.

3727. Skinner, Robert E. *The Hard-Boiled Explicator: A Guide to the Study of Dashiell Hammett, Raymond Chandler and Ross Macdonald.* Metuchen, N.J.: Scarecrow Press, 1985.

3728. Symons, Julian. *Dashiell Hammett.* New York: Harcourt Brace Jovanovich, 1985.

3729. Whitley, John S. "Stirring Things Up: Dashiell Hammett's Continental Op." *Journal of American Studies* 14 (December 1980): 443–55.

3730. Wolfe, Peter. *Beams Falling: The Art of Dashiell Hammett.* Bowling Green, Ohio: Bowling Green State University Popular Press, 1980.

3731. Ruppert, Jim. "Paula Gunn Allen and Joy Harjo: Closing the Distance Between Personal and Mythic Space." *American Indian Quarterly* 7 (1983): 27–40.

BRET HARTE

3732. Barnett, Linda D. *Bret Harte: A Reference Guide.* Boston: G.K. Hall, 1980.

3733. Beisman, Emmeline B. "The Prospector and the Pioneer: A Key to the Selected Short Stories of Bret Harte." Doctoral dissertation, University of New Mexico, 1975

3734. Boggan, J. R. "The Regeneration of 'Roaring Camp.'" *Nineteenth-Century Fiction* 22 (December 1967): 271–80.

3735. Boynton, Henry W. *Bret Harte.* New York: McClure, Phillips, 1903.

3736. Brady, Duer S. "A New Look at Bret Harte and the *Overland Monthly.*" Doctoral dissertation, University of Arkansas, 1962.

3737. Buckland, Roscoe. "Jack Hamlin: Bret Harte's Romantic Rogue." *Western American Literature* 8 (Fall 1973): 111–22.

3738. Conner, William F. "The Euchring of Tennessee: A Reexamination of Bret Harte's 'Tennessee's Partner.'" *Studies in Short Fiction* 17 (Spring 1980): 113–120.

3739. Duckett, Margaret. "Bret Harte and the Indians of Northern California." *Huntington Library Quarterly* 18 (November 1954): 59–83.

3740. ———. "Bret Harte's Portrayal of Half-Breeds." *American Literature* 25 (May 1953): 193–212.

3741. ———. *Mark Twain and Bret Harte.* Norman: University of Oklahoma Press, 1964.

3742. ———. "Plain Language from Bret Harte." *Nineteenth-Century Fiction* 11 (March 1957): 241–60.

3743. Gardner, Joseph H. "Bret Harte and Dickensian Mode in America." *Canadian Review of American Studies* 2 (Fall 1971): 89–101.

3744. Glover, Donald E. "The Later Career of Bret Harte: 1880–1902." Doctoral dissertation, University of Virginia, 1965.

3745. ———. "A Reconsideration of Bret Harte's Later Work." *Western American Literature* 8 (Fall 1973): 143–51.

3746. Harrison, Joseph B., ed. *Bret Harte: Representative Selections.* New York: American Book, 1941.

3747. Harte, Bret. *The Letters of Bret Harte.* Ed. Geoffrey Bret Harte. Boston: Houghton Mifflin, 1926.

3748. Harte, John Bret. "A Dedication to the Memory of Francis Bret Harte, 1836–1902." *Arizona and the West* 18 (Spring 1976): 1–4.

3749. Hazard, Lucy L. "Eden to Eldorado." *University of California Chronicle* 35 (January 1933): 107–21.

3750. Kolb, Harold H., Jr. "The Outcast of Literary Flat: Bret Harte as Humorist." *American Literary Realism 1870–1910* 23 (Winter 1991): 52–63.

3751. May, Charles E. "Bret Harte's 'Tennessee's Partner': The Reader Euchred." *South Dakota Review* 15 (Spring 1977): 109–17.

3752. May, Ernest. "Bret Harte and the *Overland Monthly*." *American Literature* 22 (November 1950): 260–71.

3753. Merwin, Henry C. *The Life of Bret Harte*. Boston: Houghton Mifflin, 1911.

3754. Morrow, Patrick. *Bret Harte*. Western Writers Series, No. 5. Boise, Idaho: Boise State College, 1972.

3755. ———. "Bret Harte and the Perils of Pop Poetry." *Journal of Popular Culture* 13 (Spring 1980): 476–82.

3756. ———. *Bret Harte: Literary Critic*. Bowling Green, Ohio: Bowling Green State University Popular Press, 1979.

3757. ———. "Bret Harte, Popular Fiction, and the Local Color Movement." *Western American Literature* 8 (Fall 1973): 123–31.

3758. ———. *The Works of Bret Harte*. Cassette. Deland, Fla.: Everett/ Edwards, 1974.

3759. Murphy, Brenda, and George Monteiro. "The Unpublished Letters of Bret Harte to John Hay." *American Literary Realism 1870–1910* 12 (Spring 1979): 77–110.

3760. O'Connor, Richard. *Bret Harte: A Biography*. Boston: Little, Brown, 1966.

3761. Oliver, Egbert S. "The Pig-Tailed China Boys Out West." *Western Humanities Review* 12 (Spring 1958): 159–78.

3762. *Overland Monthly* [Special Bret Harte Number] 40 (September 1902).

3763. Pattee, Fred Lewis. "Bret Harte." *The Development of the American Short Story*. New York: Harper Brothers, 1923, 220–44 passim.

3764. Scharnhorst, Gary. *Bret Harte*. New York: Twayne, 1992.

3765. ———. "Whatever Happened to Bret Harte?" *American Realism and the Canon*. Eds. Tom Quirk and Gary Scharnhorst. Newark: University of Delaware Press, 1994, 201–11.

3766. ———, ed. *Bret Harte's California Letters to the Springfield Republican and Christian Register, 1866–67.* Albuquerque: University of New Mexico Press, 1990.

3767. Stegner, Wallace. "The West Synthetic: Bret Harte." *The Sound of Mountain Water.* Garden City, N.Y.: Doubleday, 1969, 23–36.

3768. Stewart, George R., Jr. "A Bibliography of the Writings of Bret Harte in the Magazines and Newspapers of California, 1857–1871." *University of California Publications in English* 3 (September 30, 1933): 119–70. Repr. Norwood, Pa.: Norwood Editions, 1977.

3769. ———. *Bret Harte: Argonaut and Exile.* Boston: Houghton Mifflin, 1931; Port Washington, N.Y.: Kennikat Press, 1968.

3770. Thomas, Jeffrey F. "Bret Harte." *American Literary Realism 1870–1910* 8 (1975): 266–70. Analysis of dissertations on Harte.

3771. ———. "Bret Harte and the Power of Sex." *Western American Literature* 8 (Fall 1973): 91–109.

3772. Walterhouse, Roger R. *Bret Harte, Joaquin Miller, and the Western Local Color Story: A Study in the Origins of Popular Fiction.* Chicago: University of Chicago Libraries, 1939.

GERALD HASLAM

3773. Locklin, Gerald. *Gerald Haslam.* Western Writers Series, No. 77. Boise, Idaho: Boise State University, 1987.

WALTER HAVIGHURST

3774. Jones, Joel M. "To Feel the Heartland's Pulse: The Writing of Walter Havighurst." *Kansas Quarterly* 2 (Spring 1970): 88–96.

JOHN HAY

3775. Clymer, Kenton J. "John Hay and Mark Twain." *Missouri Historical Review* 67 (April 1973): 397–406.

3776. Gale, Robert L. *John Hay.* Boston: Twayne, 1978.

3777. Sloane, David E. "John Hay (1838–1905)." *American Literary Realism 1870–1910* 3 (Spring 1970): 178–88.

3778. Thayer, William Roscoe. *The Life and Letters of John Hay.* 2 vols. Boston: Houghton Mifflin, 1915.

3779. Thurman, Kelley. *John Hay as a Man of Letters.* Reseda, Calif.: Mojave, 1974.

ERNEST HAYCOX

3780. DeVoto, Bernard. "Phaëthon on Gunsmoke Trail." *Harpers* 209 (December 1954): 10–11, 14, 16.

3781. "Ernest Haycox Memorial Number." *Call Number* 25 (1963–64): 1–31. Includes bibliography, 5–27.

3782. Etulain, Richard W. *Ernest Haycox.* Western Writers Series, No. 86. Boise, Idaho: Boise State University, 1988.

3783. ———. "Ernest Haycox: Popular Novelist of the Pacific Northwest." *Northwest Perspectives: Essays on the Culture of the Pacific Northwest.* Eds. Edwin R. Bingham and Glen A. Love. Seattle: University of Washington Press, 1979, 137–50.

3784. ———. "Ernest Haycox: The Historical Western, 1937–43." *South Dakota Review* 5 (Spring 1967): 35–54.

3785. ———. "The Literary Career of a Western Writer: Ernest Haycox 1899–1950." Doctoral dissertation, University of Oregon, 1966.

3786. Fargo, James. "The Western and Ernest Haycox." *Prairie Schooner* 26 (Summer 1952): 177–84.

3787. Garfield, Brian. "Ernest Haycox: A Study in Style." *Roundup* 21 (February 1973): 1–3, 5.

3788. Nesbitt, John D. "A New Look at Two Popular Western Classics." *South Dakota Review* 18 (Spring 1980): 30–42.

3789. Newton, D. B. "After Haycox: Whither Go We?" *Roundup* 21 (November 1973): 4–8.

3790. ———. "The Legend of Ernest Haycox." *Roundup* 21 (October 1973): 8–11.

3791. "A Special Ernest Haycox Anniversary Issue." *Roundup* 21 (October 1973).

ERNEST HEMINGWAY

3792. Arnold, Lloyd R. *Hemingway: High on the Wild.* New York: Grosset Dunlap, 1977.

3793. Bovey, Seth. "The Western Code of Hemingway's Gambler." *North Dakota Quarterly* 58 (Summer 1990): 86–93.

3794. Durham, Philip. "Ernest Hemingway's Grace Under Pressure: The Western Code." *Pacific Historical Review* 45 (August 1976): 425–32.

3795. Fleming, Robert E. "American Nightmare: Hemingway and the West." *Midwest Quarterly* 30 (Spring 1989): 361–71.

3796. ———. "The Hills Remain: The Mountain West of Hemingway's *Islands* Manuscript." *North Dakota Quarterly* 58 (Summer 1990): 79–85.

3797. Johnston, Kenneth G. "Hemingway's 'Wine of Wyoming': Disappointment in America." *Western American Literature* 9 (November 1974): 159–67.

3798. Love, Glen A. "Hemingway's Indian Virtues: An Ecological Reconsideration." *Western American Literature* 22 (November 1987): 201–13.

3799. Martin, Lawrence H., Jr. "Odd Exception or Mainstream Tradition: 'The Shot' in Context." *Western American Literature* 24 (February 1990): 313–20.

3800. Meyers, Jeffrey. "Hemingway's Primitivism and 'Indian Camp.'" *Twentieth Century Literature* 34 (Summer 1988): 211–22.

3801. Price, Alan. "'I'm Not an Old Fogey and You're Not a Young Ass': Owen Wister and Ernest Hemingway." *Hemingway Review* 9 (Fall 1989): 82–90.

3802. Putnam, Alan. "'Wine of Wyoming' and Hemingway's Hidden West." *Western American Literature* 22 (May 1987): 17–32.

3803. Spilka, Mark. *Hemingway's Quarrel with Androgyny.* Lincoln: University of Nebraska Press, 1990.

3804. Westbrook, Max. "Text, Ritual and Memory: Hemingway's 'Big Two-Hearted River.'" *North Dakota Quarterly* 60 (Summer 1992): 14–25.

3805. Winslow, Richard. "'A Good Country': Hemingway at the L Bar T Ranch, Wyoming." *Fitzgerald/Hemingway Annual 1975.* Englewood, Colo.: Microcard Editions, 1975, 259–72.

ALICE CORBIN HENDERSON

3806. Bynner, Witter, and Oliver La Farge, eds. "Alice Corbin: An Appreciation." *New Mexico Quarterly Review* 19 (Spring 1949): 34–79.

3807. Pearce, T. M. *Alice Corbin Henderson.* Southwest Writers Series, No. 21. Austin, Tex.: Steck-Vaughn, 1969.

O. HENRY

See William Sydney Porter

WILL HENRY

See Henry Wilson Allen

ELLA HIGGINSON

3808. Goodman, Susan. "Ella Rhoads Higginson (c. 1862–1940)." *Legacy* 6 (Spring 1989): 59–68.

3809. Vore, Elizabeth. "Ella Higginson, A Successful Pacific Coast Writer." *Overland* 33 (May 1899): 434–36.

EDWIN B. HILL

3810. Myers, John Myers. "A Checklist of Items Published by the Private Press of Edwin B. Hill." *American Book Collector* 18 (October 1967): 22–27.

RUTH BEEBE HILL

3811. Medicine, Bea. "*Hanta Yo:* A New Phenomenon." *Indian Historian* 12 (Summer 1979): 2–5.

TONY HILLERMAN

3812. Engel, Leonard. "Landscape and Place in Tony Hillerman's Mysteries." *Western American Literature* 28 (August 1993): 111–22.

3813. Erisman, Fred. "Hillerman's Uses of the Southwest." *Roundup Quarterly* 1 (Summer 1989): 9–18.

3814. ———. *Tony Hillerman.* Western Writers Series, No. 87. Boise, Idaho: Boise State University, 1989.

3815. ———. "Tony Hillerman's Jim Chee and the Shaman's Dilemma." *Lamar Journal of the Humanities* 17 (June 1992): 5–16.

3816. Greenberg, Martin, ed. *The Tony Hillerman Companion.* New York: HarperCollins, 1994.

3817. Hillerman, Tony, and Ernie Bulow. *Talking Mysteries: A Conversation with Tony Hillerman.* Albuquerque: University of New Mexico Press, 1991.

3818. ———. *Words, Weather and Wolfmen: Conversations with Tony Hillerman.* Gallup, N.M.: Southwesterner Books, 1989.

3819. Roush, Jan. "The Developing Art of Tony Hillerman." *Western American Literature* 28 (August 1993): 99–110.

3820. Schneider, Jack W. "Crime and Navajo Punishment: Tony Hillerman's Novels of Detection." *Southwest Review* 67 (Spring 1982): 151–60.

3821. Strenski, Ellen, and Robley Evans. "Ritual and Murder in Tony Hillerman's Indian Detective Novels." *Western American Literature* 16 (Fall 1981): 205–16.

ROLANDO HINOJOSA

3822. Saldívar, José David. "Our Southwest: An Interview with Rolando Hinojosa." *The Rolando Hinojosa Reader: Essays Historical and Critical.* Ed. José David Saldívar. Houston: Arte Público Press, 1985, 180–90.

3823. ———, ed. *The Rolando Hinojosa Reader: Essays Historical and Critical.* Houston: Arte Público Press, 1985.

EDWARD HOAGLAND

3824. Fontana, Ernest L. "The Territory of the Past in Hoagland's *Notes from the Century Before.*" *Western American Literature* 9 (May 1974): 45–51.

ERIC HOFFER

3825. Wild, Peter. "Eric Hoffer: Frontiersman in Montaigne's Clothing." *North Dakota Quarterly* 57 (Winter 1989): 11–22.

LINDA HOGAN

3826. Schöler, Bo. "A Heart Made Out of Crickets: An Interview with Linda Hogan." *Journal of Ethnic Studies* 16 (Spring 1988): 107–17.

RAY HOGAN

3827. Rupert, Marc S. "Mr. Western: Ray Hogan." *Roundup* 34 (October 1986): 4–8; (November/December 1986): 6–8; 35 (January 1987): 16–19.

PAUL HORGAN

3828. Biebel, Charles D. "Paul Horgan's Early Albuquerque: Notes on a Southwest City in Transition." *New Mexico Humanities Review* 3 (Summer 1980): 35–45.

3829. Carter, Alfred. "On the Fiction of Paul Horgan." *New Mexico Quarterly* 7 (August 1937): 207–16.

3830. Cooper, Guy L. "Paul Horgan: American Synthesis." Doctoral dissertation, University of Arkansas, 1971.

3831. Day, James M. *Paul Horgan.* Southwest Writers Series, No. 8. Austin, Tex.: Steck-Vaughn, 1967.

3832. Donchak, Stella Cassano. "Paul Horgan: Craftsman and Literary Artist." Doctoral dissertation, Case Western Reserve University, 1970.

3833. Gish, Robert F. "Albuquerque as Recurrent Frontier in Paul Horgan's *The Common Heart.*" *New Mexico Humanities Review* 3 (Summer 1980): 23–33.

3834. ———. "Calliope and Clio: Paul Horgan's River Muses." *Southwest Review* 69 (Winter 1984): 2–15.

3835. ———. "*'New Mexico's Own Chronicle'* Revisited." *Southwestern American Literature* 14 (Fall 1988): 5–18.

3836. ———. *Paul Horgan.* Boston: Twayne, 1983.

3837. Hansen, Terry L. "The Experience of Paul Horgan's *The Peach Stone.*" *South Dakota Review* 22 (Summer 1984): 71–85.

3838. Kraft, James. "About Paul Horgan's *Things as They Are.*" *Canadian Review of American Studies* 2 (Spring 1971): 48–52.

3839. ———. "No Quarter Given: An Essay on Paul Horgan." *Southwestern Historical Quarterly* 80 (July 1976): 1–32.

3840. Lindenau, Judith W. "Paul Horgan's *Mountain Standard Time.*" *South Dakota Review* 1 (May 1964): 57–64.

3841. McConnell, Richard M. M., and Susan A. Frey. *Paul Horgan's Humble Powers: A Bibliography.* Washington, D.C.: Information Resources Press, 1971.

3842. Powell, Lawrence D. "Letter from the Southwest." *Westways* 67 (January 1975): 22–26.

3843. Reeve, Frank D. "A Letter to Clio." *New Mexico Historical Review* 31 (April 1956): 102–32.

EMERSON HOUGH

3844. Downey, Linda K. "Woman on the Trail: Hough's *North of 36.*" *Western American Literature* 14 (Fall 1979): 217–20.

3845. Gaston, Edwin W., Jr. *The Early Novel of the Southwest.* Albuquerque: University of New Mexico Press, 1961.

3846. Grahame, Pauline. "A Novelist of the Unsung." *Palimpsest* 11 (February 1930): 67–77.

3847. Grover, Dorys C. "Emerson Hough and J. Frank Dobie." *Southwestern American Literature* 5 (1975): 100–110.

3848. ———. "W. H. D. Koerner and Emerson Hough: A Western Collaboration." *Montana: The Magazine of Western History* 29 (April 1979): 2–15.

3849. Hutchinson, W. H. "Grassfire on the Great Plains." *Southwest Review* 41 (Spring 1956): 181–85.

3850. Johnson, Carole McCoole. "Emerson Hough and the American West: A Biographical and Critical Study." Doctoral dissertation, University of Texas, Austin, 1975.

3851. ———. "Emerson Hough's American West." *Books at Iowa* 21 (November 1974): 26–42.

3852. ———. "Emerson Hough's *The Story of the Outlaw*: A Critique and a Judgement." *Arizona and the West* 17 (Winter 1975): 309–26.

3853. Miller, John H. "Emerson Hough: Merry Christmas. Sued You Today." *Indiana University Bookman* 8 (March 1967): 23–35.

3854. Wylder, Delbert E. *Emerson Hough*. Southwest Writers Series, No. 19. Austin, Tex.: Steck-Vaughn, 1969.

3855. ———. *Emerson Hough*. Boston: Twayne, 1981.

JAMES D. HOUSTON

3856. Raskin, Jonah. *James D. Houston*. Western Writers Series, No. 99. Boise, Idaho: Boise State University, 1991.

ROBERT ERWIN HOWARD

3857. Lord, Glenn. *The Last Celt: A Bio-Bibliography of Robert Erwin Howard*. West Kingston, R.I.: Donald M. Grant, 1976.

3858. Schweitzer, Darrell. *Conan's World and Robert E. Howard*. Popular Writers of Today. San Bernardino, Calif.: Borgo, 1978.

3859. Walker, Dale L. "Pulp King of the Post Oaks." *Western American Literature* 11 (February 1977): 349–52.

EDGAR WATSON HOWE

3860. Albertini, Virgil. "Edgar Watson Howe and *The Story of a Country Town*." *Northwest Missouri State University Studies* 35 (February 1975): 19–29.

3861. ———. "Religious Miseries in Edgar Watson Howe's *The Story of a Country Town*." *American Renaissance and American West*. Eds. Christopher S. Durer, et al. Laramie: University of Wyoming, 1982, 49–58.

3862. Brune, Ruth E. "The Early Life of Edgar Watson Howe." Doctoral dissertation, University of Colorado, 1949.

3863. Bucco, Martin. *E. W. Howe*. Western Writers Series, No. 26. Boise, Idaho: Boise State University, 1977.

3864. Cosgrove, Robert William. "Joseph Kirkland and Edgar Watson Howe: A Reappraisal of Their Fiction With Emphasis on Their Realism." Doctoral dissertation, Purdue University, 1974.

3865. Dick, Everett. "Ed Howe, a Notable Figure on the Sod-House Frontier." *Nebraska History Magazine* 18 (April–June 1937): 138–43.

3866. Eichelberger, Clayton L. "Edgar Watson Howe and Joseph Kirkland: More Critical Comment." *American Literary Realism 1870–1910* 4 (Summer 1971): 279–90.

3867. ———. "EWH: Critical Bibliography of Secondary Comment." *American Literary Realism 1870–1910* 2 (Spring 1969): 1–49.

3868. Mayer, Charles W. "Realizing 'A Whole Order of Things': E.W. Howe's *The Story of a Country Town*." *Western American Literature* 11 (May 1976): 23–36.

3869. Pickett, Calder M. "Edgar Watson Howe and the Kansas Scene." *Kansas Quarterly* 2 (Spring 1970): 39–45.

3870. ———. "Edgar Watson Howe: Legend and Truth." *American Literary Realism 1870–1910* 2 (Spring 1969): 70–73.

3871. ———. *Ed Howe: Country Town Philosopher*. Lawrence: University Press of Kansas, 1968.

3872. Powers, Richard. "Tradition in E.W. Howe's *The Story of a Country Town*." *Midcontinent American Studies Journal* 9 (Fall 1968): 51–62.

3873. Ropp, Philip H. "Edgar Watson Howe." Doctoral dissertation, University of Virginia, 1949.

3874. Sackett, S. J. *E.W. Howe*. New York: Twayne, 1972.

3875. Schorer, C. E. "Growing Up with the Country." *Midwest Journal* 6 (Fall 1954): 12–26.

WILLIAM DEAN HOWELLS

3876. Bucco, Martin. "*The Rise of Silas Lapham*: The Western Dimension." *Western American Literature* 23 (Winter 1989): 291–310.

3877. Dean, James L. "The Wests of Howells and Crane." *American Literary Realism 1870–1910* 10 (Summer 1977): 254–66.

LOIS PHILLIPS HUDSON

3878. Peters, E. Roxanne. "Lois Phillips Hudson: Reaper of the Dust." *North Dakota Quarterly* 44 (Autumn 1976): 18–29.

3879. Putnam, Ann. "Betrayal and Redemption in the Fiction of Lois Phillips Hudson." *South Dakota Review* 26 (Autumn 1988): 10–23.

3880. Allen, Michael. "'Because Poems Are People': An Interview with Richard Hugo." *Ohio Review* 19 (Winter 1978): 74–90.

3881. ———. "'Only the eternal nothing of space': Richard Hugo's West." *Western American Literature* 15 (May 1980): 25–35.

3882. ———. *We Are Called Human: The Poetry of Richard Hugo.* Fayetteville: University of Arkansas Press, 1982.

3883. Bense, James. "Richard Hugo: A Bibliography." *Bulletin of Bibliography* 40 (September 1983): 148–62.

3884. Bevis, William W. "Hugo's Poetry." *Ten Tough Trips: Montana Writers and the West.* Seattle: University of Washington Press, 1990, 143–60.

3885. Dillon, David. "Gains Made in Isolation: An Interview with Richard Hugo." *Southwest Review* 62 (Spring 1977): 101–15.

3886. Garber, Frederick. "Fat Man at the Margin: The Poetry of Richard Hugo." *Iowa Review* 3 (1972): 58–67. Followed by Hugo's comments, 67–76.

3887. ———. "Large Man in the Mountains: The Recent Work of Richard Hugo." *Western American Literature* 10 (November 1975): 205–18.

3888. Gardner, Thomas. "An Interview with Richard Hugo." *Contemporary Literature* 22 (Spring 1981): 139–52.

3889. Gerstenberger, Donna. *Richard Hugo.* Western Writers Series, No. 59. Boise, Idaho: Boise State University, 1983.

3890. Helms, Alan. "Writing Hurt: The Poetry of Richard Hugo." *Modern Poetry Studies* 9 (Autumn 1978): 106–18.

3891. Howard, Richard. "Richard Hugo." *Alone With America: Essays on the Art of Poetry in the United States Since 1950.* New York: Atheneum, 1969, 232–46.

3892. Hugo, Richard. *The Triggering Town: Lectures and Essays on Poetry and Writing.* New York: Norton, [1979].

3893. Lindholdt, Paul J. "Richard Hugo's Language: The Poem as 'Obsessive Musical Deed.'" *Concerning Poetry* 16 (No. 2, 1983): 67–75.

3894. Lockwood, William J. "Richard Hugo's Return to the Pacific Northwest: Early and Recent Poems." *The Westering Experience in American Literature: Bicentennial Essays.* Eds. Merrill Lewis and L. L. Lee. Bellingham: Bureau for Faculty Research, Western Washington University, 1977, 161–71.

3895. Pinsker, Sanford. *Three Pacific Northwest Poets: William Stafford, Richard Hugo, and David Wagoner.* Boston: Twayne, 1987.

3896. "Special Richard Hugo Issue." *Slackwater Review* [Lewiston, Idaho] (1978): 7–195.

3897. "The Third Time the World Happens: A Dialogue on Writing Between Richard Hugo and William Stafford." *Northwest Review* 13 (March 1974): 26–47.

WILLIAM HUMPHREY

3898. Grammer, John M. "Where the Sun Draws Up to a Stop: The Fiction of William Humphrey." *Mississippi Quarterly* 44 (Winter 1990/1991): 5–21.

3899. Lee, James W. *William Humphrey.* Southwest Writers Series, No. 7. Austin, Tex.: Steck-Vaughn, 1967.

3900. Winchell, Mark Royden. *William Humphrey.* Western Writers Series, No. 105. Boise, Idaho: Boise State University, 1992.

DAVID HENRY HWANG

3901. Dickey, Jerry R. "'Myths of the East, Myths of the West': Shattering Racial and Gender Stereotypes in the Plays of David Henry Hwang." *New West–Old West: Centennial Essays.* Ed. Barbara Howard Meldrum. Moscow: University of Idaho Press, 1993, 272–80.

3902. Street, Douglas. *David Henry Hwang.* Western Writers Series, No. 90. Boise, Idaho: Boise State University, 1989.

LUIS INCLÁN

3903. Paredes, Americo. "Luis Inclán: First of the Cowboy Writers." *American Quarterly* 12 (Spring 1960): 55–70.

WILLIAM INGE

3904. Armato, Philip M. "The Bum as Scapegoat in William Inge's *Picnic.*" *Western American Literature* 10 (February 1976): 273–82.

3905. Bailey, Jeffrey. "William Inge: An Appreciation in Retrospect." *Kansas Quarterly* 18 (Fall 1986): 139–47.

3906. Donovan, Robert Kent. "The Dionysiac Dance in William Inge's *Picnic.*" *Dance Chronicle* 7 (No. 4, 1985): 413–34.

3907. Gale, Steven H. "Small Town Images in Four Plays by William Inge." *Kansas Quarterly* 18 (Fall 1986): 89–100.

3908. Knudsen, James. "Last Words: The Novels of William Inge." *Kansas Quarterly* 18 (Fall 1986): 121–29.

3909. Lange, Jane W. "'Forces Get Loose': Social Prophecy in William Inge's *Picnic.*" *Kansas Quarterly* 18 (Fall 1986): 57–70.

3910. Leeson, Richard M. *William Inge: A Research and Production Sourcebook*. Westport, Conn.: Greenwood Press, 1994.

3911. McClure, Arthur F., and C. David Rice, eds. *A Bibliographical Guide to the Works of William Inge*. Lewiston, N. Y.: E. Mellen, 1991.

3912. McIlrath, Patricia. "William Inge, Great Voice of the Heart of America." *Kansas Quarterly* 18 (Fall 1986): 45–53.

3913. Manley, Francis. "William Inge: A Bibliography." *American Book Collector* 16 (1965): 13–21.

3914. Miller, Jordan Y. "William Inge: Last of the Realists?" *Kansas Quarterly* 2 (Spring 1970): 17–26.

3915. Mitchell, Marilyn. "The Teacher as Outsider in the Works of William Inge." *Midwest Quarterly* 17 (Summer 1976): 385–93.

3916. Reilingh, Maarten. "William Inge." *American Playwrights Since 1945*. Ed. Philip C. Kolin. New York: Greenwood Press, 1989, 190–208.

3917. Shuman, R. Baird. *William Inge*. Rev ed. New York: Twayne, 1989.

3918. Voss, Ralph Frederick. *A Life of William Inge: The Strains of Triumph*. Lawrence: University Press of Kansas, 1989.

3919. Wentworth, Michael. "The Convergence of Fairy Tale and Myth in William Inge's *Picnic*." *Kansas Quarterly* 18 (Fall 1986): 75–85.

WASHINGTON IRVING

3920. Antelyes, Peter. *Tales of Adventurous Enterprise: Washington Irving and the Poetics of Western Expansion*. New York: Columbia University Press, 1990.

3921. Bowden, Mary W. *Washington Irving*. Boston: Twayne, 1981.

3922. ———. *Washington Irving: Bibliography*. Boston: Twayne, 1989.

3923. Brodwin, Stanley, ed. *The Old and New World Romanticism of Washington Irving*. New York: Greenwood Press, 1986.

3924. Bukoski, Anthony. "Grandeur in Washington Irving's 'A Tour on the Prairies.'" *Illinois Quarterly* 43 (Summer 1981): 5–15.

3925. Clark, William Bedford. "How the West Won: Irving's Comic Inversion of the Westering Myth in *A Tour on the Prairies*." *American Literature* 50 (November 1978): 335–47.

3926. Cracroft, Richard H. "The American West of Washington Irving." Doctoral dissertation, University of Wisconsin, 1970.

3927. ———. *Washington Irving: The Western Works*. Western Writers Series, No. 14. Boise, Idaho: Boise State University, 1974.

3928. Dervin, James Allen. "Washington Irving Tours the Frontier: A New Yorker Sees and Shapes the Raw Materials of Frontier Life." Doctoral dissertation, University of North Carolina, Chapel Hill, 1974.

3929. Dula, Martha. "Audience Response to *A Tour on the Prairies* in 1835." *Western American Literature* 8 (Spring–Summer 1973): 68–74.

3930. Egan, Hugh. "The Second-Hand Wilderness: History and Art in Irving's *Astoria.*" *American Transcendental Quarterly* 2 (December 1988): 253–70.

3931. Franklin, Wayne. "The Misadventures of Irving's Bonneville: Trapping and Being Trapped in the Rocky Mountains." *The Westering Experience in American Literature: Bicentennial Essays.* Eds. Merrill Lewis and L.L. Lee. Bellingham: Bureau for Faculty Research, Western Washington University, 1977, 122–28.

3932. Gardner, J. H. "One Hundred Years Ago in the Region of Tulsa." *Chronicles of Oklahoma* 11 (June 1933): 765–85.

3933. Hudson, Ruth. "A Literary 'Area of Freedom' Between Irving and Twain." *Western Humanities Review* 13 (Winter 1959): 46–60.

3934. Irving, Washington. *A Tour of the Prairies.* Ed. with intro., John Francis McDermott. Norman: University of Oklahoma Press, 1956.

3935. ———. *The Western Journals of Washington Irving.* Ed. and annotated, John Francis McDermott. Norman: University of Oklahoma Press, 1944.

3936. Keiser, Albert. *The Indian in American Literature.* New York: Oxford University Press, 1933, 52–64.

3937. Kime, Wayne R. "The Author as Professional: Washington Irving's 'Rambling Anecdotes' of the West." *Critical Essays on Washington Irving.* Ed. Ralph M. Aderman. Boston: G. K. Hall, 1990, 237–53.

3938. ———. "The Completeness of Washington Irving's *A Tour on the Prairies.*" *Western American Literature* 8 (Spring–Summer 1973): 55–65.

3939. ———. "Washington Irving and Frontier Speech." *American Speech* 42 (February 1967): 5–18.

3940. ———. "Washington Irving's *Astoria*: A Critical Study." Doctoral dissertation, University of Delaware, 1968.

3941. ———. "Washington Irving's Revision of the *Tonquin* Episode in *Astoria.*" *Western American Literature* 4 (Spring 1969): 51–59.

3942. Lee, Robert Edson. *From West to East.* Urbana: University of Illinois Press, 1966, 58–69.

3943. Lyon, Thomas J. "Washington Irving's Wilderness." *Western American Literature* 1 (Fall 1966): 167–74.

3944. McDermott, John Francis. "Washington Irving and the Journal of Captain Bonneville." *Mississippi Valley Historical Review* 43 (December 1956): 459–67.

3945. MacGregor, Alan Leander. "'Lords of the Ascendant': Mercantile Biography and Irving's *Astoria*." *Canadian Review of American Studies* 21 (Summer 1990): 15–30.

3946. MacLaren, I. S. "Washington Irving's Problems with History and Romance in *Astoria*." *Canadian Review of American Studies* 21 (Summer 1990): 1–13.

3947. Myers, Andrew B. "Washington Irving, Fur Trade Chronicler: An Analysis of *Astoria* with Notes for a Corrected Edition." Doctoral dissertation, Columbia University, 1964.

3948. Pochmann, Henry A. "Washington Irving." *Fifteen American Authors Before 1900: Bibliographic Essays on Research and Criticism*. Eds. Robert A. Rees and Earl N. Harbert. Madison: University of Wisconsin Press, 1971, 245–61.

3949. Rust, Richard D. "Irving Rediscovers the Frontier." *American Transcendental Quarterly* 18 (Spring 1973): 40–44.

3950. Scheick, William J. "Frontier Robin Hood: Wilderness, Civilization and the Half-Breed in Irving's *A Tour on the Prairies*." *Southwestern American Literature* 4 (1974): 14–21.

3951. Short, Julee. "Irving's Eden: Oklahoma, 1832." *Journal of the West* 10 (October 1971): 700–712.

3952. Spaulding, George F., ed. *On the Western Tour with Washington Irving: The Journal and Letters of Count de Pourtales*. Trans. Seymour Feiler. Norman: University of Oklahoma Press, 1968.

3953. Springer, Haskell. *Washington Irving: A Reference Guide*. Boston: G.K. Hall, 1976.

3954. Terrell, Dahlia Jewel. "A Textual Study of Washington Irving's *A Tour on the Prairies*." Doctoral dissertation, University of Texas, 1966.

3955. Todd, Edgeley W. "Washington Irving Discovers the Frontier." *Western Humanities Review* 11 (Winter 1957): 29–39.

3956. Von Frank, Albert James. "Frontier Consciousness in American Literature." Doctoral dissertation, University of Missouri, Columbia, 1976.

3957. Wagenknecht, Edward. *Washington Irving: Moderation Displayed*. New York: Oxford University Press, 1962.

3958. Williams, Stanley T. *Life of Washington Irving*. 2 vols. New York: Oxford University Press, 1935.

3959. ————, and Barbara D. Simpson, eds. *Washington Irving on the Prairie, or, A Narrative of a Tour of the Southwest in the Year 1832.* New York: American Book, 1937.

ARTURO ISLAS

3960. Sánchez, Marta E. "Arturo Islas' *The Rain God*: An Alternative Tradition." *American Literature* 62 (June 1990): 284–304.

MOLLY IVINS

3961. Bean, Judith Mattson. "'True Grit and all the Rest': The Expression of Regional Identity in Molly Ivins's Discourse." *Southwestern American Literature* 19 (Fall 1993): 35–46.

HELEN HUNT JACKSON

3962. Banning, Evelyn I. *Helen Hunt Jackson.* New York: Vanguard Press, 1973.

3963. Byers, John R., Jr. "Helen Hunt Jackson (1830–1885)." *American Literary Realism 1870–1910* 2 (Summer 1969): 143–48.

3964. ————. "The Indian Matter of Helen Hunt Jackson's *Ramona*: From Fact to Fiction." *American Indian Quarterly* 11 (Winter 1975–76): 331–46.

3965. ————, and Elizabeth S. Byers. "Helen Hunt Jackson (1830–1885): A Critical Bibliography of Secondary Comment." *American Literary Realism 1870–1910* 6 (Summer 1973): 197–241.

3966. Gordon, Joseph T., and Judith A. Pickle, eds. *Helen Hunt Jackson's Colorado.* Colorado Springs: Hulbert Center for Southwestern Studies, Colorado College, 1989.

3967. McConnell, Virginia. "'H. H.,' Colorado and the Indian Problem." *Journal of the West* 12 (April 1973): 272–80.

3968. Marsden, Michael T. "A Dedication to the Memory of Helen Hunt Jackson, 1830–1885." *Arizona and the West* 21 (Summer 1979): 109–12.

3969. ————. "Helen Hunt Jackson: Docudramatist of the American Indian." *Markham Review* 10 (Fall/Winter 1980–81): 15–19.

3970. Mathes, Valerie Sherer. *Helen Hunt Jackson and Her Indian Reform Legacy.* Austin: University of Texas Press, 1990.

3971. May, Antoinette. *Helen Hunt Jackson: A Lonely Voice of Conscience.* San Francisco: Chronicle Books, 1987.

3972. Nevins, Allan. "Helen Hunt Jackson, Sentimentalist vs. Realist." *American Scholar* 10 (Summer 1941): 269–85.

3973. Odell, Ruth. *Helen Hunt Jackson.* New York: D. Appleton-Century, 1939.

3974. Schmudde, Carol E. "Sincerity, Secrecy, and Lies: Helen Hunt Jackson's No Name Novels." *Studies in American Fiction* 21 (Spring 1993): 51–66.

3975. Whitaker, Rosemary. *Helen Hunt Jackson.* Western Writers Series, No. 78. Boise, Idaho: Boise State University, 1987.

GEORGE WHARTON JAMES

3976. Bourdon, Roger Joseph. "George Wharton James: Interpreter of the Southwest." Doctoral dissertation, University of California, Los Angeles, 1965.

3977. Wild, Peter. *George Wharton James.* Western Writers Series, No. 93. Boise, Idaho: Boise State University, 1990.

WILL JAMES

3978. Amaral, Anthony. "A Dedication to the Memory of Will James, 1892–1942." *Arizona and the West* 10 (Autumn 1968): 206–10.

3979. ———. *Will James: The Gilt Edged Cowboy.* Los Angeles: Westernlore Press, 1967; rev ed. *Will James: The Last Cowboy Legend.* Reno: University of Nevada Press, 1980, 1993.

3980. Bell, William Gardner. *Will James: The Life and Works of a Lone Cowboy.* Flagstaff, Ariz.: Northland Press, 1987.

3981. Bramlett, Jim. *Ride for the High Points: The Real Story of Will James.* Missoula, [Mont.]: Mountain Press Publishing, 1987.

3982. Neil, J. M., ed. *Will James: The Spirit of the Cowboy.* Casper, Wyoming: Nicolaysen Art Museum, 1985.

MITCHELL F. JAYNE

3983. Lawson, Lewis A. "Old Fish Hawk: From Stereotype to Archetype." *American Indian Quarterly* 3 (Winter 1977–78): 321–33.

ROBINSON JEFFERS

3984. Adamic, Louis. *Robinson Jeffers, a Portrait.* Seattle: University of Washington Book Store, 1929.

3985. Alexander, John R. "Conflict in the Narrative Poetry of Robinson Jeffers." *Sewanee Review* 80 (Winter 1972): 85–99.

3986. Antoninus, Brother. *Robinson Jeffers: Fragments of an Older Fury.* Berkeley. Calif.: Oyez, 1968.

3987. Bartlett, Jeffrey. "Jeffers and California Today." *North Dakota Quarterly* 57 (Spring 1989): 19–25.

3988. Beers, Terry. "Robinson Jeffers and the Canon." *American Poetry* 5 (Fall 1987): 4–16.

3989. Beilke, Marlan. *Shining Clarity: Man and God in the Works of Robinson Jeffers.* Amador City, Calif.: Quintessence Publications, 1977.

3990. Bennett, Melba B. *The Stone Mason of Tor House: The Life and Work of Robinson Jeffers.* [Menlo Park, Calif.]: Ward Ritchie, 1966.

3991. Boswell, Jeanetta. *Robinson Jeffers and the Critics, 1912–1983: A Bibliography of Secondary Sources with Selective Annotations.* Metuchen, N.J.: Scarecrow Press, 1986.

3992. Boyers, Robert. "A Sovereign Voice: The Poetry of Robinson Jeffers." *Sewanee Review* 78 (July–September 1969): 487–507.

3993. Brophy, Robert J. *In Search of Robinson Jeffers: A Selected Bibliography.* Carmel, Calif.: Tor House Foundation, 1981.

3994. ———. "Jeffers Theses and Dissertations: A Summary Listing." *Robinson Jeffers Newsletter* 45 (June 1976): 8–10.

3995. ———. "The Prose of Robinson Jeffers: An Annotated Checklist." *Robinson Jeffers Newsletter* 46 (September 1976): 14–36.

3996. ———. "Robinson Jeffers." *Western American Literature* 20 (Summer 1985): 133–50.

3997. ———. *Robinson Jeffers.* Western Writers Series, No. 19. Boise, Idaho: Boise State University, 1975.

3998. ———. *Robinson Jeffers: Myth, Ritual and Symbol in His Narrative Poems.* Cleveland: Case Western Reserve University Press, 1973; 2d ed. Hamden, Conn.: Archon Press, 1976.

3999. ———, ed. *Robinson Jeffers: Poetry and Response: A Centennial Tribute.* Los Angeles: Occidental College, 1987.

4000. ———, and John Ahouse. *A Ward Ritchie Checklist: Works by and about Robinson Jeffers.* Long Beach, Calif., 1979.

4001. Butterfield, R. W. "Robinson Jeffers." *American Writers.* Ed. A. Walton Litz. New York: Scribner's, 1980, 2d supplement, part 2, 413–40.

4002. Carpenter, Frederic I. "The Inhumanism of Robinson Jeffers." *Western American Literature* 16 (Spring 1981): 19–25.

4003. ———. "'Post Mortem': The Poet is Dead." *Western American Literature* 12 (May 1977): 3–10.

4004. ———. *Robinson Jeffers*. New York: Twayne, 1962.

4005. ———. "Robinson Jeffers Today: Beyond Good and Beneath Evil." *American Literature* 49 (March 1977): 88–96.

4006. Coffin, Arthur B. *Robinson Jeffers*. Madison: University of Wisconsin Press, 1971.

4007. Cokinos, Christopher. "If We Can Be Saved: Robinson Jeffers Today and Tomorrow." *North Dakota Quarterly* 57 (Spring 1989): 26–39.

4008. DeMott, Robert. "Robinson Jeffers' 'Tamar.'" *The Twenties: fiction, poetry, drama*. Ed. Warren French. Deland, Fla.: Everett/Edwards, 1975, 405–25.

4009. Everson, William. *The Excesses of God: Robinson Jeffers as a Religious Figure*. Stanford, Calif.: Stanford University Press, 1988.

4010. Gilbert, Rudolph. *Shine, Perishing Republic: Robinson Jeffers and the Tragic Sense in Modern Poetry*. Boston: Bruce Humphries, 1936.

4011. Greenan, Edith. *Of Una Jeffers*. Los Angeles: Ward Ritchie, 1939.

4012. Hotchkiss, William. *Jeffers: The Sivaistic Vision*. Auburn, Calif.: Blue Oak Press, 1975.

4013. Houston, James D. "Necessary Ecstasy: An Afterword to *Cawdor*." *Western American Literature* 19 (August 1984): 99–112.

4014. Hunt, Tim. "A Voice in Nature: Jeffers' *Tamar and Other Poems*." *American Literature* 61 (May 1989): 230–44.

4015. Johnson, William Savage. "The 'Savior' in the Poetry of Robinson Jeffers." *American Literature* 15 (May 1943): 159–68.

4016. Kafka, Robb. "Robinson Jeffers' Published Writings, 1903–1911." *Robinson Jeffers Newsletter* 53 (June 1979): 47–68.

4017. Karman, James. *Robinson Jeffers: Poet of California*. San Francisco: Chronicle Books, 1987.

4018. ———, ed. *Critical Essays on Robinson Jeffers*. Boston: G.K. Hall, 1990.

4019. Keller, Karl. "California, Yankees, and the Death of God: The Allegory in Jeffers' *Roan Stallion*." *Texas Studies in Literature and Language* 12 (Spring 1970): 111–20.

4020. ———. "Jeffers' Pace." *Robinson Jeffers Newsletter* 32 (July 1972): 7–17.

4021. Lewis, Joel. "'Oh, Lovely Rock': The Recovery of the Poetry of Robinson Jeffers." *Literary Review* 32 (Winter 1989): 181–92.

4022. Lyon, Horace. *Jeffers Country: The Seed Plots of Robinson Jeffers' Poetry*. San Francisco: Scrimshaw, 1971.

4023. Monjian, Mercedes C. *Robinson Jeffers: A Study in Inhumanism.*
Pittsburgh: University of Pittsburgh Press, 1958.

4024. Murphy, Patrick D. "Reclaiming the Power: Robinson Jeffers's Verse
Novels." *Western American Literature* 22 (Summer 1987): 125–48.

4025. ———. "Robinson Jeffers' Macabre and Darkly Marvelous Double
Axe." *Western American Literature* 20 (November 1985): 195–209.

4026. Nickerson, Edward A. "The Holy Light in Jeffers' Poetry." *Robinson
Jeffers Newsletter* 47 (December 1976): 19–28.

4027. ———. "The Return to Rhyme." *Robinson Jeffers Newsletter* 39 (July
1974): 12–21.

4028. ———. "Robinson Jeffers and the Paeon." *Western American Literature* 10 (November 1975): 189–93.

4029. ———. "Robinson Jeffers: Apocalypse and His 'Inevitable Place.'"
Western American Literature 11 (August 1977): 111–22.

4030. ———. "Robinson Jeffers, Poet of Apocalypse." Doctoral dissertation, State University of New York, Albany, 1973.

4031. Nolte, William H. *The Merrill Guide to Robinson Jeffers.* Columbus,
Ohio: Charles E. Merrill, 1970.

4032. ———. *Rock and Hawk: Robinson Jeffers and the Romantic Agony.*
Athens: University of Georgia Press, 1979.

4033. Nuwer, Henry. "Jeffers' Influence upon Walter Van Tilburg Clark."
Robinson Jeffers Newsletter 44 (March 1976): 11–17.

4034. Parker, Jean Louise. "Robinson Jeffers: A Study of the Phenomena of
Human Consciousness." Doctoral dissertation, Pennsylvania State
University, 1970.

4035. Plott, David Alexander. "Feasting Gods: The Early Narrative Poems
of Robinson Jeffers." Doctoral dissertation, Harvard University,
1984.

4036. Powell, Lawrence Clark. "The Double Marriage of Robinson Jeffers."
Southwest Review 41 (Summer 1956): 278–82.

4037. ———. *Robinson Jeffers: The Man and His Work.* Pasadena, Calif.:
San Pasqual Press, 1940.

4038. Quigley, Peter S. "The Ground of Resistance: Nature and Power in
Emerson, Melville, Jeffers, and Snyder." Doctoral dissertation, Indiana University of Pennsylvania, 1990.

4039. Redinger, Ellsworth L. "The Poetic Dramas of Robinson Jeffers."
Doctoral dissertation, University of Southern California, 1971.

4040. Ridgeway, Ann N., ed. *The Selected Letters of Robinson Jeffers,
1897–1962.* Baltimore: Johns Hopkins Press, 1968.

4041. *Robinson Jeffers Newsletter.* Edited by Melba B. Bennett (nos. 1–22) and Robert J. Brophy (nos. 23–). Los Angeles: Robinson Jeffers Committee, Occidental College, 1962–.

4042. Rogers, Covington. "A Checklist of Robinson Jeffers' Poetical Writings Since 1934." *Robinson Jeffers Newsletter* 48 (March 1977): 11–24.

4043. ———, and John Meador. *The Robinson Jeffers Collection at the University of Houston.* University of Houston, 1975. A 32-page checklist.

4044. Schweizer, Harold. "Robinson Jeffers' Excellent Action." *American Poetry* 5 (Fall 1987): 35–58.

4045. Scott, Robert I. "The Ends of Tragedy: Robinson Jeffers' Satires on Human Importance." *Canadian Review of American Studies* 10 (Fall 1979): 231–41.

4046. ———. "Robinson Jeffers' Tragedies as Rediscoveries of the World." *Rocky Mountain Review* 29 (Autumn 1975): 147–65.

4047. Sessions, George. "Spinoza and Jeffers on Man in Nature." *Inquiry* 20 (1977): 481–528.

4048. Shebl, James. *In This Wild Water: Suppressed Poems of Robinson Jeffers.* Pasadena, Calif.: Ward Ritchie, 1976.

4049. Shiglas, Jerry Ashburn. "The Divided Mind of Robinson Jeffers." Doctoral dissertation, Duke University, 1972.

4050. Short, R.W. "The Tower Beyond Tragedy." *Southern Review* 7 (Summer 1941): 132–44.

4051. Squires, Radcliffe. *The Loyalties of Robinson Jeffers.* Ann Arbor: University of Michigan Press, 1956.

4052. ———. "Robinson Jeffers: The Anatomy of Violence." *Modern American Poetry: Essays in Criticism.* Ed. Guy Owens. Deland, Fla. Everett/Edwards, 1975.

4053. Sterling, George. *Robinson Jeffers, the Man and the Artist.* New York: Boni and Liveright, 1926.

4054. Turlish, Molly S. "Story Patterns from Greek and Biblical Sources in the Poetry of Robinson Jeffers." Doctoral dissertation, University of Michigan, 1971.

4055. Van Dam, Danis. "Greek Shadows on the Monterey Coast: Environment in Robinson Jeffers' Poetry." *Robinson Jeffers Newsletter* 40 (November 1974): 9–17.

4056. Vardamis, Alex A. *The Critical Reputation of Robinson Jeffers: A Bibliographical Study.* Hamden, Conn.: Archon Books, 1972.

4057. Vaughn, Eric. "'Dear Judas': Time and the Dramatic Structure of the

Dream." *Robinson Jeffers Newsletter* 51 (July 1978): 7–22.

4058. Waggoner, Hyatt Howe. *The Heel of Elohim: Science and Values in Modern Poetry.* Norman: University of Oklahoma Press, 1950, 105–32.

4059. Watts, Harold H. "Multivalence in Robinson Jeffers." *College English* 3 (November 1941): 109–20.

4060. ———. "Robinson Jeffers and Eating the Serpent." *Sewanee Review* 49 (January 1941): 39–55.

4061. White, Kenneth. *The Coast Opposite Humanity: An Essay on the Poetry of Robinson Jeffers.* Dyfed, England: Unicorn, 1975.

4062. Young, Vernon. "Such Counsels He Gave to Us: Jeffers Revisited." *Parnassus* 6 (Fall/Winter 1977): 178–97.

4063. Zaller, Robert. *The Cliffs of Solitude: A Reading of Robinson Jeffers.* New York: Cambridge University Press, 1983.

4064. ———. "Land and Value: The Ecology of Robinson Jeffers." *Western American Literature* 26 (May 1991): 9–20.

4065. ———, ed. *Centennial Essays for Robinson Jeffers.* Newark: University of Delaware Press, 1991.

DOROTHY M. JOHNSON

4066. Alter, Judy. *Dorothy Johnson.* Western Writers Series, No. 44. Boise, Idaho: Boise State University, 1980.

4067. Mathews, Sue. "Pioneer Women in the Works of Two Montana Authors: Interviews with Dorothy M. Johnson and A. B. Guthrie, Jr." *Women and Western American Literature.* Eds. Helen Winter Stauffer and Susan J. Rosowski. Troy, N.Y.: Whitston, 1982, 124–31.

4068. ———, and James W. Healey. "The Winning of the Western Fiction Market: An Interview with Dorothy M. Johnson." *Prairie Schooner* 52 (Summer 1978): 158–67.

4069. Meldrum, Barbara Howard. "Dorothy M. Johnson's Short Fiction: The Pastoral and the Uses of History." *Western American Literature* 17 (November 1982): 213–26.

4070. Smith, Stephen. *The Years and the Wind and the Rain: A Biography of Dorothy M. Johnson.* Missoula, Mont.: Pictorial Histories Publishing, 1984.

NARD JONES

4071. Venn, George. "Introduction," to Nard Jones, *Oregon Detour.* Corvallis: Oregon State University Press, 1990, vii–xxxi.

PRESTON JONES

4072. Busby, Mark. *Preston Jones.* Western Writers Series, No. 58. Boise, Idaho: Boise State University, 1983.

4073. Reynolds, R. C. "Humor, Dreams and the Human Condition in Preston Jones's 'A Texas Trilogy.'" *Southern Quarterly* 24 (Spring 1986): 14–24.

WELDON KEES

4074. Nemerov, Howard. "On Weldon Kees, An Introduction to His Critical Writings." *Prairie Schooner* 61 (Winter 1987): 33–36.

GARRISON KEILLOR

4075. Lee, Judith Yaross. *Garrison Keillor: A Voice of America.* Jackson: University Press of Mississippi, 1991.

4076. Michelson, Bruce. "Keillor and Rölvaag: and the Art of Telling the Truth." *American Studies* 30 (Spring 1989): 21–34.

4077. Wilbers, Stephen. "Lake Wobegon: Mythical Place and the American Imagination." *American Studies* 30 (Spring 1989): 5–20.

ELMER KELTON

4078. Alter, Judy. *Elmer Kelton and West Texas.* Denton: University of North Texas Press, 1989.

4079. Clayton, Lawrence. *Elmer Kelton.* Western Writers Series, No. 73. Boise, Idaho: Boise State University, 1986.

4080. ———. "Elmer Kelton: A Serious Western Novelist." *Southwestern American Literature* 8 (Spring 1983): 5–11.

4081. ———. "The End of the West Motif in the Work of Edward Abbey, Jane Kramer, and Elmer Kelton." *RE: Artes Liberales* 6 (Fall 1979): 11–18.

4082. ———. "Kelton's Charlie Flagg as Modern Western Hero." *RE: Artes Liberales* 14 (Fall 1987): 13–20.

4083. Erisman, Fred. "Elmer Kelton's 'Other' West." *Western American Literature* 28 (Winter 1994): 291–99.

4084. Grover, Dorys C. "Elmer Kelton and the Popular Western Novel." *Southwest Heritage* 8 (Summer 1978): 8–19.

4085. Lee, Billy C. "Elmer Kelton: A *PQ* Interview." *Paperback Quarterly* 1 (Summer 1978): 16–30.

4086. "Special Edition: The Works of Elmer Kelton." *Southwest American Literature* 9 (Spring 1984): 5–52. Includes essays by Lawrence Clayton, Bob J. Frye, Dorys Crow Grover, and Ken Hammes.

JACK KEROUAC

4087. Askew, Melvin W. "Quests, Cars, and Kerouac." *University of Kansas City Review* 28 (Spring 1962): 231–40.

4088. Ball, Vernon Francis. "Of Glory Obscur'd: Beatific Vision in the Narrative of Jack Kerouac." Doctoral dissertation, Ball State University, 1976.

4089. Berrigan, Ted, et al. "The Art of Fiction XLI: Jack Kerouac." *Paris Review* 43 (Summer 1968): 60–105.

4090. Cassady, Carolyn. *Heart Beat: My Life with Jack Neal.* Berkeley, Calif.: Creative Arts, 1976.

4091. ———. *Off the Road: My Years with Cassady, Kerouac, and Ginsberg.* New York: William Morrow, 1990.

4092. Challis, Chris. *Quest for Kerouac.* Boston: Faber Faber, 1984.

4093. Charters, Ann. *A Bibliography of Works by Jack Kerouac 1939–1975.* New York: Phoenix Book Shop, 1967; rev ed., 1975.

4094. ———. *Kerouac: A Biography.* San Francisco: Straight Arrow Books, 1973.

4095. ———. "Kerouac's Literary Method and Experiments: The Evidence of the Manuscript Notebooks in the Berg Collection." *Bulletin of Research in the Humanities* 84 (Winter 1981): 431–51.

4096. Clark, Tom. *Jack Kerouac.* San Diego: Harcourt Brace Jovanovich, 1984.

4097. ———. *Jack Kerouac: A Biography.* New York: Paragon House, 1990.

4098. Cook, Bruce. *The Beat Generation.* New York: Charles Scribner's Sons, 1971.

4099. Dardess, George. "The Delicate Dynamics of Friendship: A Reconsideration of Kerouac's *On the Road.*" *American Literature* 46 (May 1974): 200–206.

4100. ———. "The Logic of Spontaneity: A Reconsideration of Kerouac's 'Spontaneous Prose Method.'" *Boundary 2* (1975): 729–43.

4101. Davenport, Stephen M. "Complicating 'a very masculine aesthetic': Positional Sons and Double Husbands, Kinship and Careening in Jack Kerouac's Fiction." Doctoral dissertation, University of Illinois, Urbana-Champaign, 1992.

4102. Donaldson, Scott, ed. *Jack Kerouac, On the Road: Text and Criticism.* New York: Penguin Books, 1979.

4103. Duffey, Bernard. "The Three Worlds of Jack Kerouac." *Recent American Fiction.* Ed. Joseph J. Waldmeir. Boston: Houghton Mifflin, 1963, 175–84.

4104. Feied, Frederick. *No Pie in the Sky: The Hobo as American Cultural Hero in the Works of Jack London, John Dos Passos, and Jack Kerouac.* New York: Citadel, 1964.

4105. French, Warren. *Jack Kerouac.* Boston: Twayne, 1986.

4106. Frohock, W. M. "Jack Kerouac and the Beats." *Strangers to This Ground.* Dallas: Southern Methodist University Press, 1961, 132–47.

4107. Gelfant, Blanche H. "Jack Kerouac." *Contemporary Literature* 15 (Summer 1974): 415–22.

4108. Gifford, Barry. *Kerouac's Town.* Santa Barbara, Calif.: Capra Press, 1973; Berkeley, Calif.: Creative Arts, 1977.

4109. ————, and Lawrence Lee. *Jack's Book: An Oral Biography of Jack Kerouac.* New York: St. Martin's Press, 1978.

4110. Gussow, Adam. "Bohemia Revisited: Malcolm Cowley, Jack Kerouac, and *On the Road.*" *Georgia Review* 38 (Summer 1984): 291–311.

4111. Hart, John E. "Future Hero in Paradise: Kerouac's *The Dharma Bums.*" *Critique* 14 (1973): 52–62.

4112. Hipkiss, Robert A. *Jack Kerouac: Prophet of the New Romanticism.* Lawrence: Regents Press of Kansas, 1976.

4113. ————. "*On the Road*: Kerouac's Transport." *Kansas Quarterly* 21 (Fall 1989): 17–21.

4114. Holmes, John Clellon. *Gone in October: Last Reflections on Jack Kerouac.* Hailey, Idaho: Limberlost Press, 1985.

4115. Huebel, Harry Russell. *Jack Kerouac.* Western Writers Series, No. 39. Boise, Idaho: Boise State University, 1979.

4116. Hull, Keith N. "A Dharma Bum Goes West to Meet the East." *Western American Literature* 11 (February 1977): 321–29.

4117. Hunt, Tim. *Kerouac's Crooked Road: Development of a Fiction.* Hamden, Conn.: Archon, 1980.

4118. "Jack Kerouac and Neal Cassady." *Transatlantic Review* 33–34 (Winter 1969–1970): 115–25.

4119. Jarvis, Charles D. *Visions of Kerouac: The Life of Jack Kerouac.* 2d ed. Lowell, Mass.: Ithaca Press, 1974.

4120. Knight, Arthur, and Kit Knight, eds. *Kerouac and the Beats: A Primary Source Book.* New York: Paragon House, 1988.

4121. LePellec, Yves. "Jack Kerouac and the American Critics–a Selected Bibliography." *Caliban* 10 (1973): 77–92.

4122. McDarrah, Fred W., comp. *Kerouac and Friends: A Beat Generation Album.* New York: William Morrow, 1985.

4123. McKelly, James C. "The Artist and the West: Two Portraits by Jack Kerouac and Sam Shepard." *Western American Literature* 26 (February 1992): 293–301.

4124. McNally, Dennis. *Desolate Angel: Jack Kerouac, The Beat Generation, and America.* New York: Random House, 1979.

4125. Milewski, Robert J. *Jack Kerouac: An Annotated Bibliography of Secondary Sources, 1944–1979.* Metuchen, N.J.: Scarecrow, 1980.

4126. Nicosia, Gerald. *Memory Babe: A Critical Biography of Jack Kerouac.* New York: Grove Press, 1983.

4127. Nisonger, Thomas Evans. "Jack Kerouac: A Bibliography of Biographical and Critical Material, 1950–1979." *Bulletin of Bibliography* 37 (January/March 1980): 23–32.

4128. Øverland, Örm. "West and Back Again." *Jack Kerouac, On the Road: Text and Criticism.* Ed. Scott Donaldson. New York: Penguin Books, 1979, 451–64.

4129. Primeau, Ronald. "'The Endless Poem': Jack Kerouac's Midwest." *Great Lakes Review* 2 (Winter 1976): 19–26.

4130. *Review of Contemporary Fiction* 3 (Summer 1983): 4–95. Kerouac special issue.

4131. Robertson, David. "Real Matter, Spiritual Mountain: Gary Snyder and Jack Kerouac on Mt. Tamalpais." *Western American Literature* 27 (November 1992): 209–26.

4132. Stanley, David. "The Kerouac Boom." *Western American Literature* 16 (Summer 1981): 138–41.

4133. Tallman, Warren. "Kerouac's Sound." *Tamarack Review* 11 (Spring 1959): 58–74.

4134. Tytell, John. *Naked Angels: The Lives and Literature of the Beat Generation.* New York: McGraw-Hill, 1976.

4135. Vopat, Carole Gottlieb. "Jack Kerouac's *On the Road*: A Reevaluation." *Midwest Quarterly* 14 (July 1973): 385–407.

4136. Weinreich, Regina. *The Spontaneous Poetics of Jack Kerouac.* Carbondale: Southern Illinois Press, 1987.

4137. Williams, Bruce Keith. "The Shrouded Traveller on the Road: Death and the Work of Jack Kerouac." Doctoral dissertation, Claremont Graduate School, 1977.

4138. Yu, Beoncheon. *The Great Circle: American Writers and the Orient.* Detroit: Wayne State University Press, 1983.

4139. Baurecht, William C. "Separation, Initiation, and Return: Schizo-phrenic Episode in *One Flew Over the Cuckoo's Nest.*" *Midwest Quarterly* 23 (Spring 1982): 279–93.

4140. Beidler, Peter G., and John W. Hunt, eds. "Perspectives on a Cuckoo's Nest: A Symposium on Ken Kesey." *Lex et Scientia: International Journal of Law Science* 13 (1977).

4141. Billingsley, Ronald G. "The Artistry of Ken Kesey: A Study of *One Flew Over the Cuckoo's Nest* and of *Sometimes a Great Notion.*" Doctoral dissertation, University of Oregon, 1971.

4142. Blessing, Richard. "The Moving Target: Ken Kesey's Evolving Hero." *Journal of Popular Culture* 4 (Winter 1971): 615–27.

4143. Carnes, Bruce. *Ken Kesey.* Western Writers Series, No. 12. Boise, Idaho: Boise State University, 1974.

4144. Cowley, Malcolm. "Ken Kesey at Stanford." *Kesey.* Ed. Michael Strelow, et al. Eugene, Oreg.: Northwest Review Books, 1977, 1–4.

4145. Drout, Michael D. C. "Hoisting the Arm of Defiance: Beowulfian Elements in Ken Kesey's *Sometimes a Great Notion.*" *Western American Literature* 28 (August 1993): 131–41.

4146. Fick, Thomas H. "The Hipster, the Hero, and the Psychic Frontier in *One Flew Over the Cuckoo's Nest.*" *Rocky Mountain Review of Language and Literature* 43 (1989): 19–34.

4147. Fiedler, Leslie. *The Return of the Vanishing American.* New York: Stein and Day, 1965, 159–87.

4148. Flora, Joseph M. "Westering and Women: A Thematic Study of Kesey's *One Flew Over the Cuckoo's Nest* and Fisher's *Mountain Man.*" *Heritage of Kansas* 10 (Spring 1977): 3–14.

4149. Forrey, Robert. "Ken Kesey's Psychopathic Savior: A Rejoinder." *Modern Fiction Studies* 21 (Summer 1975): 222–30.

4150. Foster, John Wilson. "Hustling to Some Purpose: Kesey's *One Flew Over the Cuckoo's Nest.*" *Western American Literature* 9 (August 1974): 115–29.

4151. Handy, William J. "Chief Bromden: Kesey's Existentialist Hero." *North Dakota Quarterly* 48 (Autumn 1980): 72–82.

4152. Hauck, Richard B. "The Comic Christ and the Modern Reader." *College English* 31 (February 1970): 498–506.

4153. Hill, Richard Allen. "The Law of Ken Kesey." Doctoral dissertation, Emory University, 1976.

4154. Hoge, James O. "Psychedelic Stimulation and the Creative Imagination: The Case of Ken Kesey." *Southern Humanities Review* 6 (1972): 381–91.

4155. Knapp, James F. "Tangled in the Language of the Past: Ken Kesey and Cultural Revolution." *Midwest Quarterly* 19 (1978): 398–412.

4156. Krassner, Paul. "An Impolite Interview with Ken Kesey." *Realist* 90 (May–June 1971): 1, 46–53.

4157. Kunz, Don R. "Mechanistic and Totemistic Symbolization in Kesey's *One Flew Over the Cuckoo's Nest*." *Studies in American Fiction* 3 (Spring 1975): 65–82.

4158. Leeds, Barry H. *Ken Kesey*. New York: Ungar, 1981.

4159. ———. "Theme and Technique in *One Flew Over the Cuckoo's Nest*." *Connecticut Review* 7 (April 1974): 35–50.

4160. Lish, Gordon, ed. "What the Hell You Looking in Here For, Daisy Mae: An Interview with Ken Kesey." *Genesis West* 2 (Fall 1963): 17–29.

4161. Madden, Fred. "Sanity and Responsibility: Big Chief as Narrator and Executioner." *Modern Fiction Studies* 32 (Summer 1986): 203–17.

4162. Marsden, James Douglas. "Modern Echoes of Transcendentalism: Kesey, Snyder, and Other Counter Cultural Authors." Doctoral dissertation, Brown University, 1977.

4163. Martin, Terence. "*One Flew Over the Cuckoo's Nest* and the High Cost of Living." *Modern Fiction Studies* 19 (Spring 1973): 43–55.

4164. Olderman, Raymond M. *Beyond the Waste Land: A Study of the American Novel in the Nineteen-Sixties*. New Haven, Conn.: Yale University Press, 1972.

4165. Pearson, Carol. "The Cowboy Saint and the Indian Poet: The Comic Hero in Kesey's *One Flew Over the Cuckoo's Nest*." *Studies in American Humor* 1 (1974): 91–98.

4166. Porter, M. Gilbert. *The Art of Grit: Ken Kesey's Fiction*. Columbia: University of Missouri Press, 1982.

4167. ———. *One Flew Over the Cuckoo's Nest: Rising to Heroism*. Boston: Twayne, 1989.

4168. Pratt, John Clark. "On Editing Kesey: Confessions of a Straight Man." *Kesey*. Ed. Michael Strelow, et al. Eugene, Oreg.: Northwest Review Books, 1977, 5–16.

4169. ———, ed. *One Flew Over the Cuckoo's Nest: Text and Criticism*. New York: Viking Press, 1973.

4170. Safer, Elaine B. "The Absurd Quest and Black Humor in Ken Kesey's *Sometimes a Great Notion*." *Critique* 24 (Summer 1983): 228–40.

4171. ————. *The Contemporary American Comic Epic: The Novels of Barth, Pynchon, Gaddis, and Kesey.* Detroit: Wayne State University Press, 1988.

4172. Searles, George J., ed. *A Casebook on Ken Kesey's "One Flew Over the Cuckoo's Nest."* Albuquerque: University of New Mexico Press, 1992.

4173. Sherman, W. D. "The Novels of Ken Kesey." *Journal of American Studies* 5 (August 1971): 185–96.

4174. Sherwood, Terry G. "*One Flew Over the Cuckoo's Nest* and the Comic Strip." *Critique* 13 (No. 1, 1971): 96–109.

4175. Singer, Barnett. "Outsider Versus Insider: Malamud's and Kesey's Pacific Northwest." *South Dakota Review* 13 (Winter 1975–76): 127–44.

4176. Stein, Howard F. "The Cuckoo's Nest, the Banality of Evil and the Psychopath as Hero." *Journal of American Culture* 2 (Winter 1980): 635–45.

4177. Strelow, Michael, et al. *Kesey.* Eugene, Oreg.: Northwest Review Books, 1977.

4178. Sullivan, Ruth. "Big Mama, Big Papa, and Little Sons in Ken Kesey's *One Flew Over the Cuckoo's Nest.*" *Literature and Psychology* 25 (No. 1, 1975): 34–44.

4179. Sutherland, Janet. "A Defense of Ken Kesey's *One Flew Over the Cuckoo's Nest.*" *English Journal* 61 (January 1972): 28–36.

4180. Tanner, Stephen L. *Ken Kesey.* Boston: Twayne, 1983.

4181. ————. "Salvation Through Laughter: Ken Kesey and the Cuckoo's Nest." *Southwest Review* 58 (Spring 1973): 125–37.

4182. Tanner, Tony. *City of Words: American Fiction 1950–1970.* New York: Harper and Row, 1971.

4183. Waldmeir, Joseph J. "Two Novelists of the Absurd: Heller and Kesey." *Wisconsin Studies in Contemporary Literature* 5 (Autumn 1964): 192–204.

4184. Weixlmann, Joseph. "Ken Kesey: A Bibliography." *Western American Literature* 10 (November 1975): 219–31.

4185. Widmer, Kingsley. "*One Flew Over the Cuckoo's Nest.*" *Twentieth Century American Novel.* Cassette. Deland, Fla.: Everett/Edwards, 1970.

4186. Wolfe, Tom. *The Electric Kool-Aid Acid Test.* New York: Farrar, Straus, and Giroux, 1968.

4187. Zashin, Elliot M. "Political Theorist and Demiurge: The Rise and Fall of Ken Kesey." *Centennial Review* 17 (Spring 1973): 199–213.

CHARLES KING

4188. Burton, Wilfred C. "The Novels of Charles King, 1844–1933." Doctoral dissertation, New York University, 1962.

4189. Peterson, Clell T. "Charles King: Soldier and Novelist." *American Book Collector* 16 (December 1965): 9–12.

4190. Sackett, S. J. "Captian Charles King, U.S.A." *Midwest Quarterly* 3 (October 1961): 69–80.

CLARENCE KING

4191. Burich, Keith R. "'Something Newer and Nobler Is Called into Being': Clarence King, Catastrophism, and California." *California History* 72 (Fall 1993): 235–49, 302.

4192. Crosby, Harry. "So Deep a Trail: A Biography of Clarence King." Doctoral dissertation, Stanford University, 1953.

4193. Dickason, David H. "Clarence King's First Western Journey." *Huntington Library Quarterly* 7 (November 1943): 71–87.

4194. ———. "Henry Adams and Clarence King: The Record of a Friendship." *New England Quarterly* 17 (June 1944): 229–54.

4195. Hoebzema, Loren. "The Literary Landscape of Clarence King's *Mountaineering in the Sierra Nevada*." *Exploration* 4 (1977): 17–23.

4196. Long, Barbara N. Messner. "An Edition of *Mountaineering in the Sierra Nevada* by Clarence King." Doctoral dissertation, University of Pennsylvania, 1973.

4197. Shebl, James M. *King, of the Mountains.* Pacific Center for Western Historical Studies, Monograph No. 5. Stockton, Calif.: University of the Pacific, 1974.

4198. Wild, Peter. *Clarence King.* Western Writers Series, No. 48. Boise, Idaho: Boise State University, 1981.

4199. Wilkins, Thurman, and Caroline Lawson Hinkley. *Clarence King: A Biography.* Rev and enlg. Albuquerque: University of New Mexico Press, 1988.

4200. Wilson, Richard B. "American Vision and Landscape: The Western Images of Clarence King and Timothy O'Sullivan." Doctoral dissertation, University of New Mexico, 1979.

MAXINE HONG KINGSTON

4201. Cheung, King–Kok. "'Don't Tell': Imposed Silences in *The Color Purple* and *The Woman Warrior*." *PMLA* 103 (March 1988): 162–74.

4202. Chun, Gloria. "The High Note of the Barbarian Reed Pipe: Maxine Hong Kingston." *Journal of Ethnic Studies* 19 (Fall 1991): 85–94.

4203. Wong, Sau-Ling Cynthia. "Necessity and Extravagance in Maxine Hong Kingston's *The Woman Warrior*: Art and the Ethnic Experience." *MELUS* 15 (Spring 1988): 3–26.

RUDYARD KIPLING

4204. Espey, David B. "Kipling's Colorado Hero." *South Dakota Review* 13 (Summer 1975): 82–90.

CAROLINE KIRKLAND

4205. Merish, Lori. "'The Hand of Refined Taste' in the Frontier Landscape: Caroline Kirkland's *A New Home, Who'll Follow?* and the Feminization of American Consumerism." *American Quarterly* 45 (December 1993): 485–523.

JOSEPH KIRKLAND

4206. Flanagan, John T. "Joseph Kirkland, Pioneer Realist." *American Literature* 11 (November 1939): 273–84.

4207. Henson, Clyde E. "Joseph Kirkland (1830–1894)." *American Literary Realism 1870–1910* 1 (Fall 1967): 67–70.

4208. ———. *Joseph Kirkland*. New York: Twayne, 1962.

4209. Holaday, Clayton A. "Joseph Kirkland: Biography and Criticism." Doctoral dissertation, Indiana University, 1950.

4210. Lease, Benjamin. "Realism and Joseph Kirkland's *Zury*." *American Literature* 23 (January 1952): 464–66.

CAROLYN KIZER

4211. Chappell, Fred. "'I'm in the Racket': Carolyn Kizer's Poetry." *St. Andrew's Review* 1 (Fall–Winter 1971): 13–16.

4212. Howard, Richard. *Alone with America: Essays on the Art of Poetry in the United States Since 1950*. New York: Atheneum, 1969, 272–80.

KY KOIKE

4213. Zabilski, Carol. "Dr. Ky Koike, 1878–1947: Physician, Poet, Photographer." *Pacific Northwest Quarterly* 68 (April 1977): 73–79.

HERBERT KRAUSE

4214. Huseboe, Arthur R.. *Herbert Krause.* Western Writers Series, No. 66. Boise, Idaho: Boise State University, 1985.

4215. ———, and William Geyer. "Herbert Krause and the Western Experience." *Where the West Begins.* Eds. Arthur R. Huseboe and William Geyer. Sioux Falls, S. Dak.: Center for Western Studies Press, 1978, 5–12.

4216. Janssen, Judith M. "'Black Frost in Summer': Central Themes in the Novels of Herbert Krause." *South Dakota Review* 5 (Spring 1967): 55–65.

4217. Paulson, Kristoffer F. "Ole Rölvaag, Herbert Krause, and the Frontier Thesis of Frederick Jackson Turner." *Where the West Begins.* Eds. Arthur R. Huseboe and William Geyer. Sioux Falls, S. Dak.: Center for Western Studies Press, 1978, 24–33.

4218. Steensma, Robert C. "'Our Comings and Goings': Herbert Krause's *Wind Without Rain.*" *Where the West Begins.* Eds. Arthur R. Huseboe and William Geyer. Sioux Falls, S. Dak.: Center for Western Studies Press, 1978, 13–23.

JOSEPH WOOD KRUTCH

4219. Holtz, William. "Homage to Joseph Wood Krutch: Tragedy and the Ecological Imperative." *American Scholar* 43 (Spring 1974): 267–79.

4220. Lehman, Anthony L. "Joseph Wood Krutch." *Quarterly Newsletter of the Book Club of California* 37 (Summer 1972): 51–63.

4221. Margolis, John D. *Joseph Wood Krutch: A Writer's Life.* Knoxville: University of Tennessee Press, 1980.

4222. Pavich, Paul N. *Joseph Wood Krutch.* Western Writers Series, No. 89. Boise, Idaho: Boise State University, 1989.

4223. ———. "Joseph Wood Krutch: Persistent Champion of Man and Nature." *Western American Literature* 13 (Summer 1978): 151–58.

4224. Powell, Lawrence C. "Joseph Wood Krutch's *The Desert Year.*" *Westways* 63 (June 1971): 14–17, 66–67.

GREG KUZMA

4225. Brummels, J. V. "An Interview with Greg Kuzma." *On Common Ground: The Poetry of William Kloefkorn, Ted Kooser, Greg Kuzma, and Don Welch.* Eds. Mark Sanders and J. V. Brummels. Ord, Nebr.: Sandhills Press, 1983, 147–64.

4226. deAuilar, Helene J. F. "Greg Kuzma: A National Poet." *On Common Ground: The Poetry of William Kloefkorn, Ted Kooser, Greg Kuzma, and Don Welch.* Eds. Mark Sanders and J. V. Brummels. Ord, Nebr.: Sandhills Press, 1983, 135–47.

PETER B. KYNE

4227. Bode, Carl. "Cappy Ricks and the Monk in the Garden." *PMLA* 64 (March 1949): 59–69.

OLIVER LA FARGE

4228. Bunker, Robert. "Oliver La Farge: The Search for Self." *New Mexico Quarterly* 20 (Summer 1950): 211–24.
4229. Byrd, Charles Lively. "A Descriptive Bibliography of the Oliver La Farge Collection at the University of Texas." Doctoral dissertation, University of Texas, Austin, 1974.
4230. Gillis, Everett A. *Oliver La Farge.* Southwest Writers Series, No. 9. Austin, Tex.: Steck-Vaughn, 1967.
4231. Hecht, Robert A. *Oliver La Farge and the American Indian: A Biography.* Metuchen, N.J.: Scarecrow Press, 1991.
4232. Kleinpoppen, Paul Steven. "The Indian Fiction of Oliver La Farge." Doctoral dissertation, Columbia University, 1985.
4233. McNickle, D'Arcy. *Indian Man: A Life of Oliver La Farge.* Bloomington: Indiana University Press, 1971.
4234. Mansfield-Kelley, Deane. "Oliver La Farge and the Indian Woman in American Literature." Doctoral dissertation, University of Texas, Austin, 1979.
4235. Pearce, T. M. *Oliver La Farge.* New York: Twayne, 1972.

LOUIS L'AMOUR

4236. Bulow, Ernest L. "Still Tall in the Saddle: Louis L'Amour's Classic Western Hero." *Possible Sack* 3 (June–July 1972): 1–8.
4237. Cozzens, Darin. "History and Louis L'Amour's Cowboy." *Journal of American Culture* 14 (Summer 1991): 42–52.
4238. Gale, Robert L. *Louis L'Amour.* Rev ed. New York: Twayne, 1992.
4239. ———. "Sack Time: Problems of Chronology in Louis L'Amour's Sackett Novels." *Southwestern American Literature* 10 (Spring 1985): 25–34.
4240. Gonzalez, Arturo F. "Louis L'Amour: Writing High in the Bestseller Saddle." *Writer's Digest* 60 (December 1980): 22–29.

4241. Hall, Halbert W. *The Work of Louis L'Amour: An Annotated Bibliography and Guide.* San Bernardino, Calif.: Borge Press, 1991.

4242. Hinds, Harold E., Jr. "Mexican and Mexican-American Images in the Western Novels of Louis L'Amour." *Latin American Literary Review* 5 (Spring–Summer 1977): 129–41.

4243. Jackson, Donald Dale. "World's Fastest Literary Gun: Louis L'Amour." *Smithsonian* 18 (May 1987): 154–70.

4244. Keith, Harold. "Louis L'Amour: Man of the West." *Roundup* 23 (December 1975): 1–2, 4, 12; 24 (January 1976): 8–9, 11; (February 1976): 4–5.

4245. Klaschus, Candace. "Louis L'Amour: The Writer as Teacher." Doctoral dissertation, University of New Mexico, 1983.

4246. Marsden, Michael T. "The Concept of Family in the Fiction of Louis L'Amour." *North Dakota Quarterly* 46 (Summer 1978): 12–21.

4247. ———. "A Conversation with Louis L'Amour." *Journal of American Culture* 2 (Winter 1980): 646–58.

4248. ———. "The Popular Western Novel as a Cultural Artifact." *Arizona and the West* 20 (Autumn 1978): 203–14.

4249. ———. "Remarks Upon an Honorary Doctor of Literature Awarded Posthumously to Louis L'Amour By Bowling Green State University on November 4, 1988." *Journal of Popular Culture* 23 (Winter 1989): 179–90.

4250. Matchie, Thomas. "Two North Dakota Writers." *North Dakota Quarterly* 50 (Winter 1982): 19–27.

4251. Nesbitt, John D. "Change of Purpose in the Novels of Louis L'Amour." *Western American Literature* 13 (Spring 1978): 65–81.

4252. ———. "Louis L'Amour – Paper Mâché Homer?" *South Dakota Review* 19 (Autumn 1981): 37–48.

4253. ———. "A New Look at Two Popular Western Classics." *South Dakota Review* 18 (Spring 1980): 30–42.

4254. Sullivan, Tom R. *Cowboys and Caudillos: Frontier Ideology of the Americas.* Bowling Green, Ohio: Bowling Green State University Popular Press, 1990, 15–28.

4255. ———. "Westward to Stasis with Louis L'Amour." *Southwest Review* 69 (Winter 1984): 78–87.

4256. Terrie, Philip G. "*Last of the Breed*: Louis L'Amour's Survivalist Fantasy." *Journal of Popular Culture* 25 (Spring 1992): 23–33.

4257. Thoene, Bodie. "L'Amour of the West: A Storyteller to Rival the Wednesday-Night Bowling League." *American West* 23 (November–December 1986): 18–25.

4258. Weinberg, Robert, ed. *The Louis L'Amour Companion.* Kansas City, Mo.: Andrews and McNeel, 1992.

ROSE WILDER LANE

4259. Holtz, William. *The Ghost in the Little House: A Life of Rose Wilder Lane.* Columbia: University of Missouri Press, 1993.

4260. ———. "Rose Wilder Lane's *Free Land*: The Political Background." *South Dakota Review* 30 (Spring 1992): 46–60.

4261. ———. "Rose Wilder Lane's *Old Home Town*." *Studies in Short Fiction* 26 (Fall 1989): 479–87.

RONALD LANNER

4262. Glotfelty, Cheryll Burgess. "Western, Yes, But is it Literature?: Teaching Ronald Lanner's *The Piñon Pine*." *Western American Literature* 17 (February 1993): 303–10.

CLINTON F. LARSON

4263. "A Conversation with Clinton F. Larson." *Dialogue* 4 (Autumn 1969): 74–80.

D. H. LAWRENCE

4264. Axelrad, Allan M. "Wish Fulfillment in the Wilderness: D. H. Lawrence and *The Leatherstocking Tales*." *American Quarterly* 39 (Winter 1987): 563–85.

4265. Foster, Joseph. *D. H. Lawrence in Taos.* Albuquerque: University of New Mexico Press, 1971.

4266. Halperin, Irving. "Unity in *St. Mawr*." *South Dakota Review* 4 (Summer 1966): 58–60.

4267. Merrild, Knud. *With D. H. Lawrence in New Mexico: A Memoir of D.H.Lawrence.* New York: Barnes and Noble, 1965.

4268. Smith, Bob L. "D. H. Lawrence's *St. Mawr*: Transposition of a Myth." *Arizona Quarterly* 24 (Autumn 1968): 197–208.

4269. Waters, Frank. "Quetzalcoatl Versus D. H. Lawrence's *Plumed Serpent*." *Western American Literature* 3 (Summer 1968): 103–13.

TOM LEA

4270. Antone, Evan H. "Tom Lea: A Study of His Life and Work." Doctoral dissertation, University of California, Los Angeles, 1971.

4271. ———. *Tom Lea: His Life and Work*. El Paso: Texas Western Press, 1988.

4272. Bennett, Patrick. "Wells of Sight and Sound: An Interview with Tom Lea." *Southwest Review* 65 (Spring 1980): 113–27.

4273. Grover, Doris Crow. "Tom Lea's Cloudrock Country." *Southwestern American Literature* 18 (Fall 1992): 31–35.

4274. Hjerter, Kathleen Gee, comp. *The Art of Tom Lea*. College Station: Texas A M University Press, 1989.

4275. Rodenberger, Lou. "Tom Lea, Artist and Novelist: Interpreter of Southwest Border Life." *Southwest Heritage* (Summer 1980): 2–5, 17.

4276. West, John O. *Tom Lea: Artist in Two Mediums*. Southwest Writers Series, No. 5. Austin, Tex.: Steck-Vaughn, 1967.

URSULA K. LE GUIN

4277. Bittner, James W. *Approaches to the Fiction of Ursula Le Guin*. Ann Arbor, Mich.: UMI Research Press, 1984.

4278. Bucknall, Barbara J. *Ursula K. Le Guin*. New York: Ungar, 1981.

4279. Clarke, Amy Michaela. "A Woman Writing: Feminist Awareness in the Work of Ursula K. Le Guin." Doctoral dissertation, University of California, Davis, 1992.

4280. Cogell, Elizabeth Cummins. *Ursula K. Le Guin: A Primary and Secondary Bibliography*. Boston: G.K. Hall, 1983.

4281. Cummins, Elizabeth. *Understanding Ursula K. Le Guin*. Columbia: University of South Carolina Press, 1990.

4282. Harper, Mary Catherine. "Spiraling around the Hinge: Working Solutions in *Always Coming Home*." *Old West–New West: Centennial Essays*. Ed. Barbara Howard Meldrum. Moscow: University of Idaho Press, 1993, 241–57.

4283. Mellor, Anne. "Ursula Le Guin." *Women Writers of the West Coast: Speaking of Their Lives and Careers*. Ed. Marilyn Yalom. Santa Barbara, Calif.: Capra, 1983, 68–78.

4284. Spivack, Charlotte. *Ursula K. Le Guin*. Boston: Twayne, 1984.

4285. Wickes, George, and Louise Westling. "Dialogue with Ursula Le Guin." *Northwest Review* 20 (Nos. 2–3, 1982): 147–59.

ALAN LEMAY

4286. Calder, Jenni. *There Must Be a Lone Ranger: The American West in Film and in Reality*. New York: Taplinger, 1974.

ELMORE LEONARD

4287. Hynes, Joseph. "High Noon in Detroit: Elmore Leonard's Career." *Journal of Popular Culture* 25 (Winter 1991): 181–87.

MERIDEL LE SUEUR

4288. Gelfant, Blanche H. "Meridel Le Sueur's 'Indian' Poetry and the Quest/ion of Feminine Form." *Women Writing in America: Voices in Collage.* Hanover, N.H.: University Press of New England, 1984, 71–91.

4289. Pratt, Linda Ray. "Woman Writer in the CP: The Case of Meridel Le Sueur." *Women's Studies* 14 (February 1988): 247–64.

4290. Rabinowitz, Paula. "Maternity as History: Gender and the Transformation of Genre in Meridel Le Sueur's *The Girl.*" *Contemporary Literature* 29 (Winter 1988): 538–48.

ALFRED HENRY LEWIS

4291. Boyer, M. G., ed. *Arizona in Literature.* Glendale, Calif.: Arthur H. Clark, 1934.

4292. Filler, Louis. "The West Belongs to All of Us." *Old Wolfville: Chapters from the Fiction of Alfred Henry Lewis.* Yellow Springs, Ohio: Antioch Press, 1968, vii–xii.

4293. ———. "Wolfville." *New Mexico Quarterly Review* 13 (Spring 1943): 35–47.

4294. Manzo, Flournoy D. "Alfred Henry Lewis: Western Storyteller." *Arizona and the West* 10 (Spring 1968): 5–24.

4295. Ravitz, Abe C. *Alfred Henry Lewis.* Western Writers Series, No. 32. Boise, Idaho: Boise State University, 1978.

JAMES FRANKLIN LEWIS

4296. Lund, Mary Graham. "James Franklin Lewis, Transhumanist." *University Review* 33 (June 1967): 307–12.

JANET LEWIS

4297. Crow, Charles L. *Janet Lewis.* Western Writers Series, No. 41. Boise, Idaho: Boise State University, 1980.

4298. Davie, Donald. "The Historical Novels of Janet Lewis." *Southern Review* 2, N. S. (Winter 1966): 40–60.

4299. Hofheins, Roger, and Dan Tooker. "A Conversation with Janet Lewis." *Southern Review* 10 (April 1974): 329–41.

4300. Inglis, Fred. "The Novels of Janet Lewis." *Critique* 7 (No. 2, 1965): 47–64.

4301. Killoh, Ellen. "Patriarchal Women: A Study of Three Novels by Janet Lewis." *Southern Review* 10 (April 1974): 342–64.

4302. Stern, Richard. "Janet Lewis." *Virginia Quarterly Review* 69 (Summer 1993): 532–43.

MERIWETHER LEWIS

(Lewis and Clark)

4303. Bakeless, John E. *Lewis and Clark: Partners in Discovery.* New York: William Morrow, 1947.

4304. Criswell, Elijah H. *Lewis and Clark: Linguistic Pioneers.* Columbia: University of Missouri Press, 1940.

4305. DeVoto, Bernard, ed. *The Journals of Lewis and Clark.* Boston: Houghton Mifflin, 1953.

4306. Dillon, Richard. *Meriwether Lewis: A Biography.* New York: Coward-McCann, 1965.

4307. Furtwangler, Albert. *Acts of Discovery: Visions of America in the Lewis and Clark Journals.* Urbana: University of Illinois Press, 1993.

4308. Jackson, Donald, ed. *Letters of the Lewis and Clark Expedition with Related Documents, 1783–1854.* Urbana: University of Illinois Press, 1962.

4309. Lee, Robert Edson. *From West to East.* Urbana: University of Illinois Press, 1966, 11–38.

4310. Moulton, Gary E. "The Missing Journals of Meriwether Lewis." *Montana: The Magazine of Western History* 35 (Summer 1985): 28–39.

4311. Nichols, William. "Lewis and Clark Probe the Heart of Darkness." *American Scholar* 49 (Winter 1979–80): 94–101.

4312. Seelye, John. "Beyond the Shining Mountains: The Lewis and Clark Expedition as an Enlightenment Epic." *Virginia Quarterly Review* 63 (Winter 1987): 36–53.

4313. Steffen, Jerome O. *William Clark: Jeffersonian Man on the Frontier.* Norman: University of Oklahoma Press, 1977.

4314. Stevenson, Elizabeth. "Meriwether and I." *Virginia Quarterly Review* 43 (Autumn 1967): 580–91.

4315. Thwaites, Reuben Gold, ed. *Original Journals of the Lewis and Clark Expedition, 1804–1806.* 8 vols. New York: Dodd, Mead, 1904–1905.

4316. Austin, Allen. "An Interview with Sinclair Lewis." *University of Kansas City Review* 24 (March 1958): 199–210.

4317. Baker, Joseph E. "Sinclair Lewis, Plato, and the Regional Escape." *English Journal* [college edition] 28 (June 1939): 460–72.

4318. Brown, Daniel R. "Lewis's Satire–A Negative Emphasis." *Renascence* 18 (Winter 1966): 63–72.

4319. Bucco, Martin. *Main Street: The Revolt of Carol Kennicott.* New York: Twayne, 1993.

4320. ———. "The Serialized Novels of Sinclair Lewis." *Western American Literature* 4 (Spring 1969): 29–37.

4321. ———, ed. *Critical Essays on Sinclair Lewis.* Boston: G. K. Hall, 1986.

4322. Carpenter, Frederic I. "Sinclair Lewis and the Fortress of Reality." *College English* 16 (April 1955): 416–23.

4323. Connaughton, Michael, ed. *Sinclair Lewis at 100: Papers Presented at a Centennial Conference.* St. Cloud, Minn.: St. Cloud State University, 1986.

4324. Conroy, Stephen S. "Sinclair Lewis's Sociological Imagination." *American Literature* 42 (November 1972): 348–62.

4325. Derleth, August. "Three Literary Men: A Memoir of Sinclair Lewis, Sherwood Anderson, and Edgar Lee Masters." *Arts in Society 1* (Winter 1959): 11–46.

4326. DeVoto, Bernard. *The Literary Fallacy.* Boston: Little, Brown, 1949, 95–123.

4327. Dooley, D. J. *The Art of Sinclair Lewis.* Lincoln: University of Nebraska Press, 1967.

4328. Douglas, George H. "*Main Street* After Fifty Years." *Prairie Schooner* 44 (Winter 1970–71): 338–48.

4329. Eby, Clare Virginia. "*Babbitt* as Veblenian Critique of Manliness." *American Studies* 34 (Fall 1993): 5–23.

4330. Fife, Jim L. "Two Views of the American West." *Western American Literature* 1 (Spring 1966): 34–43.

4331. Fisher, Joel. "Sinclair Lewis and the Diagnostic Novel: *Main Street* and *Babbitt.*" *Journal of American Studies* 20 (December 1986): 421–33.

4332. Flanagan, John T. "A Long Way to Gopher Prairie: Sinclair Lewis's Apprenticeship." *Southwest Review* 32 (Autumn 1947): 403–13.

4333. ———. "The Minnesota Backgrounds of Sinclair Lewis's Fiction." *Minnesota History* 37 (March 1960): 1–13.

4334. Fleming, Robert E. "Recent Research on Sinclair Lewis." *Modern Fiction Studies* 31 (Autumn 1985): 609–16.

4335. ———. "A Sinclair Lewis Checklist: 1976–1985." *Sinclair Lewis at 100: Papers Presented at a Centennial Conference.* Ed. Michael Connaughton. St. Cloud, Minn.: St. Cloud State University, 1985, 191–99.

4336. ———. "Sinclair Lewis vs. Zane Grey: *Mantrap* as Satirical Western." *Midamerica* 9 (1982): 124–38.

4337. ———, with Esther Fleming. *Sinclair Lewis: A Reference Guide.* Boston: G. K. Hall, 1980.

4338. *From Main Street to Stockholm: Letters of Sinclair Lewis, 1919–1930.* Ed. with intro. Harrison Smith. New York: Harcourt, Brace, 1952.

4339. Geismar, Maxwell. *The Last of the Provincials: The American Novel, 1915–1925.* Boston: Houghton Mifflin, 1947, 69–150.

4340. Grabbe, Hans-Jürgen. "The Ideal Type of the Small Town: *Main Street* in a Social Science Context." *Amerikastudien* 32 (1987): 181–90.

4341. Grebstein, Sheldon Norman. *Sinclair Lewis.* New York: Twayne, 1962.

4342. Hartwick, Harry. "The Village Virus." *The Foreground of American Fiction.* New York: American Book, 1934, 250–81.

4343. Hilfer, Anthony Channell. *The Revolt from the Village.* Chapel Hill: University of North Carolina Press, 1969, 158–92.

4344. Hutchisson, James M. "'*Babbitt* in Overalls': Sinclair Lewis's Abandoned Labor Novel." *South Dakota Review* 29 (Winter 1991): 5–22.

4345. ———. "Sinclair Lewis, Paul DeKruif, and the Composition of *Arrowsmith*." *Studies in the Novel* 24 (Spring 1992): 48–66.

4346. Lewis, Grace Hegger. *With Love from Gracie.* New York: Harcourt, Brace, 1955.

4347. Lewis, Robert W. "*Babbitt* and the Dream of Romance." *North Dakota Quarterly* 40 (Winter 1972): 7–14.

4348. Light, Martin. "H. G. Wells and Sinclair Lewis: Friendship, Literary Influence, and Letters." *English Fiction in Transition (1880–1920)* 5 (1962): 1–20.

4349. ———. "The 'Poetry and Tragedy' of the Car in Sinclair Lewis's Novels." *Kansas Quarterly* 21 (Fall 1989): 23–33.

4350. ———. *The Quixotic Vision of Sinclair Lewis.* West Lafayette, Ind.: Purdue University Press, 1975.

4351. Love, Glen A. *Babbitt: An American Life*. Boston: Twayne, 1993.

4352. ———. "New Pioneering on the Prairies: Nature, Progress, and the Individual in the Novels of Sinclair Lewis." *American Quarterly* 25 (December 1973): 558–77.

4353. Lundquist, James. *The Merrill Checklist of Sinclair Lewis*. Columbus: Charles E. Merrill Publishing, 1970.

4354. ———. *The Merrill Guide to Sinclair Lewis*. Columbus: Charles E. Merrill Publishing, 1970.

4355. ———. *Sinclair Lewis*. New York: Ungar, 1973.

4356. ———, ed. *Sinclair Lewis Newsletter*. St. Cloud State College [Minnesota], 1969–76.

4357. Manfred, Frederick F. "Sinclair Lewis: A Portrait." *American Scholar* 23 (Spring 1954): 162–84.

4358. Marovitz, Sanford E. "Ambivalences and Anxieties: Character Reversals in Sinclair Lewis' *Mantrap*." *Studies in American Fiction* 16 (Autumn 1988): 229–44.

4359. O'Connor, Richard. *Sinclair Lewis*. New York: McGraw-Hill, 1971.

4360. Parry, Sally E. "The Changing Fictional Faces of Sinclair Lewis' Wives." *Studies in American Fiction* 17 (Spring 1989): 65–79.

4361. Petrullo, Helen B. "*Babbitt* as Situational Satire." *Kansas Quarterly* 1 (Summer 1969): 89–97.

4362. ———. "*Main Street, Cass Timberlane* and Determinism." *South Dakota Review* 7 (Winter 1969–70): 30–42.

4363. Rosenberg, Charles E. "Martin Arrowsmith: The Scientist as Hero." *American Quarterly* 15 (Fall 1963): 447–58.

4364. Schorer, Mark. *Sinclair Lewis*. Minneapolis: University of Minnesota, 1963.

4365. ———. *Sinclair Lewis: An American Life*. New York: McGraw-Hill, 1961.

4366. ———, ed. *Sinclair Lewis: A Collection of Critical Essays*. Englewood Cliffs, N.J.: Prentice-Hall, 1962.

4367. Sheean, Vincent. *Dorothy and Red*. Boston: Houghton Mifflin, 1963.

4368. Simon, Tobin. "The Short Stories of Sinclair Lewis." Doctoral dissertation, New York University, 1972.

4369. *South Dakota Review* 7 (Winter 1969–70): 3–78. Special issue.

4370. Spindler, Michael. *American Literature and Social Change: William Dean Howells to Arthur Miller*. Bloomington: Indiana University Press, 1983, 168–82.

4371. Tanner, Stephen L. "Sinclair Lewis and Fascism." *Studies in the Novel* 22 (Spring 1990): 57–66.

4372. ———. "Sinclair Lewis and the New Humanism." *Modern Age* 33 (Spring 1990): 33–41.

4373. Thompson, Dorothy. "The Boy and Man from Sauk Centre." *Atlantic* 206 (November 1960): 39–48.

4374. Wagenaar, Dick. "The Knight and the Pioneer: Europe and America in the Fiction of Sinclair Lewis." *American Literature* 50 (May 1978): 230–49.

4375. Wilson, Christopher P. "Sinclair Lewis and the Passing of Capitalism." *American Studies* 24 (Fall 1983): 95–108.

FRANK B. LINDERMAN

4376. Bevis, William W. "Linderman and Plenty-Coups." *Ten Tough Trips: Montana Writers and the West.* Seattle: University of Washington Press, 1990, 79–91.

4377. Merriam, H. G. "The Life and Work of Frank B. Linderman." *Montana Adventure: The Recollections of Frank B. Linderman.* Lincoln: University of Nebraska Press, 1968, 199–214.

4378. ———. "Sign-Talker with Straight Tongue: Frank Bird Linderman." *Montana: Magazine of Western History* 12 (Summer 1962): 2–20.

4379. Van de Water, F. F. "The Work of Frank B. Linderman." *Frontier and Midland* 19 (Spring 1939): 148–52.

4380. White, C. "Bibliography of the Writings of Frank Bird Linderman." *Frontier and Midland* 19 (Spring 1939): 147–48.

VACHEL LINDSAY

4381. Avery, Emmett L. "Vachel Lindsay in Spokane." *Pacific Spectator* 3 (1949): 338–53.

4382. ———. "Vachel Lindsay's 'Poem Games' in Spokane." *Research Studies of Washington State University* 30 (Summer 1962): 109–14.

4383. ———. "Vachel Lindsay: Spokane Journalist." *Research Studies of the State College of Washington* 25 (March 1957): 101–10.

4384. Gilliland, Marshall A. "Vachel Lindsay: Poet and Newspaper Columnist in Spokane, 1924–1929." Doctoral dissertation, Washington State University, 1968.

4385. Massa, Ann. *Vachel Lindsay: Fieldworker for the American Dream.* Bloomington: Indiana University Press, 1970.

4386. Peeders, Kenneth Peder. "Vachel Lindsay: The Dispersed and Prepared Audience." Doctoral dissertation, University of North Dakota, 1981.

4387. Ruggles, Eleanor. *The West-Going Heart: A Life of Vachel Lindsay.* New York: Norton, 1959.

4388. Taylor, Marjorie Anne. "The Folk Imagination of Vachel Lindsay." Doctoral dissertation, Wayne State University, 1976.

4389. Trombly, A. E. "Listeners and Readers: The Unforgetting of Vachel Lindsay." *Southwest Review* 47 (August 1962): 294–302.

4390. Ward, John Chapman. "Vachel Lindsay Is 'Lying Low.'" *College Literature* 12 (Fall 1985): 233–45.

4391. Wertheim, Stanley. "Vachel Lindsay's American Dream." *Columbia Library Columns* 37 (May 1988): 13–24.

CAROLINE LOCKHART

4392. Furman, Necah Stewart. *Caroline Lockhart: Her Life and Legacy.* Seattle: University of Washington Press, 1994.

4393. ———. "Western Author Caroline Lockhart and Her Perspectives on Wyoming." *Montana: The Magazine of Western History* 36 (Winter 1986): 50–59.

4394. Yates, Norris. *Caroline Lockhart.* Western Writers Series, No. 116. Boise, Idaho: Boise State University, 1994.

JOHN A. LOMAX

4395. Clayton, Lawrence R. "John A. Lomax's *Cowboy Songs and Other Frontier Ballads:* A Critical Study." Doctoral dissertation, Texas Tech University, 1974.

4396. Gillis, Everett A., Jack D. Wages, Lawrence R. Clayton. "John A. Lomax and the Songs of the West." *Southwestern American Literature* 5 (1975): 14–21.

JACK LONDON

4397. Baskett, Sam S. "Jack London on the Oakland Waterfront." *American Literature* 27 (November 1955): 363–71.

4398. ———. "Jack London's Heart of Darkness." *American Quarterly* 10 (Spring 1958): 66–77.

4399. ———. "*Martin Eden*: Jack London's Poem of the Mind." *Modern Fiction Studies* 22 (Spring 1976): 23–36.

4400. ———. "Sea Change in *The Sea-Wolf.*" *American Literary Realism 1870–1910* 24 (Winter 1992): 5–22.

4401. Bennett, Kenneth I. "Jack London: The Quest for an Ethic." Doctoral dissertation, Kent State University, 1977.

4402. Birchard, Richard S. "Jack London and the Movies." *Film History* 1 (No. 1, 1987): 15–37.

4403. Buske, Frank E. "The Wilderness, the Frontier, and the Literature of Alaska to 1914: John Muir, Jack London, and Rex Beach." Doctoral dissertation, University of California, Davis, 1976.

4404. Cain, William E. "Socialism, Power, and the Fate of Style: Jack London in His Letters." *American Literary History* 3 (Fall 1991): 603–13.

4405. Collins, Billy Gene. "The Frontier in the Stories of Jack London." Doctoral dissertation, Kansas State University, 1970.

4406. Crow, Charles L. "Homecoming in the California Visionary Romance." *Western American Literature* 24 (May 1989): 3–19.

4407. Dodson, Mary Kay. "Naturalism in the Works of Jack London." *Jack London Newsletter* 4 (September–December 1971): 130–39.

4408. Drizari, Nelo. "Jack London and the 'Impossible Dream.'" *Pacific Historian* 21 (Spring 1977): 36–46.

4409. Ellis, James. "A Rereading of *The Sea Wolf*." *Western American Literature* 2 (Summer 1967): 127–34.

4410. Erbentraut, Edwin B. "The Intellectual Undertow in *Martin Eden*." *Jack London Newsletter* 3 (January–April 1970): 12–24.

4411. Etulain, Richard W. "The Lives of Jack London." *Western American Literature* 11 (Summer 1976): 149–64.

4412. ———, ed. *Jack London on the Road: The Tramp Diary and Other Hobo Writings*. Logan: Utah State University Press, 1979.

4413. Fleming, Becky London. "Memories of My Father, Jack London." *Pacific Historian* 18 (Fall 1974): 5–10.

4414. Foner, Philip S. *Jack London: American Rebel*. New York: Citadel, 1947, 1964.

4415. Fusco, Richard. "On Primitivism in *The Call of the Wild*." *American Literary Realism 1870–1910* 20 (Fall 1987): 76–80.

4416. Gatti, Susan Irwin. "Jack London on the Job: A Writer's Representation of Work." Doctoral dissertation, University of Pittsburgh, 1989.

4417. Geismar, Maxwell. *Rebels and Ancestors: The American Novel, 1890–1915*. Boston: Houghton Mifflin, 1953, 139–216.

4418. Gower, Ronald A. "The Creative Conflict: Struggle and Escape in Jack London's Fiction." *Jack London Newsletter* 4 (May–August 1971): 77–114.

4419. Graham, Don. "Jack London's Tale Told by a High-Grade Feeb." *Studies in Short Fiction* 15 (Fall 1978): 429–33.

4420. Gurian, Jay. "The Romantic Necessity in Literary Naturalism: Jack London." *American Literature* 38 (March 1966): 112–20.

4421. Hamilton, David Mike. "Some Chin-Chin and Tea–Jack London in Japan." *Pacific Historian* 23 (Summer 1979): 19–25.

4422. ———. *'The Tools of My Trade': The Annotated Books in Jack London's Library.* Seattle: University of Washington Press, 1987.

4423. Harpham, Geoffrey. "Jack London and the Tradition of Superman Socialism." *American Studies* 16 (Spring 1975): 23–33.

4424. Hedrick, Joan D. "London's Life in Letters." *Resources for American Literary Study* 18 (No. 2, 1992): 146–53.

4425. ———. *Solitary Comrade: Jack London and His Work.* Chapel Hill: University of North Carolina Press, 1982.

4426. Hendricks, King. *Jack London: Master Craftsman of the Short Story.* Logan: Utah State University, 1966.

4427. ———, and Irving Shepard, eds. *Letters from Jack London, Containing an Unpublished Correspondence between London and Sinclair Lewis.* New York: Odyssey, 1965.

4428. Hensley, Dennis E. "Jack London's Use of Maritime History in *The Sea Wolf.*" *Pacific Historian* 23 (Summer 1979): 1–8.

4429. Holtz, William. "Jack London's First Biographer." *Western American Literature* 27 (May 1992): 21–36.

4430. Johnston, Carolyn. *Jack London: An American Radical?* Westport, Conn.: Greenwood Press, 1984.

4431. Kingman, Russ. *Jack London: A Definitive Chronology.* Los Angeles: David Rejl, 1992.

4432. ———. *A Pictorial Life of Jack London.* New York: Crown, 1979.

4433. Koenig, Jacqueline. "Irving Stone's Jack London." *Pacific Historian* 22 (Fall 1978): 246–49.

4434. Labor, Earle. "From 'All Gold Canyon' to *The Acorn-Planter*: Jack London's Agrarian Vision." *Western American Literature* 11 (Summer 1976): 83–101.

4435. ———. "Jack London, 1876–1976: A Centennial Recognition." *Modern Fiction Studies* 22 (Spring 1976): 3–7.

4436. ———. "Jack London's 'Planchette': The Road Never Taken." *Pacific Historian* 21 (Summer 1977): 138–46.

4437. ———. "Jack London's Symbolic Wilderness: Four Versions." *Nineteenth-Century Fiction* 18 (Summer 1962): 149–61.

4438. ———, and Jeanne Campbell Reesman. *Jack London.* Rev ed. New York: Twayne, 1994.

4439. ———, Robert C. Leitz, III, and I. Milo Shephard, eds. *The Letters of Jack London.* 3 vols. Stanford, Calif.: Stanford University Press, 1988.

4440. ———, eds. *The Complete Short Stories of Jack London.* 3 vols. Stanford, Calif.: Stanford University Press, 1993.

4441. Lachtman, Howard. "Criticism of Jack London: A Selected Checklist." *Modern Fiction Studies* 22 (Spring 1976): 107–26.

4442. ———. "Four Horses, A Wife and a Valet: Up the California Coast With Jack London." *Pacific Historian* 21 (Summer 1977): 103–34.

4443. ———. "Jack and George: Notes on a Literary Friendship." *Pacific Historian* 22 (Summer 1978): 27–42. George Sterling.

4444. ———. "Man and Superwoman in Jack London's 'The Kanaka Surf.'" *Western American Literature* 7 (Summer 1972): 101–10.

4445. ———. "Revisiting Jack London's Valley of the Moon." *Pacific Historian* 24 (Summer 1980): 141–56.

4446. ———. "The Wide World of Jack London." Doctoral dissertation, University of the Pacific, 1974.

4447. Lessa, Richard. "Character and Perception in *The Sea-Wolf.*" *Jack London Newsletter* 15 (September–December 1982): 119–27.

4448. Littell, Katherine M. "The 'Nietzschean' and the Individualist in Jack London's Socialist Writings." *Jack London Newsletter* 15 (May–August 1982): 76–91.

4449. London, Charmian. *The Book of Jack London.* 2 vols. New York: Century, 1921.

4450. London, Joan. *Jack London and His Daughters.* Berkeley: Heyday Books, 1990.

4451. ———. *Jack London and His Times: An Unconventional Biography.* New York: Doubleday, Doran, 1939; Seattle: University of Washington, 1968.

4452. Lundquist, James. *Jack London: Adventures, Ideas, and Fiction.* New York: Ungar, 1987.

4453. Lynn, Kenneth S. *The Dream of Success.* Boston: Little, Brown, 1955, 75–118.

4454. McClintock, James I. "Jack London's Use of Carl Jung's Psychology of the Unconscious." *American Literature* 62 (November 1970): 336–47.

4455. ———. *White Logic: Jack London's Short Stories.* Grand Rapids, Mich.: Wolf House Books, 1975.

4456. Martin, Stoddard. *California Writers: Jack London, John Steinbeck, The Tough Guys*. New York: St. Martin's Press, 1983.

4457. Mills, Gordon. "Jack London's Quest for Salvation." *American Quarterly* 7 (Spring 1955): 3–14.

4458. ———. "The Symbolic Wilderness: James Fenimore Cooper and Jack London." *Nineteenth-Century Fiction* 13 (March 1959): 329–40.

4459. ———. "The Transformation of Material in a Mimetic Fiction." *Modern Fiction Studies* 22 (Spring 1976): 9–22.

4460. Mitchell, Lee Clark. "'Keeping His Head': Repetition and Responsibility in London's 'To Build a Fire.'" *Journal of Modern Literature* 13 (March 1986): 76–96.

4461. Moreland, David A. "The Quest that Failed: Jack London's Last Tales of the South Seas." *Pacific Studies* 8 (Fall 1984): 48–70.

4462. ———. "Violence in the South Sea Fiction of Jack London." *Jack London Newsletter* 16 (January–April 1983): 1–35.

4463. Noto, Sal. "Homage to Jack London: The House of Happy Walls." *Pacific Historian* 22 (Summer 1978): [Jack London Insert] 1–11.

4464. ———. "Jack London as Social Critic." *Jack London Newsletter* 4 (September–December 1971): 145–50.

4465. Nuernberg, Susan Marie. "The Call of Kind: Race in Jack London's Fiction." Doctoral dissertation, University of Massachusetts, 1990.

4466. O'Connor, Richard. *Jack London: A Biography*. Boston: Little, Brown, 1964.

4467. Ownbey, Ray Wilson, ed. *Jack London: Essays in Criticism*. Santa Barbara, Calif.: Peregrine Smith, 1978.

4468. Pankake, Jon Allan. "The Broken Myths of Jack London: Civilization, Nature, and the Self in the Major Works." Doctoral dissertation, University of Minnesota, 1975.

4469. ———. "Jack London's Wild Man: The Broken Myths of *Before Adam*." *Modern Fiction Studies* 22 (Spring 1976): 37–50.

4470. Pearsall, Robert Brainard. "Elizabeth Barrett Meets Wolf Larsen." *Western American Literature* 4 (Spring 1969): 3–13.

4471. Pizer, Donald. "Jack London: The Problem of Form." *Studies in the Literary Imagination* 16 (Fall 1983): 107–15.

4472. Price, Starling. "Jack London's America." Doctoral dissertation, University of Minnesota, 1970.

4473. Qualtiere, Michael. "Nietzschean Psychology in London's *The Sea Wolf*." *Western American Literature* 16 (Winter 1982): 261–78.

4474. Reesman, Jeanne C. "Jack London's New Woman in a New World: Saxon Brown Roberts' Journey into the Valley of the Moon." *American Literary Realism 1870–1910* 24 (Winter 1992): 40–54.

4475. ———. "The Problem of Knowledge in Jack London's 'The Water Baby.'" *Western American Literature* 23 (November 1988): 201–15.

4476. Robinson, Forrest G. "The Eyes Have It: An Essay on Jack London's *The Sea Wolf.*" *American Literary Realism 1870–1910* 18 (Spring–Fall 1985): 178–95.

4477. Rothberg, Abraham. "Old Stock: Jack London and His Valley of the Moon." *Southwest Review* 62 (Autumn 1977): 361–68.

4478. Sherman, Joan R. *Jack London: A Reference Guide.* Boston: G. K. Hall, 1977.

4479. Shivers, Alfred S. "Jack London: Not a Suicide." *Dalhousie Review* 49 (Spring 1969): 43–57.

4480. ———. "The Romantic in Jack London: Far Away from Frozen Places." *Alaskan Review* 1 (Winter 1963): 38–47.

4481. Silet, Charles L. P. "Upton Sinclair to Jack London: A Literary Friendship." *Jack London Newsletter* 5 (May–August 1972): 49–76.

4482. Sinclair, Andrew. *Jack: A Biography of Jack London.* New York: Harper and Row, 1977.

4483. Skipp, Frances E. "Jack London." *American Literary Realism 1870–1910* 8 (Autumn 1975): 299–306. Evaluates doctoral dissertations on London.

4484. Stanley, David H. "Jack London's Biographical Legend." *American Literary Realism 1870–1910* 17 (Spring 1984): 67–88.

4485. Stasz, Clarice. *American Dreamers: Charmian and Jack London.* New York: St. Martin's, 1988.

4486. ———. "Androgyny in the Novels of Jack London." *Western American Literature* 11 (Summer 1976): 121–33.

4487. ———. "The Social Construction of Biography: The Case of Jack London." *Modern Fiction Studies* 22 (Spring 1976): 51–72.

4488. Stone, Irving. *Sailor on Horseback: The Biography of Jack London.* Boston: Houghton Mifflin, 1938; reprinted in *Irving Stone's Jack London.* Garden City, N.Y.: Doubleday, 1977, 9–305.

4489. Tavernier-Courbin, Jacqueline. "Social Myth as Parody in Jack London's Northern Tales." *Thalia* 9 (Fall and Winter 1987): 3–14.

4490. ———, ed. *Critical Essays on Jack London.* Boston: G. K. Hall, 1983.

4491. Teich, Nathaniel. "Marxist Dialectics in Content, Form, Point of View: Structures in Jack London's *The Iron Heel.*" *Modern Fiction Studies* 22 (Spring 1976): 85–100.

4492. Tierney, William. "Jack London's California Ranch Novels." *Pacific Historian* 21 (Summer 1977): 147–58.

4493. Van Der Beets, Richard. "Nietzsche of the North: Heredity and Race in London's *The Son of the Wolf.*" *Western American Literature* 2 (Fall 1967): 229–33.

4494. Walcutt, Charles Child. *American Literary Naturalism, A Divided Stream.* Minneapolis: University of Minnesota Press, 1956, 87–113.

4495. ———. *Jack London.* Minneapolis: University of Minnesota Press, 1966.

4496. Walker, Dale L. *The Alien Worlds of Jack London.* Grand Rapids, Mich.: Wolf House Books, 1973. London's fantasy fiction.

4497. ———. "Jack London (1876–1916)." *American Literary Realism 1870–1910* 1 (Fall 1967): 71–78.

4498. ———, and James E. Sisson. *The Fiction of Jack London: A Chronological Bibliography.* El Paso: Texas Western Press, 1972.

4499. Walker, Franklin. "Ideas and Action in Jack London's Fiction." *Essays on American Literature in Honor of Jay Hubell.* Ed. Clarence Gohdes. Durham, N.C.: Duke University Press, 1967.

4500. ———. *Jack London and the Klondike.* San Marino, Calif.: Huntington Library, 1966.

4501. ———. "Jack London, *Martin Eden.*" *The American Novel from James Fenimore Cooper to William Faulkner.* Ed. Wallace Stegner. New York: Basic Books, 1965.

4502. ———. "Jack London's Use of Sinclair Lewis Plots, Together with a Printing of Three of the Plots." *Huntington Library Quarterly* 17 (November 1953): 59–74.

4503. Ward, Susan Eileen. "Ideas into Fiction: Popular Rhetoric in the Fiction of Jack London." Doctoral dissertation, University of Connecticut, 1975.

4504. ———. "Jack London's Women: Civilization vs The Frontier." *Jack London Newsletter* 9 (May–August 1976): 81–85.

4505. ———. "Social Philosophy as Best-Seller: Jack London's *The Sea Wolf.*" *Western American Literature* 17 (Winter 1983): 321–32.

4506. Watson, Charles N., Jr. "The Composition of *Martin Eden.*" *American Literature* 53 (November 1981): 397–408.

4507. ———. *The Novels of Jack London–A Reappraisal*. Madison: University of Wisconsin Press, 1983.

4508. Wilcox, Earl J. "Jack London and the Tradition of American Literary Naturalism." Doctoral dissertation, Vanderbilt University, 1966.

4509. ———. "Jack London's Naturalism: The Example of *The Call of the Wild*." *Jack London Newsletter* 2 (September–December 1969): 91–101.

4510. ———. "'The Kipling of the Klondike': Naturalism in London's Early Fiction." *Jack London Newsletter* 6 (January–April 1973): 1–12.

4511. ———. "Le Milieu, Le Moment, La Race: Literary Naturalism in Jack London's *White Fang*." *Jack London Newsletter* 3 (May–August 1970): 42–55.

4512. Williams, James. "The Composition of Jack London's Writings." *American Literary Realism 1870–1910* 23 (Winter 1991): 64–86.

4513. Williams, Tony. "Memories of Jack: An Interview with Becky London." *Jack London Newsletter* 19 (January–April 1986): 1–10.

4514. ———. "*The Mutiny of the Elsinore*–A Reevaluation." *Jack London Newsletter* 19 (January–April 1986): 13–41.

4515. Willson, Carolyn Johnston. "London Album: A California Legend at Work and Play." *California Historical Quarterly* 15 (Fall 1976): 218–45.

4516. ———. "'Rattling the Bones': Jack London, Socialist Evangelist." *Western American Literature* 11 (Summer 1976): 135–48.

4517. Winslow, Cedric Reimers. "The Crisis of Liberalism in the Novels of Theodore Dreiser, Frank Norris, and Jack London." 3 vols. Doctoral dissertation, New York University, 1977.

4518. Woodbridge, Hensley C. "Jack London's Current Reputation Abroad." *Pacific Historian* 21 (Summer 1977): 166–77.

4519. ———, ed. *Jack London Newsletter*. Carbondale: Southern Illinois University Library, 1967–88.

4520. ———, John London, and George H. Tweney, comps. *Jack London: A Bibliography*. Calif.: Talisman Press, 1966; enl ed. Millwood, N.Y.: Kraus, 1973.

4521. Yoder, Jon A. "Jack London as Wolf Barleycorn." *Western American Literature* 11 (Summer 1976): 103–19.

4522. Zamen, Mark E. *Standing Room Only: Jack London's Controversial Career as a Public Speaker*. New York: Peter Lang, 1990.

HANIEL LONG

4523. Almon, Bert. "Woman as Interpreter: Haniel Long's *Malinche*." *Southwest Review* 59 (Summer 1974): 221–39.

4524. Burlingame, Robert. "Haniel Long: His Seasons." *Southwest Review* 65 (Winter 1981): 21–38.

4525. Sarton, May. "The Leopard Land: Haniel and Alice Long's Santa Fe." *Southwest Review* 57 (1972): 1–14.

BARRY LOPEZ

4526. Aton, Jim. "An Interview with Barry Lopez." *Western American Literature* 21 (May 1986): 3–17.

4527. Nunnally, Patrick. "An Interview with Barry Lopez." *North Dakota Quarterly* 56 (Winter 1988): 98–107.

4528. Wild, Peter. *Barry Lopez*. Western Writers Series, No. 64. Boise, Idaho: Boise State University, 1984.

MABEL DODGE LUHAN

4529. Brett, Dorothy E. "Autobiography: My Long and Beautiful Journey." *South Dakota Review* 5 (Summer 1967): 11–71.

4530. Frazer, Winnifred L. *Mabel Dodge Luhan*. Boston: Twayne, 1984.

4531. Hahn, Emily. *Mabel: A Biography of Mabel Dodge Luhan*. Boston: Houghton Mifflin Company, 1977.

4532. Morrill, Claire. "Three Women of Taos: Frieda Lawrence, Mabel Luhan, and Dorothy Brett." *South Dakota Review* 2 (Spring 1965): 3–22.

4533. Nelson, Jane. *Mabel Dodge Luhan*. Western Writers Series, No. 55. Boise, Idaho: Boise State University, 1982.

4534. Rudnick, Lois P. "Mabel Dodge Luhan and Robinson Jeffers." *Robinson Jeffers Newsletter* 49 (June 1977): 21–49.

4535. ———. "Mabel Dodge Luhan and the Myth of the Southwest." *Southwest Review* 68 (Summer 1983): 205–21.

4536. ———. *Mabel Dodge Luhan: New Woman, New Worlds*. Albuquerque: University of New Mexico Press, 1984.

CHARLES FLETCHER LUMMIS

4537. Bingham, Edwin R. *Charles F. Lummis: Editor of the Southwest*. San Marino, Calif.: Huntington Library, 1955.

4538. Byrkit, James W., ed. *Charles Lummis: Letters from the Southwest.* Tucson: University of Arizona Press, 1989.

4539. Clark, Frank M. *Sandpapers: The Lives and Letters of Eugene Manlove Rhodes and Charles Fletcher Lummis.* Santa Fe, N.Mex.: Sunstone, 1993.

4540. Fiske, Turbesé Lummis, and Keith Lummis. *Charles F. Lummis: The Man and His West.* Norman: University of Oklahoma Press, 1975.

4541. Fleming, Robert E. *Charles F. Lummis.* Western Writers Series, No. 50. Boise, Idaho: Boise State University, 1981.

4542. Gordon, Dudley C. *Charles F. Lummis: Crusader in Corduroy.* Los Angeles: Cultural Assets Press, 1972.

4543. Newmark, Marco. "Charles Fletcher Lummis." *Historical Society of Southern California Quarterly* 32 (March 1950): 45–60.

4544. Powell, Lawrence Clark. "Song of the Southwest." *Westways* 64 (May 1973): 44–47, 82–87.

4545. Simmons, Marc. *Two Southwesterners: Charles Lummis and Amado Chaves.* Cerillos, N.Mex.: San Marcos Press, 1968.

HARRIS MERTON LYON

4546. Lyon, Zoe. "Harris Merton Lyon: Early American Realist." *Studies in Short Fiction* 5 (Summer 1968): 368–77.

CORMAC MCCARTHY

4547. Arnold, Edwin T., and Dianne C. Luce, eds. *Perspectives on Cormac McCarthy.* Jackson: University Press of Mississippi, 1993.

4548. Bell, Vereen. *The Achievement of Cormac McCarthy.* Baton Rouge: Louisiana State University Press, 1988.

4549. Luce, Dianne C. "Cormac McCarthy: A Bibliography." *Southern Quarterly* 30 (Summer 1992): 143–51.

4550. Pilkington, Tom. "Fate and Free Will on the American Frontier: Cormac McCarthy's Western Fiction." *Western American Literature* 27 (February 1993): 311–22.

MICHAEL MCCLURE

4551. Clements, Marshall. *A Catalog of Works by Michael McClure.* New York: Phoenix Book Shop, 1965.

4552. Lynch, Michael. "A Broad Silk Banner." *Parnassus* 4 (Spring–Summer 1976): 156–65.

4553. Fine, David. "Beginning in the Thirties: The Los Angeles Fiction of James M. Cain and Horace McCoy." *Los Angeles in Fiction: A Collection of Original Essays.* Ed. David Fine. Albuquerque: University of New Mexico Press, 1984, 43–66.

4554. Sturak, John Thomas. "Horace McCoy's Objective Lyricism." *Tough Guy Writers of the Thirties.* Ed. David Madden. Carbondale: Southern Illinois University Press, 1968, 137–62.

4555. ———. "The Life and Writings of Horace McCoy." Doctoral dissertation, UCLA, 1966.

4556. Winchell, Mark Royden. *Horace McCoy.* Western Writers Series, No. 51. Boise, Idaho: Boise State University, 1982.

WILMA ELIZABETH MCDANIEL

4557. Haslam, Gerald. "'Gravy Says A Lot': The Poetry of Wilma Elizabeth McDaniel." *Western American Literature* 13 (Summer 1978): 159–64.

ROSS MACDONALD

See Kenneth Millar

THOMAS MCGRATH

4558. Butwin, Joseph. "The Last Laugh: Thomas McGrath's Comedy." *North Dakota Quarterly* 55 (Winter 1987): 31–40.

4559. Engel, Bernard F. "Thomas McGrath's Dakota." *Midwestern Miscellany* 4 (1976): 3–7.

4560. Matchie, Thomas. "The Function of the Hopi Kachina in Tom McGrath's *Letter to an Imaginary Friend.*" *South Dakota Review* 22 (Autumn 1984): 7–21.

4561. Rogers, James H. "Vision and Feeling: An Interview with Thomas McGrath." *North Dakota Quarterly* 53 (Winter 1985): 29–43.

4562. Smeall, Joseph F. S. "Thomas McGrath: A Review Essay." *North Dakota Quarterly* 40 (Winter 1972): 29–38.

4563. Stern, Frederick C. "'The Delegate for Poetry': McGrath as Communist Poet." *Where the West Begins.* Eds. Arthur R. Huseboe and William Geyer. Sioux Falls, S. Dak.: Center for Western Studies Press, 1978, 119–27.

4564. ———, ed. *The Revolutionary Poet in the United States: The Poetry of Thomas McGrath.* Columbia: University of Missouri Press, 1988.

4565. Bonetti, Kay. "An Interview with Tom McGuane." *Missouri Review* 9 (1985–86): 73–99.

4566. Carter, Albert Howard, III. "McGuane's First Three Novels: Games, Fun, Nemesis." *Critique* 17 (No. 1, 1975): 91–104.

4567. Cook, Nancy S. "Investment in Place: Thomas McGuane in Montana." *Old West–New West: Centennial Essays*. Ed. Barbara Howard Meldrum. Moscow: University of Idaho Press, 1993, 213–29.

4568. Gregory, Sinda, and Larry McCaffery. "The Art of Fiction LXXXXIX: Thomas McGuane." *Paris Review* 97 (Fall 1985): 34–71.

4569. Klinkowitz, Jerome. *The New American Novel of Manners: The Fiction of Richard Yates, Dan Wakefield, and Thomas McGuane*. Athens: University of Georgia Press, 1986.

4570. Lear, Liz. "A Conversation with Thomas McGuane." *Shenandoah* 36 (No. 2, 1986): 12–21.

4571. McCaffery, Larry. "Thomas McGuane: A Bibliography, 1969–1978." *Bulletin of Bibliography* 35 (October–December 1978): 169–71.

4572. ———, and Sinda Gregory. "An Interview with Thomas McGuane." *Alive and Writing: Interviews with American Authors of the 1980s*. Eds. Larry McCaffery and Sinda Gregory. Urbana: University of Illinois Press, 1987, 196–221.

4573. Morris, Gregory L. "How Ambivalence Won the West: Thomas McGuane and the Fiction of the New West." *Critique* 32 (Spring 1991): 180–89.

4574. Wallace, Jon. "The Language Plot in Thomas McGuane's *Ninety-Two in the Shade*." *Critique* 29 (Winter 1988): 111–20.

4575. ———. "Speaking Against the Dark: Style as Theme in Thomas McGuane's *Nobody's Angel*." *Modern Fiction Studies* 33 (September 1987): 289–98.

4576. Welch, Dennis M. "Death and Fun in the Novels of Thomas McGuane." *University of Windsor Review* 14 (1978): 14–20.

4577. Westrum, Dexter. *Thomas McGuane*. Boston: Twayne, 1991.

MARY MACLANE

4578. Wheeler, Leslie. "Montana's Shocking 'Lit'ry Lady.'" *Montana: The Magazine of Western History* 27 (Summer 1977): 20–33.

NORMAN MACLEAN

4579. Bevis, William W. "Maclean's River." *Ten Tough Trips: Montana Writers and the West.* Seattle: University of Washington Press, 1990, 171–83.

4580. Butler, Douglas R. "Norman Maclean's 'A River Runs Through It': Word, Water, and Text." *Critique* 33 (Summer 1992): 263–73.

4581. Doig, Ivan. "Essays on the West: *A River Runs Through It*, A Review." *Montana: The Magazine of Western History* 43 (Winter 1993): 70–73.

4582. Lojek, Helen. "Casting Flies and Recasting Myths with Norman Maclean." *Western American Literature* 25 (August 1990): 145–56.

4583. McFarland, Ron. *Norman Maclean.* Western Writers Series, No. 107. Boise, Idaho: Boise State University, 1993.

4584. ———, and Hugh Nichols, eds. *Norman Maclean.* Lewiston, Idaho: Confluence Press, 1988.

4585. Simonson, Harold P. "Essays on the West: Tragedy and Beyond: Maclean's *Young Men and Fire*, A Review." *Montana: The Magazine of Western History* 43 (Spring 1993): 69–72.

4586. ———. "Norman Maclean's Two-Hearted River." *Western American Literature* 17 (Summer 1982): 149–55.

4587. Weltzien, O. Alan. "The Two Lives of Norman Maclean and The Text of Fire in *Young Men and Fire.*" *Western American Literature* 29 (May 1994): 3–24.

NORMAN MACLEOD

4588. Trusky, A. Thomas. "Norman Wicklund MacLeod, Poet from the West." *Prairie Schooner* 50 (Fall 1976): 257–68.

4589. Wald, Alan. "Tethered to the Past: The Poetry of Norman MacLeod." *Minnesota Review* 11 (1978): 107–11.

LARRY MCMURTRY

4590. Ahearn, Kerry. "Morte D'Urban: The Texas Novels of Larry McMurtry." *Texas Quarterly* 19 (Autumn 1976): 109–29.

4591. Busby, Mark. "Damn the Saddle on the Wall: Anti-Myth in Larry McMurtry's *Horseman, Pass By.*" *New Mexico Humanities Review* 3 (Summer 1980): 5–10.

4592. Cox, Diana H. "*Anything for Billy*: A Fiction Stranger than Truth." *Journal of American Culture* 14 (Summer 1991): 75–81.

4593. Davis, Kenneth W. "The Themes of Initiation in the Work of Larry McMurtry and Tom Mayer." *Arlington Quarterly* 2 (Winter 1969–1970): 29–43.

4594. Degenfelder, E. Pauline. "McMurtry and the Movies: *Hud* and *The Last Picture Show*." *Western Humanities Review* 29 (Winter 1975): 81–91.

4595. England, D. Gene. "Rites of Passage in Larry McMurtry's *The Last Picture Show*." *Heritage of Kansas* 12 (Winter 1979): 37–48.

4596. Folsom, James K. "*Shane* and *Hud*: Two Stories in Search of a Medium." *Western Humanities Review* 24 (Autumn 1970): 359–72.

4597. Graham, Don. "*Lonesome Dove*: Butch and Sundance Go on a Cattledrive." *Southwestern American Literature* 12 (Fall 1986): 7–12.

4598. Granzow, Barbara. "The Western Writer: A Study of Larry McMurtry's *All My Friends Are Going To Be Strangers*." *Southwestern American Literature* 4 (1974): 37–52.

4599. Landess, Thomas. *Larry McMurtry*. Southwest Writers Series, No. 23. Austin, Tex.: Steck-Vaughn, 1969.

4600. Lich, Lera Patrick Tyler. *Larry McMurtry's Texas: Evolution of the Myth*. Austin: Eakin Press, 1987.

4601. Morrow, Patrick D. "Larry McMurtry: The First Phase." *Seasoned Authors for a New Season: The Search for Standards in Popular Writing*. Ed. Louis Filler. Bowling Green, Ohio: Bowling Green State University Popular Press, 1980, 70–82.

4602. Neinstein, Raymond L. *The Ghost Country: A Study of the Novels of Larry McMurtry*. Berkeley, Calif.: Creative Arts, 1976.

4603. Peavy, Charles D. *Larry McMurtry*. Boston: Twayne, 1977.

4604. ———. "A Larry McMurtry Bibliography." *Western American Literature* 3 (Fall 1968): 235–48.

4605. Phillips, Billie. "McMurtry's Women: 'Eros [Libido, Caritas, and Philia] in [and out of] Archer County.'" *Southwestern American Literature* 4 (1974): 29–36.

4606. Phillips, Raymond C., Jr. "The Ranch as Place and Symbol in the Novels of Larry McMurtry." *South Dakota Review* 13 (Summer 1975): 27–47.

4607. Pilkington, William T. "The Dirt Farmer and the Cowboy: Notes on Two Texas Essayists." *RE: Arts and Letters* 30 (Fall 1969): 42–54.

4608. ———. "The Recent Southwestern Novel." *Southwestern American Literature* 1 (January 1971): 12–15.

4609. Reynolds, Clay, ed. *Taking Stock: A Larry McMurtry Casebook*. Dallas: Southern Methodist University Press, 1989.

4610. Schmidt, Dorey, ed. *Larry McMurtry: Unredeemed Dreams*. Edinburg, Tex.: Pan American University, 1978.

4611. Sewell, Ernestine P. "McMurtry's Cowboy-God in *Lonesome Dove*." *Western American Literature* 21 (November 1986): 219–25.

4612. Sonnichsen, C. L. "The New Style Western." *South Dakota Review* 4 (Summer 1966): 22–28.

4613. Stout, Janis P. "Cadillac Larry Rides Again: McMurtry and the Song of the Open Road." *Western American Literature* 24 (November 1989): 243–51.

4614. ———. "Journeying as a Metaphor for Cultural Loss in the Novels of Larry McMurtry." *Western American Literature* 11 (May 1976): 37–50.

4615. Summerlin, Tim. "Larry McMurtry and the Persistent Frontier." *Southwestern American Literature* 4 (1974): 22–28.

4616. Tangum, Marion. "Larry McMurtry's *Lonesome Dove*: This is What We Call Home." *Rocky Mountain Review of Language and Literature* 45 (1991): 61–73.

4617. Thurn, Thora Flack. "The Quest for Freedom in the Changing West of Edward Abbey and Larry McMurtry." Doctoral dissertation, Texas Christian University, 1990.

4618. Woodward, Daniel. "Larry McMurtry's *Texasville*: A Comic Pastoral of the Oilpatch." *Huntington Library Quarterly* 56 (Spring 1993): 167–80.

CHARLES L. MCNICHOLS

4619. Berner, Robert L. "Charles L. McNichols and *Crazy Weather*: A Reconsideration." *Western American Literature* 6 (Spring 1971): 39–51.

D'ARCY MCNICKLE

4620. Bevis, William W. "McNickle: Homing In." *Ten Tough Trips: Montana Writers and the West*. Seattle: University of Washington Press, 1990, 92–108.

4621. Hans, Birgit. "Surrounded: The Fiction of D'Arcy McNickle." Doctoral dissertation, University of Arizona, 1988.

4622. Larson, Charles R. *American Indian Fiction*. Albuquerque: University of New Mexico Press, 1978, 68–78.

4623. Owens, Louis. "The 'Map of the Mind': D'Arcy McNickle and the American Indian Novel." *Western American Literature* 19 (February 1985): 275–83.

4624. ———. "The Red Road to Nowhere: D'Arcy McNickle's *The Surrounded* and 'The Hungry Generations.'" *American Indian Quarterly* 13 (Summer 1989): 239–48.

4625. Parker, Dorothy R. *Singing an Indian Song: A Biography of D'Arcy McNickle.* Lincoln: University of Nebraska Press, 1992.

4626. Purdy, John Lloyd. *Word Ways: The Novels of D'Arcy McNickle.* Tucson: University of Arizona Press, 1990.

4627. Ruppert, James. *D'Arcy McNickle.* Western Writers Series, No. 83. Boise, Idaho: Boise State University, 1988.

4628. ———. "Politics and Culture in the Fiction of D'Arcy McNickle." *Rocky Mountain Review of Language and Literature* 42 (1988): 185–95.

JOHN MCPHEE

4629. Maher, Susan Naramore. "Deep Time, Human Time, and the Western Quest: John McPhee's *Rising From the Plains.*" *South Dakota Review* 30 (Spring 1992): 36–45.

4630. Stull, James. "Self and the Performance of Others: The Pastoral Vision of John McPhee." *North Dakota Quarterly* 59 (Summer 1991): 182–200.

4631. Terrie, Philip G. "River of Paradox: John McPhee's 'The Encircled River.'" *Western American Literature* 23 (May 1988): 3–15.

CAREY MCWILLIAMS

4632. Crister, Greg. "The Making of a Cultural Rebel: Carey McWilliams, 1924–1930." *Pacific Historical Review* 55 (May 1986): 226–55.

NORMAN MAILER

4633. Evans, Timothy. "Boiling the Archetypal Plot: Norman Mailer's American Dream." *Southwest Review* 60 (Spring 1975): 159–70.

4634. Witt, Grace. "The Bad Man as Hipster: Norman Mailer's Use of Frontier Metaphor." *Western American Literature* 4 (Fall 1969): 202–17.

4635. Astro, Richard. "In the Heart of the Valley: Bernard Malamud's *A New Life.*" *Bernard Malamud: A Collection of Critical Essays.* Eds. Leslie A. Field and Joyce W. Field. Englewood Cliffs, N.J.: Prentice-Hall, 1975, 143–55.

4636. Barsness, John A. "*A New Life:* The Frontier Myth in Perspective." *Western American Literature* 3 (Winter 1969): 297–302.

4637. Fiedler, Leslie A. "Malamud's Travesty Western." *Novel: A Forum on Fiction* 10 (Spring 1977): 212–19.

4638. Kosofsky, Rita Nathalie. *Bernard Malamud: An Annotated Checklist.* Kent, Ohio: Kent State University Press, 1969.

4639. Mandel, Ruth. "Bernard Malamud's *The Assistant and A New Life:* Ironic Affirmation." *Critique* 7 (Writer 1964–65): 110–22.

4640. Mellard, James M. "Academia and the Wasteland: Bernard Malamud's *A New Life* and His Views of the University." *The American Writer and the University.* Ed. Ben Siegel. Newark: University of Delaware Press, 1989, 54–67.

4641. Richman, Sidney. *Bernard Malamud.* New York: Twayne, 1966, 78–97.

4642. Schulz, Max F. "Malamud's *A New Life:* The New Wasteland of the Fifties." *Western Review* 6 (Summer 1969): 37–44.

4643. Singer, Barnett. "Outsider Versus Insider: Malamud's and Kesey's Pacific Northwest." *South Dakota Review* 13 (Winter 1975–76): 127–44.

4644. Solotaroff, Theodore. "Bernard Malamud's Fiction: The Old Life and the New." *Commentary* 30 (March 1962): 197–204.

4645. Witherington, Paul. "Malamud's Allusive Design in *A New Life.*" *Western American Literature* 10 (August 1975): 114–23.

JAMES C. MALIN

4646. Bell, Robert G. "James C. Malin and the Grasslands of North America." *Agricultural History* 46 (July 1972): 414–24.

4647. ———. "James C. Malin: A Study in American Historiography." Doctoral dissertation, University of California, Los Angeles, 1968.

4648. Bogue, Allan G. "The Heirs of James C. Malin: A Grasslands Historiography." *Great Plains Quarterly* 1 (Spring 1981): 105–31.

4649. ———. "James C. Malin: A Voice from the Grassland." *Writing Western History: Essays on Major Western Historians.* Ed. Richard W. Etulain. Albuquerque: University of New Mexico Press, 1991, 215–43.

4650. LeDuc, Thomas H. "An Ecological Interpretation of Grasslands History: The Work of James C. Malin as Historian and as Critic of Historians." *Nebraska History* 31 (September 1950): 226–33.

4651. Swierenga, Robert P., ed. *James C. Malin: History and Ecology: Studies of the Grassland.* Lincoln: University of Nebraska Press, 1984.

FREDERICK FEIKEMA MANFRED

See Frederick Feikema

EDWIN MARKHAM

4652. Arlt, G. O. "Poet Laureate: Edwin Markham." *Historical Society of Southern California Quarterly* 34 (September 1952): 199–212.

4653. Chase, Don M. "Edwin Markham California Prophet." *Pacific Historian* 20 (Summer 1976): 167–76.

4654. Clemens, Cyril, et al. "Edwin Markham Number." *Mark Twain Quarterly* 4 (Spring 1941): 1–20.

4655. Filler, Louis. *The Unknown Edwin Markham: His Mystery and Its Significance.* Yellow Springs, Ohio: Antioch Press, 1966.

4656. Goldstein, Jessie S. "Edwin Markham, Ambrose Bierce, and 'The Man with the Hoe.'" *Modern Language Notes* 58 (March 1943): 165–75.

4657. ———. "Escapade of a Poet." *Pacific Historical Review* 13 (September 1944): 303–13.

4658. ———. "Life of Edwin Markham." Doctoral dissertation, New York University, 1945.

4659. ———. "Two Literary Radicals: Garland and Markham in Chicago, 1893." *American Literature* 17 (May 1945): 152–60.

4660. Grose, G. R. "Edwin Markham: Poet of the Social Conscience." *Personalist* 17 (April 1936): 149–56.

4661. Haaland, C. Carlyle. "The Mystique of Markham's California: The Culmination of the Millenial Motif in America." *Markham Review* 4 (February 1975): 89–95.

4662. Slade, Joseph W. "'Putting You in the Papers': Ambrose Bierce's Letters to Edwin Markham." *Prospects: An Annual Journal of American Cultural Studies.* Vol. I. Ed. Jack Salzman. New York: Burt Franklin, 1975, 335–68.

4663. Synnestvedt, Sigfried T. "Bread, Beauty, and Brotherhood: The Ethical Consciousness of Edwin Markham." Doctoral dissertation, University of Pennsylvania, 1959.

ALICE MARRIOTT

4664. Kohler, Turner S. *Alice Marriott.* Southwest Writers Series, No. 27. Austin, Tex.: Steck-Vaughn, 1969.

4665. ———. "Alice Marriott: The Anthropologist as Artist." *Southwestern American Literature* 1 (May 1971): 72–79.

FRANCIS S. MARRYAT

4666. LeRoy, Bruce. "Frank Marryat, *Mountains and Molehills.*" *Book Club of California Quarterly News-Letter* 38 (Summer 1973): 51–62.

FREDERICK MARRYAT

4667. Maher, Susan Naramore. "Receding Frontiers: Frederick Marryat's West in *A Diary in America.*" *South Dakota Review* 29 (Spring 1991): 36–46.

JOHN JOSEPH MATTHEWS

4668. Larson, Charles R. *American Indian Fiction.* Albuquerque: University of New Mexico Press, 1978, 34–37, 55–65.

4669. Richter, Sara Jane. "The Life and Literature of John Joseph Matthews: Contributions of Two Cultures." Doctoral dissertation, Oklahoma State University, 1985.

TOM MAYER

4670. Davis, Kenneth W. "The Theme of Initiation in the Works of Larry McMurtry and Tom Mayer." *Arlington Quarterly* 2 (Winter 1969–70): 29–43.

H. L. MENCKEN

4671. Love, Glen A. "Stemming the Avalanche of Tripe; Or, How H. L. Mencken and Friends Reformed Northwest Literature." *Thalia: Studies in Literary Humor* 4 (Spring–Summer 1981): 46–53.

4672. Schwartz, Gerald. "The West as Gauged by H. L. Mencken's *American Mercury.*" *Menckeniana* 89 (1984): 1–11.

RITA MENDOZA

4673. Lewis, Marvin A. "Rita Mendoza: Chicana Poetess." *Latin American Literary Review* 5 (Spring–Summer 1977): 79–85.

OSCAR MICHEAUX

4674. Fontenot, Chester J., Jr. "Oscar Micheaux, Black Novelist and Film Maker." *Vision and Refuge: Essays on the Literature of the Great Plains.* Eds. Virginia Faulkner with Frederick C. Luebke. Lincoln: University of Nebraska Press, 1982, 109–25.

4675. Hebert, Janis. "Oscar Micheaux: A Black Pioneer." *South Dakota Review* 11 (Winter 1973–74): 62–69.

JAMES MICHENER

4676. Day, A. Grove. *James Michener.* 2d ed. Boston: Twayne, 1977.

4677. Kings, John. *In Search of "Centennial": A Journey with James A. Michener.* New York: Random House, 1978.

4678. Michener, James. *About 'Centennial': Some Notes on the Novel.* New York: Random House, 1974.

GEORGE MILBURN

4679. Disbrow, Jimmie L. "The Local-Color Artistry of George Milburn." Doctoral dissertation, Oklahoma State University, 1972.

4680. Downs, Alexis. "George Milburn: Ozark Folklore in Oklahoma Fiction." *Chronicles of Oklahoma* 55 (Fall 1977): 309–23.

4681. Turner, Steven. *George Milburn.* Southwest Writers Series, No. 28. Austin, Tex.: Steck-Vaughn, 1970.

KENNETH MILLAR

(Ross Macdonald)

4682. Browne, Ray B. "Ross Macdonald: Revolutionary Author and Critic; Or the Need for the Oath of Macdonald." *Journal of Popular Culture* 24 (Winter 1990): 101–11.

4683. Bruccoli, Matthew J. *Ross Macdonald.* San Diego: Harcourt Brace Jovanovich, 1984.

4684. ———. *Ross Macdonald/Kenneth Millar: A Descriptive Bibliography.* Pittsburgh: University of Pittsburgh Press, 1983.

4685. Busch, Susan Runholt. "Ross Macdonald as Chronicler of Southern California." *South Dakota Review* 24 (Spring 1986): 111–20.

4686. Mahan, Jeffrey Howard. *A Long Way from Solving That One: Psycho/Social and Ethical Implications of Ross Macdonald's Lew Archer Tales.* Lanham, Md.: University Press of America, 1990.

4687. Pry, Elmer. "Ross Macdonald's Violent California: Imagery Patterns in *The Underground Man*." *Western American Literature* 9 (November 1974): 197–203.

4688. Schopen, Bernard A. *Ross Macdonald*. Boston: Twayne, 1990.

4689. Sipper, Ralph B., ed. *Inward Journey: Ross Macdonald*. Santa Barbara, Calif.: Cordelia Editions, 1984.

4690. Skenazy, Paul. "Bringing It All Back Home: Ross Macdonald's California." *South Dakota Review* 24 (Spring 1986): 68–109.

4691. Skinner, Robert E. *The Hard-Boiled Explicator: A Guide to The Study of Dashiell Hammett, Raymond Chandler and Ross Macdonald*. Metuchen, N.J.: Scarecrow Press, 1985.

4692. Snodgrass, Richard. "Down These Streets, I Mean, A Man Must Go." *South Dakota Review* 24 (Spring 1986): 7–27.

4693. *South Dakota Review* 24 (Spring 1986). Special issue on Macdonald.

4694. Speir, Jerry. *Ross Macdonald*. New York: Ungar, 1978.

4695. ———. "The Ultimate Seacoast: Ross Macdonald's California." *Los Angeles in Fiction: A Collection of Original Essays*. Ed. David Fine. Albuquerque: University of New Mexico Press, 1984, 133–44.

4696. Steiner, T. R. "The Mind of the Hardboiled: Ross Macdonald and the Roles of Criticism." *South Dakota Review* 24 (Spring 1986): 29–53.

4697. Wolfe, Peter. *Dreamers Who Live Their Dreams: The World of Ross Macdonald's Novels*. Bowling Green, Ohio: Bowling Green State University Popular Press, 1976.

CINCINNATUS (JOAQUIN) HINER MILLER

4698. Allen, Merritt P. *Joaquin Miller: Frontier Poet*. New York: Harper and Brothers, 1932.

4699. Buchanan, L.E. "Joaquin Miller in the Passing of the Old West." *Research Studies of Washington State University* 32 (1964): 326–33.

4700. Frost, O.W. *Joaquin Miller*. New York: Twayne, 1967.

4701. Haight, Mary M. "Joaquin Miller in Oregon, 1852–54 and 1857–70." Doctoral dissertation, University of Washington, 1936.

4702. Hapke, Laura. *Girls Who Went Wrong: Prostitutes in American Fiction, 1885–1917*. Bowling Green, Ohio: Bowling Green State University Popular Press, 1989.

4703. Lawson, Benjamin S. *Joaquin Miller*. Western Writers Series, No. 43. Boise, Idaho: Boise State University, 1980.

4704. Longtin, Ray C. *Three Writers of the Far West: A Reference Guide*. Boston: G.K. Hall, 1980.

4705. Marberry, M. Marion. *Splendid Poseur: Joaquin Miller–American Poet.* New York: Thomas Y. Crowell, 1953.

4706. Miller, Juanita. *My Father, C. H. Joaquin Miller, Poet.* Oakland, Calif.: Tooley-Towne, [1941].

4707. Peterson, Martin Severin. *Joaquin Miller: Literary Frontiersman.* Palo Alto, Calif.: Stanford University Press, 1937.

4708. Richards, John S., ed. *Joaquin Miller: His California Diary.* Seattle: F. McCaffrey, 1936.

4709. Rosenus, A. H. "Joaquin Miller and His 'Shadow.'" *Western American Literature* 10 (May 1976): 51–59.

4710. ———, ed. *Selected Writings of Joaquin Miller.* Eugene, Oreg.: Urion Press, 1977.

4711. Thompson, H.C. "Reminiscences of Joaquin Miller and Canyon City." *Oregon Historical Quarterly* 45 (December 1944): 326–36.

4712. Wagner, Harr. *Joaquin Miller and His Other Self.* San Francisco: Harr Wagner, 1929.

4713. Walker, Franklin. *San Francisco's Literary Frontier.* New York: Alfred A. Knopf, 1939.

4714. Walterhouse, Roger R. "Bret Harte, Joaquin Miller, and the Western Local Color Story." Doctoral dissertation, University of Chicago, 1936.

4715. White, Bruce A. "The Liberal Stances of Joaquin Miller." *Rendezvous* 19 (Fall 1983): 86–94.

ENOS MILLS

4716. Abbott, Carl. "'To Arouse Interest in the Outdoors': The Literary Career of Enos Mills." *Montana: The Magazine of Western History* 31 (April 1981): 2–15.

4717. Wild, Peter. *Enos Mills.* Western Writers Series, No. 36. Boise, Idaho: Boise State University, 1979.

JOHN R. MILTON

4718. Haslam, Gerald. "An Interview with John R. Milton." *Western American Literature* 19 (August 1984): 113–24.

4719. Milton, John. "Coincidentally: A Brief Memoir." *South Dakota Review* 24 (Spring 1986): 130–36.

4720. Pavich, Paul N. "Myth and Paramyth in John R. Milton's *Notes to a Bald Buffalo." Where the West Begins*. Eds. Arthur R. Huseboe and William Geyer. Sioux Falls, S. Dak.: Center for Western Studies Press, 1978, 80–85.

4721. Sanford, Geraldine. "Mountain Climbing with Milton." *Dakota Arts Quarterly* (Fall 1979): 4–7.

4722. ———. "To Pay A Little Blood: Pursuit of the Vision in *Notes to a Bald Buffalo." Heritage of Kansas* 11 (Winter 1978): 28–34.

VILHELM MOBERG

4723. Robb, Kenneth A. "A Swedish Emigrant in the Land of Oranges." *Itinerary: Criticism, Essays on California Writers*. Ed. Charles L. Crow. Bowling Green, Ohio: University Press, 1978, 79–87.

N. SCOTT MOMADAY

4724. Aithal, S.K. "The Redemptive Return: Momaday's *House Made of Dawn." North Dakota Quarterly* 53 (Spring 1985): 160–72.

4725. Arant, Tommy Joe. "'House Made of Dawn' and the Social Context of Contemporary Native American Literature." Doctoral dissertation, Duke University, 1991.

4726. Barry, Nora Baker. "The Bear's Son Folk Tale in *When the Legends Die* and *House Made of Dawn." Western American Literature* 12 (Winter 1978): 275–87.

4727. Berner, Robert L. "N. Scott Momaday: Beyond Rainy Mountain." *American Indian Culture and Research Journal* 3 (1979): 57–67.

4728. Billingsley, R. G. "*House Made of Dawn*: Momaday's Treatise on the Word." *Southwestern American Literature* 5 (1975): 81–87.

4729. Bloodworth, William. "Neihardt, Momaday, and the Art of Indian Autobiography." *Where the West Begins*. Eds. Arthur R. Huseboe and William Geyer. Sioux Falls, S. Dak.: Center for Western Studies Press, 1978, 152–60.

4730. Davis, Jack L. "Language and Consciousness in *House Made of Dawn." New America* 3 (Summer–Fall 1977): 56–59.

4731. ———. "The Whorf Hypothesis and Native American Literature." *South Dakota Review* 14 (Summer 1976): 59–72.

4732. Dickinson-Brown, Roger. "The Art and Importance of N. Scott Momaday." *Southern Review* 14 (January 1978): 30–45.

4733. Evers, Lawrence J. "Words and Place: A Reading of *House Made of Dawn*." *Western American Literature* 11 (February 1977): 297–320.

4734. Hirsch, Bernard A. "Self-Hatred and Spiritual Corruption in *House Made of Dawn*." *Western American Literature* 17 (Winter 1983): 307–20.

4735. Hylton, Marion Willard. "On a Trail of Pollen: Momaday's *House Made of Dawn*." *Critique* 14 (No. 2, 1972): 60–69.

4736. Kerr, Blaine. "The Novel as Sacred Text: N. Scott Momaday's Mythmaking Ethic." *Southwest Review* 63 (Spring 1978): 172–79.

4737. Kousaleos, Peter G. "A Study of the Language, Structure, and Symbolism in Jean Toomer's *Cane* and N. Scott Momaday's *House Made of Dawn*." Doctoral dissertation, Ohio University, 1973.

4738. Larson, Charles R. *American Indian Fiction*. Albuquerque: University of New Mexico Press, 1978, 78–95, 165–72.

4739. McAllister, H. S. "Be a Man, Be a Woman: Androgyny in *House Made of Dawn*." *American Indian Quarterly* 11 (Spring 1975): 14–22.

4740. ———. "Incarnate Grace and the Paths of Salvation in *House Made of Dawn*." *South Dakota Review* 12 (Winter 1974–75): 115–25.

4741. ———. "The Topology of Remembrance in *The Way to Rainy Mountain*." *Denver Quarterly* 12 (Winter 1978): 19–31.

4742. Mason, Kenneth D. "Beautyway: The Poetry of N. Scott Momaday." *South Dakota Review* 18 (Summer 1980): 61–83.

4743. Nelson, Margaret Faye. "Ethnic Identity in the Prose Works of N. Scott Momaday." Doctoral dissertation, Oklahoma State University, 1979.

4744. Nicholas, Charles A. "*The Way to Rainy Mountain*: N. Scott Momaday's Hard Journey Back." *South Dakota Review* 13 (Winter 1975–76): 149–58.

4745. Oleson, Carole. "The Remembered Earth: Momaday's *House Made of Dawn*." *South Dakota Review* 11 (Spring 1973): 59–78.

4746. Raymond, Michael W. "Tai-Me, Christ, and the Machine: Affirmation Through Mythic Pluralism in *House Made of Dawn*." *Studies in American Fiction* 11 (Spring 1983): 61–71.

4747. Roemer, Kenneth M., ed. *Approaches to Teaching Momaday's <u>The Way to Rainy Mountain</u>*. New York: Modern Language Association of America, 1988.

4748. Scarberry-García, Susan. *Landmarks of Healing: A Study of <u>House Made of Dawn</u>*. Albuquerque: University of New Mexico Press, 1990.

4749. Schein, Marie. "Identity in Leslie Marmon Silko's *Ceremony* and N. Scott Momaday's *The Ancient Child*." *Southwestern American Literature* 18 (Spring 1993): 19–25.

4750. Schubnell, Matthias. *N. Scott Momaday: The Cultural and Literary Background*. Norman: University of Oklahoma Press, 1985.

4751. Trimble, Martha Scott. *N. Scott Momaday*. Western Writers Series, No. 9. Boise, Idaho: Boise State College, 1973.

4752. Trimmer, Joseph F. "Native Americans and the America Mix: N. Scott Momaday's *House Made of Dawn*." *Indiana Social Studies Quarterly* 28 (1975): 75–91.

4753. Velie, Alan R. "Cain and Abel in N. Scott Momaday's *House Made of Dawn*." *Journal of the West* 17 (April 1978): 55–62.

4754. ———. *Four American Indian Literary Masters: N. Scott Momaday, James Welch, Leslie Marmon Silko, and Gerald Vizenor*. Norman: University of Oklahoma Press, 1982.

4755. Watkins, Floyd C. *In Time and Place: Some Origins of American Fiction*. Athens: University of Georgia Press, 1977, 133–71. *House Made of Dawn*.

4756. Weiler, Dagmar. "N. Scott Momaday: Story Teller." *Journal of Ethnic Studies* 16 (Spring 1988): 118–26.

4757. Winters, Yvor. *Forms of Discovery*. Chicago: Alan Swallow, 1967, 279–84.

4758. Woodward, Charles L. *Ancestral Voice: Conversations with N. Scott Momaday*. Lincoln: University of Nebraska Press, 1989.

4759. ———. "The Concept of the Creative Word in the Writings of N. Scott Momaday." Doctoral dissertation, University of Oklahoma, 1975.

4760. Zachrau, Thekla. "N. Scott Momaday: Towards an Indian Identity." *American Indian Culture and Research Journal* 3 (1979): 39–56.

WRIGHT MORRIS

4761. Albers, Randall K. "The Female Transformation: The Role of Women in Two Novels by Wright Morris." *Prairie Schooner* 53 (Summer 1979): 95–115.

4762. Arnold, Marilyn. "Wright Morris's *Plains Song*: Women's Search for Harmony." *South Dakota Review* 20 (Autumn 1982): 50–62.

4763. Baumbach, Jonathan. "Wake Before Bomb: *Ceremony in Lone Tree*." *Critique* 4 (Winter 1961–62): 56–71.

4764. Bird, Roy K. *Wright Morris: Memory and Imagination.* New York: Peter Lang, 1985.

4765. Booth, Wayne C. "The Shaping of the Prophecy: Craft and Idea in the Novels of Wright Morris." *American Scholar* 31 (Autumn 1962): 608–26.

4766. ———. "The Two Worlds in the Fiction of Wright Morris." *Sewanee Review* 65 (Summer 1957): 375–99.

4767. Bredahl, A. Carl. "The Outsider as Sexual Center: Wright Morris and the Integrated Imagination." *Studies in the Novel* 18 (Spring 1986): 66–73.

4768. Brenner, Jack. "Wright Morris's West: Fallout from a Pioneer Past." *Denver Quarterly* 10 (Winter 1976): 63–75.

4769. Burns, Leslie Edward. "A Psychological Reading of Wright Morris' Early Novels." Doctoral dissertation, New York University, 1978.

4770. Carlisle, Olga, and Jodie Ireland. "Wright Morris: The Art of Fiction CXXV." *Paris Review* 120 (Fall 1991): 52–94.

4771. Carpenter, Frederic I. "Wright Morris and the Territory Ahead." *College English* 21 (December 1959): 147–56.

4772. Cohn, Jack Rice. "Wright Morris: The Design of the Midwestern Fiction." Doctoral dissertation, University of California, Berkeley, 1970.

4773. Crump, G. B. *The Novels of Wright Morris: A Critical Interpretation.* Lincoln: University of Nebraska Press, 1978.

4774. ———. "Wright Morris, Author in Hiding." *Western American Literature* 25 (May 1990): 3–14.

4775. Dymond, Richard Bruce. "The Impoverished Self: A Study of Selected Fiction of Wright Morris." Doctoral dissertation, University of Rochester, 1973.

4776. Eisinger, Chester E. *Fiction of the Forties.* Chicago: University of Chicago Press, 1963, 328–41.

4777. Flanagan, John T. "The Fiction of Wright Morris." *Studia Germanica Gandensia* 3 (1961): 209–31.

4778. Guettinger, Roger J. "The Problem with Jigsaw Puzzles: Form in the Fiction of Wright Morris." *Texas Quarterly* 11 (Spring 1968): 209–20.

4779. Hafer, Jack. "Setting and Theme in Wright Morris's *Ceremony in Lone Tree.*" *Heritage of Kansas* 10 (Summer 1977): 10–20.

4780. Harper, Robert D. "Wright Morris's *Ceremony in Lone Tree*: A Picture of Life in Middle America." *Western American Literature* 11 (November 1976): 199–213.

4781. Hicks, Granville. "Introduction." *Wright Morris: A Reader.* New York: Harper and Row, 1970.

4782. ———. "Wright Morris." *Literary Horizons: A Quarter Century of American Fiction.* New York: New York University Press, 1970, 7–47.

4783. Howard, Leon. *Wright Morris.* Minneapolis: University of Minnesota Press, 1968.

4784. Hunt, John W., Jr. "The Journey Back: The Early Novels of Wright Morris." *Critique* 5 (Spring–Summer 1962): 41–60.

4785. Jacobson, Joanne. "Time and Vision in Wright Morris's Photographs of Nebraska." *Great Plains Quarterly* 7 (Winter 1987): 3–21.

4786. Klein, Marcus. *After Alienation.* New York: World, 1964, 196–246.

4787. Knoll, Robert E. *Conversations with Wright Morris.* Lincoln: University of Nebraska Press, 1977.

4788. Lewis, Linda M. "*Plains Song*: Wright Morris's New Melody for Audacious Female Voices." *Great Plains Quarterly* 8 (Winter 1988): 29–37.

4789. Madden, David. "Character as Revealed Cliché in Wright Morris's Fiction." *Midwest Quarterly* 22 (Summer 1981): 319–36.

4790. ———. "Morris' *Cannibals*, Cain's *Serenade*: The Dynamics of Style and Technique." *Journal of Popular Culture* 8 (Summer 1974): 59–70.

4791. ———. *Wright Morris.* New York: Twayne, 1964.

4792. ———. "Wright Morris' *In Orbit*: An Unbroken Series of Poetic Gestures." *Critique* 10 (Fall 1968): 102–19.

4793. ———, et al. "Wright Morris Issue." *Critique* 4 (Winter 1961–62): 5–87.

4794. Miller, Ralph N. "The Fiction of Wright Morris: The Sense of Ending." *MidAmerica* 3 (1976): 56–76.

4795. Morris, Wright. *A Cloak of Light: Writing My Life.* New York: Harper Row, 1985.

4796. ———. *Will's Boy: A Memoir.* New York: Harper Row, 1981.

4797. Neinstein, Raymond L. "Wright Morris: The Metaphysics of Home." *Prairie Schooner* 53 (Summer 1979): 121–54.

4798. Nelson, Carolyn W. "The Spiritual Quest in the Works of Wright Morris." Doctoral dissertation, University of Chicago, 1966.

4799. Nemanic, Gerald. "A Ripening Eye: Wright Morris and the Field of Vision." *MidAmerica* 1 (1974): 120–31.

4800. ———, and Harry White. "GLR/Interview: Wright Morris." *Great Lakes Review* 1 (1975): 1–29.

4801. Rook, Constance Merriam. "Character in the Early Fiction of Wright Morris." Doctoral dissertation, University of North Carolina, Chapel Hill, 1973.

4802. Shetty, M. Nalini. "The Fiction of Wright Morris." Doctoral dissertation, University of Pittsburgh, 1967.

4803. Trachtenberg, Alan. "The Craft of Vision." *Critique* 4 (Winter 1961–62): 41–55.

4804. Waldeland, Lynne. "The Deep Sleep: The Fifties in the Novels of Wright Morris." *Silhouettes on the Shade: Images of the 50s Reexamined.* Muncie, Ind.: Ball State University, 1973, 25–43.

4805. ———. "*Plains Song*: Women's Voices in the Fiction of Wright Morris." *Critique* 24 (Fall 1982): 7–20.

4806. ———. "Wright Morris: His Theory and Practice of the Craft of Fiction." Doctoral dissertation, Purdue University, 1970.

4807. Waterman, Arthur E. "The Novels of Wright Morris: An Escape from Nostalgia." *Critique* 4 (Winter 1961–62): 24–40.

4808. Westdal, Lincoln Wesley. "Consciousness in the Novels of Wright Morris." Doctoral dissertation, University of Nevada, Reno, 1976.

4809. Wilson, J.C. "Wright Morris and the Search for the 'Still Point.'" *Prairie Schooner* 49 (Summer 1975): 154–63.

4810. Wydeven, Joseph J. "Focus and Frame in Wright Morris's *The Works of Love*." *Western American Literature* 23 (August 1988): 99–112.

4811. ———. "Images and Icons: The Fiction and Photography of Wright Morris." *Under the Sun: Myth and Realism in Western American Literature.* Ed. Barbara Howard Meldrum. Troy, N.Y.: Whitston, 1985, 176–203.

4812. ———. "Wright Morris, Women, and American Culture." *Women and Western American Literature.* Eds. Helen Winter Stauffer and Susan J. Rosowski. Troy, N.Y.: Whitston, 1982, 212–29.

SIDNEY MOSS

See Emerson Bennett-Sidney Moss

MOURNING DOVE

See Christine Quintasket

4813. Badé, William F. *The Life and Letters of John Muir.* Boston: Houghton Mifflin, 1924.

4814. Cohen, Michael P. "John Muir's Public Voice." *Western American Literature* 10 (November 1975): 177–87.

4815. ———. *The Pathless Way: John Muir and the American Wilderness.* Madison: University of Wisconsin Press, 1984.

4816. Fleck, Richard F. "John Muir's Evolving Attitudes Toward Native American Cultures." *American Indian Quarterly* 4 (February 1978): 19–31.

4817. Foerster, Norman. "Muir." *Nature in American Literature.* New York: Russell and Russell, 1958.

4818. Hadley, Edith. "John Muir's Views of Nature and Their Consequences." Doctoral dissertation, University of Wisconsin, 1956.

4819. Lankford, Scott. "John Muir and the Nature of the West: An Ecology of American Life, 1864–1914." Doctoral dissertation, Stanford University, 1991.

4820. Limbaugh, Ronald H. "John Muir and Modern Environmental Education." *California History* 71 (Summer 1992): 170–77.

4821. Lyon, Thomas J. *John Muir.* Western Writers Series, No. 3. Boise, Idaho: Boise State College, 1972.

4822. Merritt, J. I. "Turning Point: John Muir in the Sierra, 1871." *American West* 16 (July/August 1979): 4–15, 62–63.

4823. Miller, Sally M., ed. *John Muir: Life and Work.* Albuquerque: University of New Mexico Press, 1993.

4824. Nash, Roderick. *Wilderness and the American Mind.* 3d ed. New Haven: Yale University Press, 1982.

4825. O'Grady, John P. *Pilgrims to the Wild: Everett Ruess, Henry David Thoreau, John Muir, Clarence King, Mary Austin.* Salt Lake City: University of Utah Press, 1993.

4826. Simonson, Harold P. "The Tempered Romanticism of John Muir." *Western American Literature* 13 (Fall 1978): 227–41.

4827. Smith, Herbert F. *John Muir.* New York: Twayne, 1965.

4828. Teale, Edwin May, ed. *The Wilderness World of John Muir.* Boston: Houghton Mifflin, 1954.

4829. Terrie, Philip G. "John Muir on Mount Ritter: A New Wilderness Aesthetic." *Pacific Historian* 31 (Spring 1987): 35–44.

4830. Turner, Frederick. *Rediscovering America: John Muir in His Time and Ours.* New York: Viking, 1985.

4831. Weber, Daniel B. "John Muir: The Function of Wilderness in an Industrial Society." Doctoral dissertation, University of Minnesota, 1964.

4832. Wolfe, Linnie Marsh. *Son of the Wilderness: The Life of John Muir.* Boston: Houghton Mifflin, 1954.

4833. ———, ed. *John of the Mountains: The Unpublished Journals of John Muir.* Boston: Houghton Mifflin, 1938.

4834. Wyatt, David. "John Muir and the Possession of Landscape." *Sewanee Review* 92 (Winter 1984): 149–60.

CLARENCE MULFORD

4835. Alderman, Taylor. "*The Great Gatsby* and *Hopalong Cassidy.*" *Fitzgerald/Hemingway Annual 1975.* Englewood, Colo.: Microcard Editions Books, 1975, 83–87.

4836. Bloodworth, William A., Jr. "Mulford and Bower: Myth and History in the Early Western." *Great Plains Quarterly* 1 (Spring 1981): 95–104.

4837. Drew, Bernard. *Hopalong Cassidy: The Clarence E. Mulford Story.* Metuchen, N. J.: Scarecrow Press, 1991.

4838. Durham, Philip. "Jay Gatsby and Hopalong Cassidy." *Themes and Directions in American Literature: Essays in Honor of Leon Howard.* Eds. Ray B. Browne and Donald Pizer. Lafayette, Ind.: Purdue University Press, 1969, 163–70.

4839. Nevins, Francis M. *Bar-20: The Life of Clarence Mulford, Creator of Hopalong Cassidy....* Jefferson, N.C.: McFarland, 1993.

AMADO JESUS MURO

See Chester Seltzer

ABRAHAM NASATIR

4840. Fireman, Janet R. "Abraham Nasatir, Dean of Documents." *Pacific Historical Review* 56 (November 1987): 513–25.

CHARLES NEIDER

4841. Tatum, Stephen. "Historical Realism and the American West: The Example of Charles Neider's *The Authentic Death of Hendry Jones.*" *Under the Sun: Myth and Realism in Western American Literature.* Ed. Barbara Howard Meldrum. Troy, N.Y.: Whitston, 1985, 30–48.

JOHN G. NEIHARDT

See also Nicholas Black Elk

4842. Aly, Lucile F. *John G. Neihardt: A Critical Biography.* Amsterdam: Rodopi, 1977.

4843. ———. "John G. Neihardt and the American Epic." *Western American Literature* 13 (Winter 1979): 309–25.

4844. ———. *John Neihardt.* Western Writers Series, No. 25. Boise State University, 1976.

4845. ———. "Poetry and History in Neihardt's *Cycle of the West.*" *Western American Literature* 16 (Spring 1981): 3–18.

4846. Arthur, Anthony. "Manfred, Neihardt, and Hugh Glass: Variations on an American Epic." *Where the West Begins.* Eds. Arthur R. Huseboe and William Geyer. Sioux Falls, S.Dak.: Center for Western Studies Press, 1978, 99–109.

4847. Black, W. E. "Ethic and Metaphysic: A Study of John G. Neihardt." *Western American Literature* 2 (Fall 1967): 205–12.

4848. Bloodworth, William. "Neihardt, Momaday, and the Art of Indian Autobiography." *Where the West Begins.* Eds. Arthur R. Huseboe and William Geyer. Sioux Falls, S.Dak.: Center for Western Studies Press, 1978, 152–60.

4849. Copeland, Marion W. "*Black Elk Speaks* and Leslie Silko's *Ceremony*: Two Visions of Horses." *Critique* 24 (Spring 1983): 158–72.

4850. Deloria, Vine, Jr., ed. *A Sender of Words: Essays in Memory of John G. Neihardt.* Salt Lake City: Howe Brothers, 1984.

4851. DeLowry, Linda Diane. "Dynamic Patterns: A Thematic Study of the Works of John G. Neihardt." Doctoral dissertation, University of Pittsburgh, 1975.

4852. DeMallie, Raymond J. *The Sixth Grandfather: Black Elk's Teaching Given to John G. Neihardt.* Lincoln: University of Nebraska Press, 1984.

4853. Flanagan, John T. "John G. Neihardt, Chronicler of the West." *Arizona Quarterly* 21 (Spring 1965): 7–20.

4854. Kay, Arthur Murray. "The Epic Intent and the American Dream: The Westering Theme in Modern American Narrative Poetry." Doctoral dissertation, Columbia University, 1961, 158–84.

4855. Lee, Fred L. "John G. Neihardt: The Man and His Western Writings: The Bancroft Years, 1900–1921." *Trail Guide* 17 (September–December 1973): 3–35.

4856. McCluskey, Sally. "*Black Elk Speaks*: and So Does John Neihardt." *Western American Literature* 6 (Winter 1972): 231–42.

4857. ———. "Image and Idea in the Poetry of John G. Neihardt." Doctoral dissertation, Northern Illinois University, 1974.

4858. Milton, John R. *The Works of John G. Neihardt.* Cassette. Deland, Fla.: Everett/Edwards, 1974.

4859. Neihardt, John G. *All Is But a Beginning: Youth Remembered–1881–1901.* New York: Harcourt Brace Jovanovich, 1972.

4860. ———. *Patterns and Coincidences: A Sequel to "All Is But a Beginning."* Columbia: University of Missouri Press, 1978.

4861. Olson, Paul A. "*Black Elk Speaks* as Epic and Ritual Attempt to Reverse History." *Vision and Refuge: Essays on the Literature of the Great Plains.* Eds. Virginia Faulkner with Frederick C. Luebke. Lincoln: University of Nebraska Press, 1982, 3–27.

4862. Richards, John Thomas. "John G. Neihardt as Critic and Reviewer." Doctoral dissertation, University of Missouri, Columbia, 1976.

4863. ———. *Luminous Sanity: Literary Criticism Written by John G. Neihardt.* Cape Girardeau, Mo.: Concordia Publishing House, 1973.

4864. ———. *Rawhide Laureate: John G. Neihardt: A Selected Annotated Bibliography.* Metuchen, N.J.: Scarecrow Press, 1983.

4865. Rothwell, Kenneth S. "In Search of a Western Epic: Neihardt, Sandburg and Jaffe as Regionalists and 'Astoriadists.'" *Kansas Quarterly* 2 (Spring 1970): 53–63.

4866. Wahlstrom, Billie Joyce. "Transforming Fact: The Poetics of History in John G. Neihardt's *Cycle of the West.*" Doctoral dissertation, University of Michigan, 1975.

4867. Whitney, Blair. *John G. Neihardt.* Boston: Twayne, 1976.

JOHN NICHOLS

4868. Blessing, Richard A. "For Pookie, With Love and Good Riddance: John Nichols' *The Sterile Cuckoo.*" *Journal of Popular Culture* 7 (Summer 1973): 124–35.

4869. Márquez, Antonio. "An Interview with John Nichols." *New America* 3 (Spring 1979): 28–33.

4870. Pellow, C. Kenneth. "John Nichols, Regionalist and Reformer." *Writers' Forum* 12 (Fall 1986): 41–57.

4871. Vigil, Ralph H. "The Way West: John Nichols and Historical Reality." *Journal of the West* 24 (April 1985): 54–63.

4872. Ward, Dorothy Patricia. "Literature of Conscience: The Novels of John Nichols." Doctoral dissertation, University of North Texas, 1990.

4873. Wild, Peter. *John Nichols.* Western Writers Series, No. 75. Boise, Idaho: Boise State University, 1986.

CHARLES NORRIS

4874. Goldsmith, Arnold L. "Charles and Frank Norris." *Western American Literature* 2 (Spring 1967): 30–49.

FRANK NORRIS

4875. Ahnebrink, Lars. *The Beginnings of Naturalism in American Fiction.* Upsala: Upsala University Press, 1950.

4876. Bauer, Walter John, Jr. "The Man-Woman Relationship in the Novels of Frank Norris." Doctoral dissertation, New York University, 1973.

4877. Bell, Michael Davitt. "Frank Norris, Style, and the Problem of American Naturalism." *Studies in the Literary Imagination* 16 (Fall 1983): 93–106.

4878. Bevilacqua, Winifred Farrant. "From the Ideal to Its Reverse: Key Sociocultural Concepts in *McTeague.*" *Centennial Review* 33 (Winter 1989): 75–88.

4879. Borus, Daniel H. *Writing Realism: Howells, James, and Norris in the Mass Market.* Chapel Hill: University of North Carolina Press, 1989.

4880. Caron, James E. "Grotesque Naturalism: The Significance of the Comic in *McTeague.*" *Texas Studies in Literature and Language* 31 (Summer 1989): 288–317.

4881. Cassuto, Leonard. "'Keeping Company' with the Old Folks: Unravelling the Edges of McTeague's Deterministic Fabric." *American Literary Realism 1870–1910* 25 (Winter 1993): 46–55.

4882. Clark, William Joseph. "Naturalism, Revitalization, and the Fiction of Frank Norris." 2 vols. Doctoral dissertation, University of Minnesota, 1991.

4883. Crisler, Jesse Shattuck. "A Critical and Textual Study of Frank Norris's *McTeague.*" Doctoral dissertation, University of South Carolina, 1973.

4884. ———, and Joseph R. McElrath, Jr. *Frank Norris: A Reference Guide.* Boston: G.K. Hall, 1974.

4885. Crow, Charles L. "The Real Vanamee and His Influence on Frank Norris' *The Octopus.*" *Western American Literature* 9 (August 1974): 131–39.

4886. Davison, Richard Allen. "Frank Norris and the Arts of Social Criticism." *American Literary Realism 1870–1910* 14 (Spring 1981): 77–89.

4887. ———. "Frank Norris' *The Octopus*: Some Observations on Vanamee, Shelgrim, and St. Paul." *Literature and Ideas in America.* Ed. Robert Falk. Columbus: Ohio University Press, 1976, 182–203.

4888. ———, ed. *The Merrill Studies in The Octopus.* Ohio: Charles E. Merrill, 1969.

4889. Dawson, Hugh J. "McTeague as Ethnic Stereotype." *American Literary Realism 1870–1910* 20 (Fall 1987): 34–44.

4890. Dean, Thomas Keith. "Domestic Horizons: Gender, Genre, and Narrative Structure in the Fiction of Frank Norris." Doctoral dissertation, University of Iowa, 1991.

4891. Dillingham, William B. "Frank Norris." *Fifteen American Authors Before 1900: Bibliographic Essays on Research and Criticism.* Eds. Robert A. Rees and Earl N. Harbert. Madison: University of Wisconsin Press, 1971, 307–32.

4892. ———. *Frank Norris: Instinct and Art.* Lincoln: University of Nebraska Press, 1969; Boston: Houghton Mifflin, 1969.

4893. Duncan, Charles. "If Your View Be Large Enough: Narrative Growth in *The Octopus*." *American Literary Realism 1870–1910* 25 (Winter 1993): 56–66.

4894. Epperson, Martin Barry. "Frank Norris and the Heroic Tradition." Doctoral dissertation, University of Southwest Louisiana, 1981.

4895. French, Warren. *Frank Norris.* New York: Twayne, 1962.

4896. ———. "Frank Norris (1870–1902)." *American Literary Realism 1870–1910* 1 (Fall 1967): 84–89.

4897. Frohock, W. M. *Frank Norris.* Minneapolis: University of Minnesota Press, 1969.

4898. Gardner, Joseph H. "Dickens, Romance, and *McTeague*: A Study in Mutual Interpretation." *Essays in Literature* 1 (Spring 1974): 69–82.

4899. Geismar, Maxwell. *Rebels and Ancestors: The American Novel, 1890–1915.* Boston: Houghton Mifflin, 1953, 3–66.

4900. Goldman, Suzy Bernstein. "*McTeague*: The Imagistic Network." *Western American Literature* 7 (Summer 1972): 83–99.

4901. Goldsmith, Arnold L. "Charles and Frank Norris." *Western American Literature* 2 (Spring 1967): 30–49.

4902. ———. "The Development of Frank Norris's Philosophy." *Studies in Honor of John Wilcox.* Eds. A. Dayle Wallace and Woodburn O. Ross. Detroit: Wayne State University Press, 1958, 175–94.

4903. Graham, Don B. *The Fiction of Frank Norris – The Aesthetic Context.* Columbia: University of Missouri Press, 1978.

4904. ———, ed. *Critical Essays on Frank Norris.* Boston: G.K. Hall, 1980.

4905. Hart, James D., ed. *A Novelist in the Making.* Cambridge, Mass.: Harvard University Press, 1970.

4906. Heddendorf, David. "The 'Octopus' in *McTeague*: Frank Norris and Professionalism." *Modern Fiction Studies* 37 (Winter 1991): 677–88.

4907. Hill, John S. *Checklist of Frank Norris.* Columbus: Charles E. Merrill Publishing, 1970.

4908. Hochman, Barbara. *The Art of Frank Norris, Storyteller.* Columbia: University of Missouri Press, 1988.

4909. ———. "Loss, Habit, Obsession: The Governing Dynamic of *McTeague*." *Studies in American Fiction* 14 (Autumn 1986): 179–90.

4910. ———. "*Vandover and the Brute*: The Decisive Experience of Loss." *Western American Literature* 19 (May 1984): 3–15.

4911. Hug, William J. "*McTeague* as Metafiction? Frank Norris' Parodies of Bret Harte and the Dime Novel." *Western American Literature* 26 (November 1991): 219–28.

4912. Johnson, George W. "Frank Norris and Romance." *American Literature* 33 (March 1961): 52–63.

4913. ———. "The Frontier Behind Frank Norris' *McTeague*." *Huntington Library Quarterly* 26 (November 1962): 91–104.

4914. Kaplan, Charles. "Norris's Use of Sources in *The Pit*." *American Literature* 25 (March 1953): 75–84.

4915. Katz, Joseph. "The Elusive Criticism Syndicated by Frank Norris." *Proof* 3 (1973): 221–51.

4916. ———. "Eroticism in American Literary Realism." *Studies in American Fiction* 5 (Spring 1977): 35–50.

4917. ———. "The Shorter Publications of Frank Norris: A Checklist." *Proof* 3 (1973): 155–220.

4918. Kwiat, Joseph J. "Frank Norris: The Novelist as Social Critic and Literary Theorist." *Arizona Quarterly* 18 (Winter 1962): 319–28.

4919. ———. "The Social Responsibilities of the American Painter and Writer: Robert Henri and John Sloan; Frank Norris and Theodore Dreiser." *Centennial Review* 21 (Winter 1977): 19–35.

4920. Lohf, Kenneth A., and Eugene P. Sheehy. *Frank Norris: A Bibliography.* Los Gatos, Calif.: Talisman Press, 1959.

4921. Love, Glen A. "Frank Norris's Western Metropolitans." *New Americans: The Westerner and the Modern Experience in the American Novel.* Lewisburg, Pa.: Bucknell University Press, 1982, 30–66.

4922. Lundy, Robert D. "The Making of *McTeague* and *The Octopus.*" Doctoral dissertation, University of California, 1956.

4923. Lynn, Kenneth S. *The Dream of Success.* Boston: Little, Brown, 1955, 158–207.

4924. McElrath, Joseph R., Jr. "A Critical Edition of Frank Norris's *Moran of the Lady Letty: A Story of Adventure off the California Coast.*" Doctoral dissertation, University of South Carolina, 1973.

4925. ———. "The Erratic Design of Frank Norris's *Moran of the Lady Letty.*" *American Literary Realism 1870–1910* 10 (Spring 1977): 114–24.

4926. ———. "Frank Norris." *American Literary Realism 1870–1910* 8 (Autumn 1975): 307–19. Reviews dissertations on Norris.

4927. ———. "Frank Norris: A Bibliographical Essay." *American Literary Realism 1870–1910* 11 (Autumn 1978): 219–34.

4928. ———. *Frank Norris: A Descriptive Bibliography.* Pittsburgh: University of Pittsburgh Press, 1992.

4929. ———. *Frank Norris and the Wave: A Bibliography.* New York: Garland, 1988.

4930. ———. "Frank Norris: Biographical Data from *The Wave,* 1891–1901." *Frank Norris Studies* 10 (Fall 1990): 1–12.

4931. ———. "Frank Norris: Early Posthumous Responses." *American Literary Realism 1870–1910* 12 (Spring 1979): 1–76.

4932. ———. *Frank Norris Revisited.* New York: Twayne, 1992.

4933. ———. "Frank Norris's *Vandover and the Brute*: Narrative Technique and the Socio-Critical Viewpoint." *Studies in American Fiction* 4 (Spring 1976): 27–43.

4934. ———, and Katherine Knight, eds. *Frank Norris: The Critical Reception.* New York: Burt Franklin, 1981.

4935. McFatter, Susan Prothro. "Parody and Dark Projections: Medieval Romance and the Gothic in *McTeague.*" *Western American Literature* 26 (August 1991): 119–35.

4936. Machor, James L. "Epic, Romance, and Norris' *The Octopus.*" *American Literary Realism 1870–1910* 18 (Spring–Fall 1985): 42–54.

4937. Marchand, Ernest. *Frank Norris: A Study.* Stanford, Calif.: Stanford University Press, 1942.

4938. Messenger, Christian. "Frank Norris and the College Sportsman." *American Literary Realism 1870–1910* 12 (Autumn 1979): 288–94.

4939. Micklus, Robert. "Ambivalent Warriors in *The Octopus.*" *Western American Literature* 16 (Summer 1981): 115–23.

4940. Miller, Edwin Haviland. "The Art of Frank Norris in *McTeague*." *Markham Review* 8 (Summer 1979): 61–66.

4941. Mitchell, Lee Clark. *Determined Fictions: American Literary Naturalism*. New York: Columbia University Press, 1989.

4942. Mitchell, Mark L., and Joseph R. McElrath, Jr. "Frank Norris's *The Pit*: Musical Elements as Biographical Evidence." *Papers on Language and Literature* 23 (Spring 1987): 161–74.

4943. Morgan, H. Wayne. *American Writers in Rebellion: From Mark Twain to Dreiser*. New York: Hill and Wang, 1965.

4944. Morsberger, Robert E. "The Inconsistent *Octopus*." *Western American Literature* 16 (Summer 1981): 105–13.

4945. Mottram, Ron. "Impulse Toward the Visible: Frank Norris and Photographic Representation." *Texas Studies in Literature and Language* 25 (Winter 1983): 574–96.

4946. Murthy, Sikha S. "Frank Norris and Scott Fitzgerald: Some Parallels in Their Thoughts and Art." Doctoral dissertation, University of Utah, 1976.

4947. Pizer, Donald. "The Concept of Nature in Frank Norris' *The Octopus*." *American Quarterly* 14 (Spring 1962): 73–80.

4948. ———. "Evolutionary Ethical Dualism in Frank Norris' *Vandover and the Brute* and *McTeague*." *PMLA* 76 (December 1961): 552–60.

4949. ———. "Frank Norris' Definition of Naturalism." *Modern Fiction Studies* 8 (Winter 1962–63): 408–10.

4950. ———. *The Novels of Frank Norris*. Bloomington: Indiana University Press, 1966.

4951. ———. "Synthetic Criticism and Frank Norris: Or, Mr. Marx, Mr. Taylor, and *The Octopus*." *American Literature* 34 (January 1963): 532–41.

4952. ———, ed. *The Literary Criticism of Frank Norris*. Austin: University of Texas Press, 1964.

4953. Ryder, Mary R. "'All Wheat and No Chaff': Frank Norris' *Blix* and Willa Cather's Literary Vision." *American Literary Realism 1870–1910* 22 (Fall 1989): 17–30.

4954. Schneider, Robert W. *Five Novelists of the Progressive Era*. New York: Columbia University Press, 1965.

4955. Vance, William L. "Romance in *The Octopus*." *Genre* 3 (June 1970): 111–36.

4956. Walcutt, Charles Child. *American Literary Naturalism: A Divided Stream*. Minneapolis: University of Minnesota Press, 1956, 114–56.

4957. Walker, Don D. "The Western Naturalism of Frank Norris." *Western American Literature* 2 (Spring 1967): 14–29.

4958. Walker, Franklin. *Frank Norris: A Biography.* New York: Doubleday, Doran, 1932; London: Russell Russell, 1963.

4959. ———, ed. *The Letters of Frank Norris.* San Francisco: Book Club of California, 1956.

4960. Winslow, Cedric Reimers. "The Crisis of Liberalism in the Novels of Theodore Dreiser, Frank Norris, and Jack London." 3 vols. Doctoral dissertation, New York University, 1977.

4961. Wyatt, David. "Norris and the Vertical." *Southern Review* 19 (Autumn 1983): 749–64.

KATHLEEN NORRIS

4962. Gumina, Deanna Paoli. "The Apprenticeship of Kathleen Norris." *California History* 66 (March 1987): 40–48, 72–73.

EDGAR WILSON NYE

(Bill Nye)

4963. Bakerville, Barnet. "19th Century Burlesque of Oratory." *American Quarterly* 20 (Winter 1968): 726–43.

4964. Blair, Walter. "The Background of Bill Nye in American Humor." Doctoral dissertation, University of Chicago, 1931.

4965. Davidson, Levette J. "Bill Nye and *The Denver Tribune.*" *Colorado Magazine* 4 (January 1928): 13–18.

4966. Hasley, Louis, ed. *The Best of Bill Nye's Humor.* New Haven, Conn.: College and University Press, 1972.

4967. Kesterson, David B. *Bill Nye.* Boston: Twayne, 1981.

4968. ———. *Bill Nye: The Western Writings.* Western Writers Series, No. 22. Boise, Idaho: Boise State University, 1976.

4969. Lanier, Doris. "Bill Nye in the South." *Annals of Wyoming* 46 (Fall 1974): 253–62.

4970. Larson, T. A., ed. *Bill Nye's Western Humor.* Lincoln: University of Nebraska Press, 1968.

4971. Nye, Frank Wilson, ed. *Bill Nye: His Own Life.* New York: Century, 1926.

4972. Pribek, Thomas. "Bill Nye as Comic Lecturer, 1885." *Old Northwest* 13 (Summer 1987): 131–41.

4973. Rush, Nixon Orwin, ed. *Letters of Edgar Wilson Nye.* Laramie: University of Wyoming Library, 1950.

4974. Saum, Lewis O. "Bill Nye in the Pacific Northwest." *Pacific Northwest Quarterly* 84 (July 1993): 82–90.

DAN O'BRIEN

4975. Poland, Tim. "'The Picture Written in the Dirt': The Old and New West in Dan O'Brien's *Spirit of the Hills*." *Western American Literature* 25 (November 1990): 233–42.

JOHN OKADA

4976. Inada, Lawson Fusao. "The Vision of America in John Okada's *No-No Boy*." *Proceedings of the Comparative Literature Symposium* (Lubbock, Tex.) 9 (1978): 275–87.

TILLIE OLSEN

4977. Burkom, Selma, and Margaret Williams. "De'Riddling Tillie Olsen's Writings." *San Jose Studies* 2 (February 1976): 65–83.

4978. Faulkner, Mara. *Protest and Possibility in the Writing of Tillie Olsen.* Charlottesville: University Press of Virginia, 1993.

4979. Martin, Abigail. *Tillie Olsen.* Western Writers Series, No. 65. Boise, Idaho: Boise State University, 1984.

4980. Orr, Elaine Neil. *Tillie Olsen and a Feminist Spiritual Vision.* Jackson: University Press of Mississipi, 1987.

4981. Pearlman, Mickey, and Abby H. P. Werlock. *Tillie Olsen.* Boston: Twayne, 1991.

4982. Rose, Ellen Cronan. "Lemning: Or Why Tillie Writes." *Hollins Critic* 13 (1976): 1–13.

4983. Rosenfelt, Deborah. "From the Thirties: Tillie Olsen and the Radical Tradition." *Feminist Studies* 7 (Fall 1981): 371–406.

4984. Staub, Michael. "The Struggle for 'Selfness' Through Speech in Olsen's *Yonnondio: From the Thirties*." *Studies in American Fiction* 16 (Autumn 1988): 131–39.

4985. Trensky, Anne. "The Unnatural Silences of Tillie Olsen." *Studies in Short Fiction* 27 (Fall 1990): 509–16.

SIGURD OLSON

4986. Hertzel, Leo J. "What About Writers in the North?" *South Dakota Review* 5 (Spring 1967): 3–19.

D. J. O'MALLEY

4987. White, John I. "'Kid' O'Malley: Montana's Cowboy Poet." *Montana: The Magazine of Western History* 17 (July 1967): 60–73.

SIMON ORTIZ

4988. Gingerich, Willard. "The Old Voices of Acoma: Simon Ortiz's Mythic Indigenism." *Southwest Review* 64 (Winter 1979): 18–30.

4989. Wiget, Andrew. *Simon Ortiz.* Western Writers Series, No. 74. Boise, Idaho: Boise State University, 1986.

JOHN MILTON OSKISON

4990. Larson, Charles R. *American Indian Fiction.* Albuquerque: University of New Mexico Press, 1978, 34–37, 46–55.

4991. Strickland, Arney L. "John Milton Oskison: A Writer of the Transitional Period of the Oklahoma Indian Territory." *Southwestern American Literature* 2 (Winter 1972): 125–34.

MARTHA OSTENSO

4992. Lenoski, Daniel S. "Martha Ostenso's *Wild Geese:* The Language of Silence." *North Dakota Quarterly* 52 (Summer 1984): 279–96.

NINA OTERO-WARREN

4993. Whaley, Charlotte. *Nina Otero-Warren of Santa Fe.* Albuquerque: University of New Mexico Press, 1994.

WAYNE D. OVERHOLSER

4994. Marsden, Michael T. "The Taming of Civilization in the Western Fiction of Wayne D. Overholser." *Kansas Quarterly* 10 (Fall 1978): 105–11.

4995. Overholser, Stephen. "Wayne D. Overholser: A Critical Memoir." *Roundup Quarterly* 3 (Winter 1990): 5–12.

4996. Pronzini, Bill, and Martin H. Greenberg, eds. *The Best Western Stories of Wayne D. Overholser.* Carbondale: Southern Illinois University Press, 1984.

4997. Pilkington, William T. *William A. Owens.* Southwest Writers Series, No. 17. Austin, Tex.: Steck-Vaughn, 1968.

FRANCIS PARKMAN

4998. Beaver, Harold. "Parkman's Crack-Up: A Bostonian on the Oregon Trail." *New England Quarterly* 48 (March 1975): 84–103.

4999. Doughty, Howard. *Francis Parkman.* New York: Macmillan, 1962.

5000. Feltskog, E. N., ed. *The Oregon Trail.* Madison: University of Wisconsin Press, 1969.

5001. Jacobs, Wilbur R. *Francis Parkman, Historian as Hero: The Formative Years.* Austin: University of Texas Press, 1991.

5002. Jennings, F. P. "A Vanishing Indian: Francis Parkman Versus His Sources." *Pennsylvania Magazine of History and Biography* 87 (July 1963): 306–23.

5003. Lee, Robert Edson. *From West to East.* Urbana: University of Illinois Press, 1966, 69–81.

5004. Levin, David. "Francis Parkman: *The Oregon Trail.*" *Landmarks of American Writing.* Ed. Hennig Cohen. New York: Basic Books, 1969, 79–89.

5005. ———. *History as Romantic Art.* Stanford, Calif.: Stanford University Press, 1959.

5006. Neal, Charles R. "In Pursuit of Parkman." *Journal of the West* 25 (October 1986): 49–61.

5007. Pease, Otis. *Parkman's History: The Historian as Literary Artist.* New Haven, Conn.: Yale University Press, 1953.

5008. Scherting, Jack. "Tracking the *Pequod* Along *The Oregon Trail*: The Influence of Parkman's Narrative on Imagery and Characters in *Moby Dick.*" *Western American Literature* 22 (May 1987): 3–15.

5009. Thacker, Robert. "The Plains, Parkman, and *The Oregon Trail.*" *Nevada Historical Society Quarterly* 28 (Winter 1985): 262–70.

5010. Townsend, Kim. "Francis Parkman and the Male Tradition." *American Quarterly* 38 (Spring 1986): 97–113.

5011. Tribble, Joseph L. "The Paradise of the Imagination: The Journeys of The Oregon Trail." *New England Quarterly* 46 (December 1973): 523–42.

5012. Wade, Mason. *Francis Parkman: Heroic Historian.* New York: Viking, 1942.

5013. ———, ed. *The Journals of Francis Parkman*. 2 vols. New York: Harper, 1947.

VERNON LOUIS PARRINGTON

5014. Hall, Helen L. "Vernon Louis Parrington: The Genesis and Design of *Main Currents in American Thought*." Doctoral dissertation, Yale University, 1979.

5015. Hall, H. Lark. "V. L. Parrington's Oklahoma Years, 1897–1908." *Pacific Northwest Quarterly* 72 (January 1981): 20–28.

5016. ———. *V.L. Parrington: Through the Avenue of Art*. Kent, Ohio: Kent State University Press, 1994.

5017. Harrison, Joseph B. *Vernon Louis Parrington: American Scholar*. Seattle: University of Washington Book Store, 1929.

5018. Hofstadter, Richard. *The Progressive Historians: Turner, Beard, Parrington*. New York: Alfred A. Knopf, 1968.

5019. Reinitz, Richard. "Vernon Louis Parrington as Historical Ironist." *Pacific Northwest Quarterly* 68 (July 1977): 113–19.

5020. Singer, Barnett. "Judging Vernon Louis Parrington." *Research Studies* 43 (1975): 209–21.

KENNETH PATCHEN

5021. Clodd, Alan, ed. *Tribute to Kenneth Patchen*. London: Enitharmon, 1977.

5022. Detro, Gene. *Patchen: The Last Interview*. Santa Barbara, Calif.: Capra, 1976.

5023. Glicksberg, Charles I. "The World of Kenneth Patchen." *Arizona Quarterly* 7 (Autumn 1951): 263–75.

5024. Hack, Richard. "Memorial Poetry Reading for Kenneth Patchen...." *Chicago Review* 24 (No. 2, 1972): 65–80.

5025. Morgan, Richard G., ed. *Kenneth Patchen: A Collection of Essays*. New York: AMS, 1977.

5026. Nelson, Raymond John. *Kenneth Patchen and American Mysticism*. Chapel Hill: University of North Carolina Press, 1984.

5027. See, Carolyn. "The Jazz Musician as Patchen's Hero." *Arizona Quarterly* 17 (Summer 1961): 136–46.

5028. Smith, Larry R. *Kenneth Patchen*. Boston: Twayne, 1978.

5029. Veres, Peter. *The Argument of Innocence: A Selection from the Arts of Kenneth Patchen*. San Francisco: Scrimshaw Press, 1976.

JAMES OHIO PATTIE

5030. Batman, Richard. *American Ecclesiastes: The Stories of James Pattie.* San Diego: Harcourt Brace Jovanovich, 1984.

5031. ———. *James Pattie's West: The Dream and the Reality.* Norman: University of Oklahoma Press, 1986.

5032. Wild, Peter. "Rescuing James Ohio Pattie, Littérateur." *North Dakota Quarterly* 53 (Winter 1985): 49–59.

RODMAN W. PAUL

5033. Etulain, Richard W. "Rodman Wilson Paul, Historical Perspectives of an Adopted Westerner." *Pacific Historical Review* 56 (November 1987): 527–44.

JAMES KIRKE PAULDING

5034. Alderman, Ralph M. "James Kirke Paulding on Literature and the West." *American Literature* 27 (March 1955): 97–101.

5035. Person, Leland S., Jr. "James Kirke Paulding: Myth and the Middle Ground." *Western American Literature* 16 (Spring 1981): 39–54.

FREDERIC LOGAN PAXSON

5036. Etulain, Richard W. "After Turner: The Western Historiography of Frederic Logan Paxson." *Writing Western History: Essays on Major Western Historians.* Ed. Richard W. Etulain. Albuquerque: University of New Mexico Press, 1991, 137–65.

5037. Pomeroy, Earl. "Frederic Logan Paxson and His Approach to History." *Mississippi Valley Historical Review* 39 (March 1953): 673–92.

THOMAS BROWER PEACOCK

5038. Pady, Donald S. "Thomas Brower Peacock." *Bulletin of Bibliography* 28 (April–June 1971): 37–40.

GEORGE SESSIONS PERRY

5039. Alexander, Stanley G. *George Sessions Perry.* Southwest Writers Series, No. 13. Austin, Tex.: Steck-Vaughn, 1967.

5040. Bradford, M. E. "Making Time Run: The Rich Harvest of George Sessions Perry." *Southwestern American Literature* 1 (September 1971): 129–36.

5041. Cowser, Robert C. "A Biographical and Critical Interpretation of George Sessions Perry." Doctoral dissertation, Texas Christian University, 1965.

5042. Hairston, Maxine C. *George Sessions Perry: His Life and Works.* Austin, Tex.: Jenkins, 1973.

LEVI PETERSON

5043. England, Eugene. "Wilderness as Salvation in Peterson's *The Canyons of Grace." Western American Literature* 19 (May 1984): 17–28.

JOHN PHOENIX

See George H. Derby

ALBERT PIKE

5044. Allsopp, Frederick William. *Albert Pike: A Biography.* Little Rock, Ark.: Parke-Harper, 1928.

5045. Boyden, William L. *Bibliography of the Writings of Albert Pike: Prose, Poetry, Manuscript.* Washington, D.C.: n.p., 1921.

5046. Riley, Susan B. "The Life and Works of Albert Pike to 1860." Doctoral dissertation, George Peabody College, 1934.

ROBERT PIRSIG

5047. Rodino, Richard H. "Irony and Earnestness in Robert Pirsig's *Zen and the Art of Motorcycle Maintenance." Critique* 22 (No. 1, 1980): 21–31.

CHIEF SIMON POKAGON

5048. Larson, Charles R. *American Indian Fiction.* Albuquerque: University of New Mexico Press, 1978, 34–46, 62–65.

EARL POMEROY

5049. Lamar, Howard R. "Earl Pomeroy, Historian's Historian." *Pacific Historical Review* 56 (November 1987): 547–60.

5050. Malone, Michael P. "Earl Pomeroy and the Reorientation of Western American History." *Writing Western History: Essays on Major Western Historians.* Ed. Richard W. Etulain. Albuquerque: University of New Mexico Press, 1991, 311–34.

KATHERINE ANNE PORTER

5051. Baker, Howard. "The Upward Path: Notes on the Work of Katherine Anne Porter." *Southern Review* 4 (January 1968): 1–19.

5052. Baldeshwiler, Eileen. "Structural Patterns in Katherine Anne Porter's Fiction." *South Dakota Review* 11 (Summer 1973): 45–53.

5053. Becker, Laurence A. "'The Jilting of Granny Weatherall': The Discovery of Pattern." *English Journal* 55 (December 1966): 1164–69.

5054. Bloom, Harold, ed. *Modern Critical Views: Katherine Porter.* New York: Chelsea House, 1986.

5055. Brinkmeyer, Robert H., Jr. "'Endless Remembering': The Artistic Vision of Katherine Anne Porter." *Mississippi Quarterly* 40 (Winter 1986–1987): 5–19.

5056. ———. *Katherine Anne Porter's Artistic Development: Primitivism, Traditionalism, and Totalitarianism.* Baton Rouge: Louisiana State University Press, 1993.

5057. Bunkers, Suzanne Lillian. "Katherine Anne Porter: A Re-assessment." Doctoral dissertation, University of Wisconsin, Madison, 1980.

5058. Cheatham, George. "Death and Repetition in Porter's Miranda Stories." *American Literature* 61 (December 1989): 610–24.

5059. ———. "Fall and Redemption in *Pale Horse, Pale Rider.*" *Renascence* 39 (Spring 1987): 396–405.

5060. DeMouy, Jane Krause. *Katherine Anne Porter's Women: The Eye of Her Fiction.* Austin: University of Texas Press, 1983.

5061. Emmons, Winfred S. *Katherine Anne Porter: The Regional Stories.* Southwest Writers Series, No. 6. Austin, Tex.: Steck-Vaughn, 1967.

5062. Farrington, Thomas Arthur. "The Control of Imagery in Katherine Anne Porter's Fiction." Doctoral dissertation, University of Illinois at Urbana- Champaign, 1972.

5063. Givner, Joan. "'Her Great Art, Her Somber Craft': Katherine Anne Porter's Creative Process." *Southwest Review* 62 (Summer 1977): 217–30.

5064. ———. *Katherine Anne Porter: A Life*. Rev ed. Athens: University of Georgia Press, 1991.

5065. ———, ed. *Katherine Anne Porter: Conversations*. Jackson: University Press of Mississippi, 1987.

5066. ———, et al. "Katherine Anne Porter." *American Women Writers: Bibliographical Essays*. Eds. Maurice Duke, et al. Westport, Conn.: Greenwood Press, 1983, 201–31.

5067. Groff, Edward. "'Noon Wine': A Texas Tragedy." *Descant* 22 (1977): 39–47.

5068. Hardy, John Edward. *Katherine Anne Porter*. New York: Ungar, 1973.

5069. Hartley, Lodwick, and George Core, eds. *Katherine Anne Porter: A Critical Symposium*. Athens: University of Georgia Press, 1969.

5070. Hendrick, Willene, and George Hendrick. *Katherine Anne Porter*. Rev ed. Boston: Twayne, 1988.

5071. Hilt, Kathryn, and Ruth M. Alvarez. *Katherine Anne Porter: An Annotated Bibliography*. New York: Garland, 1990.

5072. Jensen, Lucile Rae. "The Ideas of Failure and Affirmation in the Short Fiction of Katherine Anne Porter." Doctoral dissertation, University of Utah, 1984.

5073. Kiernan, Robert F. *Katherine Anne Porter and Carson McCullers: A Reference Guide*. Boston: G.K. Hall, 1976.

5074. Levy, Helen Fiddyment. *Fiction of the Home Place: Jewett, Cather, Glasgow, Porter, Welty, and Naylor*. Jackson: University Press of Mississippi, 1992.

5075. Liberman, M. M. *Katherine Anne Porter's Fiction*. Detroit: Wayne State University Press, 1971.

5076. Lopez, Enrique Hank. *Conversations with Katherine Anne Porter: Refugee from Indian Creek*. Boston: Little, Brown, 1981.

5077. Lugg, Bonelyn. "Mexican Influences on the Work of Katherine Anne Porter." Doctoral dissertation, Pennsylvania State University, 1976.

5078. Machann, Clinton, and William Bedford Clark, eds. *Katherine Anne Porter and Texas: An Uneasy Relationship*. College Station: Texas A M University Press, 1990.

5079. Miles, Lee Robert. "Unused Possibilities: A Study of Katherine Anne Porter." Doctoral dissertation, University of California, Los Angeles, 1973.

5080. Mooney, Harry John, Jr. *The Fiction and Criticism of Katherine Anne Porter*. Rev ed. Pittsburgh: University of Pittsburgh Press, 1967.

5081. Nance, William L. *Katherine Anne Porter and the Art of Rejection.* Chapel Hill: University of North Carolina Press, 1964.

5082. Partridge, Colin. "'My Familiar Country': An Image of Mexico in the Work of Katherine Anne Porter." *Studies in Short Fiction* 7 (Fall 1970): 597–614.

5083. Stout, Janis P. "Katherine Anne Porter and the Reticent Style." *Strategies of Reticence: Silence and Meaning in the Works of Jane Austen, Willa Cather, Katherine Anne Porter, and Joan Didion.* Charlottesville: University Press of Virginia, 1990, 112–46.

5084. Tanner, James T. F. *The Texas Legacy of Katherine Anne Porter.* Denton: University of North Texas Press, 1991.

5085. Thompson, Barbara. "Katherine Anne Porter: An Interview." *Paris Review* 29 (Winter–Spring 1963): 87–114.

5086. Unrue, Darlene Harbour. *Truth and Vision in Katherine Anne Porter's Fiction.* Athens: University of Georgia Press, 1985.

5087. ———. *Understanding Katherine Anne Porter.* Columbia: University of South Carolina Press, 1988.

5088. ———, ed. *"This Strange, Old World" and Other Book Reviews.* Athens: University of Georgia Press, 1991.

5089. Waldrip, Louise, and Shirley Ann Bauer. *A Bibliography of the Works of Katherine Anne Porter and A Bibliography of the Criticism of the Works of Katherine Anne Porter.* Metuchen, N.J.: Scarecrow Press, 1969.

5090. Walsh, Thomas F. *Katherine Anne Porter and Mexico: The Illusion of Eden.* Austin: University of Texas Press, 1992.

5091. ———. "The Making of 'Flowering Judas.'" *Journal of Modern Literature* 12 (March 1985): 109–30.

5092. Walter, James. "Revolution and Time: Laura in 'Flowering Judas.'" *Renascence* 38 (Autumn 1985): 26–38.

5093. Warren, Robert Penn. "Uncorrupted Consciousness: The Stories of Katherine Anne Porter." *Yale Review* 55 (Winter 1966): 280–90.

5094. ———, ed. *Katherine Anne Porter: A Collection of Critical Essays.* Englewood Cliffs, N.J.: Prentice-Hall, 1979.

5095. Welty, Eudora. "The Eye of the Story." *Yale Review* 55 (Winter 1966): 265–74.

5096. West, Ray B., Jr. *Katherine Anne Porter.* Minneapolis: University of Minnesota Press, 1963.

5097. Young, Vernon A. "The Art of Katherine Anne Porter." *New Mexico Quarterly* 15 (Autumn 1945): 326–41.

WILLIAM SYDNEY PORTER

(O. Henry)

5098. Blansfield, Karen Charmaine. *Cheap Rooms and Restless Hearts: A Study of Formula in the Urban Tales of William Sydney Porter.* Bowling Green, Ohio: Bowling Green State University Popular Press, 1988.

5099. Current-Garcia, Eugene. *O. Henry.* New York: Twayne, 1965.

5100. ———. *O. Henry: A Study of the Short Fiction.* New York: Twayne, 1993.

5101. Davis, Robert H., and Arthur B. Maurice. *The Caliph of Bagdad.* New York: D. Appleton, 1931.

5102. Gallegly, J. S. *From Alamo Plaza to Jack Harris's Saloon: O. Henry and the Southwest He Knew.* The Hague: Mouton, 1971.

5103. Harris, Richard C. *William Sydney Porter.* Boston: Twayne, 1980.

5104. Kramer, Dale. *The Heart of O. Henry.* New York: Rinehart, 1954.

5105. Langford, Gerald. *Alias O. Henry: A Biography of William Sydney Porter.* New York: Macmillan, 1957.

5106. Long, E. Hudson. *O. Henry: American Regionalist.* Southwest Writers Series, No. 3, Austin, Tex.: Steck-Vaughn, 1969.

5107. ———. *O. Henry: The Man and His Work.* Philadelphia: University of Pennsylvania Press, 1949; New York: A. J. Barnes, 1960.

5108. ———. "O. Henry (William Sydney Porter)." *American Literary Realism 1870–1910* 1 (Fall 1967): 93–99.

5109. O'Quinn, Trueman. "O. Henry in Austin." *Southwestern Historical Quarterly* 43 (October 1939): 143–57.

5110. ———, and Jenny Lind Porter, eds. *Time to Write: How William Sidney [sic] Porter Became O. Henry.* Austin, Tex.: Eakin Press, 1986.

5111. Payne, L. W., Jr. "The Humor of O. Henry." *Texas Review* 4 (October 1918): 18–37.

5112. Peel, Donald F. "A Critical Study of the Short Stories of O. Henry." *Northwest Missouri State College Studies* 25 (November 1961): 3–24.

5113. Robinson, Duncan, et al. "O. Henry's Austin." *Southwest Review* 24 (July 1939): 388–410.

5114. Sibley, M. A. "Austin's First National and the Errant Teller." *Southwestern Historical Quarterly* 74 (April 1971): 478–506.

5115. Van Doren, Carl. "O. Henry." *Texas Review* 2 (January 1917): 248–59.

CHARLES PORTIS

5116. Ditsky, John. "True 'Grit' and *True Grit.*" *Ariel* 4 (April 1973): 18–31.

5117. Shuman, R. Baird. "Portis' *True Grit*: Adventure Story or *Entwicklungsroman?*" *English Journal* 49 (March 1970): 367–70.

LOUISE POUND

5118. Yost, Nellie Snyder. "Nebraska's Scholarly Athlete: Louise Pound." *Nebraska History* 64 (Winter 1983): 477–90.

JOHN WESLEY POWELL

5119. Aton, James M. *John Wesley Powell.* Western Writers Series, No. 114. Boise, Idaho: Boise State University, 1994.

5120. Stegner, Wallace. *Beyond the Hundredth Meridian: John Wesley Powell and the Second Opening of the West.* Boston: Houghton Mifflin, 1954.

LAWRENCE CLARK POWELL

5121. Haslam, Gerald. *Lawrence Clark Powell.* Western Writers Series, No. 102. Boise, Idaho: Boise State University, 1992.

J. F. POWERS

5122. Hertzel, Leo J. "What About Writers in the North?" *South Dakota Review* 5 (Spring 1967): 3–19.

5123. Stewart, D. H. "J. F. Powers' *Morte D'Urban* as Western." *Western American Literature* 5 (Spring 1970): 31–44.

5124. Wedge, G. F. "Two Bibliographies: Flannery O'Connor, J. F. Powers." *Critic* 2 (Fall 1958): 59–70.

THOMAS PYNCHON

5125. Abernethy, Peter L. "Entropy in Pynchon's *The Crying of Lot 49.*" *Critique* 14 (No. 2, 1972): 18–33.

5126. Carpenter, Richard C. "State of Mind: The California Setting of *The Crying of Lot 49.*" *Itinerary: Criticism, Essays on California Writers.* Ed. Charles L. Crow. Bowling Green, Ohio: University Press, 1978, 105–13.

5127. Chambers, Judith. *Thomas Pynchon.* Boston: Twayne, 1992.

5128. Eddins, Dwight. *The Gnostic Pynchon.* Bloomington: Indiana University Press, 1990.

5129. Henkle, Roger B. "Pynchon's Tapestries on the Western Wall." *Modern Fiction Studies* 17 (Summer 1971): 207–20.

5130. Horvath, Brooke. "Linguistic Distancing in *Gravity's Rainbow.*" *Pynchon Notes* 8 (February 1982): 5–22.

5131. Kharpertian, Theodore D. *A Hand to Turn the Time: The Menippean Satires of Thomas Pynchon.* Rutherford, N.J.: Fairleigh Dickinson University Press, 1990.

5132. McHoul, Alex, and David Wills. *Writing Pynchon: Strategies in Fictional Analysis.* Urbana: University of Illinois Press, 1990.

5133. Newman, Robert D. *Understanding Thomas Pynchon.* Columbia: University of South Carolina Press, 1986.

5134. Seed, David. *The Fictional Labyrinths of Thomas Pynchon.* Iowa City: University of Iowa Press, 1988.

5135. Stark, John O. *Pynchon's Fictions: Thomas Pynchon and the Literature of Information.* Athens: Ohio University Press, 1981.

5136. Tanner, Tony. *Thomas Pynchon.* New York: Methuen, 1982.

5137. Van Delden, Maarten. "Modernism, The New Criticsm, and Thomas Pynchon's *V.*" *Novel* 23 (Winter 1990): 117–36.

5138. Weixlmann, Joseph. "Thomas Pynchon: A Bibliography." *Critique* 14 (No. 2, 1972): 34–43.

HERBERT QUICK

5139. Bogue, Allan G. "Herbert Quick's Hawkeye Trilogy." *Books at Iowa* 15 (April 1972): 3–13.

5140. Keen, Carl L. "The Fictional Writings of Herbert Quick." Doctoral dissertation, Michigan State University, 1968.

5141. Morain, Frederick G. "Herbert Quick, Iowa Democrat." Doctoral dissertation, Yale University, 1970.

CHRISTINE QUINTASKET

(Mourning Dove)

5142. Brown, Alanna Kathleen. "The Choice to Write: Mourning Dove's Search for Survival." *Old West–New West: Centennial Essays.* Ed. Barbara Howard Meldrum. Moscow: University of Idaho Press, 1993, 261–71.

5143. Miller, Jay, ed. *Mourning Dove: A Salishan Autobiography.* Lincoln: University of Nebraska Press, 1990.

WILLIAM MACLEOD RAINE

5144. "Git Along, Ol' Typewriter." *Time* 64 (July 19, 1954): 82–84.

5145. Gressley, Gene M. "Mr. Raine, Mammon, and the Western." *Arizona and the West* 25 (Winter 1983): 313–28.

5146. Loomis, C. Grant. "Folk Language in William MacLeod Raine's West." *Tennessee Folklore Society Bulletin* 24 (December 1958): 131–48.

5147. Scamehorn, Lee. "Dedication to William MacLeod Raine, 1871–1954." *Arizona and the West* 24 (Spring 1982): 1–4.

OPIE READ

5148. Baird, Reed M. "Opie Read (1852–1939): An Introduction." *Mark Twain Journal* 19 (1977–78): 11–13.

5149. ———. "Opie Read (1852–1939): A Study in Popular Culture." Doctoral dissertation, University of Michigan, 1966.

5150. Linneman, William. "Opie Read and *The Arkansas-Traveler*: The Trials of a Regional Humor Magazine." *Midwest Folklore* 10 (Spring 1960): 5–10.

ISHMAEL REED

See Emmett Coleman

MAYNE REID

5151. Billington, Ray Allen. *Land of Savagery/Land of Promise: The European Image of the American Frontier in the Nineteenth Century.* New York: Norton, 1981, 43–44, 46–47, 142–44 passim.

5152. Maher, Susan Naramore. "Westering Crusoes: Mayne Reid's *The Desert Home* and the Plotting of the American West." *Journal of the Southwest* 35 (Spring 1992): 93–105.

5153. Meyer, Roy W. "The Western Fiction of Mayne Reid." *Western American Literature* 3 (Summer 1968): 115–32.

5154. Steele, Joan. "Mayne Reid: A Revised Bibliography." *Bulletin of Bibliography* 29 (July–September 1972): 95–100.

FREDERIC REMINGTON

5155. Allen, E. Douglas. "Frederic Remington–Author and Illustrator–A List of His Contributions to American Periodicals." *Bulletin of the New York Public Library* 49 (December 1945): 895–912.

5156. Alter, Judith. "Frederic Remington's Major Novel: *John Ermine.*" *Southwestern American Literature* 2 (Spring 1972): 42–46.

5157. ———. "The Western Myth in American Painting and Fiction of the Late 19th and Early 20th Centuries." Doctoral dissertation, Texas Christian University, 1970.

5158. Dippie, Brian W. "Frederic Remington's Wild West." *American Heritage* 26 (April 1975): 7–23, 76–79.

5159. Dykes, Jeff C. "Tentative Bibliographic Check Lists of Western Illustrators: 26, Frederic Remington (1861–1909)." *American Book Collector* 16 (November 1965): 20–31; (December 1965): 22–31; (January 1966): 26–31; (February 1966): 34–39; (March 1966): 21–27; (April 1966): 23–35.

5160. Erisman, Fred. *Frederic Remington.* Western Writers Series, No. 16. Boise, Idaho: Boise State University, 1975.

5161. ———. "Frederic Remington: The Artist as Local Colorist." *South Dakota Review* 12 (Winter 1974–75): 76–88.

5162. ———. "Remington the Author." *Persimmon Hill* 10 (No. 3, 1980): 24–35.

5163. Hassrick, Peter H. *Frederic Remington.* New York: Abrams, 1973.

5164. ———. "Remington in the Southwest." *Southwestern Historical Quarterly* 76 (January 1973): 297–314.

5165. McCracken, Harold. *Frederic Remington: Artist of the Old West.* Philadelphia: Lippincott, 1947.

5166. Manley, Atwood. *Frederic Remington in the Land of His Youth.* Ogdensburg, N.Y.: Northern New York Publishing Company, 1961.

5167. Nemerov, Alexander. "Past Knowing: Frederic Remington's Old West." Doctoral dissertation, Yale University, 1992.

5168. Rush, N. Orwin. "Frederic Remington and Owen Wister: The Story of a Friendship, 1893–1909." *Probing the American West: Papers from the Santa Fe Conference.* Ed. K. Ross Toole, et al. Santa Fe: Museum of New Mexico, 1962, 148–57.

5169. Samuels, Peggy, and Harold Samuels. *Frederic Remington: A Biography.* Garden City, N.Y.: Doubleday, 1982.

5170. Vorpahl, Ben Merchant. *Frederic Remington and the West: With the Eye of the Mind.* Austin: University of Texas Press, 1978.

5171. ———. *"My Dear Wister": The Frederic Remington-Owen Wister Letters.* Palo Alto, Calif.: American West, 1972.

5172. White, G. Edward. *The Eastern Establishment and the Western Experience: The West of Frederic Remington, Theodore Roosevelt, and Owen Wister.* New Haven, Conn.: Yale University Press, 1968.

5173. Bartlett, Lee. *Kenneth Rexroth.* Western Writers Series, No. 84. Boise, Idaho: Boise State University, 1988.

5174. ————, ed. *Kenneth Rexroth and James Laughlin: Selected Letters.* New York: New Directions, 1991.

5175. Foster, Richard. "The Voice of a Poet: Kenneth Rexroth." *Minnesota Review* 2 (Spring 1962): 377–84.

5176. Garren, Samuel Baity. "Quest for Value: A Study of the Collected Longer Poems of Kenneth Rexroth." Doctoral dissertation, Louisiana State University, 1976.

5177. Gibson, Morgan. *Kenneth Rexroth.* New York: Twayne, 1972.

5178. ————. *Revolutionary Rexroth: Poet of East-West Wisdom.* Hamden, Conn.: Archon Books, 1986.

5179. Grigsby, Gordon K. "The Presence of Reality: The Poetry of Kenneth Rexroth." *Antioch Review* 31 (Fall 1971): 405–22.

5180. Gutierrez, Donald. "Keeping an Eye on Nature: Kenneth Rexroth's 'Falling Leaves and Early Snow.'" *American Poetry* 1 (Winter 1984): 60–64.

5181. ————. "Kenneth Rexroth: Poet, Radical Man of Letters of the West." *Northwest Review* 30 (No. 2, 1992): 142–55.

5182. ————. "Natural Supernaturalism: The Nature Poetry of Kenneth Rexroth." *Literary Review* 26 (Spring 1983): 405–22.

5183. Hamalian, Leo. "Scanning the Self: The Influence of Emerson on Kenneth Rexroth." *South Dakota Review* 27 (Summer 1989): 3–14.

5184. Hamalian, Linda. "Early Version of 'The Homestead Called Damascus.'" *North Dakota Quarterly* 56 (Winter 1988): 131–47.

5185. ————. *A Life of Kenneth Rexroth.* New York: Norton, 1991.

5186. Hartzell, James, and Richard Zumwinkle, comps. *Kenneth Rexroth: A Checklist of His Published Writings.* Los Angeles: Friends of the UCLA Library, 1967.

5187. "An Interview with Kenneth Rexroth." *Critique* 10 (Summer 1969): 313–31.

5188. "Kenneth Rexroth." *Sagetrieb* 2 (Winter 1983). Special issue.

5189. Knabb, Ken. *The Relevance of Rexroth.* Berkeley: Bureau of Public Secrets, 1990.

5190. McKenzie, James J., and Robert W. Lewis. "'That Rexroth—He'll Argue You into Anything': An Interview with Kenneth Rexroth." *North Dakota Quarterly* 44 (Summer 1976): 7–33.

5191. Parkinson, Thomas. "Kenneth Rexroth, Poet." *Ohio Review* 17 (1976): 54–67.

5192. Sakurai, Emiko. "The Oriental Tradition in the Poetry of Kenneth Rexroth. Doctoral dissertation, University of Alabama, 1973.

5193. Woodcock, George. "Realms beyond the Mountains: Notes on Kenneth Rexroth." *Ontario Review* 6 (1977): 39–48.

EUGENE MANLOVE RHODES

5194. Busby, Mark. "Eugene Manlove Rhodes: Ken Kesey Passed by Here." *Western American Literature* 15 (Summer 1980): 83–92.

5195. Clark, Frank M. *Sandpapers: The Lives and Letters of Eugene Manlove Rhodes and Charles Fletcher Lummis.* Santa Fe, N.Mex.: Sunstone, 1993.

5196. Day, Beth F. *Gene Rhodes, Cowboy.* New York: Julian Messner, 1954.

5197. DeVoto, Bernard. "The Novelists of the Cattle Country," in May Davison Rhodes, *The Hired Man on Horseback.* Boston: Houghton Mifflin, 1938, xix–xliv.

5198. Dobie, J. Frank. "Gene Rhodes: Cowboy Novelist." *Atlantic* 183 (June 1949): 75–77.

5199. Fife, Jim Lawrence. "Eugene Manlove Rhodes: Spokesman for Romantic Frontier Democracy." Doctoral dissertation, University of Iowa, 1965.

5200. ———. "Two Views of the American West." *Western American Literature* 1 (Spring 1966): 34–43.

5201. Folsom, James K. "A Dedication to the Memory of Eugene Manlove Rhodes: 1869–1934." *Arizona and the West* 2 (Winter 1969): 310–14.

5202. Gaston, Edwin W., Jr. *Eugene Manlove Rhodes: Cowboy Chronicler.* Southwest Writers Series, No. 11. Austin, Tex.: Steck-Vaughn, 1967.

5203. Hutchinson, W. H. *A Bar Cross Liar. Bibliography of Eugene Manlove Rhodes Who Loved the West-That-Was When He Was Young.* Stillwater, Okla.: Redlands Press, 1959.

5204. ———. *A Bar Cross Man: The Life and Personal Writings of Eugene Manlove Rhodes.* Norman: University of Oklahoma Press, 1956.

5205. ———. "I Pay for What I Break." *Western American Literature* 1 (Summer 1966): 91–96.

5206. ———. "New Mexico Incident: An Episode in the Life of Western Writer Eugene Manlove Rhodes." *American West* 14 (November–December 1977): 4–7, 59–63.

5207. ———. "The West of Eugene Manlove Rhodes." *Arizona and the West* 9 (Autumn 1967): 211–18.

5208. Keleher, William A. *The Fabulous Frontier.* Santa Fe, N. Mex.: Rydal Press, 1945, 137–49.

5209. Knibbs, Henry Herbert. "Gene Rhodes," in Eugene Manlove Rhodes, *The Proud Sheriff.* Boston: Houghton Mifflin, 1935, iii–xxxviii.

5210. Raine, William MacLeod. "Eugene Manlove Rhodes, American." *1945 Brand Book.* Denver, 1946, 47–58.

5211. Rhodes, May Davison. *The Hired Man on Horseback: My Story of Eugene Manlove Rhodes.* Boston: Houghton Mifflin, 1938.

5212. Skillman, Richard, and Jerry C. Hoke. "The Portrait of the New Mexican in the Fiction of Eugene Rhodes." *Western Review* 6 (Spring 1969): 26–36.

CONRAD RICHTER

5213. Barnes, Robert J. *Conrad Richter.* Southwest Writers Series, No. 14. Austin, Tex.: Steck-Vaughn, 1968.

5214. Carpenter, Frederic I. "Conrad Richter's Pioneers: Reality and Myth." *College English* 12 (November 1950): 77–83.

5215. Edwards, Clifford D. *Conrad Richter's Ohio Trilogy: Its Ideas, Themes and Relationship to Literary Tradition.* The Hague: Mouton, 1971.

5216. Flanagan, John T. "Conrad Richter: Romancer of the Southwest." *Southwest Review* 43 (Summer 1958): 189–96.

5217. ———. "Folklore in the Novels of Conrad Richter." *Midwest Folklore* 2 (Spring 1952): 5–14.

5218. Friesen, Paul. "The Use of Oral Tradition in the Novels of Conrad Richter." Doctoral dissertation, Texas Tech University, 1978.

5219. Gaston, Edwin W., Jr. *Conrad Richter.* Rev ed. Boston: Twayne, 1989.

5220. Harris, Jim R. "New Mexico History: A Transient Period in Conrad Richter's *The Sea of Grass.*" *Southwestern American Literature* 5 (1975): 62–67.

5221. Kohler, Dayton. "Conrad Richter: Early Americana." *College English* 8 (February 1947): 221–27.

5222. LaHood, Marvin J. *Conrad Richter's America.* The Hague: Mouton, 1975.

5223. Meldrum, Barbara. "Conrad Richter's Southwestern Ladies." *Women, Women Writers, and the West.* Eds. Lawrence L. Lee and Merrill E. Lewis. Troy, N. Y.: Whiston, 1980, 119–29.

5224. Richter, Conrad. "*The Sea of Grass*–A New Mexico Novel." *New Mexico Magazine* 43 (February 1965): 12–15.

5225. Richter, Harvena. *Writing to Survive: The Private Notebooks of Conrad Richter.* Albuquerque: University of New Mexico Press, 1988.

5226. Sutherland, Bruce. "Conrad Richter's Americana." *New Mexico Quarterly Review* 15 (Winter 1945): 413–22.

5227. Wilson, Dawn M. "Conrad Richter: The Novelist as Philosopher." Doctoral dissertation, Kent State University, 1971.

5228. ———. "The Influence of the West on Conrad Richter's Fiction." *Old Northwest* 1 (1975): 375–89.

5229. Young, David Lee. "The Art of Conrad Richter." Doctoral dissertation, Ohio State University, 1964.

EDWARD F. RICKETTS

5230. Astro, Richard. *Edward F. Ricketts.* Western Writers Series, No. 21. Boise, Idaho: Boise State University, 1976.

5231. ———. *John Steinbeck and Edward Ricketts: The Shaping of a Novelist.* Minneapolis: University of Minnesota Press, 1973.

5232. Fontenrose, Joseph. "Sea of Cortez." *John Steinbeck: An Introduction and Interpretation.* New York: Holt, Rinehart and Winston, 1962, 84–97.

5233. Hedgpeth, Joel W. "Philosophy on Cannery Row." *Steinbeck: The Man and His Work.* Eds. Richard Astro and Tetsumaro Hayashi. Corvallis: Oregon State University Press, 1971, 89–129.

5234. Perez, Betty L. "The Collaborative Role of John Steinbeck and Edward F. Ricketts in the Narrative Section of *Sea of Cortez.*" Doctoral dissertation, University of Florida, 1972.

5235. ———. "Steinbeck, Ricketts and *Sea of Cortez*: Partnership or Exploitation?" *Steinbeck Quarterly* 7 (Summer–Fall 1974): 73–79.

5236. Steinbeck, John. "About Ed Ricketts." *The Log from the Sea of Cortez.* New York: Viking Press, 1951, i–lxvii.

JOHN ROLLIN RIDGE

5237. Parins, James W. *John Rollin Ridge: His Life Works.* Lincoln: University of Nebraska Press, 1991.

5238. Aughtry, Charles. "Lynn Riggs at the University of Oklahoma." *Chronicles of Oklahoma* 37 (Autumn 1959): 280–84.

5239. ———. "Lynn Riggs, Dramatist: A Critical Biography." Doctoral dissertation, Brown University, 1959.

5240. Benton, Joseph. "Some Personal Remembrances about Lynn Riggs." *Chronicles of Oklahoma* 34 (Autumn 1956): 296–301.

5241. Braunlich, Phyllis Cole. "*The Cherokee Night* of R. Lynn Riggs." *Midwest Quarterly* 30 (Autumn 1988): 45–59.

5242. ———. *Haunted by Home: The Life and Letters of Lynn Riggs.* Norman: University of Oklahoma Press, 1988.

5243. Erhard, Thomas A. *Lynn Riggs: Southwest Playwright.* Southwest Writers Series, No. 29. Austin, Tex.: Steck-Vaughn, 1970.

5244. Roth, Henry. "Lynn Riggs and the Individual." *Folk-Say: A Regional Miscellany 1930.* Ed. B.A. Botkin. Norman: University of Oklahoma Press, 1930, 386–95.

5245. Wentz, John C. "American Regional Drama, 1920–40: Frustration and Fulfillment." *Modern Drama* 6 (December 1963): 286–93.

5246. Wilson, Eloise. "Lynn Riggs: Oklahoma Dramatist." Doctoral dissertation, University of Pennsylvania, 1957.

MARY ROBERTS RINEHART

5247. Dowing, Sybil, and Jane Valentine Barker. *Crown of Life: The Story of Mary Roberts Rinehart.* Niwot, Colo.: Roberts Rinehart, 1992.

TOMÁS RIVERA

5248. Grajeda, Ralph F. "Tomás Rivera's Appropriation of the Chicano Past." *Modern Chicano Writers.* Eds. Joseph Sommers and Tomás Ybarra-Frausto. Englewood Cliffs, N.J.: Prentice-Hall, 1979, 74–85.

5249. Lattin, Vernon E., Rolando Hinojosa, and Gary D. Keller, eds. *Tomás Rivera 1935–1984: The Man and His Work.* Tempe, Ariz.: Bilingual Review, 1988.

5250. Olivares, Julián, ed. *International Studies in Honor of Tomás Rivera.* Houston: Arte Público, 1986. Reprints special issue of *Revista Chicano-Riqueña* 13 (Fall–Winter 1985).

5251. Pino, Frank, Jr. "The Outsider and 'El Otro' in Tomás Rivera's '...y no se lo tragó la tierra.'" *Books Abroad* 49 (Summer 1975): 453–59.

5252. Rocard, Marcienne. "The Cycle of Chicano Experience in '... *and the earth did not part*' by Thomas Rivera." *Caliban* 10 (1974): 141–51.

5253. Rodríguez, Juan. "The Problematic in Tomás Rivera's ... *And the Earth Did Not Part*." *Revista Chicano-Riqueña* 6 (1978): 42–50.

5254. Sommers, Joseph. "Interpreting Tomás Rivera." *Modern Chicano Writers*. Eds. Joseph Sommers and Tomás Ybarra-Frausto. Englewood Cliffs, N.J.: Prentice-Hall, 1979, 94–107.

5255. Testa, Daniel P. "Narrative Technique and Human Experience in Tomás Rivera." *Modern Chicano Writers*. Eds. Joseph Sommers and Tomás Ybarra-Frausto. Englewood Cliffs, N.J.: Prentice-Hall, 1979, 86–93.

TOM ROBBINS

5256. Anderson, Bette Bacon, and William Burke. "Tom Robbins' *Another Roadside Attraction* and the Second Coming." *Slackwater Review* 3 (Winter 1979–80): 69–76.

5257. Gross, Beverly. "Misfits: Tom Robbins' *Even Cowgirls Get the Blues*." *North Dakota Quarterly* 50 (Summer 1982): 36–51.

5258. McCaffery, Larry, and Sinda Gregory. "An Interview with Tom Robbins." *Alive and Writing: Interviews with American Authors of the 1980s*. Eds. Larry McCaffery and Sinda Gregory. Urbana: University of Illinois Press, 1987, 222–39.

5259. Nadeau, Robert. "Physics and Cosmology in the Fiction of Tom Robbins." *Critique* 20 (1978): 63–74.

5260. Siegel, Mark. *Tom Robbins*. Western Writers Series, No. 42. Boise, Idaho: Boise State University, 1980.

MARILYNNE ROBINSON

5261. Burke, William M. "Border Crossings in Marilynne Robinson's *Housekeeping*." *Modern Fiction Studies* 37 (Winter 1991): 716–24.

5262. Florby, Gunilla. "Escaping this World: Marilynne Robinson's Variation on an Old American Motif." *Moderna Språk* 78 (No. 3, 1984): 211–16.

5263. Gernes, Sonia. "Transcendent Women: Uses of the Mystical in Margaret Atwood's *Cat's Eye* and Marilynne Robinson's *Housekeeping*." *Religion and Literature* 23 (Autumn 1991): 143–65.

5264. Geyh, Paula E. "Burning Down the House? Domestic Space and Feminine Subjectivity in Marilynne Robinson's *Housekeeping.*" *Contemporary Literature* 34 (Spring 1993): 103–22.

5265. Mallon, Anne-Marie. "Sojourning Women: Homelessness and Transcendence in *Housekeeping.*" *Critique* 30 (Winter 1989): 95–105.

5266. O'Brien, Sheila Ruzycki. "*Housekeeping*: New West Novel, Old West Film." *Old West–New West: Centennial Essays.* Ed. Barbara Howard Meldrum. Moscow: University of Idaho Press, 1993, 173–83.

5267. Ravits, Martha. "Extending the American Range: Marilynne Robinson's *Housekeeping.*" *American Literature* 61 (December 1989): 644–66.

5268. Toles, George. "'Sighs Too Deep for Words': Mysteries of Need in Marilynne Robinson's *Housekeeping.*" *Arizona Quarterly* 47 (Winter 1991): 137–56.

5269. Van Dyke, Annette. "Marilynne Robinson's *Housekeeping*: A Landscape of Discontent." *The Big Empty: Essays on Western Landscapes as Narratives.* Ed. Leonard Engel. Albuquerque: University of New Mexico Press, 1994, 147–63.

RICHARD RODRIGUEZ

5270. Márquez, Antonio C. "Richard Rodriguez's *Hunger of Memory* and the Poetics of Experience." *Arizona Quarterly* 40 (Summer 1984): 130–41.

THEODORE ROETHKE

5271. Alkalay, Karen. "The Poetry of Theodore Roethke." Doctoral dissertation, University of Rochester, 1974.

5272. Balakian, Peter. *Theodore Roethke's Far Fields: The Evolution of His Poetry.* Baton Rouge: Louisiana State University Press, 1989.

5273. Blessing, Richard A. *Theodore Roethke's Dynamic Vision.* Bloomington: Indiana University Press, 1974.

5274. Bogen, Don. "'Intuition' and 'Craftsmanship': Theodore Rocthke at Work." *Papers on Language and Literature* 18 (Winter 1982): 58–76.

5275. ———. *A Necessary Order: Theodore Roethke and the Writing Process.* Athens: Ohio University Press, 1991.

5276. Bowers, Neal. *Theodore Roethke: The Journey From I to Otherwise.* Columbia: University of Missouri Press, 1982.

5277. ———. "Theodore Roethke: The Manic Vision." *Modern Poetry Studies* 11 (1982): 152–64.

5278. Breslin, Glenna Louise. "Form as Process in the Poetry of Theodore Roethke." Doctoral dissertation, University of Minnesota, 1973.

5279. Burke, Kenneth. "The Vegetal Radicalism of Theodore Roethke." *Language as Symbolic Action.* Berkeley: University of California Press, 1966, 254–81.

5280. Chaney, Norman. *Theodore Roethke: The Poetics of Wonder.* Washington, D.C.: University Press of America, 1981.

5281. Foster, Ann Tucker. "A Field for Revelation: Mysticism in the Poetry of Theodore Roethke." Doctoral dissertation, Florida State University, 1977.

5282. Freer, Coburn. "Theodore Roethke's Love Poetry." *Northwest Review* 11 (Summer 1971): 42–66.

5283. Gardner, Thomas. "Far from the Crash of the Long Swell: Theodore Roethke's 'North American Sequence.'" *Discovering Ourselves in Whitman: The Contemporary American Long Poem.* Urbana: University of Illinois Press, 1989, 78–98.

5284. ———. "'North American Sequence': Theodore Roethke and the Contemporary American Long Poem." *Essays in Literature* 11 (Fall 1984): 237–52.

5285. Heilman, Robert. "Theodore Roethke: Personal Notes." *Shenandoah* 16 (Autumn 1964): 55–64.

5286. Heyen, William. *Profile of Theodore Roethke.* Columbus, Ohio: Charles E. Merrill Company, 1971.

5287. Kalaidjian, Walter B. *Understanding Theodore Roethke.* Columbia: University of South Carolina Press, 1987.

5288. Kramer, Hilton. "The Poetry of Theodore Roethke." *Western Review* 18 (Winter 1954): 131–46.

5289. Kunitz, Stanley. "Roethke: Poet of Transformations." *New Republic* 152 (January 23, 1965): 23–29.

5290. LaBelle, Jenijoy. *The Echoing Wood of Theodore Roethke.* Princeton, N.J.: Princeton University Press, 1976.

5291. Lane, Gary, ed. *A Concordance to the Poems of Theodore Roethke.* Metuchen, N.J.: Scarecrow Press, 1972.

5292. Lorimer, William Lund. "Ripples from a Single Stone: An Archetypal Study of Theodore Roethke's Poetry." Doctoral dissertation, University of Notre Dame, 1976.

5293. McLeod, James Richard. *Theodore Roethke: A Bibliography.* Kent, Ohio: Kent State University, 1973.

5294. ———. *Theodore Roethke: A Manuscript Checklist.* Kent, Ohio: Kent State University Press, 1971.

5295. McMichael, James. "The Poetry of Theodore Roethke." *Southern Review* 5 (Winter 1969): 4–25.

5296. ———. "Roethke's North America." *Northwest Review* 11 (Summer 1971): 149–59.

5297. Malkoff, Karl. *Theodore Roethke: An Introduction to the Poetry.* New York: Columbia University Press, 1966.

5298. Martz, William J. *The Achievement of Theodore Roethke.* Glenview, Ill.: Scott, Foresman, 1966.

5299. Mazzaro, Jerome. "Theodore Roethke and the Failures of Language." *Modern Poetry Studies* 1 (July 1970): 73–96.

5300. Meredith, William. "A Steady Storm of Correspondences: Theodore Roethke's Long Journey Out of the Self." *Shenandoah* 16 (Autumn 1964): 41–54.

5301. Mills, Ralph J., Jr. *Theodore Roethke.* Minneapolis: University of Minnesota Press, 1963.

5302. ———. "Theodore Roethke: The Lyric of the Self." *Poets in Progress: Critical Prefaces to Ten Contemporary Americans.* Ed. Edward Hungerford. Evanston: Northwestern University Press, 1962, 3–23.

5303. ———, ed. *On the Poet and His Craft: Selected Prose of Theodore Roethke.* Seattle: University of Washington Press, 1965.

5304. ———, ed. *Selected Letters of Theodore Roethke.* Seattle: University of Washington Press, 1968.

5305. Moul, Keith R. *Theodore Roethke's Career: An Annotated Bibliography.* Boston: G.K. Hall, 1977.

5306. Rohrkemper, John. "'When the Mind Remembers All': Dream and Memory in Theodore Roethke's 'North American Sequence.'" *Journal of the Midwest Modern Language Association* 21 (Spring 1988): 28–37.

5307. Schumacker, Paul J. "The Unity of Being: A Study of Theodore Roethke's Poetry." *Ohio University Review* 12 (1970): 20–40.

5308. Scott, Nathan A. "The Example of Roethke." *The Wild Prayer of Longing and the Sacred.* New Haven, Conn.: Yale University Press, 1971, 76–118.

5309. Seager, Allan. *The Glass House: The Life of Theodore Roethke.* New York: McGraw-Hill, 1968.

5310. ———, Stanley Kunitz, and John Ciardi. "An Evening with Ted Roethke." *Michigan Quarterly Review* 6 (Fall 1967): 227–45.

5311. Staples, Hugh. "The Rose in the Sea-Wind: A Reading of Theodore Roethke's North American Sequence." *American Literature* 36 (May 1964): 189–203.

5312. Stein, Arnold, ed. *Theodore Roethke: Essays on the Poetry.* Seattle: University of Washington Press, 1965.

5313. Stiffler, Randall. *Theodore Roethke: The Poet and His Critics.* Chicago: American Library Association, 1986.

5314. Sullivan, Rosemary. *Theodore Roethke: The Garden Master.* Seattle: University of Washington Press, 1975.

5315. Tuten, Nancy Lewis. "Theodore Roethke and Galway Kinnell: Voices in Contemporary American Romanticism." *Northwest Review* 29 (1991): 126–42.

5316. Vanderbilt, Kermit. "Theodore Roethke as a Northwest Poet." *Northwest Perspectives: Essays on the Culture of the Pacific Northwest.* Eds. Edwin R. Bingham and Glen A. Love. Seattle: University of Washington Press, 1979, 187–216.

5317. Wain, John. "Theodore Roethke." *Critical Quarterly* 6 (Winter 1964): 322–38.

5318. Williams, Harry. *"The edge is what I have": Theodore Roethke and After.* Cranbury, N.J.: Bucknell University Press, 1977.

WILL ROGERS

5319. Alworth, E. Paul. *Will Rogers.* New York: Twayne, 1974.

5320. Brown, William R. *Imagemaker: Will Rogers and the American Dream.* New York: Columbia University Press, 1970.

5321. *Chronicles of Oklahoma* 57 (Fall 1979). Special issue on Will Rogers.

5322. Clark, Blue. "The Literary Will Rogers." *Chronicles of Oklahoma* 57 (Fall 1979): 385–94.

5323. Day, Donald. *Will Rogers, A Biography.* New York: David McKay, 1962.

5324. Roach, Samuel Frederick, Jr. "Lariat in the Sun: The Story of Will Rogers." Doctoral dissertation, University of Oklahoma, 1972.

5325. Rogers, Will. *The Autobiography of Will Rogers.* Ed. Donald Day. Boston: Houghton Mifflin, 1949.

5326. Wertheim, Arthur Frank. *Will Rogers at the Ziegfield Follies.* Norman: University of Oklahoma Press, 1992.

5327. Yagoda, Ben. *Will Rogers: A Biography.* New York: Knopf, 1993.

OLE RÖLVAAG

5328. Anderson, Carol Jane. "Narrative Techniques in Selected Novels by Ole Edvart Rölvaag." Doctoral dissertation, University of Arkansas, 1979.

5329. Bjork, Kenneth O. "The Unknown Rölvaag: Secretary in the Norwegian-American Historical Association." *Norwegian-American Studies and Records* 11 (1940): 114–49.

5330. Boynton, Percy H. "O.E. Rölvaag and the Conquest of the Pioneer." *English Journal* 18 (September 1929): 535–42.

5331. De Grazia, Emilio. "The Great Plain: Rölvaag's New World Sea." *South Dakota Review* 20 (Autumn 1982): 35–49.

5332. Dittmann, Erling. "The Immigrant Mind: A Study of Rölvaag." *Christian Liberty* 1 (October 1952): 7–47.

5333. Eckstein, Neil T. "*Giants in the Earth* as Saga." *Where the West Begins.* Eds. Arthur R. Huseboe and William Geyer. Sioux Falls, S. Dak.: Center for Western Studies Press, 1978, 34–41.

5334. ————. *The Marginal Man as Novelist: The Norwegian-American Writers, H. H. Boyesen and Ole Rölvaag, as Critics of American Institutions.* New York: Garland, 1990.

5335. ————. "The Social Criticism of Ole Edvart Rölvaag." *Norwegian-American Studies* 24 (1970): 112–36.

5336. Geyer, Carolyn. "An Introduction to Ole Rölvaag (1876–1931)." *Big Sioux Pioneers.* Ed. Arthur R. Huseboe. Sioux Falls, S. Dak.: Norland Heritage Foundation, 1980, 54–62.

5337. Grider, Sylvia. "Madness and Personification in *Giants in the Earth.*" *Women, Women Writers, and the West.* Eds. Lawrence L. Lee and Merrill E. Lewis. Troy, N.Y.: Whitston, 1978.

5338. Gvåle, Gudrun Hovde. *Ole Edvart Rölvaag: Nordmann og Amerikanar.* Oslo: Aschehoug, 1962.

5339. Hahn, Steve. "Vision and Reality in *Giants in the Earth.*" *South Dakota Review* 17 (Spring 1979): 85–100.

5340. Haugen, Einar. "O.E. Rölvaag: Norwegian-American." *Norwegian-American Studies and Records* 7 (1933): 53–73.

5341. ————. *Ole Edvart Rölvaag.* Boston: Twayne, 1983.

5342. Heitmann, John. "Ole Edvart Rölvaag." *Norwegian-American Studies and Records* 12 (1941): 144–66.

5343. Homola, Priscilla Hepler. "Following a Leg of Mutton: The Pastoral in Rölvaag's *Giants in the Earth*." Doctoral dissertation, University of North Dakota, 1985.

5344. ———. "The Indian Hill in Rölvaag's *Giants in the Earth*." *South Dakota Review* 27 (Spring 1989): 55–61.

5345. ———. "Rölvaag's Beret as Spiritual Descendent of Ibsen's Brand." *South Dakota Review* 24 (Summer 1986): 63–70.

5346. Jordahl, Owen. "Folkloristic Influences upon Rölvaag's Youth." *Western Folklore* 34 (January 1975): 1–15.

5347. Jorgenson, Theodore, and Nora O. Solum. *Ole Edvart Rölvaag: A Biography*. New York: Harper and Brothers, 1939.

5348. Meyer, Roy W. *The Middle Western Farm Novel in the Twentieth Century*. Lincoln: University of Nebraska Press, 1965.

5349. Moseley, Ann. *Ole Edvart Rölvaag*. Western Writers Series, No. 80. Boise, Idaho: Boise State University, 1987.

5350. Olson, Julius E. "Ole Edvart Rölvaag, 1876–1931: In Memoriam." *Norwegian-American Studies and Records* 7 (1933): 121–30.

5351. ———. "Rölvaag's Novels of Norwegian Pioneer Life in the Dakotas." *Scandinavian Studies and Notes* 9 (1927): 45–55.

5352. Parrington, Vernon. "Ole Rölvaag's 'Giants in the Earth.'" *The Beginnings of Critical Realism in America: 1860–1920*. New York: Harcourt Brace and World, 1930, 387–96.

5353. Paulson, Kristoffer F. "Ole Rölvaag, Herbert Krause, and the Frontier Thesis of Frederick Jackson Turner." *Where the West Begins*. Eds. Arthur R. Huseboe and William Geyer. Sioux Falls, S. Dak.: Center for Western Studies Press, 1978, 24–33.

5354. ———. "What Was Lost: Ole Rølvaag's *The Boat of Longing*." *MELUS* 7 (Spring 1980): 51–60.

5355. Reigstad, Paul. "Mythic Aspects of *Giants in the Earth*." *Vision and Refuge: Essays on the Literature of the Great Plains*. Eds. Virginia Faulkner with Frederick C. Luebke. Lincoln: University of Nebraska Press, 1982, 64–70.

5356. ———. *Rölvaag: His Life and Art*. Lincoln: University of Nebraska Press, 1972.

5357. Ruud, Curtis Duane. "The Dakota Prairie as Changing Force in Rölvaag's *Giants in the Earth*." Doctoral dissertation, University of Nebraska, Lincoln, 1977.

5358. Simonson, Harold P. *The Closed Frontier: Studies in American Literary Tragedy.* New York: Holt, Rinehart, and Winston, 1970, 77–97.

5359. ———. *Prairies Within: The Tragic Trilogy of Ole Rölvaag.* Seattle: University of Washington Press, 1987.

5360. ———. "Rölvaag and Kierkegaard." *Scandinavian Studies* 49 (Winter 1977): 67–80.

5361. Skårdal, Dorothy Burton. "Life on the Great Plains in Scandinavian-American Literature." *Vision and Refuge: Essays on the Literature of the Great Plains.* Eds. Virginia Faulkner with Frederick C. Luebke. Lincoln: University of Nebraska Press, 1982, 71–92.

5362. Steensma, Robert. "Rölvaag and Turner's Frontier Thesis." *North Dakota Quarterly* 27 (Autumn 1959): 100–104.

5363. Stevens, Robert. "Ole Edvart Rölvaag: A Critical Study of His Norwegian-American Novels." Doctoral dissertation, University of Illinois, 1955.

5364. Suderman, Elmer F. "An Experiment in Reading *Giants in the Earth.*" *Minnesota English Journal* 8 (Winter 1972): 30–41.

5365. Thorson, Gerald, ed. *Ole Rölvaag: Artist and Cultural Leader.* Northfield, Minn.: St. Olaf College Press, 1975.

5366. Tweet, Ella Valborg. "Recollections of My Father, O. E. Rölvaag." *Minnesota English Journal* 8 (Winter 1972): 4–16.

5367. White, George Leroy. "O.E. Rölvaag–Prophet of a People." *Scandinavian Themes in American Fiction.* Philadelphia: University of Pennsylvania Press, 1937, 97–108.

THEODORE ROOSEVELT

5368. Barsness, John A. "Theodore Roosevelt as Cowboy: The Virginian as Jacksonian Man." *American Quarterly* 21 (Fall 1969): 609–19.

5369. Collins, Michael L. *That Damned Cowboy: Theodore Roosevelt and the American West, 1883–1898.* New York: P. Lang, 1989.

5370. Dornbusch, Clyde H. "Theodore Roosevelt's Literary Taste and Relationships with Authors." Doctoral dissertation, Duke University, 1957.

5371. Fenton, Charles. "Theodore Roosevelt as a Man of Letters." *Western Humanities Review* 13 (August 1959): 369–74.

5372. Lewis, Merrill E. "American Frontier History as Literature: Studies in Historiography of George Bancroft, Frederick Jackson Turner, and Theodore Roosevelt." Doctoral dissertation, University of Utah, 1968.

5373. Moers, Ellen. "Teddy Roosevelt: Literary Feller." *Columbia University Forum* 6 (Summer 1963): 10–16.

5374. Norton, Aloysius A. *Theodore Roosevelt.* Boston: Twayne, 1980.

5375. Slotkin, Richard. "Theodore Roosevelt's Frontier Hypothesis." *The American West, as Seen by Europeans and Americans.* Ed. Rob Kroes. Amsterdam: Free University Press, 1989, 44–71.

5376. Walker, Don D. "Wister, Roosevelt and James: A Note on the Western." *American Quarterly* 12 (Fall 1960): 358–66.

5377. White, G. Edward. *The Eastern Establishment and the Western Experience: The West of Frederic Remington, Theodore Roosevelt, and Owen Wister.* New Haven, Conn.: Yale University Press, 1968.

JEROME ROTHENBERG

5378. Clements, William M. "Faking the Pumpkin: On Jerome Rothenberg's Literary Offenses." *Western American Literature* 16 (Fall 1981): 193–204.

5379. Paul, Sherman. *In Search of the Primitive: Rereading David Antin, Jerome Rothenberg, and Gary Snyder.* Baton Rouge: Louisiana State University Press, 1986.

JOSIAH ROYCE

5380. Clendenning, John. *The Life and Thought of Josiah Royce.* Madison: University of Wisconsin Press, 1985.

5381. ———, ed. *The Letters of Josiah Royce.* Chicago: University of Chicago Press, 1970.

5382. Hine, Robert V. "The American West as Metaphysics: A Perspective on Josiah Royce." *Pacific Historical Review* 58 (August 1989): 267–91.

5383. ———. *Josiah Royce: From Grass Valley to Harvard.* Norman: University of Oklahoma Press, 1992.

5384. ———. "Josiah Royce: The West as Community." *Writing Western History: Essays on Major Western Historians.* Ed. Richard W. Etulain. Albuquerque: University of New Mexico Press, 1991, 19–41.

5385. Kuklick, Bruce. *Josiah Royce: An Intellectual Biography.* Indianapolis: Bobbs-Merrill, 1972.

5386. Pomeroy, Earl. "Josiah Royce, Historian in Quest of Community." *Pacific Historical Review* 40 (February 1971): 1–20.

5387. Starr, Kevin. *Americans and the California Dream 1850–1915.* New

York: Oxford University Press, 1973, 142–71.

EVERETT RUESS

5388. O'Grady, John P. *Pilgrims to the Wild: Everett Ruess, Henry David Thoreau, John Muir, Clarence King, Mary Austin.* Salt Lake City: University of Utah Press, 1993.

DAMON RUNYON

5389. Bayard, Charles J. "Me and Mr. Finch in Denver." *Colorado Magazine* 52 (Winter 1975): 22–33.

CHARLES M. RUSSELL

5390. Adams, Ramon F., and Homer E. Britzman. *Charles M. Russell, The Cowboy Artist.* Pasadena, Calif.: Trail's End, 1948.

5391. Brunvand, Jan Harold. "From Western Folklore to Fiction in the Stories of Charles M. Russell." *Western Review* 5 (Summer 1968): 41–49.

5392. Conrad, Barnaby, III. "C.M. Russell and the Buckskin Paradise of the West." *Horizon* 22 (May 1979): 42–49.

5393. Cristy, Raphael. "Charlie's Hidden Agenda: Realism and Nostalgia in C. M. Russell's Stories About Indians." *Montana: The Magazine of Western History* 43 (Summer 1993): 2–15.

5394. Dippie, Brian W. "Charles Russell's Lost West." *American Heritage* 24 (April 1973): [4]–21, 89.

5395. ———, ed. *Charles M. Russell, Word Painter: Letters 1887–1926.* New York: Abrams, 1993.

5396. Ellsberg, William. "Charles, Thou Art a Rare Blade." *American West* 6 (March 1969): 4–9; (May 1969): 40–43, 62.

5397. Gale, Robert L. *Charles Marion Russell.* Western Writers Series, No. 38. Boise, Idaho: Boise State University, 1979.

5398. Linderman, Frank Bird. *Recollections of Charles Russell.* Norman: University of Oklahoma Press, 1963.

5399. McCracken, Harold. *The Charles M. Russell Book: The Life and Work of the Cowboy Artist.* Garden City, N.Y.: Doubleday, 1957.

5400. Renner, Frederic G. "Rangeland Rembrandt: The Incomparable Charles Marion Russell." *Montana: The Magazine of Western History* 7 (Autumn 1957): 15–28.

5401. Renner, Ginger. *A Limitless Sky: The Work of Charles M. Russell in the Collection of the Rockwell Museum, Corning, New York.* Flagstaff, Ariz.: Northland, 1986.

5402. Russell, Austin. *C.M.R.: Charles M. Russell: Cowboy Artist: A Biography.* New York: Twayne, 1957.

5403. Shelton, Lola. *Charles Marion Russell: Cowboy, Artist, Friend.* New York: Dodd, Mead, 1962.

5404. Woodcock, Lyle S. "The St. Louis Heritage of Charles Marion Russell." *Gateway Heritage* 2 (Spring 1982): 2–15.

5405. Yost, Karl, and Frederic G. Renner. *Bibliography of the Published Works of Charles M. Russell.* Lincoln: University of Nebraska Press, 1971.

GEORGE F. RUXTON

5406. Barrick, Mac E. "Ruxton's Western Proverbs." *Western Folklore* 34 (July 1975): 215–25.

5407. Cracroft, Richard H. "*The Big Sky*: A. B. Guthrie's Use of Historical Sources." *Western American Literature* 6 (Fall 1971): 163–76.

5408. ———. "'Half Froze for Mountain Doin's: The Influence and Significance of George F. Ruxton's *Life in the Far West.*" *Western American Literature* 10 (May 1975): 29–43.

5409. Gaston, Edwin W., Jr. *The Early Novel of the Southwest.* Albuquerque: University of New Mexico Press, 1961.

5410. Hafen, LeRoy, et al., eds. *Ruxton of the Rockies.* Norman: University of Oklahoma Press, 1950.

5411. Lambert, Neal. *George Frederick Ruxton.* Western Writers Series, No. 15. Boise, Idaho: Boise State University, 1974.

5412. Poulsen, Richard L. "Black George, Black Harris, and the Mountain Man Vernacular." *Rendezvous* 8 (Summer 1973): 15–23.

5413. Sutherland, Bruce. "George Frederick Ruxton in North America." *Southwest Review* 30 (Autumn 1944): 86–91.

5414. Voelker, Frederic E. "Ruxton of the Rocky Mountains." *Missouri Historical Bulletin* 5 (January 1949): 79–90.

5415. Walker, Don D. "The Mountain Man as Literary Hero." *Western American Literature* 1 (Spring 1966): 15–25.

EDWARD L. SABIN

5416. Jordan, Philip D. "Edwin L. Sabin: Literary Explorer of the West." *Books at Iowa* 22 (April 1975): 3–19, 24–25.

THOMAS SANCHEZ

5417. Bonetti, Kay. "An Interview with Thomas Sanchez." *Missouri Review* 14 (No. 2, 1991): 75–95.

5418. Marovitz, Sanford E. "The Entropic World of the Washo: Fatality and Self-Deception in *Rabbit Boss*." *Western American Literature* 19 (November 1984): 219–30.

MARI SANDOZ

5419. Bohling, Beth. "Mari Sandoz' Saddlebags." *Platte Valley Review* 17 (Winter 1989): 84–91.

5420. Clark, LaVerne Harrell. "The Indian Writings of Mari Sandoz: 'A Lone One Left from the Old Times.'" *American Indian Quarterly* 1 (Autumn 1974): 183–92; (Winter 1974–75): 269–80.

5421. ———. *Re-visiting the Plains Indian Country of Mari Sandoz.* Marvin, S. Dak.: Blue Cloud Quarterly Chapbook, No. 5, 1977.

5422. Doher, Pam. "The Idioms and Figures of *Cheyenne Autumn*." *Where the West Begins.* Eds. Arthur R. Huseboe and William Geyer. Sioux Falls, S. Dak.: Center for Western Studies Press, 1978, 143–51.

5423. Graulich, Melody. "Every Husband's Right: Sex Roles in Mari Sandoz's *Old Jules*." *Western American Literature* 18 (May 1983): 3–20.

5424. Greenwell, Scott L. "A Descriptive Guide to the Mari Sandoz Collection." *University of Nebraska Studies* 63 (1980): 1–109.

5425. ———. "Fascists in Fiction: Two Early Novels of Mari Sandoz." *Western American Literature* 12 (August 1977): 133–43.

5426. ———. "The Literary Apprenticeship of Mari Sandoz." *Nebraska History* 57 (Summer 1976): 248–72.

5427. Hill, Michael R. "Mari Sandoz' Sociological Imagination: *Capital City* as an Ideal Type." *Platte Valley Review* 17 (Winter 1989): 102–22.

5428. Kurth, Robert H. "Frontier Medicine as Perceived by Mari Sandoz." *Platte Valley Review* 17 (Winter 1989): 33–40.

5429. Limbaugh, Elaine E. "A Feminist Reads *Old Jules*." *Platte Valley Review* 17 (Winter 1989): 41–50.

5430. Lowe, David. "A Meeting with Mari Sandoz." *Prairie Schooner* 42 (Spring 1968): 21–26.

5431. Mason, Katherine A. "Greed and the Erosion of the Pioneer Ethic: Selected Novels of Mari Sandoz." *Platte Valley Review* 17 (Winter 1989): 92–101.

5432. Mattern, Claire. "Mari Sandoz: Her Use of Allegory in *Slogum House*." Doctoral dissertation, University of Nebraska, Lincoln, 1981.

5433. ———. "Rebels, Aliens, Outsiders, and the Nonconformist in the Writing of Mari Sandoz." *CEA Critic* 49 (Winter 1986–Summer 1987): 102–13.

5434. Moon, Myra Jo, and Rosemary Whitaker. "A Bibliography of Works by and about Mari Sandoz." *Bulletin of Bibliography* 38 (April–June 1981).

5435. Morton, Beatrice K. "A Critical Appraisal of Mari Sandoz' *Miss Morissa*: Modern Woman on the Western Frontier." *Heritage of Kansas* 10 (Fall 1977): 37–45.

5436. Nicoll, Bruce H. "Mari Sandoz: Nebraska Loner." *American West* 2 (Spring 1965): 32–36.

5437. Oehlschlaeger, Fritz. "The Art of Mari Sandoz's 'The Smart Man.'" *South Dakota Review* 19 (Winter 1982): 65–75.

5438. ———. "Passion and Denial in Mari Sandoz's *Peachstone Basket*." *Great Plains Quarterly* 2 (Spring 1982): 106–13.

5439. Pifer, Caroline Sandoz. *Making of an Author: From the Mementoes of Mari Sandoz*. Gordon, Nebr.: Mari Sandoz Corporation, 1972.

5440. Powell, Peter J. "Bearer of Beauty: Woman of the Sand Hills." *Platte Valley Review* 17 (Winter 1989): 3–16.

5441. Rice, Minnie C. "Mari Sandoz: Biographer of the Old West." *Midwest Review* (Spring 1960): 44–49.

5442. Rippey, Barbara. "Mari Sandoz' Historical Perspective: Linking Past and Present." *Platte Valley Review* 17 (Winter 1989): 60–68.

5443. ———. "Mari Sandoz: Novelist as Historian." Doctoral dissertation, University of Nebraska, Lincoln, 1989.

5444. ———. "Toward a New Paradigm: Mari Sandoz's Study of Red and White Myth in *Cheyenne Autumn*." *Women and Western American Literature*. Eds. Helen Winter Stauffer and Susan Rosowski. Troy, N.Y.: Whitston, 1982, 247–66.

5445. Stauffer, Helen Winter. *Mari Sandoz*. Western Writers Series, No. 63. Boise, Idaho: Boise State University, 1984.

5446. ———. "Mari Sandoz and Western Biography." *Women, Women Writers, and the West*. Eds. Lawrence L. Lee and Merrill E. Lewis. Troy, N.Y.: Whitston, 1978.

5447. ———. *Mari Sandoz, Story-Catcher of the Plains*. Lincoln: University of Nebraska Press, 1982.

5448. ————. "Narrative Voice in Sandoz's *Crazy Horse*." *Western American Literature* 18 (November 1983): 223–37.

5449. ————. "Two Authors and a Hero: Neihardt, Sandoz, and Crazy Horse." *Great Plains Quarterly* 1 (January 1981): 54–66.

5450. ————. "Two Massacres on the Sappa River – Cause and Effect in Mari Sandoz's *Cheyenne Autumn*." *Platte Valley Review* 19 (Winter 1991): 25–43.

5451. ————, ed. *Letters of Mari Sandoz*. Lincoln: University of Nebraska Press, 1992.

5452. Switzer, Dorothy. "Mari Sandoz's Lincoln Years." *Prairie Schooner* 45 (Summer 1971): 107–15.

5453. Walton, Kathleen O'Donnell. "Mari Sandoz: An Initial Critical Appraisal." Doctoral dissertation, University of Delaware, 1970.

5454. Whitaker, Rosemary. "Violence in *Old Jules* and *Slogum House*." *Western American Literature* 16 (Fall 1981): 217–24.

5455. Yost, Nellie Snyder. "The Mari Sandoz I Knew." *Persimmon Hill* 13 (Fall 1983): 24–35.

ROSS SANTEE

5456. Dykes, Jeff C. "Tentative Bibliographic Check Lists of Western Illustrators: 28, Ross Santee (1888–1965)." *American Book Collector* 16 (Summer 1966): 23–28.

5457. Houston, Neal B. *Ross Santee*. Southwest Writers Series, No. 18. Austin, Tex.: Steck-Vaughn, 1968.

5458. Powell, Lawrence Clark. "Southwest Classics Reread: How He Pictured the West." *Westways* 65 (March 1973): 46–50, 84.

WILLIAM SAROYAN

5459. Bedrosian, Margaret. "William Saroyan and the Family Matter." *MELUS* 9 (Winter 1982): 13–24.

5460. Burgum, Edwin B. "The Lonesome Young Man on the Flying Trapeze." *Virginia Quarterly Review* 20 (Summer 1944): 392–403.

5461. Calonne, David Stephen. *William Saroyan: My Real Work Is Being*. Chapel Hill: University of North Carolina Press, 1983.

5462. Carpenter, Frederic I. "The Time of Saroyan's Life." *Pacific Spectator* 1 (Winter 1947): 88–96.

5463. Everding, Robert George. "The Dissolution Process in the Early Plays of William Saroyan." Doctoral dissertation, Stanford University, 1976.

5464. Floan, Howard R. *William Saroyan*. New York: Twayne, 1966.

5465. Foard, Elisabeth C. *William Saroyan: A Reference Guide*. Boston: G.K. Hall, 1989.

5466. Foster, Edward Halsey. *William Saroyan*. Western Writers Series, No. 61. Boise, Idaho: Boise State University, 1984.

5467. ———. *William Saroyan: A Study of the Short Fiction*. New York: Twayne, 1991.

5468. Hamalian, Leo, ed. *William Saroyan: The Man and the Writer Remembered*. Rutherford, N.J.: Fairleigh Dickinson University Press, 1987.

5469. Kherdian, David. *A Bibliography of William Saroyan, 1934–1964*. San Francisco: Roger Beacham, 1965.

5470. Krickel, Edward. "Cozzens and Saroyan: A Look at Two Reputations." *Georgia Review* 24 (Fall 1970): 281–96.

5471. Lee, Lawrence, and Barry Gifford. *Saroyan: A Biography*. New York: Harper Row, 1984.

5472. Mills, John A. "'What. What-not.' Absurdity in Saroyan's *The Time of Your Life*." *Midwest Quarterly* 26 (Winter 1985): 139–59.

5473. Nathan, George Jean. "Saroyan: Whirling Dervish of Fresno." *American Mercury* 51 (November 1940): 303–8.

5474. Rahv, Philip. "William Saroyan: A Minority Report." *American Mercury* 57 (September 1943): 371–77.

5475. Remenyi, Joseph. "William Saroyan: A Portrait." *College English* 6 (November 1944): 92–100.

5476. Saroyan, Aram. *Last Rites: The Death of William Saroyan*. New York: William Morrow, 1982.

5477. ———. *William Saroyan*. San Diego: Harcourt Brace Jovanovich, 1983.

5478. Schulberg, Budd. "Saroyan: Ease and Unease on the Flying Trapeze." *Esquire* 54 (October 1960): 85–91.

5479. Shinn, Thelma J. "William Saroyan: Romantic Existentialist." *Modern Drama* 15 (September 1972): 185–94.

5480. Wattenberg, Richard. "'Old West'/'New West': The New Frontier in Sherwood's *The Petrified Forest* (1934) and Saroyan's *The Time of Your Life* (1939)." *Journal of American Drama and Theatre* 1 (Fall 1989): 17–33.

5481. Wilson, Edmund. "The Boys in the Back Room." *A Literary Chronicle: 1920–1950*. Garden City, N.Y.: Doubleday, 1956, 222–27.

WALTER SATTERTHWAIT

5482. Satterthwait, Walter, and Ernie Bulow. *Sleight of Hand: Conversations with Walter Satterthwait.* Albuquerque: University of New Mexico Press, 1993.

THOMAS SAVAGE

5483. Scheckter, John. "Thomas Savage and the West: Roots of Compulsion." *Western American Literature* 20 (May 1985): 35–49.

DOROTHY SCARBOROUGH

5484. Neatherlin, James William. "Dorothy Scarborough: Form and Milieu in the Work of a Texas Writer." Doctoral dissertation, University of Iowa, 1973.

5485. Palmer, Pamela Lynn. "Dorothy Scarborough and Karle Wilson Baker: A Literary Friendship." *Southwestern Historical Quarterly* 91 (July 1987): 19–32.

5486. Quissell, Barbara. "Dorothy Scarborough's Critique of the Frontier Experience in *The Wind*." *Women, Women Writers, and the West.* Eds. Lawrence L. Lee and Merrill E. Lewis. Troy, N.Y.: Whitston, 1978.

5487. Slade, Carole. "Authorship and Authority in Dorothy Scarborough's *The Wind*." *Studies in American Fiction* 14 (Spring 1986): 85–91.

JACK SCHAEFER

5488. Cleary, Michael. "Jack Schaefer: The Evolution of Pessimism." *Western American Literature* 14 (Spring 1979): 33–47.

5489. Erisman, Fred. "Growing Up With the American West: Fiction of Jack Schaefer." *Journal of Popular Culture* 7 (Winter 1973): 710–16.

5490. ———. "Jack Schaefer: The Writer as Ecologist." *Western American Literature* 13 (Spring 1978): 3–13.

5491. Folsom, James K. "*Shane* and *Hud*: Two Stories in Search of a Medium." *Western Humanities Review* 24 (Autumn 1970): 359–72.

5492. Haslam, Gerald. *Jack Schaefer.* Western Writers Series, No. 20. Boise, Idaho: Boise State University, 1975.

5493. ———. "Sacred Sources in *The Canyon*." *Western American Literature* 14 (Spring 1979): 49–55.

5494. ———. *The Works of Jack Schaefer.* Cassette. Deland, Fla.: Everett/Edwards, 1974.

5495. Johnson, Dorothy M. "Jack Schaefer's People," in Jack Schaefer, *The Short Novels of Jack Schaefer*. Boston: Houghton Mifflin, 1967.

5496. Marsden, Michael T. "Savior in the Saddle: The Sagebrush Testament." *Illinois Quarterly* 36 (December 1973): 5–15.

5497. ———. "*Shane*: From Magazine Serial to American Classic." *South Dakota Review* 15 (Winter 1977–78): 59–69.

5498. Mikkelsen, Robert. "The Western Writer: Jack Schaefer's Use of the Western Frontier." *Western Humanities Review* 8 (Spring 1954): 151–55.

5499. Nuwer, Hank. "An Interview with Jack Schaefer." *South Dakota Review* 11 (Spring 1973): 48–58.

5500. Rankin, Chuck. "Clash of Frontiers: A Historical Parallel to Jack Schaefer's *Shane*." *Shane: The Critical Edition*. Ed. James C. Work. Lincoln: University of Nebraska Press, 1984, 3–15.

5501. Robinson, Forrest G. "Heroism, Home, and the Telling of *Shane*." *Arizona Quarterly* 45 (Spring 1989): 72–100.

5502. Simmons, Marc. "A Salute to *Shane*." *Roundup* 23 (May 1974): 1–2, 9–11.

5503. Work, James C. "Settlement Waves and Coordinate Forces in *Shane*." *Western American Literature* 14 (Fall 1979): 191–200.

5504. ———, ed. *Shane: The Critical Edition*. Lincoln: University of Nebraska Press, 1984.

MARK SCHORER

5505. Bluefarb, Sam. "What We Don't Know *Can* Hurt Us." *Studies in Short Fiction* 5 (Spring 1968): 269–74.

JAMES WILLARD SCHULTZ

5506. Hanna, Warren. *The Life and Times of James Willard Schultz (Apikuni)*. Norman: University of Oklahoma Press, 1986.

HARVEY SCOTT

5507. Nash, Lee. "Scott of the *Oregonian*: Literary Frontiersman." *Pacific Historical* Review 45 (August 1976): 357–78.

5508. ———. "Scott of the *Oregonian*: The Editor as Historian." *Oregon Historical Quarterly* 70 (1969): 197–232.

CHARLES SEALSFIELD

5509. Grunzweig, Walter. *Charles Sealsfield.* Western Writers Series, No. 71. Boise, Idaho: Boise State University, 1985.

5510. Schuchalter, Jerry. *Frontier and Utopia in the Fiction of Charles Sealsfield: A Study of the Lebensbilder aus der westlichen Hemisphäre.* Frankfort am Main and New York: Peter Lang, 1986.

JOHN SEELYE

5511. Cleary, Michael. "John Seelye's *The Kid*: Western Satire and Literary Reassessment." *South Dakota Review* 17 (Winter 1979–80): 23–43.

CHESTER SELTZER

(Amado Jesus Muro)

5512. Gegenheimer, Albert F. "'Amado Muro.'" *Arizona Quarterly* 34 (Autumn 1978): 197–203.

5513. Haslam, Gerald. "The Enigma of Amado Jesus Muro." *Western American Literature* 10 (May 1975): 3–9.

5514. "The Short Stories of 'Amado Muro': A Checklist." *Arizona Quarterly* 34 (Autumn 1978): 217–18.

ROBERT W. SERVICE

5515. Bucco, Martin. "Folk Poetry of Robert W. Service." *Alaska Review* 2 (Fall 1965): 16–26.

ERNEST THOMPSON SETON

5516. Anderson, H. Allen. *The Chief: Ernest Thompson Seton and the Changing West.* College Station: Texas A M University Press, 1986.

5517. Keller, Betty. *Black Wolf: The Life of Ernest Thompson Seton.* Vancouver: Douglas McIntyre, 1984.

5518. Wadland, John Henry. *Ernest Thompson Seton: Man in Nature and the Progressive Era, 1880–1915.* New York: Arno Press, 1978.

RICHARD SHELTON

5519. Contoski, Victor. "Richard Shelton: A Voice in the Wilderness." *Western American Literature* 14 (Spring 1979): 3–17.

5520. Amidon, Rick E. "An American Odyssey: Kinship and Cowboys in Sam Shepard's Drama." Doctoral dissertation, Michigan State University, 1986.

5521. Auerbach, Doris. *Sam Shepard, Arthur Kopit and the Off-Broadway Theater*. Boston: Twayne, 1982.

5522. Bigsby, C.W.E. "Sam Shepard: Imagining America." *Modern American Drama, 1945–1990*. Cambridge: Cambridge University Press, 1992, 162–94.

5523. Blau, Herbert. "The American Dream in American Gothic: The Plays of Sam Shepard and Adrienne Kennedy." *Modern Drama* 27 (December 1984): 520–39.

5524. Collins, Robert Hammond. "American Realism and the Plays of Sam Shepard: A Study of Theme and Form." Doctoral dissertation, University of Minnesota, 1984.

5525. Daniels, Barry V., ed. *Joseph Chaikin and Sam Shepard: Letters and Texts, 1972–1984*. New York: New American Library, 1989.

5526. Demastes, William W. "Understanding Sam Shepard's Realism." *Comparative Drama* 21 (Fall 1987): 229–48.

5527. DeRose, David J. *Sam Shepard*. New York: Twayne, 1992.

5528. Dugdale, John. *File on Shepard*. London: Methuen Drama, 1989.

5529. Erben, Rudolf. "In Search of the Ancient West: Sam Shepard's Exile Plays." *South Dakota Review* 29 (Spring 1991): 162–74.

5530. ———. "True Western: Sam Shepard's Early Plays." *Southwestern American Literature* 18 (Fall 1992): 37–48.

5531. Ganz, Arthur. "Sam Shepard: Iconographer of the Depths." *The Play and Its Critic: Essays for Eric Bentley*. Ed. Michael Bertin. Lanham, Md.: University Press of America, 1986, 211–38.

5532. Grant, Gary. "Writing as a Process of Performing the Self: Sam Shepard's Notebooks." *Modern Drama* 34 (December 1991): 549–65.

5533. Hart, Lynda. *Sam Shepard's Metaphorical Stages*. New York: Greenwood Press, 1987.

5534. ———. "Sam Shepard's Pornographic Visions." *Studies in the Literary Imagination* 21 (Fall 1988): 69–82.

5535. Heilman, Robert B. "Shepard's Plays: Stylistic and Thematic Ties." *Sewanee Review* 100 (Fall 1992): 630–44.

5536. Holstein, Suzy Clarkson. "'All Growed Up' in the *True West*, or Huck and Tom Meet Sam Shepard." *Western American Literature* 29 (May 1994): 41–50.

5537. King, Kimball, ed. *Sam Shepard: A Casebook.* New York: Garland, 1988.

5538. Kleb, William. "Sam Shepard." *American Playwrights Since 1945.* Ed. Philip C. Kolin. New York: Greenwood Press, 1989, 387–419.

5539. Luedtke, Luther S. "From Fission to Fusion: Sam Shepard's Nuclear Families." *Costerus* 76 (New Series, 1989): 143–66.

5540. Lyons, Charles R. "Text as Agent in Sam Shepard's *Curse of the Starving Class.*" *Comparative Drama* 24 (Spring 1990): 24–33.

5541. McKelly, James C. "The Artist and the West: Two Portraits by Jack Kerouac and Sam Shepard." *Western American Literature* 26 (February 1992): 293–301.

5542. Malkin, Jeanette R. "Sam Shepard: The Tooth of Crime." *Verbal Violence in Contemporary Drama.* Cambridge: Cambridge University Press, 1992, 198–223.

5543. Mottram, Ron. *Inner Landscapes: The Theater of Sam Shepard.* Columbia: University of Missouri Press, 1984.

5544. Orbison, Tucker. "Mythic Levels in Shepard's *True West.*" *Modern Drama* 27 (December 1984): 506–19.

5545. Oumono, Ellen. *Sam Shepard: The Life and Work of an American Dreamer.* New York: St. Martin's, 1986.

5546. Parker, Dorothy, ed. *Essays on Modern American Drama: Williams, Miller, Albee and Shepard.* Toronto: University of Toronto Press, 1987.

5547. Patraka, Vivian M., and Mark Richard Siegel. *Sam Shepard.* Western Writers Series, No. 69. Boise, Idaho: Boise State University, 1985.

5548. Podol, Peter L. "Dimensions of Violence in the Theater of Sam Shepard: *True West* and *Fool for Love.*" *Essays in Theatre* 7 (May 1989): 149–58.

5549. Procter, Elizabeth Clifton. "The Art of Sam Shepard." Doctoral dissertation, University of North Carolina, Chapel Hill, 1985.

5550. Shewey, Don. *Sam Shepard.* New York: Dell, 1985.

5551. Siegel, Mark. "Holy Ghosts: The Mythic Cowboy in the Plays of Sam Shepard." *Rocky Mountain Review of Language and Literature* 36 (1982): 235–46.

5552. Simard, Rodney. "American Gothic: Sam Shepard's Family Trilogy." *Theatre Annual* 4 (1986): 21–36.

5553. Tucker, Martin. *Sam Shepard.* New York: Continuum, 1992.

5554. Wattenberg, Richard. "'The Frontier Myth' on Stage: From Nineteenth Century to Sam Shepard's *True West.*" *Western American Literature* 24 (November 1989): 225–41.

5555. Wetzsteon, Ross. "Sam Shepard: Escape Artist." *Partisan Review* 49 (1982): 253–61.

GORDON D. SHIRREFFS

5556. Cox, Carole Shirreffs. "Gordon D. Shirreffs: An Interview with a Western Writer." *English Journal* 75 (April 1986): 40–48.

LUKE SHORT

See Frederick Glidden

FORREST SHREVE

5557. Bowers, Janice Emily. *A Sense of Place: The Life and Work of Forrest Shreve.* Tucson: University of Arizona Press, 1988.

LESLIE MARMON SILKO

5558. Allen, Paula Gunn. "Special Problems in Teaching Silko's *Ceremony.*" *American Indian Quarterly* 14 (Fall 1990): 379–86.

5559. Benediktsson, Thomas E. "The Reawakening of the Gods: Realism and the Supernatural in Silko and Hulme." *Critique* 33 (Winter 1992): 121–31.

5560. Blicksilver, Edith. "Traditionalism vs. Modernity: Leslie Silko on American Indian Women." *Southwest Review* 64 (Spring 1979): 149–60.

5561. Brown, Patricia Claire. "The Spiderweb: A Time Structure in Leslie Silko's *Ceremony.*" Doctoral dissertation, East Texas State University, 1986.

5562. Copeland, Marion W. "*Black Elk Speaks* and Leslie Silko's *Ceremony*: Two Visions of Horses." *Critique* 24 (Spring 1983): 158–72.

5563. Crow, Stephen Monroe. "The Works of Leslie Marmon Silko and Teaching Contemporary Native American Literature." Doctoral dissertation, University of Michigan, 1986.

5564. Ekra, Soumalay Marie-Olga. "Native American Religion in the Work of Leslie Marmon Silko." Doctoral dissertation, Indiana University, 1988.

5565. Evers, Lawrence J., and Dennis W. Carr, eds. "A Conversation with Leslie Marmon Silko." *Sun Tracks* 3 (Fall 1976): 28–33.

5566. Graulich, Melody, ed. *"Yellow Woman": Leslie Marmon Silko*. New Brunswick, N.J.: Rutgers University Press, 1993.

5567. Hirsch, Bernard A. "'The Telling Which Continues': Oral Tradition and the Written Word in Leslie Marmon Silko's *Storyteller*." *American Indian Quarterly* 12 (Winter 1988): 1–26.

5568. Hobbs, Michael. "Living In-Between: Tayo as Radical Reader in Leslie Marmon Silko's *Ceremony*." *Western American Literature* 28 (Winter 1994): 301–12.

5569. Hoilman, Dennis R. "'A World Made of Stories': An Interpretation of Leslie Silko's *Ceremony*." *South Dakota Review* 17 (Winter 1979–80): 54–66.

5570. Krumholz, Linda Joan. "Ritual, Reader, and Narrative in the Works of Leslie Marmon Silko and Toni Morrison." Doctoral dissertation, University of Wisconsin, Madison, 1991.

5571. Larson, Charles R. *American Indian Fiction*. Albuquerque: University of New Mexico Press, 1978, 150–61.

5572. Ruoff, A. LaVonne. "Ritual and Renewal: Keres Traditions in the Short Fiction of Leslie Silko." *MELUS* 5 (Winter 1978): 2–17.

5573. Ruppert, James. "Dialogism and Mediation in Leslie Silko's *Ceremony*." *Explicator* 51 (Winter 1993): 129–34.

5574. ———. "The Reader's Lessons in *Ceremony*." *Arizona Quarterly* 44 (Spring 1988): 78–85.

5575. ———. "Story Telling: The Fiction of Leslie Silko." *Journal of Ethnic Studies* 9 (Spring 1981): 53–58.

5576. St. Andrews, B. A. "Healing the Witchery in Silko's *Ceremony*." *Arizona Quarterly* 44 (Spring 1988): 86–94.

5577. Sands, Kathleen M., ed. "A Special Symposium Issue on Leslie Marmon Silko's *Ceremony*." *American Indian Quarterly* 5 (February 1979): 1–75.

5578. Schein, Marie. "Identity in Leslie Marmon Silko's *Ceremony* and N. Scott Momaday's *The Ancient Child*." *Southwestern American Literature* 18 (Spring 1993): 19–25.

5579. Seyersted, Per. *Leslie Marmon Silko*. Western Writers Series, No. 45. Boise, Idaho: Boise State University, 1980.

5580. Slowik, Mary. "Henry James Meets Spider Woman: A Study of Narrative Form in Leslie Silko's *Ceremony*." *North Dakota Quarterly* 57 (Spring 1989): 104–20.

5581. Truesdale, C. W. "Tradition and *Ceremony*: Leslie Marmon Silko as an American Novelist." *North Dakota Quarterly* 59 (Fall 1991): 200–228.

5582. Wright, Anne, ed. *The Delicacy and Strength of Lace: Letters between Leslie Marmon Silko and James Wright.* Saint Paul, Minn.: Graywolf Press, 1986.

UPTON SINCLAIR

5583. Bloodworth, William A., Jr. *Upton Sinclair.* Boston: Twayne, 1977.

5584. Blumenthal. W. A. "Prolific: Writer's Cramp versus Literary Fecundity." *American Book Collector* 8 (May 1958): 3–10.

5585. Buitenhuis, Peter. "Upton Sinclair and the Socialist Response to World War I." *Canadian Review of American Studies* 14 (Summer 1983): 121–30.

5586. Gottesman, Ronald. *Upton Sinclair: An Annotated Checklist.* Kent, Ohio: Kent State University Press, 1973.

5587. ———, and Charles L. P. Silet. *The Literary Manuscripts of Upton Sinclair.* Columbus: Ohio State University Press, 1972.

5588. Graham, John. "Upton Sinclair and the Ludlow Massacre." *Colorado Quarterly* 21 (Summer 1972): 55–67.

5589. Harris, Leon. *Upton Sinclair: American Rebel.* New York: Thomas Y. Crowell, 1975.

5590. Herms, Dieter, ed. *Upton Sinclair: Literature and Social Reform.* New York: Peter Lang, 1990.

5591. Hicks, Granville. "The Survival of Upton Sinclair." *College English* 4 (January 1943): 213–20.

5592. Koerner, J. D. "The Last of the Muckrake Men." *South Atlantic Quarterly* 55 (April 1956): 221–32.

5593. Mitchell, Greg. *The Campaign of the Century: Upton Sinclair's E.P.I.C. Race for Governor of California and the Birth of Media Politics.* New York: Random House, 1992.

5594. Mookerjee, R. N. *Art for Social Justice: The Major Novels of Upton Sinclair.* Metuchen, N.J.: Scarecrow Press, 1988.

5595. Remley, David. "The Correspondence of H. L. Mencken and Upton Sinclair: 'An Illustration of How Not to Agree.'" Doctoral dissertation, Indiana University, 1967.

5596. Silet, Charles L. P. "The Upton Sinclair Archives." *Southern California Quarterly* 4 (Winter 1974): 407–14.

5597. ———, ed. "Upton Sinclair to Jack London: A Literary Friendship." *Jack London Newsletter* 5 (May–August 1972): 49–76.

5598. Soderbergh, Peter A. "Upton Sinclair and Hollywood." *Midwest Quarterly* 11 (January 1970): 173–91.

5599. Whittemore, Reed. *Six Literary Lives: The Shared Impiety of Adams, London, Sinclair, Williams, Dos Passos, and Tate.* Columbia: University of Missouri Press, 1993.

5600. Yoder, Jon. "Decades of Decay: Upton Sinclair and American Liberalism After World War II." Doctoral dissertation, University of New Mexico, 1970.

5601. ———. *Upton Sinclair.* New York: Ungar, 1975.

CHARLES A. SIRINGO

5602. Hammond, John Hays. "Strong Men of the West." *Scribner's Magazine* 77 (February, March 1925): 115–25, 246–56.

5603. Peavy, Charles D. *Charles A. Siringo: A Texas Picaro.* Southwest Writers Series, No. 3. Austin, Tex.: Steck-Vaughn, 1967.

5604. Pingenot, Ben E. *Siringo.* College Station: Texas A & M University Press, 1989.

5605. Sawey, Orlan. *Charlie Siringo.* Boston: Twayne, 1981.

AGNES SMEDLEY

5606. MacKinnon, Janice R., and Stephen R. MacKinnon. *Agnes Smedley, the Life and Times of an American Radical.* Berkeley: University of California Press, 1988.

5607. Nichols, Kathleen L. "The Western Roots of Feminism in Agnes Smedley's *Daughter of Earth.*" *Women and Western American Literature.* Eds. Helen Winter Stauffer and Susan J. Rosowski. Troy, N.Y.: Whitston, 1982, 114–23.

HENRY NASH SMITH

5608. Bridgman, Richard. "The American Studies of Henry Nash Smith." *American Scholar* 56 (Spring 1987): 259–68.

5609. Kuklick, Bruce. "Myth and Symbol in American Studies." *American Quarterly* 24 (October 1972): 435–50.

5610. Marks, Barry. "The Concept of Myth in *Virgin Land.*" *American Quarterly* 5 (Spring 1953): 71–76.

5611. Mitchell, Lee Clark. "Henry Nash Smith's Myth of the West." *Writing Western History: Essays on Major Western Historians.* Ed. Richard W. Etulain. Albuquerque: University of New Mexico Press, 1991, 247–75.

5612. Smith, Henry Nash. "Symbol and Idea in *Virgin Land.*" *Ideology and Classic American Literature.* Eds. Sacvan Bercovitch and Myra Jehlen. Cambridge: Cambridge University Press, 1986, 21–35.

5613. Voloshin, Beverly R., ed. *American Literature, Culture, and Ideology: Essays in Memory of Henry Nash Smith.* New York: Peter Lang, 1990. Includes Henry F. May, "The Rough Road to Virgin Land," 1–23, and a selected list of Smith's publications.

JEDEDIAH SMITH

5614. Morgan, Dale. *Jedediah Smith and the Opening of the West.* Indianapolis: Bobbs-Merrill, 1953; Lincoln: University of Nebraska Press, 1964.

5615. Walker, Don D. "The Western Explorer as a Literary Hero: Jedediah Smith and Ludwig Leichhardt." *Western Humanities Review* 29 (Summer 1975): 243–59.

GARY SNYDER

5616. Almon, Bert. *Gary Snyder.* Western Writers Series, No. 37. Boise, Idaho: Boise State University, 1979.

5617. ———. "The Imagination of Gary Snyder." Doctoral dissertation, University of New Mexico, 1971.

5618. Altieri, Charles. "Gary Snyder's Lyric Poetry: Dialectic as Ecology." *Far Point* 4 (Spring–Summer 1970): 55–65.

5619. ———. "Gary Snyder's *Turtle Island*: The Problem of Reconciling the Roles of Seer and Prophet." *Boundary* 24 (Spring 1976): 761–77.

5620. Bartlett, Lee. "Gary Snyder's Han-shan." *Sagetrieb* 2 (Spring 1983): 105–10.

5621. ———. "Gary Snyder's *Myth Texts* and the Monomyth." *Western American Literature* 17 (Summer 1982): 137–48.

5622. ———. "Interview: Gary Snyder." *California Quarterly* 9 (Spring 1975): 43–50.

5623. Bly, Robert. "The Work of Gary Snyder." *The Sixties* 6 (Spring 1962): 25–42.

5624. Carpenter, David A. "Gary Snyder's Inhumanism, from *Riprap* to *Axe Handles.*" *South Dakota Review* 26 (Spring 1988): 110–38.

5625. Dean, Tim. *Gary Snyder and the American Unconscious: Inhabiting the Ground.* New York: St. Martin's Press, 1991.

5626. Faas, Ekbert. *Towards a New American Poetics: Essays and Interviews.* Santa Barbara, Calif.: Black Sparrow Press, 1978, 87–142.

5627. Folsom, L. Edwin. "Gary Snyder's Descent to Turtle Island: Searching for Fossil Love." *Western American Literature* 15 (Summer 1980): 103–21.

5628. Geneson, Paul. "An Interview with Gary Snyder." *Ohio Review* 18 (Fall 1977): 67–105.

5629. Gitzen, Julian. "Gary Snyder and the Poetry of Compassion." *Critical Quarterly* 15 (Winter 1973): 341–57.

5630. Hunt, Anthony. "'Bubbs Creek Haircut': Gary Snyder's 'Great Departure' in *Mountains and Rivers Without End.*" *Western American Literature* 15 (Fall 1980): 163–75.

5631. Jungels, William J. "The Use of Native-American Mythologies in the Poetry of Gary Snyder." Doctoral dissertation, State University of New York, Buffalo, 1973.

5632. Kern, Robert. "Clearing the Ground: Gary Snyder and the Modernist Imperative." *Criticism* 19 (Spring 1977): 158–77.

5633. ———. "Recipes, Catalogues, Open Form Poetics: Gary Snyder's Archetypal Voice." *Contemporary Literature* 18 (Spring 1977): 173–97.

5634. Kraus, James W. "Gary Snyder's Biopoetics: A Study of the Poet As Ecologist." Doctoral dissertation, University of Hawaii, 1986.

5635. Lavazzi, Tom. "Pattern of Flux: The 'Torsion Form' in Gary Snyder's Poetry." *American Poetry Review* 18 (July–August 1989): 41–47.

5636. Leach, Thomas James, Jr. "Gary Snyder: Poet as Mythographer." Doctoral dissertation, University of North Carolina, Chapel Hill, 1974.

5637. Lin, Jyan-lung. "Gary Snyder's Poetry: A Study of the Formation and Transformation of His Enlightened Vision." Doctoral dissertation, Michigan State University, 1992.

5638. Lyon, Thomas J. "The Ecological Vision of Gary Snyder." *Kansas Quarterly* 2 (Spring 1970): 117–24.

5639. ———. "Gary Snyder, a Western Poet." *Western American Literature* 3 (Fall 1968): 207–16.

5640. McNeil, Katherine, comp. *Gary Snyder: A Bibliography.* New York: Phoenix Book Shop, 1983.

5641. Martin, Julia. "The Pattern Which Connects: Metaphor in Gary Snyder's Later Poetry." *Western American Literature* 22 (Summer 1987): 99–123.

5642. ———. "Practising Emptiness: Gary Snyder's Playful Ecological Work." *Western American Literature* 27 (May 1992): 3–19.

5643. Molesworth, Charles. *Gary Snyder's Vision: Poetry and the Real Work.* Columbia: University of Missouri Press, 1983.

5644. Murphy, Patrick D. "Beyond Humanism: Mythic Fantasy and Inhumanist Philosophy in the Long Poems of Robinson Jeffers and Gary Snyder." *American Studies* 30 (Spring 1989): 53–71.

5645. ———. "Two Different Paths in the Quest for Place: Gary Snyder and Wendell Berry." *American Poetry* 2 (Fall 1984): 60–68.

5646. ———. *Understanding Gary Snyder.* Columbia: University of South Carolina Press, 1992.

5647. ———, ed. *Critical Essays on Gary Snyder.* Boston: G.K. Hall, 1990.

5648. Nelson, Rudolph L. "'Riprap on the Slick Rock of Metaphysics': Religious Dimensions in the Poetry of Gary Snyder." *Soundings* 57 (Summer 1974): 206–21.

5649. Norton, Jody. "The Importance of Nothing: Absence and Its Origins in the Poetry of Gary Snyder." *Contemporary Literature* 28 (Spring 1987): 41–66.

5650. Okada, Roy. "Zen and the Poetry of Gary Snyder." Doctoral dissertation, University of Wisconsin, 1973.

5651. Parkinson, Thomas. "The Poetry of Gary Snyder." *Sagetrieb* 3 (Spring 1984): 49–61.

5652. ———. "The Poetry of Gary Snyder." *Southern Review* 4 (Summer 1968): 616–32.

5653. ———. "The Theory and Practice of Gary Snyder." *Journal of Modern Literature* 2 (1971–72): 448–52.

5654. Paul, Sherman. "From Lookout to Ashram: The Way of Gary Snyder." *Repossessing and Renewing: Essays in the Green American Tradition.* Baton Rouge: Louisiana State University Press, 1976, 195–235.

5655. ———. *In Search of the Primitive: Rereading David Antin, Jerome Rothenberg, and Gary Snyder.* Baton Rouge: Louisiana State University Press, 1986.

5656. Pickett, Rebecca A. "Gary Snyder and the Mythological Present." Doctoral dissertation, University of Nebraska, Lincoln, 1981.

5657. Quigley, Peter S. "The Ground of Resistance: Nature and Power in Emerson, Melville, Jeffers, and Snyder." Doctoral dissertation, Indiana University of Pennsylvania, 1990.

5658. Robertson, David. "Gary Snyder Riprapping in Yosemite, 1955." *American Poetry* 2 (Fall 1984): 52–59.

5659. ———. "Real Matter, Spiritual Mountain: Gary Snyder and Jack Kerouac on Mt. Tamalpais." *Western American Literature* 27 (November 1992): 209–26.

5660. Rothberg, Abraham. "A Passage to More Than India: The Poetry of Gary Snyder." *Southwest Review* 61 (Winter 1976): 26–38.

5661. Schuler, Robert Jordan. "Journeys Toward the Original Mind: The Longer Poems of Gary Snyder." Doctoral dissertation, University of Minnesota, 1989.

5662. Schultz, Robert, and David Wyatt. "Gary Snyder and the Curve of Return." *Virginia Quarterly Review* 62 (Autumn 1986): 681–94.

5663. Steuding, Bob. *Gary Snyder.* Boston: Twayne, 1976.

5664. Weisner, Kenneth Robert. "Gary Snyder's 'Myths Texts' and the Poetry of Constituency." Doctoral dissertation, University of California, Santa Cruz, 1992.

5665. Williamson, Alan. "Gary Snyder, An Appreciation." *New Republic* 173 (November 1, 1975): 11–21.

5666. Windham, Steve. "Unity and Power of Imagination in Gary Snyder's 'The Elwha River.'" *Western American Literature* 14 (Winter 1980): 317–19.

5667. Yamazato, Katsunori. "Seeking a Fulcrum: Gary Snyder and Japan (1956–1975)." Doctoral dissertation, University of California, Davis, 1987.

C. L. SONNICHSEN

5668. Roach, Joyce Gibson. *C. L. Sonnichsen.* Western Writers Series, No. 40. Boise, Idaho: Boise State University, 1979.

5669. Walker, Dale. *C. L. Sonnichsen, Grassroots Historian.* El Paso: Texas Western Press, 1972.

VIRGINIA SORENSEN

5670. Bradford, Mary L. "Virginia Sorensen: A Saving Remnant." *Dialogue* 4 (Autumn 1969): 56–64.

5671. Lee, L. L., and Sylvia B. Lee. *Virginia Sorensen.* Western Writers Series, No. 31. Boise, Idaho: Boise State University, 1978.

5672. Lee, Sylvia B. "The Mormon Novel: Virginia Sorensen's *The Evening and the Morning.*" *Women, Women Writers, and the West.* Eds. Lawrence L. Lee and Merrill E. Lewis. Troy, N.Y.: Whitston, 1978.

JACK SPICER

5673. Chamberlain, Lori. "Ghostwriting the Text: Translation and the Poetics of Jack Spicer." *Contemporary Literature* 26 (Winter 1985): 426–42.

5674. Foster, Edward Halsey. *Jack Spicer.* Western Writers Series, No. 97. Boise, Idaho: Boise State University, 1991.

5675. "Jack Spicer." *Boundary* 6 (1977). Special issue.

5676. Sadler, Frank. "The Frontier in Jack Spicer's 'Billy the Kid.'" *The Westering Experience in American Literature: Bicentennial Essays.* Eds. Merrill Lewis and L. L. Lee. Bellingham: Bureau for Faculty Research, Western Washington University, 1977, 154–60.

JEAN STAFFORD

5677. Avila, Wanda Ellen. "The Ironic Fiction of Jean Stafford." Doctoral dissertation, University of Maryland, 1980.

5678. ———. *Jean Stafford: A Comprehensive Bibliography.* New York: Garland, 1983.

5679. Burns, Stuart L. "Counterpoint in Jean Stafford's *The Mountain Lion.*" *Critique* 9 (No. 2, 1967): 20–32.

5680. Flagg, Nancy. "People to Stay." *Shenandoah* 30 (No. 3, 1979): 65–76.

5681. Goodman, Charlotte Margolis. *Jean Stafford: The Savage Heart.* Austin: University of Texas Press, 1990.

5682. Hassan, Ihab H. "Jean Stafford: The Expense of Style and the Scope of Sensibility." *Western Review* 19 (Spring 1955): 185–203.

5683. Hulbert, Ann. *The Interior Castle: The Art and Life of Jean Stafford.* New York: Alfred A. Knopf, 1992.

5684. Jensen, Sid. "The Noble Wicked West of Jean Stafford." *Western American Literature* 7 (Winter 1973): 261–70.

5685. Leary, William G. "Checkmate: Jean Stafford's 'A Slight Maneuver.'" *Western American Literature* 21 (August 1986): 99–109.

5686. ———. "Grafting onto Her Roots: Jean Stafford's 'Woden's Day.'" *Western American Literature* 23 (August 1988): 129–39.

5687. ———. "Jean Stafford: The Wound and the Bow." *Sewanee Review* 98 (Summer 1990): 333–49.

5688. ———. "Native Daughter: Jean Stafford's California." *Western American Literature* 21 (November 1986): 195–205.

5689. Oates, Joyce Carol. "The Interior Castle: The Art of Jean Stafford's Short Fiction." *Shenandoah* 30 (No. 3, 1979): 61–64.

5690. Roberts, David. *Jean Stafford: A Biography.* Boston: Little, Brown, 1988.

5691. Ryan, Maureen. *Innocence and Estrangement in the Fiction of Jean Stafford.* Baton Rouge: Louisiana State University Press, 1987.

5692. Sheed, Wilfred. "Miss Jean Stafford." *Shenandoah* 30 (No. 3, 1979): 92–99.

5693. Straus, Dorothea. "Jean Stafford." *Shenandoah* 30 (No. 3, 1979): 85–91.

5694. Taylor, Peter. "A Commemorative Tribute to Jean Stafford...." *Shenandoah* 30 (No. 3, 1979): 56–60.

5695. Vickery, Olga W. "The Novels of Jean Stafford." *Critique* 5 (Spring–Summer 1962): 14–26.

5696. Walsh, Mary Ellen Williams. *Jean Stafford.* Boston: Twayne, 1985.

5697. ———. "The Young Girl in the West: Disenchantment in Jean Stafford's Short Fiction." *Women and Western American Literature.* Eds. Helen Winter Stauffer and Susan J. Rosowski. Troy, N.Y.: Whitston, 1982, 230–43.

5698. White, Barbara A. *Growing Up Female: Adolescent Girlhood in American Fiction.* Westport, Conn.: Greenwood Press, 1985.

5699. Wilson, Mary Ann. "In Another Country: Jean Stafford's Literary Apprenticeship in Baton Rouge." *Southern Review* 29 (Winter 1993): 58–66.

WILLIAM STAFFORD

5700. Carpenter, David A. *William Stafford.* Western Writers Series, No. 72. Boise, Idaho: Boise State University, 1986.

5701. "A Conversation between William Stafford and Primus St. John." *Voyages* 3 (Spring 1970): 70–79.

5702. Dickinson-Brown, Roger. "The Wise, the Dull, the Bewildered: What Happens in William Stafford." *Modern Poetry Studies* 6 (Spring 1975): 30–38.

5703. Ellsworth, Peter. "A Conversation with William Stafford." *Chicago Review* 30 (Summer 1978): 94–100.

5704. Gerber, Philip L., and Robert J. Gemmett, eds. "Keeping the Lines Wet: A Conversation with William Stafford." *Prairie Schooner* 44 (Summer 1970): 123–36.

5705. Gitzen, Julian. "The Listener: William Stafford." *Modern Poetry Studies* 11 (1983): 274–86.

5706. Greiner, Charles F. "Stafford's 'Traveling Through the Dark': A Discussion of Style." *English Journal* 55 (November 1966): 1015–18.

5707. Heyen, William. "William Stafford's Allegiances." *Modern Poetry Studies* 1 (No. 6, 1970): 307–18.

5708. Holden, Jonathan. *The Mark to Turn: A Reading of William Stafford's Poetry.* Lawrence: University Press of Kansas, 1976.

5709. Hugo, Richard. "Problems with Landscapes in Early Stafford Poems." *Kansas Quarterly* 2 (Spring 1970): 33–38.

5710. ———, and William Stafford. "The Third Time the World Happens: A Dialogue in Writing." *Northwest Review* 13 (March 1973): 26–47.

5711. Kitchen, Judith. *Understanding William Stafford.* Columbia: University of South Carolina Press, 1989.

5712. Kramer, Lawrence. "In Quiet Language." *Parnassus* 6 (Spring–Summer 1978): 101–17.

5713. Kyle, Carol. "Point of View in 'Returned to Say' and the Wilderness of William Stafford." *Western American Literature* 7 (Fall 1972): 191–201.

5714. Lauber, John. "World's Guest – William Stafford." *Iowa Review* 5 (Spring 1974): 88–101.

5715. Leavens, Norman Dennis. "Herald and Oracle: The Poetics of William Stafford." Doctoral dissertation, University of Notre Dame, 1983.

5716. Lensing, George S. "William Stafford: Mythmaker." *Modern Poetry Studies* 6 (Spring 1975): 1–18.

5717. Lofsness, Cynthia. "An Interview with William Stafford." *Iowa Review* 3 (Summer 1972): 92–107.

5718. Lynch, Dennis Daley. "Journeys in Search of Oneself: The Metaphor of the Road in William Stafford's *Traveling Through the Dark* and *The Rescued Year.*" *Modern Poetry Studies* 7 (Autumn 1976): 122–31.

5719. Marshall, Gary Thomas. "William Stafford: A Writer Writing." Doctoral dissertation, Southern Illinois University, Carbondale, 1990.

5720. Moran, Ronald, and George Lensing. "The Emotive Imagination: A New Departure in American Poetry." *Southern Review* 3 (January 1967): 51–67.

5721. Mukerji, Malovika. "The Forgiving Landscape: The Poetry of William Stafford." Doctoral dissertation, Louisiana State University Agricultural Mechanical College, 1981.

5722. Nordström, Lars. "Willingly Local: A Conversation with William Stafford about Regionalism and Northwest Poetry." *Studia Neophilolgica* 59 (No. 1, 1987): 41–57.

5723. *Northwest Review* 13 (No. 3, 1973): 1–92. Special issue on William Stafford.

5724. Pinsker, Sanford. *Three Pacific Northwest Poets: William Stafford, Richard Hugo, and David Wagoner.* Boston: Twayne, 1987.

5725. Roberts, J. Russell, Sr. "Listening to the Wilderness with William Stafford." *Western American Literature* 3 (Fall 1968): 217–26.

5726. Stafford, William E. "A Poet Responds." *Oregon Historical Quarterly* 81 (Summer 1980): 172–79.

5727. Stewart, David, and Michael Smetzer. "Interview with William Stafford." *Cottonwood Review* (Fall 1975): 21–34.

5728. Sumner, D. Nathan. "The Poetry of William Stafford." *Research Studies* 36 (September 1968): 187–95.

5729. Tammaro, Thomas Michael. "To Love What is Near: Self, Language and the World in the Poetry of William Stafford." Doctoral dissertation, Ball State University, 1980.

5730. Wagner, Linda W. "William Stafford's Plain-Style." *Modern Poetry Studies* 6 (Spring 1975): 19–30.

5731. Weatherhead, A. K. "William Stafford's Recent Poetry." *Concerning Poetry* 16 (1983): 71–78.

PATIENCE STAPLETON

5732. Dalton, Joann. "Patience Stapleton: A Forgotten Frontier Writer." *Colorado Magazine* 53 (Summer 1976): 261–76.

WILBUR DANIEL STEELE

5733. Bucco, Martin. *Wilbur Daniel Steele.* New York: Twayne, 1972.

WALLACE STEGNER

5734. Ahearn, Kerry. "*The Big Rock Candy Mountain* and *Angle of Repose*: Trial and Culmination." *Western American Literature* 10 (May 1975): 11–27.

5735. ———. "Heroes vs. Women: Conflict and Duplicity in Stegner." *Women, Women Writers, and the West.* Eds. Lawrence L. Lee and Merrill E. Lewis. Troy, N.Y.: Whitston, 1978.

5736. ———. "Stegner's Short Fiction." *South Dakota Review* 23 (Winter 1985): 70–86.

5737. ———. "Wallace Stegner and John Wesley Powell: The Real – and Maimed – Western Spokesman." *South Dakota Review* 15 (Winter 1977–78): 33–43.

5738. Arthur, Anthony, ed. *Critical Essays on Wallace Stegner.* Boston: G.K. Hall, 1982.

5739. Benson, Jackson J. "'Eastering': Wallace Stegner's Love Affair with Vermont in *Crossing to Safety.*" *Western American Literature* 25 (May 1990): 27–33.

5740. ———. "Finding a Voice of His Own: The Story of Wallace Stegner's Fiction." *Western American Literature* 29 (August 1994): 99–122.

5741. ———. "Wallace Stegner and the Battle against Rugged Individualism." *North Dakota Quarterly* 61 (Spring 1993): 5–18.

5742. Berry, Wendell. "Wallace Stegner and the Great Community." *South Dakota Review* 23 (Winter 1985): 10–18.

5743. Burrows, James Russell. "The Pastoral Convention in the California Novels of Wallace Stegner." Doctoral dissertation, Bowling Green State University, 1987.

5744. ———. "Wallace Stegner's Version of Pastoral." *Western American Literature* 25 (May 1990): 15–25.

5745. Canzoneri, Robert. "Wallace Stegner: Trial by Existence." *Southern Review* 9 (Autumn 1973): 796–827.

5746. Clayton, James L. "From Pioneers to Provincials: Mormonism as Seen by Wallace Stegner." *Dialogue* 1 (Winter 1966): 105–14.

5747. Colberg, Nancy. *Wallace Stegner: A Descriptive Bibliography.* Lewiston, Idaho: Confluence Press, 1990.

5748. Cracroft, Richard H. "'A Profound Sense of Community': Mormon Values in Wallace Stegner's *Recapitulation.*" *Dialogue* 24 (Spring 1991): 101–13.

5749. Dillon, David. "Time's Prisoners: An Interview with Wallace Stegner." *Southwest Review* 61 (Summer 1976): 252–67.

5750. Eisinger, Chester E. *Fiction of the Forties.* Chicago: University of Chicago Press, 1963, 324–28.

5751. "Essays on the West: Tribute to Wallace Stegner." *Montana: The Magazine of Western History* 43 (Autumn 1993): 52–76. Collection of eight brief essays.

5752. Etulain, Richard W. "Western Fiction and History: A Reconsideration." *The American West: New Perspectives, New Dimensions.* Ed. Jerome O. Steffen. Norman: University of Oklahoma Press, 1979, 152–74.

5753. Ferguson, Suzanne. "History, Fiction and Propaganda: The Man of Letters and the American West: An Interview with Wallace Stegner." *Literature and the Visual Arts in Contemporary Society.* Eds. Suzanne Ferguson and Barbara Groseclose. Columbus: Ohio State University Press, 1985, 3–22.

5754. Flora, Joseph M. "Stegner and Hemingway as Short Story Writers: Some Parallels and Contrasts in Two Masters." *South Dakota Review* 30 (Spring 1992): 104–19.

5755. ———. "Vardis Fisher and Wallace Stegner: Teacher and Student." *Western American Literature* 5 (Summer 1970): 122–28.

5756. Graulich, Melody. "The Guides to Conduct that a Tradition Offers: Wallace Stegner's *Angle of Repose*." *South Dakota Review* 23 (Winter 1985): 87–106.

5757. Hairston, Joe B. "Wallace Stegner and the Great Community." *South Dakota Review* 12 (Winter 1974–75): 31–42.

5758. ———. "The Westerner's Dilemma." Doctoral dissertation, University of Minnesota, 1971.

5759. Hepworth, James R. "The Art of Fiction CXVIII: Wallace Stegner." *Paris Review* 115 (Summer 1990): 58–90.

5760. Hofheins, Roger, and Dan Tooker. "Interview with Wallace Stegner." *Southern Review* 11 (Autumn 1975): 794–801.

5761. Hudson, Lois Phillips. "*The Big Rock Candy Mountain*: No Roots and No Frontier." *South Dakota Review* 9 (Spring 1971): 3–13.

5762. "Interview [with] Wallace Stegner." *Great Lakes Review* 2 (Summer 1975): 1–25.

5763. Jensen, Sid [Sidney LaMarr]. "The Compassionate Seer: Wallace Stegner's Literary Artist." *BYU Studies* 14 (Winter 1974): 248–62.

5764. ———. "The Middle Ground: A Study of Wallace Stegner's Use of History in Fiction." Doctoral dissertation, University of Utah, 1972.

5765. Lewis, Merrill. *The Works of Wallace Stegner*. Cassette. Deland, Fla.: Everett/Edwards, 1974.

5766. ——— and Lorene Lewis. *Wallace Stegner*. Western Writers Series, No. 4. Boise, Idaho: Boise State College, 1972.

5767. Maguire, James H. "Stegner vs. Brautigan; Recapitulation or Deconstruction?" *Pacific Northwest Forum* 11 (Spring 1986): 23–28.

5768. Mason, Kenneth C. "*The Big Rock Candy Mountain*: The Consequences of a Delusory American Dream." *Great Plains Quarterly* 6 (Winter 1986): 34–43.

5769. Milton, John. "Conversation with Wallace Stegner." *South Dakota Review* 10 (Spring 1971): 45–57; 23 (Winter 1985): 107–18.

5770. Olsen, Brett J. "Wallace Stegner and the Environmental Ethic: Environmentalism as a Rejection of Western Myth." *Western American Literature* 29 (August 1994): 123–42.

5771. Otis, John Whitacre. "The Purified Vision: The Fiction of Wallace Stegner." Doctoral dissertation, Drake University, 1977.

5772. Peterson, Audrey C. "Narrative Voice in Wallace Stegner's *Angle of Repose.*" *Western American Literature* 10 (August 1975): 125–33.

5773. Putnam, Jackson K. "Wallace Stegner and Western History: Some Historiographical Problems in *Angle of Repose.*" *vis-a-vis* 3 (September 1975): 51–60.

5774. Robertson, Jamie. "Henry Adams, Wallace Stegner, and the Search for a Sense of Place in the West." *The Westering Experience in American Literature: Bicentennial Essays.* Eds. Merrill Lewis and L. L. Lee. Bellingham: Bureau for Faculty Research, Western Washington University, 1977, 135–43.

5775. Robinson, Forrest G. "A Usable Heroism: Wallace Stegner's *Beyond the Hundredth Meridian.*" *South Dakota Review* 23 (Winter 1985): 58–69.

5776. ————. "Wallace Stegner's Family Saga: From *The Big Rock Candy Mountain* to *Recapitulation.*" *Western American Literature* 17 (Summer 1982): 101–16.

5777. ————, and Margaret G. Robinson. *Wallace Stegner.* Boston: Twayne, 1977.

5778. ————. "Wallace Stegner: An Interview." *Quarry* 4 (1975): 72–84.

5779. Ronald, Ann. "Stegner and Stewardship." *Writer's Forum* 17 (Fall 1991): 3–16.

5780. Singer, Barnett. "The Historical Ideal in Wallace Stegner's Fiction." *South Dakota Review* 15 (Spring 1977): 28–44.

5781. Socolofsky, Homer E., R. David Edmunds, and Joseph C. Porter. "Western History Association Prize Recipient, 1991: Wallace Stegner." *Western Historical Quarterly* 22 (Spring 1991): 137–41.

5782. Stegner, Wallace, and Richard W. Etulain. *Conversations with Wallace Stegner on Western History and Literature.* Rev ed. Salt Lake City: University of Utah Press, 1990.

5783. Swingrover, Elizabeth Anne. "'The Way Things Are': The Later Novels of Wallace Stegner." Doctoral dissertation, University of Nevada, Reno, 1988.

5784. Topping, Gary. "Wallace Stegner and the Mormons." *South Dakota Review* 23 (Winter 1985): 25–41.

5785. Tyburski, Susan J. "Wallace Stegner's Vision of Wilderness." *Western American Literature* 18 (August 1983): 133–42.

5786. Tyler, Robert L. "The I.W.W. and the West." *American Quarterly* 12 (Summer 1960): 175–87.

5787. Watkins, T. H. "Bearing Witness for the Land: The Conservation Career of Wallace Stegner." *South Dakota Review* 23 (Winter 1985): 42–57.

5788. White, Robin, and Ed McClanahan. "An Interview with Wallace Stegner." *Per Se* 3 (Fall 1968): 28–35.

5789. Willreich, Patricia Rowe. "A Perspective on Wallace Stegner." *Virginia Quarterly Review* 67 (Spring 1991): 240–59.

5790. Zahlan, Anne Ricketson. "Cities of the Living: Disease and the Traveler in *Collected Stories* by Wallace Stegner." *Studies in Short Fiction* 29 (Fall 1992): 509–15.

JOHN STEINBECK

5791. Alexander, Stanley. "*Cannery Row*: Steinbeck's Pastoral Poem." *Western American Literature* 2 (Winter 1968): 281–95.

5792. ———. "The Conflict of Form in *Tortilla Flat*." *American Literature* 40 (March 1968): 58–66.

5793. Allen, Mary. "The Cycle of Death: John Steinbeck." *Animals in American Literature*. Urbana: University of Illinois Press, 1983, 115–34.

5794. Anderson, Arthur Commins. "The Journey Motif in the Fiction of John Steinbeck – The Traveler Discovers Himself." Doctoral dissertation, Fordham University, 1976.

5795. Apthorp, Elaine S. "Steinbeck, Guthrie, and Popular Culture." *San Jose Studies* 16 (Winter 1990): 19–39.

5796. Astro, Richard. "From the Tidepool to the Stars: Steinbeck's Sense of Place." *Steinbeck Quarterly* 10 (Winter 1977): 5–11.

5797. ———. *John Steinbeck and Edward F. Ricketts: The Shaping of a Novelist*. Minneapolis: University of Minnesota Press, 1973.

5798. ———. "John Steinbeck and the Tragic Miracle of Consciousness." *San Jose Studies* 1 (November 1975): 61–72.

5799. ———. "Something That Happened: A Non-Teleological Approach to 'The Leader of the People.'" *Steinbeck Quarterly* 6 (Winter 1973): 19–23.

5800. ———. "Steinbeck's Bittersweet Thursday." *Steinbeck Quarterly* 4 (Spring 1971): 36–48.

5801. ———. "Travels With Steinbeck: The Laws of Thought and the Laws of Things." *Steinbeck Quarterly* 8 (Spring 1975): 35–44.

5802. ———, and Tetsumaro Hayashi, eds. *Steinbeck: The Man and His Work*. Corvallis: Oregon State University Press, 1971.

5803. Autrey, Max L. "Men, Mice, and Moths: Gradation in Steinbeck's 'The Leader of the People.'" *Western American Literature* 10 (November 1975): 195–204.

5804. Benson, Jackson J. "Hemingway the Hunter and Steinbeck the Farmer." *Michigan Quarterly Review* 24 (Summer 1985): 441–60.

5805. ———. "John Steinbeck: Novelist as Scientist." *Novel: A Forum on Fiction* 10 (Spring 1977): 248–64.

5806. ———. "John Steinbeck's *Cannery Row*: A Reconsideration." *Western American Literature* 12 (May 1977): 11–40.

5807. ———. *Looking for Steinbeck's Ghost*. Norman: University of Oklahoma Press, 1988.

5808. ———. "Steinbeck – A Defense of Biographical Criticism." *College Literature* 16 (Spring 1989): 107–16.

5809. ———. "Through a Political Glass, Darkly: The Example of John Steinbeck." *Studies in American Fiction* 12 (Spring 1984): 45–59.

5810. ———. "'To Tom, Who Lived It': John Steinbeck and the Man from Weedpatch." *Journal of Modern Literature* 5 (April 1976): 151–94. See also "An Afterword and An Introduction," 194–210.

5811. ———. *The True Adventures of John Steinbeck, Writer: A Biography*. New York: Viking Press, 1984.

5812. ———, ed. *The Short Novels of John Steinbeck: Critical Essays with a Checklist to Steinbeck Criticism*. Durham, N.C.: Duke University Press, 1990.

5813. ———, and Anne Loftis. "John Steinbeck and Farm Labor Unionization: The Background of *In Dubious Battle*." *American Literature* 52 (May 1980): 194–223.

5814. Benton, Robert M. "Realism, Growth, and Contrast in 'The Gift.'" *Steinbeck Quarterly* 6 (Winter 1973): 3–9.

5815. Bloom, Harold, ed. *Modern Critical Views: John Steinbeck*. New York: Chelsea House, 1992.

5816. ———. *Modern Critical Views: John Steinbeck's* Grapes of Wrath. New York: Chelsea House, 1988.

5817. Bowron, Bernard. "*The Grapes of Wrath*: A 'Wagons West' Romance." *Colorado Quarterly* 3 (Summer 1954): 84–91.

5818. Bracher, Frederick. "Steinbeck and the Biological View of Man." *Pacific Spectator* 2 (1948): 14–29.

5819. Brasch, James D. "*The Grapes of Wrath* and Old Testament Skepticism." *San Jose Studies* 3 (1977): 16–27.

5820. Britch, Carroll, and Cliff Lewis. "Shadow of 'The' Indian in the Fiction of John Steinbeck." *MELUS* 11 (Summer 1984): 39–58.

5821. Burns, Stuart L. "The Turtle or the Gopher: Another Look at the Ending of *The Grapes of Wrath*." *Western American Literature* 9 (May 1974): 53–57.

5822. Busch, Christopher Scott. "John Steinbeck and the Frontier West." Doctoral dissertation, University of Notre Dame, 1993.

5823. Carpenter, Frederic I. "The Philosophic Joads." *College English* 2 (December 1941): 315–25.

5824. Carr, Duane Ralph. "John Steinbeck: Twentieth Century Romantic: A Study of the Early Works." Doctoral dissertation, University of Tulsa, 1975.

5825. ———. "Steinbeck's Blakean Vision in *The Grapes of Wrath*." *Steinbeck Quarterly* 8 (Summer–Fall 1975): 67–73.

5826. Chametzky, Jules. "The Ambivalent Endings of *The Grapes of Wrath*." *Modern Fiction Studies* 11 (Spring 1965): 34–44.

5827. Champney, Freeman. "John Steinbeck, Californian." *Antioch Review* 7 (1947): 345–62.

5828. Coers, Donald V. *John Steinbeck as Propagandist: The Moon is Down Goes to War*. Tuscaloosa: University of Alabama Press, 1991.

5829. Cox, Martha Heasley. "The Conclusion of *The Grapes of Wrath*: Steinbeck's Conception and Execution." *San Jose Studies* 1 (November 1975): 73–81.

5830. ———. "In Search of John Steinbeck: His People and His Land." *San Jose Studies* 1 (November 1975): 41–60.

5831. ———. "Remembering John Steinbeck." *San Jose Studies* 1 (November 1975): 109–27.

5832. Crouch, Steve. *Steinbeck Country*. Palo Alto, Calif.: American West, 1973.

5833. Davis, Robert Con, ed. *The Grapes of Wrath: A Collection of Critical Essays*. Englewood Cliffs, N.J.: Prentice–Hall, 1982.

5834. Davis, Robert Murray. "The World of John Steinbeck's Joads." *World Literature Today* 64 (Summer 1990): 401–40.

5835. ———, ed. *Steinbeck: A Collection of Critical Essays*. Englewood Cliffs, N.J.: Prentice-Hall, 1972.

5836. DeMott, Robert. *Steinbeck's Reading: A Catalogue of Books Owned and Borrowed*. New York: Garland, 1984.

5837. ———. "Toward a Redefinition of *To A God Unknown*." *University of Windsor Review* 8 (Spring 1973): 34–53.

5838. ———. "'Working Days and Hours': Steinbeck's Writing of *The Grapes of Wrath*." *Studies in American Fiction* 18 (Spring 1990): 3–15.

5839. ———, ed. *Working Days: The Journals of The Grapes of Wrath, 1938–1941.* New York: Viking, 1989.

5840. Dillman, Mary Alice. "Contexts of Development in John Steinbeck's *The Journals of the Grapes of Wrath* and *Journal of a Novel.*" Doctoral dissertation, Ohio State University, 1992.

5841. Ditsky, John. *Essays on "East of Eden."* Steinbeck Monograph Series, No. 7. Muncie, Ind.: Ball State University, 1977.

5842. ———. "*The Grapes of Wrath*: A Reconsideration." *Southern Humanities Review* 13 (Summer 1979): 215–20.

5843. ———. *John Steinbeck: Life, Work, and Criticism.* Fredericton, Canada: York Press, 1985.

5844. ———. "John Steinbeck – Yesterday, Today, and Tomorrow." *Steinbeck Quarterly* 23 (Winter–Spring 1990): 5–16.

5845. ———. "Music from a Dark Cave: Organic Form in Steinbeck's Fiction." *Journal of Narrative Technique* 1 (January 1971): 59–67.

5846. ———. "Rowing from Eden: Closure in the Later Steinbeck Fiction." *North Dakota Quarterly* 60 (Summer 1992): 87–100.

5847. ———. "'Some Sense of Mission': Steinbeck's *The Short Reign of Pippin IV* Reconsidered." *Steinbeck Quarterly* 16 (Summer–Fall 1983): 73–89.

5848. ———. "Steinbeck's 'Flight': The Ambiguity of Manhood." *Steinbeck Quarterly* 5 (Summer–Fall 1972): 80–85.

5849. ———. "Steinbeck's *Travels with Charley*: The Quest That Failed." *Steinbeck Quarterly* 8 (Spring 1975): 45–50.

5850. ———. "*The Wayward Bus*: Love and Time in America." *San Jose Studies* 1 (November 1975): 89–101.

5851. ———, ed. *Critical Essays on Steinbeck's The Grapes of Wrath.* Boston: G.K. Hall, 1989.

5852. Donohue, Agnes McNeill, ed. *A Casebook on The Grapes of Wrath.* New York: Thomas Y. Crowell, 1968.

5853. Eddy, Darlene. "To Go A-Buccaneering and Take a Spanish Town: Some Seventeenth-Century Aspects of *A Cup of Gold.*" *Steinbeck Quarterly* 8 (Winter 1975): 3–12.

5854. Everest, Beth, and Judy Wedeles. "The Neglected Rib: Women in *East of Eden.*" *Steinbeck Quarterly* 21 (Winter–Spring 1988): 13–23.

5855. Falkenberg, Sandra. "A Study of Female Characterization in Steinbeck's Fiction." *Steinbeck Quarterly* 8 (Spring 1975): 50–56.

5856. Fensch, Thomas. *Steinbeck and Covici: The Story of a Friendship.* Middlebury, Vt.: Paul S. Eriksson, 1979.

5857. ———, ed. *Conversations with John Steinbeck.* Jackson: University Press of Mississippi, 1988.

5858. Fiedler, Leslie. "Looking Back After 50 Years." *San Jose Studies* 16 (Winter 1990): 54–64.

5859. Fontenrose, Joseph. *John Steinbeck: An Introduction and Interpretation.* New York: Barnes and Noble, 1963.

5860. Fossey, W. Richard. "The End of the Western Dream: *The Grapes of Wrath* and Oklahoma." *Cimarron Review* 22 (January 1973): 25–34.

5861. French, Warren G. "The 'California Quality' of Steinbeck's Best Fiction." *San Jose Studies* 1 (November 1975): 9–19.

5862. ———. "'Johnny Bear' – Steinbeck's 'Yellow Peril' Story." *Steinbeck Quarterly* 5 (Summer–Fall 1972): 101–7.

5863. ———. "John Steinbeck." *Fifteen Modern American Authors.* Ed. Jackson R. Bryer. Durham, N.C.: Duke University Press, 1969, 369–87; *Sixteen Modern American Authors.* New York: W. W. Norton, 1973, 499–527; *Sixteen Modern American Authors: Volume 2: A Survey of Research and Criticism.* Durham, N.C.: Duke University Press, 1990, 582–622.

5864. ———. *John Steinbeck.* 2d ed., rev. Boston: Twayne, 1975.

5865. ———. "John Steinbeck, the Model T Ford, and the Theory of the Anglo-Saxon Home." *Kansas Quarterly* 21 (Fall 1989): 7–13.

5866. ———, ed. *A Companion to <u>The Grapes of Wrath</u>.* New York: Penguin, 1989.

5867. Gerstenberger, Donna. "Steinbeck's Waste Land." *Modern Fiction Studies* 11 (Spring 1965): 59–65.

5868. Goldhurst, William. "*Of Mice and Men*: John Steinbeck's Parable of the Curse of Cain." *Western American Literature* 6 (Summer 1971): 123–35.

5869. Goboni, Mark William. "'Symbols for the Wordlessness': A Study of John Steinbeck's *East of Eden.*" Doctoral dissertation, Ohio University, 1978.

5870. Gray, James. *John Steinbeck.* Minneapolis: University of Minnesota Press, 1971.

5871. Griffin, R. J., and W. A. Freedman. "Machines and Animals: Pervasive Motifs in *The Grapes of Wrath.*" *Journal of English and Germanic Philology* 62 (July 1963): 569–80.

5872. Grommon, A. H. "Who Is 'The Leader of the People'?" *English Journal* 48 (November 1959): 449–61.

5873. Gurko, Leo. "*Of Mice and Men*: Steinbeck as Manichean." *University of Windsor Review* 8 (Spring 1973): 11–23.

5874. Harmon, Robert B. *The Grapes of Wrath: A Fifty Year Bibliographic Survey*. San Jose: Steinbeck Research Center, San Jose State University, 1990.

5875. ————. *Steinbeck Bibliographies: An Annotated Guide*. Metuchen, N.J.: Scarecrow Press, 1987.

5876. Hartrangt, Marshall V. *Grapes of Gladness*. Los Angeles: DeVorss, 1939. An "answer" to *Grapes of Wrath*.

5877. Hayashi, Tetsumaro. *John Steinbeck: A Dictionary of His Fictional Characters*. Metuchen, N.J.: Scarecrow Press, 1976.

5878. ————. *John Steinbeck: A Guide to the Doctoral Dissertations (1946–1969)*. Steinbeck Monograph Series, No. 1. Muncie, Ind.: Ball State University, 1971.

5879. ————. *A New Steinbeck Bibliography, 1929–1971*. Metuchen, N.J.: Scarecrow Press, 1973.

5880. ————. *A New Steinbeck Bibliography: Supplement One, 1971–1981*. Metuchen, N.J.: Scarecrow Press, 1983.

5881. ————. *Steinbeck's Women: Essays in Criticism*. Muncie, Ind.: Steinbeck Society of America, 1979.

5882. ————. *A Study Guide to Steinbeck: A Handbook of His Major Works*. Metuchen, N.J.: Scarecrow Press, 1974.

5883. ————. *A Study Guide to Steinbeck (Part II)*. Metuchen, N.J.: Scarecrow Press, 1979. Companion to *A Handbook of His Major Works*.

5884. ————, ed. *John Steinbeck on Writing*. Muncie, Ind.: Steinbeck Research Institute, Ball State University, 1988.

5885. ————, ed. *Steinbeck Quarterly* (1968–). Ball State University, Muncie, Ind.

5886. ————, ed. *Steinbeck's Literary Dimension: A Guide to Comparative Studies*. Metuchen, N.J.: Scarecrow Press, 1991.

5887. ————, ed. *Steinbeck's The Grapes of Wrath: Essays in Criticism*. Muncie, Ind.: Steinbeck Research Institute, Ball State University, 1990.

5888. ————, and Thomas J. Moore, eds. *Steinbeck's Posthumous Work: Essays in Criticism*. Muncie, Ind.: Steinbeck Research Institute, Ball State University, 1989.

5889. ————, eds. *Steinbeck's The Red Pony: Essays in Criticism*. Muncie, Ind.: Steinbeck Research Institute, Ball State University, 1988.

5890. Heavilin, Barbara Anne. "Hospitality, the Joads, and the Stranger Motif: Structural Symmetry in John Steinbeck's *The Grapes of Wrath*." *South Dakota Review* 29 (Summer 1991): 142–52.

5891. Hecker, David Alan. "John Steinbeck: America's Isaiah." Doctoral dissertation, Washington State University, 1983.

5892. Hedgpeth, Joel W. "Genesis of the *Sea of Cortez*." *Steinbeck Quarterly* 6 (Summer 1973): 74–80.

5893. Hopkins, Karen J. "Steinbeck's *East of Eden*: A Defense." *Itinerary: Criticism, Essays on California Writers*. Ed. Charles L. Crow. Bowling Green, Ohio: University Press, 1978, 63–78.

5894. Houghton, Donald E. "'Westering' in 'Leader of the People.'" *Western American Literature* 4 (Summer 1969): 117–24.

5895. Hughes, R. S. *Beyond the Red Pony: A Reader's Companion to Steinbeck's Complete Short Stories*. Metuchen, N.J.: Scarecrow Press, 1987.

5896. ———. *John Steinbeck: A Study of the Short Fiction*. Boston: Twayne, 1989.

5897. "Interview with John Steinbeck." *Paris Review* 63 (Fall 1975): 180–94.

5898. Kiernan, Thomas. *The Intricate Music: A Biography of John Steinbeck*. Boston: Little, Brown, 1979.

5899. Kinney, Arthur F. "The Arthurian Cycle in *Tortilla Flat*." *Modern Fiction Studies* 11 (Spring 1965): 11–20.

5900. Koloc, Frederick Joseph. "John Steinbeck's *In Dubious Battle*: Backgrounds, Reputation, and Artistry." Doctoral dissertation, University of Pittsburgh, 1974.

5901. Krause, Sydney J. "*The Pearl* and 'Hadleyburg': From Desire to Renunciation." *Steinbeck Quarterly* 7 (Winter 1974): 3–18.

5902. Levant, Howard. *The Novels of John Steinbeck: A Critical Study*. Columbia: University of Missouri Press, 1974.

5903. ———. "*Tortilla Flat*: The Shape of John Steinbeck's Career." *PMLA* 85 (October 1970): 1087–95.

5904. Lewis, Cliff, and Carroll Britch, eds. *Rediscovering Steinbeck: Revisionist Views of His Art, Politics, and Intellect*. Lewiston, N.Y.: E. Mellen, 1989.

5905. Lieber, Todd M. "Talismanic Patterns in the Novels of John Steinbeck." *American Literature* 44 (May 1972): 262–75.

5906. Lisca, Peter. "John Steinbeck: A Literary Biography." *Steinbeck and His Critics: A Record of Twenty-five Years*. Eds. E. W. Tedlock, Jr., and C. V. Wicker. Albuquerque: University of New Mexico Press, 1957, 3–22.

5907. ———. *John Steinbeck: Nature and Myth*. New York: Thomas Y. Crowell, 1978.

5908. ———. "Steinbeck and Hemingway: Suggestions for a Comparative Study." *Steinbeck Newsletter* 2 (Spring 1969): 9–17.

5909. ———. "Steinbeck's Image of Man and His Decline as a Writer." *Modern Fiction Studies* 11 (Spring 1965): 3–10.

5910. ———. *The Wide World of John Steinbeck.* New Brunswick, N.J.: Rutgers University Press, 1958.

5911. ———, ed. *John Steinbeck, The Grapes of Wrath: Text and Criticism.* New York: Viking Press, 1972.

5912. ———, et al., eds. "John Steinbeck Special Number." *Modern Fiction Studies* 11 (Spring 1965): 3–103.

5913. Loftis, Anne. "Steinbeck and the Federal Migrant Camps." *San Jose Studies* 16 (Winter 1990): 76–90.

5914. McCarthy, Paul. *John Steinbeck.* New York: Ungar, 1979.

5915. McDaniel, Barbara Albrecht. "Self-Alienating Characters in the Fiction of John Steinbeck." Doctoral dissertation, North Texas State University, 1974.

5916. McMahan, Elizabeth E. "'The Chrysanthemums': Study of a Woman's Sexuality." *Modern Fiction Studies* 14 (Winter 1968–69): 453–58.

5917. McWilliams, Carey. "A Man, A Place, and A Time." *American West* 7 (May 1970): 4–8, 38–40, 62–64.

5918. Mangelsdorf, Tom. *A History of Steinbeck's Cannery Row.* Santa Cruz, Calif.: Western Tanager Press, 1986.

5919. Marcus, Mordecai. "The Lost Dream of Sex and Childbirth in 'The Chrysanthemums.'" *Modern Fiction Studies* 11 (Spring 1965): 54–58.

5920. Marks, Lester Jay. "*East of Eden*: 'Thou Mayest.'" *Steinbeck Quarterly* 4 (Winter 1971): 3–18.

5921. ———. *Thematic Design in the Novels of John Steinbeck.* The Hague: Mouton, 1970.

5922. Marovitz, Sanford E. "The Cryptic Raillery of 'Saint Katy the Virgin.'" *Steinbeck Quarterly* 5 (Summer–Fall 1972): 107–12.

5923. ———. "The Expository Prose of John Steinbeck." *Steinbeck Quarterly* 7 (Spring 1974): 41–53; (Fall 1974): 88–102.

5924. Martin, Bruce K. "'The Leader of the People' Reexamined." *Studies in Short Fiction* 8 (Summer 1971): 423–32.

5925. Martin, Stoddard. *California Writers: Jack London, John Steinbeck, the Tough Guys.* New York: St. Martin's Press, 1983.

5926. May, Charles E. "Myth and Mystery in Steinbeck's 'The Snake': A Jungian View." *Criticism* 15 (Fall 1973): 322–35.

5927. Miller, William V. "Sexual and Spiritual Ambiguity in 'The Chrysanthemums.'" *Steinbeck Quarterly* 5 (Summer–Fall 1972): 68–75.

5928. Millichap, Joseph R. *Steinbeck and Film*. New York: Ungar, 1983.

5929. Mitchell, Marilyn L. "Steinbeck's Strong Women: Feminine Identity in the Short Stories." *Southwest Review* 61 (Summer 1976): 303–15.

5930. Moore, Harry Thornton. *The Novels of John Steinbeck: A First Critical Study*. Chicago: Normandie House, 1939; Port Washington, N.Y.: Kennikat, 1968.

5931. Morsberger, Robert E. "*Cannery Row* Revisited." *Steinbeck Quarterly* 16 (Summer–Fall 1983): 89–95.

5932. Motley, Warren. "From Patriarchy to Matriarchy: Ma Joad's Role in *The Grapes of Wrath*." *American Literature* 54 (October 1982): 397–412.

5933. Nelson, H.S. "Steinbeck's Politics Then and Now." *Antioch Review* 27 (Spring 1967): 118–33.

5934. O'Connor, Richard. *John Steinbeck*. New York: McGraw-Hill, 1970.

5935. Okerland, Arlene N., ed. "Steinbeck Special Issue." *San Jose Studies* 1 (November 1975).

5936. Ortego, Philip D. "Fables of Identity: Stereotype and Caricature of Chicanos in Steinbeck's *Tortilla Flat*." *Journal of Ethnic Studies* 1 (Spring 1973): 39–43.

5937. Ouderkirk, Bruce J. "Children in Steinbeck: Barometers of the Social Condition." Doctoral dissertation, University of Nebraska, Lincoln, 1990.

5938. Owens, Louis D. *The Grapes of Wrath: Trouble in the Promised Land*. Boston: Twayne, 1989.

5939. ———. *John Steinbeck's Re-Vision of America*. Athens: University of Georgia Press, 1985.

5940. ———. "John Steinbeck's *The Pastures of Heaven*: Illusions of Eden." *Arizona Quarterly* 41 (Autumn 1985): 197–214.

5941. ———. "Steinbeck's 'Flight': Into the Jaws of Death." *Steinbeck Quarterly* 10 (Summer–Fall 1977): 103–8.

5942. ———, and Hector Torres. "Dialogic Structure and Levels of Discourse in Steinbeck's *The Grapes of Wrath*." *Arizona Quarterly* 45 (Winter 1989): 75–94.

5943. Pearce, Howard D. "Steinbeck's 'Leader of the People': Dialectic and Symbol." *Publications in Language and Literature* 8 (Fall 1972): 415–26.

5944. Peterson, Richard F. "The Grail Legend and Steinbeck's 'The Great Mountains.'" *Steinbeck Quarterly* 6 (Winter 1973): 9–15.

5945. Pratt, John Clark. *John Steinbeck*. Grand Rapids, Mich.: Eerdmans, 1970.

5946. Pratt, Linda Ray. "Imagining Existence: Form and History in Steinbeck and Agee." *Southern Review* 11 (Winter 1975): 84–98.

5947. ———. "In Defense of Mac's Dubious Battle." *Steinbeck Quarterly* 10 (Spring 1977): 36–44.

5948. Renner, Stanley. "The Real Woman Inside the Fence in 'The Chrysanthemums.'" *Modern Fiction Studies* 31 (Summer 1985): 305–17.

5949. ———. "Sexual Idealism and Violence in 'The White Quail.'" *Steinbeck Quarterly* 17 (Summer–Fall 1984): 76–87.

5950. Rombold, Tamara. "Biblical Inversion in *The Grapes of Wrath*." *College Literature* 14 (Spring 1987): 146–66.

5951. Rundell, Walter, Jr. "Steinbeck's Image of the West." *American West* 1 (Spring 1964): 4–17, 79.

5952. St. Pierre, Brian. *John Steinbeck: The California Years*. San Francisco: Chronicle Books, 1983.

5953. Sargent, Raymond Matthews. "Social Criticism in the Fiction of John Steinbeck." Doctoral dissertation, Arizona State University, 1981.

5954. Satyanarayana, M. R. *John Steinbeck: A Study in the Theme of Compassion*. Hyderabad, India: Satyanarayana, 1977.

5955. Schmidt, Gary D. "Steinbeck's 'Breakfast': A Reconsideration." *Western American Literature* 26 (February 1992): 303–11.

5956. Schmitz, Anne-Marie. *In Search of Steinbeck*. Los Altos, Calif.: Hermes Publications, 1978.

5957. Shaw, Patrick W. "Tom's Other Trip: Psycho-Physical Questing in *The Grapes of Wrath*." *Steinbeck Quarterly* 16 (Winter–Spring 1983): 17–25.

5958. Shillinglaw, Susan, ed. "*The Grapes of Wrath*, A Special Issue." *San Jose Studies* 16 (Winter 1990).

5959. Short, John D., Jr. "John Steinbeck: A 1930's Photo-Recollection." *San Jose Studies* 2 (May 1976): 74–82.

5960. Shuman, R. Baird. "Initiation Rites in Steinbeck's *The Red Pony*." *English Journal* 59 (December 1970): 1252–55.

5961. Simmonds, Roy S. "Steinbeck and World War II: The Moon Goes Down." *Steinbeck Quarterly* 17 (Winter–Spring 1984): 14–34.

5962. ———. *Steinbeck's Literary* Achievement. Muncie, Ind.: Ball State University, 1976.

5963. Simpson, Hassell A. "Steinbeck's Anglo-Saxon 'Wonder-Words' and the American Paradox." *American Literature* 62 (June 1990): 310–17.

5964. Slade, Leonard A., Jr. "The Use of Biblical Allusions in *The Grapes of Wrath*." *CLA Journal* 11 (March 1968): 241–47.

5965. Spilka, Mark. "Of George and Lennie and Curley's Wife: Sweet Violence in Steinbeck's Eden." *Modern Fiction Studies* 20 (Summer 1974): 169–79.

5966. Steinbeck, Elaine, and Robert Wallsten, eds. *Steinbeck: A Life in Letters.* New York: Viking Press, 1975.

5967. Street, Webster. "Remembering John Steinbeck." Ed. Martha Heasley Cox. *San Jose Studies* 1 (November 1975): 109–27.

5968. Taylor, Walter Fuller. "*The Grapes of Wrath* Reconsidered." *Mississippi Quarterly* 12 (Summer 1959): 136–44.

5969. Tedlock, E. W., Jr., and C. V. Wicker, eds. *Steinbeck and His Critics: A Record of Twenty-Five Years.* Albuquerque: University of New Mexico Press, 1957.

5970. TeMaat, Agatha. "John Steinbeck: On the Nature of the Creative Process in the Early Years." Doctoral dissertation, University of Nebraska, Lincoln, 1975.

5971. Timmerman, John H. "Comic Vision in *The Grapes of Wrath.*" *San Jose Studies* 16 (Winter 1990): 133–41.

5972. ———. *The Dramatic Landscape of Steinbeck's Short Stories.* Norman: University of Oklahoma Press, 1990.

5973. ———. *John Steinbeck's Fiction: The Aesthetics of the Road Taken.* Norman: University of Oklahoma Press, 1986.

5974. ———. "John Steinbeck's Use of the Bible: A Descriptive Bibliography of the Critical Tradition." *Steinbeck Quarterly* 21 (Winter–Spring 1988): 24–39.

5975. Trachtenberg, Stanley. "John Steinbeck: The Fate of Protest." *North Dakota Quarterly* 41 (Spring 1973): 5–11.

5976. Tuttleton, James W. "Steinbeck in Russia: The Rhetoric of Praise and Blame." *Modern Fiction Studies* 11 (Spring 1965): 79–89.

5977. Valjean, Nelson. *John Steinbeck the Errant Knight: An Intimate Biography of His California Years.* San Francisco: Chronicle Books, 1975.

5978. Watt, F. G. *John Steinbeck.* New York: Grove Press; Edinburgh: Oliver and Boyd, 1962.

5979. Weisiger, Marsha L. "The Reception of *The Grapes of Wrath* in Oklahoma: A Reappraisal." *Chronicles of Oklahoma* 70 (Winter 1992–93): 394–415.

5980. West, Philip J. "Steinbeck's 'The Leader of the People': A Crisis in Style." *Western American Literature* 5 (Summer 1970): 137–41.

5981. White, Ray Lewis. "*The Grapes of Wrath* and the Critics of 1939." *Resources for American Literary Study* 13 (Autumn 1983): 134–64.

5982. Wollenberg, Charles. *The Harvest Gypsies: On the Road to the "Grapes of Wrath."* Berkeley: Heyday Books, [1988].

5983. Woodress, James. "John Steinbeck: Hostage to Fortune." *South Atlantic Quarterly* 63 (Summer 1964): 385–97.

5984. Woodward, Robert H. "San Jose Studies: The Steinbeck Research Center at San Jose State University: A Descriptive Catalogue." *San Jose Studies* 11 (Winter 1985): 1–128.

5985. ———. "Steinbeck's 'The Promise.'" *Steinbeck Quarterly* 6 (Winter 1973): 15–19.

5986. Work, James C. "Coordinate Forces in 'The Leader of the People.'" *Western American Literature* 16 (February 1982): 279–89.

5987. Wyatt, Bryant N. "Experimentation as Technique: The Protest Novels of John Steinbeck." *Discourse* 12 (Spring 1969): 143–53.

5988. Wyatt, David, ed. *New Essays on "The Grapes of Wrath."* New York: Cambridge University Press, 1990.

5989. Yarmus, Marcia D. "John Steinbeck and the Hispanic Influence." *Steinbeck Quarterly* 10 (Summer–Fall 1977): 97–102.

5990. Zane, Nancy Elizabeth. "Steinbeck's Heroes: 'The Individual Mind and Spirit of Man.'" Doctoral dissertation, Ohio University, 1982.

ALLAN STEPHENS

5991. Markos, Donald W. "Allan Stephens: The Lineaments of the Real." *Southern Review* 11 (Spring 1975): 331–56.

GEORGE STERLING

5992. Angoz, Charles, ed. *George Sterling: A Centenary Memoir Anthology.* South Brunswick, Maine: A. S. Barnes, 1969.

5993. Benediktsson, Thomas E. *George Sterling.* Boston: Twayne, 1980.

5994. Brazil, John R. "Ambrose Bierce, Jack London, and George Sterling: Victorians between Two Worlds." *San Jose Studies* 4 (February 1978): 19–33.

5995. Cross, Dalton, ed. "Seventeen George Sterling Letters." *Jack London Newsletter* 1 (July–December 1968): 41–61.

5996. Duke, Maurice. "Letters of George Sterling to James Branch Cabell." *American Literature* 44 (March 1972): 146–53.

5997. Dunbar, John R. "Letters of George Sterling to Carey McWilliams." *California Historical Society Quarterly* 46 (September 1967): 235–52.

5998. Fleming, Donald R. "The Last Bohemian." *Book Club of California Quarterly Newsletter* 37 (Fall 1972): 75–95.

5999. Johnson, Cecil, ed. *A Bibliography of the Writing of George Sterling.* Folcroft, Pa.: Folcroft Press, 1969.

6000. Longtin, Ray C. *Three Writers of the Far West: A Reference Guide.* Boston: G. K. Hall, 1980.

6001. Slade, Joseph W. "George Sterling, 'Prophet of the Suns.'" *Markham Review* 1 (May 1968): 4–10.

6002. ———, ed. "The Testament of an American Schopenhauer: George Sterling's 'Pleasure and Pain!'" *Resources for American Literary Study* 3 (Autumn 1973): 230–48.

6003. Stevenson, Lionel. "George Sterling's Place in Modern Poetry." *University of California Chronicle* 31 (October 1929): 401–21.

JAMES STEVENS

6004. Clare, Warren L. "Big Jim Stevens: A Study in Pacific Northwest Literature." Doctoral dissertation, Washington State University, 1967.

6005. ———. "James Stevens: The Laborer and Literature." *Research Studies* 4 (December 1964): 355–67.

6006. ———. "'Posers, Parasites, and Pismires': *Status Rerum*, by James Stevens and H. L. Davis." *Pacific Northwest Quarterly* 61 (January 1970): 22–30.

6007. Maunder, Elwood R. "An Interview with James Stevens: The Making of a Folklorist." *Forest History* 7 (Winter 1964): 2–19.

ROBERT LOUIS STEVENSON

6008. Baumgarten, Murray. "Between Geology and History: An Interpretation of Robert Louis Stevenson's *Silverado Squatters*." *Book Club of California Quarterly News-Letter* 38 (Fall 1973): 75–83.

6009. Issler, Anne Roller. "Robert Louis Stevenson in Monterey." *Pacific Historical Review* 34 (August 1965): 305–21.

6010. Thomas, Phillip D. "From Old World to New with Robert Louis Stevenson: The Famous Scottish Author Reports on Life in Steerage and Emigrant Train During an 1879 Trip to the Far West." *American West* 12 (May 1975): 28–31, 60–61.

ELINORE PRUITT STEWART

6011. George, Susanne K. *The Adventures of The Woman Homesteader: The Life and Letters of Elinore Pruitt Stewart.* Lincoln: University of Nebraska Press, 1992.

6012. ———. "A Patchwork of Friends: The Female Community of Elinore Pruitt Stewart." *Platte Valley Review* 17 (Winter 1989): 51–59.

GEORGE R. STEWART

6013. Beeler, Madison S. "George R. Stewart, Toponymist." *Names* 24 (June 1976): 77–85.

6014. Caldwell, John. *George R. Stewart.* Western Writers Series, No. 46. Boise, Idaho: Boise State University, 1981.

6015. Cogell, Elizabeth Cummin. "The Middle-Landscape Myth in Science Fiction." *Science Fiction Studies* 5 (July 1978): 134–42.

6016. Stegner, Wallace. "George R. Stewart, Western Writer: An Appreciation of a Remarkable Author." *American West* 19 (March/Aprill 1982): 64, 67–69.

CHARLES WARREN STODDARD

6017. Baird, James R. "The Noble Polynesian." *Pacific Spectator* 4 (Autumn 1950): 452–65.

6018. Bentzon, Théodore. [Marie Thérèse Blanc] "Un Loti américain: Charles Warren Stoddard." *Revue des Deux Mondes* 138 (December 1, 1896): 615–44.

6019. Gale, Robert L. *Charles Warren Stoddard.* Western Writers Series, No. 30. Boise, Idaho: Boise State University, 1977.

6020. Grenander, M. E. "Ambrose Bierce and Charles Warren Stoddard: Some Unpublished Correspondence." *Huntington Library Quarterly* 23 (May 1960): 261–92.

6021. Longtin, Ray C. *Three Writers of the Far West: A Reference Guide.* Boston: G. K. Hall, 1980.

6022. McGinty, Brian. "Charles Warren Stoddard: The Pleasure of His Company." *California Historical Quarterly* 52 (Summer 1973): 153–69.

6023. Stroven, Carl G. "A Life of Charles Warren Stoddard." Doctoral dissertation, Duke University, 1939.

HYEMEYOHSTS STORM

6024. Larson, Charles R. *American Indian Fiction.* Albuquerque: University of New Mexico Press, 1978, 112–27, 130–32, 165–72.
6025. Peyer, Bernd. "Reconsidering Native American Fiction." *Amerikastudien/American Studies* 24 (No. 2, 1979): 264–74.

MICHAEL STRAIGHT

6026. Graham, Don. "Tragedy and Western American Literature: The Example of Michael Straight's *A Very Small Remnant.*" *Denver Quarterly* 12 (Winter 1978): 59–66.
6027. Milton, John R. *Three West: Conversations with Vardis Fisher, Max Evans, Michael Straight.* Vermillion, S. Dak.: Dakota Press, 1970.

IDAH MEACHAM STROBRIDGE

6028. Amaral, Anthony. "Idah Meacham Strobridge: First Woman of Nevada Letters." *Nevada Historical Society Quarterly* 10 (Fall 1967): 5–12; 30 (Summer 1987): 102–10.

RUTH SUCKOW

6029. Baker, Joseph E. "Regionalism in the Middle West." *American Review* 5 (March 1935): 603–14.
6030. DeMarr, Mary Jean. "Ruth Sukow's Iowa 'Nice Girls.'" *Midamerica* 13 (1986): 69–83.
6031. Frederick, John T. "Ruth Suckow and the Middle Western Literary Movement." *English Journal* 20 (January 1931): 1–8.
6032. Hamblen, Abigail Ann. *Ruth Suckow.* Western Writers Series, No. 34. Boise, Idaho: Boise State University, 1978.
6033. Kiesel, Margaret Matlack. "Iowans in the Arts: Ruth Suckow in the Twenties." *Annals of Iowa* 45 (Spring 1980): 257–87.
6034. Kissane, Leedice. "D. H. Lawrence, Ruth Suckow, and 'Modern Marriage.'" *Rendezvous* 4 (Spring 1969): 39–45.
6035. ———. *Ruth Suckow.* New York: Twayne, 1969.
6036. McAlpin, Sara. "Englightening the Commonplace: The Art of Sarah Jewett, Willa Cather and Ruth Suckow." Doctoral dissertation, University of Pennsylvania, 1971.
6037. Martin, Abigail Ann. "*The Folks:* Anatomy of Rural Life and Shifting Values." *North Dakota Quarterly* 53 (Fall 1985): 173–79.

6038. Mott, Frank Luther. "Ruth Suckow." *A Book of Iowa Authors*. Ed. Johnson Brigham. Des Moines: Iowa State Teachers Association, 1930, 21–24, 54.

6039. Muehl, Lois B. "Ruth Suckow's Art of Fiction." *Books at Iowa* 13 (November 1970): 3–12.

6040. Nuhn, Ferner. "The Orchard Apiary: Ruth Suckow in Earlville." *Iowan* 20 (Summer 1972): 21–24, 54.

6041. ———, ed. "Cycle of the Seasons in Iowa: Unpublished Diary of Ruth Suckow." *Iowan* 9 (October–November 1960; December–January 1960–61; April–May 1961).

6042. Oehlschlaeger, Fritz. "The Art of Ruth Suckow's 'A Start in Life.'" *Western American Literature* 15 (Fall 1980): 177–86.

6043. ———. "A Book of Resolutions: Ruth Suckow's *Some Others and Myself*." *Western American Literature* 21 (August 1986): 111–21.

6044. Omrcanin, Margaret Stewart. *Ruth Suckow: A Critical Study of Her Fiction*. Philadelphia: Dorrance, 1972.

6045. Paluka, Frank. "Ruth Suckow: A Calendar of Letters." *Books at Iowa* 1 (October 1964): 34–40; 2 (April 1965): 31–40.

6046. White, Barbara A. *Growing Up Female: Adolescent Girlhood in American Fiction*. Westport, Conn.: Greenwood Press, 1985, 65–88.

RONALD SUKENICK

6047. Bellamy, Joe David. "Imagination as Perception: An Interview with Ronald Sukenick." *Chicago Review* 23 (Winter 1972): 59–72.

6048. Cheuse, Alan. "Way Out West: The Exploratory Fiction of 'Ronald Sukenick.'" *Itinerary: Criticism, Essays on California Writers*. Ed. Charles L. Crow. Bowling Green, Ohio: University Press, 1978, 115–21.

6049. Klinkowitz, Jerome. "Getting Real: Making It (up) with Ronald Sukenick." *Chicago Review* 23 (Winter 1972): 73–82.

6050. Kutnik, Jerzy. *The Novel as Performance: The Fiction of Ronald Sukenick and Raymond Federman*. Carbondale: Southern Illinois University Press, 1986.

6051. Noel, Daniel C. "Tales of Fictive Power: Dreaming and Imagination in Ronald Sukenick's Postmodern Fiction." *Boundary* 5 (Fall 1976): 117–35.

MARTHA SUMMERHAYES

6052. Powell, Lawrence C. "Martha Summerhayes' *Vanished Arizona.*" *Westways* 63 (July 1971): 16–19, 60–61.

ALAN SWALLOW

6053. Claire, William F., ed. *Publishing in the West: Alan Swallow.* Santa Fe, N. Mex.: Lightning Tree, 1974.

6054. McConnell, Virginia. "Alan Swallow and Western Writers." *South Dakota Review* 5 (Summer 1967): 88–97.

6055. North, Dennis D. "Alan Swallow: A Bibliographical Checklist." *Denver Quarterly* 2 (Spring 1967): 63–72.

6056. Ross, Morton L. "Alan Swallow and Modern, Western American Poetry." *Western American Literature* 1 (Summer 1966): 97–104.

6057. Waters, Frank. "Notes on Alan Swallow." *Denver Quarterly* 2 (Spring 1967): 16–25.

GLENDON SWARTHOUT

6058. Robertson, Richard. "Book's End: The Modern Western Hero and Glendon Swarthout's *The Shootist.*" *Heritage of the Great Plains* 13 (Winter 1980): 20–27.

ALEXANDER SWEET

6059. Speck, Ernest B. "Alex. Sweet, Texas Humorist." *Southwestern American Literature* 3 (1973): 49–60.

MAY SWENSON

6060. Gadomski, Kenneth E. "May Swenson's Poetry: A Discussion with Checklist." Doctoral dissertation, University of Delaware, 1984.

JOHN SWETT

6061. Polos, Nicholas C. "Early California Poetry." *California Historical Society Quarterly* 48 (September 1969): 243–55.

BELLA FRENCH SWISHER

6062. Dickey, Imogene. "Bella French Swisher: Texas Editor and Litterateur." *Southwestern American Literature* 1 (January 1971): 8–11.

AMY TAN

6063. Shear, Walter. "Generational Differences and the Diaspora in *The Joy Luck Club.*" *Critique* 34 (Spring 1993): 193–99.

BAYARD TAYLOR

6064. Doughty, Nanelia S. "Bayard Taylor: First California Booster." *Western Review* 7 (Spring 1970): 22–27.

6065. ———. "Bayard Taylor's Second Look at California (1859)." *Western Review* 8 (Winter 1971): 51–55.

6066. Luedtke, Luther S., and Patrick D. Morrow. "Bret Harte on Bayard Taylor: An Unpublished Tribute." *Markham Review* 3 (May 1973): 101–5.

6067. Schwartz, Thomas D. "Bayard Taylor's 'The Prophet': Mormonism as Literary Taboo." *BYU Studies* 14 (Winter 1974): 235–47.

6068. Wermuth, Paul C. *Bayard Taylor.* New York: Twayne, 1973.

DOUGLAS THAYER

6069. Jorgensen, B. W. "Romantic Lyric Form and Western Mormon Experience in the Stories of Douglas Thayer." *Western American Literature* 22 (May 1987): 33–49.

JOHN WILLIAM THOMASON, JR.

6070. Graves, John. "The Old Breed: A Note on John W. Thomason, Jr." *Southwest Review* 54 (Winter 1969): 36–46.

6071. Norwood, W. D. *John W. Thomason, Jr.* Southwest Writers Series, No. 25. Austin, Tex.: Steck-Vaughn, 1969.

6072. Willock, Roger. *Lone Star Marine: A Biography of the Late Colonel John W. Thomason, Jr., U.S.M.C.* Princeton, N.J.: Roger Willock, 1961.

THOMAS BANGS THORPE

6073. Blair, Walter. "The Technique of 'The Big Bear of Arkansas.'" *Southwest Review* 28 (Summer 1943): 426–35.

6074. Current-Garcia, Eugene. "Thomas Bangs Thorpe and the Literature of the Ante-Bellum Southwestern Frontier." *Louisiana Historical Quarterly* 39 (April 1956): 199–222.

6075. Estes, David C. "Thomas Bangs Thorpe's Backwoods Hunters: Culture Heroes and Humorous Failures." *University of Mississippi Studies in English* 5 (1984–1987): 158–71.

6076. ———, ed. *A New Collection of Thomas Bangs Thorpe's Sketches of the Old Southwest.* Baton Rouge: Louisiana State University Press, 1989.

6077. Higgs, Robert J. "The Sublime and the Beautiful: The Meaning of Sport in Collected Sketches of Thomas B. Thorpe." *Southern Studies* 25 (Fall 1986): 235–56.

6078. Lemay, J. A. Leo. "The Text, Tradition, and Themes of 'The Big Bear of Arkansas.'" *American Literature* 47 (November 1975): 321–42.

6079. Petry, Alice Hall. "The Common Doom: Thorpe's 'The Big Bear of Arkansas.'" *Southern Quarterly* 21 (Winter 1983): 24–31.

6080. Rickels, Milton. *Thomas Bangs Thorpe: Humorist of the Old Southwest.* Baton Rouge: Louisiana State University Press, 1962.

6081. Simoneaux, Katherine G. "Symbolism in Thorpe's 'The Big Bear of Arkansas.'" *Arkansas Historical Quarterly* 25 (Fall 1966): 240–47.

WALLACE THURMAN

6082. Haslam, Gerald. "Wallace Thurman: A Western Renaissance Man." *Western American Literature* 6 (Spring 1971): 53–59.

6083. McIver, Dorothy Jean Palmer. "Stepchild in Harlem: The Literary Career of Wallace Thurman." Doctoral dissertation, University of Alabama, 1983.

6084. Perkins, Huel D. "Renaissance 'Renegade'? Wallace Thurman." *Black World* 25 (1976): 29–35.

6085. West, Dorothy. "Elephant's Dance: A Memoir of Wallace Thurman." *Black World* 20 (1970): 77–85.

6086. Wright, Shirley Haynes. "A Study of the Fiction of Wallace Thurman." Doctoral dissertation, East Texas State University, 1983.

JEAN TOOMER

6087. Quirk, Tom, and Robert E. Fleming. "Jean Toomer's Contributions to the *New Mexico Sentinel*." *CLA Journal* 29 (June 1976): 524–32.

BERICK TRAVEN TORSVAN

(B. Traven)

6088. Baumann, Michael L. *B. Traven: An Introduction*. Albuquerque: University of New Mexico Press, 1976.

6089. ———. "B. Traven: Realist and Prophet." *Virginia Quarterly Review* 53 (Winter 1977): 73–85.

6090. Chankin, Donald O. *Anonymity and Death: The Fiction of B. Traven*. University Park: Pennsylvania State University Press, 1975.

6091. Gutierrez, Donald. "Maker Versus Profit-Maker: B. Traven's 'Assembly Line.'" *Studies in Short Fiction* 17 (Winter 1980): 9–14.

6092. Hanson, George Steven. "The Short Stories of B. Traven." Doctoral dissertation, University of California, San Diego, 1980.

6093. Mezo, Richard Eugene. "The Journey to Solipaz: A Study of B. Traven's Fiction." Doctoral dissertation, University of North Dakota, 1978.

6094. Miller, Charles, and R. E. Lujan, eds. "B. Traven." *Texas Quarterly* 6 (1963): 161–211.

6095. Payne, K. "Americans and Indians: Cultural Commentary in B. Traven's *The Treasure of the Sierra Madre*." *Dutch Quarterly Review of Anglo-American Letters* 18 (No. 1, 1988): 46–58.

6096. Pearson, Sheryl Marie Sherman. "The Anglo–American Novel of the Mexican Revolution, 1910–1940: D. H. Lawrence, B. Traven, Graham Greene." Doctoral dissertation, University of Michigan, 1976.

6097. Ponick, Terrence Lee. "The Novels of B. Traven: Literature and Politics in the American Editions." Doctoral dissertation, University of South Carolina, 1976.

6098. Schürer, Ernst, and Philip Jenkins, eds. *B. Traven: Life and Work*. University Park: Pennsylvania State University Press, 1987.

6099. Stone, Judy. "The Mystery of B. Traven." *Ramparts* 6 (1967): 31–49, 55–69 ff.

6100. Warner, John M. "Tragic Vision in B. Traven's 'The Night of the Visitor.'" *Studies in Short Fiction* 7 (Summer 1970): 377–84.

6101. Wyatt, Will. *The Secret of the Sierra Madre: The Man Who Was B. Traven*. Garden City, N. Y.: Doubleday, 1980.

JAMES TOWNSEND

6102. Dwyer, Richard A., and Richard E. Lingenfelter. *Lying on an Eastern Slope: James Townsend's Comic Journalism on the Mining Frontier.* Miami: University Presses of Florida, 1984.

JOHN K. TOWNSEND

6103. Walker, Don D. "Townsend's *Narrative*: A Note on Its Literary Features." *Possible Sack* 4 (October 1973): 15–20.

B. TRAVEN

See Berick Traven Torsvan

FREDERICK JACKSON TURNER

6104. Bennett, James D. *Frederick Jackson Turner.* Boston: Twayne, 1975.

6105. Benson, Lee. *Turner and Beard: American Historical Writing Reconsidered.* Glencoe, Ill.: Free Press, 1960.

6106. Billington, Ray A. *The American Frontier Thesis: Attack and Defense.* Washington, D.C.: American Historical Association, 1971.

6107. ———. *Frederick Jackson Turner: Historian, Scholar, Teacher.* New York: Oxford University Press, 1973.

6108. Bonazzi, Tiziano. "Frederick Jackson Turner's Frontier Thesis and the Self-Consciousness of America." *Journal of American Studies* 27 (August 1993): 149–71.

6109. Boyle, Thomas E. "Frederick Jackson Turner and Thomas Wolfe: The Frontier as History and Literature." *Western American Literature* 4 (Winter 1970): 273–85.

6110. Carpenter, Ronald H. *The Eloquence of Frederick Jackson Turner.* San Marino, Calif.: Huntington Library, 1983.

6111. ———. "Frederick Jackson Turner and the Rhetorical Impact of the Frontier Thesis." *Quarterly Journal of Speech* 63 (April 1977): 117–29.

6112. ———. "Style in Discourse as an Index of Frederick Jackson Turner's Historical Creativity: Conceptual Antecedents of the Frontier Thesis in His 'American Colonization.'" *Huntington Library Quarterly* 40 (May 1977): 269–77.

6113. Cronon, William. "Revisiting the Vanishing Frontier: The Legacy of Frederick Jackson Turner." *Western Historical Quarterly* 18 (April 1987): 157–76.

6114. ———. "Turner's First Stand: The Significance of Significance in American History." *Writing Western History: Essays on Major Western Historians.* Ed. Richard W. Etulain. Albuquerque: University of New Mexico Press, 1991, 73–101.

6115. Ducey, Cathryn Annette. "The Development of a Frontier Thesis: Mark Twain, Domingo Faustino Sarmineto, and Frederick Jackson Turner." Doctoral dissertation, University of Hawaii, 1975.

6116. Ellis, Richard J., and Alan Munslow. "Narrative, Myth and the Turner Thesis." *Journal of American Culture* 9 (Summer 1986): 9–16.

6117. Gressley, Gene M. "The Turner Thesis: A Problem in Historiography." *Agricultural History* 32 (October 1958): 227–49.

6118. Hofstadter, Richard. *The Progressive Historians: Turner, Beard, Parrington.* New York: Alfred A. Knopf, 1968.

6119. Holtgrieve, Donald G. "Frederick Jackson Turner as a Regionalist." *Professional Geographer* 26 (May 1974): 159–76.

6120. Jacobs, Wilbur R. "The Many-Sided Frederick Jackson Turner." *Western Historical Quarterly* 1 (October 1970): 363–72.

6121. ———. *On Turner's Trail: 100 Years of Writing Western History.* Lawrence: University Press of Kansas, 1994.

6122. Jensen, Richard. "On Modernizing Frederick Jackson Turner: The Historiography of Regionalism." *Western Historical Quarterly* 11 (July 1980): 307–22.

6123. Lamar, Howard R. "Frederick Jackson Turner." *Pastmasters: Some Essays on American Historians.* Eds. Marcus Cunliffe and Robin Winks. New York: Harper and Row, 1969, 74–109, 419–26.

6124. Lewis, Merrill E. "American Frontier History as Literature: Studies in Historiography of George Bancroft, Frederick Jackson Turner, and Theodore Roosevelt." Doctoral dissertation, University of Utah, 1968.

6125. ———. "The Art of Frederick Jackson Turner: The Histories." *Huntington Library Quarterly* 35 (May 1972): 241–55.

6126. ———. "Language, Literature, Rhetoric, and the Shaping of the Historical Imagination of Frederick Jackson Turner." *Pacific Historical Review* 45 (August 1976): 399–424.

6127. Mattson, Vernon E., and William E. Marion. *Frederick Jackson Turner: A Reference Guide.* Boston: G.K. Hall, 1985.

6128. Mood, Fulmer. "The Development of Frederick Jackson Turner as a Historical Thinker." *Transactions of the Colonial Society of Massachusetts* 34 (December 1943): 283–352.

6129. Nash, Gerald D. *Creating the West: Historical Interpretations, 1890–1990*. Albuquerque: University of New Mexico Press, 1991.

6130. Nichols, David A. "Civilization over Savage: Frederick Jackson Turner and the Indian." *South Dakota History* 2 (Fall 1972): 383–405.

6131. Noble, David W. "American Studies and the Burden of Frederick Jackson Turner: The Case of Henry Nash Smith and Richard Hofstadter." *Journal of American Culture* 4 (Winter 1981): 34–45.

6132. Paulson, Kristoffer F. "Ole Rölvaag, Herbert Krause, and the Frontier Thesis of Frederick Jackson Turner." *Where the West Begins*. Eds. Arthur R. Huseboe and William Geyer. Sioux Falls, S. Dak.: Center for Western Studies Press, 1978, 24–33.

6133. Putnam, Jackson K. "The Turner Thesis and the Westward Movement: A Reappraisal." *Western Historical Quarterly* 7 (October 1976): 377–404.

6134. Ridge, Martin. "Frederick Jackson Turner and His Ghost: The Writing of Western History." *Proceedings of the American Antiquarian Society* 101 (April 1990): 65–76.

6135. ———. "Introduction," to *History, Frontier, and Section: Three Essays by Frederick Jackson Turner*. Albuquerque: University of New Mexico, 1993, 1–26.

6136. ———. "The Life of an Idea: The Significance of Frederick Jackson Turner's Frontier Thesis." *Montana: The Magazine of Western History* 40 (Winter 1991): 3–13.

6137. ———, et al. "A Centennial Symposium on the Significance of Frederick Jackson Turner." *Journal of the Early Republic* 13 (Summer 1993): 133–249.

6138. Simonson, Harold P. "Frederick Jackson Turner: Frontier History as Art." *Antioch Review* 24 (Summer 1964): 201–11.

6139. Steiner, Michael C. "Frederick Jackson Turner and Western Regionalism." *Writing Western History: Essays on Major Western Historians*. Ed. Richard W. Etulain. Albuquerque: University of New Mexico Press, 1991, 103–35.

6140. ———. "The Significance of Turner's Sectional Thesis." *Western Historical Quarterly* 10 (October 1979): 437–66.

6141. White, Richard. "Frederick Jackson Turner." *Historians of the American Frontier: A Bio-Bibliographical Sourcebook*. Ed. John R. Wunder. Westport, Conn.: Greenwood Press, 1988, 660–81.

MARK TWAIN

See Samuel Clemens

I.L. UDELL

6142. Jason, Rick. "Udell." *South Dakota Review* 7 (Spring 1969): 5–7.

6143. Milton, John R. "Udell–The Taos Man." *South Dakota Review* 7 (Spring 1969): 107–23.

ALBERTO URISTA

(Alurista)

6144. Ybarra-Frausto, Tomás. "Alurista's Poetics: The Oral, The Bilingual, The Pre-Columbian." *Modern Chicano Writers.* Eds. Joseph Sommers and Tomás Ybarra-Frausto. Englewood Cliffs, N.J.: Prentice-Hall, 1979, 117–32.

JOHN C. VAN DYKE

6145. Wild, Peter. "John C. Van Dyke: A Western Esthetician as His Own Outlier." *South Dakota Review* 29 (Spring 1991): 7–23.

6146. ———. *John C. Van Dyke: The Desert.* Western Writers Series, No. 82. Boise, Idaho: Boise State University, 1988.

6147. ———. "'My Dear Van Dyke'; 'My Dear Brownell': New Perspectives On Our Foremost (and Most Coy) Desert Writer." *New Mexico Humanities Review* 35 (1991): 131–48.

6148. ———. "A Western Sun Sets in the East: The Five 'Appearances' Surrounding John C. Van Dyke's *The Desert.*" *Western American Literature* 25 (November 1990): 217–31.

6149. ———, and Neil Carmony. "The Trip Not Taken: John C. Van Dyke, Heroic Doer or Armchair Seer?" *Journal of Arizona History* 34 (Spring 1993): 65–80.

FRANCES FULLER VICTOR

6150. Martin, Jim. *A Bit of Blue: The Life and Work of Frances Fuller Victor.* Salem, Oreg: Deep Well Publishing Company, 1992.

6151. Mills, Hazel Emery. "The Emergence of Frances Fuller Victor – Historian." *Oregon Historical Quarterly* 62 (December 1961): 309–36.

6152. Bruce-Novoa, [Juan]. "Interview with José Antonio Villarreal." *Revista Chicano-Riqueña* 4 (Spring 1976): 40–48.

6153. ———. "*Pocho* as Literature." *Aztlán* 7 (Spring 1976): 65–77.

6154. Luedtke, Luther S. "*Pocho* and the American Dream." *Minority Voices* 1 (Fall 1977): 1–16.

6155. Padilla, Genaro Miguel. "The Progression from Individual to Social Consciousness in Two Chicano Novelists: José Antonio Villarreal and Oscar Zeta Acosta." Doctoral dissertation, University of Washington, 1981.

6156. Shirley, Carl. "*Pocho*: Bildungsroman of a Chicano." *Revista Chicano-Riqueña* 7 (Spring 1979): 63–68.

GERALD VIZENOR

6157. Blaeser, Kimberly Marie. "Gerald Vizenor: Writing – in the Oral Tradition." Doctoral dissertation, University of Notre Dame, 1990.

R. G. VLIET

6158. Gish, Robert. "R. G. Vliet's Lonesome Cowboys: Language and Lyricism in the Contemporary Western Novel." *Southwestern American Literature* 9 (Fall 1983): 5–21.

6159. Wright, Charlotte. "Sex and Violence in the West: Forbidden Territory in the Works of R. G. Vliet." *Roundup Quarterly* 4 (Fall 1991): 37–42.

6160. Wright, Kay Hetherly. "R. G. Vliet's *Soledad*: Rewriting the Southwest." *Southwestern American Literature* 18 (Fall 1992): 13–30.

DAVID WAGONER

6161. Cording, Robert Kenneth. "A New Lyricism: David Wagoner and the Instructional Voice." Doctoral dissertation, Boston College, 1976.

6162. "David Wagoner, Special Issue." *Slackwater Review.* Lewiston, Idaho: Confluence Press, 1981.

6163. Lieberman, Laurence. *Unassigned Frequencies: American Poetry in Review 1964–1977.* Urbana: University of Illinois Press, 1977, 152–81.

6164. McAulay, Sara. "'Getting There' and Going Beyond: David Wagoner's Journey Without Regret." *Literary Review* 28 (Fall 1984): 93–98.

6165. McFarland, Ron. *David Wagoner*. Western Writers Series, No. 88. Boise, Idaho: Boise State University, 1989.

6166. ———. "David Wagoner's Comic Westerns." *Critique* 28 (Fall 1986): 5–18.

6167. Peters, Robert. "Thirteen Ways of Looking at David Wagoner's New Poems." *Western Humanities Review* 35 (Autumn 1981): 267–72.

6168. Pinsker, Sanford. "The Achievement of David Wagoner." *Connecticut Review* 8 (October 1974): 42–47.

6169. ———. "On David Wagoner." *Salmagundi* 22–23 (Spring–Summer 1973): 306–14.

6170. ———. *Three Pacific Northwest Poets: William Stafford, Richard Hugo, and David Wagoner*. Boston: Twayne, 1987.

6171. Schafer, William J. "David Wagoner's Fiction: In the Mills of Satan." *Critique* 9 (No. 1, 1966): 71–89.

STANLEY WALKER

6172. Milner, Jay. "Stanley Walker: The Retread Texan." *Arlington Quarterly* 2 (Summer 1969): 7–21.

ANNA LEE WALTERS

6173. Carroll, Rhonda. "The Values and Vision of a Collective Past: An Interview with Anna Lee Walters." *American Indian Quarterly* 16 (Winter 1992): 63–73.

ARTEMUS WARD

See Charles Farrar Browne

MAY WARD

6174. Snipes, Helen Joann. "May Ward: Poet of the Prairie and its People." Doctoral dissertation, Kansas State University, 1973.

EUGENE FITCH WARE

6175. Malin, James C. "The Burlington, Iowa, Apprenticeship of the Kansas Poet Eugene Fitch Ware, 'Ironquill.'" *Iowa Journal of History* 57 (July 1959): 193–230.

6176. ———. "Eugene F. Ware, Master Poet...." *Kansas Historical Quarterly* 32 (Winter 1966): 401–25.

6177. ———. "Eugene F. Ware's Literary Chronology." *Kansas Historical Quarterly* 37 (August 1971): 314–32.

6178. ———. "Notes on the Poetic Debts of Eugene F. Ware – Ironquill." *Kansas Historical Quarterly* 35 (Summer 1969): 165–81.

FRANK WATERS

6179. Adams, Charles L. "Frank Waters's 'Symbols and Sacred Mountains.'" *Nevada Historical Society Quarterly* 29 (Winter 1986): 266–80.

6180. ———. "The Genesis of *Flight From Fiesta*." *Western American Literature* 22 (November 1987): 195–200.

6181. Blackburn, Alexander. "Frank Waters: Preface and Bibliography." *Writers' Forum* [Colorado College Symposium] 11 (Fall 1985): 164–70.

6182. ———. "Frank Waters's *The Lizard Woman* and the Emergence of the Dawn Man." *Western American Literature* 24 (August 1989): 121–36.

6183. ———. "Pastoral, Myth, and Humanity in *People of the Valley*." *South Dakota Review* 28 (Spring 1990): 5–18.

6184. ———. *A Sunrise Brighter Still: The Visionary Novels of Frank Waters*. Athens: Ohio University Press, 1991.

6185. Bucco, Martin. *Frank Waters*. Southwest Writers Series, No. 22. Austin, Tex.: Steck-Vaughn, 1969.

6186. Colley, Joanne. "Hollywood and the American Indian Motif: *The Man Who Killed the Deer*." *Southwestern American Literature* 16 (Fall 1990): 12–20.

6187. Davis, Jack L. "Frank Waters' *Mexico Mystique*: The Ontology of the Occult." *South Dakota Review* 15 (Autumn 1977): 17–24.

6188. ———, and June H. Davis. "Frank Waters and the Native American Consciousness." *Western American Literature* 9 (May 1974): 33–44.

6189. Deloria, Vine, ed. *Frank Waters: Man and Mystic*. Athens: Swallow Press, Ohio University Press, 1993.

6190. "Frank Waters Issue." *South Dakota Review* 15 (Autumn 1977): 5–153.

6191. Grider, Daryl Aleck. "Rightness with the Land: Spirit of Place in the Novels of Frank Waters." Doctoral dissertation, University of Tennessee, 1980.

6192. Grigg, Quay. "The Kachina Characters of Frank Waters' Novels." *South Dakota Review* 11 (Spring 1973): 6–16.

6193. Hoy, Christopher. "The Archetypal Transformation of Martiniano in *The Man Who Killed the Deer*." *South Dakota Review* 13 (Winter 1975–76): 43–56.

6194. Lyon, Thomas J. *Frank Waters*. New York: Twayne, 1973.

6195. ———. "On *The Man Who Killed the Deer*." *Writers' Forum* [Colorado College Symposium] 11 (Fall 1985): 180–94.

6196. Malpezzi, Frances M. "Meru, the Voice of the Mountain." *South Dakota Review* 27 (Summer 1989): 27–35.

6197. ———. "A Study of the Female Protagonist in Frank Waters' *People of the Valley* and Rudolfo Anaya's *Bless Me, Ultima*." *South Dakota Review* 14 (Summer 1976): 102–10.

6198. Milton, John. "Conversation with Frank Waters." *South Dakota Review* 26 (Winter 1988): 33–44.

6199. ———. *The Novel of the American West*. Lincoln: University of Nebraska Press, 1980, 264–97.

6200. ———, ed. *Conversations with Frank Waters*. Chicago: Swallow Press, 1972.

6201. Pilkington, William T. "Character and Landscape: Frank Waters' Colorado Trilogy." *Western American Literature* 2 (Fall 1967): 183–93.

6202. Rogers, Gary Wade. "Frank Waters: Author of Vision in the American Tradition of Emerson, Melville, and Faulkner." Doctoral dissertation, Texas Christian University, 1993.

6203. Swallow, Alan. "The Mavericks." *Critique* 2 (Winter 1959): 74–92.

6204. Tanner, Terence. *Frank Waters: A Bibliography with Relevant Selections from His Correspondence*. Glenwood, Ill.: Meyerbooks, 1983.

6205. Waters, Frank, ed. "Bibliography of the Works of Frank Waters." *South Dakota Review* 4 (Summer 1966): 77–78.

6206. Young, Vernon. "Frank Waters: Problems of the Regional Imperative." *New Mexico Quarterly Review* 19 (Autumn 1949): 353–72.

WINSTON WEATHERS

6207. Kidney-Wells, Jennifer. "The Writer in His Region: An Interview with Winston Weathers." *Kansas Quarterly* 9 (Spring 1977): 11–18.

6208. Sale, Richard B. "The Several Worlds of Winston Weathers." *Southwestern American Literature* 1 (May 1971): 93–97.

GORDON WEAVER

6209. Kennedy, Thomas E. "This Intersection Time: The Fiction of Gordon Weaver." *Hollins Critic* 22 (February 1985): 1–11.

6210. Barzun, Jacques. "Walter Prescott Webb and the Fate of History." *Essays on Walter Prescott Webb and the Teaching of History.* Eds. Dennis Reinhartz and Stephen E. Maizlish. College Station: Texas A M University Press, 1985, 11–35.

6211. Billington, Ray A. "Frederick Jackson Turner and Walter Prescott Webb: Frontier Historians." *Essays on the American West.* Eds. Harold M. Hollingsworth and Sandra L. Myers. Austin: University of Texas Press, 1969, 89–114.

6212. Butler, Anne M., and Richard A. Baker. "Walter Prescott Webb: The Legacy." *Essays on Walter Prescott Webb and the Teaching of History.* Eds. Dennis Reinhartz and Stephen E. Maizlish. College Station: Texas A M University Press, 1985, 61–78.

6213. Frantz, Joe B. "Walter Prescott Webb." *Turner, Bolton, and Webb: Three Historians of the American Frontier.* Seattle: University of Washington Press, 1965, 1979, 75–108.

6214. Friend, Llerena. "Walter Prescott Webb and Book Reviewing." *Western Historical Quarterly* 4 (October 1973): 381–404.

6215. Furman, Necah Stewart. *Walter Prescott Webb: His Life and Impact.* Albuquerque: University of New Mexico Press, 1976.

6216. Morris, Margaret. "Walter Prescott Webb, 1888–1963: A Bibliography." *Essays in the American Civil War.* Eds. William F. Holmes and Harold M. Hollingsworth. Austin: University of Texas Press, 1968.

6217. Owens, William A. *Three Friends: Bedichek, Dobie, Webb: A Personal History.* Garden City, N.Y.: Doubleday, 1969.

6218. Philp, Kenneth R., and Elliott West, eds. *Essays on Walter Prescott Webb.* Austin: University of Texas Press, 1976. Collects essays by Joe B. Frantz, W. Eugene Hollon, George Wolfskill, and Walter Rundell, Jr.

6219. Pickens, Donald K. "Westward Expansion and the End of American Exceptionalism: Sumner, Turner, and Webb." *Western Historical Quarterly* 12 (October 1981): 409–18.

6220. Rundell, Walter, Jr. *Walter Prescott Webb.* Austin, Tex.: Steck-Vaughn, 1971.

6221. ———. "Walter Prescott Webb: Product of Environment." *Arizona and the West* 5 (Spring 1963): 4–28.

6222. ———. "W. P. Webb's *Divided We Stand*: A Publishing Crisis." *Western Historical Quarterly* 13 (October 1982): 391–407.

6223. Shannon, Fred A. *An Appraisal of Walter Prescott Webb's The Great Plains: A Study in Institutions and Environment.* New York: Social Sciences Research Council, 1940.

6224. Tobin, Gregory M. "Landscape, Region, and the Writing of History: Walter Prescott Webb in the 1920s." *American Studies International* 16 (Summer 1978): 7–18.

6225. ———. *The Making of a History: Walter Prescott Webb and "The Great Plains."* Austin: University of Texas Press, 1976.

6226. ———. "Walter Prescott Webb." *Historians of the American Frontier: A Bio-Bibliographical Sourcebook.* Ed. John R. Wunder. New York: Greenwood Press, 1988, 713–28.

6227. West, Elliott. "Walter Prescott Webb and the Search for the West." *Writing Western History: Essays on Major Western Historians.* Ed. Richard W. Etulain. Albuquerque: University of New Mexico Press, 1991, 167–91.

NATHAN WALLENSTEIN WEINSTEIN

(Nathanael West)

6228. Atheneos, Michael Anthony. "Nathanael West: Progressive Pessimist." Doctoral dissertation, University of Northern Colorado, 1976.

6229. Banta, Martha. "American Apocalypses: Excrement and Ennui." *Studies in Literary Imagination* 7 (Spring 1974): 1–30.

6230. Baxter, Charles Morley. "Nathanael West: Dead Letters and the Martyred Novelist." *West Coast Review* 9 (October 1974): 3–11.

6231. Beaver, Harold. "Nathanael West's 'Chamber of American Horrors.'" *The Modern American Novella.* Ed. A. Robert Lee. New York: St. Martin's Press, 1989, 85–96.

6232. Briggs, Arlen John. "Nathanael West and Surrealism." Doctoral dissertation, University of Oregon, 1972.

6233. Brown, Daniel R. "The War Within Nathanael West: Naturalism and Existentialism." *Modern Fiction Studies* 20 (Summer 1974): 181–202.

6234. Clark, Neill Wilson, III. "The Metaphor of Apocalypse in the Fiction of Nathanael West." Doctoral dissertation, Emory University, 1976.

6235. Comerchero, Victor. *Nathanael West: The Ironic Prophet.* Syracuse, N.Y.: Syracuse University Press, 1964; Seattle: University of Washington Press, 1967.

6236. Conroy, Mark. "Letters and Spirit in *Miss Lonelyhearts.*" *University of Windsor Review* 17 (Fall–Winter 1982): 5–20.

6237. Dardis, Tom. "Nathanael West: The Scavenger of the Back Lots." *Some Time in the Sun.* New York: Charles Scribner's Sons, 1976, 151–81.

6238. Ellenberger, Matthew. "The 'Middle Westerners' in *Day of the Locust*: An Examination of Their History in Los Angeles and Their Role in Nathanael West's Novel." *Southern California Quarterly* 65 (Fall 1983): 227–50.

6239. Evans, Calvin Weakley. "Nathanael West as Satirist." Doctoral dissertation, Southern Illinois University, Carbondale, 1981.

6240. Fine, David M. "Landscape of Fantasy: Nathanael West and Los Angeles Architecture of the Thirties." *Itinerary: Criticism, Essays on California Writers.* Ed. Charles L. Crow. Bowling Green, Ohio: University Press, 1978, 49–62.

6241. ———. "Nathanael West, Raymond Chandler, and the Los Angeles Novel." *California History* 68 (Winter 1989/90): 196–201.

6242. Galloway, David D. "Nathanael West's Dream Dump." *Critique* 6 (Winter 1963–64): 46–63.

6243. Gerkey, Stephen Joseph. "You Only Have Time to Explode: Technique and Structure in Nathanael West's Narratives." Doctoral dissertation, Indiana University, 1977.

6244. Gorak, Jan. *God the Artist: American Novelists in a Post-Realist Age.* Urbana: University of Illinois Press, 1987.

6245. Hansell, William H. "Miss Lonelyhearts: A Sculptor Grown Angry With His Clay." *CLA Journal* 34 (March 1991): 340–53.

6246. Herbst, Josephine. "Nathanael West." *Kenyon Review* 23 (Autumn 1961): 611–30.

6247. Hyman, Stanley Edgar. *Nathanael West.* Minneapolis: University of Minnesota Press, 1962.

6248. Jones, Beverly. "Shrike as the Modernist Anti-Hero in Nathanael West's *Miss Lonelyhearts*." *Modern Fiction Studies* 36 (Summer 1990): 218–24.

6249. Klug, M. A. "Nathanael West: Prophet of Failure." *College Literature* 14 (Winter 1987): 17–31.

6250. Light, James F. *Nathanael West: An Interpretive Study.* 2d ed. Evanston, Ill.: Northwestern University Press, 1971.

6251. ———. "Varieties of Satire in the Art of Nathanael West." *Studies in American Humor* 2 (April 1975): 46–60.

6252. Long, Robert Emmet. *Nathanael West.* New York: Ungar, 1985.

6253. Madden, David, ed. *Nathanael West: The Cheaters and the Cheated: A*

Collection of Critical Essays. Deland, Fla.: Everett/Edwards, 1973. Includes an annotated bibliography by Helen R. Taylor, 323–41.

6254. Malin, Irving. *Nathanael West's Novels.* Carbondale: Southern Illinois University Press, 1972.

6255. Martin, Jay. *Nathanael West: The Art of His Life.* New York: Farrar, Straus, and Giroux; London: Secker and Warburg, 1971.

6256. ————, ed. *Nathanael West: A Collection of Critical Essays.* Englewood Cliffs, N.J.: Prentice-Hall, 1971.

6257. Michaels, I. Lloyd. "A Particular Kind of Joking: Nathanael West and Burlesque." Doctoral dissertation, State University of New York, Buffalo, 1972.

6258. Reid, Randall. *The Fiction of Nathanael West: No Redeemer, No Promised Land.* Chicago: University of Chicago Press, 1971.

6259. Ross, Alan. "The Dead Centre: An Introduction to Nathanael West." *Horizon* 18 (October 1948): 284–96.

6260. Schoenewolf, Carroll Robert. "The Novels of Nathanael West." Doctoral dissertation, University of Oklahoma, 1973.

6261. Scott, Nathan A., Jr. *Nathanael West: A Critical Essay.* Grand Rapids, Mich.: Eerdmans, 1971.

6262. Smith, Marcus. "Religious Experience in *Miss Lonelyhearts.*" *Contemporary Literature* 9 (Spring 1968): 172–88.

6263. Strychacz, Thomas. "Making Sense of Hollywood: Mass Discourses and the Literary Order in Nathanael West's *The Day of the Locust.*" *Western American Literature* 22 (Summer 1987): 149–62.

6264. Trachtenberg, Stanley. "West's Locusts: Laughing at the Laugh." *Michigan Quarterly Review* 14 (1975): 187–98.

6265. Vannatta, Dennis P. *Nathanael West: An Annotated Bibliography of the Scholarship and Works.* New York: Garland, 1976.

6266. Wexelblatt, Robert. "*Miss Lonelyhearts* and the Rhetoric of Disintegration." *College Literature* 16 (Fall 1989): 219–31.

6267. White, William. *Nathanael West: A Comprehensive Bibliography.* Kent, Ohio: Kent State University Press, 1975.

6268. Widmer, Kingsley. *Nathanael West.* Boston: Twayne, 1982.

6269. ————. "Twisting American Comedy: Henry Miller and Nathanael West, Among Others." *Arizona Quarterly* 43 (Autumn 1987): 218–30.

6270. Wisker, Alistair. *The Writing of Nathanael West.* New York: St. Martin's Press, 1990.

6271. Zlotnik, Joan. "Nathanael West and the Pictorial Imagination." *Western American Literature* 9 (November 1974): 177–85.

6272. Ballard, Charles. "The Question of Survival in *Fools Crow*." *North Dakota Quarterly* 59 (Fall 1991): 251–59.

6273. Barnett, Louise K. "Alienation and Ritual in *Winter in the Blood*." *American Indian Quarterly* 4 (May 1978): 123–30.

6274. Barry, Nora. "'The Lost Children' in James Welch's *The Death of Jim Loney*." *Western American Literature* 25 (May 1990): 35–48.

6275. ———. "*Winter in the Blood* as Elegy." *American Indian Quarterly* 4 (May 1978): 149–57.

6276. Beidler, Peter G., ed. "A Special Symposium Issue on James Welch's *Winter in the Blood*." *American Indian Quarterly* 4 (May 1978).

6277. ———, and A. LaVonne Ruoff, eds. "A Discussion of *Winter in the Blood*." *American Indian Quarterly* 4 (May 1978): 159–68.

6278. Bevis, William W. "Welch's Winters and Bloods." *Ten Tough Trips: Montana Writers and the West*. Seattle: University of Washington, 1990, 117–39.

6279. Bovey, Seth. "Whitehorns and Blackhorns: Images of Cattle Ranching in the Novels of James Welch." *South Dakota Review* 29 (Spring 1991): 129–39.

6280. Brenner, Jack. "Beyond Myth: Welch's *Winter in the Blood*." *Under the Sun: Myth and Realism in American Literature*. Ed. Barbara Howard Meldrum. Troy, N.Y.: Whitston, 1985, 206–19.

6281. Gish, Robert F. "Word Medicine: Storytelling and Magic Realism in James Welch's *Fools Crow*." *American Indian Quarterly* 14 (Fall 1990): 349–54.

6282. Horton, Andrew. "The Bitter Humor of *Winter in the Blood*." *American Indian Quarterly* 4 (May 1978): 131–39.

6283. Kunz, Don. "Lost in the Distance of Winter: James Welch's *Winter in the Blood*." *Critique* 20 (No. 1, 1978): 93–99.

6284. Larson, Charles R. *American Indian Fiction*. Albuquerque: University of New Mexico Press, 1978, 140–49.

6285. Orlandini, Roberta. "Variations on a Theme: Traditions and Temporal Structure in the Novels of James Welch." *South Dakota Review* 26 (Autumn 1988): 37–52.

6286. Owens, Louis. "Earthboy's Return – James Welch's Act of Recovery in *Winter in the Blood*." *Wicazo SA Review* 6 (Fall 1990): 27–37.

6287. Purdy, John. "'He Was Going Along': Motion in the Novels of James Welch." *American Indian Quarterly* 14 (Spring 1990): 133–45.

6288. Ruoff, A. LaVonne. "Alienation and the Female Principle in *Winter in the Blood.*" *American Indian Quarterly* 4 (May 1978): 107–22.

6289. Sands, Kathleen M. "Alienation and Broken Narrative in *Winter in the Blood.*" *American Indian Quarterly* 4 (May 1978): 97–105.

6290. Smith, William F. "*Winter in the Blood*: The Indian Cowboy as Everyman." *Michigan Academician* 10 (1978): 299–306.

6291. Tatum, Stephen. "'Distance,' Desire, and the Ideological Matrix of *Winter in the Blood.*" *Arizona Quarterly* 46 (Summer 1990): 73–100.

6292. Thackeray, William W. "'Crying for Pity' in *Winter in the Blood.*" *MELUS* 7 (Spring 1980): 61–78.

6293. Vangen, Kathryn Winona Shanley. "'Only An Indian': The Prose and Poetry of James Welch." Doctoral dissertation, University of Michigan, 1987.

6294. Velie, Alan R. "James Welch's Poetry." *American Indian Culture and Research Journal* 3 (1979): 19–38.

6295. ———. "*Winter in the Blood* as Comic Novel." *American Indian Quarterly* 4 (May 1978): 141–47.

6296. Welch, James. "A Conversation with James Welch." *South Dakota Review* 28 (Spring 1990): 103–10.

6297. Westrum, Dexter Lyle. "The Art of Survival in the Contemporary West: The Fictions of Thomas McGuane, James Welch, and Edward Abbey." Doctoral dissertation, University of Minnesota, 1985.

6298. ———. "James Welch's *Fools Crow*: Back to the Future." *San Jose Studies* 14 (Spring 1988): 49–58.

6299. Wild, Peter. *James Welch.* Western Writers Series, No. 57. Boise, Idaho: Boise State University, 1983.

LEW WELCH

6300. Allen, Donald, ed. *I Remain: The Letters of Lew Welch and the Correspondence of His Friends.* Vol. I: 1949–1960; Vol. II: 1960–1971. Bolinas, Calif.: Grey Fox Press, 1980.

6301. Saroyan, Aram. *Genesis Angels: The Saga of Lew Welch and the Beat Generation.* New York: William Morrow, 1979.

6302. Shaffer, Eric Paul. "Inhabitation in the Poetry of Robinson Jeffers, Gary Snyder, and Lew Welch." *Robinson Jeffers Newsletter* 78 (October 1990): 28–40.

JESSAMYN WEST

6303. Farmer, Ann Dahlstrom. *Jessamyn West.* Western Writers Series, No. 53. Boise, Idaho: Boise State University, 1982.

6304. Shivers, Alfred S. *Jessamyn West.* Rev ed. New York: Twayne, 1992.

NATHANAEL WEST

See Nathan Wallenstein Weinstein

ALBERT RICHARD WETJEN

6305. Corning, Howard McKinley. "A. R. Wetjen: British Seaman in the Western Sunrise." *Oregon Historical Quarterly* 74 (June 1973): 145–78.

STEWART EDWARD WHITE

6306. Alter, Judy. *Stewart Edward White.* Western Writers Series, No. 18. Boise, Idaho: Boise State University, 1975.

6307. Aufderheide, Lawrence Richard. "American Literary Primitivists: Owen Wister, Stewart Edward White and Jack London." Doctoral dissertation, University of Michigan, 1973.

6308. Butte, Edna Rosemary. "Stewart Edward White: His Life and Literary Career." Doctoral dissertation, University of Southern California, 1960.

6309. Powell, Lawrence Clark. "Southwest Classics Reread: A Land to Know, A West to Love." *Westways* 64 (December 1972): 28–31, 50, 52–53.

6310. Underwood, John Curtis. "Stewart Edward White and All Outdoors." *Literature and Insurgency: Ten Studies in Racial Evolution.* New York: Michell Kinnerley, 1914, 254–98.

WILLIAM ALLEN WHITE

6311. Dubbert, Joe L. "William Allen White: Reflections on an American Life." *Markham Review* 4 (May 1974): 41–47.

6312. ———. "William Allen White's American Adam." *Western American Literature* 7 (Winter 1973): 271–78.

6313. Elkins, William R. "William Allen White's Early Fiction." *Heritage of Kansas* 8 (Winter 1975): 5–17.

6314. Griffith, Sally Foreman. *Home-Town News: William Allen White and the Emporia Gazette*. New York: Oxford University Press, 1989.

6315. ———, ed. *The Autobiography of William Allen White*. 2d ed., rev. Lawrence: University Press of Kansas, 1990.

6316. Groman, George L. "The Political Fiction of William Allen White: A Study in Emerging Progressivism." *Midwest Quarterly* 8 (October 1966): 79–93.

6317. Jernigan, E. Jay. *William Allen White*. Boston: Twayne, 1983.

6318. Johnson, W., and P. Pantle. "Bibliography of the Published Works of William Allen White." *Kansas Historical Quarterly* 15 (February 1947): 22–41.

6319. McKee, John DeWitt. *William Allen White: Maverick in Main Street*. Westport, Conn.: Greenwood Press, 1975.

6320. Pady, Donald S. "A Bibliography of the Poems of William Allen White." *Bulletin of Bibliography* 25 (January–April 1971): 44–46.

6321. Quantic, Diane Dufva. *William Allen White*. Western Writers Series, No. 109. Boise, Idaho: Boise State University, 1993.

6322. Resh, Richard W. "GLR Bibliography: William Allen White." *Great Lakes Review* 5 (Summer 1978): 49–66.

6323. ———. "A Vision in Emporia: William Allen White's Search for Community." *Midcontinent American Studies Journal* 10 (Fall 1969): 19–35.

OPAL WHITELEY

6324. Bede, Elbert. *Fabulous Opal Whiteley: From Logging Camp to Princess of India*. Portland, Oreg.: Binfords and Mort, 1954

6325. Holbrook, Stewart H. *Far Corner: A Personal View of the Pacific Northwest*. New York: Macmillan, 1952, 209–19.

6326. Whiteley, Opal. *Opal/Opal Whiteley*. Arranged and adapted by Jane Boulton. New York: Macmillan, 1976.

WALT WHITMAN

6327. Allen, Gay Wilson. *The Solitary Singer: A Critical Biography of Walt Whitman*. New York: Macmillan, 1955

6328. ———. *Walt Whitman Handbook*. New York: Packard, 1946.

6329. Canby, Henry Seidel. *Walt Whitman: An American*. Boston: Houghton Mifflin, 1943.

6330. Coffman, S. K., Jr. "Form and Meaning in Whitman's 'Passage to India.'" *PMLA* 70 (June 1955): 337–49.

6331. Eitner, Walter H. *Walt Whitman's Western Jaunt.* Lawrence: Regent's Press of Kansas, 1981.

6332. Erkkila, Betsy. *Whitman the Political Poet.* New York: Oxford University Press, 1989.

6333. Folsom, Ed. *Walt Whitman's Native Representatives.* New York: Cambridge University Press, 1994.

6334. Fussell, Edwin. *Frontier: American Literature and the American West.* Princeton, N. J.: Princeton University Press, 1965, 397–441.

6335. Greenspan, Ezra. *Walt Whitman and the American Reader.* New York: Cambridge University Press, 1990.

6336. Hubach, Robert R. "Walt Whitman and the West." Doctoral dissertation, Indiana University, 1943.

6337. ———. "Western Newspaper Accounts of Whitman's 1879 Trip to the West." *Walt Whitman Review* 18 (June 1972): 56–62.

6338. Huffstickler, Star. "Walt Whitman as a Precursor of Frederick Jackson Turner." *Walt Whitman Review* 8 (March 1962): 3–8.

6339. Hutchinson, George B. *The Ecstatic Whitman: Literary Shamanism and the Crisis of the Union.* Columbus: Ohio State University Press, 1986.

6340. Lovell, John, Jr. "Appreciating Whitman: 'Passage to India.'" *Modern Language Quarterly* 21 (June 1960): 131–41.

6341. Miller, James E., Jr. *A Critical Guide to Leaves of Grass.* Chicago: University of Chicago Press, 1957.

6342. Moon, Michael. *Disseminating Whitman: Revision and Corporeality in "Leaves of Grass."* Cambridge, Mass.: Harvard University Press, 1991.

6343. Nathanson, Tenney. *Whitman's Presence: Body, Voice, and Writing in Leaves of Grass.* New York: New York University Press, 1992.

6344. Nelson, Herbert B. "Walt Whitman and the Westward Movement." Doctoral dissertation, University of Washington, 1945.

6345. Smith, Henry Nash. *Virgin Land: The American West as Symbol and Myth.* Cambridge, Mass.: Harvard University Press, 1950, 1970.

6346. Steensma, Robert C. "Whitman and General Custer." *Walt Whitman Review* 10 (June 1964): 41–42.

6347. Trimble, Martha Scott. "The Westering of Walt Whitman." *Heritage of Kansas* 10 (Summer 1977): 42–51.

PETER WILD

6348. Butscher, Edward. *Peter Wild*. Western Writers Series, No. 106. Boise, Idaho: Boise State University, 1992.

6349. Maguire, James H. "Discovering Peter Wild: Contemporary Poet of the Southwest." *New Mexico Humanities Review* 32 (1989): 16–25.

LAURA INGALLS WILDER

6350. Adam, Kathryn. "Laura, Ma, Mary, Carrie, and Grace: Western Women as Portrayed by Laura Ingalls Wilder." *The Women's West.* Eds. Susan Armitage and Elizabeth Jameson. Norman: University of Oklahoma Press, 1987, 95–110.

6351. Anderson, William. *Laura Ingalls Wilder: A Biography*. New York: HarperCollins, 1992.

6352. ———. "The Literary Apprenticeship of Laura Ingalls Wilder." *South Dakota History* 13 (Winter 1983): 285–331.

6353. ———, and Leslie A. Kelly. *Laura Ingalls Wilder Country*. New York: HarperCollins, 1990.

6354. Erisman, Fred. "*Farmer Boy*: The Forgotten 'Little House' Book." *Western American Literature* 28 (August 1993): 123–30.

6355. ———. *Laura Ingalls Wilder*. Western Writers Series, No. 112. Boise, Idaho: Boise State University, 1994.

6356. ———. "The Regional Vision of Laura Ingalls Wilder." *Studies in Medieval, Renaissance, and American Literature: A Festschrift*. Ed. Betsy Colquitt. Fort Worth: Texas Christian Press, 1971, 165–71.

6357. Giff, Patricia Reilly. *Laura Ingalls Wilder: Growing Up in the Little House*. New York: Viking Kestrel, 1987.

6358. Holtz, William. "Closing the Circle: The American Optimism of Laura Ingalls Wilder." *Great Plains Quarterly* 4 (Spring 1984): 79–90.

6359. Jacobs, W. J. "Frontier Faith Revisited: The Little House Books of Laura Ingalls Wilder." *Horn Book Magazine* 41 (October 1965): 465–73.

6360. Miller, John E. "Freedom and Control in Laura Ingalls Wilder's De Smet." *Great Plains Quarterly* 9 (Winter 1989): 27–35.

6361. ———. *Laura Ingalls Wilder's Little Town: Where History and Literature Meet*. Lawrence: University Press of Kansas, 1994.

6362. ———. "Place and Community in the 'Little Town on the Prairie': De Smet in 1883." *South Dakota History* 16 (Winter 1986): 351–72.

6363. Moore, Rosa Ann. "Laura Ingalls Wilder's Orange Notebooks and the Art of the Little House Books." *Children's Literature* 4 (1975): 105–19.

6364. Romines, Ann. "Writing the *Little House*: The Architecture of a Series." *Great Plains Quarterly* 14 (Spring 1994): 107–15.

6365. Rosenblum, Dolores. "'Intimate Immensity': Mythic Space in the Works of Laura Ingalls Wilder." *Where the West Begins*. Eds. Arthur R. Huseboe and William Geyer. Sioux Falls, S. Dak.: Center for Western Studies Press, 1978, 72–79.

6366. Spaeth, Janet. *Laura Ingalls Wilder*. Boston: Twayne, 1987.

6367. Wolfe, Virginia. "The Symbolic Center: *Little House in the Big Woods*." *Children's Literature in Education* 13 (Autumn 1982): 107–14.

6368. Zochert, Donald. *Laura: The Life of Laura Ingalls Wilder*. Chicago: Regnery, 1976.

JEANNE WILLIAMS

6369. Alter, Judy. *Jeanne Williams*. Western Writers Series, No. 98. Boise, Idaho: Boise State University, 1991.

JOHN WILLIAMS

6370. Brenner, Jack. "*Butcher's Crossing*: The Husks and Shells of Exploitation." *Western American Literature* 7 (Winter 1973): 243–59; *Denver Quarterly* 20 (Winter 1986): 78–95.

6371. McCabe, Victoria. "John Williams: Fixed Star Writer." *South Dakota Review* 29 (Spring 1991): 123–28.

HARRY LEON WILSON

6372. Kummer, George. *Harry Leon Wilson: Some Accounts of the Triumphs and Tribulations of an American Popular Writer*. Cleveland: Press of Western Reserve University, 1963.

LANFORD WILSON

6373. Barnett, Gene A. *Lanford Wilson*. Boston: Twayne, 1987.

6374. Busby, Mark. *Lanford Wilson*. Western Writers Series, No. 81. Boise, Idaho: Boise State University, 1987.

6375. Cooperman, Robert. "Lanford Wilson: A Bibliography." *Bulletin of Bibliography* 48 (September 1991): 125–35.

6376. Herman, William. *Understanding Contemporary American Drama.* Columbia: University of South Carolina Press, 1987.

6377. Jacobi, Martin J. "The Comic Vision of Lanford Wilson." *Studies in the Literary Imagination* 21 (Fall 1988): 119–34.

YVOR WINTERS

6378. Abood, Edward. "Some Observations on Yvor Winters." *Chicago Review* 11 (Autumn 1957): 51–66.

6379. Bagchee, Shyamal. "The Western-ness of Yvor Winters's Poetry." *South Dakota Review* 24 (Winter 1986): 148–65.

6380. Barish, Jonas A. "Yvor Winters and the Antimimetic Prejudice." *New Literary History* 2 (Spring 1971): 419–44.

6381. Davie, Donald. "Winters and Leavis: Memories and Reflections." *Sewanee Review* 87 (Fall 1959): 608–18.

6382. Davis, Dick. *Wisdom and Wilderness: The Achievement of Yvor Winters.* Athens: University of Georgia Press, 1983.

6383. Fraser, Shirley S. "Yvor Winters: The Critic as Moralist." Doctoral dissertation, Louisiana State University, 1972.

6384. Graff, Gerald. "Yvor Winters of Stanford." *American Scholar* 44 (Spring 1975): 291–98.

6385. Holloway, John. "The Critical Theory of Yvor Winters." *Critical Quarterly* 7 (Spring 1965): 54–66.

6386. Kaye, Howard. "The Post-Symbolist Poetry of Yvor Winters." *Southern Review* 7 (January 1971): 176–97.

6387. Levin, David. "Yvor Winters at Stanford." *Virginia Quarterly Review* 54 (Summer 1978): 454–73.

6388. Lohf, Kenneth A., and E. P. Sheehy. "Yvor Winters: A Bibliography." *Twentieth Century Literature* 5 (April 1959): 27–51.

6389. Marsh, Robert. "Observations on the Criticism of Ivor Winters." *Spectrum* 4 (Fall 1960): 146–62.

6390. Parkinson, Thomas, ed. *Hart Crane and Yvor Winters: Their Literary Correspondence.* Berkeley: University of California Press, 1978.

6391. Powell, Grosvenor E. "Mythical and Smoky Soil: Imagism and the Aboriginal in the Early Poetry of Yvor Winters." *Southern Review* 11 (April 1975): 300–317.

6392. ———. "Solipsism and the Absolute in Yvor Winters' Poetry." *Compass* 1 (1977): 44–59.

6393. ———. "Yvor Winters' Greek Allegories." *Southern Review* 14 (Spring 1978): 262–80.

6394. Ramsey, Paul. "Yvor Winters: Some Abstractions Against Abstrac-
tion." *Sewanee Review* 73 (Summer 1965): 451–64.

6395. Robson, W. W. "The Literary Criticism of Yvor Winters." *Cambridge
Quarterly* 6 (No. 2, 1973): 189–200.

6396. Stephens, Alan. "The *Collected Poems* of Yvor Winters." *Twentieth
Century Literature* 9 (October 1963): 127–39.

6397. Van Deusen, Marshall. "In Defense of Yvor Winters." *Thought* 32
(Autumn 1957): 409–36.

6398. Wellek, René. "Yvor Winters Rehearsed and Reconsidered." *Denver
Quarterly* 10 (Autumn 1975): 1–27.

6399. Zaniello, Thomas A. "The Early Career of Yvor Winters: The Imagist
Movement and the American Indian." *Studies in the Humanities* 6
(1977): 5–10.

SOPHUS K. WINTHER

6400. Meldrum, Barbara. "Duality and Dream in S. K. Winther's Grimsen
Trilogy." *Prairie Schooner* 49 (Winter 1975–76): 311–19.

6401. ———. *Sophus K. Winther.* Western Writers Series, No. 60. Boise,
Idaho: Boise State University, 1983.

6402. ———. "Structure and Meaning in S. K. Winther's *Beyond the Garden Gate.*" *Western American Literature* 6 (Fall 1971): 191–202.

6403. Mossberg, Christer Lennart. *Scandinavian Immigrant Literature.*
Western Writers Series, No. 47. Boise, Idaho: Boise State University,
1981.

6404. Powell, Desmond. "Sophus Winther: The Grimsen Trilogy." *American Scandinavian Review* 36 (June 1948): 144–47.

6405. Whicher, George F. "Dane in America." *Forum* 106 (November
1946): 450–54.

OWEN WISTER

6406. Agnew, S. M. "Destry Goes on Riding: *The Virginian.*" *Publisher's
Weekly* 157 (August 23, 1952): 746–51.

6407. Alter, Judy. "The Virginian Rides On." *Southwestern American Literature* 5 (1975): 68–72.

6408. Aufderheide, Lawrence Richard. "American Literary Primitivists:
Owen Wister, Stewart Edward White, and Jack London." Doctoral
dissertation, University of Michigan, 1973.

6409. Barsness, John A. "Theodore Roosevelt as Cowboy: The Virginian as
Jacksonian Man." *American Quarterly* 21 (Fall 1969): 609–19.

6410. Boatright, Mody C. "The American Myth Rides the Range: Owen Wister's Man on Horseback." *Southwest Review* 36 (Summer 1951): 157–63.

6411. Bode, Carl. "Henry James and Owen Wister." *American Literature* 26 (May 1954): 250–52.

6412. Bogard, William J. "Wister's Journals and *The Virginian*: From Static to Dynamic." *South Dakota Review* 28 (Summer 1990): 22–33.

6413. Branch, Douglas. *The Cowboy and His Interpreters*. New York: D. Appleton, 1926.

6414. Cady, Edwin H. *The Light of Common Day: Realism in American Fiction*. Bloomington: Indiana University Press, 1971, 171–73, 182–92.

6415. Cawelti, John G. *Adventure, Mystery, and Romance: Formula Stories as Art and Popular Culture*. Chicago: University of Chicago Press, 1976, 230–41.

6416. Cobbs, John L. *Owen Wister*. Boston: Twayne, 1984.

6417. Cooper, Frederic Taber. "Owen Wister." *Some American Story Tellers*. New York: Henry Holt, 1911, 265–94.

6418. Davis, Robert Murray, ed. *Owen Wister's West: Selected Articles*. Albuquerque: University of New Mexico Press, 1987.

6419. Donahue, John. "Nature in *Don Segundo Sombra* and *The Virginian*." *Great Plains Quarterly* 7 (Summer 1987): 166–77.

6420. Durham, Philip. "Introduction" and "Textual Note" to Owen Wister, *The Virginian: A Horseman of the Plains*. Boston: Houghton Mifflin, 1968.

6421. Etulain, Richard W. *Owen Wister*. Western Writers Series, No. 7. Boise, Idaho: Boise State College, 1973.

6422. Fiske, Horace Spencer. *Provincial Types in American Fiction*. Chautauqua, N.Y.: Chautauqua Press, 1903, 215–41.

6423. Gripp, Gary. "Point of View in Wister's *Red Man and White*." *Possible Sack* 5 (April 1974): 7–17.

6424. Houghton, Donald E. "Two Heroes in One: Reflections Upon the Popularity of *The Virginian*." *Journal of Popular Culture* 4 (Fall 1970): 497–506.

6425. Lambert, Neal. "A Cowboy Writes to Owen Wister." *American West* 2 (Fall 1965): 31–36.

6426. ———. "Owen Wister's 'Hank's Woman': The Writer and His Comment." *Western American Literature* 4 (Spring 1969): 39–50.

6427. ———. "Owen Wister's Lin Mclean: The Failure of the Vernacular Hero." *Western American Literature* 5 (Fall 1970): 219–32.

6428. ———. "Owen Wister – The 'Real Incident' and the 'Thrilling Story.'" *The American West: An Appraisal.* Ed. Robert G. Ferris. Santa Fe: Museum of New Mexico Press, 1963, 191–200.

6429. ———. "Owen Wister's Virginian: The Genesis of a Cultural Hero." *Western American Literature* 6 (Summer 1971): 99–107.

6430. ———. "The Values of the Frontier: Owen Wister's Final Assessment." *South Dakota Review* 9 (Spring 1971): 76–87.

6431. ———. "The Western Writing of Owen Wister: The Conflict of East and West." Doctoral dissertation, University of Utah, 1966.

6432. Lewis, Marvin. "Owen Wister: Caste Imprints in Western Letters." *Arizona Quarterly* 10 (Summer 1954): 147–56.

6433. Marovitz, Sanford E. "Owen Wister: An Annotated Bibliography of Secondary Material." *American Literary Realism 1870–1910* 7 (Winter 1974): 1–110.

6434. ———. "Testament of a Patriot: The Virginian, the Tenderfoot, and Owen Wister." *Texas Studies in Literature and Language* 15 (Fall 1973): 551–75.

6435. ———. "Unseemly Realities in Owen Wister's Western/American Myth." *American Literary Realism 1870–1910* 17 (Autumn 1984): 209–15.

6436. Mason, Julian. "Owen Wister and World War I: Appeal for Pentecost." *Pennsylvania Magazine of History and Biography* 101 (January 1977): 89–102.

6437. ———. "Owen Wister, Boy Librarian." *Quarterly Journal of the Library of Congress* 26 (October 1969): 201–12.

6438. Mitchell, Lee Clark. "'When You Call Me That...': Tall Talk and Male Hegemony in *The Virginian*." *PMLA* 102 (January 1987): 66–77.

6439. Mogen, David. "Owen Wister's Cowboy Heroes." *Southwestern American Literature* 5 (1975): 47–61.

6440. Nesbitt, John D. "Owen Wister's Achievement in Literary Tradition." *Western American Literature* 18 (November 1983): 199–208.

6441. Payne, Darwin. *Owen Wister: Chronicler of the West, Gentleman of the East.* Dallas: Southern Methodist University Press, 1985.

6442. Price, Alan. "'I'm Not an Old Fogey and You're Not a Young Ass': Owen Wister and Ernest Hemingway." *Hemingway Review* 9 (Fall 1989): 82–90.

6443. Robinson, Forrest G. "The Roosevelt-Wister Connection: Some Notes on the West and the Uses of History." *Western American Literature* 14 (Summer 1979): 95–114.

6444. ———. "The Virginian and Molly in Paradise: How Sweet Is It?" *Western American Literature* 21 (May 1986): 27–38.

6445. Scharnhorst, Gary. "The Virginian as Founding Father." *Arizona Quarterly* 40 (Autumn 1984): 227–41.

6446. Seelye, John. "When West Was Wister." *New Republic* 167 (September 2, 1972): 28–33.

6447. Solensten, John M. "Richard Harding Davis, Owen Wister, and *The Virginian*: Unpublished Letters and a Commentary." *American Literary Realism 1870–1910* 5 (Spring 1972): 122–33.

6448. Stokes, Frances Kemble Wister. *My Father, Owen Wister, and Ten Letters Written by Owen Wister to his Mother during his First Trip to Wyoming in 1885.* Laramie: University of Wyoming Library, 1952.

6449. Thompson, Gerald. "Musical and Literary Influences on Owen Wister's *The Virginian*." *South Atlantic Quarterly* 85 (Winter 1986): 40–55.

6450. ———. "Owen Wister and His Critics: Realism and Morality in *The Virginian*." *Annals of Wyoming* 64 (Winter 1992): 2–10.

6451. Trimmer, Joseph F. "*The Virginian*: Novel and Films." *Illinois Quarterly* 35 (December 1972): 5–18.

6452. Vorpahl, Ben M. "Henry James and Owen Wister." *Pennsylvania Magazine of History and Biography* 95 (July 1971): 291–338.

6453. ———. "*My Dear Wister*": The Frederic Remington-Owen Wister Letters. Palo Alto, Calif.: American West, 1972.

6454. ———. "Very Much Like a Firecracker: Owen Wister on Mark Twain." *Western American Literature* 6 (Summer 1971): 83–98.

6455. Walker, Don D. "Wister, Roosevelt and James: A Note on the Western." *American Quarterly* 22 (Fall 1960): 358–66.

6456. Watkins, George T. "Owen Wister and the American West: A Biographical and Critical Study." Doctoral dissertation, University of Illinois, 1959.

6457. ———. "Wister and 'The Virginian.'" *Pacific Northwesterner* 2 (Fall 1958): 49–52.

6458. Westbrook, Max. "Afterword," to Owen Wister, *The Virginian.* New York: Signet Books, 1979, 318–31.

6459. ———. "Bazarov, Prince Hal, and the Virginian." *Western American Literature* 24 (August 1989): 103–11.

6460. Whipp, Leslie T. "Owen Wister: Wyoming's Influential Realist and Craftsman." *Great Plains Quarterly* 10 (Fall 1990): 245–59.

6461. White, G. Edward. *The Eastern Establishment and the Western Experience: The West of Frederic Remington, Theodore Roosevelt, and Owen Wister.* New Haven, Conn.: Yale University Press, 1968.

6462. White, John I. "Owen Wister and the Dogies." *Journal of American Folklore* 82 (January–March 1969): 66–69.

6463. ———. "The Virginian." *Montana: The Magazine of Western History* 16 (October 1966): 2–11.

6464. Wister, Fanny K. "Letters of Owen Wister, Author of *The Virginian.*" *Pennsylvania Magazine of History and Biography* 83 (January 1959): 3–28.

6465. ———. "Owen Wister Out West." *Midway* 10 (April 1962): 24–49.

6466. ———. "Owen Wister's West." *Atlantic Monthly* 195 (May 1955): 29–35; (June 1955): 52–57.

6467. ———, ed. *That I May Tell You: Journals and Letters of the Owen Wister Family.* Wayne, Pa.: Haverford House, 1979.

6468. Wister, Owen. *Owen Wister Out West: His Journals and Letters.* Ed. Fanny Kemble Wister. Chicago: University of Chicago Press, 1958.

LARRY WOIWODE

6469. Scheick, William J. "Memory in Larry Woiwode's Novels." *North Dakota Quarterly* 53 (Summer 1985): 29–40.

THOMAS WOLFE

6470. Barth, Daniel. "Thomas Wolfe's Western Journeys." *Western American Literature* 26 (May 1991): 39–48.

6471. Boyle, Thomas E. "Frederick Jackson Turner and Thomas Wolfe: The Frontier as History and Myth." *Western American Literature* 4 (Winter 1970): 273–85.

6472. Chittick, V. L. O. "Thomas Wolfe's Farthest West." *Southwest Review* 48 (Spring 1963): 93–110.

6473. Cracroft, Richard H. "Through Utah and the Western Parks: Thomas Wolfe's Farewell to America." *Utah Historical Quarterly* 37 (Summer 1969): 291–306.

6474. Powell, Desmond. "Of Thomas Wolfe." *Arizona Quarterly* 1 (Spring 1945): 28–36.

6475. Wolfe, Thomas. *A Western Journal.* Pittsburgh: University of Pittsburgh Press, 1951.

CHARLES ERSKINE SCOTT WOOD

6476. Bingham, Edwin R. *Charles Erskine Scott Wood.* Western Writers Series, No. 94. Boise, Idaho: Boise State University, 1990.

6477. ———. "Experiment in Launching a Biography: Three Vignettes of Charles Erskine Scott Wood." *Huntington Library Quarterly* 35 (May 1972) 221–39.

6478. ———. "Oregon's Romantic Rebels: John Reed and Charles Erskine Scott Wood." *Pacific Northwest Quarterly* 50 (July 1959): 77–90.

6479. ———. "Shaping a Region's Culture: Charles Erskine Scott Wood in Oregon." *Oregon Rainbow* 1 (Number 4): 13–20.

STANLEY WOOD

6480. Kedro, Milan James. "Stanley Wood and the Great Divide: Rocky Mountain Literary Promotion in the Late Nineteenth Century." Doctoral dissertation, University of Denver, 1977.

JOHN WOODS

6481. Smith, Dave. "Fifty Years, Mrs. Carter: The Poetry of John Woods." *Midwest Quarterly* 17 (Summer 1976): 410–31.

DAVID WRIGHT

6482. Jorgensen, Bruce W. "The Vocation of David Wright: An Essay in Analytic Biography." *Dialogue* 11 (Summer 1978): 38–52.

HAROLD BELL WRIGHT

6483. Gaston, Edwin W., Jr. *The Early Novel of the Southwest.* Albuquerque: University of New Mexico Press, 1961.

6484. Ifkovic, Edward. "Harold Bell Wright and The Minister of Man: The Domestic Romancer at the End of the Genteel Age." *Markham Review* 4 (February 1974): 21–26.

6485. Oehlschlaeger, Fritz H. "Civilization as Emasculation: The Threatening Role of Women in the Frontier Fiction of Harold Bell Wright and Zane Grey." *Midwest Quarterly* 22 (Summer 1981): 346–60.

6486. Tagg, Lawrence V. "A Dedication to the Memory of Harold Bell Wright, 1872–1944." *Arizona and the West* 22 (Winter 1980): 303–6.

6487. ———. *Harold Bell Wright.* Western Writers Series, No. 115. Boise, Idaho: Boise State University, 1994.

JAMES ARLINGTON WRIGHT

6488. McMaster, Belle M. "James Arlington Wright: A Checklist." *Bulletin of Bibliography* 31 (April–June 1974): 71–82, 88.

HISAYE YAMAMOTO

6489. Yogi, Stan. "Legacies Revealed: Uncovering Buried Plots in the Stories of Hisaye Yamamoto." *Studies in American Fiction* 17 (Autumn 1989): 169–81.

BRIGHAM YOUNG

6490. Jessee, Dean C. "The Writings of Brigham Young." *Western Historical Quarterly* 4 (July 1973): 273–94.

RAY A. YOUNG BEAR

6491. Gish, Robert F. "Memory and Dream in the Poetry of Ray A. Young Bear." *Minority Voices* 2 (1978): 21–29.

ANN ZWINGER

6492. Rea, Paul W. "An Interview with Ann Zwinger." *Western American Literature* 24 (May 1989): 21–36.
6493. Trimble, Stephen, ed. "Ann Zwinger." *Words from the Land: Encounters with Natural History Writing.* Salt Lake City: Peregrine Smith, 1988, 78–91.
6494. Wild, Peter. *Ann Zwinger.* Western Writers Series, No. 111. Boise, Idaho: Boise State University, 1993.

Index

Biebel, Charles D. 3828
Bier, Jesse 2977
Bigsby, C. W. E. 5522
Billick, David J. 1868
Billingsley, Ronald G. 4141, 4728
Billington, Ray Allen 289, 540, 5151, 6106, 6107, 6211
Bingham, Edwin R. 290, 541, 950, 4537, 6476–6479
Bingham, June 1972
Birchard, Richard S. 4402
Bird, Roy K. 4764
Bishop, Elizabeth 1422
Bishop, Jack 3318
Bishop, John Peale 3438
Bittner, James W. 4277
Bjork, Kenneth O. 5329
Black, W. E. 4847
Blackburn, Alexander 175, 1134, 6181–6184
Black Elk, Wallace 2315
Blacker, Irwin R. 176
Blaeser, Kimberly Marie 6157
Blaine, Harold A. 291
Blair, Walter 292, 2406, 2785–2788, 4964, 6073
Blaisdell, Gus 2962
Blake, Forrester 188
Blakely, Carolyn F. 2373
Blanck, Jacob 11, 12
Blanding, Paul J. 153, 500
Blansfield, Karen Charmaine 5098
Blatt, Muriel Rosen 293
Blau, Herbert 5523
Blend, Benay 1869, 2195
Blessing, Richard A. 4142, 4868, 5273
Blevins, Richard Lowell 2147
Blevins, Winfred 294
Blicksilver, Edith 5560
Blodgett, E. D. 2025, 2026
Bloodworth, William A. 1135, 1423, 1424, 2316, 2364, 3346, 3347, 3622, 4729, 4836, 4848, 5583
Bloom, Edward A. 2489
Bloom, Harold 2789, 5054, 5815, 5816
Bloom, Lillian D. 2489, 2490
Blouet, Brian W. 951
Bluefarb, Sam 3430, 5505
Bluestone, George 1136, 1259, 2742
Blumenthal, W. A. 5584
Bly, Robert 5623

Boag, Peter G. 542
Boatright, Mody C. 295, 543–547, 1137–1139, 1260, 1261, 6410
Bode, Carl 4227, 6411
Bode, Winston 3213
Bogard, William J. 296, 6412
Bogdanovich, Peter 1262
Bogen, Don 5274, 5275
Boggan, J. R. 3734
Bogue, Allan G. 4648, 4649, 5139
Bohling, Beth 2491, 5419
Bohlke, L. Brent 2492–2496
Bold, Christine 297, 548, 1140–1142
Bonazzi, Tiziano 6108
Bonetti, Kay 3256, 3323, 4565, 5417
Bonora, Diane Christine 952
Booth, Wayne C. 4765, 4766
Borgman, Paul 2497
Borus, Daniel H. 4879
Bostwick, Prudence 189
Boswell, Jeanetta 3991
Botkin, Benjamin A. 177, 953, 954
Bouquet, Sarah 1870
Bourdon, Roger Joseph 3976
Bovee, John R. 3242
Bovey, Seth 3793, 6279
Bowden, Mary W. 3921, 3922
Bowen, Catherine Drinker 3175
Bowers, Janice Emily 5557
Bowers, Neal 5276, 5277
Bowman, John S. 13, 2441
Bowron, Bernard 5817
Bowser, Eileen 1263
Boyden, William L. 5045
Boyer, Jay 2374, 2955
Boyer, Mary G. 178, 3703, 4291
Boyers, Robert 3992
Boyle, Thomas E. 6109, 6471
Boyling, Mary Ellen F. 3176
Boynton, Henry W. 3735
Boynton, Percy H. 298, 5330
Bracher, Frederick 549, 955, 5818
Bradford, Curtis 2498
Bradford, Mary L. 5670
Bradford, M. E. 3613, 3614, 3701, 5040
Bradley, Jennifer 2177
Bradshaw, Michael 956
Bradsher, Frieda Katherine 1871
Brady, Duer S. 3736
Brady, H. Jennifer 3192

Goble, Danney 3626
Goboni, Mark William 5869
Goetzmann, William H. 346, 649, 1297
Goetzmann, William N. 346, 1297
Gohdes, Clarence 71, 72, 1003
Golden, Catherine 3574
Goldhurst, William 5868
Goldie, Terry 2048
Goldman, Harold Raymond 1988
Goldman, Suzy Bernstein 4900
Goldsmith, Arnold L. 4874, 4901, 4902
Goldstein, Bernice 1298
Goldstein, Jessie S. 2289, 4656–4659
Gonzales, Arturo F. 4240
Gonzáles, Sylvia A. 1647
Gonzales-Berry, Erlinda 1648, 1649, 1932
Gonzalez, Maria Carmen 1650
Gonzalez-T, Cesar A. 2163
Goodman, Charlotte Margolis 5681
Goodman, Susan 3808
Goodwyn, Frank 650
Goodykoontz, Colin B. 1192
Gorak, Jan 6244
Gordon, Dudley C. 4542
Gordon, Joseph T. 3966
Gordon-McCutchan, R. C. 651
Gorrell, Robert 2748
Gossett, Louise Y. 3609
Gottesman, Ronald 5586, 5587
Gottfried, Herbert Wilson 347
Goulart, Ron 1193
Gould, Lewis L. 1785
Gower, Ronald A. 4418
Grabbe, Hans-Jürgen 4340
Graber, Kay 3298
Grace, Sherrill E. 2049
Graff, Gerald 6384
Graham, Don B. 348, 652, 1004, 1005, 1299–1301, 1355, 2134, 2393, 2447, 2448, 3216, 3285, 4419, 4597, 4903, 4904, 6026
Graham, Ina Agnes 2964
Graham, John 5588
Grahame, Pauline 3846
Grajeda, Rafael Francisco 1651
Grajeda, Ralph F. 5248
Grammer, John M. 3898
Grant, Gary 5532

Granzow, Barbara 4598
Grattan, C. Hartley 2290
Graulich, Melody 1889, 2202, 5423, 5566, 5756
Graves, John 6070
Gray, James 5870
Greb, Gordon 2326
Grebstein, Sheldon Norman 4341
Green, Douglas B. 653
Green, Martin 350, 2846
Green, Rayna 73, 199, 1472, 1473, 1890, 1891
Green, Timothy 654
Greenan, Edith 4011
Greenberg, Martin H. 1170, 3816, 4996
Greene, Donald 2050
Greenspan, Ezra 6335
Greenway, John 200
Greenwell, Scott L. 5424–5426
Gregg, Barbara 201
Gregg, John J. 201
Gregg, Josiah 3617
Gregory, Horace 1194
Gregory, James N. 351
Gregory, Sinda 3720, 4568, 4572, 5258
Greiner, Charles F. 5706
Greiner, Francis F. 3152
Greiner, Patricia 1786
Grenander, M. E. 2291, 2292, 6020
Gressley, Gene M. 655, 656, 1006, 5145, 6117
Grey, Loren 3627
Grey, Zane 3628
Gribben, Alan 2847
Grider, Daryl Aleck 6191
Grider, Sylvia 5337
Griego y Maestas, José 202
Griffin, R. J. 5871
Griffin, Shaun T. 203
Griffin, Susan 1787, 1892
Griffith, Sally Foreman 6314, 6315
Griffith, Thomas 1007
Grigg, Quay 6192
Grigsby, Gordon K. 5179
Gripp, Gary 6423
Griswold, Jerry 2249
Groff, Edward 5067
Groman, George L. 6316
Grommon, A. H. 5872
Grose, G. R. 4660

Gross, Barry 3472
Gross, Beverly 5257
Gross, David S. 3091
Grossman, James 2994
Grossman, Mark 1788
Grover, Dorys C. 1893, 3449–3452,
    3615, 3847, 3848, 4084, 4273
Gruber, Frank 1195, 3629
Grumbach, Doris 2546
Grunzweig, Walter 5509
Gubar, Susan 1886
Guettinger, Roger J. 4778
Gumina, Deanna Paoli 4962
Gunn, Drewey Wayne 2848
Gurian, Jay 352, 657–659, 2266, 4420
Gurko, Leo 5873
Gurpegui, José Antonio 61, 1641
Gussow, Adam 4110
Gustafson, Antoinette McCloskey 353
Guthrie, A. B., Jr. 660, 661, 3680
Gutiérrez, David G. 1652
Gutierrez, Donald 5180–5182, 6091
Gutiérrez, Ramón 1653
Gvåle, Gudrun Hovde 5338
Gwynn, R. S. 1008

Haaland, C. Carlyle 4661
Hack, Richard 5024
Hackenberry, Charles 2378
Hacker, Peter R. 3177
Hadley, Edith 4818
Hafen, LeRoy 5410
Hafer, Jack 4779
Hafer, John William 354
Hagedorn, Jessica 204
Hagen, Lyman B. 2403
Hahn, Emily 4531
Hahn, Stephen 3587
Hahn, Steve 5339
Haight, Mary M. 4701
Haines, John 1789
Hairston, Joe B. 355, 3681, 5757, 5758
Hairston, Maxine C. 5042
Hakac, John 1009
Hall, Blaine H. 41
Hall, Halbert W. 4241
Hall, H[elen] Lark 5014–5016
Halliburton, David 3092
Halperin, Irving 4266
Halpert, Sam 2459
Hamalian, Leo 5183, 5468

Hamalian, Linda 1010, 5184, 5185
Hamblen, Abigail Ann 6032
Hamilton, Cynthia S. 1196, 3630
Hamilton, David Mike 4421, 4422
Hamilton, Ian 356
Hamilton, W. I. 1474
Hammond, John Hays 5602
Hampsten, Elizabeth 1894, 1895
Hancock, Joel 1654
Hand, Richard A. 74
Handy, William J. 4151
Hanna, Archibald 75
Hanna, Warren 5506
Hans, Birgit 4621
Hansell, William H. 6245
Hansen, Terry L. 3837
Hanson, Elizabeth I. 1475, 1476, 2157
Hanson, George Steven 6092
Hapke, Laura 4702
Harbert, Earl N. 76
Harding, Eugene 3506
Hardwick, Bonnie Skell 357
Hardy, John Edward 5068
Hardy, Phil 1302
Harline, Paula Kelly 1896
Harmon, Robert B. 5874, 5875
Harney, Steve 1989
Harper, Mary Catherine 4282
Harper, Robert D. 4780
Harpham, Geoffrey 4423
Harrell, David 2547
Harrington, John 1303
Harriott, Esther 358
Harris, Charles W. 1197
Harris, Jeane 2548
Harris, Jim R. 5220
Harris, Leon 5589
Harris, Richard C. 5103
Harris, Stephen L. 2233
Harris, Susan K. 2849
Harrison, Cynthia E. 77, 1897
Harrison, Dick 2051–2056
Harrison, Joseph B. 3746, 5017
Harrison, Stanley R. 3522
Hart, James D. 78, 359, 3138, 4905
Hart, John E. 4111
Hart, Lynda 5533, 5534
Hart, William S. 1304
Harte, Bret 3747
Harte, John Bret 3748
Harter, Carol C. 3233

McFarland, Dorothy Tuck 2570
McFarland, Ron 4583, 4584, 6165, 6166
McFarland, Ronald E. 227
McFatter, Susan Prothro 4935
McGinity, Sue Simmons 1679, 3400
McGinty, Brian 6022
MacGregor, Alan Leander 3945
Machann, Clinton 5078
Machlis, Paul 2881, 2882
Machor, James L. 4936
McHoul, Alex 5132
Maciel, David R. 1330
McIlrath, Patricia 3912
McIntosh, Kenneth W. 3163
McIver, Dorothy Jean Palmer 6083
Mack, Effie Mona 2883
McKee, Irving 2411
McKee, John DeWitt 2884, 6319
McKelly, James C. 399, 4123, 5541
McKenzie, James J. 5190
McKinney, Doug 1331
MacKinnon, Janice R. 5606
MacKinnon, Stephen R. 5606
McKnight, Jeannie 1913
MacLaren, I. S. 3946
McLay, Catherine M. 2068, 2571
McLean, Austin J. 3573
MacLean, H. N. 3098
McLean, Kenneth Hugh 2069
McLeod, Gordon Duncan 2070
McLeod, James Richard 5293, 5294
Macleod, Norman 1048
McMahan, Elizabeth E. 2885, 5916
McMaster, Belle M. 6488
McMichael, James 5295, 5296
McMurtry, Larry 400, 731, 732, 1332
McNally, Dennis 4124
McNamee, Gregory 228, 2109
McNamee, Lawrence F. 102
McNeil, Katherine 5640
McNickle, D'Arcy 4233
McPheron, William 103, 3251
McReynolds, Douglas J. 733
McRobbie, Kenneth 2032
MacShane, Frank 2715
McTaggart, Fred 1521
McVicker, Mary Louis 3218
McWilliams, Carey 734, 735, 1049, 1050, 2294, 5917
Madden, David 2437, 2438, 4789–4793, 6253
Madden, Fred 4161
Madrid-Barela, Arturo 1680
Magalaner, Marvin 3329
Maguire, James H. 104, 173, 229, 736, 737, 3494, 5767, 6349
Magnaghi, R. M. 2359
Mahan, Jeffrey Howard 4686
Maher, Susan Naramore 2423, 4629, 4667, 5152
Mahon, Robert Lee 401
Mailer, Norman 2001
Mainiero, Lina 105, 1914
Major, Mabel 106, 230
Malin, Irving 6254
Malin, James C. 6175–6178
Malkin, Jeanette R. 5542
Malkoff, Karl 5297
Malley, Terence 2386
Mallon, Anne-Marie 5265
Mallon, Thomas 3201
Malone, Michael P. 107, 738, 739, 791, 5050
Malpezzi, Frances M. 2164, 6196, 6197
Manchel, Frank 1333
Manchester, John 2396
Mandel, Eli 2071–2073
Mandel, Ruth 4639
Manfred, Frederick 740, 1093, 3365, 4357
Mangelsdorf, Tom 5918
Manley, Atwood 5166
Manley, Francis 3913
Mansfield-Kelley, Deane 4234
Manso, Peter 2387
Manzo, Flournoy D. 4294
Maples, Donna Elaine 1915
Marberry, M. Marion 4705
March, John 2572
Marchand, Ernest 741, 4937
Marcus, Mordecai 5919
Mares, E. A. 1681
Margolis, John D. 4221
Marín, Mariana 2175
Marion, William E. 6127
Marken, Jack W. 108, 1522, 1523
Markos, Donald W. 5991
Marks, Barry A. 742, 2886, 5610
Marks, Lester Jay 5920, 5921
Marling, William 2716, 3723
Marotti, Maria Ornella 2887

Marovitz, Sanford E. 72, 402, 743–745, 3099, 4358, 5418, 5922, 5923, 6433–6435
Márquez, Antonio C. 1682, 4869, 5270
Márquez, María Teresa 1683, 1932
Marsden, James Douglas 4162
Marsden, Michael T. 1181, 1213, 1214, 1334, 1335, 3968, 3969, 4246–4249, 4994, 5496, 5497
Marsh, Robert 6389
Marshall, Gary Thomas 5719
Marshall, Ian 746
Marshall, Susan Elaine 1336
Martin, Abigail Ann 2144, 4979, 6037
Martin, Bruce K. 5924
Martin, Calvin 1809
Martin, Jay 6255, 6256
Martin, Jim 6150
Martin, Julia 5641, 5642
Martin, Lawrence H., Jr. 3799
Martin, Reginald 2958
Martin, Russell 231, 232
Martin, Stoddard 1051, 4456, 5925
Martin, Terence 2573, 3004, 3005, 4163
Martínez, Eliud 2176
Martínez, Julio A. 109, 110, 1684, 1685
Martz, William J. 5298
Marx, Leo 1810, 2888, 2889
Mason, Julian 6436, 6437
Mason, Katherine A. 5431
Mason, Kenneth C. 5768
Mason, Kenneth D. 4742
Mason, Theodore O., Jr. 2959
Mass, Roslyn 1337
Massa, Ann 4385
Matchie, Thomas 3258, 3330, 4250, 4560
Mathes, Valerie Sherer 3970
Mathews, Sue 4067, 4068
Matlack, Anne 3317
Mattern, Claire 5432, 5433
Matthews, Eleanor H. 3706
Mattson, Vernon E. 6127
Maule, Harry E. 233
Maunder, Elwood R. 6007
Maurice, Arthur B. 5101
Mawer, Randall Ray 1052
Maxwell, Margaret F. 3716
May, Antoinette 3971

May, Charles E. 3751, 5926
May, Ernest 3752
May, Judith Stinson 3006
Mayberry, Susan Neal 2574
Mayer, Charles W. 3868
Maynard, John Arthur 2002
Mazzaro, Jerome 5299
Mead, S. Jean 111
Meador, John 4043
Medicine, Bea 3811
Medoff, Jeslyn 2575
Meier, A. Mabel 2145
Meine, Franklin J. 292
Meinig, D. W. 1053
Melada, Ivan 3007
Meldrum, Barbara Howard 403, 404, 747–749, 1916, 1917, 2325, 3456, 3457, 4069, 5223, 6400–6402
Mellard, James M. 4640
Melling, Philip H. 750
Mellor, Anne 4283
Meltzer, David 234, 2003
Merchant, Carolyn 1811, 1812
Meredith, William 5300
Merish, Lori 4205
Merlock, Raymond J. 3008
Merren, John 3191
Merriam, C. Hart 1524
Merriam, H. G. 4377, 4378
Merrild, Knud 4267
Merrill, Thomas 3591
Merritt, J. I. 4822
Merwin, Henry 3753
Messenger, Christian 4938
Meyer, Adam 2460
Meyer, Harold 2890
Meyer, Roy W. 112, 405, 751–754, 2367, 3538, 3563, 5153, 5348
Meyer, William Claus 3009
Meyer, William E. H., Jr. 3639
Meyer, William R. 1338
Meyering, Sheryl L. 2576, 3576
Meyers, Jeffrey 3800
Mezo, Richard Eugene 6093
Michaels, I. Lloyd 6257
Michelson, Bruce 2891, 4076
Michener, James 4678
Micklus, Robert 4939
Middleton, Jo Ann 2577
Mignon, Charles W. 2508, 2509
Mikkelsen, Hubert Aage 3010

Motley, Warren 3012, 3541, 5932
Mott, Frank Luther 6038
Mottram, Ron 4945, 5543
Moul, Keith R. 5305
Moulton, Gary E. 4310
Movalli, Charles Joseph 3013
Movshovitz, Howard 1341
Moynihan, Ruth Barnes 3275
Muehl, Lois B. 6039
Muggli, Mark Z. 3203
Mukerji, Malovika 5721
Mulder, Rodney J. 3371
Muller, Marcia 237
Munden, Kenneth J., M.D. 1218
Munslow, Alan 6116
Murphy, Brenda 3759
Murphy, John J. 1918, 2587–2598
Murphy, Miriam B. 2451
Murphy, Patrick D. 4024, 4025,
    5644–5647
Murray, David 1531
Murray, John A. 2115
Murthy, Sikha S. 4946
Musser, Charles 1342
Muszynska-Wallace, E. Soteris 3014
Myers, Andrew B. 3947
Myers, Edward 2963
Myers, George, Jr. 2346
Myers, John Myers 3810
Myers, Samuel L. 3704

Nachbar, Jack 1343–1346
Nadeau, Robert 5259
Nagel, Gwen L. 115
Nagel, James 115, 3542
Namias, June 1919
Nance, William I. 5081
Nash, Gerald D. 419, 776–779, 6129
Nash, Lee 5507, 5508
Nash, Roderick 1814, 1815, 4824
Nathan, George Jean 5473
Nathanson, Tenney 6343
Neal, Charles R. 5006
Neale, Walter 2295
Neatherlin, James William 5484
Neihardt, John G. 4859, 4860
Neil, J. M. 3982
Neinstein, Raymond L. 1059, 4602,
    4797
Nelson, Barney 420
Nelson, Carolyn W. 4798

Nelson, Doris 1920
Nelson, F. C. 780
Nelson, H. S. 5933
Nelson, Herbert B. 421, 2229, 2230,
    2258, 6344
Nelson, Howard 2347, 2348
Nelson, Jane 4533
Nelson, Margaret Faye 4743
Nelson, Nancy Owen 3361, 3372–3374
Nelson, Raymond John 5026
Nelson, Rudolph L. 5648
Nelson, Solveig Leraas 422
Nemanic, Gerald 116, 4799, 4800
Nemerov, Alexander 5167
Nemerov, Howard 4074
Nesbitt, John D. 1219, 1220, 1921,
    3641, 3788, 4251–4253, 6440
Nesset, Kirk 2461
Neumann, Edwin J. 3543
Nevins, Allan 3972
Nevins, Francis M. 4839
Nevius, Blake 3015
New, W. H. 2075–2077
Newlin, Keith 2717
Newman, Robert D. 5133
Newmark, Marco 4543
Newton, Dwight B. 2468, 3789, 3790
Niatum, Duane 1532
Nibbelink, Harman 2896
Nicholas, Charles A. 4744
Nicholl, James R. 781
Nichols, David A. 6130
Nichols, Hugh 4584
Nichols, Kathleen L. 5607
Nichols, Roger L. 117, 1533
Nichols, William 4311
Nickerson, Edward A. 4026–4030
Nicoll, Bruce H. 5436
Nicosia, Gerald 4126
Nilon, Charles II. 118
Nisonger, Thomas Evans 4127
Noble, David W. 423, 3016, 6131
Noel, Daniel C. 6051
Noel, Mary 424
Nolan, Paul T. 3120–3122
Nolan, William F. 3351
Nolte, William H. 4031, 4032
Nomura, Gail M. 119, 782
Nordström, Lars 1816, 5722
Norell, Irene P. 783
North, Dennis D. 6055

Norton, Aloysius A. 5374
Norton, Jody 5649
Norwood, Vera 1817–1819, 1922
Norwood, W. D. 6071
Nostrand, Richard L. 146
Noto, Sal 4463, 4464
Novak, Frank G., Jr. 2599
Nuernberg, Susan Marie 4465
Nuhn, Ferner 6040, 6041
Nunnally, Patrick DeWitt 1820, 4527
Nussbaum, Martin 1221, 1222
Nutt, Francis Dorothy 3705
Nuwer, Henry [Hank] 4033, 5499
Nye, Frank Wilson 4971
Nye, Naomi Shihab 1008
Nye, Russel 1223

Oaks, Priscilla 121, 1534
Oates, Joyce Carol 5689
O'Brien, Lynne Woods 1535, 3294
O'Brien, Sharon 2600–2602
O'Brien, Sheila Ruzycki 5266
O'Connell, Nicholas 425, 783, 1060
O'Conner, John Joseph William 2078
O'Connor, Carol A. 407
O'Connor, John E. 1347
O'Connor, Margaret Anne 2603
O'Connor, Richard 2296, 3760, 4359,
    4466, 5934
O'Dell, Charles A. 3123
Odell, Ruth 3973
Odum, Howard W. 1061
Oehlschlaeger, Fritz H. 2604, 3642,
    5437, 5438, 6042, 6043, 6485
Oelschlaeger, Max 1821
Officer, James E. 1644
Ogden, Dunbar H. 426
Oglesby, Richard E. 2311
O'Grady, John P. 2209, 4825, 5388
Okada, Roy 3252, 5650
Okerland, Arlene N. 5935
Olafson, Robert B. 3643
Oldenburg, Ray 1062
Olderman, Raymond M. 4164
Oldham, John N. 1063
Olendorf, Donna 3204
Oleson, Carole 4745
Oliva, Leo E. 1536, 2271
Olivares, Julián 5250
Oliver, Egbert S. 785, 3761
Oliver, Lawrence J. 2297, 3577

Olsen, Brett J. 5770
Olsen, T. V. 3603
Olson, Alan M. 2476
Olson, James C. 786
Olson, Julius E. 5350, 5351
Olson, Paul A. 787, 2321, 4861
Omrcanin, Margaret Stewart 6044
Oppewall, Peter 3375
O'Quinn, Trueman 5109, 5110
Orbison, Tucker 5544
Orenstein, Gloria Feman 1771
Orians, G. Harrison 1114
Orlandini, Roberta 6285
Orr, Elaine Neil 4980
Ortega, Adolfo 1688
Ortego y Gasca, Philip D. [Felipe de]
    238, 1689–1692, 5936
Ortiz, Simon J. 1537
Osborn, M. Elizabeth 1693
Osborne, Stephen Douglas 1538
Ossman, David 2004
Ostwalt, Conrad E., Jr. 2605
Otero, Rosalie 1694
Otis, John Whitacre 5771
Ouderkirk, Bruce J. 5937
Oumono, Ellen 5545
Overholser, Stephen 4995
Øverland, Örm 3017, 4128
Owens, Louis D. 39, 1445, 1539, 4623,
    4624, 5938–5942, 6286
Owens, William A. 788, 2256, 6217
Ownbey, Ray Wilson 4467

Packer, Warren M. 789
Padget, Martin 427
Padilla, Genaro M. 1653, 1695, 1696,
    2128, 2730, 6155
Pady, Donald S. 5038, 6320
Paine, Albert Bigelow 2897
Paine, Gregory 790, 3018
Palmer, Frederick A. 595
Palmer, Pamela Lynn 5485
Palmieri, Rory Albert Joseph 1348
Paluka, Frank 122, 6045
Pankake, Jon Allan 4468, 4469
Pantle, P. 6318
Papanikolas, Zeese 174
Paredes, Américo 1697–1699, 3903
Paredes, Raymund A. 1699–1701,
    2129, 3102
Parins, James W. 100, 1516, 5237

Ravitz, Abe C. 2251, 4295
Rawls, James J. 3182
Ray, Charles Eugene 3688
Raymond, Catherine E. 1070
Raymond, Michael W. 4746
Rea, Paul W. 2119, 6492
Reamer, Owen J. 3551
Rebolledo, Tey Diana 243, 1709–1711, 1932
Reck, Tom S. 2439
Reddin, Paul Laverne 445
Redekop, Ernest H. 1553, 3026
Redfern, Bernice 131, 1933
Redinger, Ellsworth L. 4039
Reed, John Q. 2413, 2899
Reed, Mary E. 2399
Rees, Robert A. 76
Rees, Ronald 2083
Reesman, Jeanne C. 4438, 4474, 4475
Reeve, Frank Durer 3843
Reeve, Kay Aiken 446, 447
Reid, Randall 6258
Reigelman, Milton M. 1072
Reigstad, Paul 5355, 5356
Reilingh, Maarten 3916
Rein, David 3461
Reinitz, Richard 5019
Reiter, Joan Govan 3473
Remenyi, Joseph 5475
Remley, David A. 1934, 3395, 5595
Renner, Frederic G. 5400, 5405
Renner, Ginger 5401
Renner, Stanley 5948, 5949
Resh, Richard W. 6322, 6323
Rexroth, Kenneth 2011–2013
Réyes, Luis 1360, 1712
Reynard, Grant 2611
Reynolds, Clay 1073, 4609
Reynolds, Quentin 1227, 3352
Reynolds, R. C. 4073
Rhode, Robert D. 1074
Rhodelhamel, Josephine DeWitt 2966
Rhodes, May Davison 5211
Rice, C. David 3911
Rice, Julian 1554, 2322, 3166–3169
Rice, Minnie C. 5441
Richards, John S. 4708
Richards, John Thomas 4862–4864
Richards, Robert F. 3419–3423
Richardson, Darrell C. 3353
Richey, Elinor 2186

Richman, Sidney 4641
Richter, Conrad 5224
Richter, Harvena 5225
Richter, Sara Jane 4669
Rickels, Milton 6080
Ricou, Laurence R. 813, 2084, 2085
Rideout, Walter B. 2444
Ridge, Martin 814, 1075, 2312, 2313, 3244, 6134–6137
Ridgeway, Ann N. 4040
Rieupeyrout, Jean-Louis 1361, 1362
Riley, Glenda 815, 1935, 1936
Riley, Susan B. 5046
Ringe, Donald A. 3027, 3028
Ringler, Donald P. 2216
Rippey, Barbara 5442–5444
Rivera, Tomás 1713–1715
Rivero, Eliana S. 243, 1711
Rizzo, Fred F. 3344
Roach, Joyce Gibson 5668
Roach, Samuel Frederick, Jr. 5324
Robb, Kenneth A. 4723
Robbins, J. Albert 133
Robbins, William G. 816–818, 1076, 1828, 3235
Roberson, William H. 2351
Roberts, David 5690
Roberts, J. Russell, Sr. 5725
Roberts, Thomas J. 1228
Robertson, David 1829, 2014, 4131, 5658, 5659
Robertson, Jamie 3103, 5774
Robertson, Kirk 819
Robertson, Richard 1363, 6058
Robertson, R. M. 2612
Robinson, Barbara J. 1716
Robinson, Cecil 448, 449, 1717–1719, 3407
Robinson, Chandler A. 3702
Robinson, Duncan 5113
Robinson, Forrest G. 820, 1229, 2900–2904, 3029, 4476, 5501, 5775–5778, 6443, 6444
Robinson, J. Cordell 1716
Robinson, John W. 821
Robinson, Margaret G. 5777, 5778
Robinson, Phyllis C. 2613
Robinson, William Hedges, Jr. 2905
Robson, W. W. 6395
Rocard, Marcienne 1720, 5252
Rocha, Mark William 3552

Schweizer, Harold 4044
Schwind, Jean 2644
Scott, James F. 2017
Scott, Kenneth W. 3648
Scott, Nathan A., Jr. 5308, 6261
Scott, Robert I. 4045, 4046
Seager, Allan 5309, 5310
Seale, Jan Epton 1008
Searles, George J. 4172
See, Carolyn P. 460, 5027
Seed, David 5134
Seelye, John 461, 1834, 4312, 6446
Segade, Gustavo 1733
Seibel, George 2645
Seigel, Catharine F. 3067
Seitz, Don C. 2414
Sellars, Richard West 832
Seller, Maxine Schwartz 462
Selzer, John L. 2646
Sennett, Ted 1369
Sequeira, Isaac 3034
Sergeant, Elizabeth Shepley 2647
Sessions, George 4047
Settle, Elizabeth A. 2960
Settle, Thomas A. 2960
Settle, William A., Jr. 1232
Sevillano, Mando 1573
Sewell, Ernestine P. 3320, 3321, 4611
Seydor, Paul 1370
Seyersted, Per 5579
Shadoian, Jack 833, 1371
Shaffer, Eric Paul 6302
Shames, Priscilla 1574
Shannon, Fred A. 6223
Shaughnessy, Mary Rose 3393
Shaul, Lawana J. 834
Shaw, Patrick W. 2648, 2649, 5957
Shear, Walter 6063
Shebl, James M. 4048, 4197
Sheean, Vincent 4367
Sheed, Wilfred 5692
Sheehy, Eugene P. 4920, 6388
Sheller, Harry L. 2302
Shelton, Frank W. 3231
Shelton, Lola 5403
Shepard, Irving 4427
Shepard, Paul 1835
Shephard, I. Milo 4439, 4440
Sheppard, Jocelyn 103
Sheppard, Keith S. 3035
Sherman, Caroline B. 835–837

Sherman, Joan R. 4478
Sherman, W. D. 4173
Sherwood, Terry G. 4174
Shetty, M. Nalini 4802
Shewey, Don 5550
Shiglas, Jerry Ashburn 4049
Shillinglaw, Susan 5958
Shinn, Thelma J. 5479
Shirley, Carl R. 1676, 1734, 1735,
    3063, 6156
Shirley, Paula W. 1735
Shiveley, JoEllen 1372
Shively, James R. 2650
Shivers, Alfred S. 4479, 4480, 6304
Shockley, Martin 245
Short, John D., Jr. 5959
Short, Julee 3951
Short, R. W. 4050
Shortridge, James R. 1083
Showalter, Dennis E. 1353
Showalter, Elaine 1949
Shumaker, Conrad 3582, 3583
Shuman, R. Baird 3917, 5117, 5960
Shute, Kathleen Westfall 2464
Sibley, M. A. 5114
Siegel, Mark R. 5260, 5547, 5551
Silber, Irwin 246
Silet, Charles L. P. 3555, 4481, 5587,
    5596, 5597
Silver, Charles 1373
Silver, Marilyn Brick 463
Simard, Rodney 5552
Simmen, Edward 247, 1736, 1737
Simmonds, Roy S. 5961, 5962
Simmons, Marc 1950, 4545, 5502
Simmons, Michael K. 1233, 3689
Simon, Tobin 4368
Simoneaux, Katherine G. 6081
Simons, John L. 1374
Simonson, Harold P. 464, 465, 838,
    839, 1084, 3236, 4585, 4586, 4826,
    5358–5360, 6138
Simpson, Barbara D. 3959
Simpson, Claude M., Jr. 1085, 3556
Simpson, Elizabeth 3237, 3238
Simpson, Hassell A. 5963
Sinclair, Andrew 1375, 4482
Singer, Barnett 840, 2276, 4175, 4643,
    5020, 5780
Singh, Jane 142
Sipper, Ralph B. 4689

Sisson, James E. 4498
Skaggs, Merrill Maguire 2651, 2652
Skårdal, Dorothy Burton 466, 841, 1086, 5361
Skau, Michael W. 2018, 3068, 3414, 3415
Skelley, Grant Teasdale 1087
Skenazy, Paul 2440, 2719, 3726, 4690
Skerl, Jennie 2427
Skillman, Richard 5212
Skinner, Robert E. 2720, 3727, 4691
Skipp, Frances E. 4483
Skjelver, Mabel R. 1235
Slade, Carole 5487
Slade, Joseph W. 4662, 6001, 6002
Slade, Leonard A., Jr. 5964
Sloan, Karin Ramspeck 1088
Sloane, David E. E. 2917, 2918, 3777
Slote, Bernice 2653–2659, 3105, 3106
Slotkin, Richard 467–469, 1376, 1836, 5375
Slovic, Scott Harlan 1837
Slowik, Mary 5580
Smeall, Joseph F. S. 4562
Smetzer, Michael 5727
Smith, Annick 212
Smith, Bob L. 4268
Smith, Caroline 470
Smith, Dave 3571, 6481
Smith, David Douglas 2240
Smith, Duane A. 3435
Smith, Dwight L. 143, 144, 1575
Smith, Edwin B. 842
Smith, Goldie Capers 843
Smith, Harriet Elinor 2919
Smith, Henry Nash 471, 844–852, 1236, 2219, 2920, 2921, 3036, 3037, 5612, 6345
Smith, Herbert F. 4827
Smith, Johanna M. 2721
Smith, Larry R. 3416, 5028
Smith, Marcus 6262
Smith, Norman D. 1738, 2130
Smith, Patricia Clark 1838, 1951
Smith, Paul 1377
Smith, Richard Cándida 472
Smith, Robert W. 3378
Smith, Stephen 4070
Smith, William F., Jr. 1576, 6290
Smorkaloff, Pamela Maria 853
Snell, George 3462

Snell, Joseph W. 1237
Snipes, Helen Joann 6174
Snodgrass, Richard 4692
Snook, Donald Gene 3038
Snyder, Gary 854, 1839
Snyder, Richard C. 2504
Socolofsky, Homer E. 5781
Soderbergh, Peter A. 5598
Solensten, John M. 6447
Solomon, Eric 3107
Solomon, Roger B. 2922
Solotaroff, Theodore 4644
Solum, Nora O. 5347
Sommers, Joseph 182, 1629, 1739, 1740, 5254
Sondrup, Steven P. 855
Sonnichsen, C. L. 248–250, 473, 474, 856–862, 1238, 1239, 1378, 1577, 1741, 2449, 3463, 4612
Soto, Gary 251
Spaeth, Janet 6366
Spaulding, George F. 3952
Spears, Jack 1379, 1380
Speck, Ernest B. 2354, 2355, 2450, 6059
Speir, Jerry 2722, 4694, 4695
Spencer, Benjamin T. 1090–1092
Spencer, Betty Lee 3390
Spencer, Marcia C. 563
Sper, Felix 476
Spies, George H. 3380
Spilka, Mark 3803, 5965
Spiller, Robert E. 3039, 3040
Spindler, Michael 4370
Spivack, Charlotte 4284
Spotts, Carl B. 477
Springer, Haskell 1952, 3953
Springer, Marlene 1952
Sproxton, Birk 2086
Squires, Radcliffe 4051, 4052
Stafford, Bart Lanier, III 214
Stafford, William E. 215, 478, 1093, 3345, 5710, 5726
Stall, Lindon 3127
Stallman, R. W. 3108, 3109
Standiford, Lester A. 1578
Stanley, David 4132
Stanley, David H. 4484
Staples, Hugh 5311
Stark, John O. 5135
Starobin, Christina Fijan 3041

Starr, Kevin 479–481, 2187, 3210, 5387

Starrett, Vincent 2303, 2304

Stasz, Clarice 4485–4487

Staub, Michael 4984

Stauffer, Helen Winter 482, 1953, 5445–5451

Stavrakis, Kathryn 221

Stearns, Peter N. 483

Steckmesser, Kent L. 864, 865, 1240

Stedman, Raymond William 1381

Steele, Joan 5154

Steensma, Robert C. 866, 4218, 5362, 6346

Steeves, Harrison R. 3569

Steffen, Jerome O. 4313

Steffens, Lincoln 2220

Stegner, Page 1095

Stegner, Wallace 484–486, 867, 868, 1094, 1095, 1840–1843, 2087, 2660, 2661, 2763, 3184–3189, 3767, 5120, 5782, 6016

Stein, Arnold 5312

Stein, Howard F. 4176

Stein, Paul 2764

Stein, Rita 487

Stein, Robert A. 3128

Stein, W. B. 3042

Steinbeck, Elaine 5966

Steinbeck, John 5236

Steinberg, Alan L. 1579, 3043

Steinbrink, Jeffrey 2924

Steiner, Michael C. 145, 1096, 6139, 6140

Steiner, Stan 1608, 1756

Steiner, T. R. 4696

Steinmetz, Lee 869

Stekler, Paul 1382

Steltenkamp, Michael F. 2323

Stensland, Anna Lee 1580–1582, 3295

Stephens, Alan 6396

Stephens, D. G. 2088

Stephens, Edna Buell 3476

Stephenson, Gregory 2019

Sterling, George 252, 4053

Stern, Daniel 3612

Stern, Frederick C. 4563, 4564

Stern, Richard 4302

Steuding, Bob 5663

Stevens, A. Wilbur 253

Stevens, James 3160, 3161

Stevens, Peter 2089

Stevens, Robert 5363

Stevenson, Dorothy 870

Stevenson, Elizabeth 4314

Stevenson, Lionel 6003

Stewart, David 5727

Stewart, D. H. 5123

Stewart, Donald C. 3690, 3691

Stewart, George R., Jr. 871, 1097, 3173, 3768, 3769

Stewart, Robert 3597

Stich, Klaus Peter 2090

Stiffler, Randall 5313

Stine, Peter 1807

Stineback, David C. 2662, 2663, 3205, 3692

Stineman, Esther Lanigan 2221

Stoddard, Ellwyn R. 146

Stokes, Frances Kemble Wister 6448

Stone, Albert E., Jr. 2925

Stone, Irving 4488

Stone, Judy 6099

Stone, Paul C. 3222

Stonely, Peter 2926

Story, Norah 2091

Stott, Graham St. John 3649

Stouck, David 872, 2092, 2664–2671

Stouck, Mary-Ann 2670, 2671

Stout, Janis P. 2672, 2673, 3206, 4613, 4614, 5083

Stowell, Peter 1383

Straight, Michael 873, 1241

Stratton, David H. 1098

Straus, Dorothea 5693

Street, Douglas 3902

Street, Webster 5967

Strelow, Michael 254, 4177

Strenski, Ellen 3821

Strickland, Arney L. 4991

Strong, Lester 3464

Stroven, Carl G. 6023

Strychacz, Thomas 6263

Studebaker, William 227

Stuhr, Margaret D. 488

Stull, James 4630

Stull, William L. 2389, 2458, 2465, 2466

Sturak, John Thomas 4554, 4555

Suckow, Ruth 1099

Suderman, Elmer F. 3044, 5364

Sugg, Richard P. 2353

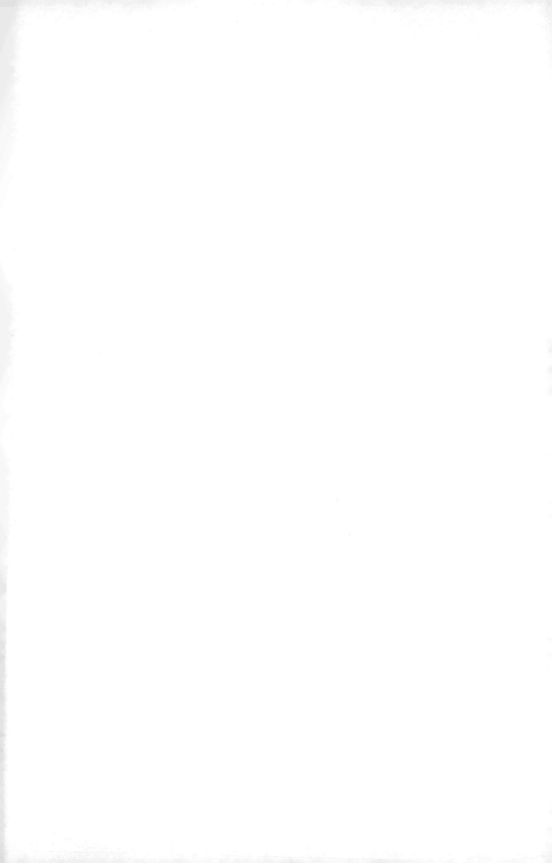